Care and Administration of Heritage Monuments in India (1784-1904)

Care and Administration of Heritage Monuments in India (1784-1904)

Dhirendra Kumar Pant

Aryan Books International
New Delhi

Care and Administration of Heritage Monuments in India (1784-1904)

ISBN: 978-81-7305-420-4

Published in **2012** by
ARYAN BOOKS INTERNATIONAL
Pooja Apartments, 4B, Ansari Road, Darya Ganj, New Delhi-110 002 (India)
Tel.: 23287589, 23255799; Fax: 91-11-23270385
E-mail: aryanbooks@gmail.com
www.aryanbooks.co.in

Printed in India at Mudrak, Delhi-110091

In Memory of My Mother

Kamala Pant

सर्वमङ्गलमङ्गल्ये शिवे सर्वार्थसाधिके।
शरण्ये त्र्यम्बके गौरि नारायणि नमोऽस्तु ते।।

Foreword

I have the greatest pleasure to associate myself with the book entitled *Care and Administration of Heritage Monuments in India, 1784-1904* written by Dr. Pant. The earlier books written on the history of Archaeology in India have been based on the published literature. Of course, A. Ghosh, Sourendra Nath Roy and Dilip K. Chakrabarti have written on the subject but this book appears to be the first one which has encompassed the field from 1784 to 1904 purely on archival sources. Both these dates are very crucial from the point of view of the development of history of Archaeology in India. While the establishment of Asiatic Society at Calcutta, 1784 is the beginning of the emergence of a consciousness 'to explore, document and preserve' the ancient heritage of India, the enactment of The Ancient Monuments Preservation Act 1904 was a culmination of the spirit to 'dig, discover and preserve the heritage'. All these years witness the birth and growth of the 'Archaeological Consciousness' among the people and its urge to protect and preserve the monuments by the State leading to a permanent footing of the Archaeological Survey of India. The beginnings of the State's anxiety for the preservation of ancient monuments could be gleaned from Bengal Regulation 1810, Madras Regulation 1817 and the Treasure Trove Act. But the Monuments Preservation Act 1904 clearly shows that the State intervention in the archaeological persuits had taken a concrete shape. With the vision of Lord Curzon and execution of the archaeological works in the field by Sir John Marshall, the then Director General gave permanent footing to the Archaeological Survey of India which was in future years to grow in to a large department having several circles and branches all over the country.

Dr. Pant has rightly chosen the subject as he was associated with Sourendra Nath Roy who used to spend considerable time in the library of National Achives of India where young Pant was serving. Dr. Pant developed an admiration for this great scholar who advised him to take up the subject of writing on the administrative history of the growth and care of heritage during the period 1784 to 1904 after a detailed examination of the archival records of National Archives and other State Archives and also records of India Office, London, which Dr. Pant has carried out arduously. The book is well divided into fifteen chapters. This aspect is well reflected at the end of each chapter where a large number of original references appear. The study covers very well the periods of Lytton and Curzon during which maximum state support was received by Archaeology in India. In this connection, the private archives are a source of most important information so far as archaeology is concerned. Some other interesting aspects are for example Burgess' Memorandum on the reorganization of the Archaeological Survey of India, the controversy regarding the Amaravati sculptures between Burgess and Cole, the debate on ancient monuments preservation bill in the Central Assembly, etc. which are quite fascinating. Cole's general observation in connection with the preservation of historical monuments is yet another aspect which deserves attention. Curzon's speech at the Bengal Asiatic Society on 7th Feb. 1900 has been reproduced, which is a thought-provoking address.

Interesting names like Bhim Singh Lat, now called Asokan Pillar Fort at Allahabad and Senapoor caves, i.e., Ajanta Caves have shown how the names started changing during the British period.

The tributes paid to Lord Curzon in Chapter XV make the study very memorable.

Dr. Pant has dealt with the subject with considerable objectivity and has brought out the development of care of heritage in a lucid way based on records and the study stands out as a pioneering contribution. He deserves congratulations for this interesting study. I hope the book will be received well by the students, scholars and heritage managers.

(Jagat Pati Joshi)
Director General (Retd.)
Archaeological Survey of India

Preface

The invitation to write this book was both gratifying and somewhat challenging. I was inspired to undertake this study by late Shri Sourindranath Roy, the doyen amongst archivists during last century.

I was keenly aware of the huge range and high quality of unpublished sources available on this subject at the National Archives of India with which I was associated for three decades. Although Shri Sourindranath Roy had documented this subject in his book published in 1961 as *The Story of Indian Archaelogy, 1784-1947* and also by Shri Dilip K. Chakrabarti's *A History of Indian Archaeology from the Beginning to 1947*, but they had not made extensive use of untapped record material on the subject which are available in the National Archives of India and other States Archives as is evident by their own admission.

In addition, I was confronted with the dilemma where I should begin and where should I end? I soon decided that I should approach the enterprise by limiting the chronology, starting in the mid-eighteenth century with the advent of the company's rule and limiting it to 1904. It also seemed to me that rather than attempting a vast narrative history I should select a number of administrative efforts of British Indian authorities for framing a sound policy towards care of archaeological heritage which would be examined and assessed in a documentation that was both scholarly and accessible. In the process, I do hope that the reader might gain certain insights into the essential nature of British archaeological experience. Inevitably, some points of the story have been compressed and briefly summarized. I hope this work will be a useful aid to the understanding of one of the greatest historical phenomena.

My regret has been that my mother Smt. Kamala Pant did not live to see my book in the present form and with due deference, I dedicate this work to her memory. She has been a constant source of strength all through my endeavours. My thought also goes to my maternal grand father late Pandit Bhola Dutt Joshi and father Late Pandit Nand Kishore Pant who have been a constant source of strength. Among those I wish to thank for their encouragement and support from start to finish are the archivists and historians. I must express my gratitude to late Shri Sourindranath Roy, Deputy Director who inspired me to undertake this work and

Dr. S.N. Prasad, former Director General of National Archives of India and Joint Secretary. Ministry of Defence who encouraged all those who joined the archival profession for dabbling in research pursuits.

Shri Duli Chand, an eminent Archivist, was a constant source of inspiration all through my research activities, always coming up with solutions to the problems I had confronted while consulting record wealth. I would be failing in my duty if I do not record sincere appreciation of the constant editorial efforts put forth by him.

Amongst others from whom I received academic support and guidance were Professor Bhupen Qanungo, Banaras Hindu University; Professor Ajay S. Rawat, Kumaon University who was my mentor and able supervisor and gave valuable suggestions for improvement of thesis for publication. Shri B.M. Pande, former Director, Archaeological Survey of India, helped me in many ways during my research pursuits, my maternal uncle late Krishna Chandra Joshi, Department of Political Science, Allahabad University provided copious information on various archaeological legislations. Shri Munish Joshi, former Director-General, Archaeological Survey of India, gave innumerable suggestions for enhancing the scope of this publication, but could not live to see this work due to his untimely death. I am indeed indebted to late Dr. Jagatpati Joshi, former Director-General, Archaeological Survey of India for contributing a foreword to this book and giving insights to hitherto unknown facets of the care of archaeological monuments.

My friends who lent financial support were Kunwar Rajender Singh, microphotographist, National Archives of India and Pandit Mohanlal Sharma of village Samalka, New Delhi. I am really grateful to them for their generosity.

Among others who deserve my grateful thanks during my research activities were Shri N.P. Sharma, Shri Rajesh Verma, Assistant Directors; Dr. Mahesh Narayan Sharma, Shri Ashok Kaushik, Choudhary V.S. Rana, Shri J.B.Balani, Shri Probir Roy, Shri Rajmani, Dr. Faizan Ahmed, Archivists; Shri Harish Chand Sharma, UDC; Shri Dhaneshwar Kumar Record Attendent in the National Archives of India and Shri Rakesh Uppal of Navjivan Books, Delhi.

I am also grateful to my neighbours as well as friends, viz., Shri Venkatraman Padmanabhan and Shri Madan Mohan Batra.

Besides, I must acknowledge the help and professional support received from the staff of Research Section, Record Division and library of the National Archives.I also wish to thank all those individuals, librarians, archivists who have helped me at various stages in variety of ways. I have not been able to thank them individually, but their kind help is gratefully acknowledged.

My family members who provided emotional support and encouragement are my maternal uncles late Shri Pitabmer Dutt Joshi, Dr. Kundal Chandra Joshi; my brothers-in-law late Shri Mohan Chandra Joshi, Shri Puran Chandra Joshi; my brother Shri Dharni Dhar Pant; my nephews Shri Girish Chandra Joshi, Shri Raj Joshi, Shri Khajan Chandra Joshi, Shri Dhiraj Pant, Shri Apurv Pant and my son-in-law late Shri Jayant Pande.

My wife Smt. Kusum Pant, son Vaibhav Pant and daughter-in-law Smt. Neha Pant understood my enthusiasm and provided emotional support when it was most needed.

The publication of this volume was mainly due to interest taken by Shri Vikas Arya of Aryan Books International and special thanks to his staff who took care of all the mistakes and inconsistencies in the manuscript.

D-1/C, 19-C, JanakPuri
New Delhi-110058.

Dhirendra Kumar Pant

Contents

Introduction

The British efforts to safeguard the monumental heritage is indeed remarkable. The central administration of the Company's Government and, subsequently, that of Crown took keen interest in the care of monuments besides implementation of programmes for safeguarding the edifices of our rich cultural past. The present study chronicles the administrative policy of English East India Company and the British Crown towards the neglect of monuments and pursuance of their concerted efforts in shaping a definitive policy for arresting their further decay. The study is divided into fifteen chapters, keeping in view to document the development and shaping of a definitive policy towards care of monuments in India which was considered an importance aspect of governance based on original records.

The first three chapters give the historical retrospect (1784-1858), thus documenting the efforts of early European travellers from all over the world, Asiatic Society and the East India Company. The early European travellers documented the ancient Indian monuments in the middle of the 18th century. These travellers published their travel accounts, which were replete with plans and drawing of cities, forts, temples, etc. These travelogues were potential publications of their accounts of the country and its monumental wealth. Accounts of a few early European travellers give detailed study of our cultural past. Travel accounts and translations of Indian literacy works helped European scholars to understand India in its social, economic, political, religious and geographical aspects which were hitherto unknown at that point of time. Later, the Asiatic Society in Calcutta was founded on 15 January 1784 which afforded the British to know different aspects of India and Asia in detail. The Asiatic Society was actively encouraged and patronised by Warren Hastings, the then Governor-General. The official journal of the Asiatic Society, *Asiatic Researches*, launched in 1788 became an ideal forum for framing a well-knit programme for the care of monuments. The Company's Government, however, was alarmed by the neglect of the monuments. The efforts of the Company's Government to document the extant of repairs, dimensions and drawings of the edifices provided a forum for framing a policy in the days to come. The first major effort for the care of monuments was undertaken during the tenure of Lord Minto I when a Taj Committee was constituted in 1808 to undertake conservation and repairs to the Taj. However, the major projects during the Company's period were confined to clearing the environs and upkeep of the monuments of Taj and Moti Masjid at Agra. Besides, repair works and breaches in the Akbar's Tomb at Sikandra were also carried out.

The Old Mosque at Allahabad, Qutb Minar, Bhim Singh Lat at Allahabad and Buddhist Pillar in Raja Hindu Rao's Garden in Delhi, Agra Fort, etc. were brought under the ambit of repair works, which were undertaken by the Company. Elsewhere, the Company also effected repairs to the Tomb of Begampur, the Black Pagoda (Sun Temple) at Konarak and Sher Shah's Mausoleum at Sahasram (Bihar). The Somnath temple, which was vandalised by Mahmud of Ghazni in the 11th century, was restored. The Company also introduced two regulations – Bengal Regulation XIX of 1810 and Madras Regulation VII of 1817 – for ensuring the proper upkeep of monuments in India and took measures for preventing any monument from misuse by private individuals, which is in itself a major step in the beginning of a consciousness for the governmental care of monuments.

The most important assignment was, however, in the field of care of cave temples, viz., Ajanta and Ellora. The Company with the help of the Asiatic Society and Provincial Governments drew up an elaborate plan for care of monuments in India. However, the funds allocated for preservation of monumental edifices were not sufficient. The funds were not adequate and there was always a need felt towards the care of monumental heritage.

After the promulgation of the Government of India Act 1858, the Government of Canning was concerned towards the care of monuments and took adequate measures for their conservation. However, later, they introduced Act XX of 1863, which invested them the authority to "prevent injury to and preserve building remarkable for their antiquity for their historical and architectural value". This augured ushering of an era in the history of Indian archaeology. Besides, the invention of photography facilitated the task of British Indian Government which was introduced in fairly large scale for documenting the monumental heritage.

Besides the advent of photography and its importance in the field of care of monuments, aerial photography was also experimented in photographing archaeological sites at Agra in 1891. Sir Charges Close, Lieutenant in the Survey of India, had proposed that balloons fitted with cameras should be introduced. This scheme was approved by the Surveyor General of India. It resulted in some aerial photographs but none related to archaeological monuments. However, the plans relating to aerial photographs bore fruits after the Second World War.*

The responsibility of archaeological excavations and of upkeep of monuments was entrusted to Alexander Cunningham on 1 December 1861 and he was required to furnish the progress report of the excavations and archaeological objects found during his investigations. However, care of monuments was kept outside the purview of the functions of Director General, Archaeology. However, the Government of India issued a circular on 13 February 1873, thereby assigning to local governments the responsibility towards care and preservation of all buildings and monuments of historical and architectural interest. The Government of India's priority was inventorisation of monuments which were eventually classified and published after the preparation of their descriptive inventory.

* Roy, Sourin, *The Story of Indian Archaeology*, New Delhi, p. 76.

After Lytton assumed the charge of Governor-General in 1876, he enacted the Treasure Trove Act of 1878 which authorized the Government to claim possession of any treasure thus unearthed which exceeded ten rupees in value. Besides, Lytton decentralized the Archaeological Survey and made the local governments responsible for the preservation of national monuments under their respective jurisdiction.

The activities towards care of monuments in India got a fillip after H.H. Cole was appointed as Curator of Ancient Monuments in 1881. During his tenure as Curator of Ancient Monuments, restoration and conservation works were effected to monuments in Sanchi and Agra, Mathura and Brindavan. Cole also emphasised the need of constituting a separate department or organization under the charge of Public Works Department in each province. He was of the view that repair and conservation work could be entrusted to them. Cole's tenure also witnessed a spurt in the conservation activities in many monuments. He prepared a list of monuments of intrinsic nature, which were worthy of repair and conservation and submitted to the Government for their concurrence.

After Cole's tenure had come to an end, the administrative functions relating to care and conservation of ancient monuments was transferred from Home Department to Public Works Department on 16 December 1884. However, this decision was recorded by the Governor-General on 4 February 1885 and vested the powers of allocation of funds by the Home Department for execution of the work relating to conservation of monuments by Public Works Department. Meanwhile, A. Cunningham retired from service. He had submitted a Memorandum on the Archaeological Department and on the care and conservation of ancient monuments. The Memorandum was to guide the future course of action with regard to care and conservation of monuments of archaeological importance.

On 15 March 1886, the Government of India appointed James Burgess as Director General, Archaeological Survey of India and he assumed his office on 25 March 1886. Burgess had a positive approach towards care and conservation of archaeological monuments. As Cunningham's activities in the field of conservation of monuments were confined to North India, Burgess concentrated on the archaeological edifices in South India. He performed his task with great zeal and enthusiasm, and undertook care and conservation work of dilapidated monuments in South India as well as in North India, especially in Punjab and North West Provinces. However, after his retirement on 1 June 1889, the Government of India took a decision for not filling the post of Director General of Archaeological Survey of India.

After Burgess' retirement, followed a decade of inactivity towards care of monuments. The Government of India, however, instructed the Provincial Governments periodically and drew their attention to the need of conserving monumental edifices which were in a dilapidated condition. Besides, the Asiatic Society, antiquarians and orientalists played a prominent role by giving their suggestions to the Government of India with regard to conservation of monuments. The Government of India reorganized the Archaeological Survey of India on 15 May 1890 and reviewed the functions of the Archaeological Survey of India during 1895 and 1899. The reorganization thus effected had a positive effect on initiative and responsibility towards the care and conservation of archaeological monuments.

The period of apathy and inactivity came to end with the assumption of Lord Curzon as the Viceroy on 6 January 1899. Curzon and John Marshall, whom he brought as Director General, together gave importance to the promotion of archaeological research and conservation of monuments as a "part of our Imperial obligation to India". Curzon evinced personal interest in archaeology in general and care and preservation of monuments in particular. A major step towards this direction was an enactment of "The Ancient Monuments Preservation Act, 1904" (VII of 1904). This Act was a landmark in the history of archaeology in India and in the field of care of monuments.

With the enactment of Ancient Monuments Act, 1904, the Government of India took keen interest towards establishment of the Archaeological Department on a permanent basis. The constitution of the Archaeological Survey Department on a permanent basis was an important landmark in the history of Indian archaeology. The efforts of Lord Curzon gave archaeology a status of scientific discipline which was so necessary towards the mission of conservation of monuments for posterity.

The study, based primarily on records of National Archives of India, reveals how the sense of care of heritage developed that included governmental participation, development and control of the care of monuments and its various enactments. Besides, the records throw considerable light on the deliberations of the central legislature for enacting the legislation.

CHAPTER I

Historical Retrospect, 1784-1807

Before we discuss the background of conservation/protection of monuments, it is imperative to state that the care of the monuments is a significant facet of archaeological studies. Conservation of monuments is undoubtedly the soul of archaeology. Archaeology is a study of scientific discipline and has made our country conscious of her glorious past by bringing forth the rich and chequered past of achievements in the field of monuments. Monuments in India have a highly significant role to play in recalling our cultural and glorious past.

Before surveying the administrative measures of the Company's Government during the 18th and 19th centuries, it is worthwhile discussing the etymon 'monuments'. Monument means anything that serves to commemorate any structure, building, statue, column, edifice, etc., primarily to keep alive the memory of a person or event in a country. It can also be attributed to mean a piece of scholarship, work of literature or science of lasting value and objects of special historical value. Historians and archeologists to define and determine the etymon of a monument put changing definitions and attribute determinants forth.

Some lexicographers defined monument to encompass "all immovable or movable objects, which have been handed down from a bygone period of civilization, and as characteristic production of their time have a special significance for the comprehension of art and art industry and their development for the knowledge of antiquity and for historical investigation in general, as well as for keeping alive the remembrance of events of outstanding interest".

According to yet another popular definition, "Monument is made to include all remains of bygone artistic periods, be they purely historical, as for example, inscriptions; or of importance for the understanding of past phases of civilization and art (pre-historic tombs, weapons and the like); or again of picturesque significance for the general effect of a scene or a landscape, as towers, gates, etc., or of value as a model for the present time in the domain of the formative arts or of handicrafts. The worth of a monument does not always reside in its importance for the art or the history of the whole land, but not seldom in its value for a much smaller area, or for the actual place where it stands (wall, ramparts, etc.)."

However, giving an altogether new dimension to monuments' definition, Prof. G. Baldwin Brown in the Department of Fine Arts in the University of Edinburgh had stated in July 1905 that the description of monuments includes, "not only buildings and other immovable objects but also movable objects of an artistic kind as small as examples of goldsmith's work, and historical relics equally portable, such as manuscripts. The monument is something that gives us pause, that bids us reflect and is a reminder of past or absent thing".[1]

The definition indicates one common ground and an important aspect that monuments are communication vehicles that bridge one generation to another and should be the primary duty of every Government in the world to make all round efforts for ensuring their protection. G. Baldwin Brown has aptly pointed out that, "these are heirlooms from the past and appeal to the piety and patriotism of the present. Their number can never be increased, but on the contrary as time goes on, they must necessarily become fewer. As the decay or destruction of any of them involves an increase of value in those that endure, so the care of them will become every year a matter of more and more urgent duty."[2]

It may be mentioned here that this study confines primarily to the care of old historical buildings of architectural significance along with cave temples. It, however, does not dwell on the study of technical aspects but covers the significant contribution of the Government of times towards administrative care of monuments in India.

MONUMENTS IN INDIA

India is renowned for the cultural tradition of heritage and civilization. It has magnificent historical monuments, similar to those in England, Germany, France, Egypt, Greece, Italy, Portugal, etc.

In the words of Lord Lytton, Governor-General (1876-80), they are "for the variety, extent, completeness and beauty unsurpassed perhaps unequalled in the world".[3] According to Lord Curzon, Governor-General (1899-1905), "I have often stated my opinion that in the range, the variety, the historical interest and artistic beauty of its ancient monuments India stands first of all countries in the world."[4]

The monuments have afforded a special status to India, which has become an indisputable custodian of knowledge and tradition and, therefore, commands respectable status in the comity of nations. The architectural edifices have become an integral part of our country's heritage.

There were instances relating to monuments conservation during the ancient period of Indian history and in Mahabharata there is a reference to the protection of endowments of lands for religious establishment and duties of the rulers for the preservation of relics relating to heritage.

One of the oldest examples relating to preservation and maintenance of monuments was during the reign of Asoka. Asoka had drawn up an elaborate plan for the conservation of monuments and 84,000 stupas for the preservation of Buddha's relics. He achieved this through governmental decree and financial support.

Besides, King Kharavela of Kalinga carried out repair works of the structures that had been damaged due to ravages of weather and time. Another example was the preservation of a bund of Sudarshan Lake in Junagodh which was carried out by the Greek Governor of the State. The purpose of carrying out the repair works or *jirnoddhara* was essentially for public utility and welfare. During AD 1001, the circumbulatory passage around the *garbha griha* in Brihadisvara temple at Tanjore in Tamil Nadu was repaired by Rajaraya Chola.

The attempts towards conservation had religious motivation for repairs and renovation rather than their preservation in the pristine form.

Ever since times immemorial down to the reign of Shah Jahan, the Mughal Emperor, beautiful monuments came into existence. Although the rulers gave adequate attention towards their conservation and preservation, the edifices were also subject to occasional vandalism. Akbar was conscious of the rampant vandalism of the monuments when he built a magnificent temple in Kashmir; he had inscribed the following inscription which served as a warning to the bigots and vandals. He warned, "He who from insincere motives destroys the temple, should first destroy his own places of worship; if we follow the dictates of the heart, we must bear up with all men; but if we look to the externals, we find everything proper to be destroyed."[5]

Unfortunately, Shah Jahan's successors were not enthusiastic towards preservation of monuments. However, Francois Bernier mentions in his monumental work *Travels in the Mogul Empire (1659-1667)* that Aurangzeb made sincere attempts to organize regular conservation and repair works for Jama Masjid[6] in Delhi for the purpose of congregational prayers every Friday. There were, however, no signs of cultural awareness towards monuments. The physical state of monuments in the country was also not very encouraging.

Early Travellers' Account

Many foreign travellers visited India from time to time before the establishment of the Asiatic Society of Bengal. Travellers evinced interest in India which acted as a catalyst to the antiquarian interest of Europeans who were drawn towards India's rich cultural past. The discovery of India's cultural heritage should, however, be credited to travellers who traversed the distance to India for a variety of reasons from their respective homelands.

These travellers established India's classical image. They came to India in the garb of merchants, ambassadors, conquerors, rulers, chaplains, administrators, soldiers, poets and missionaries in search of philosophy and religion of the country. Many of these travellers recorded their impressions through lively tales, anecdotes and travel accounts. They came from all directions, especially from China, Russia, Arab, Turkey, Italy, Tibet, Germany, Holland, England, etc.[7] Their travel accounts exist in many languages and are scattered in different archives and libraries all over the world.

Abdul Razzak (1442) and Khondamir (1527) arrived from Herat Afghanistan. Abdul Razzak testifies to the prosperity of the Deccan and speaks of the grandeur of Vijaynagar with unfounded admiration. He observes, "The city is such that eye has not seen nor ear heard of any place resembling it upon the whole earth."

Ibn-Batuta (1333) arrived from Morocco, Africa. He wrote an account of his travels in his *Rahia* or journal. He speaks of the wealth and fertility of Bengal and of the extensive foreign trade of Calicut. He noticed the practice of *Sati*.

There were many travellers from Arab such as Sulaiman (c.AD 851), Al-Biladuri (c.AD 870) Abu Ishak Al Istakhri (c.AD 951), Al-Idrisi (c.AD 1150), etc. but the main was Alberuni (Albiruni) (c.AD 1017), author of *Tarik-i-Hind*. He came to India in the train of Sultan Mahmud and applied his scholarly tastes to the mastery of the Sanskrit language. He made a thorough study of Hindu philosophy and other branches of Indian Science. He proved himself to be one of the most gifted scientific men known to history. His special subjects were mathematics, astronomy, physics, chemistry and mineralogy. According to S. Roy, "The one Muslim historian to show a true scientific understanding and an objective approach was Al-Beruni. But the great Khwarizmian scholar preoccupied himself with the literary antiquities of the Hindus and scarcely directed any attention to their material relics."

Bairam Khan (1535), a Turk by birth and author of a *Diwan,* accompanied Humayun from Persia. He was a distinguished officer in the Mughal Court. Another traveller from Turkey was Sidi Ali Reis, who wrote *Mirat ul Memalik.*

Hafiz of Shiraz (14th century) came from Iran and wrote a *Diwan.* Mir Sayyad Ali Tabrizi and Khwaja Abd-us-Samod Shirazi (16th century), both painters, accompanied Humayun to India. Muhammad Kasim Farishta, a historian wrote *Tarikhi-i-Farishta* and another traveller, Mulla Zuhuri (17th century), wrote *Mina Bazar* and *Saqi-Nama.*

Chinese travellers such as Fah-Hien (c.AD 401), Sung Yun (518), Hieun-Tsang (630), I-tsing (675) and Hui-chao were the main. Fa-hien and Hieun-Tsang visited the *Kusanagra,* the place with a temple containing a large image of the dying Buddha lying facing west. Hieun-Tsang made two long sojourns. He testifies to the prevalence of the practice of *Jirnoddhara* by using old material of the earlier structure built in the first century BC. Fa-hien's account of his travels gives much information about temples and monasteries and repeats many Buddhist legends. Early in the fifteenth century, a Chinese traveller, Mauhan visited Bengal and was greatly impressed by the wealth of the Province.

After the discovery of the Cape route, there was an influx of European travellers to India. Their memoirs and travelogues about India became popular in their respective countries and provided necessary support to poets and playwrights who were in search of information about distant and unknown countries. After the discovery of the Cape route by Vasco Da Gama, European contacts in India became regular.

Numerous travel accounts and scholarly works were produced. During 18th-19th centuries, the activities of travellers from Europe to India could be gauged by the numerous guide books on India published by them.[8] Besides these, the travellers were potential publishers of their accounts of the country they had visited. These travel accounts were replete with plans and drawings of cities, forts, temples, etc. and stimulated an urge for further research about our country's cultural past. They vividly described the social, religious and political life prevalent in India and also the architectural splendour and the physical state of monuments.

Unfortunately, there were no methods with which these travellers could capture their insights during their travels as photography was not in existence then. Whatever experiences the travellers gained in the country were vividly described through their travel accounts. This led to insatiable curiosity amongst intellectuals. They read and evinced interest in India and its monuments in particular. These monuments also drew the attention of intellectuals in Europe towards India's rich cultural heritage. Indologists and social scientists were influenced a great deal and they undertook the study of our cultural heritage in a detailed manner. Accounts of a few early European travellers are replete with detailed study of our cultural past.

After the invasion of India by Alexander the Great and his successor Seleucus Nikatur around 300 BC, India had mostly remained elusive to the Europeans until 15th century. However, travel accounts of Marco Polo, the Venetian were written in AD 1295, which had innumerable references to India. Marco Polo hailed India as "the greater, the richest province world". Influenced by Marco Polo, the influx of European travellers to India continued unabated.

However, Portugal is to be given credit for exploring India by sea route after years of "stubborn endeavour and heroic perseverance" when Vasco da Gama anchored off the coast of Calicut in May 1498.[9]

The travel accounts of Portuguese travellers, viz., Domingo Paes, Fernao Nuniz and Mannuel Barradas who wrote extensively on the kingdom of Vijaynagar evinced interest amongst the intellectuals in Europe. Besides, Abdul Razzak had earlier written about Vijaynagar in early fifteenth century. *Dacadas da Asia (1602-45)* in 12 volumes was authored by Diogo do Couto, which contain detailed description of the country. Garcia da Orta (1535-1570) described the Elephanta Caves off Bombay coast "a very fine sight",[10] while another traveller Dom Joao de Castro who came to India in 1538 was impressed with the amazing work at Kanheri which in his view was one of the seven wonders of the world. Other notable Portuguese travellers were Fernao Lopez de Castanheda (1500-59), Father Antonio Monserrate (1580) and Father Jerome Xavier (1595) whose accounts contributed a great deal towards further exploration of India by European travellers.

A vivid description of the temples and architectural splendour of Goa and Cochin was given by Jan Hyghen Van Linschton (1583), a Dutch traveller. He wrote extensively on Kanheri and Elephanta caves. Other Dutch travellers were Abraham Rojernis (c.1650), Philippus Baldaeus (c.1660) and Daniel Havart (c.1680) who not only extensively described the religion, places and languages, but gave a vivid description of the monuments in South India.

After the establishment of Danish East India Company in 1616, Admiral Ove Gjedde, a Danish traveller, undertook an expedition to Tranquebar in 1618 and his travel accounts were published in 1622. In 1678, Federik Balling, another Danish traveller, published an account of his Indian expedition. Whereas, Carsten Niebuhr described the Elephanta Caves in detail which he had visited in 1763.

Walter Balthosar Reinhardt, 'Sombre' (c.1757) a German traveller, who served in the Court of Shah Alam II gave a lucid narrative of important events in the Court. Other notable travellers from Germany were Martin Behim (1498), Johannes Muller (1498), Hans Mayer (1505), Balthasar Sprenger (1505), Martin Wintergiest (c.1670), John Earnest Haxleden (c.1700), John Phillip Fabricius (c.1770), Christian Breithaupt (c.1770) and Johann Peter Rotter (1770) who wrote extensively about life in India. The contributions of German travellers towards description of India cannot be underestimated.

Nikitin (1470), a Russian merchant, gave a vivid description of Indian art and architecture and described the palace of the Sultan of Bidar thus, "... the palace is very beautiful with fretwork and its every stone is fretted and gilt all over it and very beautifully painted in gold and inside the palace there are sundry vessels". Besides, Johawn Philipp Wesdin (1774), a monk from Austria, gave a vivid description of India in his treatise, *Viaggio alle India Orientali.*

In 1616, W.P. Kirwritzer, a Czech traveller who was a mathematician by profession, recounted his travel accounts in his memoirs. Other Czech travellers Karel Prikryl, a theologian, and Vaclav Prutky – Remedius, a monk, also visited India in 1749 and 1753, respectively and gave description of Indian heritage in their memoirs.

Polish travellers also evinced interest in India. Pawl Palezewksi's accounts of the Indian society were published in 1610. Besides, Maksymilian Wiklinski, another prominent Polish traveller, visited India during the eighteenth century and recorded the life and activities of people in Pondicherry and Calcutta in his diary.

The Venetian merchant Marco Polo (1295), the first European to traverse and record the route across Asia, added much accurate information about the East.

Italian travellers also recounted their impressions about India. Nicolo dei Conti (c.1419) described the magnificence of Vijaynagar kingdom, whereas Ludovico de Vorthema (1505) gave a detailed account about Calicut, Malabar Coast, Cannanore and Vijaynagar. Andrea Corsali's (1515) correspondence with Duke Guliano de Medici of Florence lamented the destruction of an ancient temple in Goa by the Portuguese. Whereas, Pietro della Valle (1622) gave a vivid description of some temples in Cambay & Ahinely and also elaborated on the plans of some temples.

Niccolao Manucci (1656) as a 'Doctor'[11] was very close to the Mughals. He vividly described many great buildings that were under construction. His most valuable contribution was the description of monuments at Delhi and Agra.[12] His description of the city of Delhi, especially the Red Fort, in his *Storia do Major* is a major historical treatise during the period. He also described Sikandra near Agra in this treatise.[13]

Giovanni Francesea Gamelli Careri (c.1693), a prominent Italian traveller, focussed on the Elephanta and Kanheri caves. His description of the Kanheri caves contained intricate details and objectively described. There were other Italian travellers as Odorico da Pordenone (1321), Gerolamo di Santo Stefano (c.1499), Giovanni da Emploi (1503) and Fillippo Sassetti (1582) who wrote elaborately about India and its heritage.

Early French travellers, viz., Parmentier Brothers (Jean and Paul) (1529), Francois Martin de Vitre (1602), Francois Pyrard de Laval (1602) and Jean Mocquet (c.1615) visited India during sixteenth and early seventeenth centuries, and these travel accounts primarily focussed on Maldives, Chittagong, Calicut and Goa. The important travel accounts of Jean Baptiste Tavernier who visited India in 1631 makes for an interesting reading. In his *Les six Voyages de Jean Baptiste Tavernier,* he vividly described the flora and fauna of the country which encompassed the entire species. As he was a jeweller in the Court of Shah Jahan, he gave details on some magnificent jewels and description of monuments. He described the grandeur of the edifices of Bijapur, Delhi and Agra. He also described the city of Madras albeit briefly.

Francois Bernier (1656) as a Physician at the Mughal Court wrote extensively on the physical state of monuments in his monumental work *Histoire de La dermere revolution des etats du gran Mogul*. In his *Travels in the Mogul Empire (1659-1667),* he gave a description of the Red Fort of Delhi. Besides, he also gave a detailed description of the Jama Masjid. However, he was not favourably disposed towards the Indian painters. He stated, "The Indian painters are chiefly deficient in just proportions, and in the expression of the face; but these defects would soon be corrected if they possessed good masters, and were instructed in the rules of art."

Bernier, however, was the first European traveller who evinced interest in Sanskrit texts, especially *Rajtarangini* written by Kalhana, a Kashmiri litterateur during the 11th century.[14] Jean de Thevenot (1666) described the life, customs, murals and monuments in Delhi and Agra. He also appreciated the Indian painters. Other early French travellers who deserve mention include: Abbe Caire (1672), Francois Martin (c.1690), Abraham Duquesne (1690), Luillier-Lagaudiers (c.1700), Jean Baptiste (1752), Joseph Gentil (1752) and Comte Duprat (c.1770) whose travel accounts attracted the attention of many European intellectuals towards India.

Magasthenese (302 BC), author of Indica was the noteworthy traveller from Greece. He described the richly painted, columned palace and royal garden of Patliputra (modern Patna). A.L. Basham describes in his book *The Wonder that was India* that "Megasthenes wrote a detailed account of India which became the standard text book on the subject for later classical writers. Unfortunately no manuscript of Megasthenes' description of India has survived, but many Greek and Latin authors made abundant use of it and from their works it may be partially reconstructed. The record of the Megesthenes is of great importane as the first authentic and connected description of India by a foreign traveller."

Nearchus (326 BC), Dionysius (3rd cent. BC) and Cosmas Indicopleustes (AD 535-547) were other Greek travellers.

John Stewart (1763) arrived India from Scotland and wrote "Travellers to Discover the Source of Moral Motion".

Early travellers from England kindled an interest amongst the British towards the rich cultural heritage of India. The reports about wealth and prosperity of India by Ralph Fitch (1583) and Thomas Stephens (1579) along with the publications of the eastern expeditions of their European counterparts instilled in them a desire to share the lucrative trade of India. Subsequently, a body of London merchants applied to Queen Elizabeth I for a Charter granting them the privileges to trade in the East. The Queen acceded to their request and granted them a charter on 31 December 1600 incorporating the East India Company under the title of "The Governor and Company of Merchants of London trading into the East Indies."

Ralph Fitch portrayed the grandeur of Benaras, Agra, Fatehpur Sikri, Bijapur, Goa and Patna in a graphic manner while John Mildenhall (Midnell) (1603) despatched interesting accounts of Lahore, Agra and Ajmer to England.

William Finch (1608) was yet another English traveller to have a rare distinction of being the first European to discover the Ashok Pillars at Delhi and Allahabad. He left behind a journal which embodies one of the best accounts of architectural wealth of Delhi, Agra, Lahore, Gwalior, Mandu and a host of other places of historical interest.[15] He was, however, not attracted towards pagodas, which he described as "stone images of monstrous men fearful to behold, but adored by the Indians with flowers and offerings".[16]

William Hawkins' (1608) description of the Akbar's tomb in Sikandra may be counted as one of the rarest monuments of the world.[17] Besides Sikandra, Hawkins also described the architecture of Surat and Burhanpur.

Nicholas Withington (1612) also described the architectural marvels of Agra, Delhi, Ahmedabad, Tatta (Sind), Ajmer and Surat, whereas Thomas Roe (1615) described the pillar at Chittorgarh.[18]

Thomas Coryat (1616) visited Lahore, Delhi, Agra, Ajmer, Hardwar, Jwala Mukhi temple in Kangra, Mandu and Surat. S. Roy, the author of *History of Indian Archaeology* observed that "he hiked all the way from Alappo to Ajmer and did not leave a pillar or a tomb nor character unobserved in all Asia".[19]

Peter Mundy (1628) in his *Travels in Europe and Asia* (1608-67) described the garden layout in Taj Mahal and Sikandra very elaborately. He also gave a detailed description of the edifices at Goa. Henry Lord (1630) devoted his energy to the study of Hindu and Parsi culture, while John Burnell (1655) focussed on the monuments at Bombay.

John Marshall (1668) is regarded as the first Englishman to undertake the study of Indian antiquities. The first Englishman to have pursued Indian studies on a non-religious, non-political plane was John Marshall.[20]

John Ovington (1689) took active interest in Parsi art and culture and gave a detailed account of the Elephanta Caves. He gave a new dimension to the definition of the term 'pagoda'. He described it as "...the heathen temple or a place dedicated to the worship of their false gods, and it borrows its name from the Persian word 'pout' which signifies idol; hence 'pout Gluida', a temple of false gods, and from thence 'pagoda'".[21]

John Henry Grose (1750) in his *A Voyage to the East Indies* has hailed the Elephanta Caves as "a far more bold attempt than that of the Pyramids of Egypt".

Other English travellers, viz., William Hickey (1769), Patrick Russell (1781), David Price (1781), Donald Campbell (1781), John Malcolm (1782), Edward Moor (1782), James Forbes (1765), John Burnell (1655), Henry Middleton (1611) wrote extensively about the edifices and monuments in India.

William Hodges, a landscape artist, travelled to India under the patronage of Warren Hastings in 1778. He remained in India for six years and described the painting of various schools of Islamic and Hindu style. His select views on India contain a set of magnificent aquatints of scenic beauty which attracted other painters to India. He extended the knowledge of India to Europeans through drawings and aquatints of landscapes drawn on the spot. [22]

After he left India, he thanked Warren Hastings through a letter dated 13 November 1783 for extending patronage to him.[23] In 1783, Hodges presented to the East India Company five scenic landscapes of the Agra and Gwalior forts, Akbar's tomb at Fatehpur Sikri and the palace of Nawab Vizier at Lucknow. He was of the view that these landscapes "have not yet been represented by any artist who has travelled that part of India".[24]

Translations of Hindu and Muslim literary treatises were rendered into European languages particularly in English and were made available to the Europeans. This invoked the curiosity of European intellectuals about India's rich cultural past. Antiquarian awareness and consciousness had already pervaded in Europe but in India it took some time.

ESTABLISHMENT OF THE ASIATIC SOCIETY OF BENGAL

Travel accounts and translations of Indian literary works helped European scholars to understand India in social, economic, political, religious and geographical spheres.

Britishers were, however, front-runners in this field. Yet, they were aware of the evils and weaknesses prevalent in the Indian society. However, they were influenced by the spiritual, philosophical and cultural heritage of India. They had respect for the learning and culture of the country and undertook the study of law, philosophy, religion and literature in a systematic manner and study of architectural monuments. British scholars such as Alexander Daw, Nathaniel Halhed, Francis Gladwin, Charles Wilkins, John Zephaniah and Holwell, all studied Indology in its broader aspects and were aware of the inherent dangers of superficial studies of alien culture.

Dr. Samuel Johnson who undertook pioneering antiquarian efforts to promote antiquarian spirit in the Indian soil advocated investigation of India's past vestiges. On 30 March 1774, he recommended to Warren Hastings, the Governor-General, for the need for improving the methodology of surveying the remains of the ancient edifices in India and trace the vestiges of its ruined cities. "I can only wish for information, and hope that a mind comprehensive like yours will find leisure amidst the cares of your important station to enquire into many subjects, of which the European would either thinks not at all, or thinks with deficient intelligence and uncertain conjecture. I shall hope that he who once intended to increase the learning of his country by the introduction of the Persian language, will examine nicely the tradition and histories of the East that he will survey the remains of its ancient edifices and trace the vestiges of its ruined cities; and that at his return we shall know the arts and the opinions of a race of men from whom very little has hitherto been derived."[25]

Warren Hastings endorsed his views as he was conversant with Persian and Bengali languages and took a keen interest in art and literature. He encouraged the study of Sanskrit literature by European scholars and helped William Jones for the establishment of the Royal

Asiatic Society. Incidentally, William Jones was a friend of Samuel Johnson. He founded the Asiatic Society on 15 January 1784 in Calcutta*.[26] The establishment of a literary society in Bombay in 1804 and Madras in 1818 were modeled on the Asiatic Society, Calcutta. However, the Asiatic Society of Bengal was the first research institute to conduct researches in the field of history, science, archaeology and anthropology. In fact, this society proved to be an excellent training ground for educated Indians seeking to undertake researches both in arts and science streams. The Society had the active support and encouragement of Warren Hastings. After the establishment of the Asiatic Society, travellers from all over the world continued to visit India till the 20th century. Their travel accounts are still considered as authentic and original source for writing Indian history. The details of travellers visiting India after 1784 could be seen in H.N. Kaul *Travellers' India – An Anthology* (New Delhi, 1979).

In spite of these developments, no serious efforts were made towards the protection of monuments. Although the efforts of the Asiatic Society towards protection of monuments was almost neglible, articles were regularly contributed by the intellectuals on the state of monuments in "Asiatic Researches", which was launched in 1788 for wider dissemination for concerns regarding preservation of monuments. The articles highlighted hitherto unknown aspects of monuments elaborately. As a result, the interest enthused a great deal and people gradually became conscious on the importance of monuments. This was the Society's valuable and signal contribution.

The noteworthy personalities who contributed their articles on descriptions, survey accounts, illustrated drawings, measurements of monuments, etc. in "Asiatic Researches" and other publications were James Hoare, J.H. Harrington, Duncan, Moustuart Elphinstone, E. Fell, James T. Blunt, James Tod, Charles Warre Malet, Salt, Mool, James Macintosh, J. Goldingham, Mackenzie William Champers, etc. A museum was founded in 1814 to house the objects collected by the Society.

Thomas Daniell, a celebrated landscape artist, travelled extensively from Garhwal in the north to Cape Comorin in the south. He published *Oriental Scenery* with 144 Indian sketches; and *A Picturesque Voyage to India*. To him, India owes a wonderful graphic presentation of Indian scenes and landscapes of nearly 200 years back. According to S. Roy, "Daniell started on a larger canvas executing water colours of representative selection of monuments. He brought to his task a true painterly vision controlled by perfect draughtsman-like skill and even today his portraits of Indian architecture bear the test of comparison with most successful photographs".[27]

The Government of India undertook the task of measuring the dimension of the monuments. However, the Government took no steps on the preservation of monuments neither by individuals nor by experts. Their work was confined to description, measurements and drawings of monuments which would serve as a reference data bank. In future, when monuments were to be repaired in a scientific manner, archaeologists and experts would consult these drawings, measurements and descriptions as an authentic source. The importance of these drawings, measurements and descriptions gave a thrust forward towards spreading consciousness on monuments.

---

* Sir William Jones, a distinguished scholar, a lawyer, a jurist, an orientalist and a linguist did much to encourage interest in Oriental Studies in the West. In 1783, he was knighted and sailed for Calcutta as judge of the Supreme Court. With the help of some colleagues he founded the 'Asiatic Society' of Bengal on 15th January 1784 in Calcutta "for enquiring into the History...the Antiquities, Arts, Sciences and Literature of Asia".

SOME ENDEAVOURS FOR THE REPAIR OF MONUMENTS

Repair of monuments, however, continued and some glaring examples for effecting repair of monuments were the Agra Fort, Sikandra, monuments in the walled city of Delhi and the palace at Padmanabhapuram. This exercise was carried out without any archeological consciousness required for effecting such repairs. In January 1804, Lt. Col. Humfray of Engineers, Allahabad obtained sanction of Lucknow Rs. 2835-6-4 (Lucknow Rupees)[28] from Secretary, Political Department, Fort William towards the repair of the tombs of Sultan Khusrau and his family.[29] Another measure of significance was the appointment of Major G. Henry of Engineers on the special orders of Lord Wellesley, Governor-General, to supervise repairs of the buildings of Murshidabad along with the Palace in June 1804.[30]

As the English East India Company was not in possession of a fortress in the dominions of Oudh, the Nawab Vizier Sadit Ali Khan of Oudh, in pursuance of a Treaty on 21 February 1798 agreed for improvements in the Fort precincts. The Nawab agreed to an advance of money amounting to Rs. 8 lakhs Oudh *sicca* rupees.[31] Nawab Ali Sadit Khan further sanctioned Rs. 3 lakhs Oudh *sicca* Rupees to carry out repair works of the Fort of Fatehgarh.[32] In Punjab, especially the French and Italian generals in the service of Maharaja Ranjit Singh carried out archaeological "investigations" though not in a scientific manner.[33]

There were also cases of vandalism at the Stupa of Sarnath, near Benaras. In 1794, Jagat Singh, Minister of Raja Chait Singh of Benaras, demolished it for reclaiming building materials. It was a case of vandalism on the part of the Raja. However, the building objects were rescued by the British Resident Jonathan Duncan and later presented to the Asiatic Society.[33] This was a glaring example of vandalism committed by the Raja.

French and Italian generals who were in the service of Maharaja Ranjit Singh also organized archaeological excavations, though not methodically in a scientific manner.[34]

Besides, when Maharaja Ranjit Singh built the Golden Temple at Amritsar, he razed building religious shrines owned by Muslims.[35]

The first major effort, however, for the preservation of monuments was undertaken in 1808 during the tenure of Lord Minto I, the Governor-General. The Taj Committee was appointed for the repair of Taj Mahal during his Governor-Generalship.

NOTES AND REFERENCES

1. "The Care of Ancient Monuments" by G. Baldwin Brown, 1905, pp. 17-18.
2. *Ibid.*, pp.3.
3. Department of Finance and Commerce, Expenditure A, December 1878, No. 570.
4. Curzon Collection, MSSEUR F 111/420 in N.A.I. Acc.No.1643 (Microfilm). Home, Archaeology and Epigraphy, Deposit, October 1905, No.15.
5. "Dara Sukoh" by K.R. Qaunungo, 1935, pp. 401-2.
6. Some authors such as Michael Alexander and Philip Davies have written it as "Jami Masjid".
7. "Travellers' India". An Anthology, edited by H.K. Kaul, 1979, pp. xxi.
8. *Ibid.*, pb. XXX.
9. "History of India under the Company and the Crown" by P.E. Roberts, pb. 14-15.
10. "Colloquies on the Simples and Drugs of India" by Gracia da Orta, 1913, pp. 444.
11. He claims to have invented the enema.
12. "Delhi and Agra; A Travellers' Companion" selected and introduced by Michael Alexander, pp. 58.
13. *Ibid.*, pp. 223.
14. "The Asiatic Society of Bengal and the discoveries of India's past" by O.P. Kejariwal, pp. 127.

15. "The story of Indian Archaeology, 1784-1947" by Sourendranath Roy, p. 7.
16. "Early travels in India, 1583-1619". Ed. by William Foster, p. 155.
17. *Ibid.*
18. "A History of Indian Archaeology", by Dilip K. Chakravarti, p. 10 (cited from Della Valle 1664), p. 355.
19. "The Story of Indian Archaeology, 1784-1947" by Sourendranath Roy, p. 7.
20. "The Asiatic Society of Bengal, 1784-1838" by O.P. Kejariwal, p. 18.
21. "A History of Indian Archaeology" by Dilip K. Chakravarti, p. 8 (cited from Gough, 1785, p. 4).
22. "Travels in India during the years, 1780-83" by William Hodges, pp. 151-153.
23. Home, Public, B. 13 November 1783, No. 50, pp. 1-5.
24. *Ibid.*
25. Original in British Museum. Additional manuscripts 29196, ib-2; microfilm copy available in the National Archives of India displayed at the Archaeological Centenary Exhibition held in New Delhi in December, 1961-January, 1962.
26. Home, Public, 20 February 1784, Nos. 90-91.
27. "History of Indian Archaeology, 1784-1947" by S. Roy, p. 19.
28. **Coins:** The currency arrangements were as yet anything but uniform. The rupees issued from the Company's mints were, at the close of this period, still of four different standards and weight. The Murshidabad or Sikka rupee, struck at the Calcutta mint, represented the old Mughal coin; the Farrukhabad mint in the upper provinces followed the standard of the Lucknow rupee struck by the wazirs of Oudh; the 'Surat' rupee was the standard of the Bombay Presidency and the 'Arcot' that of Madras; while in addition there was considerable circulation of coin struck by native sovereigns. The Company's accounts were generally kept in "current rupees, but these represented merely the estimated value of the standard coin after making allowance for wear". (General memorandum on the 'development of British Administration in India and on the origin and functions of the India Government' by W.S. Meyer, C.I.E., I.C.S., Decentralization Committee for the Royal Commission on Decentralization; 1907, p. 20).

    Uniform Coinage: In 1835, a uniform rupee coinage was introduced based on the Madras or Arcot rupee and from this period may be dated the centralized control of the Government of India over coinage matters (*Ibid.*, p. 24).
29. Foreign, Political, 17 May 1804, Nos. 70-71.
30. Foreign, Political, 21 June 1804, No. 17.
31. Hyderabad Residency, Vol. No. 16, pp. 103-104.
32. *Ibid.*
33. Asiatic Review, January 1921, pp. 82-83.
34. *Ibid.*
35. Curzon's speech delivered at a meeting of the Asiatic Society of Bengal at Calcutta, the 7th February 1900. (Proceedings, Department of Revenue and Agriculture, Archaeology & Epigraphy, January 1901, pp. 21-27, Calcutta, Office of the Superintendent of Government Printing, India, 1901).

CHAPTER II

Protection and Repair of Monuments

1. MAJOR PROJECTS DURING THE COMPANY'S PERIOD, 1808-1843

During the period, emphasis was laid on preservation of literary works on monuments. Besides, not much attention was given to the programme of preservation of monuments. Even H.T. Colebrooke, member of the Asiatic Society, admitted this fact and stated that in the absence of authentic evidence for documenting the history of Hindu race, due importance to monuments by the Company's administration should be justifiable. The scattered information on monuments could be easily gleaned from the writings on some edifices, which are readily available.[1]

A turning point, however, came when Lord Minto was appointed Governor-General on 31 July 1807.[2] Many important projects for the protection of monuments were undertaken during his tenure as Governor-General.

TAJ AND MOTI MASJID

The Company's administration authorised on 15 July 1808 an establishment and sanctioned Rs. 477.10 annas[3] per month for the upkeep of gardens in the environs of Taj Mahal and also towards cleaning the monuments twice a year.*

The actual repair works were undertaken when Lord Minto constituted a Taj Committee in 1808 for the care and protection of Taj Mahal. A considerable amount was spent exclusively for carrying out the repair works of Taj Mahal. This was the first time that any project for carrying out the repair works was undertaken in India during the Company's rule in India. Taj Mahal always remained a priority area and got serious attention in comparison with other monuments by Company's Government.

---

* The establishment thus sanctioned by the Company comprise of Daroga – Rs. 25, 2 Munshis – Rs. 6, 32 Khadims – Rs. 64, 12 pensioners – Rs. 23.10; 2 Durbans – Rs. 6; 2 bhistis – Rs. 6; 8 sweepers – Rs. 24; 1 Head *Mali* – Rs. 6; 1 *Mali* (Assistant) – Rs. 5; 30 *Malis* – Rs. 120; 12 Bullockmen – Rs. 48; Petty charges – Rs. 4; 40 Bullocks with fodder – Rs. 140 = Total: Rs. 477.10

The Taj Committee, as constituted under the orders of Lord Minto, comprised of I. Wanchope and A. Ross of Engineers and Lt. Col. G.S. Browne, who was commanding at Agra as members. Later on, T. Perry, Judge and Magistrate, Agra and R. Martin, Collector, Agra were inducted as members.[4]

On the recommendations of the Taj Committee, Lt. Steel of Engineers was asked by Lord Minto to submit a report detailing the repair works required to be instituted in Taj Mahal and also other buildings in its vicinity. Accordingly, Steel prepared a report taking into consideration all the relevant facts and submitted his report alongwith an estimate for an expenditure of Rs. 1,00,000/- approximately to be incurred for the purpose.

Lord Minto forwarded this report to Col. A. Kyd, Acting Chief Engineer for expert comments and directed him to examine the various buildings in the vicinity of Taj Mahal and tender his expert opinion to Taj Committee for carrying out the necessary repairs. Accordingly, Kyd surveyed the building in the periphery of the Taj and recorded his observations. He also submitted an estimate for Rs. 83,500/- for carrying out the repair works (Please see Appendix-I).

The report of Kyd was forwarded to Taj Committee on 24 November 1808 along with the recommendations incorporated in the report submitted by Lt. Steel of Engineers. The report thus submitted was in consonance with the report of Steel with regard to manner in which repair works to the buildings would be carried out.[5] In the opinion of Kyd, that work involved was novel indeed and correct estimates of repair works could not be given and that this estimate of Rs. 83,500/- was on a lower side while comparing with the estimate of Rs. 1,00,000/- submitted by Steel, which was definitely higher.

Kyd was in favour of keeping an establishment comprising expert workmen on a monthly salary under the supervision of an Engineer Officer. In this regard, he suggested that initially the repairs to the drain and domes of Taj to be effected and gradually in a few months' time, the repairs to the entire edifice of Taj would be completed. He was further of the opinion that this methodology would enable us to calculate the time and money taken for effecting the repair works, which in his estimate could be completed in a span of three years.[6]

After considering the report of Col. Kyd, Taj Committee expressed its views to George Dowdeswell, Secretary to Government at Fort William on 27 October 1809, thereby negating the Kyd's views on the permanent establishment for repair of Taj as unnecessary.[7] The Taj Committee apprised George Dowdeswell that they suspended the repair works for the purification of Masjid and Jumayat Khana located in the environs of Taj. This measure would avoid unnecessary expenses to be incurred by the Government.[8]

On a similar analogy, the Taj Committee discontinued the practice of payment of allowances to the establishment for conducting religious ceremonies in these monuments.[9] Finally, however, on 21 November 1809, the Vice-President in Council authorised the Taj Committee for undertaking repairs at the Taj Mahal as advised by Colonel Kyd, and ordered that the Engineer Officer stationed at Agra would execute necessary repair works and would apply for financial sanction.[10] On 6 April 1810, Lt. Joseph Taylor of Engineers was nominated to superintend the execution of repairs under the control of Captain Steel, Garrison Engineer, Agra and gave express orders to commence work without delay.[11]

Accordingly, Taylor commenced the work on the guidelines laid down by Kyd. However, Taylor felt that the amount thus sanctioned, i.e., Rs. 83,500/- was not sufficient for completion of work. This anomaly was brought to the notice of Lord Minto as well as the Court of Directors. The Court of Directors expressed their views through a despatch dated 23 February 1813 that they had already sanctioned amount and emphasised that the edifices in India were beautiful and ornamental piece of architecture and should be preserved in the best possible manner and saved from being dilapidated.[12]

In September 1813, Taylor noticed that much repair work remained to be done and that an expenditure amounting to Rs. 83,500/- as estimated by Col. Kyd was not in consonance with the estimated expenditure after completion of the repair works. It was felt that Steel's estimate, i.e., Rs. 1,00,000/- was correct. Taylor demanded additional expanses for completion of repair works. Initially, Lord Minto was not in favour of granting the requisite amount but soon sanctioned an additional expense, thus requisitioned Rs. 19,648/- as he was not in favour leaving the repair works midway in imperfect and incomplete condition.[13]

Estimates of the additional expenses was as follows:

Excess disbursed in the repair of the spire	Rs. 2,000/-
An account of the repairs of the fountains and stone network railings not included in the estimate	Rs. 5,248/-
Additional sum required by the repair of the wall on the river face	Rs. 1,500/-
For the repair of two bastions at the two ends of the river face	Rs. 5,700/-
For the repair of two pavilions connecting with the bastions	Rs. 3,700/-
Miscellaneous repair	Rs. 1,500/-
Total	**Rs. 19,648/-**

Lord Minto wanted to levy[14] a tax on the persons including Indians and European visiting the Taj. The money thus realised could be utilised for carrying out repairs and not transferred to State Exchequer for being used for other purposes.[15]

Taylor completed the remaining repair works towards the end of 1814. At his instance, a Committee with a nomenclature "Committee of Survey" was appointed by Lt. Col. Cuppage, Commanding Officer at Agra, for the purpose of inspecting and reporting about the progress of the repair works of the edifice. The Committee comprised Major D. Macleod of 11th Native Infantry as its President and Captain W. Tallemach of Artillery, Captain, A. Owen of 13th Native Infantry, Lt. I. Land of 11th Native Infantry and Lt. F.W. Fordyce as members.[16]

Lt. Taylor laid before the Survey Committee, a copy of Colonel Kyd's letter of 24 November 1808 addressed to the Taj Committee incorporating guidelines for repair and pointed out the portions of the edifice and other buildings situated in its environs which were to be repaired at the instance of the Government for carrying out the necessary repair works. Therefore, the Committee proceeded with the task of examining the several portions of the edifice which required repair works and initially commissioned the repair of roof and domes (Please see Appendix-II).

After having inspected the portions of the edifice which required repair works, the Committee lauded the repair works executed by Lt. Taylor "in the best and most substantial manner".[17]

On 10 November 1814, Lt. Taylor communicated to the local agents about the completion of civil repair works in a substantial manner and his endeavours to procure ebony wood from Bundelkhand for the new doors of Taj and his plans to procure the wood from Monghyr during his visit to Calcutta.[18]

Taylor submitted the final accounts of the expenditure towards repair works rendered by him. He indicated that the amount authorised by the Government on 21 November 1809 and

23 October 1813 amounted to Rs. 1,03,148/-. A total sum of Rs. 1,00,583/- 4 annas 11 paise was spent in the repair works leaving a balance of Rs. 2,564/-, 11 annas 1 paisa.[19] Besides, Taylor volunteered his services for any work which may be required to be executed as he had carried out at Taj Mahal.

The local agents recommended that Lt. Taylor had been authorised to procure ebony for the construction of new doors for the interior of that building and got it fabricated in Calcutta because the designs of doors which were to be made of plated copper and embellished with gilt copper moulding could not be executed by any artisan in and around Agra.[20]

The Board of Commissioners promptly endorsed the views of the local agents and duly informed the Vice-President in Council. On 26 January 1815, Secretary to Council, Ceded and Conquered Provinces informed that the Governor-General might visit the city of Agra to inspect Taj Mahal and requested him to sanction additional sum for repair and beautification of the edifice. They further added that the local agents at Agra would furnish additional information about the expenditure incurred and for additional expenditure for effecting repair and improvement of Taj Mahal may also be sanctioned.[21] Accordingly, the Vice-President in Council admitted the accounts in question as per details furnished.

Sum authorized by the Government on the 21 November 1809 and 23rd October 1813	1,03,148
Actual amount expended in the repair	1,00,583-4-11
Leaving a surplus of	2,564-11-1

He further instructed the Board of Commissioners that the balance of Rs. 2,564.11 annas 1 paisa was to be kept as reserve deposit for carrying out additional repairs or improvement as per future instructions.[22] Marquess of Hastings, Governor-General did visit Agra and inspected the monuments and he was appreciative of the efforts of Taylor in carrying out the repair works.[23] The local agents escorted the Governor-General.

On the basis of the suggestions of local agents as well as his on the spot assessment estimated, further repairs were required to be undertaken by the Government.[24]

The Governor-General left behind a memorandum comprising instructions with the local agents that a fresh estimate of the expenses likely to be incurred should be submitted in consultation with Captain Phipps, the Barrack Master. In the memorandum of instructions, Governor-General did not confine its scope to Taj Mahal and the building in its environs but also to the magnificent monuments in and around the vicinity of Agra, i.e., Moti Masjid, Sikandra, Fatehpur Sikri, the tomb of Salim Chisti, etc.[25]

As per instructions of the Governor-General, the local agents convened a meeting with Captain Phipps for assessing the extent of repairs required for the monuments and preparation of an estimate of expenses likely to be involved in the execution of repair works. The estimates thus prepared by the local agents along with Captain Phipps incorporated the instructions of the Governor-General[26].

The local agents classified several items of repairs into separate and distinct items of expenditure and those items of expenditure which were found unnecessary were excluded from the estimate. Thereafter, the estimates were submitted to the Governor-General on 4 March 1815 wherein they recommended an expenditure of Rs. 19,800/- for Taj (a surplus amount of Rs. 2,564 was already kept in deposit), Rs. 3,960/- for Moti Masjid and Rs. 20,000/- for Akbar's mausoleum at Sikandra. No amount was indicated for effecting repair works for the Salim

Chisti Dargah at Fatehpur Sikri as they felt that the Management Committee of the Dargah had in its jurisdiction numerous endowments which were adequate for the maintenance of this edifice[27] (Appendix III).

Marquess of Hastings felt that it was incumbent upon all the local governments to ensure that the monuments of national pride should not be neglected and necessary repair works should be executed, whenever it was found necessary. He was further of the view that no nation should neglect its monuments of national pride and should ensure that they remain in a state of perfection. The views of the Governor-General were conveyed by C.M. Ricketts, Secretary to the Governor-General, to Sir Edward Colebrook and John Deane, Commissioners for the Ceded and Conquered Provinces on 4 April 1815.[28]

Marquess of Hastings accepted the recommendations of the local agents for carrying out the repair works of these edifices. He, however, had certain reservations with regard to rebuilding of cupolas at the southern end of the garden for which an estimate of Rs. 10,000/- out of allocated funds amounting to Rs. 19,800/- was submitted by the local agents. The Governor-General felt that it was not necessary as it did conform to the uniformity and beauty of the garden and this item of repair work should not be executed at all.[29]

The Governor-General further instructed that Captain Phipps, the Barrack Master, should commence the repair work and the services of Lt. Taylor should also be utilised after his return to Agra from Madras. He felt that Taylor had evinced "so much of interest, science and taste".[30] On 28 April 1815, the decision of the Governor-General was promptly conveyed to Lt. Taylor.[31]

Capt. P. Phipps Barrack Master apprised the local agents about the dilapidated condition of the walls of Moti Masjid that had fallen due to seepage of water through the walls and brick masonry, and the urgent need of effecting repair works. Phipps elaborated that the stone wall of Moti Masjid had fallen and continued to fall due to disrepair. This would affect about 600 square feet superficial of the wall. Some measures were to be taken immediately before the rains.[32]

Taylor returned from Madras. Before commencing the repair work with the estimates prepared by Captain P. Phipps and local agents, he decided to request the local agents on 20 June 1815 in order to know:

> If I am to carry on these repairs according to my own judgement or that of the local agents. If of the latter, I must beg they may be made to me in writing, for the directions I have received will not, in my opinion complete them or reflect any credit on my works and the approbation His Lordship was pleased to express with regard to the Taj, I do not wish to lose in the repairs to the Moti Masjid.[33]

The local agents on 22 June 1815 gave a detailed description of the repair works of the Moti Masjid as prescribed by the Governor-General and requested that there should be no deviation from the prescribed mode of effecting repair works without the express permission of the authorities concerned.[34]

Thereafter, Lt. Taylor resumed the necessary repair works. The Taj Mahal and Moti Masjid were got cleared of roots of the overgrown plants. Besides, they were got repaired and renovated. The copper ornamentation were repaired and portions were regilted and burnished. Battlements (*Kangooras*) were polished with marble chunam. The staircases were polished. Old walls were re-plastered with slabs of marble. The terraced rooves were also got repaired.[35]

The material which were used for effecting repair works were Konkar (*Kankar*) chunam, Burrai chunam, marble chunam, *goor*, iron clamps, *moong* rope, hemp rope, *moong*, iron, gudgee, earthen pots, charcoal battasser, oil copper, hemp, pewter, borax, grease, rosin, sal, babool wood, gayroo, ghee, coconut, black paint, yellow paint, quicksilver, lake, marble and red-stone.[36]

Thereafter, Lt. Taylor on 19 August 1816, in his report detailed the repair works effected in Taj Mahal, Moti Masjid in the vicinity of Agra fort and submitted accounts of expenditure detailing each item of work effected. He also raised a demand of Rs. 9410 and paise 6 as advance money.* He further informed that an amount of Rs. 874 annas 4 paise 10 that remained due to him was expended in the repairs of the north face of the Moti Masjid. Considerable portion of that particular area had fallen apart after expenditure estimates had been submitted.

After examining the repair work which was to be carried out, he had noticed damages to the wall wherein the brick work had been fallen apart and was in a dangerous state. It was, therefore, felt necessary to remove the bricks and stones and get them replaced, for which the above-mentioned sum was expended.[37]

The local agents sought an explanation of Lt. Taylor after examining the report along with accounts of expenditure on the following day, 20 August 1816, pertaining to the repair works connected with Taj Mahal and Moti Masjid. The local agents particularly wanted to know the reasons for not taking up the cleaning of the interiors of Taj and repair works of rooms and stair cases particularly when an allocation of Rs. 2,500/- was earmarked for the purpose. Further, it was necessary to know the reasons for not furnishing the accounts for ornamental doors for which an allocation of Rs. 2,300/- was not furnished. Besides, the reasons for exceeding the expenditure beyond the sum allocated specifically for the repairs to be effected in the outer square of the edifice of Taj Mahal had to be described. Also, estimates for repair works towards Moti Masjid was prepared and an estimate amounting to Rs. 3,960/- was submitted. The local agents felt that the detailed explanation on the issues raised need to be given for consideration of the Board of Commissiners.[38]

Lt. Taylor submitted his detailed explanation on 24 August 1816 as sought by the local agents. He stated that undoubtedly he was entrusted with the responsibility to carry out the repair works of Taj Mahal and Moti Masjid on the basis of estimates submitted and sums allocated for the purpose accordingly. He contended that the estimates for repair works were drawn up in his absence and was never consulted on this particular issue of importance. He felt that rather than leaving the repair works in an unfinished state midway, especially when the expenditure exceeded the estimates, he executed the complete repair works.[39]

Lt. Taylor also added that the extent of damages to Moti Masjid was not known as the report of Capt. Phipps had no indication and information was thus not available. It was only when scaffolding was erected around the Moti Masjid for effecting repairs, the details for the damaged condition of the edifice was known. Taylor felt that the repair works could not have got executed at a lower expense as was given in the estimates made earlier.[40]

The local agents asked Taylor to submit all the relevant correspondence and the details of the estimate for carrying out the repair works in Taj and Moti Masjid.[41] The following day Taylor complied with the wishes of the local agents and sent the requisite correspondence. On receipt of the correspondence, the local agents forwarded the relevant papers concerning the

* Amount due to Lt. Taylor	-	Rs. 874-4-10
Further advance required for Moti Masjid	-	3102-4-10
Further advance required for the Taj New Doors	-	2195-2-4
For completing the outer square of Taj	-	2778-1-6
Staircase of the Taj Mahal	-	460-3-10

estimate of repair works to the Board of Commissioners on 27 September 1816 along with their observations.

The local agents reiterated that the repair works to be executed by Lt. Taylor was confined to repair of the interior of Taj along with the cleaning operations, repair works to the rooms staircases and fabrication of ornamental doors. The repair works of the outer elevation and square was outside the scope of repair works entrusted to Taylor. The spirit behind the repair works was to ensure that the interior of the edifice got a face-lift. As regards the repair of turrets was concerned, the local agents referred to the visit of Governor-General to Taj Mahal when decision was taken to postpone the repair of this item.

However, they recommended the payment of Rs. 874.4 annas 10½ paise to Taylor, which was due to him as the expenditure had exceeded the allocation.[42]

The Board of Commissioners submitted the entire correspondence, accounts, reports and explanations tendered by Lt. Taylor for exceeding the amount indicated in the estimates and also proposals regarding repair works to be executed at Taj Mahal and Moti Masjid to the Governor-General in Council.[43]

The Governor-General, however, lamented with regret that expenses for repair works executed on Taj Mahal and Moti Masjid had exceeded the estimated amount. He also observed that "it is, however, now probably too late to revert to the original design and the repair must be finished in the style in which it has been imminent". He, however, authorised Rs.6731.11 annas 3 paise as advance to Lt. Taylor on account of repair works, as detailed herein.[44]

Amount due to Taylor*	Rs. 874.4.10
* Advance regarding repair of Moti Masjid (deducting the expense of proposed doors	Rs. 2619.1.1
For completing the outer square of Taj	Rs. 2778.1.6
Staircases of Taj	Rs. 460.3.10
	Rs. 6731.11.3

* Estimated expenditure
Rs. 3,102.4.0
Deduction
Doors for Grand Entrance
Rs. 387.15.7
Doors for South Entrance
Rs. 65.6.4
Doors for North Entrance
Rs.29.13.0
Rs. 483.2.11

Remaining Balance: Rs. 3,102.4.0 – Rs. 483.2.11 = Rs. 2619.1.1

The Secretary to the Governor-General, however, informed the Board of Commissioners about the procurement of doors for Taj Mahal and Moti Masjid from Calcutta. He further advised them to give instructions to the local agents to forward plans for doors wherein the dimensions of the size had to be indicated along with the motifs for ornamentation.[45]

The local agents, on their visit to Moti Masjid on 28 February 1818, were not happy with the manner in which repairs to the interior edifice was being carried out. They noticed that workmen engaged for the repair were using rough stones with the result that the fine polish of marble was entirely destroyed. They, however, felt that it was never too late to put an end to the evil and accordingly requested Lt. Taylor to discontinue such operations connected with repair works. However, Lt. Taylor was of the view that he alone was responsible for what was being done towards the repair works of Moti Masjid. He further stated that if judgement of the local agents was superior to his own in so far as the manner in which repair works was being executed, then he would gladly follow their suggestions.[46]

The local agents further stated that since aesthetic beauty of the interior of the Moti Masjid was in stake, Lt. Taylor would be requested to discontinue the repair works inside Moti Masjid[47] (Appendix III, Statement II.2 Moti Masjid). The Board of Commissioners also apprised details of repair works undertaken by Taylor inside Moti Masjid to the Vice-President in Council. The Vice-President in turn cautioned Taylor that he should avoid any action that would have deleterious effect on the fine polish and that sheen of the original polish should be ensured in the interior of the monument.

The Vice-President advised both Taylor as well as the local agents that they should work in close coordination and shun confrontationist attitude, which could seriously jeopardise the aesthetic beauty of the concerned monument.[48]

However, after a lapse of four years, i.e., in 1822, Taylor who was promoted to the rank of Captain, created yet another controversy with regard to effecting repairs to the Taj. In a letter dated 18 March 1822 to the Company's Government, Taylor emphasised the need of having an establishment of personnel for keeping a close vigil and for effecting repairs to the monuments in Agra. He was of the view that the vegetation in form of grass and plants were found in abundance in the domes of the monument, which could have a devastating effect on the monument. Taylor, therefore, suggested that the vegetation growth should be removed periodically before they take firm roots. He suggested that this work could be achieved through erection of scaffolding.[49]

Taylor sought permission of the Government to indent strong ropes for ladders from the army magazine stationed at Agra for deploying in each of the domes of the monument concerned on a monthly sum of Rs. 100/-.[50] He also offered his services in removal of vegetation growth and ensured that the monuments would be in constant repair on a nominal allowance.

The Government immediately responded to Taylor's request. L. Lushington, Chief Secretary to the Government, instructed the local agents on 10 April 1822 to cooperate with Captain Taylor and take immediate measures to eradicate grass and plants from the monument.[51] The Government further advised the local agents to clear encroachments due to construction of several buildings in the vicinity of Taj Mahal. They were instructed to ensure that no structure was allowed to be constructed within the precincts of the Taj.[52]

The local agents, however, after inspection of the Taj and other monuments in its vicinity, assured the Governor-General in Council on 24 April 1822 that there were no encroachments and further stated that the reports lodged by Taylor were unfounded and baseless.[53]

The local agents, however, admitted the fact that there was a vegetation growth in the monuments particularly during monsoon season and to curb this menace, they recommended deployment of two masons for the purpose. They further contended that the masons thus engaged could also effect minor repairs to the monuments. Further, the local agents stated that this operation was effected in August 1820 and also in May 1821 and would continue regularly even after rains. For this, they were of the opinion that an expense of Rs. 150/- would be sufficient which is normally sanctioned by the Board of Commissioners as and when required.[54]

The local agents also brought to notice the menace of building encroachments in the vicinity of Taj Mahal. They stated that Captain Taylor was permitted to occupy one of the buildings in the periphery of the Taj, which is claimed by Taylor as his private property. The building thus occupied had an ugly appearance as it was having windowsills made out of thatched curtains and ill-conceived thatched roofs. Besides, the hearth in the kitchen was erected without permission. For his personal convenience, Taylor had removed the Baths from the fort. The local agents, however, informed that they had directed Taylor to remove thatched structures and the hearth from the building, as their appearances were not in conformity to the aesthetic beauty of Taj Mahal.[55]

Taylor was enraged with the reports of the local agents which accused him of lodging false reports to the Company's Government. He, therefore, of his own accord appointed a Special Committee of Survey to inspect the dome of Taj as well as the domes of the edifices within its environs.[56] He took permission to appoint the 'Committee' neither from local agents nor from Board of Commissioners nor from the Governor-General. This Committee comprised of Lt. Col. Sir Thomas Ramsay Bart as President and Captain John Sevinton of Pioneers and Captain I.Taylor of 2nd Battalion of 3rd Native Infantry as members. The prime objective of the Committee was to ascertain and report about the growth of vegetation on domes and terraces of Taj and other edifices within its environs. The Committee carried out the inspection and submitted their report on 29 April 1822. It contended that there was rampant growth of grass and discovered as many as 25 tufts of grass on the dome of Taj and on the domes of the other buildings also but in a smaller proportion.[57] On 29 April 1822 itself, Captain Taylor forwarded the report of the Committee to C. Lushington, Chief Secretary to the Government and stated that this report would dismiss all the allegations levelled against him by the local agents. He further clarified that the local agents were not fully equipped with the machinery to remove the grass atop domes nor they had the requisite expertise to restore the mosaic work of the interiors. He concluded by stating that it was the precise reason that an establishment comprising of skilled workmen was requisitioned.[58] Taylor also refuted the allegations levelled by the local agents with regard to removal of grass by them through means of a rope ladder, which he clarified that no such operations were carried out and that no ladders were in existence as contended by the local agents.[59]

The local agents, however, did not take the explanations of Capt. Taylor very kindly. Instead, they sought an explanation from Lt. Col. Macleod Commandant at Agra for exceeding their jurisdiction in conducting an enquiry. The local agents stated that they were themselves competent to exercise superintendence for the general upkeep of monuments in Agra as they were appointed by the Government for the purpose.[60] Col. Macleod, however, clarified his position in the Committee which was appointed at the request of Captain Taylor and further that the Committee had no intention to interfere with the authority of the local agents.[61] The local agents, having being convinced with the clarification tendered by Capt. Macleod, informed C. Lushington, Chief Secretary on 1 May 1822 that they were convinced with the contention put forth by Col. Macleod but not favourably inclined with the conduct of Capt. Taylor. The local agents were particularly unhappy with his action in centralising all the authority under his control.[62] They also refuted the submission of Taylor with regard to his assertion about the growth of vegetation in the domes and ceilings of the edifices of Taj and other monuments within its environs.[63] They particularly objected to the high-handed interference in discharge of the responsibilities entrusted to them.[64]

The Governor-General also disapproved the conduct of Capt. Taylor. In this connection, the Secretary of the Governor-General informed the local agents on 30 May 1822 that Taylor's conduct in constituting a Committee without the sanction of the local agents was irregular and unwarranted action on his part.[65]

Besides, the Secretary to the Governor-General also admonished Capt. Taylor on this account and warned him to be careful in future and exercise restraints in discharging his functions within the prescribed administrative limits.[66]

It seemed that controversy was over but that was not so. In March 1823, the Darogah of the Taj informed the local agents about damages inflicted on Taj due to incessant rains. The local agents inspected the damages thus reported to the Company's Governments about their observations and the nature and methodology of repairs to be effected. The damages were confined to inlaid ornamental work on the exteriors of the edifice of Taj which was originally ornamented with coloured stones but later when it was repaired, it was replaced with coloured **chunam** which had worn out and fallen off. It gave a bad appearance as compared to the original work of inlaid mosaic work. Besides, the joints of the marble slabs of the minarets which were originally fabricated with pieces of black stones were also repaired and replaced with coloured mortar which eventually weared off and fell thus exposing the cavities exposed to the vagaries of weather which might eventually damage the aesthetics beauty of the Taj.[67] The local agents in their report took into account details of the estimate submitted by Col. Kyd, Chief Engineer, in which it was decided to effect in economy in expenditure by improvising the repair works from the materials from dilapidated buildings. In this regard, they had suggested that the workmanship would be of prime concern and suggested to fill the joints and crevices with fresh pieces of coloured stones and marbles from the dilapidated buildings. The local agents felt that propriety of this suggestion was on the basis of experience and, therefore, this procedure of repair work should have been adopted earlier when repair work was earlier attempted and it should be done on priority basis.[68]

The Company's Government was seized of the gravity of situation in so far as repair works to be effected in Taj before the onset of rainy season and sought clarifications from the local agents about the repairs to be effected on Taj. The Government also referred to the earlier reports of the local agents in this regard and also the Report of the Taj Committee of November 1814.[69]

The local agents accordingly clarified about the repair works that commenced in 1809 and completed in 1814 and were unaware of the subsequent repair works effected on the edifice. They stated that while conducting the repair works, the old and new repair works should correspond with each other for ensuring durability and appearance in an aesthetic manner. Besides, they forwarded a sample piece of **chunam** of the dimension 3 feet by 2 feet purported to be an imitation of marble and inlaid stone that had fallen from the outer surface of Taj and from the minarets. The local agents expressed their apprehension over the durability of material thus used for the repair works as per recommendation of Col. Kyd and suggested consideration of repair works **de novo.**[70]

A Special Committee of Survey was appointed on 11 December 1823 by the orders of Lord Amherst, who assumed charge as the Governor-General on 1 August 1823.[71] This Committee was constituted to report on the state of physical condition of Taj and also the nature of repair works effected by Capt. Taylor between 1809-1814. The Committee comprised Brigadier Shuldham, Commandant. Agra and Mathura Frontier as President. Lt. Col. Anburey and Capt. R. Smith of Engineers, Lt. Col. Cartwright of 1 Battalion of the 24 Native Infantry and Capt. Thomas, Barrack Master of Agra Division as members.[72]

The Committee thus constituted met at Agra on 20 January 1824 and inspected the Taj for assessing the damages and repair works to be effected. It noticed the dilapidated mosaic work and the four minarets, which required considerable repair work. It also examined the upper roof, dome and rooms beneath the edifice. The Committee made comprehensive recommendations on the nature of the repair works that was to be effected in Taj Mahal[73] (Appendix IV).

It called upon the local agents to submit the entire correspondence that was exchanged between the local agents and Captain Taylor. In compliance the correspondence was submitted to the Committee. However, the Committee could not assess the quality of repair works as detailed by the local agents and stated, "It is not in their power to discover the causes which led to the misconception in the Remarks regarding the mosaic work, further than that the coloured cement and chunam must have been less observable when quite fresh and consequently bearing a stronger similarity to the original works."[74]

The members of this Committee were unanimous in so far as the state of preservation of Taj was concerned and also for its recommendations with regard to repair works.[75] However, two members of the Committee, viz., Lt. Col. Anburey and Capt. R. Smith, though they were in general agreement with the recommendations of the Committee, submitted a separate note to Brigadier Shuldham, President of the Committee on January 1824 on the extent of damages and the methodology of repair works.

In their minute dated 28 January 1824, Lt. Col. Anburey and Captain Smith contended that after surveying Taj and examining the repair works effected to that edifice, they felt that deterioration of the edifice was visible as the marble chunam had been used for repair works instead of stones and marbles. As a result, the joints remained exposed and state of disrepair was visible. However, Lt. Col. Anburey and Captain Smith submitted that the estimate of repairs submitted by Col. Kyd was one-third less than that submitted by Captain Steel and further Captain Taylor executed the repair works on the basis of estimates submitted by Col. Kyd. The estimates of Col. Kyd did not mention the acquisition of coloured stones and marbles for repair works, whereas Captain Steel's estimate did mention repair with coloured stones or mosaic work. They added that had Taylor carried out the repair works strictly in accordance with Kyd's estimates, the expenditure involved would have been ten times higher than that originally proposed by him in his estimates. They stated that procurement of mosaic material would have resulted in considerable loss of time and money as Captain Taylor had not been vested with any authority to purchase them and utilise them after processing with precision.

With regard to Col. Kyd's proposal for the mosaic work, he stated that fresh pieces of coloured stones could be inserted with precision and this could be achieved with little marble cement and coloured stones which could be procured from the nearby dilapidated edifices and structures since dilapidated structures did not exist in the environs of Taj. They appreciated Captain Taylor's efforts in repairing the mosaic work by employing coloured lime and gypsum for ensuring a finished surface. Captain Anburey and Captain Smith stated that Captain Taylor completed his assigned work in the best possible manner for restoring the edifice to its original beauty within his limitations.

Captain Anburey and Captain Smith in their concluding remarks stated that although the estimates submitted by Captain Steel for purposes of repair works of the mosaic at Taj was on higher side as compared to those submitted by Col. Kyd, the workmanship involved in this kind of repair work had to be taken into account for restoring the edifice in its pristine glory. In executing the work, Captain Taylor faced difficulties in acquiring and cutting stones for the proposed mosaic work which had no mention in the estimates submitted by Kyd.

Besides, Captain Anburey and Captain Smith in their dissenting note also stated that the local agents were not competent to analyse the repair works to Taj by Captain Taylor and also commented on the competence of Captain Taylor. They also contended that without a permanent establishment to inspect the edifices and report on their general condition, it was not possible to assess the physical state of monuments and the measures for their preservation could be timely undertaken. Towards this end, they proposed an establishment comprising artificers for ensuring that the monumental edifices are in a state of perfect preservation.[76] During the inspection of the Taj and other edifices, which were being undertaken by the Committee, Captain Taylor presented his case for his own defence. He stated that as the local agents had also carried out the repair works to the edifices, the Committee would not be able to report on the quantum of repair works, which remained to be executed by him. Taylor stated that the veracity of these facts could be had from Captain George Steel, Garrison Engineer to whom he had regularly submitted the accounts along with the details of the repair works effected. Taylor also gave details of the estimates for repair works submitted by Captain Kyd and also by Captain Steel. He analysed the nature of repair works as well as expenditure involved for carrying them out. He also stated that the Committee of Survey was satisfied with the repair works effected by him. The Committee had contended that there was nothing objectionable in the repair works and they themselves were aware that coloured cement had been used by Taylor for effecting the work. Taylor further contended that the Survey Report was as well forwarded to the local agents and the Company's Government who accepted the recommendations of the Committee without any objections whatsoever. Taylor also referred to the Survey Report of the Committee which mentioned that mosaic work was to be done afresh but did not comment on the nature of repairs effected through stone or coloured cement. He stated that the mosaic work was completely restored in stone as it could be easily procured and the remaining work was completed by utilising coloured cement.

Taylor also stated that the repair works to the edifice of Taj was completed in 1811, as in November 1811 he was directed to report to Army and consequently handed over the charge of the repair works to be effected by Captain Steeel as per directives of the local agents. The repair works in Taj was undertaken by Captain Steel and he completed the charge after three months on 28 February 1812.

Taylor also contended that Sir George Nugent, Commander-in-Chief visited Agra and he was appreciative of his efforts in completion of the repair works of Taj. Shortly after completion of the work in 1814, Lord Hardinge I visited Taj and expressed his satisfaction over the repair works at Taj. Besides, Lord Hardinge directed to utilise coloured cement for repair works at Sikandra as was used in Taj. This was conveyed by W.B. Bayley, Acting Secretary on 28 April 1815.[77]

Concluding his defence, Taylor revealed a contradictory statement that he had accidentally found underground a collection of stones of various kinds and stated he had made use of stones for mosaic which had been perfectly camouflaged with the cement for repairing the mosaic on the Taj. Further, the stones which were left behind in the godowns could be best utilized in future repair works and he had offered his services **gratis** in 1822 which the Company's Government did not accept.[78]

The statement of defence tendered by Taylor, however, did not satisfy the Committee as the fact was that earlier Taylor had claimed that no dilapidated buildings from which stones could be procured were in existence and admittedly that he found stones of various hues and colours, later. However, all the members of the Special Committee were unanimous in so far as the state of preservation of Taj and submitted their report to the Company's Government on 30 January 1824.

Lord Amherst, Governor-General, however, after considering all the reports, facts, complaints, allegations and counter-allegations, observed in a Resolution dated 29 April 1824 that the estimate submitted by Col. Kyd was not in consonance with the actual repair works executed by Captain Taylor. The Governor-General observed that there were lots of deviations from the original estimates and plans and Captain Taylor's statements of his defence were superficial. Lord Amberst lamented that an opportunity for repair works as recommended by Col. Kyd was lost.[79]

The Governor-General, however, exonerated Captain Taylor of his intent to conceal from the Taj Committee his action for substituting the use of cement instead of marble for carrying out the repair works and stated that it was for the Committee to determine the usage of cement in place of marble and that it should have been detected by them when the repair work was being executed.[80]

The Governor-General thereafter directed the local agents to report on the nature of repair works to be effected on Taj so that the reputation of the British Government was not tarnished in so far as ensuring preservation of the Taj edifice and also in conformity with the feelings of the Muslim population for the perfect state of Taj mausoleum.[81]

The local agents responded to the Governor-General's directives on 22 May 1824. They were of the view that at the first instance, the terracotta and mortar works should be removed and replaced with stones as recommended by Col. Kyd and the stones should be acquired from wherever they could be procured.

The floral designs which were filled with limestone on the exterior of the Taj edifice and on the minarets which were replaced by stones and black stone should be repaired in a way to ensure that marble was firmly laid in the edifice and minarets in particular. The expenses to be incurred could be considerably high but would go a long way in honouring the British tradition of preservation of monuments.

The local agents in order to enhance the appearance and majestic splendour of the Taj made concrete suggestions. These suggestions were made to suggest altering the entrance to Taj and a flight of stairs leading up to the marble terrace of the edifice.

The local agents also recalled their suggestions made earlier for the doors that were to be constructed which should be of ebony and ornamented with brass. They stated that although there were difficulties in procuring the material, but doors could be made of durable wood, which subsequently should be painted black and adorned with brass ornamentations. This exercise would greatly enhance the entrance to the edifice as the present doors were ugly and worm-eaten – a complete disfigurement to a magnificent building. The local agents further suggested that the water channels from the reservoir to the fountains should be repaired and put in functional order.[82]

C. Lushington, Secretary, Government of India promptly conveyed to the local agents on 17 June 1824 that these suggestions would be favourably considered and recommended to Captain Turner, Fort Adjutant stationed at Agra for executing the repair works of the Taj.[83]

Subsequently, the local agents informed Lushington on 19 July 1824 that the material required for carrying out the repair works of Taj could be conveniently procured from Jaipur and Delhi and stated that since it was an extensive repair work, the Local Mahajans would easily supply the requisite material for repair works at the site itself.[84]

However, the local agents prepared a list indicating the different varieties of stones along with the estimated price.

Marble Stone	-	4 Rupees per maund
Sung Soorkh	-	28 Rupees per 100 maund
Sung Moosah	-	4 Rupees 8 annas per maund
Sung Sulleman	-	1 Rupee 12 annas per seer
Sauz Burrutt	-	20 Rupees per seer
Sung Urree	-	2½ seers per rupee
Sung Patteney	-	3 Rupees 8 annas per maund
Ruttuck	-	4 Rupees 8 annas per seer
Sung Baddul	-	7 Rupees per maund
Sung Ukkeek	-	1 Rupee per seer
Khulloo	-	9 Rupees per maund[85]

The local agents, however, on 23 August 1824 regretted their inability to submit estimate for expenditure to be incurred in building material and expenditure required for the man power to carry out the repair works of this nature as particularly required for Taj.[86]

The local agents pledged their cooperation to Captain Turner appointed to execute the repair works on Taj. They, however, gave their opinion on the competence of Captain Turner, Fort Adjutant to repair the Taj as per directions of the Government although they felt Captain Turner did not have any scientific education.[87] On 9 September 1824, Captain Turner was appointed and entrusted with the responsibility to carry out the repair works on Taj. He was asked by the Company's Government to prepare an estimate of the expenditure to be incurred in that direction as the local agents had regretted their inability to furnish. He was also authorised to seek technical advice on the matter from engineers posted in Agra. However, the Secretary sought details of the availability of marbles from the dilapidated ruins in the Taj environs from the local agents and requested them to apprise Captain Turner accordingly.[88]

On 8 August 1824, Taj and Moti Masjid were struck by lightning followed by a severe storm. The local agents assessed the damages caused to the edifice as severe. The edifice of Taj was struck by lightning at two spots, i.e., on the dome on the north-west and north-east direction. On the north-west direction of the dome, the lightning struck the centre of a block that measured five inch thick. It then struck perpendicularly down and penetrated the inner dome comprising roof over the tombs in the inner chamber of Taj and struck down some portions of marble. The marble was broken and dislodged from its place and the crack was visible as it went up to the dome. However, in the north-east side the damage was less inflicted. Here, a large block of marble was struck and was dislodged from its original place, and crack was visible up to a considerable height. However, the lightning did not penetrate further.[89]

The main edifice of Moti Masjid was, however, not struck by lightning but one of the large cupolas to the south of the entrance gateway was severely struck. The spire was damaged and fell in the ground, and thus lightning penetrated into the dome and split it from top to bottom. The local agents undertook the responsibility of repairing the damaged portions and sent an estimate for the expenditure amounting to Rs. 500-700.[90] Lord Amherst promptly authorised the local agents to effect the repair works on Taj and Moti Masjid and advised them to take care that the expenditure did not exceed Rs. 700/-.[91]

It was soon realised that Captain Turner, who was entrusted with the responsibility of effecting repair to Taj, was indisposed due to ill health and possessed no knowledge and experience to undertake such repair works as he possessed no qualifications essential for executing the repair works as contemplated for the Taj and Moti Masjid edifices. Besides, Captain Turner could not even prepare an estimate of expenditure to be incurred for executing such repairs.[92]

At this juncture, Captain Craggier, Secretary, Military Board requested the Secretary, Government of India on 14 June 1824 to once again consider enlisting the services of Captain Taylor of Engineers who was now the Executive Officer, Agra Division. He requested the Secretary, Government of India to call upon Captain Taylor to send an estimate of the expenditure for repair works of Taj and was subsequently entrusted with the execution of repair works.

The Secretary, Government of India was not favourably inclined towards enlisting the services of Captain Taylor once again as he was embroiled in controversies. He, however, requested the Military Board to select another officer instead.[93] The Military Board recommended Captain Cheape of Engineers, Lt. Cantley of Artillery, Captain William Grant, Barrack Master of Meerut Division, Captain Thomas, Barrack Master, Agra Division and Lt. Berkett, Executive Officer but eventually they were not approved by the Company's Government. Ultimately, the matter pertaining to repair works of Taj was entrusted to the Military Board as it was the wish of the Government to have Taj put into a complete state of repair as recommended by General Kyd.[94] The Military Board, however, expressed its inability on 26 September 1826 as it was not qualified to prepare an estimate on the suggestions by Col. Kyd. The Board also felt as the plans of the building were unavailable and the work involved was tremendous, its execution and expenditure could not be effectively monitored by the Military Board.[95]

At this juncture, the Governor-General appointed Lt. Boileau, Garrison Engineer for the purpose and issued instructions to prepare an estimate of repair works to be effected on Taj and other edifices within its environs.[96] An advance sum of Rs. 20,000/- was placed at the disposal of Lt. Boileau so as to enable him to commence repair works to the Taj edifice. It was also decided by the Company's Government that Lt. Boileau would seek the help of the Committee comprising Lt. Col. Anburey and Captain R. Smith of Engineers as these officers were conversant with the architecture of Taj and well-versed with the techniques of repair works. Anburey and Smith were also keen on the repair works to be effected on Taj and were in favour of an estimate for ensuring the restoration of the beauty of the monument.[97] However, all these efforts taken were in vain. Due to non-availability of funds with the Company's Government, the execution of repair works was kept in abeyance.[98] An amount of Rs. 20,000/- which was kept at the disposal of Lt. Boileau for effecting repairs to the Taj was now to be expended on petty repairs of public building. The Governor-General sanctioned an amount of Rs. 3044.3.4¾ for renewing the bridge near the Taj edifice as he felt that the vicinity and surroundings of Taj should not be ugly and shabby as it badly reflected on the environs of Taj.[99]

Major I. Craggie, Secretary Military Board, requested a permanent establishment of workmen for executing repair works to the Taj as proposed earlier by Lt. Boileau. He also recommended the removal of scaffolding erected to the dome of Taj as he felt it could endanger the edifice. Besides, the Military Board recommended precautionary measures to prevent the buildings suffering from further decadence.[100]

Lord Amherst was succeeded by Lord William Bentinck as Governor-General on 13 March 1828.[101] The Secretary, Government of India on 10 April 1828 conveyed to Major Craggie, Secretary, Military Board, the observations of the Governor-General in effecting an economy of expenditure in carrying out the repair works to the edifices of Taj. Though, the Governor-General was in not in favour of any expenditure to be involved in dismantling of scaffolding and also the permanent establishment of workmen to effect repair works of Taj. The Governor-General, however, allowed petty repairs to be executed which were absolutely essential.[102]

It is worthwhile mentioning the fact that no major repair works were effected on the edifice of Taj after 1814. On the contrary, the Taj was on the verge of being demolished for the value of its marbles during the tenure of Lord William Bentinck as Governor-General.[103]

SIKANDRA

The first major repair work at Sikandra was undertaken during the tenure of Lord Minto in 1809. A Committee was constituted under the chairmanship of Lt. Col. H. Grace which was appointed in September 1809 for the restoration of Akbar's mausoleum and other edifices in its environs at Sikandra to its original form before it was occupied by the British Regiment of Dragoon. The Committee was entrusted with the task of removing all remnants of barracks which were constructed within its premises and restore the monument with the marbles and stones from the ruins. The Committee, however, confined its activities to the levelling of temporary wall, strengthening of pillars and removal of barracks within its precincts and clearing of filth and garbage left behind by the residing troops. Besides, it also carried out removal of building material strewn all over and repaired the breaches in the wall and filled up holes with masonry in edifices situated in its environs. The Committee also proposed the future course of action for the preservation of the edifice along with the structures within its environs.[104]

Lt. Col. Brown, Commanding Officer at Agra forwarded his suggestions on the Committee's proposals on restoration to Lt. Col. Worsley, Adjutant General on 24 November 1809. He suggested that the monument of Sikandra should be placed under the superintendence of Taj Committee without hurting the sentiments of Muslims. He also suggested that the monument be looked after by six to eight *khadims* (persons appointed to preserve the sanctity of tomb) belonging to the Taj Establishment for the upkeep of tombs and placed under the charge of a *Darogha* of Taj. For this arrangement, an expenditure amounting to Rs.15-20 per month be allowed for the additional duties.[105]

The Military Board gave instructions to remove temporary walls and enclosures erected by the British troops at Sikandra. The estimated expenditure amounted to Rs. 4399-1 anna 2 paise (Sonnet Rupees), which was approved by the Company's Government on 2 January 1810.

The serviceable material, viz., logs, doors along with their frames, windows, etc. which were salvaged from the razed structures were to be utilised for repairs to the monuments within the jurisdiction of the Agra Fort.[106] The necessary orders were issued for placing charge of the mausoleum under the Taj Committee as proposed by Lt. Col. Brown on 24 November 1809.[107] The Court of Directors, however, proposed that the repairs to be effected on the edifice of Sikandra should be effected in a similar manner as was done in the Taj. They further proposed to display a plan for its restoration at Sikandra. They were also of the view that Colonel Kyd's estimate of repair work should serve as a guiding force along with the Col. Steel's repair estimates.[108]

Marques of Hastings, Governor-General, instructed the local agents to prepare an estimate of expenditure involved in restoring Sikandra in consultation with Captain Phipps, Barrack Master. Hastings was of the opinion that Sikandra was a magnificent monument and it was desirable that the Company's Government should undertake its restoration.[109]

The local agents prepared an estimate of Rs. 20,000 for the repair of the monument and for preparing the same, they had taken into account the observations of the Governor-General on his visit to Agra[110] (Appendix III). The local agents, however, felt that the estimated amount would not be sufficient for restoring the ornamental designs which had been removed since 1804 in the tomb, but would be sufficient for repairing the damages to the edifice.[111]

Marquess of Hastings, Governor-General, accordingly granted the funds thus requisitioned by the local agents on 4 April 1815. While sanctioning the amount of Rs. 20,000/- as requisitioned, Hastings observed that the amount was only sufficient to effect minor repairs and not for the restoration of the monument to its original state.[112] He directed the Military Board and the local agents to ensure proper utilisation of funds and take measures for avoiding its further dilapidation which had been particularly due to the long stay of the Regiment of Dragoons, a British regiment. The repairs thus effected should bring the tomb to its original form and restore its pristine glory, he added and agreed that he would sanction further sum at an appropriate opportunity for carrying out the repairs. The Governor-General was of the view that "our Government is called upon to make some sacrifices for the preservation of this grand Mausoleum ... No step that could be taken by Government it is conceived will be felt more warmly by the natives than the attention to the tomb of Akbar".[113] The petty repair works were carried out by the local agents. However, six years later on 3 August 1821, Hastings observed that Captain Taylor should attend to the mausoleum of Akbar at Sikandra under the supervision of the Superintendent Barrack Division, to which Sikandra belongs, which had been particularly due to the long stay of the Regiment of Dragoons, a British regiment.[114]

The Secretary, Government of India addressed a communication to Captain Cobbe, Secretary, Military Board on 3 August 1821 itself. In this communication, the Secretary spelled out the guidelines to be followed by Captain Taylor for effecting repair works at Sikandra. The Secretary felt that the work should be carried out under the supervision of the Military Board and to be conducted under the general regulations of the Barrack Department.[115] Captain Taylor, however, assured C. Lushington, Secretary, Government of India that he would carry out this task with great care and attention, and would prove worthy of the Governor-General's confidence as reposed in him.[116]

Captain Taylor undertook the repair works at Sikandra in 1822 and he was placed under the superintendence of Colonel Penson, Superintendent, Buildings, Upper Provinces. A sum of Rs. 10,000 (Sonnet rupees) was granted for the purpose.[117] A. Cobbe, Secretary, Military Board instructed Captain Taylor on 12 February 1822 to undertake repairs at Akbar's mausoleum at Sikandra and also addressed a communication to Col. Penson for ensuring that Captain Taylor completes his assigned work at Sikandra and further that accounts and progress report of work are regularly submitted to him for inspection.

The local agents also permitted Taylor to commence the repair works in Sikandra and instructed him not to get himself embroiled in any controversy as was in the case of the Taj. They particularly instructed him not to construct any structure for his personal use as was done in the Taj.[118]

Taylor commenced the repair works of the mausoleum and utilised the material from other edifices which were in ruins for carrying out repair works at Sikandra. The local agents somehow were not in favour of this methodology adopted by Taylor for carrying out the repair works. Taylor, however, explained that he had taken the prior consent of the Governor-General.

The local agents, however, on 4 May 1822 addressed a communication to Captain Taylor that it was reported to them by Shaikh Mohammad and Shaikh Munna, Khadims at the mausoleum at Sikandra that the edifice Baradari Mulk Jahan had been razed for utilising the material and advised him to avoid such acts. They also stated that prior permission of the Government should be obtained before initiating such arrangements.[119]

Taylor, however, stated in his letter to the local agents on 6 May 1822 that the stones of the dilapidated edifices were earmarked for repair at Sikandra and were meant to be utilised for repair by the express sanction of the Government and hence it was not possible to stop the work at this stage.[120] On 8 May 1822, the local agents received a representation from Sajeewan Lall, a resident of Agra, that he was appalled to notice that the Baradari of Mallika Jahan Begam near Sikandra was ordered to be demolished by Captain Taylor and the debris of the edifice was removed at the instance of Captain Taylor. This fact was well known to the local populace of the Sikandra village.[121]

On the same day, i.e., 8 May 1822, the local agents instructed Captain Taylor to desist from carrying out the demolition of the edifice of Baradari of Mallika Jahan Begam and removal of the debris of the demolished edifice without the permission of the competent authority. They also drew the attention of Captain Taylor to the instructions with regard to the demolition of buildings issued by the Company's Government and utilisation of the debris for other buildings for repair works of monuments. The local agents firmly instructed to avoid such actions in future.[122]

They even wrote a letter of complaint to C. Lushington, Chief Secretary on 9 May 1822 wherein they stated the demolition of edifices in the precincts of Sikandra, especially the Baradari of Malika Jehan Begam carried out by Captain Taylor for utilising the material to carry out repair works at Sikandra. This was followed by a request to the Company's Government to restrain Captain Taylor to carry out such demolitions. Although there was no permission granted by the Government to Taylor, the local agents had complied with the request of Captain Taylor to carry out repair works but permission to carry out the entire demolition of the structure was not apparent against the letter and spirit of the Government's approval.[123]

Besides, Boodh (Bhood) Singh, a Nazul Chaprasi reported to the local agents on 13 May 1822 about continuance of the demolition of Baradari Malika Jahan Begam and when he objected to such work being carried out, he was informed that Captain Taylor had authorised them to carry out the demolition operations. Further, Boodh Singh represented his case to Crainee (Copyist or Clerk in a Public Office of Eurasian descent) who after consultations with Taylor directed Boodh Singh to report the matter to the local agents.[124]

The local agents addressed a communication to Captain Taylor on 14 May 1822 along with the translation of the deposition of Boodh Singh for carrying out the demolition operation and warned Taylor that eventually he alone would be responsible to carry out the restoration of Baradari Malika Jahan Begam.[125]

Thereafter, the local agents lodged a complaint to Henry Graham, Acting Judge and Magistrate in which the details of the case were enumerated and requested for a guard comprising provincial sepoys to be posted on guard duty for ensuring the security of the Baradari. They stated that "the buildings near Secundera form a part of the charge entrusted to the local agents at this station and by the Regulation: 19 of 1810"[126] (Appendix VII).

On the following day, 15 May 1822 Henry Graham, the Acting Magistrate addressed a letter to Col. Macleod, Commander at Agra to restrain Captain Taylor from carrying out the demolition operations of Baradari, thereby avoiding the posting of a guard of provincial sepoys for guarding the Baradari.[127] At the same time, Henry Graham assured the local agents that if a guard of provincial sepoys was still required, it would be sent immediately.[128]

The local agents also complained to the Company's Government on the conduct of Captain Taylor and measures taken to curb the demolition operations. They stated that they had desisted themselves from writing to Taylor as it would have created an unprecedented controversy.[129] In the meantime, Captain Taylor also lodged a complaint to C. Lushington, Secretary, Government of India on 16 May 1822 wherein he reported the gross interference of the local agents which was a great hindrance in carrying out the repair works at Sikandra. He stated that the material from the demolition of Baradari Mallika Jahan Begam was mentioned in his estimates for repair works submitted to the Government and it had the Government's express sanction on the matter. Besides, Taylor was also disturbed by the conduct of the local agents in requisitioning a guard of sepoys for guard duty at Baradari. He lamented that these acts of the local agents tantamounted to gross interference and were an impediment in carrying out his assigned duties. He requested the Government to restrain the local agents from such interference.[130] Taylor also forwarded to the Government the extracts of his report on the repair works and enclosed the estimates which he had earlier submitted to the Government. He even showcased that he had the sanction of the Government. He apprised the Government about the careless selection of 'redstone' that were of inferior quality and that they had been removed and replaced with good quality stones from the ruins of the neighbourhood of Sikandra. He particularly indicated the procurement of 14934 maunds of 'redstone' to be collected from the debris of ruins around Sikandra and transported to the restoration site at Rs. 6¼ annas per 100 maunds.[131]

The Secretary to the Governor-General addressed a letter to the local agents on 30 May 1822 and lamented the procedure adopted by Captain Taylor in destroying Baradari and using the material for repairing the Akbar's mausoleum. He felt that Taylor had exceeded his discretionary powers vested in him. The Governor-General also felt that he had hurt the sentiments of the local people, who held the monument as a sanctified edifice. The Governor-General described the actions of Captain Taylor as "reprehensible act".[132]

On the same day, the Secretary to the Governor-General conveyed the displeasure of the Governor-General in Council to Captain Taylor about the growing discontent and confrontations with the local agents.[133] Similar views were already expressed earlier to Captain Taylor by the Governor-General over his differences with the local agents on Taj Mahal's repair. The Governor-General also apprised the Court of Directors and condemned Taylor's conduct in defying the local agents.[134] The repair works, however, continued unabated. On 18 July 1822, the Governor-General conveyed approval of the recommendation of Military Board and sanctioned Sonnet Rs. 161 per month for the establishment towards repair of Akbar's mausoleum at Sikandra.[135]

Meanwhile, Lord Amherst was appointed Governor-General on 1 August 1823.[136] On the request of the local agents at Agra, he conveyed his approval of an expenditure Rs. 4,347.4.3 (Lucknow Sicca) on 6 November 1823 for the repair of a boundary wall at Sikandra which had crumbled down.[137] Taylor was displeased with the conduct of the local agents in executing the repair works without taking him into confidence. The local agents, however, maintained that they were directed by the Government on 6 November 1823 to execute such repairs and this did not amount to interference with the functions assigned to Captain Taylor.[138]

Besides, they also apprised C. Lushington, Secretary, Company's Government about the state of preservation of the Sikandra monument. They referred to the dilapidated state of the minarets and the deteriorating condition of the structures on both sides of the monuments. They particularly referred to the inlaid stones falling from these structures and laid emphasis on their restoration. The local agents further referred to the submission of accounts and progress of the repair work to the Military Board and stated that it was not necessary to submit these accounts to them. With regard to exercise of administrative control over Captain Taylor, the local agents were of the opinion that the copy of instructions and directives given to Captain Taylor should as well be endorsed to them and a monthly report of the progress of the repair works should be submitted so as to ensure exercising effective control over him.[139]

No positive response was forthcoming from C. Lushington, Secretary, Company's Government on the observations of the local agents. However, the Military Board apprised the Governor-General in Council on 21 September 1824 about the progress made in the direction of effecting repairs to Sikandra by Captain Taylor.[140]

Lord Amherst, the Governor-General expressed his satisfaction with the views expressed by the Secretary, Military Board on the repair works thus executed on Sikandra monument. On 17 January 1825, Captain Taylor reported about the completion of the repair works at Sikandra to the Military Board. The Military Board directed the Officer Commanding at Agra to assess the repair works completed by Captain Taylor. The Board gave directions to have it examined and inspected by a "Special Committee of Officers".[141]

Accordingly, a survey was conducted on the repair effected by Captain Taylor to the mausoleum. The Committee reported that the repair works to Sikandra were well executed by Captain Taylor and recommended an establishment comprising two bricklayers, two stone-cutters, six *beldars* and six coolies for ensuring that the monument was in perfect state and in perpetual repair.[142] A sum of Rs. 74 per month was sanctioned for the purpose.[143]

The local agents, however, objected to the Committee's proposal for maintaining a permanent establishment for keeping the monument in perfect condition. In their communication to the Secretary, Company's Government on 11 August 1825, the local agents were particularly in favour of reduction of the proposed establishment and suggested that having a permanent establishment of personnel for the upkeep of monument would result in expenditure of no consequence and lot of money had to be incurred on material and engaging temporary workmen viz. bhistis, etc.[144] The Governor-General on 1 September 1825 approved the modified establishment for the maintenance of the mausoleum as proposed by the local agents.[145]

After the repair works were effected at the Sikandra monument, Captain Taylor forwarded a bill on 25 May 1825 amounting to Rs. 57616.6.6 towards expenditure incurred in the repair of the mausoleum. While forwarding the bill, Captain Taylor expected a reward for executing the repair works as assured by C. Lushington, Secretary, Government of India in his letter dated 10 April 1822. Taylor also reported that he had utilised the marble blocks buried at the Agra Fort for effecting repairs. He also stated that these marble blocks were part of the consignment used for constructing the palace at the Agra Fort during the reign of Shah Jahan. These marbles were valued at Rs. 4680 (Sonnet rupees) by a Committee formed by the orders of Lt. Col. Macleod, Commandant at the Fortress. Taylor further informed that he was duly authorised to use these marble blocks for repairs at Sikandra, as this could effect a saving of a considerable amount and no marbles would be required to be purchased. He, therefore, demanded a share of its value for effecting such savings. Taylor also drew up a plan for effecting further repair works at Sikandra and for ensuring that the monument remained in perfect state of preservation. He recommended that inlay work of the south gate as well as portions of the monument on the east and west sides should be repaired by replacing their inlay work with red stone after being properly sculpted. He was of the opinion that the minarets at the gateway should be rebuilt to their original height. He added that marble for the purpose could be procured from the quarries of Sikandra in the province of Ajmer. He was of the opinion that a sum of Rs. 35,000 to Rs. 45,000 would be incurred for effecting such repairs though it was not possible to frame exact estimates for effecting a work of this nature.[146]

Captain Roberts promptly forwarded the bill sent to him by Taylor to Major Craggie, Secretary Military Board on 7 June 1825 and appreciated the efforts of Captain Taylor in effecting the repair works to the Sikandra monument.[147] The Military Board forwarded this case to C. Lushington, Secretary, Government of India with a recommendation that a bill of Rs. 57616.6.6 be approved and also recommended a honorarium of 15 per cent of the amount, i.e., Rs. 8642.7.4 for payment to Captain Taylor. The Secretary, Government of India recommended that for labour involved in the execution of repair works at Sikandra, Captain Taylor should be adequately compensated.[148]

The Governor-General approved the payment of bill amounting to Rs. 57616 annas 6 paise 6 towards expenses in effecting repair works at Sikandra. Besides, the Governor-General also sanctioned a remuneration of 15 per cent on the outlay amount as proposed by the Military Board.[149]

The petty repair works continued to be undertaken in Sikandra. During the tenure of Lord William Bentinck as Governor-General, it was proposed in 1831 to lease the gardens at Sikandra to the Executive Engineer at Agra for cultivation purposes.[150]

Fatehpur Sikri

When Lord Hastings (Earl of Moira) was the Governor-General, it was reported to him about the endowments attached to the shrine of Salim Chisti which were considered fully adequate for ensuring maintenance of the monument. The pecuniary aid from the Company's Government was, therefore, considered unnecessary. The Governor-General, however, felt that the local agents should exercise perfect vigil and supervision in order to ensure that the amount sanctioned under these endowments was not misappropriated[151] (Appendix III).

Agra Fort

Agra Fort required repair works on a larger scale along with the Moti Masjid within its precincts. The monument was noticed by the Company's Government during the tenure of Lord Minto I as the Governor-General. Inspection of certain portions of the fortress was undertaken by Lt. H. Grace and Lt. Steel of Engineers. A report was submitted to the Military Board on 17 September 1809 in which a specific recommendation was made for carrying out repairs of the Agra Fort. In pursuance of the recommendations of the Committee, Lt. Col. Brown, Commandant, Agra requested A. Greene, Secretary, Military Board on 20 September 1809 to initiate action on carrying out the repair works.[152]

A Survey Committee was thus constituted with a view to assess the repair works required to be executed at Agra Fort. A Special Committee was also constituted for the purpose of repair works on 30 October 1809 comprising Lt. Col. H. Grace as President and Captain G. Pennington, Captain H. Green and Captain H. Starke of the Artillery as members. Lt. Steel, Garrison, Engineer was also entrusted with the responsibility of survey work.[153] With the direction of the Military Board, Lt. Col. Brown instructed the Committee on 2 November 1809 to carry out the survey of repair works thus effected in a comprehensive manner.[154] Besides, the Vice-President in Council authorised a sum of Rs. 466.7.8 for repairing the two cavaliers of the Agra Fort on the river face.[155]

The Committee commenced its work, inspected the entire area of the Fort and prepared a detailed report suggesting repairs, alterations, erections and demolitions, etc. where they thought it was necessary and such repairs had to be effectively carried out. A Report was thus submitted to Lt. Col. Brown, Commandant, Agra on 10 March 1810 (Appendix V).

Besides, some suggestions were also tendered by Lt. Col. Horsford, Commandant of Artillery for carrying out repairs at the Agra Fort effectively. These recommendations/suggestions were similar to the recommendations of the Special Committee, which were submitted by them on 10 March 1810.

These recommendations related to the construction of a ditch/moat on the bastion, repair of gates and bridges, clearing of encroachments, repairs of the staircases, building of walls and parapets, construction of magazines in bastions, repair works of Amar Singh Gate and Bengali bastion of the fort, clearing of vegetation of the fort, construction of roads in the fort and delegation of authority to Col. Brown to get the repair works executed.[156]

Col. John Garsten of Engineers also gave his suggestions on the state of repairs and his views for carrying out the repair works at Agra Fort.[157]

Thereafter, Lt. Col. Brown, Commandant, Agra forwarded the Committee's report to A. Greene, Secretary, Military Board on 1 April 1810. He was in agreement with the recommendations of the Committee but differed with the Committee's specific recommendation on the repairs, alterations, erections and demolition to be effected in the Agra Fort. He felt that an estimate of Rs. 1,00,000 submitted by the Committee was not realistic and at least Rs. 4,00,000 would be required to carry out the repair works at Agra Fort in keeping with the recommendations of the Committee. He, however, appreciated the efforts of the Committee who had surveyed the repair works required to be effected in the Agra Fort.[158]

Thereafter, A. Greene, Secretary, Military Board forwarded the papers to John Adams, Secretary, Military Department on 24 July 1810 for the concurrence of the Government to carry out the repair works at Agra Fort and sanction Rs. 4,00,000/- for effecting the repair works. Greene was for the present enthusiastic only about repairs and not about other works such as alterations, demolitions, lodgments for troops, erection of walls/new rooms, etc. in the buildings. He was of the opinion that "I would keep the Fort of Agra in good repair, but not lay out a Rupee on works that are not absolutely necessary for its defence and I would call for an estimate of repairs only".[159]

On 6 August 1810, Lord Hastings concurred in the recommendations of the Committee relating to repair works in Agra Fort besides keeping the Fort in a perfect state of repair.[160]

Later, Lord Minto I, Governor-General also approved plans for repair works as indicated by Lt. Col. Horsford, Commandant of Artillery, earlier. The work was to be executed in consultation with Col. Brown and Captain Steel.[161] This was the first major step taken for the preservation of Agra Fort.

Towards the beginning of 1815, it was noticed that some urgent repairs had to be made at Agra Fort. These repair works related to the repair of water-gate and gateway besides rebuilding a well on the left bank of the water-gate. To effect these repairs, Rs. 181.4.0 (Sonnet Rupees) were required. For building a wall near the ditch sluice gate for ensuring prevention of water escaping from the ditch, an additional amount of Rs. 1285.3.2 was recommended. However, these works could not be executed at that time as Captain Smith and Lt. Taylor to whom the Governor-General wanted to entrust these assignments were pre-occupied with other important assignments.[162]

On 20 October 1820, Lord Hastings proposed to assign the work relating to removal of marbles from the Bath of Agra Palace to Captain Taylor. Hastings felt that preservation of rare and exquisite works of art could always be considered a great achievement of glory by the Hon'ble Court of Directors of the English East India Company. He compared the inlaid bath chambers and its workmanship at Agra Fort to Taj and thought of transporting them to England via river navigation to Calcutta. Hastings particularly wanted to have a sculpture of the Duke of Wellington to be fashioned out from the marbles of baths at Agra Fort. He felt that the sculpture of the Duke of Wellington could be placed at the Wellington square for public admiration as a tribute to the memory of a man who brought glory to Great Britain for humbling Napoleon Bonaparte at the Battle of Waterloo. For effecting this particular assignment, Hastings thought of no other person than Captain Taylor, who had ample experience in carrying out the restoration of the Taj.[163]

Captain Taylor was, accordingly, entrusted with the task of transporting the marbles from the Bath at Agra Fort to Calcutta. He was authorised to draw an allowance of Rs. 44 per month for the purpose.[164] A few marble stones buried in the Agra Fort were also discovered by Captain Taylor in 1821.[165]

Old Mosque At Allahabad

During the tenure of Lord Hastings as the Governor-General, the dilapidated state of the mosque at Allahabad was brought to the notice of the Court of Directors by the Company's Government. Earlier, Courtney Smith, the Second Judge of the Benaras Court of Circuit through an Appendix to the Report 15 December 1815 also drew their attention to the ruinous condition of the mosque. The Court of Directors sanctioned an amount proposed by the Government rather hesitatingly on 26 April 1820.

The Court of Directors while sanctioning funds had observed that the ruinous state of the mosque at Allahabad was primarily due to the fact that it had become a private dwelling unit of Col. Kyd after it was given to him by Nawab Vizier of Oudh. It was sold to Col. Humfrays by Col. Kyd and again sold to Col. Ochterlony.

After a petition of the local Muslim population, the mosque was bought for Rs. 12,000 from Col. Ochterlony by the Company. Later, military authorities raised doubt about the security threats to Allahabad Fort as it was in close proximity to this mosque. Thereafter, doors and other building materials of the mosque were taken out and sold off. The mosque then remained in a state of ruin from 1811-1814.

Later, when Mr. Smith and his attendants addressed a letter to Dowdeswell, Secretary about the antiquity and beautiful structure of the mosque, it was restored to a place of worship to the Muslim inhabitants at an expense of Rs. 4,000.[166] Mr. Smith stated that the mosque was constructed two hundred years ago and it served as a Jama Masjid of the Subah of Allahabad which constituted the fifteenth part of Akbar's empire.[167] The Court of Directors added that the mosque should serve as a place of worship for Muslims and should be restored to its pristine glory as was done in the case of restoring Taj and other monuments of Agra, viz., Sikandra and Agra Fort. The Court concluded by stating that it was essentially the duty of the Government to protect the religious rights and freedom of the Muslim and Hindu population and, therefore, the same should be respected and maintained on all occasions.[168]

Qutab Minar

In 1826, Lord Amherst, Governor-General discovered that Qutab Minar was in a state of utter disrepair and ordered that repair works of the monument should be taken up immediately. However, actual repair to this monument was undertaken during the tenure of Lord William Bentinck who assumed the charge of Governor-General on 13 March 1828.[169] It was for the first time that major repair works were carried out at Qutab Minar. The charge of carrying out the repair works was entrusted to Major Robert Smith of Engineers. The repair works of all the storeys of Qutab Minar were thus carried out under his supervision. An amount of Rs. 22,262.2.1½ (Sonnet Rupees) was expended towards repair works by Major Smith.

Later, a Committee of Survey was constituted by the Company's Government for the purpose of assessing the repair works executed at Qutab Minar. The Committee comprised Captain John Wilson, 17th Regiment Native Infantry as its President, Lt. F. Mackeson of 14th Regiment, Native Infantry and Ensign C. Black of 17th Regiment Native Infantry as its members. This Committee surveyed the repair works meticulously and approved the work done by Major Smith. During the course of survey, Major Smith also attended the deliberations of the Committee[170] (Appendix VI for details).

The plans for tackling the future repairs at Qutab Minar were apprised to Edward Colebrooke, Resident, Delhi on 26 March 1829 by Major Robert Smith. He also gave valuable advice on any event of natural calamity striking the edifice of Qutab Minar, especially during floods and earthquakes, and suggested keeping the balconies of the monument in perpetual repair.[171]

On 28 March 1829, Edward Colebrook informed George Sevinton, Chief Secretary, Political Department regarding the completion of repair works executed by Major Smith and stated the amount of Rs. 22,262.2.1½ spent towards repairs was in perfect consonance with the estimated expenditure.[172] Colebrook also recommended an establishment for carrying out the maintenance of the monument so as to ensure its perfect preservation. Besides, encroachments in future by khadins and fakirs in the neighborhood were to be checked through this proposed arrangement. He stated that the area round the pillar was cleared and the lanes leading to the site were opened. The Hindu antiquities were cleared and trees were planted in the vicinity. The area was also cleared of khadims and fakirs who inhabited the place. Besides, haphazard constructed inhabitations of mud partition walls in thatched huts were cleared so as to ensure perfect symmetry. It could now be compared to the modern inhabitations of brass and metal covering of the monuments which were now renovated.[173]

A proposal for having an establishment by Major Smith was also submitted to Lord William Bentinck for consideration by Colebrook that involved an expenditure of Rs. 25 per month. Besides, Colebrook also submitted a set of draft rules for creating awareness for the monuments amongst the general public:

> (1) All visitors, European and Native are requested to abstain from mutilating or otherwise injuring the Minar of Kutub in any of its parts, the adjoining Mosques and Hindoo antiquities or other objects connected with the Palace including the trees, shrubs and their fences.
>
> (2) The whole of the Buildings, Mosques, Tombs and Grounds immediately adjoining and to the east of Minar having been laid open for general access and inspection are not to be occupied at any time by any description of persons, cattle carriages or camp equipage.

(3) The Surae (Inn) adjoining to and opening into the Kootub grounds is available in its Kootrees and apartments for all parties, cattle and carriages requiring cover.

(4) The places for encampment are **1st** the old Encamping Surae (Inn) or enclosure between the Bazar and the Tomb of Adam Khan **2nd** To the north of Adam Khan's Tomb on the Ridge **3rd** on the high ground adjoining the Bunglow south of the Lat and **4th** in the new Surae (Inn) or outside to the north of it; but all the open ground in front of the Minar to the eastward is reserved for a general free use and communication and not to be supplied in any part to encampments.

(5) Sowaries and Sowarree carriages have passing through the Kutub ground road, but all common carriages, cattle and ordinary traffic to keep the high road through the Surae.

(6) Groups of natives of the lower classes are not to ascend the Minar in a number exceeding 10 at a time and are not allowed to make any stay in the Minar.*

(7) No Fakeers, Beggars or Vagrants are allowed to take up their Post and demand money about the Kutub.[174]

Establishment for Kutub as suggested by Major R. Smith:[175]

		Rs.	A.	P.
For the change and preservation of good order of the place and the young trees which require care and watering the tree fences, cleaning the roads and ground of jungle weeds and rank vegetation included.	1 chowkidar per month 1 Maly 2 Bistees @4 Rs. 2 Coolies @3½ Rs. Moonji string and petty expense on trees	5 4 8 7 -	- 8 8	-
Total Sonnet Rupees		25		

Lord William Bentinck, Governor-General on 25 April 1829 had approved the accounts of expenditure submitted by Major Smith amounting to Rs. 22,262, 2.1½ sanctioned for Rs. 25/- p.m. maintaining an establishment for ensuring that the monument remains in perfect condition and in perpetual repair.[176]

Nine years later, Lord Auckland who had assumed the charge of the Governor-General on 4 March 1836 stressed in his minute dated 7 March 1838 the need for preservation of monuments in Delhi. Auckland was of the opinion that the Company's Government should preserve Qutab Minar and other monuments in its vicinity in pristine glory. This was essential to arouse interest amongst the Indian subjects to the Government's efforts in ensuring their preservation. Auckland was particularly interested in the maintenance of Qutab Minar and issued orders to the officials for its upkeep. He particularly wanted Captain Thomson to inspect the monument periodically and order removal of vegetation and other outgrowth in the monument. He also instructed that remedial measures be taken to avoid accumulation of rain water and ensure proper sanitation. Auckland particularly drew the attention of Captain Thomson to the sinking keystones of the arches of the gateways to Qutab Minar. He personally ensured that the Qutab Minar was in good state of preservation during his tenure as Governor-General till he laid down his office on 28 February 1842.[177]

* The draft rules were prophetic as a stampede had occurred at Qutab Minar on 4 December 1981 when a large number of visitors entered the Qutab Minar which resulted in death and injury to children and women which also included foreign tourists.

Bhim Singh Lat Allahabad

Major repair works at the monument of Bhim Singh Lat at Allahabad was undertaken after Lord Auckland assumed charge as Governor-General on 4 March 1836.[178]

It was at the meeting of the Asiatic Society held on 7 September 1836 that the stone pillars, commonly known as "Bhim Singh Lat" at Allahabad, were crumbling gradually and were in neglected condition. The pillars were also partly buried in the swamps and saline soil of Allahabad Fort. Reacting to this news, James Prinsep, Secretary, Asiatic Society addressed a communication on 10 September 1836 to H.J. Prinsep, Secretary, Company's Government on the preservation of the monument, especially the ancient inscriptions on the pillars.[179]

In a similar vein, it was suggested in the meeting of the Asiatic Society on 7 September 1836 that a representation should be made before the Supreme Court on the subject wherein the value of the ancient edifice should be brought before the Hon'ble Court for taking immediate measures for restoration and preservation of the monument within the premises of the Allahabad Fort and that the Government should make appropriate recommendations for its preservation.

Further, James Prinsep, Secretary, Asiatic Society was of the view that the value and importance of the monument should be brought to the notice of the Governor-General in Council and several memorials on the importance of the monument, submitted by Lt. Burt of Engineers, Captain Troyer, Secretary, Government Sanskrit College, and Rev. Dr. Mill, which were also published in the journal of the Asiatic Society in 1834 should also be placed before the Governor-General in Council for their information. Prinsep also was of the view that inscriptions found in the pillar at Allahabad has since excited and ignited antiquarian interest of similar pillars found elsewhere in the country.[180]

The Governor-General forwarded a copy of the letter received from the Secretary, Asiatic Society to the Military Board with orders that the Executive Officer, Allahabad Division should furnish an estimate on expenditure likely to be involved in the erection of pillar. It was found be an expensive proposition, the officer should suggest a comprehensive plan for preserving the pillars and ensure that they remain in perfect state of preservation.[181]

Captain Edward Smith of Engineers, who was entrusted with this task, prepared six elegant designs of the monument which were exhibited at the Asiatic Society and considered in its meeting held on 6 October 1837. Thereafter, a Special Committee was constituted comprising Col. D. Macleod, Chief Engineer, Captain W.N. Forbes, Captain W.P. Grant and Captain A. Cunningham. The Committee was primarily constituted to assess the design prepared by Captain Smith. The Committee examined the six designs and selected the third design as the most appropriate one. With regard to Captain Smith's design on the Lion Capital, the Committee felt that it was an elegant design.* It was also suggested that for fixing the Pillar, a platform was to be constructed from covering an octagon stone of 6½ feet diameter and 2 feet width to be procured from Chunar for the erection of the pillar. The Committee approved the design.[182] The Asiatic Society at its meeting convened on 4 October 1837 unanimously adopted the report of the Committee.

Thereafter, James Prinsep, Secretary, Asiatic Society addressed a communication to Captain E. Sanders of Engineers, Secretary, Military Board on 15 October 1837 on the selection of a design by Captain Smith (Design No. 3) as most appropriate. The design is based on the inscription

---

* The Lion capital design of Sarnath was adopted by the Government of India as its insignia on 26 January 1950 when India became a Republic.

of Ashoka during 3rd century BC and efforts for restoration by the Society was as well taken by the Company's Government.[183] Prinsep also referred to the design for the restoration of the pillar by Lt. Kittoe in 1836 in which the surmounting Lion or *Singha* on a pedestal was introduced.[184]

The Military Board promptly recommended the adoption of Design No. 3 with modifications and informed Hon'ble Alexander Ross, President, Council of India, Fort William on 31 October 1837 about the designs by Captain Smith, the Executive Officer, i.e., Designs 1, 2 and 6 at the cost of Rs. 4227.6.2 and Designs 3, 4 and 5 at the cost of Rs. 2183.13.3. The Military Board further stated the selection of Design No. 3 which commensurated with consistency and economy in expenditure.

The Military Board added that the Asiatic Society also endorsed the selection of Design No. 3. The Board also recommended that the Design No. 7, which was based on the blue print delineated by Lt. Kittoe, was also of intrinsic and superior quality, but as it was received quite late, selection of the design as submitted by Captain Smith was eventually made.[185]

The Board was of the view that the restoration of the Lion on the 'Capital' of the pillar would correspondingly increase the height of the basement and would, therefore, result in the increase of amount as mentioned in the estimates submitted by Captain Smith. They requested the Company's Government for a sanction of Rs. 2,500/- for the purpose. The estimates submitted by Captain Smith for erecting the Bhim Singh Lat in the Fort of Allahabad, commonly known as Ashok Lat, amounted to Rs. 2183.13.1.[186]

The Governor-General in his letter dated 7 December 1837 had a preference for Design No. 3 with certain modifications of the design by supplementing it with a 'capital' and 'lion' as per Lt. Kittoe's design. An expenditure of Rs. 2500/- was sanctioned for executing the work and Captain Smith was asked to undertake the work.[187] This position was also apprised to the Court of Directors on 13 March 1839.[188]

Captain Smith undertook the work of restoration of Bhim Singh Lat. The Governor-General, however, was not satisfied with the progress and he apprised the Military Board of his apprehensions in this regard on 12 August 1840. He called upon the Military Board to monitor the progress and report every month about the restoration work.[189]

He, however, attributed the delay to torrential rains and administrative difficulties. He also experienced technical difficulties in executing the restoration work.

He apprised the Military Board about the progress on 12 September 1840 as following:

ERECTION OF LION CAPITAL

"(1) The supporting wall, dome and platform of brick masonry have been finished some months and are now set.

(2) The body of the stonework which is to form the Base and surround and enclose the bottom of the pillar when erected has been quarried and the several pieces are cut, trimmed, filled and arranged for immediate application to the Pillar where raised.

(3) The external casing of finally wrought stone with the cornices and ornamental pieces are in great part cut. Thus all the masonry for receiving the Pillar, and for upholding it when raised and for forming and finishing its base are built or nearly ready for use.

(4) For raising the pillar the machine was ready at the spot. Being a massive wooden frame weighing 4 tons working on an axis and similar in nature to that used in lowering the Luxor Obelisk now standing in Paris.

(5) The 6 capstans for raising the machine and Pillar are in part made and can at once be put together for setting into the spindles or axles on which they are to work.
(6) The Blocks and the Ropes are mostly provided, prepared and arranged.
(7) The 6 guns, which hold the spindles of the powerful capstans, have been let into blocks of masonry sunk in the ground.
(8) The Kerbs, the pieces connecting them and the other portions of the casing, which is to go over, the Lat are prepared in their several parts and ready to be attached to the Pillar. Thus, there are ready or prepared for application all the means of erecting the Lat. The pieces of the Capital, which is all remaining for completing the work after erection are partly cut."[190]

Besides, Smith also explained his efforts in the restoration and effecting the repair works of the pillar. He stated that the pillar could not be erected due to rainy season and that was the precise reason he deferred its erection after the rainy season.[191]

The Governor-General was satisfied with the explanation thus tendered by Smith. The work was finally completed towards the end of May 1841 and the Court of Directors were accordingly informed on 28 July that "the celebrated Pillar of antiquity, Bhim Singh Lat, at Allahabad has at length been set up".[192]

Buddhist Pillar in Raja Hindu Rao's Garden

A broken column was noticed on the estate of W. Fraser in Raja Hindu Rao's garden near Delhi, which comprised five pieces of stone which could not be restored. The broken ends prevented its restoration logically in its totality.

It was at the meeting of the Asiatic Society held on 6 December 1837, the matter relating to the broken column attracted the attention of the members of the Society. It was decided that Major L. Pew of Artillery would convince Raja Hindu Rao to hand over the fragments of the broken column for possible realignment for restoration.[193]

Thereafter, J. Prinsep, Secretary, Asiatic Society apprised W.H. Macnaughten, Secretary, North Western Provinces and also the Governor-General on 15 December 1837 about the broken column which had an inscription and was worthy of preservation. Prinsep requested for the transportation of the pillar to Calcutta and if it was not possible to send the entire pillar, the fragment containing the inscription could be sent.[194]

Major Pew informed the Society that the Buddhist Pillar would incur considerable expenses for its repair and transport. However, James Prinsep, Secretary, Asiatic Society promptly informed W.H. Macnaughten, Secretary, North-West Provinces about the need and importance of repairing the Buddhist pillar at the cost of the public exchequer. He further suggested the mode of transport through ordnance store boats to Calcutta.[195]

At this juncture, Macnaughten requested Captain George Thomson, Executive Engineer, Delhi on 2 January 1838 for an estimate of the cost involved in transporting the pillar to Calcutta.[196] Thomson, in turn, requested Captain Burt, Bengal Engineers on 21 April 1838 to examine the broken column. Captain Burt apprised Thomson on 27 April 1838 about his observations of the pillar. He stated that the pillar where the inscription appears could be sent to Asiatic Society at Calcutta instead of sending the entire pillar as it weighed 4/¼ tons and he had made arrangements for its transport through military boats and gun carriage trucks. In this process, the cost of transport would considerably be reduced from Rs. 2,000 to 200.[197] However, Thomson replied to the letter of Macnaughten dated 2 January 1838 on 30 April 1838 describing the pillar which comprised four pieces, each measuring 8 feet in length and the girth measuring 8 to 10 feet. He also informed that due to vagaries of weather, the inscriptions had been defaced and the pillar could not be restored logically and hence should not be transported to Calcutta.[198]

As Thomson was not acquainted with the importance of inscriptions on the pillar, he sought Captain Burt's opinion on the matter. It may be recalled that Burt had taken a facsimile of the inscription of the pillar before it had been cut and sawed and had proposed its transportation to Calcutta at the cost of Rs. 200/-.[199] Besides, Captain Burt pointed out to Macnaughten on 3 May 1838 that the facsimile of the inscription of the pillar was incomplete due to the presence of abrasions and obliterations, which prevented the task of piecing the portion of stone together where the inscription appeared. He also apprised Macnaughten whether the cost involved in transporting the portion of pillar containing the inscription would be justifiable for its preservation at Asiatic Society.

James Prinsep, however, stated that they were aware of the incomplete inscription of the dilapidated pillar and an account had since been published in the Journal of Asiatic Society on the basis of the facsimiles taken by Major Pew of Artillery. Prinsep also stated that the inscription appearing in the Pillar was unique and the matter of fragmented inscription could be reconstructed with the help of numerous inscriptions available in the Asiatic Society. He also stated that the broken pillar was invaluable and they would gladly accept the fragments of the pillar as a valuable gift from Raja Hindu Rao.[200] Princep once again pleaded fervently for transporting the pillar containing inscriptions through an agency which would exercise care and economy during its transportation to Calcutta. He particularly recommended Captain Burt to be entrusted with this task.[201]

Besides, Prinsep also proposed deputing one officer from the Asiatic Society for the purpose.[202] At last, Lord Auckland, Governor-General on June 1838 ordered that the portion of dilapidated pillar containing inscriptions should be transported to Calcutta and presented to the Asiatic Society by Raja Hindu Rao. This assignment had to be effectively completed by Captain Thomson, Executive Engineer, Delhi with the help of Captain Burt.[203]

Tomb of Begampur

On 15 April 1838, G. Wingate, Assistant Collector in-charge of Mohole and Marah requested P. Stuart, Acting Sub-Collector, Sholapur for sanctioning an expenditure of Rs. 600/- towards the repair works of the tomb of Begampur. He justified this expenditure by stating that this would enable him to repair the wall which would secure the foundation of the tomb erected by Emperor Aurangzeb at the town of Begampur. He also stated that the tomb was prone to destruction by floods in river Bumma which posed a danger to its foundation. The tomb was erected in a walled enclosure and is a good example of Mughal architecture. As a work of art in the Deccan region, it was worthy of preservation.

Wingate also a gave historical importance of the tomb. He stated that Aurangzeb while on a Bijapur expedition had encamped for 12 years on the banks of river Bumma, and had a tomb in the memory of the daughter of his Minister Ghazi Nildeen who died and had founded the town of Begampur. The site of Begampur formed part of the adjoining village of Ghoreshwar which was purchased from the headman by the Emperor and assigned its revenues amounting to Rs. 300 along with revenues of two neighbouring villages in the Mohole taluka for the support of the tomb. The revenues from the villages continued till the agents of Nizam transferred them to Company. Since this transaction was kept outside the purview of Nizam's knowledge at

Hyderabad, it was proper to apprise the Nizam of the arrangement of revenues from the villages for the upkeep of the tomb at Begampur. Wingate also apprised the Nizam about the Begam who happened to be the daughter of his ancestor Ghazi Nildeen.

Besides, Wingate also appealed to the Company's Government on behalf of the inhabitants of Begampur towards the upkeep and safety of the tomb and to ensure its preservation. The residents of Begampur had expended a sum of Rs. 500 towards the maintenance of the edifice. Accordingly, Wingate requested for a sanction of Rs. 500/- for ensuring that the tomb was kept in a perfect state of repair.[204]

G.H. Burton, Assistant Collector, Sholapur requested Richard Mills, Principal Collector, Poona for a sanction of Rs. 600 as requested by Wingate, Lt. Governor for the upkeep of the tomb of Begampur erected by Emperor Aurangzeb.[205] Mills recommended the grant of expenditure and asked the Revenue Commissioner, Poona to sanction the requisite amount.[206] Williamson asked Mills on 4 May 1838 whether the tomb had lodging arrangements for travellers or for official use in Poona district. [207] To this, Wingate clarified that although considerable accommodation was available for the use of travellers but travellers normally would like to lodge themselves in adjoining towns.[208] Mills promptly informed the Revenue Commissioner on 15 June 1838 that as informed by Wingate, the tomb was not used as lodging house for the travellers.[209]

However, I. Williamson, the Revenue Commissioner observed in his communication to the Acting Secretary, Bombay Government on 5 July 1838 that he was not in favour of granting any amount for repairs of a tomb as it did not come under the purview of religious character.[210] However, W.S. Boyd, who was officiating as the Secretary to the Government of Bombay, recommended an expenditure of Rs. 600 to the Government of India towards the upkeep of the tomb at Begampur situated in the Sholapur sub-collectorate.[211]

After a protracted correspondence, the Home Department conveyed that the Government could only sanction part of the amount as sufficient funds were available under the head "endowment of lands" which could be utilised for maintenance and upkeep of the tomb.[212]

Black Pagoda or Konark Temple

For the repair of the Black Pagoda, R. Kerr, Magistrate, Cuttack in his communication dated 27 March 1806 to George Dowdeswell, Secretary, Judicial Department, Fort William Council, Calcutta had sought orders for restituting illegal removal of stones from the precincts of the Black Pagoda at Konark. He had reiterated the Resolution of the Governor-General in Council, which was thus:

"The Governor-General in Council under the circumstances stated by the magistrate of Cuttuck does not think it advisable to authorize any repairs to be made to the Black Pagoda at Juggunath.

Ordered that the Magistrate be at the same time directed to continue to prevent any further removal of the materials of the Pagoda.

Ordered that an Extract from the proceedings be sent to the Public Department, in reply to the reference from that Department under date the 23rd January last."[213]

After a lapse of 32 years, James Prinsep, Secretary, Asiatic Society recommended on 18 August 1838 to T. Maddock, Secretary, Judicial Department that the Raja of Khurda, acting under the misconceived order of Mr. Williamson, Commissioner, was destroying the Black Pagoda and urgent measures should be taken by removing statues to his residence in order to save the grand edifice from destruction. James Prinsep requested the Government to stall further destruction to the monument by the local government. He also recommended restoration of the monument thus destroyed and few specimens of its sculptures to be transferred to the Asiatic Society for being exhibited in their museum.[214]

The Secretary, Home Department directed I.I. Halliday, Secretary, Government of Bengal on 20 August 1838 for obtaining necessary orders from the Deputy Governor of Bengal.[215]

Acting on the communication, A. Forbes, Magistrate Cuttack reported to H. Rickett, Commissioner, 19th Division, Cuttack on 27 October 1838 about the ownership of the Black Pagoda. He stated that the ownership rights are vested with the Company's Government, although the Raja of Khurda along with zamindars on whose lands the Black Pagoda was situated claim as their private property. The Thana Daroga had been vested with powers to prevent the removal of debris and building material from the monument.

It was in January 1837, the Raja of Khurda requested permission to remove some of the black and white stones with an ostensible motive to repair the Jagannath Temple. The Collector had acceded to his request and accordingly instructed the Daroga and zamindars to that effect. The white stones with which the temple was constructed was lying in the temple premises. Besides, black stones of the doorways were also available. When the Raja of Khurda did not find enough black stones, he dislodged the **Navgriha** structure and carried its stones to Puri where they were processed for use in the repairs of the Jagannath temple. Forbes attributed this mishap to the wrongly worded order of the Magistrate and he sought an explanation from the Daroga who managed his transfer to another Thana, an excuse for not giving an explanation.[216]

Henry Ricketts, Commissioner, Cuttack Division reported to the Secretary, Judicial Department on 31 October 1838 the circumstances leading to the dismantling of Black Pagoda as reported to him by A. Forbes, Magistrate, Cuttack. Ricketts particularly recommended restoration of the Black Pagoda and suggested it should be rebuilt at a height so as to regain its glory as a landmark monument.[217]

A copy of this communication from the Commissioner, Cuttack to Secretary, Government of India was as well forwarded to Mr. Maddock on 20 November 1838.

The Governor-General approved the measures taken for stoppage of further dismantling of the Black Pagoda. In this connection, the Secretary, Judicial Department, Government of India addressed a communication to Halliday, Secretary, Government of Bengal on 10 December 1838, wherein he instructed the Deputy Governor of Bengal to prevent further dismantling of the Black Pagoda and reprimanded the Magistrate for his irresponsible order which encouraged the Raja of Khurda to exceed his brief in dismantling the Navagriha edifice within the precincts of the Black Pagoda. He further instructed to raise the height of the edifice of the Black Pagoda in consultation with the Marine Board so that the Black Pagoda retains its position as a landmark monument.[218]

Besides, the Secretary, Government of India also informed the Secretary, Asiatic Society on 10 December 1838 about the measures taken by the local authorities to prevent further dismantling of the Black Pagoda.[219]

C.B. Greenlam, Secretary, Marine Board also addressed a communication to M. Ricketts, Commissioner, Cuttack on 23 January 1839 requesting the deputation of Mr. Bond, Master Attendant to the site of the Black Pagoda for assessing the cost estimate of elevating the edifice to a lofty height. He also advised that the Navgriha (Navigrihur) should be restored to its original position since if it is raised to a greater height, it would give the same appearance and would not have its distinct entity vis-á-vis the Black Pagoda.[220]

A. Bond, Master Attendant, Marine Office was accordingly deputed to Konark after the inspection of the edifice reported to A. Mills, Officiating Commissioner, Cuttack on 17 February 1839. Bond stated that the Black Pagoda was situated in a land which was 1½ miles away from the area. The western side of the temple had crumbled down leaving the eastern side of the temple intact in a diameter 10 feet above the temple, which was likely to fall over the eastern temple. The height of the eastern temple was 84 feet and 22 feet above the sea level. The Black Pagoda is a landmark for ships, which sail 17 miles away to the west of the Jagannath temple. The eastern temple lies in ruinous condition and the remaining portions of the western temple would eventually fall over it. The dome of the temple has also developed cracks in three places in the centre and the southern doorway had also weakened and, consequently, it was not advisable to effect repairs as the stones weighed from 10 maunds to 2 to 4 tons.

The **Navgriha** or Great Stone at the base of the temple at the eastern doorway measured 19 feet 10 inch in length by 4 feet 3 inch square (nearly) in breadth and weighed 10-12 tons each. The temple as such could be a distinct landmark for maritime purposes.

In order to prevent the crumbling of the portion of the western temple, Bond suggested that the wall of the western temple should be razed and the doorways of the eastern temple should be blocked with debris and the centre should also be filled up with debris material so that the temple could be prevented from falling down and this would prevent undertaking major alterations in the temple. The expenses involved should not exceed Rs. 1,000/- whereas undertaking major repairs should increase the expenses five times the sum proposed.

For filling up of the eastern temple, Bond proposed the utilisation of stones lying in the precincts of the Black Pagoda. He stated that stones weighed from 10 maunds to 4 tons each and the stones from the western temple weighed 4 to 10 maunds each, which could be utilised for filling up of the eastern temple.[221]

The communications from Bond, Master Attendant was forwarded to the Secretary, Marine Board by A. Maffalt Mills, Commissioner, 19th Division with regard to the physical condition of the Black Pagoda.[222]

Besides, the Marine Board also recommended to Mr. Morison, Deputy Governor on 15 March 1839 that the edifice of the Black Pagoda had been a landmark for all the Calcutta bound vessels during the south-west monsoons and it should be maintained at a moderate expense.

With regard to Bond's proposal for blocking the eastern temple with the debris of western temple at an expense of Rs. 1,000/- Marine Board recommended the sanction of the requisite amount as the proposal was considered justified.[223]

Responding to Marine Board's proposal, H.J. Prinsep, Secretary, Government of Bengal informed the Marine Board on 27 March 1839 about the decision of the Deputy Governor of Bengal for not incurring any expenses on the repair and alterations of the Black Pagoda for effecting its position as a distinguished landmark.[224] Besides, the Secretary, Government of Bengal also apprised I.P. Grant, Secretary, Government of India on 16 April 1839 about the decision of the Deputy Governor, Bengal for not incurring any expenses towards alterations and repairs of the Black Pagoda. It may, however, be mentioned that the Government of India appeared to be silent on this subject but, however, repairs to the Black Pagoda monument were carried out periodically.[225]

Sher Shah's Mausoleum at Sahasaram

During the tenure of Lord Auckland as Governor-General, large scale repairs were undertaken of the Sher Shah's mausoleum at Sahasaram. In this connection, T.E. Ravenshaw, Officiating Commissioner, Patna addressed a communication to Mr. Halliday, Secretary, Government of Bengal informing him of the dilapidated condition of the mausoleum of Sher Shah Suri and recommended urgent steps to be taken for preservation of the mausoleum. Ravenshaw personally visited the mausoleum and reported about rampant growth of vegetation in the tomb which had taken roots in the dome of the mausoleum and stated that if urgent steps for their removal were not taken, the entire monument would be prone to destruction.

Ravenshaw referred to the efforts of the Company's Government in restoring and carrying of conservation work at Taj, Kutab Minar and other monuments, which were distinguished edifices of architectural beauty. He stated that the mausoleum of Sher Shah was also a remarkable and celebrated specimen of Pathan architecture to which the people attach much importance and look up with pride and reverence. He recommended that the mausoleum should be placed under the charge of the Executive Engineer stationed at Dinapur or Hazaribagh for ensuring that it was kept in a perfect state of repair and adequate measures must be taken to prevent its dilapidation. He also recommended that the cupola on the dome, which was destroyed due to lightning earlier, should be replaced. With the annual inspection of the monument by the Executive Engineer, the expenses on repair to the mausoleum should be brought down considerably and the monument should be preserved in a perfect condition.

The expenditure for the repairs in the mausoleum could be spent from the proceeds of the endowments of Shah Kubeerodeen.[226] The Secretary, Government of Bengal forwarded the proposal of Ravenshaw to the Secretary, Government of India. Besides, Lt. P. Alcock, Superintendent of Roads also forwarded an estimate of the expenditure for removal of vegetation growth in Sher Shah's mausoleum to Ravenshaw and requested an amount of Rs. 893/- for the purpose.[227] However, Ravenshaw in his communication to Halliday, Secretary, Government of Bengal, recommended an expenditure of Rs. 200/- and suggested that Lt. Alcock should submit a detailed report and expenditure estimates after the stones inflicted with vegetation growth in the tomb were taken down, and ascertain the extent of penetration of the roots of vegetation, especially **peepal** trees.[228]

He also forwarded this proposal to Lord Auckland, Governor-General and the Secretary, Government of India addressed a communication to the Secretary, Government of Bengal authorising requisite expenditure for repair works of Sher Shah's tomb.[229]

Besides, it was also decided that in order to keep the tomb in perfect condition, the proceeds of the wakf (trust) of Shah Kubeeroodeen should be utilised.

Return of Gate of Somnath Temple

On 8 January 1026, Mahmud of Ghazni destroyed the Somnath temple during his 14th expedition to India. Mahmud took away the sandalwood gates of the city. In 1842, Lord Ellenborough, the Governor-General decided to get the gates back from Ghazni to India.

A Committee was thus appointed under the orders of Major General Nott to report on the condition of the gates to be brought back from Ghazni. The Committee comprised Major Edward Sanders of Engineers as President, Capatin C. Blood, Artillery, John Studdart of Engineers and C.F. North of Engineers as members. The Committee submitted its report on 8 November 1842 stating that in spite of the fact that the gates had been displaced from Somnath temple and transported to Ghazni, they were in good condition. These gates were buried during the invasion of Afghanistan by Chengiz Khan to save them from being vandalised by his troops. Further, great care had been taken after their removal from the tomb of Mahmud of Ghazni and they have not sustained any damage during their transport back to India. The Committee was further of the opinion that the tomb of the Mahmud of Ghazni had been a centre of pilgrimage and adored by the Muslims. The gates merited special attention. The lower portions of the gates within the reach of human hand had, of course, been damaged. The carvings of the gates in some places have disappeared and some portions of the gates have been vandalised and taken as relics. The pieces of carved wood have been used to replace with original carvings and in other portions of the gates, artisans were deployed to restore the carvings. The Committee further was of the opinion that the upper portion of the gate has the original carving intact and was in a good state of preservation. The gates have been decorated with plates of precious metal fixed by small clips of iron. Many of these iron clips still remain in regular pattern over the upper portion of the gates. However, the patterns have disappeared in the lower portion. The Committee further stated that the gates were surrounded by a frame comprising small pieces of carved wood and held together by numerous joints in regular pattern. The exterior dimension of the frames were 16½ feet in height and 13½ feet in width. The frames were in good state of preservation except in the lower portion, which has shrunk due to constant friction. Though the Committee felt that it was difficult to restore the entire portion of the gates, if logical judgement could be applied in repair and restoration work, it could be restored to its original state.[230]

Captain Harris was entrusted with the charge of transporting the gates to Bawda State. Sayaji Rao Gaekwar received these gates for being preserved at Somnath temple. This was the first archaeological reinstalment of removed artefact, which was our integral cultural heritage of immense significance. The Governor-General felt that if these gates were erected at the temple, the enthusiasm of devotees would have an adverse impact and the gates could be damaged. He suggested that the gates could be preserved as relics in the Somnath temple and placed on an elevated platform of marble supported by lattice work of marble and surmounted by an Imperial Crown. This should be done in consultation with the Hindus, and their aesthetics and wishes should be carried out in entirety.[231]

The Governor-General desired that adequate steps should be taken for publicity among the Hindus and in this connection the Secretary, Government of Bombay addressed a communication to T.H. Maddock, Secretary, Government of India on 5 December 1842 for publicising the restoration and investiture of gates of Somnath temple as desired by the Governor-General to the Hindu populace of Bombay Presidency and also to the Hindu princes, chieftains and *jagirdars*.[232]

Sayaji Rao Gaekwar had all praises in his letter of 8 January 1843 for Lord Ellenborough's efforts in salvaging the gates of Somnath temple from Ghazni, which had brought joy and happiness to the Hindus of India and also to the princely chiefs of the states in India. He concluded in his letter thus,

> No king or ruler of any country can be compared to your Lordship for valor, gaining of victories and for untying the knots of difficulty and for arranging matters in the permanent style thus accomplished, for which God be praised. From your great wisdom and pure intentions, you have been enabled to carry your intentions into effect, all this has the good wishes of your Lordship's friends. Your fame has spread far and wide. Your letters state that it gives you great pleasure in whatever affords joy to the princes and chiefs of Hindustan. Be assured, that your Lordship's

welfare is the wish of my heart as well as the good name of the Hon'ble Company. May your fame and prosperity daily increase.[233]

Introduction of Regulations

The East India Company introduced two regulations for ensuring the proper upkeep of the monuments in India and vested with the powers to intervene or to save any monument from misuse by private individuals. The two regulations were: Bengal Code-XIX in 1810 (Appendix VII) and the Madras Code VII in 1817 (Appendix VIII).

With the enactment of these legislations, the conservation of monuments remained with the Management Board, which had been especially set up for the purpose. The upkeep of the monuments was to be managed from earnings and accruals of revenue coming from land holdings attached to these monuments. If in case any monument was found in dilapidated condition and could not be repaired from the revenue accruals, the Government was vested with the authority to auction the land holdings thus attached to the concerned monument. However, this did not extend to monuments, which were in private ownership. Unfortunately, the law was ineffective when state officials ordered the demolition of an ancient edifice or when a Governor-General was party to gross acts of vandalism.[234]

It was under the tenure of Lord Hastings as Governor-General that a decision was taken to gift marble bath in Shah Jahan's palace. This was sold by public auction on the orders of Lord William Bentinck. During Bentinck's tenure as Governor-General (1828-1835), the Taj was on the point of being demolished for the value of its marbles. Besides, in 1831 it was proposed to lease the gardens at Sikandra to the Executive Engineer at Agra for the purposes of speculative cultivation.[235]

NOTES AND REFERENCES

1. Paper on 'Ancient Monuments' presented to the Asiatic Society in 1807. *Asiatic Researches*, Vol. IX, p. 389.
2. *Hyderabad Residency*, Vol. No. 34, p. 381.
3. Home, Public, 26 October 1830, No. 14.
4. Judicial, 24 November 1809, No. 9.
5. *Ibid.*
6. *Ibid.*
7. Judicial, 24 November 1809, No. 8.
8. *Ibid.*
9. *Ibid.*
10. Judicial, 24 November 1809, No. 10.
11. Judicial, 6 April 1810, No. 13.
12. Judicial letter from Court, 23 February 1813, para 26.
13. Revenue, 30 October 1813, No. 36.
14. *Ibid.*
15. *Ibid.*
16. Revenue, 26 January 1815, No. 66.
17. *Ibid.*
18. *Ibid.*
19. Revenue, 26 January 1815, No. 65.
20. Revenue, 26 January 1815, No. 66.
21. Revenue, 26 January 1815, No. 67.

22. Revenue, 26 January 1815, No. 68.
23. Revenue, 28 April 1815, No. 50 E.
24. Revenue, 28 April 1815, No. 50 D.
25. *Ibid.*
26. Revenue, 28 April 1815, No. 50 B.
27. *Ibid.*
28. Revenue, 28 April 1815, No. 50 D.
29. *Ibid.*
30. *Ibid.*
31. Revenue, 28 April 1815, No.50 E.
32. Revenue, 9 May 1817, No. 37.
33. *Ibid.*
34. *Ibid.*
35. Revenue, 9 May 1817, No. 38.
36. Revenue, 9 May 1817, No. 40-43.
37. Revenue, 9 May 1817, No. 37.
38. *Ibid.*
39. *Ibid.*
40. *Ibid.*
41. *Ibid.*
42. Revenue, 9 May 1817, No. 36.
43. Revenue, 9 May 1817, No. 35.
44. Revenue, 9 May 1817, No. 44.
45. *Ibid.*
46. Revenue, 15 May 1818, No. 60.
47. *Ibid.*
48. Revenue, 15 May 1818, No. 61.
49. Public, 10 April 1822, No. 83.
50. *Ibid.*
51. Public, 10 April 1822, No. 86.
52. *Ibid.*
53. Public, 30 May 1822, No. 36.
54. *Ibid.*
55. *Ibid.*
56. Public, 30 May 1822, No. 40
57. *Ibid.*
58. Public, 30 May 1822, No. 46.
59. *Ibid.*
60. Public, 30 May 1822, No. 39.
61. *Ibid.*
62. Public, 30 May 1822, No. 38
63. *Ibid.*
64. *Ibid.*
65. Public, 30 May 1822, No. 49.
66. Public, 30 May 1822, No. 50.
67. Public, 30 July 1823, No. 35.
68. *Ibid.*
69. Public, 30 July 1823, No. 36.
70. Public, 4 December 1823, No. 30.

71. Hyderabad Residency, Vol. No. 62, p. 675.
72. Public, 29 April 1824, Nos. 3-4.
73. Public, 29 April 1824, No. 5.
74. *Ibid.*
75. Public, 29 April 1824, No. 6.
76. Public, 29 April 1824, No. 7.
77. Public, 29 April 1824, No. 9.
78. *Ibid.*
79. Public, 29 April 1824, No. 10.
80. *Ibid.*
81. *Ibid.*
82. Public, 17 June 1824, No. 29.
83. Public 17 June 1824, No. 30.
84. Public, 5 August 1824, No. 12.
85. *Ibid.*
86. Public, 9 September 1824, No. 13.
87. Public, 5 August 1824, No. 12.
88. Public, 9 September 1824, No.14.
89. Public, 2 September 1824, No. 35.
90. Public, 2 September 1824, No. 36.
91. Public, 2 September, 1824, No. 37.
92. Public, 21 October 1824, No. 8.
93. Public, 23 June 1825, Nos. 9-10.
94. Public, 29 June 1826, No. 61.
95. Public, 5 October 1826, No. 8.
96. Public, 4 August 1826, No. 75.
97. Public, 27 December 1827, No. 31.
98. Public, 27 December 1827, No. 32.
99. Public, 20 March 1828, Nos. 25-26.
100. Public, 10 April 1828, No. 25.
101. *Hyderabad Residency*, Vol. No. 67, p. 45.
102. Public, 10 April 1828, No. 26.
103. First Report of the Curator of Ancient Monuments in India for the year 1881-82. Government Central Branch Press, 1882, p. 5.
104. Military Department, 2 January 1810, No. 62.
105. *Ibid.*
106. Military Department, 2 January 1810, No. 65.
107. Military Department, 2 January 1810, No. 66.
108. Judicial letter from Court of Directors, 23 February 1813, para 26.
109. Revenue, 28 April 1815, No. 50 D.
110. Revenue, 28 April 1815, No. 50 B.
111. *Ibid.*
112. Revenue, 28 April 1815, No. 50 D.
113. *Ibid.*
114. Public, 3 August 1821, No. 56.
115. Public, 3 August, 1821, No. 58.
116. Public, 3 August 1821, No. 57.
117. Public, 23 May 1822, No. 3.
118. Public, 30 May 1822, No. 37.

119. Public, 30 May 1822, No. 42.
120. *Ibid.*
121. Public, 30 May 1822, No. 43.
122. Public, 30 May 1822, No. 42.
123. Public, 30 May 1822, No. 41.
124. Public, 30 May 1822, No. 45.
125. *Ibid.*
126. *Ibid.*
127. *Ibid.*
128. *Ibid.*
129. Public, 30 May 1822, No. 44.
130. Public, 30 May 1822, No. 48.
131. *Ibid.*
132. Public, 30 May 1822, No. 49.
133. Public, 30 May 1822, No. 50.
134. Public and Law Letters to Court of Directors, No. 87 of 1822.
135. Public, 18 July 1822, Nos. 9-10.
136. *Hyderabad Residency,* Vol. No. 62, p. 675.
137. Public, 16 October 1823, No. 34; Public, 6 November 1823, No. 33.
138. Public, 24 June 1824, No. 35.
139. Public, 24 June 1824, No. 34.
140. Public, 7 October 1824, No. 10.
141. Public, 17 February 1825, No. 7.
142. Public, 14 April 185, Nos. 13-15.
143. Public, 26 May 1825, No. 22.
144. Public, 25 September 1825, No. 12.
145. Public, 25 September 1825, No. 13.
146. Public, 15 December 1825, No. 50.
147. *Ibid.*
148. *Ibid.*
149. Public, 15 December 1825, No. 51.
150. First Report of the Curator of Ancient Monuments, 1881-82, p. 5.
151. Revenue, 28 April 1815, No. 50 D.
152. Military Proceedings, 13 February 1810, No. 57.
153. Military Proceedings, 24 November 1810, No. 72.
154. *Ibid.*
155. Military, Fort William, 13 February 1810, No. 57.
156. Military, 24 November 1810, No. 73.
157. Military 24 Noveber 1810, No. 74.
158. Military, 24 Novembr 1810, No. 70.
159. Military Proceedings, 6 August 1810, Nos. 90-91.
160. Military Proceedings, 6 August 1810, No. 92.
161. Military Proceedings, 6 August, 1810, No. 90.
162. Military Proceedings, 18 February 1815, Nos. 88-89.
163. Public, 20 October 1820, No. 1.
164. Public, 20 October 1821, No. 2.
165. Public, 21 September 1821, No. 11.
166. Judicial letter from the Court, 26 February / April 1820, para 131.
167. Judicial letter from the Court, 26 April / February 1820, para 132.

168. Judicial letter from the Court, 26 April / February 1820, para 133.
169. *Hyderabad Residency*, Vol. No. 67, p. 45.
170. Political, 25 April 1829, No. 18.
171. Political, 25 April 1829, No. 17.
172. Political, 25 April 1829, No. 16.
173. Political, 25 April 1829, No. 20.
174. *Ibid.*
175. *Ibid.*
176. Political, 25 April 1829, No. 22.
177. Land Revenue, G.G. April 1838, No. 15 (Minute of Governor-General, 7 March 1838).
178. *Hyderabad Residency*, Vol. No. 72, p. 163.
179. Public, 14 September 1836, No. 20.
180. *Ibid.*
181. 14 September 1836, No. 21.
182. Public, 31 January 1838, No. 5.
183. *Ibid.*
184. *Ibid.*
185. *Ibid.*
186. *Ibid.*
187. Public, 31 January 1838, No. 8.
188. Public letter to Court No. 6 of 1839 and 13 March 1839.
189. Public, 12 August 1840, No. 33.
190. Public, 10 March 1841, No. 5.
191. *Ibid.*
192. Public letters to Court, No. 35 of 1841, para 1.
193. Public, 23 May 1838, No. 10.
194. *Ibid.*
195. *Ibid.*
196. *Ibid.*
197. *Ibid.*
198. *Ibid.*
199. *Ibid.*
200. Public, 4 July 1838, No. 11.
201. *Ibid.*
202. *Ibid.*
203. *Ibid.*
204. Public, 15 August 1838, No. 15.
205. *Ibid.*
206. *Ibid.*
207. *Ibid.*
208. *Ibid.*
209. *Ibid.*
210. *Ibid.*
211. *Ibid.*
212. Public, 15 August 1838, No. 16.
213. Public, 3 April 1806, No. 50.
214. Judicial, 20 August 1838, No. 18.
215. Judicial, 10 December 1838, No. 19.
216. Judicial, 10 December 1838, No. 17.

217. *Ibid.*
218. Judicial, 10 December 1838, No. 18.
219. Judicial, 10 December, 1838, No. 19.
220. Judicial, 6 May 1839, No. 10.
221. *Ibid.*
222. *Ibid.*
223. *Ibid.*
224. *Ibid.*
225. Judicial, 6 May 1839, No. 9.
226. Judicial, 29 April 1839, Nos. 8-9.
227. Judicial, 7 October 1839, No. 6.
228. *Ibid.*
229. Judicial, 7 October 1839, No. 7.
230. *Journal of Asiatic Society*, 1843, pp. 73-74.
231. Foreign, Political, 4 January 1843, Nos. 6-10.
232. *Ibid.*
233. Foreign, Political, 1 March 1843, Nos. 10-12.
234. *The Story of Indian Archaeology*, by S. Roy, p. 22.
235. First Report of the Curator of 'Ancient Monuments' for the year 1881-1882, p. 5.

CHAPTER III

Major Projects during Company (1844-1858)

CARE OF CAVE TEMPLES

The year 1844 was a watershed in the history of Indian archaeology. On 8 April 1844, R. Clarke, Honorary Secretary, Royal Asiatic Society of Great Britain, brought to the notice of the Court of Directors that the Royal Asiatic Society had in its possession an interesting paper on the Cave Temples of India by James Fergusson, who had conducted a meticulous research on cave temples especially in Bihar and Cuttack region as well as in western India where he had highlighted the earliest and simple forms of cave temples and wherein he had given a vivid description of designs of these structures by classifying them. The Honorary Secretary further stated that Fergusson was also well versed in deciphering inscriptions which appeared in cave temples in India and that he was conversant with the architectural features of the monuments, which were amply reflected in the paper.

He further stated that according to Fergusson, early cave temples were of Buddhist origin and classified them into two classes, i.e., the Viharas or Monastic and the **Chaitya** or temple caves. The ancient Buddhist caves were normally found in Gaya and Cuttack. Fergusson gave a detailed description of these caves that were situated along the roadside during his travels and described their architecture and importance and compared, with the Ajanta Caves in Berar region. The Honorary Secretary stated that these caves were first described in a research paper by Lt. Alexander and published in the second volume of the **Translations of the Royal Asiatic Society**. Alexander elucidated that the paintings of the caves had profuse descriptions of attires, habits and life of Indians as existed 2000 to 2500 years ago and were well-preserved paintings of the sects of Buddhists. The antiquity of Buddhism could be proved by the paintings and sculptures and their depiction exhibit a wooly haired race of Indians, which is more or less extinct in the Indian sub-continent.

The paintings also depicted the frescoes of the Buddha and his disciples with **chowries** in their hands. The colours of the paintings vary from brown, light red, blue and white, with red colour dominating the painting. The colouring fades to soften the effect of depiction and its execution is bold depicting the subject and perspective of the theme. The figures are two feet to three feet in height. The paintings in many of the caves represent interesting delineations of hunting scenes or depictions of battle. The elephants and horses were particularly well drawn besides the depiction of Lord Ram and display of cock fights. He further described that spears were peculiar in shape having three knobs near the head and an instrument resembling a lyre with three strings like a zodiac sign.

The research treatise of James Fergusson also relates interesting relics of Indian antiquity. The description of terrain encompasses details of Tapti valley in the north to the tableland of Deccan. The ghats in between these areas were ravines and in one of these ravines, the caves of Ajanta (or Ajeend) were situated. The entrance to these ravines measured a mile, which led to a cascade of seven falls, viz., Satkund and one of them measured 100 feet high; besides there were 100 more.

The entire cave complex has been covered with stucco and many of the smaller paintings on the pillars of the roof of the aisles comprise figures of the Buddha and his disciples in various postures that were in a state of ruin. There were, however, several inscriptions dating to 100 or 200 BC, the evidence of which could be relied upon by sheer conjecture.

The zodiac cave had the dimension of 64 feet x 63 feet and had 20 pillars and one of these pillars was beautiful and elegant. The paintings of these pillars had faded but one can determine its theme. The wall on the right had a painting of a procession comprising three elephants, which were painted black, red and white and these motifs also formed part of Burmese and Siamese style of paintings comprising **chatris** (umbrellas) and flags despoiled with a large retinue of men armed with spears, swords and shields. Besides, on the back of a wall was depicted a hunting scene in which a lion was depicted as a royal power as well as deer and dogs. Men on horseback and on foot were also graphically depicted.

The verandah of the cave had interesting paintings, which was circularly depicted and could be mistaken for a zodiac. The central theme of the painting was divided into eight compartments and the outer circumference into sixteen or seventeen compartments. Each of these compartments was crowded with small figures.

The Buddhist figurines were depicted on the door of the cave. The figures had details sitting cross-legged. The first four figures were black in colour, the fifth fairer the others fair and the last figure fair and adorned with a crown. The women were generally depicted as fairer than men who in turn were painted in all shades from black to sallow European complexion.

The roof was painted in various patterns in albeit inferior style of art. Fergusson further stated that the deterioration of painting was imminent and after a lapse of some time, these paintings would not be visible to connoisseurs of art. The style of the paintings could not be compared to European paintings as existed during the period but certainly superior to paintings of antiquity of that age. The details of these paintings were livid and better depicted than the Chinese paintings of the period.

The paint used for these paintings could not be determined as the colours lay on a dry surface and absorbed in the plaster.

The Royal Asiatic Society felt that the caves of Ajanta were unique specimens of Hindu painting of pre-Christian era and must have been executed by mendicants. The Society felt that both Hindus and Muslims were apathetic towards the preservation of the heritage and that there was every likelihood of these specimens of art to be lost to posterity. There was an imperative need to preserve these specimens, which amply illustrate the early history of India. The Society petitioned to the Court of Directors to save the caves from decay and "preserve the remembrance of these most curious and valuable remains of ancient art".[1]

The Court of Directors forwarded the petition of the Royal Asiatic Society to Lord Ellenborough, Governor-General on 29 May 1844 and recommended that something should be done for saving the cave temples in India from decay and deterioration. The Court of Directors suggested talented officers should be entrusted with the task of preservation and also procure copies of drawings of other caves for ensuring scientific and methodical conservation. The Court of Directors was also desirous of collecting data on "liberal and mechanic arts" in India and various tribes along with implements and costumes for their Library and the data thus collected could be used for reference purposes. Lastly, the Court of Directors directed that for ensuring accuracy of the drawing and plans, the Dolland's camera or Lucida camera could be procured for each of the Presidencies and put in proper use.[2]

The Governor-General forwarded the communication received from the Court of Directors to the Governments of Fort St. George, Bombay, Bengal and North Western Provinces on 27 July 1844 with a request that measures should be immediately taken for preserving the cave temples of India obtaining accurate delineations and procuring plans for carrying out the repair and restoration work of the sculptures and paintings.[3] These Governments took immediate measures and initiatives in this regard. They are detailed as hereunder:

I. Action Taken by the Bombay Government

The Secretary, Government of Bombay circulated on 2 August 1844 the letter from the Governor-General to various Collectorates of southern and northern division (where most of these cave temples were located) and the response was encouraging. The details are as follow:

Southern Division

David Blane, Revenue Commissioner, Southern Division received reports of implementation of the orders of Court of Directors from various Collectorates of southern division.

1. Report from A. Nash, Superintendent, Survey and Assessment, Deccan Poona on 13 August 1844.

Recommended the name of Mr. Fallen from Poona who was a Drawing Master and whose services could be utilised for the restoration of paintings at Ajanta with the assistance of an Assistant Surveyor and Builder to produce accurate representation of the paintings and make correct plans and drawings of the caves. Further, Mr. Fallen would be useful for designing the costumes of the people depicted in the paintings. He also recommended the reference of Poona figures that would convey an accurate idea of costume designing and also designs for implements of agriculture and manufacturing implements. The contingent charges could be authorised for the purpose, which were well within his jurisdiction.

Besides, Mr. Fallen suggested that these were persons in Gujarat who could build models of the temples at Abu and other places in the region and also could be entrusted with the task of building the models at Bijapur and Aurangabad, which would be eventually helpful in restoration and conservation assignments.[4]

2. Report from CEF Taylor, Superintendent of Dong Survey (Nasik).

On 15 August 1844, Taylor responded and stated that draftsman who had the requisite experience was not available. Further, he was of the opinion that the preservation of cave temples could be effectively executed by the district authorities.[5]

3. Report from D. Davidson, Superintendent, Revenue, Survey and Assessment, Ahmadnagar.

On 16 August 1844, Davidson expressed his inability to do anything "towards the accomplishment of the objects contemplated by Hon'ble Court".[6]

4. Report from Wingate, Acting Superintendent, Revenue Survey and Assistant on 11 September 1844.

On 11 September 1844, Wingate stated that there were no cave temples or any monuments of architectural significance in Belgaum or Dharwar, which would require the attention of district administration towards their upkeep. However, Wingate requested that Lucida's camera could be sent to district administration that could be employed "to greater advantage in other parts of the Presidency". As regards documentation on "the state of the liberal and mechanic arts in India", Wingate requested for additional information in this regard so that adequate action could be taken.[7]

5. Report from A. Elphinstone, Collector, Ratnagiri on 31 December 1844.

On 31 December 1844, Elphinstone stated that in the absence of any important monument or caves in the district as compared to the presence of such edifices or caves in Western India, it was not possible to furnish the detailed information in this regard. However, the Court's directives were forwarded to various sub-divisions or talukas of the district.[8] He also appended a list of cave temples in various sub-divisions of taluka of the collectorate. He further stated that Bal Gangadhar Shastri, Superintendent, Government School pays an annual visit to the district and requested the Company's Government to approach him for a report on the caves and cave temples.[9]

6. Report from H.A. Harrison, Collector, Ahmadnagar on 28 September 1844

On 28 September 1844, Harrison reported that there were no cave temples in the district and there was no competent personnel who could render any assistance with regard to ensuring conservation of cave temples.[10]

7. Report from Juveravity, Assistant Collector, Poona on 23 October 1844.

On 23 October 1844, Juveravity communicated to the Company's Government that there was no competent person available who could competently and accurately delienate the plans of the temples or paintings and sculptures.[11]

8. Report from H.W. Reives, Collector, Belgaum on 31 August 1844.

On 31 August 1844, H.W. Reives assured the Company's Government of his services towards conservation of caves and cave temples. He stated that he had since rendered assistance to Dr. Bird in deciphering inscriptions at the caves in Nasik and would continue towards this objective in future. However, he stated that for use of Lucida's camera in delineating drawings there was no able person in the district who could be entrusted with this assignment. A competent person for copying the inscriptions of Badami and other cave temples of southern Maratha region could be located and entrusted with the assignment of this nature.[12]

9. Report from E. Montgomerie, Collector, Sholapur on 14 January 1845.

On 14 January 1845, Montgomerie reported that there was no one in his district who could be entrusted with the task of this nature.[13]

Thereafter, David Blane, Revenue Commissioner, Southern Division compiled the inputs thus received from the various districts of the Southern Division and forwarded to the Secretary, Government of Bombay for information. He stated that for the preservation and conservation of caves and cave temples, encouraging replies have not been received in so far as delineation of temples was concerned, excepting Lt. Nash's suggestion for the employment of a professional artist.[14]

Northern Division

Likewise, R.K. Pringle, Revenue Commissioner, Northern Division on 19 February 1845 also forwarded a report on the subject of preservation and conservation of caves and cave temples to the Secretary, Government of Bombay. He stated that Collectors or Officers employed on surveys would not be in a position to contribute effectively towards preservation of caves or cave temples as contemplated by the Court of Directors. However, the execution of such works could be entrusted to persons possessing relevant qualifications required for the purpose. He advised that Captain Ottley, Acting Chief Engineer, Khandesh had suggested the deployment of an officer from Artillery possessing requisite qualifications for the purpose.

He further was of the opinion that only cave temples were in the Tanna Collectorate and the Acting Collector of the District, Mr. Law, had suggested that an officer from the Road and Tank Department should carry out the inspection of caves in Elephanta and precautionary measures should be taken for ensuring their preservation. He also suggested the deployment of two peons for taking care of Kanheri caves at Salsette which had since suffered onslaught of wet weather. Besides, the Commissioner also stated that the Ajanta caves were under the jurisdiction of Nizam's Government and not under Khandesh Collectorate.[15]

W. Escombe, Secretary, Government of Bombay on 19 March 1845 forwarded the reports from the Revenue Commissioners of Northern and Southern Divisions of the Bombay Presidency to Bushby, Secretary, Government of India and stated that if an officer was not appointed for making delineation of the cave temples of Western India as required by the Court of Directors, accurate delineations of the temples would not be possible.[16]

Bushby suggested on 12 April 1845 that "the services of an artist fully competent for that duty can be obtained for making delineations of the cave temples of Western India. To despatch public servant, civil or military, from his proper duties for the proposed employment would be objectionable". He further stated that the services of an artist if requisitioned should be ratified by the Supreme Government in so far as the expenses and period of employment was concerned.[17] However, efforts continued for the care and conservation of cave temples unabated.

On 1 December 1844, Captain B. Johnston, Commander, Hill Rangers addressed a communication to Brigadier M.E. Bagnold, Commandant, Aurangabad Division. He referred to the swarming of bees and wasps at the entrance of the Senapur Caves, commonly called the Ajanta Caves. Besides, he also pointed out the thorny creepers and growth of wild vegetation obstructing the entrance of the caves and his efforts to remove them with the help of three persons. He also referred to the paintings of Ajanta caves that were fading and deteriorating due to the use of smoke by the local population to drive away the bees for extracting honey.

He further stated that in order to carry out the wishes of the Court of Directors, he had suggested a plan of action for employing two Bheel labourers on a salary of Rs. 5-6 per month to carry out cleaning operations and also deploying escalating ladders to clear swallows, nests and beehives. The services of labourers should also be made to travellers visiting the caves. As regards damage inflicted to the footpaths leading to caves due to rains, he suggested that the new footpaths should be laid so as to ensure safety to the persons using them. This would result in incurring expenses by the Company's Government which would be worth incurring.[18]

A list of the Senapur Caves (Ajanta Caves) and their present state of preservation are detailed in Appendix IX.

On 14 December 1844, Brigadier M.E. Bagnold reported to W.Escombe, Secretary, Government of Bombay and stated that no officer was available under his command who was capable of undertaking the sketching of Ajanta Caves and that he was informed that the Government of Madras had actually appointed Captain Gill to carry out the sketching of caves.

He added that the caves of Ellora were in good state of preservation and despite their mutilation during the rule of Muslims, the interior of these caves have not shown any signs of damage or decay due to ageing. He concluded by stating that his experience of 37 years had led him to this belief and conclusion.

As regards vegetation growth on the exterior of the caves, he stated that the growth of vegetation especially Peepul trees have taken roots which had resulted in displacement of earth and stone. This had also resulted in the debris getting accumulated raising the mounds of debris in some places which were five or six feet in depth. The debris had to be removed and the trees had to be uprooted and burnt down.

The barrier walls to most of the lower entrances should be removed to prevent the entry of cattle as herded by the locals. The defecations of the cattle often result in heaps that are burnt by pilgrims or Bairagis inside the caves which result in infliction of damages to the cave paintings.

Ellora was under the jagir of Raja Ram Baksh, the tutelage ruler or minister at Nizam's Court at Hyderabad and if General Fraser could exercise his influence, he could obtain an order of Nizam for the preservation of caves under the protection and care of Brigadier commanding at Aurangabad.[19] Brigadier Bagnold had suggested that the removal of earth and wild vegetation growth would require incurring an expenditure of Rs. 500-1000.[20]

W. Escombe, Secretary, Government of Bombay submitted the information to G.A. Bushby, Secretary, Government of India on 13 January 1845 for consideration of Sir Henry Hardinge.[21]

The Governor-General in Council sought the information concerning cost to be involved in the preservation of Ellora Caves and for removal of trees and debris in Brigadier Bagnold's Report. The Council also suggested the need of communicating to the Nizam's Government towards this direction. Besides, the Governor-General in Council also authorised an expenditure of Rs. 500-1000 for removing the obstacles from the entrance of the gate of Ajanta Caves and the removal of debris that had accumulated in the caves, and deployment of 2 Bheel labourers for the purpose on a salary of Rs.5 to 6 each per month.[22]

With a view to ensure proper preservation of Ellora Caves, Captain W.K. Lloyd, Executive Officer, Aurangabad Division visited the caves, minutely inspected the entire area and reported to the Brigade Major on 21 April 1845. He reported that the state of preservation of Ajanta Caves were same as they were in 1794. When Sir G. Malet published an account in the *Asiatic Researches*, he categorically stated that they were generally in good state of preservation. However, he commented on the general state of caves which required thorough repair works. He recommended a sanction of expenditure of Rs. 2000/- towards their preservation and for preventing them from further dilapidation.[23]

Thereafter, the Secretary, Government of Bombay authorised Brigadier M. Bagnold on 23 April 1845 to draw money to be expended on the temple caves of Ajanta from the account of the Collector, Ahmadnagar. In response, Brigadier Bagnold requested the Government of Bombay to sanction Rs. 2,000/- to Captain W.K. Lloyd, Executive Officer stationed at Aurangabad for clearing the weeds and vegetation growth at Ellora Caves. He further requested the Government of Bombay to sanction a similar amount as was made for protection and preservation of the Ajanta Caves.[24]

Acting on this request of Brigadier Bagnold, W. Escombe, Secretary, Government of Bombay submitted the entire correspondence relating to the Ellora Caves and Ajanta Caves on 15 May

1845 to G.A. Bushby, Secretary, Government of India for being laid before the Governor-General for his consideration. Meanwhile, the entire affairs relating to preservation of Ajanta and Ellora caves was apprised to the Court of Directors by the Government of India on 24 May 1845. The Government of India particularly referred to the measures taken for clearing of vegetation and weeds from these caves; the recommendations of the Government of Bombay for appointment of an officer on Special Duty for delineations of the Cave Temples; their objections for appointment of Lt. I. Phillip of the Artillery; and reasons for not allowing attachment of officers from the regular civil and military services.[25]

The Home Department on 31 May 1845 communicated the sanction of the Governor-General in Council for authorising an expenditure of Rs. 2,000 for clearing vegetation growth in the Ellora caves and for preserving them from further dilapidation. The Governor-General in Council also allowed employment of two Bheel labourers on a salary from 5 to 6 rupees each per month for the protection and preservation of the Ellora Caves similar to that authorised for the Ajanta Caves.[26]

Besides, a copy of the concerned papers regarding the preservation of Ajanta and Ellora Caves was forwarded to the Foreign Department with a request that a communication should be made available to the Resident at Hyderabad with a primary objective for apprising the Nizam's Government.[27]

Accordingly, the Nizam's Government was apprised of the efforts made in this direction for fulfillment of this objective. Sooraj Mulk Bahadur (to whom the Ajanta Caves belong) addressed a note to Major General Fraser, Resident at Hyderabad on 4 July 1845 that since Nizamabad or Ajanta came under his dominion, the Naib of Nizamabad was directed to follow the directives of Captain Gill in so far as preservation of Ajanta Caves was concerned. As regards Ellora Caves, it was decided to address a representation to Nizam and after obtaining an appropriate order, the Naib of Nizamabad shall be accordingly addressed.[28]

To this, Fraser thanked Sooraj-ul-Mulk for instructions to the Naib of Nizamabad for carrying out the repairs at Ajanta Caves. With regard to Ellora, he requested for appropriate orders of the Nizam so that the Government of India could be apprised accordingly.[29]

The following day, i.e., 5 July 1845, Fraser forwarded the entire correspondence between Sooraj-ul-Mulk and him to Currie, Secretary, Government of India and stated that Ajanta Caves were the hereditary and private property of Sooraj-ul-Mulk. He stated that he had undertaken to bear the expenses for repair and ensure future preservation. He had also forwarded a copy of the despatch to Captain Gill who was appointed by the Government of Madras and entrusted with the work of copying the paintings of Ajanta.[30]

Thereafter, Fraser addressed a communication to Currie, Secretary on 23 July 1845 through which he informed about the restoration work of Ajanta Caves to be taken over by Sooraj-ul-Mulk for their preservation. As regards Ellora Caves, Fraser referred to the intention of the Supreme Government and the requisition of a plan of Ellora Caves by the Nizam's Government before he could decide on the matter. Fraser further stated that since there was ambiguity with regard to plans or copy of the paintings regarding Ellora Caves as desired by the Nizam, he expressed his inability to furnish the requisite information.

Fraser further elaborated that Sooraj-ul-Mulk had sent him a note stating that the Nizam was concerned with the repair works of Ellora Caves and since it was a place of worship for the Hindus, Peshwa Raja Ram Baksh Bahadur would depute a person to assess the repair works needed for restoration of caves.

Fraser sought the consent of the Company's Government about his intention about entrusting the repair works of Captain Gill but as Nizam had since declared the Caves a place of worship for Hindus, he felt it necessary for the Company's Government to initiate such measures, and orders of the Nizam for their preservation and upkeep would be quite sufficient in this regard.[31]

In the meantime, on 31 July 1845, Captain B. Gill informed Major General Fraser that not much work was effected with regard to repair works of Ellora Caves in comparison to repair works effected at Ajanta Caves. Gill felt that the arrangements for preservation as proposed by the Nizam should be the best alternative as that was declared a place of Hindu worship and the Brahmin priests at Ellora were taken into confidence. It was also decided that the Nizam would effect the preservation work through hired labourers and would "keep them in a state of cleanliness and to prevent all future injury and desecration".[32]

The observations of Captain Gill were thus conveyed to the Secretary, Government of India on 5 August 1845 by Major General Fraser. Subsequently, the Military Board, Bombay comprising Major General D. Barr, Military Auditor General, Lt. Col. George Jervies, Chief Engineer and Lt. Col. F.P. Lester, Member, Military Board made some important suggestions to the Government of Bombay on 8 August 1845 with regard to deployment of Mr. Fallen for making delineations of the cave temples and the term of his employment.

To this communication of the Military Board, Fallen had stated that this assignment was important and time-consuming. He requested the payment of a salary amounting to Rs.600 per month. With regard to the period of employment, Fraser referred to a Memorandum by Prof. Orlebar (please see Appendix X) sent by Fallen. This Memorandum incorporated the discussion between Prof. Orlebar and Fallen with regard to history, mythology and antiquities of western India, and estimated a period of 32 years as sufficient for detailed drawings of all the objects of interest in the caves by a single artist.

Prof. Orlebar had divided the sphere of operations for the delineations of the cave temples dwelling on the following districts: (1) Ajanta, (2) Ellora, (3) Kanheri, (4) Jonar, (5) Abu, (6) Palitana, (7) Bijapur and (8) Ahmedabad.

Prof. Orlebar felt four years in each district would be sufficient for such delineations of the cave temples in the aforementioned districts.

Fraser, therefore, suggested that the area of operations should be selected by the Committee as recommended by Prof. Orlebar for delineating the best caves of the area concerned. As regards the drawing of Ajanta, Prof. Orlebar contended that a period of 18 months would be adequate and thus recommended the appointment of Mr. Fallen for carrying out the task of delineations on the terms and conditions suggested by Mr. Fallen himself. Fraser was also of the opinion that Mr. Fallen should commence the work of delineation and his future assignments would depend upon the completion of work of some caves in the Salsette region. His workmanship on certain specimens of caves would be adjudged for future employment. Fallen had assured that certain specimens of his work would be shown and after they were approved, he would delineate the entire cave for Rs. 500 which would also include the drawings of pillars of one side of a cave, corresponding frieze and geometrical drawing of the pillars and different figures on the frieze. He would also be asked to execute complete drawings of one cave comprising plan, elevation details along with view of landscapes on the basis of Stuart's delineations of the temples and antiquities of Athens. He would be given a remuneration of Rs. 1,500 (one thousand five hundred only).

Fraser also apprised the Government about the communication exchanged between Lt. Nash of Engineers and Mr. Smart, Portrait Painter residing at Poona on the cave temples. He further informed that Mr. Smart has expressed his willingness to make drawings of the caves of Carlee, Bursa and Elephanta on prescribed Government rates. Besides, Nash had a high regard for and confidence on Smart's ability, and recommended the purchase of his paintings for the Committee's approval. Fraser sought the approval of the Board for entering into correspondence with Smart on the subject of cave drawings.[33]

On 22 August 1845, William Escombe, Secretary, Government of Bombay requested G.A. Bushby, Secretary, Government of India for the employment of a competent artist on terms and conditions laid by the Government of India for undertaking the work regarding delineations of the cave temples of western India.[34] Escombe further informed Bushby on 26 August 1845 that since Sooraj-ul-Mulk had undertaken the responsibility of repair and preservation of the cave temples of Ajanta, it was necessary to employ Bheel labourers for removing the accumulated debris from the caves and the grant of an amount of Rs. 500/- to Rs. 1000/- was essential to be expended on this particular repair work. On the offer of repair works to be undertaken by the Nizam's Government, Fraser sought the concurrence of the Governor-General in Council. He also informed that the Governor-in-Council was in favour of retention of Bheels labourers in the Government establishment.[35]

Thereafter, on 20 September 1845, Bushby informed W. Escombe that the Supreme Government and the Court of Directors had not contemplated such an expensive operation as recommended by the Military Board at the Government of Bombay for procuring the copies of the paintings in the Ajanta Caves and drawings of other cave temples of India. He further added that the Governor-General was of the opinion that the Court of Directors would restrict the expenses to be incurred in delineating cave drawings and limit to two dozen drawings of the best and interesting cave antiquities of western India. The Governor-General in Council sought the recommendation of the Bombay Government to determine a suitable remuneration to be given to an artist who may execute the work, although finished drawings were not required and the work executed should be artistic and commensurate with the expenses incurred.[36] He further added that since the cave temples of Ajanta were private property, expenditure sanction for clearing the debris by employing Bheel labourers should stand superseded as Sooraj-ul-Mulk has agreed to attend to the repair works.[37]

Accordingly, the Court of Directors sent a letter on 27 January 1847 to Lord Hardinge, Governor-General in which they referred to the steps taken by the Company's Government for removal of debris in the Ellora Caves and the acceptance of the responsibility of repair works by the Nizam's Government. The Court of Directors was of the opinion that the restrictions of a number of cave temples for illustrations should be guided, by principle, not only by the importance but also by their relation and bearing with each other. The yardstick to be adopted for such preservation of antiquities in the form of caves should be resorted by employing experienced and talented persons on military service by giving them honorarium and moderate remuneration for their services rendered. The Court of Directors further suggested that uniform and effective plans for conservation and restoration of antiquities should be resorted to, which should be based on scientific principles.

The Court of Directors made important suggestions for the systematic survey of the monuments with a view to provide protection and encourage conservation.

The Court of Directors felt that accurate, minute and classification of monuments should be undertaken by men who are qualified to carry out their assigned work of conservation within a prescribed time frame. A concise plan should be drawn up indicating the topography and physical features detailing mineral wealth and other botanical details. The plan should be uniformly adopted depicting the decorative details of the architecture of the monuments concerned. Besides, a general outline of sculptural embellishments and pictorial details had to be drawn up. The documents and records detailing the monuments should be collected for carrying out scientific conservation programmes. With regard to the financial implications involved with the programme of documenting the various antiquities requiring attention, the Court of Directors was of the opinion that estimated expenditure had to be drawn up and its spending should commensurate with the priorities to be adopted for conservation of such an antiquity.

After the preliminary planning is done, the persons qualified to undertake the job should be selected and put on the job. The Court of Directors was of the opinion that such measures would ensure satisfactory completion of job and economy in expenditure. The Court also felt that for the proper execution of conservation plans, a Commission could be established which would give directives to carry out such plans of conservation of caves and edifices of archaeological importance effectively.[38]

After receipt of the directives of the Court, H.M. Eliot, Secretary to the Governor-General, received a letter from the Home Department on 24 April 1847 stating that the Governor-General should be informed that the Public Department did not propose to take any cognizance of the Court's directives with regard to collection of requisite information before embarking upon conservation programmes of the antiquities relating to the cave temples. After the approval of the Governor-General, they would initiate the conservation plans as indicated in the Despatch of the Court of Directors.

However, Rs. 1,000/- was sanctioned by the Government of India to clear the debris at the entrance to the Ajanta Caves. Towards the fulfillment of this objective, two Bheel labourers were hired at Rs. 5-6 each per month for ensuring that the caves were kept in clean and neat condition and were free from vegetation growth. An amount of Rs. 2,000/- was also authorised for the caves at Ellora and an establishment comprising two labourers was also sanctioned. Besides, the Government of India was informed about orders, which were to be issued by the Nizam's Government, for cleaning and maintenance as the Ellora caves were designated places of worship by Hindus. Besides, the Government of India was also informed that Suraj-ul-Mulk had offered to attend to the repair and preservation work of Ajanta Caves.

With regard to employment of a competent artist for preparing drawings as required in the Court's Despatch, the Government of Bombay informed that Mr. Fallen had offered his services on a salary of Rs. 600 per month. Further, the Government of Bombay was also informed that this assignment would take 32 years by a single artist to encompass all the objects of historical, mythological and scientific interest in western India. The Government was of the opinion that Professor Orlebar, who was consulted by Mr. Fallen, supported Fallen's proposal.

However, the Government of India was of the opinion that the proposal of the Government of Bombay would not satisfy the Courts' contention as the expenses involved were on a higher side. The Government of India, however, felt that the expenses could be restricted by having two dozen drawings of the interesting and important cave temples in western India rather than encompassing the entire cave antiquities of western India. However, the Government of India left the entire matter to the discretion of the Government of Bombay, which ultimately did not pursue the matter.

Subsequently, the Company's Government referred to the employment of Captain Gill by the Government of Fort St. George on a monthly salary of Rs.200 in addition to his admissible allowances and an establishment of Rs. 175/- per month for delineating the drawings of the architectural remains in the Ajanta Caves.[39]

Likewise, the Bombay Branch of Royal Asiatic Society on 15 April 1848 addressed a communication to I.G. Sumesdon, Secretary, General Department, Government of Bombay wherein suggestions were made for the procurement of information pertaining to the cave temples under the jurisdiction of the Government of Bombay and likewise sought the Governments' sanction to appoint a Commission comprising its own members for collecting, receiving and requesting information for the guidance of personnel to be appointed, as contemplated in the Despatch from the Court. The Society felt that before the appointment of a Commission, a circular to Collectors/Political Agents and other local authorities should be issued wherein they should be directed to supply information with regard to cave temples in their respective jurisdiction so that the Society could facilitate its task. Thereafter, the Society would be in a position to suggest deployment of personnel with requisite experience and qualifications to undertake the job.[40]

The Government of Bombay promptly sought the Government of India's approval on 3 May 1848 for the proposal submitted by the Society.[41] This proposal of the Society was approved by the Government of India to appoint a Commission from amongst the members of the Bombay Branch of the Royal Asiatic Society for the purpose of conducting preliminary enquiries as to the number and situation of different monuments and cave temples of antiquity within Bombay Presidency and of the Commission being placed in communication with the public authorities mentioned for the execution of the task. However, it sought detailed information on such enquiries, before any expenditure was incurred for the appointment of personnel to undertake such investigations relating to the cave temples in western India.[42]

Finally, the Government of India addressed a communication to the Court of Directors on 30 November 1848 regarding measures proposed by the Society to the Government of Bombay for effectively conducting antiquarian researches in Bombay Presidency. The Government of India sought approval of the Court of Directors for addressing a communication to the district officials and Political Agents in the Bombay Presidency for facilitating the assignment of the Society.[43]

Eventually, the Government of Bombay appointed a Commission comprising Rev. Dr. Wilson, Honorary President, Dr. Stevenson, Vice-President, C.I. Erskine, Captain H.B. Lynch, Prof. John Harkness, Vinayak Gangadhar Shastri and the Secretary of the Society as members.

At the first meeting of the Commission held on 20 November 1849 and at the suggestion of Dr. Wilson, its President, it was resolved that a descriptive list of cave temples and antiquarian monuments should be drawn up and forwarded to the district officials, under whose jurisdiction the monuments existed. In this meeting, Dr. Wilson was requested to compile a summary which was completed in May 1850 and was later printed in the Society's journal under the title "Memoir on the Cave Temples and Monasteries and other ancient Buddhist and Brahmanical Remains of Western India".[44] A copy of the Memoir was as well forwarded to the district officials and the local governments in the jurisdiction of Bombay Government with a request that description of cave temples and monuments of antiquarian interest be forwarded to the Society so as to facilitate further research on the subject.[45]

The Government of Bombay approved the proceedings of the Commission and procured 60 copies of the 'Memoir' for distribution in the manner suggested by the Governor-General in Council.[46] Besides, the Government conveyed its gratitude to the Cave Temple Commission and to Dr. Wilson in particular. Thereafter, William A. Fallen, Portrait and Ancient Painter, entered into correspondence with Rev. John Wilson, Honorary President, Royal Asiatic Society, Bombay Branch, on 2 December 1850 and evince interest in paintings of Elephanta caves and offered his services to obtain the drawings of Hindu antiquities in Western India, 'deserving on account of their great merit, a more skilful pencil than mine'. Fallen offered his services on a monthly salary and stated that if the financial propositions of his proposal was considered exhorbitant, he would offer his drawings by renouncing his copyright and execute the work on salary of Rs. 400 per month.

The plan of work submitted by Fallen was divided under the following heads:

1. A study in oil similar to the specimen forwarded.
2. A plan of the cave.
3. Elevation of the plan with all its sections projected in architectural principles.
4. Sections and elevations of the caves.
5. A projection of the above serial nos. 1, 2, 3 and 4 to be done in water colour.[47]

On 14 December 1850, Henry Carter, Secretary, Bombay Branch of the Royal Asiatic Society recommended to the Secretary, Government of Bombay the grant of an honorarium amounting to Rs. 100 to the Brahmin priest who brought to light the excavations at Kuda and Khandasu and Rs. 20 to the local guide who accompanied Dr. Wilson to the excavation sites in the Garodi Hills. He also sought the Government's permission to allow the Commission to publish in the Government's Gazette, the details of prizes from Rs. 25 to Rs. 100 to any party for bringing any site of prospective excavation to their notice. The reward should commensurate with the importance of the discovery. The Commission also recommended the employment of Mr. Fallen for executing the illustrations of cave paintings in Bombay Presidency on the terms and conditions as proposed by Mr. Fallen himself. On this issue, the Commission recommended that he should be entrusted at the first instance the task of illustrating the cave temples at Elephanta.[48]

Accordingly, on 1 February 1851, H.E. Goldsmith, Secretary, Government of Bombay sought the approval of the Government of India on the appointment of Mr. Fallen.[49] Accordingly, a Resolution was adopted on 4 April 1851 through which Mr. Fallen was appointed for undertaking the illustrations of the Elephanta Caves on a salary of Rs. 400 per month.[50]

The Cave Temple Commission was satisfied with the paintings executed by Fallen and recommended the retention of Mr. Fallen for executing the remaining cave temples of western India. Accordingly, the Government of Bombay solicited the approval of the Government of India. A Resolution was adopted on 11 June 1852 by the Governor-General in Council for retaining the services of Mr. Fallen "for a further period of one year on a salary of Rs. 400 a month".[51] The Court of Directors was accordingly informed on 11 October 1852.[52]

In the meanwhile, the President of the Cave Temple Commission strongly recommended the further extension of Mr. Fallen for the purpose of illustrating the caves at Aurangabad as the work done by him could not be completed. The Government of Bombay promptly approached the Government of India on 20 February 1854 for an extension of Fallen's employment for a further period of six months from 1 January 1854 to 30 June 1854 so as to enable him "to commence the illustration of the Karlee caves near Aurangabad".[53]

A Resolution was adopted on 18 March 1854 extending the employment of Mr. Fallen to undertake the illustration of Karlee caves at Aurangabad.[54] Another extension of employment was given to Mr. Fallen through a Resolution of the Company's Government on 23 October 1854.[55]

On 9 April 1856, John Wilson, President of the Cave Temple Commission, sent a detailed note to William Hart, Secretary, Government of Bombay regarding desirability of a publication under the auspices of the Government which would contain facsimiles, decipherments, translations of cave temple inscriptions, rock inscriptions and copperplates found within the British Empire in the east. The publication of such **Corpus Inscription** was an important antiquarian documentation of Indian history which should merit the attention of the Government, learned societies and orientalists. The Cave Temple Commission sought the approval of the Government of India for obtaining the concurrence of the Court of Directors.

The Commission was of the opinion that much work in the field of antiquarian studies had been done in India and needs to be documented. It detailed the documentation of inscriptions, which had been copied, deciphered and translated, and the chronology of these inscriptions could reflect the religious and political changes that had occurred in the country through times immemorial. In the field of antiquarian studies, the three Presidencies have a great role to play. The works on the inscriptions had to be revised and perfected and the entire annotations revised after thorough decipherment and translations. The Commission particularly felt that zealous and competent men of letters were to be hardly found and orientalists and indologists, viz., Col. Sykes and Prof. H.H. Wilson were advancing in age. The Commission, therefore, recommended that as an **ad interim** measure they should be permitted to employ a learned scholar Pandit Vishnu Shastri Bapat who was well versed in the art of cave character and language script and further had also been testified by Mr. Wathen and Dr. Wilson as having considerable experience in collating the transcripts of the inscription made by Mr. Brett with the originals. Beginning from February 1856, the Pandit could be employed on a salary of Rs. 50 per month. The Commission was of the view that Bapat was on a higher salary as the Head Pandit of the Poona Sanskrit College and employed thereafter at the Revenue Department in northern Konkan. The Commission further proposed that he should be placed under the President, Cave Temple Commission and designated as Pandit to the Commission.[56]

Taking the facts into consideration as enumerated in the letter dated 9 April 1856, William Hart, Secretary, Government of Bombay sought the approval of the Government of India on 30 April 1856 on the publication of **Corpus Inscriptionum** and also the employment of Vishnu Shastri Bapat for the collection of Sanskrit inscriptions.[57]

The Government of Bombay subsequently received a letter from the Government of India on 29 May 1856 wherein it had sanctioned the employment of Pandit Vishnu Shastri Bapat with retrospective effect, i.e., from 1 February 1856 on a salary of Rs. 50 per month.[58]

II. Action taken by Madras Government

The Madras Literary Society and Auxiliary Asiatic Society began to evince interest in the field of preservation and care of monuments which had the support of the Government of Fort St. George. In his Minute, Walter Elliot, Chairman of the Committee of Management of the Madras Literary Society and Auxiliary Royal Asiatic Society referred to the Despatch of the Court of Directors dated 29 May 1844 for collection and preservation of objects of antiquarian interest which intended to throw light on India's past.

As a preliminary step, information on antiquities or areas on antiquarian interest needed to be collected and enquiry had to be initiated for collection of facts and data without incurring considerable expense.

In the process of antiquarian research, facts on early history, ascendancy of various races, religions, population trade and manufactures, statistical data, art, science and literature needed be collated and documented.

To achieve this stupendous task, the cooperation of district officials and engineers was essential to document the information succinctly and in a comprehensive manner. In this connection, the Commission outlined the undermentioned subjects on which information was required:

1. The existence of cave temples.
2. Sites of deserted cities or places of importance, which are in ruins, though still inhabitated, particularly earlier, existing states/potentates, which were the capital cities of erstwhile rulers.
3. Stones or ancient pagodas or fine architectural edifices, viz., temples at Tanjore, Gangodram, the brick structures at Negapatam and the brick remains of the palace of Cholas at Kumbakonam.
4. All palaeographic remains, stone grants and copper-plate grants.
5. Sculptured rocks or walls or stones whether monumental or commemorative of important persons or events.
6. Ancient walls, fortifications, dargahs or hill forts.
7. Mounds indicating sites of towns, fortresses or other edifices, viz., stupas.
8. Fine works of utility or irrigation works, e.g., Tungabhadra and Caveri (Kaveri) anicuts, Poneri Tank at Tiruchirapalli and the bridges at Sivasumundram and Anagundi.

The Commission also contended that a letter should be addressed by the Chief Secretary to the Government to all Collectors and Officers-in-charge of districts and to the Engineers of the 8th Division. The replies thus received should be referred to this Committee, which could suggest further measures for being considered for adoption by the Government of Fort St. George.[59]

A Circular was accordingly sent to all the districts and Local Governments by the Government of Fort St. George in which was elicited details of edifices of antiquarian interest, "with a character of interest or curiosity, but avoiding all lengthened description or detail.[60]

The Secretary, Government of India was accordingly informed about the minute and the circular. After the receipt of replies, the Government of Madras adopted measures for the preservation of archaeological remains, which were to be implemented with the help and guidance of the Madras Literary Society and Auxiliary Royal Asiatic Society.

III. Action taken by the Government of North Western Provinces

An effective and hearty response was received from the Government of North Western Provinces in the field of preservation and conservation of monuments. In this connection, J. Thornton, Secretary, Government of North Western Provinces addressed a communication to H. Rose, Collector and Magistrate, Banda on 15 September 1845 in which was enclosed an extract from the *History of India*, by Professor Wilson[61] which described the cave temples at Kalinjar which had inscriptions. Rose was requested to procure facsimiles and authorised moderate expenditure for the purpose.[62]

Besides, Rose contacted Lt. Maiscy of 67 Regiment of Native Infantry who was well acquainted with these temples for eliciting details of the temple-complex. Accordingly, Maisey informed H. Rose on 4 December 1845 that there were abundance of temple conglomerates in

Banda and if required, drawings of principal specimens could be furnished which are worth preserving. He further stated that the exquisite works of art were scattered in the region and work of that dimension would take some time. Maisey added that, in case his corps marches to another destination, he would be compelled to abandon the project mid way but assured him that he would concentrate on the architectural intricacies and details of Neelkanth temple after eliciting measurements of the edifices, drawings of which could, however, be completed at Allahabad. Maisey also sought the favour of Rose to approach the Lt. Governor on the matter regarding his accompanying the Regiment in their movements from one destination to another.[63]

Rose promptly forwarded the letter from Maisey dated 4 December 1845 to I. Thornton, Secretary, Government of North West Provinces on the issue of temple drawings and sought his advice on the matter.[64] However, Rose informed Maisey to limit his area of investigation to cave temples only as was wished by the Lt. Governor.[65] Thereafter, Rose addressed another communication to I. Thornton, Secretary to Government of North Western Provinces on 19 December 1845 and apprised him of his instructions to Lt. Maisey with regard to the drawings of the cave temples and sought his leave of absence from the Regiment through the military authorities in order to complete the job assigned.[66] In reply, Thornton had his apprehensions about Lt. Maisey's absence from his military duties and regretted that he could not be spared much longer with the temple drawings and at the same time sought detailed information on the antiquities of temples examined by Lt. Maisey.[67]

On 6 May 1846, a description of the cave temples at Kalinjar along with the illustrations as prepared by Lt. Maisey were forwarded to Thornton by Rose and he testified the accuracy of the drawings, correctness of the depictions and made recommendations for the remuneration. Rose also forwarded the unfurnished drawings by Maisey and hoped that "Mr. Maisey will be allowed to return next year to conclude what he has so well began".[68]

A sum of Rs. 454 was proposed as remuneration by Rose to be paid to Lt. Maisey and he added that Maisey had confined his operations to the Neelkanth temple and description of "caves, reservoirs and sculptures which may be said to belong to it as they all form one" series and are approached by the same gateway and descent.[69]

Thornton replied to Rose's letter and conveyed the sentiments of the Lt. Governor for the creditable work done by Maisey. He also authorised Rose to pay a sum of Rs. 454 as remuneration for the work done by Maisey.[70]

On the same day, i.e., 19 May 1846, Thornton requested H. Torrens, Secretary, Asiatic Society to lay before the Society, the report on cave temples at Kalinjar in Bundelkhand prepared by Maisey at the instance of H. Rose, Collector, Banda. The work could not be completed as he had moved with this troops to the frontier for the Sikh War. Thornton also conveyed the wishes of the Lt. Governor for a publication on the temples at Kalinjar in their journal for "the notice of those who are filled and experienced in such researches".[71]

At the same time, Thornton requested Major Frederick, commanding 67th Native Infantry on 19 September 1846, for granting leave to Lt. Maisey so as to enable him to complete the task at Kalinjar temples to "complete the drawings and designs of the cave temples in that locality on which he was engaged last year".[72]

In reply, Major Frederick requested Thornton to apprise the Lt. Governor about Maisey's application for 6 months' leave commencing from 1 November 1846 which was forwarded by him.[73] Accordingly, Maisey commenced his second tenure from 1 November 1846 for completion of art work relating to the Kalinjar group of temple caves and communicated to Thornton accordingly.[74] Thornton informed Maisey the appreciation of Lt. Governor in accomplishing the art work of Kalinjar and informed him about the remuneration amounting to Rs. 1,000 granted by the Lt. Governor.[75] Maisey was prompt in thanking Thornton for his gestures.[76]

In the meanwhile, it was brought to the notice of the Lt. Governor the discovery of some cave temples in the forested hilly tracts in south of Chunar near Mirzapur. The Hon'ble Court of Directors instructed that such archaeological sites should be explored, described and preserved. He authorised some expenditure to be incurred in this regard. Thornton approached Captain Stewart, Fort Adjutant, Chunar on 26 December 1845 for this assignment and proposed an amount of Rs. 400-500 to be sanctioned for the purpose.[77]

Captain Stewart submitted a set of plans and drawings executed by C.H. Burke who was formerly with the Revenue Survey Department and reported to Thornton on 3 November 1846 that there were three caves, viz., Beach Mandah, Rounah Mandah and Chargoodree situated in Taloogah, Shahpuri (Shapori) in pargana Burdee which was at one time part of Benaras State but subsequently merged with Rewa State through an agreement between the Rajas of Rewa and Burdee. The tract near the caves was inaccessible due to rock hills covered with dense overgrowth and interspered with villages inhabited by aboriginal tribes, information on whom was not readily available. The caves were abandoned due to wild beasts in the nearby forests. These caves were under the Balund Raja of Khurwar tribe who held the states of Agoree and Singrauli until the Chandels expelled him, emigrated from Mahoba in AD 1190 and regained control of Agoree by defeating the Balunds 50 years later. The envoys of the Balund Rajah resided in a village named Mircaus in the vicinity of Shapore Singrauli. Though dispossessed of their titular rights for nearly 600 years, they were still hopeful of regaining their control over their possession. They had taken a vow that they would don the turban after principality was restored to them.

Besides, ruins of walls and brick structures as well as a Fort were found in the Nilour Hills near a village called Benowlee, 12 miles north-west of the caves which were believed to be the ancient capital of Shahpur Singrauli and the last stronghold of the Balund. Stewart added "the former existence of a people capable of constructing such stupendous work."[78] A bill amounting to Rs. 500 was forwarded by Stewart for expenses incurred by Burke.[79] Thornton appreciated the work done by Burke and informed Stewart that the plans and sketches of the cave temples had been forwarded to the Asiatic Society in Calcutta for publication in their journal or for notice in such other shape as may appear to them expedient.[80]

Thereafter, the Secretary, Asiatic Society informed Thornton that the description of the caves had since been published in the Society's journal and the drawings would be published after the approval of the Committee of Papers. The Secretary, Asiatic Society conveyed his thanks for the material on cave temples thus sent to the Asiatic Society.[81]

The Court of Directors sanctioned Rs. 1012.12 to the Lt. Governor, North West Provinces for expenses incurred "on the preparation of accurate accounts and drawings of Cave Temples at Kalinjar and at Shahpuri, south of Chunar".[82]

On 26 January 1848, Thornton apprised the Government of India about drawings of Kalinjar temples in Bundelkhand by Lt. Maisey and Mandah temples by Burke thus forwarded to the Asiatic Society and publication of their description in the journal of the Asiatic Society. He further informed that the second set of drawings of the Kalinjar temple in Bundelkhand were forwarded to Benaras in order to decipher the inscriptions before they were forwarded to the Court of Directors. It would be desirable that they should also be sent to the Asiatic Society for assessing them for being published in the Society's journal before forwarding.[83] On 26 January 1848 itself, Thornton requested the Secretary, Asiatic Society to send the drawings and plans of cave temples to G.A. Bushby, Secretary, Government of India for onward transmission to the Court of Directors. Besides, Thornton also informed that the second set of drawing of Kalinjar temple executed by Lt. Maisey could be seen by the Asiatic Society before they were sent to the Court of Directors by the Government of India.[84]

In November 1847, Lt. Maisey was entrusted with the task of investigating the ruins at Ranode under Scindia's jurisdiction. Resident at Indore and Captain Cunningham furnished the details of these ruins. In fact, Captain Cunningham had suggested that the fallen gateways of Bhilsa Stupa should be sent to London for being exhibited in the British Museum. The Court of Directors, however, objected to this proposal and suggested to forward the drawings of the gateway. The Court felt that the removal of gateways would hurt the local sentiments.[85]

About 100 drawings of Sanchi Stupa were prepared by Lt. Maisey and submitted to the Government of India for onward transmission to the Court of Directors. In this assignment, Captain Cunningham who incidentally had published an interesting book on the subject actively helped him. Maisey was of the opinion that his work was quite different from Cunningham. Cunningham should also be considered for publication. This publication would provide complete documentation on Buddhist antiquities. He attributed the delay in his work of drawings of Sanchi to his active involvement in Burma War at Pegu.[86] Maisey also suggested that sculptures from India should be exhibited in a space at the London Crytical Palace which had been enriched by the speciments of art from Egypt-Assyria. He concluded by stating that the sculptures of India both in style and mystic import are too closely allied with the Assyrian and Egyptian sculptures.[87]

Mention may be made of M. Kittoe, who combined his functions as Archaeological Engineer and Archaeological Enquirer. On 29 September 1847, he was addressed a communication by the Court of Directors to Lord Hardings I, Governor-General about the selection of officers who were well-versed in research and knowledge of Indian antiquities for documenting the temple architecture for their eventual publication. In this connection, the Court of Directors suggested the names of Captain Kittoe and Lt. Cunningham for undertaking the documentation of antiquities of Bengal and North West Provinces, provided their services could be spared. He further contended that the drawings of sculptures at Bodh Gaya as submitted by Captain Kittoe were of considerable interest and depiction of drawings "assist to throw light upon the ancient history of the country".

The Court of Directors concluded that they would like to receive specimens of sculptures provided they could be removed "without great convenience and that their removal will not be offensive to the feelings of the people which we do not anticipate. The Court of Directors felt that the reports on the archaeological surveys would help a great deal the orientalist in Europe for documenting the publication on Indian artifacts and antiquities".[88]

Accordingly, the Home Department informed Captain Kittoe on 31 December 1847 that he was being entrusted with the task of undertaking, "the preliminary archaeological enquiries in the Provinces of Benaras and Bihar where the antiquities all or chiefly reside".[89]

A Resolution dated 31 December 1847 was drawn for the appointment of Captain M. Kittoe to undertake antiquarian researches in the Provinces of Behar and Benaras. The Home Department justified Kittoe's appointment by stating that Kittoe was engaged in superintending the construction of Benaras College building and was the most suitable person to undertake researches in the provinces of Bihar and Benaras. He would draw a salary and allowances of Rs. 200 per month over and above the salary, which he received, for Benaras college work.[90] The Court of Directors was informed about the appointment of Captain Kittoe by the Government of India on 8 January 1848. The Government of India also stated that instructions to Captain Kittoe were given for supervision of progress report on annually.[91]

Subsequently, Kittoe commenced the work and the Governor-General in Council desired that 30 copies of ancient sculptures along with a catalogue, which was earlier prepared by Mr. Laidlay, Vice-President of the Asiatic Society, be sent to the Court of Directors, as the Governor-General in Council felt that it was a signal contribution of the Society.[92]

The Home Department, thereafter, addressed a communication to the Secretary, Asiatic Society on 18 January 1850 requesting to forward to the Court of Directors for their Museum some specimens of sculptures selected by Captain Kittoe and kept in the custody of the Asiatic Society.[93]

After being packed in two cases which weighed 20 maunds, they were shipped to England under the charge of 2nd Assistant to the Master Attendant through **Asia** (ship). The details of the sculptures thus forwarded to the Court of Directors were as hereunder:

1. Figure of Sakya bearing an inscription in Maithili Nagri script "He Dharma Hetu" also inscribed the name of the donor and the maker of the statue.
2. Figure representing Nirvana or death of Sakya beneath a Sal tree with the disciples lamenting and musicians playing.
3. Shiva with his consort Parvati and his daughter Laxmi.
4. Mahadeva giving advice to his consort.
5. Standing figure of Mayadevi, mother of Sakya.[94]

IV. Action taken by Bengal Government

A circular was addressed to all the civil officials in Bengal Presidency wherein a copy of the despatch of the Court of Directors was enclosed. They were requested to report whether cave temples or monuments of antiquarian importance existed in their respective districts or divisions and if they existed, their suggestions for preserving them were invited.

The Government of Bengal assured the Government of India to carry out the wishes and suggestions of the Court of Directors on the care and preservation of cave temples keeping into consideration such temples and buildings which were not in use for worship and had no caretaker to oversee their upkeep and preservation. This was done so as to "explain the object of any researches or enquiries they may institute in consequences of these orders so as to prevent any misconception regarding them on the part of the native community". The Asiatic Society also assured that they would suggest "means for preserving the cave temples and other monuments of antiquarian value from injury or decay".[95]

Besides, Captain Kittoe, Archaeologist, requested G. Bushby, Secretary, Home Department on 8 February 1848, to elicit information on antiquarian objects mentioned in the circular of 1844 and also sent a draft circular which could be considered for issue by the Governor-General. Captain Kittoe also suggested that the magistrates should be empowered to utilise the services of under-trial prisoners for regularly clearing of garbage in the vicinity of such monuments. He referred to similar operation at Bodh Gaya where specimens of sculptures could be obtained without much effort.[96]

CIRCULAR

In accordance with the instructions received from the Hon'ble Court of Directors in their dispatch dated 27 January 1847 and appointment of Captain Kittoe for inspecting the antiquities of the Residency and also for collection of specimens of sculptures and objects for the Museum of Hon'ble Court, a circular was issued. The circular also underlined the need for enlisting the services of the magistrate of districts with regard to eliciting data on monuments and temples of antiquarian interest.[97]

It was also decided that Captain Kittoe and the magistrate should ensure especially when the sculptures and objects of antiquarian interest are removed, their description is also detailed therein.[98]

Captain Kittoe reported the progress of work done by him to G.A. Bushby, Secretary, Home Department, on 9 February 1848. He stated that after assumption of his duties as an archaeologist on 21 January 1848, he deciphered inscriptions from Bodh Gaya temple and after transcribing them in Devnagari translated them into vernacular. He induced the people to come forward to help in deciphering the inscriptions which were mutilated as were the inscriptions from Kalinjar which were forwarded under the direction of Lt. Governor, North West Provinces.[99]

Besides, Kittoe also addressed a communication to the Secretary, Home Department on 27 December 1852 informing him about the desire to visit Gaya for archaeological duties for clearing the debris in order to locate **tumulus** or Buddhist charity through which he was expected to locate valuable data in the form of relic boxes. Kittoe requested for communication of instructions to the authorities for rendering assistance in this venture. He clarified that he would require the services of 100 prisoners for 3-4 days. The distance between the jail and the temple was five miles and the Mahant of Bodh Gaya temple was ready to assist him in this venture. He further stated that the **timulus** was small and buried in debris. He discovered this in 1848-49. During his recent visit to Gwalior, he had met Major Cunningham who had encouraged locating the inscribed relic boxes.[100]

The Home Department of the Government of India requested the Under Secretary, Government of Bengal on 5 January 1853 to instruct the authorities in Gaya to facilitate Captain Kittoe's venture in conducting enquiries in Bodh Gaya Temple.[101]

However, the Under Secretary, Government of Bengal informed A.R. Young on 20 January 1853 that the services of prisoners would not be possible in view of recent orders on the subject as enlisting prisoners for archaeological work was objected by the Government. The Magistrate, Gaya, however, had been instructed to render every kind of assistance to Captain Kittoe for conducting archaeological enquiries at Bodh Gaya.[102] This decision was accordingly communicated to Major Kittoe.[103]

Thereafter, Kittoe addressed another communication to the Secretary, Home Department, Government of India on 4 February 1853 that he had prepared over 155 drawings of sculptures, architectural edifices and idols of Buddha, Jain and Hindu pantheon which he proposed to take with him to England for being delivered to the Court of Directors after classifying them into major groups enroute England. Besides, a large collection of inscriptions transcribed in modern Devanagari script as well as facsimiles and impressions in duplicates was in his possession. A large collection of sculptures in stone and bricks at Benaras had been packed for being transmitted to the Home Department as well as for Hon'ble Courts' Museum.[104]

The Secretary, Government of North West Provinces addressed a communication to I.P. Grant, Secretary, Government of India on 16 April 1853 that Major Kittoe had been engaged since 1847 in the construction of the Government College at Benaras and after completion of its construction had to leave the country due to ill health. He recommended that the Governor-General should commend the services of Major Kittoe to the Court of Directors and grant him special remuneration for his work of excellence. His staff salary as an architect during the period of his employment was only Rs. 20 per month. He further stated that during his sojourn at Benaras, his talents and experience were utilised by all those who wanted to plan such buildings. Besides, Kittoe was well-versed in church architecture, which was conspicuous in the construction of churches in the provinces especially Punjab which were designed and assistance rendered by him in their construction.

The cities of Benaras, Mirzapur and Jaunpur were improved and embellished at the instance of Kittoe and he has raised a school of workmen where their skills were honed so as to ensure architectural excellence. Concluding his remarks, Secretary, North West Provinces stated that, "his incessant and anxious labours contributed in a small degree to impair his health and consequently to drive him from this country".[105] Along with this letter, a list of important survey reports of Major Kittoe was also enclosed.[106]

Lord Dalhousie, the Governor-General concurred in the proposal of the North West Provinces and addressed a communication to the Court of Directors on 29 April 1853 recommending some award to be bestowed on Major Kittoe by the Hon'ble Court.[107]

After some time, Kittoe died. The Court of Directors granted the family of Major Kittoe £1,000 in recognition of the services rendered by him and also the dispatch of sandal-wood model of the Benaras College prepared by Kittoe for being presented to the Court of Directors and also in execution of "Benaras College and other architectural and engineering works in which he took part".[108]

USE OF PHOTOGRAPHY

After appreciating the efforts of Major Kittoe and Lt. Maisey in execution of their duties assigned to them, the Court of Directors emphasised the importance of photography in their letter to the Government of India on 7 February 1855. The Court specially highlighted the advantages of photography over employment of draughtsmen in the delineation of antiquities. It laid stress on the accuracy, economy in expenditure and time and strongly urged to employ photography to "obtain representation of objects of interest". The Court of Directors also assured to forward the necessary apparatus for use in Government.[109]

On 13 April 1855, the Government of India directed the Secretary to the Governments of Madras, Bengal and North West Provinces (N.W.P.) to consider photography "as a means by which representations of scenes and buildings may be obtained with accuracy and economy of time and money".[110]

A deciding step was thus taken following a suggestion from the Royal Asiatic Society of U.K. *vide* their circular dated 8 April 1844 mentioned earlier in this chapter. The Government of Fort St. George, Bombay, Bengal and North West Provinces took a positive initiative in introducing the marvel of photography towards preservation and conservation of monuments.

CARE OF OTHER MONUMENTS

Besides cave temples, the care of ancient structures (monuments) of antiquarian interest continued unabated. There were various instances but only a few merit special mention. In 1842, during the Governor-Generalship of Lord Auckland, the local agents at Agra were directed to assume charge of Itmad-ud-daulah's tomb and keep it in perfect repair.[111] In 1843, Viscount Hardinge authorised the local agents at Agra to grant a sum of Rs. 150 for carrying out repair works at the tomb of Itmad-ud-daulah.[112]

However in 1847, an Archaeological Society was established in Delhi.[113] Its members included British officials and Master Ram Chandra, Syed Ahmed Khan, Maulvi Ziauddin and other reputed scholars of Delhi. This was the first voluntary organisation which was devoted to the cause of archaeological works. The objectives of this organisation were "the investigation by means of plans, drawings and elevations by inspirational and historical researches of the ancient remains both Hindu and Mohammedan, in and around Delhi, and the institution of similar researches in other parts of North Western Provinces". In the Archaeological Society, discussions were held and papers were presented. The example could be cited of a paper presented jointly by Henry Cope, Secretary, Archaeological Society of Delhi and Henry Lewis, member of the Society on 9 August 1847 under the auspices of the Archaeological Society. The paper highlighted the conservation of monuments.[114]

The Secretary announced many programmes and plans for conservation of monuments but according to S. Roy, the announcement remained "no more than an idea". The reason being that the Society was short-lived but its decision was a systematic evidence in solving problems in chronology. It had an important plan in the annals of Indian archaeology.[115]

Thereafter, in 1848, Sir Bartle Frere, the erstwhile Resident at Satara, instituted a survey of the Islamic architectural remains at Bijapur. Captain Hart of the Bombay Engineers was entrusted with this responsibility.[116]

However, during the tenure of Lord Dalhousie as Governor-General, the Lt. Governor of North West Provinces in 1850 sanctioned an expenditure of Rs. 1500 from the endownment fund earmarked for the tomb of Salim Chisti at Fatehpur Sikri.[117]

In 1850, the Governor-General forwarded a memorial for consideration to Lt. Governor, North West Provinces from the trustees of the Fatehpuri Mosque, Delhi requesting that the Road Committee should be prevented from destroying any portion of the Fatehpuri Mosque. Meanwhile, the Lt. Governor had ascertained that the destruction of the Fatehpuri Masjid in Delhi had been proposed in the Road Committee at Delhi with a view to improve the Grand Trunk Road.[118]

In 1853, in his minute Lord Dalhouse, the Governor-General lamented the neglect of monuments in the vicinity of Kutub Minar, which were in ruinous condition and in a state of utter disrepair. General Sir William Maynard, the Commander-in-Chief whose camp halted for some days at Delhi, reported this. Dalhousie recalled his own instructions five years ago to this effect for preservation of these beautiful remains. Lord Dalhousie in his minute stated that the Mughal Dynasty had left these monuments that were magnificent and the Company's Government could face reproach if these monuments were neglected. He strongly pleaded for taking immediate measures for their preservation for the "admiration of ages to come".

Dalhousie directed the Military Board to send instructions to the Executive Officer at Delhi for immediately taking up the repairs at the monuments in the vicinity of Kutab and ensure their proper preservation. Lord Dalhousie made it clear that "the officers of the Department of Public Works at Agra and Delhi and in other places where such remains may exist should consider it to be a part of their duty to attend to them, if they are not otherwise cared for." Lord Dalhousie also emphasised the need to have a report of the Executive Officers and elicit details of "annual cost of preserving them from further decay as far as this is practicable".[119]

The Members of the Governor-General's Council readily concurred with the contents of the minute for Lord Dalhousie and they assured of their support and sanction of finances "to preserve those relics of a past dynasty".[120]

On 2 December 1853, G. Plowden, Officiating Secretary, Government of India conveyed to the Military Board and also entrusted with the responsibility to carry out the necessary repair and ensure proper upkeep of archaeological edifices.[121] Meanwhile, W. Muir, Secretary, North West Provinces forwarded a circular dated 7 December 1853 to the Commissioners of Rohilkhand, Allahabad, Benaras, Jaunpur, Delhi, Ajmer and Kumaon for taking adequate measures in the preservation of archaeological sites and monuments of significance. The circular also contained instructions to be transmitted to the magistrates for adopting urgent measures with a view to preserve the antiquarian monuments from neglect and destruction in their respective jurisdiction.[122]

The Commissioners and Magistrates immediately responded in a positive manner. Accordingly, W.C. Cunningham, Magistrate at Farrukhabad, addressed a communication to W.H. Tyler, Commissioner Agra Division on 2 January 1854 and recommended repair works of the Dargah of Makdum Jehma Jahangust at Kannauj. In fact, the Lt. Governor of North West Provinces had inspected the monument and had approved of its repair works at the Government's expense.[123] Likewise, C. Wingfield, Magistrate, Mathura reported to W.H. Tyler, Commissioner, Agra Division and recommended repair works of mosques in the Mathura town which was built by Abdul Nabi Khan and the Idgah situated in the outskirts of the city erected by Emperor Aurangzeh. The exterior of the mosque, built by Abdul Nabi Khan, was entirely destroyed. The Idgah Mosque built by Aurangzeb was a fine structure and the Muslims of the Mathura city had raised Rs. 2000 for repair works of the mosque. However, Wingfield felt that an equal amount should also be sanctioned to complete the repair works. He also informed about the programme of the Lt. Governor to visit Mathura who would be in a position to make on-the-spot assessment about the extent of repair works needed.[124]

On 9 August 1854, R. Drummond, Magistrate of Agra reported to H. Muvin, Commissioner of Agra Division that funds available would not be sufficient to keep the monuments in a state of perfect condition.[125]

A statement of ancient structures that required repairs along with the estimated cost of expenditure was prepared.

Details of the monuments	**Estimated cost of repair works**
Taj Mahal	Rs. 28,337.13.6
Itmad-ud-daulah	Rs. 11,817.14.0
Sikandra	Rs. 20,406.2.0
Various Buildings of Fatehpur Sikri (21)	Rs. 1,585.0.0[126]

H. Muvin, Commissioner, Agra Division addressed a communication to W. Muir, Secretary, Government of North West Provinces on 18 August 1854 on the ancient structures of exquisite beauty and grandeur, and stated that such monuments were only found in Mathura, Furrukhabad and Agra. Besides, he communicated the reaction of the Magistrates of Mathura and Farrukhabad on the repair works of the monuments to be undertaken in these two towns.

He also made reference to the list of 24 monuments in Agra as furnished by the Magistrate, Agra. Taj Mahal dominated the list and the expenses involved in carrying out the repair works of the edifice amounted to Rs. 28,337. Whereas, the Itmad-ud-daula's tomb required Rs. 11,817 for the preservation works and for the tomb of Akbar at Sikandra, a sum of Rs. 20,406 was estimated.

The Commissioner, Agra Division further suggested that Rambagh Palace should be entrusted to the care of the local agents. Although the funds at the disposal of the local agents were insufficient for effecting improvements in the edifice, but the Government's assistance was necessary to effect the repair works.[127]

Reacting to this communication, William Muir, Secretary, Government of North West Provinces communicated to the Commissioner, Agra Division, the orders relating to repair works of the Idgah at Mathura, Dargah at Farrukhabad, Taj, tomb of Akbar, Sikandra and Itmad-ud-daula's tomb at Agra. An amount of Rs. 1,000 was sanctioned to carry out the necessary repairs to the monuments at Sikri. Muir also stated that the Lt. Governor felt it necessary to allocate an outlay for carrying repair works at the Rambagh Palace.[128]

Lord Dalhouse, the Governor-General appreciated and approved preventive measures adopted by the Lt. Governor for preservation of ancient structures of aesthetic beauty in public interest in the Agra Division, in his letter dated 29 September 1854.[129]

The Court of Directors appreciated these efforts on 16 May 1855 and directed the Military Board and the Public Works Department to carry out the repair works within the environs of Kutub as stated by the Governor-General.[130]

On 22 September 1857, Colonel Cotton, Commanding at Agra constituted a Committee of Engineer officers under the command of Lt. Col. Glassford of Bombay Engineers to report on the existing defenses of Agra Fort and suggest measures to be adopted for its further improvement. Other members of the Committee were Captain Munbee, Captain Campbell, Captain Nicolls and Lt. Glover (all from Bombay Engineers). The Committee submitted its report on 18 February 1858 and suggested means for its proper preservation. The theme of the Report revolved on the measures to be adopted to prevent demolition of ancient structures.[131]

The Court of Directors initially sanctioned the repair works of Delhi's Red Fort in 1833 and partial repairs to the Fort were undertaken. After a lapse of 11 years in December 1844, the Court of Directors once again sanctioned repair works to be undertaken at the Red Fort Palace. The king of Delhi requested Metcalfe, Agent at Delhi, to complete the repair works by the Government as the Court of Directors sanctioned it.[132]

Metcalfe conveyed the request of the Sovereign King of Delhi to Sir Henry Hardinge I, Governor-General. Reacting to this, the Secretary to the Governor-General addressed a communication to the Government of North West Provinces on 5 December 1845 and contended that the Red Fort should be repaired at the expense of the Government as desired by the Sovereign King but expressed his reservations about the expenses involved in the repair work. The Secretary to the Governor-General conveyed that "His Excellency suspects, that it will cost as much to build a new Palace as to repair the old one and the Agent at Delhi should be requested to ascertain whether, in that case, His Majesty might not prefer a new Palace at the Kutub with the same exemption from which he now enjoys whereby we should get rid of the great inconvenience of having the palace and its precincts exempt from the jurisdiction of our Courts in the very centre of the popular city of Delhi."[133]

The king of Delhi did not like the developments in this regard. He, therefore, sent a *shuqqa* (Royal letter, letter from a superior) to I.F. Metcalfes Agent to the Lt. Governor on 29 January 1846 reiterating the need of repairs to the building and estimated an expenditure of Rs. 1 lakh for the purpose. He stated, "His Lordship will not think of building a new Palace. By doing this, you will do my pleasure and it will add to your good name". The king gave his own reasons for abandoning his plans for building a Palace at Kutab. He cited reasons of unnecessary expenditure and uneven, hilly and defective terrain in the vicinity at Kutab, which would be an obstacle in the building of a Palace. Besides, the King asserted that "he had a special attachment to the Palace as it was in the heart of city and on the banks of River Yamuna".[134]

In response to this *shuqqa* from the Sovereign King of Delhi, Metcalfe, Agent to the Governor of North West Provinces, addressed a communication to I. Thornton, Secretary, North West Provinces, Agra on 5 February 1846 and stated that His Majesty, the Sovereign King, was declined to accede to their proposal of building a new Palace at Kutab. Metcalfe felt the disinclination of the king was natural primarily due to vacating the residence of his ancestors. Metcalfe felt that estimate of repair amounting to Rs. one lakh was on the lower side and suggested to have an estimate to be submitted by a professional official.[135]

On 27 February 1846, Thornton replied to Metcalfe that it was essential to have an estimate for repair works prepared by the Executive Engineer to inspect the Palace and submit realistic estimates "of the sum which will be necessary to put it to a good state of repair".[136] Thornton requested Metcalfe to submit repair estimates through the Military Board. An estimate was finally prepared by Captain A. Abbot, Officiating Executive Officer at Delhi, which amounted to Rs. 50,573/- (rupees fifty thousand five hundred and seventy three only). This estimate was submitted to the Lt. Governor through the Military Board. The following areas of the Palace needed repair:

Entrance arcades; Tripolia Chowk, 6 Bazar Gates, Gotal Bar, Lal Purdah Ke Chowk, Summan Boorj, Garden; Passage from Dewan Khas to Garden; Entrance to Baths; Southern Wall near Entrance; Garden wall at the River Face; New Wall at the River Face; Moti Mahal; Rebuilding Domes on Corners; Shah Boorj; Canal in Garden; Jumma Masjid in the Palace; Khan Sumanee; Large Cook House (Burra Kussa); Small Cook House (Chota Kussa); Surrounding Wall of Palace (inside); Delhi Gate; and the surrounding walls (exterior).[137]

The Lt. Governor soon sanctioned the requisite amount.[138] Captain P. Abbot was directed to undertake the works immediately confirming the repair works which were absolutely essential.[139]

The Lt. Governor did not refer the entire episode regarding the repair works of Red Fort Palace to the Governor-General. However, when Lord Dalhousie, the Governor-General was apprised of the progress on 5 June 1849, he was unhappy over the Lt. Governor's conduct and opined, "Lt. Governor had acted beyond his powers in authorising the repairs".[140]

Finally, the Secretary, Government of India clarified that the Governor-General's approval was necessary in this regard. However, there was a similar misunderstanding on the part of the Lt. Governor. He presumed that the Governor-General had given his approval. According to I. Thornton, Secretary, Government of North West Provinces, "...the Lt. Governor would not have felt himself warranted in authorising the commencement of the repairs".[141] However, the repair work was undertaken.

After a lapse of eight years, on 21 September 1857, Major General A. Wilson, commanding the Army at Delhi sent a telegram to the Chief Commissioner, Lahore enquiring the future fate of the Red Fort Palace as its inhabitants had abandoned it. He apprised him that he had 3,300 sick and wounded and lots of munitions of war. He proposed to stay within the city wall and transport the sick and wounded, and guns and munitions, to Meerut and blow the bastions of the Fort before taking troops on to the Ganges Doab.[142]

The Chief Commissioner replied through a telegram and advised Major General Wilson that the Palace of Delhi would make a safe refuge for the small body of troops, guns and munitions of war which would help in recovering Delhi and the Company's Government's hold on the adjacent districts. The telegram further said that the occupation, rather than the destruction, of the Palace would be a political gain and advised him against the destruction pending the orders of the Government. The Chief Commissioner was of the opinion, "We can always destroy, we cannot so easily construct. It will take years to build such a magazine."[143]

On 22 September 1857, A. Brendeth, Secretary to Chief Commissioner communicated to Major General A. Wilson, who was commanding the Army at Delhi on the orders of the Chief Commissioner with regard to taking care of the sick, wounded and munitions of war, about the secure possession of the city, the Palace of Delhi and vigorous prosecution of war. The Chief Commissioner felt that these objectives could best be achieved by occupying the Palace at Delhi. Without the occupation of a Palace, the Company's forces would be confined to defensive arrangements. So long as the Palace was in occupation, no enemy would attempt to enter the city and even if they should do so, they would not do any harm.

On the other hand, if we may dismantle the Palace, the army should guard the sick and munitions of war. In this process, loss of valuable time would be detrimental to the Company's interests. The Chief Commissioner referred to the dismantling of the Fort at Multan, which was built over a period of eight years, considered that it was a mistake as after annexation of Punjab it would have been an ideal refuge for munition and soldiers. All the political objectives to be gained by the destruction of the Palace would be equally secured by its occupation. It would take several years for the Engineers to construct an arsenal, the Chief Commissioner contended.[144]

In a similar vein, A. Brendeth also addressed a communication to Edmonstone, Secretary, Foreign Department on 23 September 1857 and stated that with the arrest of the king of Delhi and death of his two sons in a battle with Lt. Hodson, the success of the Company's Government has been completed and the object to "restore our administration in the upper part of Hindustan and these latter objects can only be gained by vigorous and prompt action".[145]

Besides, R. Temple, Secretary to Chief Commissioner, Punjab on 1 March 1858 addressed a communication to W. Edmonstone, Secretary, Foreign Department focusing on the fortifications of the city and Palace of Delhi and the need for converting the Palace into a fort which would enable them to fortify the town and would serve as a safe repository for munitions of war.

After the fall of Delhi, the munitions of war and the guns recovered from the mutineers were placed in the confines of the citadel (palace) and subsequently removed to the old magazine. The Chief Commissioner wanted the Government to take a decision whether the European troops were to be permanently stationed at Delhi. He was of the opinion that the Palace could be converted into a strong fortress from the military and political point of view and the two regiments of European infantry could be perfectly controlled with this suggestion. He suggested deployment of a battery of engineers and sappers from the army for carrying out the demolition of buildings and walls in the vicinity of the fort and the city. With this measure, the city would be prone to the incursions and depredations of Goojars and Mewaties. However, this threat could be taken care of during the visits and inspections by the Governor-General and Commander-in-Chief on their visit to Delhi. The Palace should be converted into a fort for keeping the situation under control.[146]

Later, the Chief Commissioner, accompanied by Brigadier Chamberlain and Brigadier Longfield, examined the Red Fort Palace and appreciated the measures undertaken for its security and upkeep.

It was suggested by Lt. Newmarch, Executive Engineer, Delhi to Col. Glassford, Chief Engineer, Agra that the plan suggested by the Commander-in-Chief, that an Engineer Officer should be specifically deployed for the work, should be implemented. Further measures for restoration would be undertaken with a view to ensure improvement of military science in this particular project. The destruction of Vienna fortification was an example referred to the Chief Commissioner in this regard.

Besides, Major General Wilson, commanding the Division, suggested to Lt. Newmarch that it would be advisable to carry on the demolition of the walls gradually by commencing the work of dismantling them near Kashmere Gate by removing the parapets at the first instance and continuing the repair works regularly in gradual phases and stages.[147]

On 16 November 1859, Major R.C. Lawrence, Secretary, Government of Punjab in his letter to the Secretary, P.W.D. Government of India reported that a portion of the clearance of Red Fort was effected but that much remained to be executed.

The following estimated expenditure of account had been sanctioned by the Local Government and expended:

On 29 March 1859	Rs. 1259.4.3
On 14 April 1859	Rs. 5000.0.0
Total:	Rs. 6259.4.3
Amount now proposed	Rs. 9502.0.0
Grand Total:	**Rs. 15,761.4.3**

The amount thus proposed and amounting to Rs. 9502.0.0 was required to complete the work relating to clearance of the old town near the Palace of Red Fort, Delhi.

The military authorities were desirous that the work, which had been stopped for paucity and want of funds, should commence forthwith, and the allocations were since received. Consequently, a company of sappers was detained at Delhi for the clearance operations. Even the Lt. Governor felt that the clearance operations should commence forthwith and delay should not occur.[148]

Finally, on 5 December 1859, Secretary, P.W.D., communicated to the Secretary, Military Department, Government of Punjab "to communicate the approval of the Governor-General to the sanction given by the H.H. the Lt. Governor to the completion of the demolition in Delhi Palace at an entire cost of Rs. 15,761 it being".[149]

NOTES AND REFERENCES

1. *Hyderabad Residency*, Volume No. 249, pp. 405-425; Home Public Letters from Court, No. 15 of 1844.
2. *Ibid.*
3. Public, 27 July 1844, No. 29.
4. Public, 12 April 1845, No. 39.
5. *Ibid.*
6. *Ibid.*
7. *Ibid.*
8. *Ibid.*
9. *Ibid.*
10. *Ibid.*
11. *Ibid.*
12. *Ibid.*

13. *Ibid.*
14. *Ibid.*
15. Public, 12 April 1845, No. 38.
16. Public, 12 April 1845, No. 37.
17. Public, 12 April, 1845, No. 40.
18. Public, 22 February 1845, No. 10.
19. *Ibid.*; Political, 20 June 1845, No. 183.
20. *Ibid.*
21. *Ibid.*
22. Public, 22 February 1845, No. 11; Political, 20 June 1845, No. 183.
23. Public, 31 May 1845, No. 7.
24. Public, 31 May 1845, No. 6.
25. Public Letter to Court, No. 14 of 1845.
26. Public, 31 May 1845, No. 8.
27. Public, 31 May 1845, No. 9.
28. Public, 16 August 1845, No. 25; *Hyderabad Residency*, Volume No. 82, pp. 28-30.
29. *Ibid.*
30. *Ibid.*
31. Public, 16 August 1845, No. 27; *Hyderabad Residency*, Volume No. 82, pp. 134-135.
32. Public, 6 September 1845, No. 11.
33. Public, 20 September 1845, No. 64.
34. Public, 20 September 1845, No. 63.
35. Public, 20 September 1845, No. 67.
36. Public, 20 September 1845, No. 66.
37. Public, 20 September 1845, No. 68.
38. Home, Public and Ecclesiastical Letters from the Court No. 1 of 1847.
39. Public, 24 April 1847, No. 1.
40. Public, 27 May 1848, No. 17.
41. Public, 27 May 1848, No. 16.
42. Public, 27 May 1848, No. 18.
43. Public, Letter to Court 65 of 1848.
44. Public, 11 April 1851, No. 24.
45. *Ibid.*
46. Public, 11 April 1851, No. 22.
47. Public, 11 April 1851, No. 23.
48. *Ibid.*
49. Public, 11 April 1851, No. 21.
50. Public, 11 April 1851, No. 25.
51. Public, 18 June 1852, Nos. 27-28.
52. Public Letter to Court of Directors, No. 58 of 1852.
53. Public, 24 March 1854, No. 43.
54. Public, 24 March 1854, No. 44.
55. Public, B, 27 October 1854, No. 32.
56. Public, 30 May 1856, No. 7.
57. Public, 30 May 1856, No. 6.
58. *Ibid.*
59. Home, Public, 24 March 1849, No. 10 & K.W.
60. *Ibid.*
61. Wilson – *History of India*.

In some places mutilated inscriptions were found in characters said to be the same as those on the staff of Firoz Shah at Delhi. They have never been collected or published. Cave Temples also are described one of which is dedicated to the 'Neila Kantha', a form of Siva as a Singa-Kalanjara, the correct appellation of the Mountain is also a name of Siva. He who sees time itself decay and all the Hindoo traditions relating to this Hill connect it with his worship. Kalbhirov / or correctly Kala Bhairava / whose colossal image is specified by Abulfazl as existing at Kullenger is an attendant of Siva, or one of his minor.

The word Cullizer to which Kalanjar is commonly barbarously metamorphosed in Hamilton's Gazetter. A general description of the Fort and its antiquities is given in Pagson's History of the Buildilas but the latter have been but curiously imperfectly investigated.

62. Public, 5 February 1848, No. 20.
63. *Ibid.*
64. *Ibid.*
65. *Ibid.*
66. *Ibid.*
67. *Ibid.*
68. *Ibid.*
69. *Ibid.*
70. *Ibid.*
71. *Ibid.*
72. *Ibid.*
73. *Ibid.*
74. Public, 5 February 1848, No. 21.
75. *Ibid.*
76. *Ibid.*
77. Public, 5 February 1848, No. 22.
78. *Ibid.*
79. *Ibid.*
80. *Ibid.*
81. *Ibid.*
82. Home, Public and Eccls. Letters from Court No. 33 of 1847.
83. Public, 5 February 1848, No. 17.
84. Public, 5 February 1848, No. 18.
85. Public letter from Court No. 21 of 1849.
86. Public, 17 November 1854, No. 18.
87. *Ibid.*
88. Public letter from Court of Directors No. 24 of 1847 dated 29 September 1847.
89. Public, 31 December 1847, No. 2.
90. Public, 31 December 1847, No. 1.
91. Public letter to Court No. 2 of 1848, 8 January 1848.
92. Public, 7 October 1848, No. 23.
93. Public, 18 January 1850, No. 3.
94. Public, 4 April 1850, Nos. 36-37.
95. Public, 19 February 1848, No. 10.
96. *Ibid.*
97. *Ibid.*
98. *Ibid.*
99. Public, 19 February 1848, No. 11.
100. Public, 7 January 1853, No. 49.

101. Public, 7 January 1853, No. 50.
102. Public, 28 January 1853, No. 4.
103. Public, 28 January 1853, No. 5.
104. Public, 16 February 1853, No. 46 A.
105. Public, 29 April 1853, No. 11.
106. Public, 29 April 1853, No. 12.
107. Public letter to Court No. 26 of 1853.
108. Public letter to Court No. 98 of 1855.
109. Public letter from Court No. 22 of 1855.
110. Public, 13 April 1855, No. 9.
111. First Report of H.H. Cole, the Curator of Ancient Monuments for the year 1881-82, p. 5.
112. *Ibid.*
113. *Delhi Gazette*, 1847, 30 March 1847, pp. 209-10.
114. *Journal of Asiatic Society*, Bengal, September 1847, p. 971.
115. *The Story of Indian Archaeology* by S. Roy, p. 33.
116. First report of H.H. Cole, the Curator of A.Ms. for the year 1881-82, p. 5.
117. *Ibid.*
118. Public, 30 May 1850, No. 21.
119. Home, Public, 2 December 1853, No. 9.
120. *Ibid.*
121. *Ibid.*
122. Home, Public, 13 January 1854, Nos. 43-47.
123. Home, Public, 6 October 1854, No. 45.
124. Public, 6 October 1854, No. 45.
125. Public, 6 October 1854, No. 44.
126. Public, 6 October 1854, No. 43.
127. Public, 6 October 1854, No. 46.
128. Public, 6 October 1854, No. 41.
129. Public, 6 October 1854, No. 47.
130. Public letter from Court No. 54 of 1855.
131. Home, P.W.D. – Military G.G., 20 December 1858, Nos. 12-14 and K.W.
132. Foreign, Political, 13 December 1845, Nos. 124-125.
133. Foreign, Political, 13 December, 1845, No. 127.
134. Political Proceedings, 17 October 1846, No. 32.
135. Political Proceedings, 17 October 1846, No. 31.
136. Political Proceedings, 17 October 1846, No. 36.
137. Political Proceedings, 17 October 1846, No. 35.
138. Foreign, Political, 21 April 1849, Nos. 36-37.
139. Foreign, Political, 16 June 1849, No. 23.
140. Foreign, Political, 16 June 1849, No. 25.
141. Foreign, Political, 16 June 1849, No. 24.
142. Foreign, Secret, 18 December 1857, No. 439.
143. *Ibid.*
144. *Ibid.*
145. Foreign, Secret, 18 December 1857, No. 438.
146. Foreign, Secret, 25 June 1858, No. 14.
147. Foreign, Secret, 25 June 1858, No. 15.
148. P.W.D., G.G., 6 December 1859, No. 2.
149. P.W.D., G.G., 6 December 1859, No. 3.

CHAPTER IV

Systematic Efforts for Early Archaeological Survey and the Role of Alexander Cunningham, 1859-1865

The Government of India Act, 1858 changed the character of the Government of India. The control of the Government was transferred from the East India Company to the British Crown on 1 November, 1858. Lord Canning, who served the East India Company as its last Governor-General was retained and designated Viceroy and Governor-General under the Crown's administration.

The progress of archaeology in general and care of monuments in particular was slow but steady. Gradually the Government wrested its control from individuals and private bodies and associations.

Several dedicated persons devoted their lives for its development. After the first war of Independence in 1857, Alexander Cunningham, a distinguished member of the Asiatic Society appeared on the archaeological scene in 1857. From the beginning, he had been taking active, interest and was first person to realize the need of organizing a countrywide survey of archaeological remains. In 1848, he had contributed an article "**Proposed Archaeological Investigations**" in the *Journal of the Asiatic Society*,[1] wherein he had emphasized the need of undertaking archaeological survey. Although, his proposal was not taken seriously but Cunningham did not lose hope, and continued his efforts towards this direction.

CUNNINGHAM'S MEMORIAL

His efforts brought results in November 1861, when he submitted an elaborate Memorandum to Lord Canning, wherein he emphasized the importance and need for adopting of systematic investigation in the field of archaeology. The Memorandum, thus submitted was a significant milestone in the development of archaeology in India.

The Memorandum emphasized the need of conducting systematic archaeological survey in North West Provinces and Bihar. He also underlined the need to examine the ancient cities of Punjab, viz. Taxila, Sakala and Jalandhar, caves and rock paintings at Cuttack and archaeological remains at Ujjain, Bhiba Dhumnar and Kholvee in Central India.

To commence the survey, Cunningham suggested that Gaya and Rajgriha should be explored in the first instance, and thereafter Tirkoot and Benaras and extending it to Gorakhpur.

The methodology of survey was also enumerated in Cunningham's Memorandum. This involved description of each place explored and surveyed, wherein ground plan of every monument would be indicated. This would also have drawings and sections of all objects of interest. Cunningham also underlined the need of photography of archaeological remains and the apparent need to employ a Photographer for the purpose. Cunningham felt that with the facsimiles of all inscriptions of archaeological monuments would thus be prepared. This documentation when over, would furnish detailed and accurate account of the archaeological remains of Upper India".[2]

However, Cunningham undermined the important aspect of archaeology, i.e., preservation of monuments as was done by the East India Company's Government. The Company's Government, as is evident from previous chapters, had done much. It is true that work was not conducted in a centralized manner and was done in fits and starts. A large outlay of amount was alloçated and this money was spent in the field of preservation.

Lord Canning concurred with the facts stated in the Memorandum of Cunnigham and sanctioned a scheme of survey and an investigation of archaeological remains. He recorded a minute on 22 January, 1862 on the overall neglect of monuments and edifices, whichwere of architectural significance and splendour. Canning lamented about the general condition of monuments in India and stated that to avoid further deterioration a good deal of expenditure and labour would be required to ensure that they were restored to their pristine glory. Canning was of the opinion that documenting the details of a monument was to be given priority, so that the future generation would be able to know about the country's past for the sake of "intelligent and enquiring classes in European countries". He further was of the opinion that professional approach and the Government's sponsorship would be essential so that proper and thorough research was completed. He particularly referred to the need of documenting the archaeological studies of the remains of Buddist Capital in Bihar, ruins of Kannauj and ruins in the plains surrounding Delhi. He lamented that individuals and private bodies effected the documentation on these ruins, which was done "imperfectly and without system". He asserted that "It is impossible not to feel that there are European Governments, if they had held our rule in India, would not have allowed this to be said". In this connection, he referred to a representation from the Royal Asiatic Society in 1844 and another in 1847 with the detailed suggestions from Lord Hardinge, and the consequent action of the Court of Directors in accordance with a sanction for carrying out examination, delineating and recording some antiquities in India. For one reason or other, the work of this magnitude could not be completed due to the death of the investigating officer. Some drawings and plans were delineated and sent to India House in London. Some 15 out of 20 papers were contributed by Major Kittoe and Major Cunningham, and published in the ***Journal of the Asiatic Society***. The scheme appears to have been abandoned due to half hearted response of the Government within three years of its adoption.[3] However, Canning appreciated the memorandum prepared by Cunningham and stated that it was a "systematic archaeological investigation". He, however, felt that the documentation on the investigations carried out on archaeological remains would provide the basis for writing history of archaeological ruins and their "accurate description – illustrated by plans, measurements, drawings or photographs, and by copies of inscriptions – of such remains as most deserve notice, with the history of them so far as it may be traceable, and a record of the traditions that are retained regarding them". This exercise, Canning felt would not commit any expense on the part of the Company's Government on spending any money on repairs and preservation but provide a basis for such expenditure in future.[4]

Lord Canning also proposed to entrust the task of investigation to Cunningham who had a clear understanding of archaeological surveys that were essential for the fair judgement of the future utility of such documentation on archaeological monuments. He added that investigation of this kind could be entrusted to Cunningham during the ensuing winter season. Canning proposed to grant a salary of Rs. 450 per month to Cunningham along with Rs. 250 to defray the cost of surveys and measurements. He also proposed to deploy an assistant for facilitating the task of taking photographic views of such excavations under Cunningham.

Concluding his minute, Canning proposed retaining proprietary rights on such investigations by Cunningham and "interests of Cunningham should be considered in the terms upon which they may be furnished to the public".[5]

Finally, Cunningham was informed on 31 January, 1862 by Lt. Col. H. Yule, Secretary, Public Works Department that he was appointed as Archaeological Surveyor to the Government of India with retrospective effect from 1 December, 1861 on a consolidated salary of Rs. 450/- per month together with a field allowance of Rs. 250/- per month. Cunningham was instructed to furnish the progress of work every month detailing the areas excavated and objects found during the course of his investigations.[6]

Thus, the Viceroyalty of Lord Canning marked the formal establishment of the Archaeological Survey of India. It is also worth mentioning that the work of Lord Canning in the promotion of archaeological investigation in India greatly contributed to the establishment of the Archaeological Survey of India.[7]

Cunningham's work was only confined to the survey, description and for providing precise measurements of monuments. The Government was not serious in investing finances towards conservation of monuments.

However, in 1863, an Act (XX) was passed in which provisions were made for the preservation of important monuments of antiquarian nature.

> Nothing in this Act shall be held to effect the provisions of the Regulations mentioned in this Act, except in so far as they relate to Mosque, Hindu Temples and other religious establishments, or to prevent the Government from taking such steps as it may deem necessary. Under the provisions of the said Regulations, to prevent injury to and preserve building remarkable for their antiquity or for their historical or architectural value.[8]

The basic character of this Act was that no other person than those appointed by the Government were entrusted with the task of the management formed for the maintenance and conservation of monuments under the charge of the Government. The amount required for the maintenance and conservation of monuments was to be met from the revenues accrued from the lands, etc. attached to these monuments (Appendix – XI).

However, it was observed that keeping this Act in view, nothing much was done as should have been done.

However, the Act was appreciated by Sourindranath Roy and he rightly observed that "thus arranged a pronounced departure from the old policy of apathy and downright neglect and marked the opening of a new era in the history of Indian Archaeology".[9]

Within a short span of time, i.e., December 1861-January 1865, Cunningham encompassed a vast area in Northern India. He surveyed, described and reported on every monument of repute situated in the historical sites, which he had visited. He identified the Ujjain Fort in Kashipur, which was erected by the Pandawas and the Drona Sagar Tank. The Drona Sagar Tank and the Fort was dedicated by the Pandavas to their preceptor Acharya Drona after whose name the Tank was christened "Drona Sagar".[10]

Cunningham also described elaborately the caves and rock-cut *chaityas*. He appended description of each place, which he surveyed, indicating therein the position of remains along with a ground plan of every ruin with drawings and photographic views of archaeological remains with their exquisite architecture and sculptures.[11] This survey scheme was not renewed after 1864-65 and Cunningham was not entrusted with the task of preservation of monuments. He was given the responsibility of survey of historical sites for documenting their description. He highlighted the rampant vandalism of the monuments and recommended concrete measures for their preservation. The glaring examples of Cunningham's survey were that of Red Fort Palace in Delhi where the fragments of two statues in red stone and two figures of elephant in black stone were noticed in the debris of the Red Fort. He pointed this in his Memorandum submitted to the Governor-General. He highlighted the need for salvaging fragmentary remains of the figurines and statues with a view to reconstruct them, and a photograph taken of the reconstructed efforts. He recommended that Lt. Macsween of the Engineers should be entrusted with the task of reconstruction "of these statues at a small expense, say of Rs. 50 in about fortnight" (Appendix-XII). The Government of Punjab, however, took immediate measures for erecting these statues following the orders of the Governor-General.[12] On the other hand, Sir Charles Wood, the Secretary of State for India, appreciated Cunningham's work in his Despatch dated 24 June, 1844 to Sir John Lawrence, the Governor-General. He particularly appreciated the reports of his investigation for "arresting the decay of numerous" beautiful and curious monuments of Hindu and Muslim civilization".[13] Charles Wood also declared that he would approve an expenditure wherever required for the preservation of Kutub Minar, tomb of Tughlak Shah and other monuments of antiquity "or for their intrinsic merit as works of art"[14]. However, in reality not much was spent on the repair of monuments.

On 9 February, 1866, Cunningham left for England due to his indisposition. Consequently, Lord Lawrence became disinterested in continuance of the good work done by Cunningham and the survey work was abandoned, which resulted in abolition of the post of Archaeological Surveyor.

The successors of Charles Wood – Earl de Gray and Ripon – endorsed his views and appreciated Cunningham's contributions to the field of Indian archaeology. In his Despatch of 16 June, 1866 to Sir John Lawrence, the Governor-General, it was specifically mentioned about value of Cunningham's investigations.[15] He, however, felt that similar surveys should be undertaken in other parts of India as well.[16]

A few examples of the state of monuments in the country during the period are worth indicating. The block of crystal was removed from the Private Audience Hall (Diwan-i-Khas) in the Red Fort Palace for being sent to England on the plea that it was not held in reverence by the local people and further it was only meant for special occasions on state functions.[17]

On 13 May 1859, C.B. Saunders, the Commissioner of Delhi, in his communication addressed to R.H. Davies, Secretary, Government of Punjab stated that it was undoubtedly the thrones of the Kings of Delhi, "being in itself from its size and material which it is composed, a rarity".[18] Finally, on 24 June, 1859, the Governor-General ordered the Secretary, the Government of Punjab to send the crystal block to England.[19]

JAMA MASJID AND RELICS

Yet, another example was of Jama Masjid. After suppression of the Mutiny of 1857, the Government took control of Jama Masjid as it was considered the King's property along with other edifices of Delhi. Jama Masjid became an official lodging for military detachments, which were deployed for quelling the mutineers. It was suggested that the Jama Masjid should be demolished and a cathedral be built in its place. Somehow, this proposal did not materialize because the British officers were not favourably disposed to this proposal for various reasons.[20] In 1860, however, a petition was submitted by the Muslim inhabitants of Delhi, i.e., Syed Ahmad Ali and others. They pleaded that Jama Masjid should be restored to the Muslims in public interest, as it was built by the sovereign of Delhi and Muslims attached a special significance to it. The petition stated that:

> It is quite plain that Masjid was erected by the late King Shahjahan of Delhi, but it cannot be included into the property of the Ex-King of Delhi as such sort of property if built by anyone is never to be counted in the property of the builder, but it is always the duty of the man who built such things as wells and Masjids to take care of them, and to spend money from their own pocket, but still they are not to be counted in the property any one they belong to God, which act of kindness and shall every pray.[21]

Lord Canning acceded to this request of the local Muslims on a condition that they would make proper arrangements for keeping it in constant repair. However, there were fears of a possibility of outbreak of disputes concerning the arrangements of the mosque. On 3 February 1862, the Commissioner of Delhi Division addressed a communication to the Secretary, the Government of Punjab about the lurking fears of conflict between Wahabis and Bidhutis on this issue as the Wahabis denounced worship of relics and propagated worship of one God. However, the Bidhutis worshipped relics, which were kept in a casket within the mosque. It is said that the casket remained in the mosque but the relics were removed. The Bidhutis maintained that they were preserved in fact and stated that they should be restored in the casket. However, the Wahabis strongly objected to this proposal.

The Chief Commissioner maintained that the Government cannot be expected to prescribe a rule of faith and a dispute of this nature should be amicably resolved, so as to maintain peace and harmony between the two sects of Islam.[22] He, therefore, recommended that the mosque be restored and no relics or objects of veneration should be introduced in the mosque, and that all the sects of one religion should work in harmony.[23]

The Governor-General, however, objected to the clause regarding relics as proposed by the Commissioner of Delhi. He was of the opinion that the Government should not side with either sects and both the sects should approach and state categorically, "until they came before the British authorities with unanimity in their propositions, and satisfactory security for the maintenance of the peace, the mosque will not be given up at all".[24]

At last, the various sects of Muslims came up with a compromise formula about the relics and general management of the Jama Masjid. Ten reputed persons representing different sects of Muslims were appointed managers of Jama Masjid at Delhi. They signed an agreement on 24 November 1862 and assured in the form of stipulations as detailed below:

1. We are responsible that no rioting will be allowed to occur in the Masjid.
2. Should any case occur connected with the Masjid or religion, we shall settle it among ourselves.
3. Nothing seditious which may tend to contempt or be brought the interests of the Government will be allowed to occur within the mosque. Should anything accidentally occur, which may be beyond our control and power, we shall report it immediately to the Deputy Commissioner.
4. On any diminution of the number of managers from whatever cause the place of vacating number will be supplied another appointed by ourselves.
5. We agree that should any circumstances occur opposed to the pleasure of the Government, the Government has under all circumstances the power of closing the door of the Masjid and making its own arrangement.
6. We shall keep the Masjid in repair. The income for the maintenance of the mosques in repairs will be derived from the rent of the shops at the back attached to the mosque, the collections from squatters on the steps as before the mutiny and private subscriptions.[25]

Finally, the Jama Masjid was thrown open to the Muslims on the morning of 28 November 1862 for the prime objective of offering prayers.[26] The relics were kept in the coffers of the mosque at that time and were not displayed for public viewing.

As stated earlier, this period witnessed minimal spending towards repair of monuments. In 1863, Sir Bartle Frere, the Governor of Bombay sanctioned an annual grant of Rs. 2,480/- towards the archaeological ruins of Bijapur.[27]

In the preservation of monuments, archaeological consciousness was totally absent.

NOTES AND REFERENCES

1. *Journal*, Asiatic Society of Bengal XVIII, pt.i, 1848, p. 535.
2. P.W.D., General, 14 February 1862, No. 29.
3. P.W.D., General, 14 February 1862, No. 28.
4. *Ibid.*
5. *Ibid.*
6. P.W.D., General, 14 February 1862, Nos. 30-32.
7. An address was delivered by J.P. Vogel, Professor at the University of Leiden and Former Superintendent of Archaeological Survey of India on November 14, 1916 at a meeting of the Indian Society of the Hague. (*The Asiatic Review*: January 1921, p. 80).
8. Legislative Department, Act XX of 1863.
9. *The Story of Indian Archaeology 1784-1947* by S. Roy, p. 37.
10. P.W.D., General A, February 1863, Nos. 17-19.
11. P.W.D., General A, 14 February 1862, No. 29.
12. P.W.D., General, A, April 1863, Nos. 31-33.
13. P.W.D., Despatch from Secretary of State, No. 28, dated 24 June 1864.
14. P.W.D., General despatches from Secretary of State, 16 June 1866, No. 29.
15. *Ibid.*
16. Foreign, Political, 24 June 1859, Nos. 22-28 and K.W.
17. *Ibid.*

18. *Ibid.*
19. Foreign Department, Part A, April 1860, Nos. 259-262.
20. Foreign Department, General B, March 1862, Nos. 113-114.
21. Foreign Department, General B, March 1862, Nos. 116-117.
22. *Ibid.*
23. Foreign Department, General B, March 1862, No. 118.
24. Foreign General A, December 1862, Nos. 87-89. The signatories (ten respective persons) were: Mirza Ilahee Bukhsh, Mohammad Buddeerordeen Khan, Mohammad Hussain, Nasiruddin, Hafiz Daood, Mohammad Tuffuzul Hussain Khan, Mehboob Baksh, Nafiz Meer Mohammad. Two signatures were were found illegible in the brittle original document.
25. Foreign, General B, March 1862, No. 117.
26. *First Report of the Curator of Ancient Monuments in India for the year 1881-82*, p. 6.

CHAPTER V

Government's Initial Apathy and Subsequent Impetus to Care of Monuments, 1866-1870

In 1866, Sir Henry Cole, the erstwhile Secretary of the Science and Art Department, and the Director of South Kensington Museum, London instituted enquiries primarily with a view to systematic collection of illustrations of Indian architecture, in lieu of originals through photography, plans and casts.[1]

In the following year at the Paris Exhibition (1867), a large collection of photographs evinced a great interest for Indian architecture. During the exhibition, several princes of royal families of Europe entered into an agreement to assist the museums there in procuring casts and copies of national objects for the promotion of art.

Conventions for promoting re-productions of works of art universally for the benefit of Museums.

> Throughout the world every country possesses fine historical monuments of art of its own, which can easily be reproduced by casts, electrotypes, photographs and other processes, without the slightest damage to the original.
>
> (a) The knowledge of such monuments is necessary to the progress of art and the reproduction of them would be of a high value to all museums for public instruction.
>
> (b) The commencement of a system of reproducing works of art has been made by the South Kensington Museum and illustrations of it are now exhibited in the British Section of Paris Exhibition where may be seen specimens of French, Italian, Spanish, Portuguese, German, Swiss, Russian, Hindoo, Celtic and English Art.
>
> (c) The following outline of operation is suggested:
>
> 1. Each country to form its own Commission according to its own views, for obtaining such reproductions as it may desire for its own museums.

2. The Commissions of each country to correspond with one another and send information of what reproductions each causes to be made, so that every country, if disposed may take advantage of the labours of other countries at a moderate cost.
3. Each country to arrange for making exchanges of objects which it desires.
4. In order to promote the formation of the proposed Commissions in each country, and facilitate the making of the reproductions, the undersigned members of the reigning families throughout Europe, meeting at the Paris Exhibition of 1867, have signified their approval of the plan and their desire to promote the realization of it.

The following members of the royal families signed the agreement:

1. Great Britain and Ireland	Albert Edward, Prince of Wales; Alfred, Duke of Edinburgh.
2. Prussia	Frederick William, Crown Prince of Prussia.
3. Hesre	Louis, Prince of Hesre.
4. Saxony	Albert, Prince – Royal of Saxony.
5. France	Prince Napoleon (Jerome).
6. Belgium	Philippe, Comte de Flanders.
7. Russia	The Cesarewith Nicholas, Due de Leuchtenberg
8. Sweden and Norway	Oscar, Prince of Sweden and Norway.
9. Italy	Humbert, Prince – Royal of Italy; Amadevs, Duke of Aosta.
10. Austria	Charles-Louis, Archduke of Austria; Rainier, Archduke of Austria.
11. Denmark	Frederick, Crown Prince of Denmark.[2]

In this exhibition, the Princes of Great Britain and Ireland exhibited fine archaeological specimens belonging to the historical monuments of India.[3] An interest was awakened in England for Indian architecture through the medium of this exhibition. Consequently, Sir Stafford Northcote, the Secretary of State for India suggested to the Government of India to take steps for conserving and documenting the ancient monuments in India after being greatly impressed by that exhibition. He addressed a private letter to Lord Lawrence, Governor-General regarding conservation of works of art and architecture in India. In that letter Lord Lawrence was requested to kindle interest in government circles in India the urgent need for taking up the conservation of architectural structures and other works of art and evolving a procedure of taking casts and photographs of them for the benefit of students of art and architecture.[4]

In his minute dated 28 August 1867, Lord Lawrence opined that such works are generally and sufficiently cared in India. He stated that earlier there were instances of vandalism but have been taken to prevent it and considerable expense incurred with this object.[5] Lord Lawrence, however, proposed that a circular should be issued to all Governments, Administrations and Political Officers underlining the desirability for documenting the ancient architectural monuments of archaeological interest and organizing a system of photographing them for future reference use. Accordingly, a circular was issued (No. 57-4030-4039) on 29 August 1867 by E.C. Bayley, Secretary, Government of India. The circular also made stipulations with regard to the list of monuments to be sent by each Province/Local Government and a report of the measures adopted for the preservation of monuments.

With regard to photographing the monuments of archaeological interest, the circular emphasised the need of employment of photographers having professional skill as not that essential and the utilization of the services of amateurs considered with advantage.[6]

Northcote desired that photographs that should be prepared should be accompanied by accurately drawn plans as well as written descriptions of the subject of the object thus photographed. He, accordingly, addressed a letter to the Governor-General to this effect and emphasized the need of photographing structures of archaeological delight with proper description. He also desired that the negatives of the photographs should become the property of the Government and should be made available for reproduction as and when necessary.[7]

The sentiments expressed in Northcote's letter were conveyed to all the Provinces/Local Government/Political Officers on 29 August 1867. The responses from the Provinces/Local Governments were indeed heartening. The responsive attitudes of such Government are detailed below.

1. Bengal, Lower Provinces

Although the Lt. Governor had certain reservations about the results from the amateur photographs, nevertheless, an account of laterite temples at Kapuri, Bhadrak Sub-Division and three photographs of monasteries in Sikkim were forwarded. Besides, three photographs of Hindu temples in Sibsagar District by Major Davis, Executive Engineer and a Muslim tomb in Burdwan by Dr. Mantell, Civil Surgeon, two photographs of Jagannath Temple and four photographs of the Black Pagoda (Puri), three photographs of temple with description of temple at Jalpesh in Jalpaiguri District by Dr. R. Macleod, Civil Surgeon and six photographs from Bhubaneswar. The photographs thus received from Bengal were by amateurs and few were found "of much merit".[8]

2. North-West Provinces

An amalgamated list of objects of architectural interest was received. The description was brief and that Lt. Governor proposed that the list could act as a guide for the District Officers and Lt. Cole could undertake a detailed survey for description of the monuments thus listed.[9]

3. Punjab

The letter had suggestions for undertaking works in this direction in Delhi Yusufzai. Besides, archaeological objects on display at the Local Museum at Peshawar and Central Museum at Lahore were photographed. Measures were also taken for the care and preservation of the garden tank and buildings at Hasan Abdal which were of historical interest.[10]

4. Central Provinces

The list of architectural monuments requiring preservation was forwarded. The Chief Commissioner was of the opinion that majority of the archaeological remains were devoid of architectural beauty, but they, nevertheless, had antiquarian interest though it was doubtful whether many of the structures can lay claim to very great antiquity.[11]

5. Mysore

A list of 72 buildings of architectural significance and of archaeological importance was forwarded. The remains of Jain dynasty of Belal Rajahs, which reigned 700 hundred years ago, i.e., Halebid, Sravanbelagola. A list of 87 photographs of remains of a Nandidurg, Chitaldurg, Seringapatam, Halebid and Belur was as well forwarded. Major Dixon, an amateur, did the photographic views. The house where the Duke of Wellington resided, the tomb of Tipu and the Halebid temple required repair and preservation.[12]

6. Hyderabad, including Assigned Districts and Nizam's dominions

Measures taken by the administration to procure the photographs were intimated. Around 51 different photographic views furnished by Mulheran of the survey were forwarded. Many of the photographs were of Buddhist remains.[13]

7. Rajasthan

19 photographic and 15 stereographic views by Dr. Eddowes of Erinpoora Agency and 7 photographic views by Bourne and Shepherd of the palaces at Deeg were forwarded with detailed description.[14]

8. Central India Agency

A list of 55 photographic views of Gwalior, Narwar, Datia, Orchcha, Gohad and other places were forwarded.[15]

9. Madras

The Madras Government furnished no list. However, Captain Lyon was deployed to take photographs of temple structures at Madurai. Besides, he was also deployed for taking the photographs of Perur temple. The Madras Government with the sanction of the Secretary of State also paid Rs. 3,000 to Major Gill for a set of drawings, plans and photographic negatives of the caves of Ajanta. A further expenditure of Rs. 3,600 for tracing the paintings in these caves also received the sanction of the Home Department.[16]

10. Bombay

No list of structures was received from the Bombay Government. However, a sum of Rs. 1,050 was paid to Mr. H. Hinton for obtaining copies of his publication entitled *The Cave Temples of Ellora and Aurangabad*. It further announced that amateurs presenting the Government with approved negatives would receive a remuneration to be settled on the merits of each case. Captain Lyons was also assigned the task of taking photographs of the archaeological ruins at Bijapur, the cave temples at Karlee and the temple at Ambernath. Arrangements were made to obtain from Sind the negatives of certain tombs taken by Legget, a Deputy Collector.[17]

However, it is impossible from the above-mentioned reports to state the exact sum expended on account of photographs; not a very large amount seemed to have been spent except in Madras. The only negatives obtained by the Government were those of Colonel Herne in Central India and of Mr. Leggett in Sind.[18]

In the meanwhile, Norman Macleod, Assistant Secretary, Science and Art Department, South Kensignton, London addressed a communication to Sir Stafford H. Northcote, Secretary of State for India on 30 July 1867 and requested collaboration in the field of Indian architecture with a view to elicit certain illustrations for the study of art both in India and U.K. They were unaware of any organization in India which could survey the monuments and obtain plans for preparing photographs and casts of them. He particularly sought the views of the Secretary of State for sharing financial expenditure between the Government of British India and the Department of Science of Art to be incurred in the eventuality of such a collaborative affair.[19]

On behalf of the Secretary of State, H. Merivale, Under Secretary of India replied on 6 December 1867 that the Government of India had since taken steps to establish an organization primarily with a view to collect information and take photographs of various architectural monuments in India. Sir Northcote's instructions to the Government of India for collaborative efforts in preparing casts and photographs of architectural and monumental wealth in India were also conveyed.[20]

In fact, Northcote was so impressed with the suggestion of the Science and Art Department on casts that he addressed a communication to the Governor-General of India on 9 December 1867 about the proposal for collaborative efforts for the study of art in Great Britain. The proposal pertained to preparation of plaster casts of large size where the material and expertise in their preparation were in existence and thus an estimate of expenditure involved in preparation of casts could be drawn up for implementation of the proposal.[21]

Quickly responding to the proposal of the Secretary of State, a Resolution on the subject of obtaining casts and photographs of important architectural works in India was issued by the Government of India on 24 February 1868 (No. 14-930-941).

The Resolution called for provision in the Annual Administration Report, a separate chapter on archaeology. It also contained procedures for carrying out petty repairs for the preservation of monuments. The manner in which the casts and photographs are to be adopted and ancient structures, training programmes in various schools of art on this subject were also detailed. The expenditure involved in carrying out various programmes involved in casts and photographs were also detailed in the Government's Resolution. The methodology in procuring raw materials especially plaster of Paris was also included. The Resolution further made proposals for visits to the archaeological sites and monuments and for visit and inspection, a sum of Rs. 13,000 was proposed for each team. It stated that there were four teams which would involved in such survey work in the region, viz., one party in Madras, one in Bombay, one for Lower Bengal and Bihar, and another for the North-West Provinces and Central Provinces at an expenditure amounting Rs. 52,000 per annum. The Local Governments should also be given sufficient autonomy to carry out survey in their respective regions and should be allowed to carry out experiments in maintenance and preparation of models/casts. The Resolution referred to the short supply and availability of Plaster of Paris for preparation of casts, called for consultation with the School of Art at Calcutta for finding a substitute for Plaster of Paris and their efforts to import gypsum from Europe. It stated that gypsum was available in Madras and could be substituted for the imported gypsum from Europe, thus effecting economy in expenditure.

The Resolution was forwarded to the Local Governments/Administrations and also to the Foreign Department for communication to the Commissioner of Mysore and the Resident of Hyderabad. It was also sent to the Asiatic Society of Bengal. Besides, Sir Northcote, Secretary of State was informed about the action taken by the Government of India is adopting the Resolution.[22]

The conspectus of action taken under this Resolution was as follows:

1. Upper Provinces

Lt. Cole was appointed as the Superintendent but he was opposed to the scheme of obtaining casts as he felt that in the absence of training, it would not be possible to obtain adequate results. Lt. Cole recommended Kumaon as the best place to obtain results in getting casts made for architectural splendours. He was directed to visit Kashmir and he left for Murree on 29 September

1868. On return from Kashmir, he proceeded to Mathura and Vrindavan and assisted by the chaplain of Mathura, he undertook sundry survey and took photographs.

A proposal was received by the Begum of Bhopal from M. Place, French Consul at Calcutta with regard to obtaining the Gateway of Sanchi Stupa for being presented to Naploean III. The Begum of Bhopal consulted the Resident who promptly opposed such a request. Thereafter, the Begum of Bhopal offered the structure to the British Museum. This offer was also declined and the Government of India intended to have casts made of parts of the Sanchi Stupa which could be presented to the French Government.

The task was ultimately entrusted to Lt. Cole, who organized a group of trained assistants to be employed in carrying out the work at Sanchi Stupa. He proceeded to Bhilsa and made himself familiar with the structures which were to be modelled for the photo type. The services of few sappers to aid Lt. Cole's assignment were also solicited. In the meanwhile, the Government of India had decided on sending Lt. Cole to England for six months to escape from the vagaries of hot and humid weather. In May 1869, Lt. Cole left Bombay for England. The North-West Provinces Government elicited the progress of work from Cole while he was in England. On 20 July 1869, Cole intimated that the gelatine process of preparing casts was the most suitable method for casting the Sanchi Stupa gateway and was training a Corporal and two sappers of the Royal Engineers for the work. He also informed that he could be getting the requisite amount of Plaster of Paris. Cole further informed that the Secretary of State had sanctioned an expenditure amounting to Rs. 353. But the Government of North-West Provinces intimated that it had no budget provisions for that amount sanctioned to Lt. Cole.

A telegram was received thereafter from the Secretary of State on 13 October 1869 directing that six modelers should be sent to Sanchi, two each from Schools of Art at Calcutta, Bombay and Madras and arrangements for preparing the cast of gateway of Sanchi should be made accordingly.

On 29 November 1869, Lt. Cole reported his arrival at Calcutta accompanied by two Corporals and one Sergeant of the Royal Engineers. A letter was addressed to the Secretary of State on 15 February 1870 in which enquiries were made about the number of copies required of the cast of the Sanchi Gateway for U.K. or foreign countries by the Science and Art Department of the Council of Education. The letter also queried about the number of copies, estimated cost of expenditure and lastly three copies would be required by the Government of India, i.e., one for Calcutta, one for Madras and one for Bombay. It also stated that the estimated cost of making the principal parent cast of conveying it to England and making six copies as shown by Lt. Cole was Rs. 53,999.[23]

2. Lower Provinces of Bengal

A copy of instructions was forwarded to Mr. Locke, Principal, School of Art, with a view to carry out the orders of 24 February 1868 and allowed to draw Rs. 100 p.m. as an extra remuneration for the extra work connected with the cast and photographs of Bhubaneswar temples. An estimated expenditure of Rs. 5,166 was accordingly sanctioned. Mr. Locke prepared 132 casts of 119 different subjects from 10 temples; 13 plans and drawings and 30 photographs measuring 8 inches x 10 inches of 12 buildings. The expenditure for the year ending 30 April 1869 was Rs. 11,870. Although Mr. Locke extolled the casts, he was unable to provide accounts of photographs and drawings. The survey operation was carried out by Babu Rajendra Lal Mitra in Orissa between 1868 and 1869 and incorporated it in two monumental volumes entitled *Antiquities of Orissa*. This work constitutes the most difficult branches of Indian archaeology.[24]

3. Madras

Casts were taken of the finest ornaments in these pagodas, viz., Conjeevaram, Vellore and Mahabalipuram.[25]

4. Bombay

Bombay Government adopted the suggestion of the Committee of the Jeejee Bhoy School of Art. A party comprising eight students along with the Head Draughtsman and Head Moulder under the superintendence of Mr. Terry, Acting Superintendent of that Institution commenced their assigned work during the winters of 1868-69 on the Ambernath Temple in Kalyan taluka. A photographer (native) was also attached to the party. The party prepared 76 moulds, 24 plans and other architectural drawings and 35 photographic negatives. The expenditure on this account up to 31 May 1869 was Rs. 12,714.13.1.[26]

Sourindranath Roy stated that the results from these operations did not commensurate with either money, labour and time thus applied.[27] E.C. Bayley, Secretary, Home Department noticed that the functions and activities were only confined to making casts or obtaining photographs of the objects concerned which were artistic or of architectural importance. It was a fallacy rightly noticed by Bayley who besides being a civil servant was also an antiquarian of great repute. The Government of India owes much to Bayley in shaping the archaeological policy of the Government of India. Bayley was of the opinion that it was the supreme responsibility of the Government for not only conserving all historical remains that had been unearthed and explored, but also to encourage the exploration of other sites hitherto unexplored.[28]

The Government of India did not take this suggestion of Bayley seriously.

A brief Memorandum followed it in March 1869 by General Cunningham on the archaeological remains of India under the heads of architecture, sculpture, coins and inscriptions. This Memorandum detailed practical suggestions for securing the objectives that the Government of India had in its agenda.

The Memorandum underlined the need of leaving the judgement and decisions to the officers who were assigned archaeological duties.

The officers selected for these duties should possess adequate qualifications, which are usually otherwise not found in the same person. The Memorandum also highlighted the importance of photography and competent knowledge of the language, and history of the country. It mentioned that the photographers and draughtsmen should be placed under experienced Superintendents.

It further recommended uniform system of reporting to be adopted by the officers employed on this duty. The drawings and photographs of every building should be accompanied with a detailed description, giving an account of its history and tradition of people. The inscriptions should be copied in the absence of any record in a given situation, short scribbling of the visitors' or masons' marks on the stones will serve as major determinant for assessing its age.

The principal monuments of Islamic architecture should be photographed. Photographs of many such buildings could be purchased from the existing stock of professional photographers and the negatives should be acquired for the purposes of publication. Some of these negatives could be obtained from the professional photographers, especially of the edifices of Islamic architecture at Agra, Delhi and other cities. If the photographers are to be employed, it should be made clear that the negatives would become the property of the Government.

As regards edifices and monuments of Hindu architecture, Cunningham desired in his Memorandum that the ancient buildings should be photographed with details regarding dimensions. For the later monuments, it would be appropriate to make a selection of the larger and important structures which were worthy of preservation.

The officers who are deployed on these duties should make enquiries about the monuments and the topographical details of the places in which the edifices were located and they should not leave any archaeological sites or monumental edifices without being surveyed. He adopted this procedure while he conducted the surveys of monuments and in the process he became acquainted with the sites of the "celebrated cities of ancient India".

Besides, the Memorandum also suggested that photographs of the fortresses, viz., Rohtas and Multan in Punjab, Agra, Gwalior, Kalinjar and Ajaygarh in North-Western India; Chittor, Ranthambhor and Kumbhomer in Rajputana; Asirgarh on Tapti; and Rohtas in Bengal. Photographs should be taken of and all the important caves and sculptures should be taken of.

The Memorandum also referred the deployment of staff for this purpose. It was suggested for employing a larger contingent of staff for a few years in comparison to small contingent for many years. This methodology would infuse interest in the archaeological survey work otherwise, "interest in the subject which now exists has died away, and while the objects themselves are still standing, as several important monuments have disappeared altogether during my career in India".[29]

Bayley supported Cunningham's views incorporated in his Memorandum. He was of the view that General Cunningham's assertion in the Memorandum was satisfaction of the expression he had earlier urged for implementation of archaeological survey plans and conservation of monuments.

However, he made his view explicit in his notings which urged that the person chosen for this survey should be a man of ability who could systematize the survey work at a comparatively small cost. It might be useful to employ special enquiries in the field of archaeology in Kashmir, in Derajat and at Brahminabad or on the pre-determined sites of ancient Taxila and Sravasti. Bayley opined that selection of the right person for the job was fraught with difficulties and it was difficult to find a person adequately qualified to undertake the job. He indicated that there were hardly few people in the country who had competent knowledge of archaeology. He cited the examples of Gibbs, Bhao Daji at Bombay, Rajendra Lal Mitra in Calcutta, Lt. Col. Pearce at Madras, Rev. Shering at Benaras and Major Stubbs at Amritsar who had really studied the subject of archaeology, whereas Lt. Waterhouse, Captain Ayrton Pullan of the survey, Terry and Burgess of Bombay, F.S. Growse in N.W.P., Carlyle of the Agra Museum and Baden Powell of Lahore had paid some attention for the promotion of archaeological pursuits. He suggested Carlyle alone could be spared for independent employment.

Bayley also suggested to secure a Government archaeologist in consultation with Government Departments, viz., Home, PWD or new departments who can record and publish the survey and researches thus conducted. Further, he also suggested that local observers and surveyors could be deployed who should examine and report on prospective archaeological sites.

Besides, the district authorities should be entrusted with the responsibility for preservation of everything, which the Government archaeologist determines worthy of preservation and the annual reports on the condition of such monuments should be forwarded to the Government. Bayley also felt that this arrangement would work out well with the aid and cooperation of the

Asiatic Societies of Calcutta and Bombay at a moderate expense. He further suggested the appointment of General Cunningham for the task that could train a band of archaeological observers and create a team of archaeologists.

Bayley was also sceptical about the acceptance of responsibility by General Cunningham but suggested that due to failing health, he may be persuaded to accept the offer of appointment on an allowance of Rs. 1,000/- in addition to his pension. An annual outlay of Rs. 5,000 could be spent on the archaeological pursuits, till such time a band of trained archaeologist was created.

In conclusion, Bayley felt that after the appointment, the various Asiatic and oriental societies both in India and Europe would be requested to make suggestions for the survey of archaeological sites to be taken up and "attention should be directed and that in India gentlemen on the spot capable and willing to assist should be invited to do so".[30]

In fact, which Bayley had been pursuing since 1867 were ignored in its early stages. However, Argyll pointed out the failings of the Government in his Despatch No. 4 dated 11 January 1870 and felt that researches should be conducted in a systematic manner. He advised the Government to make a new beginning by establishing a Central Department, which would tackle the archaeological problems of the entire country. Argyll felt it was high time that researches should be systematically attempted without "imposing inconvenient restrictions". The archaeological operations in the country should proceed and be conducted with "some definite plan".

He also objected to the instructions of the Government on sporadic surveys without proper directions and without planning. He referred to earlier efforts of the Government in making of plans and photographs of ancient buildings and taking casts of their structures. Argyll suggested enlistment of travellers and other persons unconnected with the Government who had a flair and talent for photography and whose services could be utilized to the best advantage under proper supervision. He suggested that the photographs should be taken with economy of expenditure through this arrangement, which could hardly be expected on the part of volunteers. However, he did not favour the negatives of photographs becoming property of the Government. This arrangement was earlier suggested by Lord Northcote which did not have desired results. In fact, the Government in certain cases had been compelled to purchase them from the photographers. He also suggested the methodology to be adopted for the preparation of catalogues of archaeological interest. He said that catalogues should be compiled with care and erudition. He was of the opinion that the catalogues have exhaustive details of the archaeological objects rather than cursorily prepared description.

Argyll also referred to the report on archaeological remains at Etah forwarded by the North-West Provinces. He suggested that sculptures of stone elephant as existed in Etah should be removed to a less important place for ensuring their safety and preservation. Removing the objects to less important places has certain advantages in so far as safety of object is concerned. He further referred to demolition of the famous Palace of Akbar at Agra due to it being unsuitable for "magazine purposes". Argyll felt that decay of ancient edifices are often aggravated by man-made injuries rather than their decay through natural process.

He was apparently disturbed at the public works activity in such edifices, i.e., construction of railways. He thought such wanton destruction by the Government's own servants should be scrupulously averted in future. Argyll also referred to the enthusiasm of princely chiefs of Rajputana in survey and preservation of archaeological sites, monuments in their respective states.[31] In making these observations, Argyll was influenced by Cunningham's Memorandum on the archaeological remains in India.

Lord Mayo, the Governor-General, was entirely in agreement with the views expressed by Bayley and also with the views expressed by Argyll. He recorded in his minute dated 30 May 1870, decrying the manner in which the Government of India had conducted itself on the subject relating to archaeological research. He particularly suggested that the Government of India should divest itself of the responsibility of taking casts and authorizing indiscriminate use of photography. He also suggested taking immediate steps for the creation of a Department under the Government of India with the nomenclature Indian Archaeological Survey. This Department should be placed under the control of an experienced and an able officer under whose direction the archaeological researches should be conducted in a systematic manner. He abhorred the manner in which the Government had dealt with issues relating to photography and casting of archaeological objects. The Governor-General was of the opinion that as per Bayley's suggestion, General Cunningham could be persuaded to undertake the responsibility of overseeing archaeological responsibilities to the public advantage. The Governor-General felt that his duties should comprise investigation and research especially of monuments, which are illustrative of ethnology, history and ancient history, besides publication of the investigation for the preservation of ancient monuments.

If General Cunningham were appointed, he would be able to enlist the services of persons, both Europeans and Indians, who could undertake these studies and pursuits. He reiterated his proposal for the appointment of Cunningham for "investigations into monuments and remains, which, perhaps, are unequalled in their historical and archaeological value" and "the time has come when a great and enlightened in Government can no longer neglect contributing to the archaeological literature of the world".[32]

Basing his views as expressed in his Minute, the Governor-General sent a Despatch (No. 84 of 29 July 1870) to the Duke of Argyll, Secretary of State which detailed the general progress made in the field of archaeological survey in India. In this Despatch, he recommended the appointment of Major General A. Cunningham as Director General of Archaeological Survey of India on payment of £5,000 per annum to maintain this Central Agency, to aid local researches and to provide for the annual publication of the results attained.

The Governor-General maintained that there was no person available who was so well qualified for the post as Major General A. Cunningham as "he would accept the task of a few years, we trust that he would give an impulse to the study of archaeology which would make the future working of the scheme comparatively easy".[33]

At last, Cunningham agreed which resulted in the revival of the Archaeological Survey of India as a distinct Department of the Government and *vide* Despatch No. 111 dated 24 November 1870, the Secretary of State sanctioned the appointment of Major General A. Cunningham as Director General for the Archaeological Survey of India on a salary of Rs. 2,000/- per month in addition to his pension.[34] Major General Cunningham assumed the charge as Director General, Archaeological Survey in December 1870.[35]

During the period 1866-1870, petty repair works were done. For example, repair of buildings at Ahmedabad were taken in hand. A sum of Rs. 5,300/- had been sanctioned for the tomb of Shah Alam and Rs. 5,000/- for repairing the buildings at Sarkhej.[36]

In 1868, in Madras, Lord Napier initiated the restoration of Tirunal Nayakka's Palace and its utilization for public offices. In 1869, Rs. 3,000/- was sanctioned by the Bombay Government for the repair of palace and tank at Sarkhej, Ahmedabad.[37]

In fact, not a amount was exclusively earmarked and spent on the repair works of ancient monuments.

NOTES AND REFERENCES

1. *First Report of the Curator of Ancient Monuments in India for the year 1881-82*, p. 7.
2. Home, Public A, 19 March 1870, No. 203.
3. *Ibid.*
4. Home, Public A, September 1867, No. 41.
5. *Ibid.*
6. *Ibid.*
7. Public Despatch from Secretary of State, 9 December 1867, No. 165.
8. K.W. to Home, Public, 30 July 1870, Nos. 204-16; Home Public A, 9 January 1869, No. 139.
9. Home, Public, 5 September 1868, Nos. 28-30.
10. Home, Public, October 1867, No. 81.
11. Home, Public, 24 October 1867, Nos. 79-80.
12. Public Proceedings, 21 March 1868, Nos. 146-147.
13. Home, Public A, 6 February 1869, Nos. 199-201.
14. Public A, 9 January 1869, No. 136.
15. K.W. to Home, Public, A, 30 July 1870, Nos. 204-216.
16. *Ibid.*
17. K.W. to Public A, 30 July 1870, Nos. 204-16; Public A, 11 December 1869, Nos. 169-171.
18. *Ibid.*
19. *Ibid.*
20. *Ibid.*
21. *Ibid.*
22. Public, 29 February 1868, No. 131.
23. Foreign, General B, March 1868, Nos. 83-84; Foreign, General A, June 1868, Nos. 59-61; July 1868, Nos. 75-79; October 1868, Nos. 6-7 November 1869, Nos. 31-32; Public Proceedings, 4 July 1868, No. 111; Public A, 17 October 1868, No. 20; 15 August 1868, No. 18; 19 March 1870, 201-219; 30 July 1870, 204-216.
24. Home, Public A, August 1868, 83-85; 29 May 1869, Nos. 24-34; 4 September 1869, Nos. 75-76; 30 October 1869, Nos. 1820.
25. Public, 30 July 1870, Nos. 204-216.
26. *Ibid.*
27. *The Story of Indian Archaeology, 1784-1947* by Sourindranath Roy, p. 42.
28. Public, 6 September 1867, No. 41.
29. Public, 30 July 1870, Nos. 204-16.
30. *Ibid.*
31. *Ibid.*
32. *Ibid.*
33. *Ibid.*
34. Public, 31 December 1870, No. 117.
35. Home, Archaeology and Conservation of Monuments, September 1885, No. 46.
36. *First Report of the Curator of Ancient Monuments in India*, 1881-82, p. 7
37. *Ibid.*, p. 8.

CHAPTER VI

Establishment of the Archaeological Survey of India: Appointment of Cunningham as Director General of Archaeological Survey of India

It was towards the end of the year 1870 that Cunningham was appointed Director General of the Archaeological Survey of India from December 1870, during the tenure of Lord Mayo.[1] The Government of India adopted a Resolution on 2 February 1871 wherein instructions were issued for the guidance of Major General Cunningham for the conduct of duties as Director General of the Archaeological Survey of India.

The Resolution stated that there was no one so well qualified for superintending the operations as Cunningham, and his appointment to the post of Director General would give an impetus to the study of archaeology and ensure smooth functioning of the scheme of survey pertaining to archaeological operations. The Resolution directed attention to the functions, which were to be assigned to Cunningham. Firstly, he was to be entrusted with the task of preparing a brief summary of the survey, which was effected in the past. Much of the valuable information was incorporated in the researches and journals of the Asiatic Societies, but it was scattered in various research journals, many of which are rare and expensive and had limited accessibility to information contained therein due to their availability only in public libraries. A brief abstract of information on the research and surveys already affected would serve the time and labour of researchers or enquirers about monuments in India. Secondly, if a general scheme of systematic enquiry for the guidance of staff and assistants is attempted, it would greatly benefit them. The scheme should indicate what has already been accomplished and what remains to be done, and nature and bulk of information along with the details of the availability of illustrations of archaeological remains would go a long way in saving time and energy for the curious enquirers. The services of the local people should be gainfully employed as they would be in a better position to perform their assigned work objectively as they are likely to be conversant with the local conditions.[2]

As soon as Cunningham resumed his duties, he placed before the Government of India a proposal for the establishment of the Archaeological Survey of India. He addressed a letter to A.O. Hume, Secretary, Revenue and Agricultural Department on 7 February 1871 and apprised him of his plan of action. He envisaged division of country for the purposes of conducting archaeological survey and each division to be sub-divided into three sections as follows:

I. **Punjab** – 1. East Punjab, 2. West Punjab, 3. Sindh, and. Multan.
II. **North-West Provinces** – 1. Agra, 2. Ajmer, 3. Benaras
III. **Bengal** – 1. Bihar, 2. Bengal, 3. Assam
IV. **Bombay** – 1. Gujarat, 2. Maharashtra, 3. Berar
V. **Madras** – 1. Telengana, 2. Karnataka, 3. Dravid

By dividing the country into convenient small and compact sections, he envisaged economy of time and expenditure and the work of survey would be accomplished within three years, which could be extended to five years and subsequently to 10-12 years for ensuring survey of the entire country. Thus, enquiries and explorations will lead to fresh discoveries. The work to be done will thus grow under their hands.

Cunningham felt that in order to start with the archaeological survey would entail certain difficulties and suggested collaboration with Geological Survey for their in service assistants who could start the work immediately. In this way, he planned to train archaeologists and the survey could begin in full swing.

Cunningham was not satisfied with the outcome of archaeological excavations conducted in Yusufzai and Rawalpindi Districts by private individuals and proposed to undertake a regular archaeological survey of these districts **de novo.** He intended to tour Punjab in this connection and also visit Lahore and Peshawar Museum to assess the progress of excavations conducted in the past and decide the future course of action by enlisting the services of people who had associated themselves in "unconnected and superficial excavations". Besides, Cunningham also made enquiries in India and England for enlisting the services of persons who had knowledge of Indian antiquities and could contribute their expertise in the pursuit of archaeological researches. One such person was James Burgess whom he had met in Bombay and who was a qualified architect and because of his knowledge of local languages, training and zeal for archaeology, he was to be considered for appointment as the Superintendent of the Archaeology Survey of the Bombay Presidency. Incidentally, Burgess was being considered for appointment as Director of Bombay School of Art. Cunningham felt Burgess to be "most fit person to succeed me hereafter as Director of Archaeological Survey of India".*

Besides, the names of Dr. J.D. Beglar, Assistant Engineer, P.W.D. Bengal and A.C. Carlyle, Curator, Riddell Museum, Agra were also recommended to Cunningham for being appointed as archaeologists.[3]

The Governor-General sanctioned the proposal of Cunningham on 9 February 1871 and stated that "should any future modification of the scheme be thought desirable, it can always be made the most important; now is to let General Cunningham get to work at once."[4] Cunningham resumed the work and his main thrust was on allied fields of archaeology other than conservation. On 13 February 1873, the Government of India issued a circular assigning to Local Governments the responsibility of the preservation of all building and monuments of historical and architectural

* This prophecy became true on 25 March 1886 when Burgess assumed the office of Director General, Archeological Survey of India.

interest. He referred to para 4, Section iii, Chapter III of the Public Works Code and requested for issue of a Standing Order by incorporating this information.[5] The Governor-General in Council desired that conservation and preservation of buildings should be treated as a matter of importance and duty without expecting any special order from the Government to this effect.[6]

On 21 July 1873, a meeting of eminent persons having interest in Indian antiquities was convened at the Royal Asiatic Society in London. In that meeting, a memorial (London Memorial) signed by many notable personages[7] was submitted to the Duke of Argyll Her Majesty's Principal Secretary of State for India on 22 July 1873. The memorialists urged the Government of India to adopt measures to prevent decay of the monuments and adopt immediate remedial and curative measures. They urged immediate preservation of monuments of Islamic and Hindu architecture in their pristine glory and suggested a number of measures for ensuring proper maintenance of these monuments. Besides, they lamented that detailed documentation on monuments was not available prior to the advent of Muslim conquest of India and detailed study of the period could only be made from the coins and inscriptions, and the study of the period should be supplemented with available data on monuments of that period in Europe, which is of intrinsic nature. The memorialists also urged that the monuments in India also revealed the history of religious warfare and the ethnological relations of the races, which adopted a distinct style of architecture and penetrated from North India to South India. The monuments of the Muslim period also revealed the interplay of tribes and races in the architecture of their monuments in their respective capital cities. The memorialists further felt that these architectural splendours should not be allowed to perish in oblivion but adequate measures should be taken for their repair and conservation. The authorities in India and England should give priority for their upkeep and preservation.

The petitioners recommended classification of various monuments in India under three categories.

a. Those which should be kept for permanent repair by the Government.
b. Those which require occasional attention of the Government, the decay of which was to be arrested by clearing of vegetation growth and ensuring protection from water seepage in its walls.
c. Those monuments which were in advanced state of decay and were unimportant. Further, if, preservation of edifices of monuments was not possible, a record of the monument was to be obtained before their actual destruction was carried out.

The memorialists also suggested the employment of officers having the necessary experience for the conservation of monuments. They would not only survey and describe the monuments but also be entrusted with the responsibility of appointments of establishment required for monument care and protection and disburse expenditure grants sanctioned by the Government.

Finally, the memorialists felt that the Government of India should be authorized to make necessary provisions for allocating a fixed amount to each Presidency and Provincial Government for carrying out the stipulations as incorporated in the memorial. An estimate of annual expenditure should be prepared and presented by the Local Governments.

The memorialists appreciated the Government's action in effecting the appointment of Cunningham as the Director of Archaeological Survey of India and added that, "additional impulse must be given and measures of a more practical nature must be adopted, the nature and form of which we leave to the superior judgement of Her Majesty's Government".[8]

With regard to the proposal for employment of special officers, there was some difference of opinion. While most of them thought that their employment offered to carry out an intelligent system of conservation, others held that the task of maintenance of monuments could be entrusted to the District Officers after completion of the task and also taking up its classification and repair of monuments.

The earlier orders of August 1867 envisaged submission of lists of all existing archaeological remains of works of art in each district of India. In February 1868, the Local Governments were directed to make a special mention of archaeology in their Annual Administration Reports in which they would also highlight the condition of all works of arts and were also empowered to undertake such petty repairs as were considered necessary. All large scale repairs were to be referred to the Public Works Department. The Local Governments, except that of Bombay submitted the requisite lists. Bengal and Punjab Governments did not mention archaeology in their Administration Reports. The list thus submitted was not prepared on any uniform plan or pattern. The classification that was proposed in the London Memorial seemed to be appropriate step in the right direction. The Annual Administration Report for 1872-73 submitted by North-West Provinces Government made a similar suggestion. They highlighted the suggestion as "what is still wanted in these enquiries is a systematic classification and arrangement of the existing remains".[9]

On 27 February 1874, James Fergusson, one of the signatories of the memorial, addressed a communication to Marquis of Salisbury, Secretary of State for India and lamented over the destruction of temples and edifices in the cities of India and cited an example of temples at Halebid which were in the process of destruction and eventual extinction and requested for an earnest action by stating "that something may be done, before it is too late to arrest the destruction of many beautiful buildings which are daily disappearing in every part of India".[10]

Salisbury promptly addressed a communication to Lord Northbrook, Governor-General on 19 March 1874 and referred to a circular issued by the Government of India on 13 February 1873 undertaking the duty of Executive Engineers to report and suggest measures for the protection of any public monument or building of architectural or historical interest, whether public or private, which was prone to decay. He also referred to the steps taken by them for preservation of such works from ruin and sought views of the Governor-General for the "feasibility of some systematic plan for ensuring the preservation of Indian monuments".[11]

Lord Northbrook, Governor-General, in his notings dated 1 May 1874 pointed out that in pursuance of a memorial of the Asiatic Society which recommended for classification of Indian monuments of architectural significance; classification of monuments in India having been done, the problems of taking measures for preservation of monuments were being encountered. Northbrook contemplated that they cannot have a conservator of Ancient Monuments as they have in France. Therefore, neglect of monuments could be seen in the country. It is the practice in India that its people spend money on matters of public utility such as Post Offices and toilets, although it is not the custom in Asia to preserve ancient buildings. The Government of India should give directives to select the buildings requiring conservation. Alternatively, Northbrooke noted that the zamindar or the local officer should be entrusted to take care of such buildings after granting certain allowances for ensuring its maintenance. He also noted that the temple at Lonar in Berar region and some buildings of significance situated in the Nizam's dominions were repaired. However, Northbrooke felt that the advice of Cunningham could be sought for the classification of monuments.[12]

E.C. Bayley, Secretary, Home Department also contended similarly in regard to preservation of monuments of architectural significance. However, Bayley pointed out the fallacies in the memorial thus submitted with regard to existence of historical works and literature in existence prior to the advent of Muslims in India. Bayley referred to the existence of many such works in Sanskrit and the accounts of Chinese travellers and translations of Tibetan works of **Tara Kantha** (Nath) and many lists of sovereigns and historical facts incorporated in the entire corpus of Sanskrit literature.

Bayley felt that it was the inherent responsibility of Cunningham to give clues for further research in unearthing ancient classics. He referred to the discovery of buried ruins of Sanchi Stupa and Bharahut Stupa near Seoni, wherein the description of the celebrated monumental discoveries were indicated in the inscriptions.

However, he felt that the Asiatic Society's proposal with regard to classification of monuments and the preservation of the most important monuments would determine the extent of monuments existing in the country.

Bayley made some important suggestions with regard to discoveries of archaeological monuments by late Mr. Bellasis in Sind and three houses thus discovered were buried in the city called 'Brahmanabad' destroyed by earthquake during the invasion of Alexander the Great. Bayley asserted that these cities were unexcavated till now. He also referred to some archaeological sites unexplored at Mathura region. He felt that these areas should be carefully explored and excavated: "Here and there, it has been done, sometimes, as in railway cuttings and destructively". He further suggested that efforts should be made to remove the objects thus excavated to a Central Museum, as "it is useless to attempt to preserve the "remains on the spot". Through thus action one can ensure effectual preservation of archaeological objects. He referred to Bharahut where the stupa was in ruins and lost its archaeological importance due to its crumbling. If such remains were not taken care of, they would be destroyed and lost to future generations.

Another similar example of efforts made in Gaya was by Mr. Broadley who indulge in unauthorised collection of valuable sculptures from Nalanda and other sites in Bihar. Such collections could be lost or suffer destruction. Bayley was of the opinion that selections of the best of inscriptions, which were of great historic interest, should be made and brought to Calcutta for preservation.[13]

Later, A.P. Howell, Secretary addressed a letter to Cunningham on 2 June 1874 and referred to a memorial in which it was petitioned that the monuments in India should be classified under several heads with a view to prioritise their preservation in a phased manner and invited suggestions incorporated in the memorial. Howell requested that the requisite suggestions could be conveyed to officers who would be entrusted with the responsibility of classification of monuments in Bombay and Madras.[14]

Similarly, Northbrooke apprised Salisbury in response to a letter dated 19 March 1874 and gave a brief account of the work accomplished by the Archaeological Survey ever since its inception in 1871. He also apprised Salisbury about the Fergusson's proposal for undertaking a work on the rock-cut temples of Western India.

In Bengal, J.H. Ravenshaw, Collector of Dinajpur, had in his custody a complete set of photographic negatives pertaining to the Gaur ruins as well as ground plans of all the principal monuments along with translation of every inscription. He had also compiled a complete history of Gaur as well as an account of the rise and fall of the city. Ravenshaw was keen in handing over the documentation to the Government of India, which he had in his possession. The Government of India intended to publish a selection of photographs with a descriptive account of its location find.

The Government of India was engaged in correspondence with Cunningham for restoration of old palace edifices in the premises of the Agra Fort and agreed to restore the Diwan-i-Khas, the Mussaman Burj, Khas Mahal, Jahangiri Mahal and the marble cupola in the Machi Bhawan at an estimated cost of Rs. 1 lakh.

Besides, for the preservation and conservation of the frescoes of Ajanta caves, a sum of Rs. 5,000 was sanctioned in 1872. During 1871-72, Cunningham engaged himself in the task of conducting researches at the various places in the Gangetic Valley. Beglar and Carlyle were employed in conducting explorations at Delhi, Bundelkhand and Agra. His report for 1872-73 contains a lucid account of his explorations in Punjab, Kangra, Multan and Tusham in down South. Burgess, Director of the School of Art in Bombay Presidency, was employed as Superintendent of the Archaeological Survey in Western India and he was entrusted with the task of carrying out the assignment for obtaining copies of the frescoes of caves on the verge of decay. Later Griffiths, Decorative Artist in Bombay, was deputed by the Bombay Government to make copies of the remaining frescoes.

Cunningham visited Nagpur and Jabalpur during 1873-74 and carried out archaeological surveys of these areas. At Jabalpur, Cunningham and Beglar examined the old temple at Bheraghat adjoining the marble rocks cliffs. Cunningham described the structure of that temple and stated that the temple was small in size and apparently a reconstruction of part only of the original building. The circular colonnade surrounding the temple was adorned with a life-size female statues and perfect specimens of Hindu architecture. The temple was dedicated to Lord Shiva but a single small statue had an inscription with a legend **Ye Dharmna Hetu** inscribed on the pedestal. Cunningham felt that the circular colonnade must have had a Buddhist Stupa earlier. Each of the female statues had the name engraved on the pedestal and from the inscriptions, it could be deduced that the Buddhist altar was destroyed and Shiva temple was built at its place during the 9th or 10th century.

Cunningham also described the archaeological splendours to the north of Jabalpur where he explored the temples of Bilhari in decrepit state and of the archaeological ruins of Karnpur near Kari Talai. He also obtained fairly good copies of Ashoka inscriptions on the Rupnath rock edict.

Towards the west side of Jabalpur, Cunningham explored the city of Burhanpur, where he got the plans of Jami and Bibi Masjids, Jami Masjid being one of the finest specimens of Islamic architecture. It contains an inscription of Adil Shah Fariki along with a Sanskrit rendering and a document of Akbar detailing his conquest of Khandesh and Deccan. Another document of Akbar was procured from Asirgarh, which had an inscription of his son Daniyal. Some documents of Shah Jahan and Aurangzeb were also available.

Towards south, Cunningham explored the Buddhist caves and Brahamanical temples in Bhanduk. There he restored a valuable inscription of 6th-7th century, the find-spot of which was unknown.[15]

Lord Northbrooke concluded his letter to Salisbury, Secretary of State by stating that proposals incorporated in the memorial for classifying the monuments and preserving the best monument was a good one and as a result of Cunningham's researches, it would be possible to determine the monuments which were worthy of preservation and selection of an agency which should be entrusted and the expenditure involved in undertaking its preservation. Northbrook also informed the Secretary of State that Cunningham was instructed to undertake classification of monuments in all the provinces including Rajputana and Central Provinces, whereas Burgess was asked to undertake similar classification for monuments in Bombay and Berar.

Northbrooke further stated that it was not known as to who was assigned the similar classification of monuments in Madras Presidency. Nevertheless, the Local Governments have been addressed on the subject. After the classification of monuments was completed, definitive measures would be devised for preserving monuments, which are really worthy of preservation.[16]

On 18 October 1874, Rajendra Lal Mitra, who was entrusted with the survey operation of monuments in Orissa, suggested to A.C. Lyall, Secretary, Government of India about the yet another class of monuments which includes relics of great importance.

These relics were scattered in different parts of India mostly in uninhabitated tracts of forests. Many of such ancient monuments were dismembered to an extent that they could not be described as they have been intermingled with quarry stones, the sculptures and inscribed stones have been converted into building material or serve as raw material for domestic utensil. In this connection, Mitra referred to the discovery of a marble slab bearing an inscription by James Prinsep which had been rendered illegible in several places from the circumstances of the stone having been used as a mortar for grinding curry stuffs. Mitra stated that he received from Bodh Gaya an inscription of the ninth century that had been cut through to serve as a fulcrum for the pivot of a door hinge. Similarly, Bradley in Bihar had discovered valuable inscriptions from the walls of private house. Even Cunningham had seen several inscriptions in the same manner. It may as well be stated that stone columns and statues and some of its major portions are known to have been thrown into **nullahs** and serve as a marginal bund to protect the foundation of bridges, many of which had been broken down for the purpose of metalling roads; the shaft of an Asoka pillar bearing one of the oldest of Indian inscriptions was once converted into a street roller. Mitra, therefore, urged that the vandalism of this nature had to be stopped forthwith and measures to be adopted for the preservation of such sculptures and inscriptions which were buried in ancient ruins but are conveniently accessible. He also suggested to locate such material of intrinsic value which could be interesting to archaeologists and should be deposited in the Public Museum. He also suggested that an annual grant should be placed at the disposal of the Superintendent, Archaeological Survey of India in order to ensure that material which are considered valuable should be transferred to a Museum. Mitra felt that the Imperial Museum at Calcutta would be an appropriate place for depositing such relics and could advantageously be consulted by persons engaged in the pursuit of antiquarian studies. He felt that the Allahabad Museum was not accessible and did not have the Library situated within its premises. He strongly pleaded that collections should be located at a central place and certainly not scattered in various small depositories in the provinces.

Mitra was also sceptical about sculptures, which were valuable and had inherent difficulties faced by the archaeologists for transportation to a safer haven. He referred to the sanction of a grant amounting to Rs. 3,000/- for transporting a piece of sculpture from Konarak to the museum of the Asiatic Society. The task was so formidable that the entire amount of the grant was consumed in moving the stone only 300 yards from the original site. Mitra suggested that it would be convenient as well as economical to depute a team of moulders for obtaining a cast for being exhibited in the museum. He suggested the sites from where the archaeological objects could be located and he especially made a mention of stone objects and remnants of statues which were defaced and lying all over the Konarak temple periphery. He suggested that concerted effort should be made to centralize these objects and deposited in the Indian Museum and transporting and that handling expenses should not exceed Rs. 2,000 to Rs. 3,000.[17]

A copy of a letter from Rajendra Lal Mitra was forwarded to Alexander Cunningham for information. Reacting to this communication, Cunningham lamented that monuments, which had finest specimens of architecture, had suffered considerably due to human carelessness and vandalism. To stop this menace, Cunningham recommended that the ancient buildings that were not being utilized as a place of worship should be placed under the Chief Civil authority of the districts in which they have been located. The district authorities should be held responsible for their upkeep and preservation.

Cunningham made valuable suggestions for ensuring perfect preservation of ancient monuments. He was of the opinion that in the old stone buildings, the principal causes of ruins were the cracks developed in the beams and splitting of pillars on account of enormous pressure. He cited an example of the Jain temple in the Gwalior Fort where the main beams had cracked across and consequently the pillars had altogether crumbled due to enormous pressure. He further stated that he had effected repairs in 1844 by putting upright stones in place of missing pillars and building walls under the broken beams. These measures could be used in other Hindu temples as well. Where pillars were actually broken and had no leavings to support the roof, Cunningham recommended that either upright stones or square masonry pillars should be built in their place to strengthen the edifice. With regard to brick structures in a monument, the usual cause of decay was the gradual mouldering of the bricks in the bottom of walls primarily on account of deleterious action of saltpeter and the pernicious neglect of the people whether Hindus or Muslims by replacing decayed bricks. He suggested a remedial measure for this kind of decay by replacing the lower portion of the outer faces of the walls with good bricks set in mud plaster.[18]

The Government of India, after creation of the Archaeological Survey of India, set this organization into motion. The first priority was inventorization of monuments, which were also classified and their descriptive inventory was prepared and published. In fact, the Archaeological Survey was regarded as something, which was once done, was done for ever and it was thought that in a measurable time, the task would be accomplished and the survey ceases to have any function.

No provision was made for carrying out excavations to conduct study of the monuments. The important question of giving them a scientific treatment with a view to ensure their preservation was in fact relegated to background.

Many of the greatest buildings and monuments were steadily sinking into a deplorable condition as Sourindranath Roy had rightly observed: "A different emphasis, however, came to be placed on imperial responsibility in this respect when Lord Lytton took up the reins of the Viceregal Office in 1876."[19]

NOTES AND REFERENCES

1. Home, Archaeology and the Conservation of Monuments, September 1885, No. 46.
2. Home, Public, 18 February 1871, Nos. 28-29.
3. Home, Public A, 11 February 1871, No. 152.
4. Home, Public, 11 February 1871, Nos. 152-153.
5. **P.W. Code, Chapter III, Section III, para 4**: The term "public monument or building of architectural or historical interest" is intended to include all works that may be of public interest, whether originally public or private property. In the latter case, it will be for the Local Government to decide whether the Government shall take any further steps than endeavoring the influence the owners.
6. P.W.D. Building and Roads, Civil Buildings, February 1873, No. 13.
7. Prominent signatories were: Duleep Singh, W. Ebor, Devonshire, Lothian, Salisbury, Ripon, Derby, Stanhope, Carnarvon, Arthur Gordon, A. Grote, A.J.B. Beresford, Henry Holland, Charles Kingsley,

James Ph. Lacaita, John George Shaw-Lefevre, Stafford H. Northcote, Lawrence Peel, Stanley, Russell, Lawrence, Napier and Ettrick, Halifax, Edward Colebrook, James Fergusson, H.B.E. Frere, J.A. Froude, F.M. Gomm, Field Marshall, A.P. Phayre, Edward Ryan, Albert Sassoon, G. Gilbert Scott, Arthur, P. Stanley, George, Edmund Street, Meadows Taylor, C.S.I., Edward Thomas and C.E. Trevelyan.

8. Public, June 1874, No. 11.
9. Public, June 1874, No. 13.
10. *Ibid.*
11. Public, June 1874, No. 10.
12. Public, June 1874, No. 13.
13. *Ibid.*
14. Home, Public, June 1874, No. 12.
15. Home, Public, June 1874, No. 13.
16. *Ibid.*
17. Home, Public A, November 1874, No. 18.
18. Home, Public Proceedings, February 1875, No. 51.
19. *The Story of Indian Archaeology* by S. Roy, p. 53.

Chapter VII

Lytton and Care of Monuments

Lord Lytton assumed charge of Governor-General on 12 April 1876. A proposal for arranging the collections, comprising sculptures and antiquities, in Geological Survey of India was sent by H.B. Medlicott, Superintendent, Geological Survey of India to W.T. Blanford, Secretary, Trustees of the Indian Museum, Calcutta. In this connection, the latter was requested that it will be a great advantage to the Museum if a competent officer of the Archaeological Survey could be spared to arrange the collections of sculptures and other antiquities. Accordingly, W.T. Blanford sought the Government of India's approval for the purpose. Cunningham readily agreed to the proposal and sent his own suggestions to the Government of India on 21 July 1876. He further stated that the collections of the Geological Survey of India should be entrusted to the care of Archaeological Survey of India so that it could be classified properly and provide the discerning visitor necessary information.[1]

Cunningham prepared a short Memorandum (Appendix XIII) regarding the classification of antiquities and recommended his assistant J.D. Beglar for the task. Cunningham stated that Beglar was competent to carry out the classification as he was acquainted with all styles of script writings prevalent in different period of times and various localities. Besides, Cunningham asserted that Beglar was fully competent and possessed necessary expertise in setting of Buddhist railings and gateways from Bharahut as he had seen all the pillars in their original positions and afterwards photographed them on the spot.[2] He further suggested that sculptured and Corinthian capitals from Yusufzai district should be confined to a room and not allowed to be kept in an open space where they would be subject to vagaries of weather and eventually ruined.[3] The proposal of Cunningham for deputing Beglar was approved by the Governor-General in Council.[4]

In a communication from the Secretary, P.W.D. Government of India to Secretary, PWD North-West Provinces on 25 July 1876, it was proposed to appropriate the grant-in-aid of Rs. 35,000 from Imperial to provincial services for the restoration and preservation of works of art and antiquity in the North-West Provinces. Lytton, the Governor-General, had conveyed his approval with regard to reappropriation of Rs. 35,000 p.a. for a period of five years for works connected with the restoration of archaeological antiquities in the North-West Provinces and decided that the grant shall be sanctioned for the current official year and the continuance of the grant must depend upon the state of the finances and the report that should be submitted at the end of the year detailing what has been done during the year and whether any grant was necessary.[5]

Another instance, which was brought to the notice of the Government of India, related to the amount sanctioned by the Government of Bombay for undertaking demolition works of Guttal Fort and for filling in the ditch for levelling of the Fort's premises and also reclaiming the ditch at Gadag as famine relief works. In this connection, A.P. Howell, Secretary, Government of India addressed a communication to the Secretary, PWD, Government of Bombay on 9 August 1877 and assured that demolition orders for the buildings which were of intrinsic architectural significance or work of historical importance could not have been given by the Governor-in-Council. He also urged the Secretary to exercise restraint in ordering demolitions of such edifices and said that vigilance was needed so as to avoid destruction of such buildings by railway contractors and engineers. If they had to be removed, inscriptions and valuable artifacts, icons, etc. were to be carefully preserved.[6]

However, necessary repair works to the archaeological heritage and architecturally sound edifices were carried out. In this connection, it was reported by the Chief Engineer that during 1872-76, Rs. 87,995 and Rs. 79,588 were spent on repair works of Agra Fort and Taj Mahal respectively. Besides, Rs. 1,968 was spent for the preservation of Fatehpur Sikri. A sum of Rs. 19,533 was spent on repair of the Govind Deva Temple at Vrindavan (Mathura) of which Rs. 5,000 was provided by the Maharaja of Jaipur. On repair works alone, the Government of India granted Rs. 55,000 and the balance of Rs. 1,29,084 was provided from the revenues from provinces.[7]

The Secretary of State for India, in his despatch dated 10 May 1877, informed the Governor-General in Council that the organization of an archaeological survey of South India should be postponed, "at present juncture". This postponing was mainly attributed to climatic vagaries and due to lack of cohesive policy with regard to archaeological investigations in Madras Presidency. Besides, the Secretary of State felt that data with regard to principal archaeological monuments throughout Madras Presidency was also essential before any definite policy was adopted. The Secretary of State also felt that selection of an officer possessing the necessary qualifications for supervising such a task was of paramount importance. He further urged upon the Government of India for securing the services of the right person who was conversant with the languages of Southern India. In this connection, it was pointed out that James Fergusson had earlier recommended the name of Mr. Chisholm, who had been engaged in the survey of rock-cut temples of Mahabalipuram and therefore he urged the Governor-General to consider the proposal of Fergusson. The Secretary of State felt that any selection of this nature should be done judiciously and ensure a systematic archaeological survey of Southern India.

The Secretary of State felt that there should be no financial objection to carry into effect the scheme of archaeological survey of Southern India but stressed the need for preparation of a list of archaeological antiquities in Madras Presidency, which would form a necessary basis for initiating an exhaustive survey of the region.[8]

In the meanwhile, Major General A. Cunningham, Director General, Archaeological Survey of India on 18 October 1877 forwarded his report on the Stupa of Bharahut to the Secretary, Government of India. The Stupa of Bharahut was a Buddhist monument ornamented with numerous sculptures and which also depicted illustrations of Buddhist legends and history of the 3rd century BC. The report contained 57 illustrations in folio plates, mainly photographs, the negatives of which had been handed over to the Government by J.D. Beglar. As regards the publication of these photographs, Beglar had consulted Captain Waterhouse, in charge of the Photographic Branch of the Surveyor General's Office, and was informed that the cost of photographic printing was steep in India as compared to its cost prevalent in England. This opinion was corroborated by Cunningham's own experience when he discovered that the cost of photographic prints were half the cost prevalent in England. Cunningham suggested that the report along with illustrations should be forwarded to the Secretary of State for India for publication in London. He also stated that his documentation was critically reviewed and appreciated by the front ranking scholars of Europe. Max Mueller, the celebrated scholar and Indologist from Germany stated, "the sculptures and inscriptions of Bharahut, we shall have in future a real landmark in the religious and literary history of India and many theories held by Sanskrit scholars will have to be modified accordingly". Prof. Childers stated that "We owe to Cunningham one of the most imposing archaeological discoveries of the present century." Cunningham further stated that the opinions of two scholars were added by him to justify the need of a publication.[9]

The Government of India endorsed the views of Cunningham. Arthur Howell, Secretary, Government of India addressed a communication to him on 5 November 1877 conveying his best wishes and appreciating the Governor-General in Council on his discovery of the "Stupa of Bharahut" and stated that the documentation on the stupa was forwarded to the Secretary of State for India for publication in England. [10]

One of the principal achievements of Lord Lytton as Governor-General was to prevent the desecration of the archaeological remains by treasure hunters and the enactment of the Treasure Trove Act of 1878. This Act empowered the Government of India to claim possession of any treasure unearthed whose value exceeded ten rupees (Appendix XIV).

Lord Lytton felt that the national antiquities and art should not be exclusively left to the charge of Local Governments, as they were not "always alive to the importance of such a duty." Lieutenant Governors, who combine aesthetic culture with administrative energy, are not likely to be very common. Lytton was of the opinion that the Government of India that had essential financial resources could exercise vigil over the country's archaeological wealth and its antiquities.[11]

The views expressed by Lord Lytton were welcomed. A. Clarke fully agreed with the views put forth by the Viceroy. He felt that a systematic imperial survey of architectural buildings in India should be undertaken. Firstly, the Director General of Archaeology and various local governments and administrations should coordinate the preservation of architectural splendours. Restoration should not be undertaken as it was impossible to perfectly reproduce old work and even if were to be undertaken, it would be an expensive proposition.

Secondly, provide the means for producing a standard work on Indian architecture for being prescribed as a textbook in the Engineering Colleges and Schools in India and also for serving as a guide manual in Public Works Department.

Clarke was of the opinion that in order to assist the Governor, Lt. Governor or Chief Commissioner, a list of important monuments amongst thousands of existing monuments should be prepared and their architecture with all peculiarities should be examined from an imperial point of view. Clarke felt that the best monument in a province may not have the best style of architecture and an elaborate record of local monuments of discerning architecture needs to be prepared. In this regard, Clarke was of the opinion that a review of work done in the field of documenting architectural heritage of archaeological importance need to be undertaken before submitting definitive proposals for consideration.

He even pointed out the treatises on Indian architecture and referred to such treatise of Ram Raz, a Hindu, who had published his treatise on Hindu architecture in 1834 wherein he had discussed the rules of indigenous architecture. During the Paris exhibition of 1867, an interest was kindled in England for Indian architecture. This had led Sir Stafford Northcote to make a suggestion in 1868 for recording the ancient monuments in India with a view to conserve them. The Government of India, accordingly, adopted some measures to encourage amateur photographers to capture views of architectural buildings and offered monetary assistance. Soon after, Sir E.C. Bayley, through which survey of Bengal, Madras, Bombay and Upper Provinces was assigned to various agencies to prepare a documented treatise on the archaeological heritage, initiated a comprehensive measure. This proposal resulted in documentation of existing archaeological splendours. The results of some were got published by the Secretary of State and the Arundel Society. The South Kensington Museum obtained casts of various Indian subjects and exhibited them. As the work progressed, the Government was determined to reappoint General Cunningham in 1870. The investigation of archaeology in India and publication of his reports had thrown new light on hitherto unknown facts, while researches prosecuted by Burgess in Bombay had added to the already available information.

In 1875, Sir John Strachey organized a system of recording and restoring magnificent specimens of architecture in the North-West Provinces. Many valuable and important works for preservation had been undertaken. Besides, the Duke of Buckingham made an earnest effort to establish an Archaeological Department in Madras.

In the meantime, Fergusson's volume on *History of Eastern Architecture* was published, which constituted an exhaustive general review. He stated in the introduction of his book that without preliminary study, the subject cannot be mastered but the volume contains an outline of the archaeology in India and rightly affords an opportunely to "anyone who wishes for more information to know where to look for it, or how to appreciate it when found".

Clarke also referred to deficiencies on the survey work. He stated that the prominent architectural buildings were well known and what was required was steps to be taken for their preservation. The system adopted by the indigenous architect for construction of a particular monument of intrinsic architecture needed to be documented for agencies employed towards preservation and conservation of heritage monuments.

With regard to the importance of studying Indian architecture, Clarke was of the view that building architecture of Hindus and Muslims were being heavily influenced by European architecture, hence the need and importance of studying Indian architecture of the yore. The introduction of Hindu and Muslim architecture need to be introduced in the local engineering and other colleges in India. This type of study would suit indigenous habits and tastes, and conform to specifications which are needed for comfort and health and thereby serve as a protection from fierce heat as compared to buildings designed to suit the purpose for temperate climate. It was this precise reason that buildings of indigenous architecture were encouraged to be built in style of indigenous architecture. For example:

Temples*	Schools
Mosques*	Markets
Palaces*	Hospitals
Colleges*	Asylums

As per comforts and requirements of Europeans such as residences, churches, offices, railways and buildings, European architecture was adopted with inbuilt provisions to acclimitise the various seasons in India.

Clarke also dilated on the debasement of Indian art by European influences. He referred to evidences which had proved that European influence tended to debase Indian art. He felt that it was easy to adopt Hindu or Muslim design in a building than Gothic styles of architecture which demanded elaborate detail.

Clarke also lamented about the fact that Indian architecture was being corrupted due to wrong usage of material, i.e., use of plaster instead of stone. He was of the view that there was consistency between material and style in ancient buildings but recently "this consistency threatened to vanish". Plaster was constantly being used, which crumbled after few years due to climatic changes. He referred to Gaur ruins in Bengal, where the edifices were made of bricks, ornamented with pillars and details depicted in hard baked clay with polish. He suggested that terracotta details could be found everywhere and study of this nature should be encouraged and use of durable material should be revived and propagated.

He suggested to undertake two kinds of survey by the Archaeological Survey of India, namely,

1. Survey for purposes of preservation or repair of old fine buildings.
2. Survey for collecting information and details on styles of architecture.

With regard to methodology for the survey, he suggested that existing information should be supplemented. Besides, reports, drawings, plans, photographs and private works should be examined and information on the general condition of well known buildings should be elicited from the reports and also from Local Governments.

Thereafter, the survey should commence and material collected. As a first step in this direction, he suggested the need of procuring estimates for ascertaining the cost of preservation and undertaking repair works. He also prescribed compilation of standard text book on Indian architecture. Further, he proposed to illustrate the text book and referred to a standard book on engineering compiled by the Roorkee College. The text book should be prescribed in schools and colleges throughout India. In this way, the Government could make a good beginning to teach natives "the skilful art practiced by their ancestors – almost a tradition", he concluded.

Clarke also proposed to organize famine relief works to prevent old buildings from ruination. In carrying out these famine relief measures, the information was to be elicited from the Local Governments and there should be no interference in the work of preservation and restoration by the Government of India.

He suggested the name of Captain Cole to undertake this work. He stated that Captain Cole had many years of experience in architecture. Cole was engaged in archaeological survey of the North-West Provinces and was offered the post of Archaeological Surveyor of Southern India on Rs. 1,200 per month.[12]

---

* Clarke suggested that "Such works do not come directly within the province of the Government but it is our duty and endeavour to encourage in them a good and pure style of native architecture".

Reacting to the recommendation of Clarke, Lord Lytton, Viceroy, mentioned in his minute and emphasized the need of systematic conservation of archaeological remains in India. He referred to the minute dated 25 August 1875 of Sir John Strachey, the erstwhile Lt. Governor of North-West Provinces (Appendix XV) wherein he had recorded that conservation of monuments should be entrusted to "Curator of Ancient Monuments" who should be assisted by a complement of subordinate staff and should be placed under the administrative control of Public Works Department and also Director General of the Archaeological Survey. He referred to Clarke's proposals in revamping the Archaeological Survey in India and his suggestions to appoint a competent person for the preservation of monuments. He suggested that the same officer could be vested with the responsibility of collecting and compiling information on the ancient systems of Indian architecture along with their material and methodology of construction.

Lytton drafted a Resolution for consideration of the Governor-General in Council with regard to appointment of Captain Cole to the post of Curator.[13] E.C. Bayley, one of the members of the Governor-General in Council, hailed the Resolution for selecting Captain Cole as "a very good one". He further opined,

> the truth is the history of Indian architecture is so difficult a subject, and one so little studied hitherto, that the time has scarcely arrived preparing a manual regarding it. Little has hitherto been done beyond collecting isolated masses of information, but except recently, in the third volume of Mr. Fergusson's new work on architecture, no attempt has hitherto been made to review the subject as a whole. In fact this subject is one of such difficulty and requires such close study so much so varied knowledge, that I believe Mr. Fergusson himself, who is of all men the most competent, has shrunk from undertaking it.
>
> The country of India is so vast and has been overrun by so many differing races, of so many and such varying creeds, and varies so widely in physical conditions, all of which accidents have affected the local character of the architecture prevailing from time to time, that a pretty close attention to them and a pretty full knowledge of them, is required before any comprehensive view of the architecture of India can be arrived at.
>
> Thus for example, the Muslim architecture of the invaders in upper India was, while it preserved characteristics traceable to the physical conditions of the countries where they came, yet was at once modified to suit the materials found ready to hand in the spoils of the stone-built Hindu temples destroyed and the practices of the Hindu artisans employed and was further modified to suit the climate and the growing magnificence of the Muslim sovereigns, till at last it culminated into a style peculiar, though perfectly adapted, to its object, and which nevertheless bore traces even to the last of all the sources from which it was drawn. In Sind, the style was modified by the deficiency of materials but developed more strongly the ornaments of mosaic tiling which the character of the soil favoured.
>
> Moreover, on many points we at present literally know nothing or next to nothing. Even in South India for example, it has only recently been discovered that large megalithic monuments which in Europe it has been the custom to identify with races long before historic times, have been erected in very recent periods, some actually dating as late as the middle of the last century.
>
> As will be seen from Cunningham's last report – No. 233 dated 2 February 1878 – where it was made explicit the principal part of his final labours is designed to provide materials for such a task, much of it from districts and belonging to periods of which hitherto little or nothing has been known.
>
> It may be said that what is intended is nothing so ambitious as this, but merely an introductory manual to the study of Indian architecture, but in truth it is not possible to write a manual of a

subject which is only yet imperfectly studied. So far from being useful, such a manual could only be superficial and misleading.

If Fergusson and Cunningham would together undertake the task when the materials recently collected are made available, it is possible that a satisfactory beginning might be made. At present they are the only persons qualified to undertake such a task, and one of them at least has, as I am informed, shrunk from undertaking it alone.

I should like to modify the Resolution on this point, and to leave out all allusion to a manual. There will be for a long time, more than ample work for the Curator in his more proper duties.[14]

Cunningham also offered his opinion on the course of action to be adopted for the preservation of ancient monuments in India and lamented on the ruthless defacement of monuments due to neglect on account of official apathy.

He opined that the proposal to appoint a Curator of Ancient Monuments had given him the satisfaction and stated that

during my long career several valuable monuments have been ruthlessly defaced, whilst others have been swept away altogether. To the former class belongs the Bihar Pillar, bearing two Gupta inscriptions. This was removed by Mr. Broadley, the Deputy Magistrate of Bihar and re-erected 'upside down' in front of his own house and its blank face was barbarously covered with the names of the entire deputy Magistrates of Bihar in rude English characters. To the second class belongs the Tomb of Ibrahim Lodi who was defeated by Babar on the field of Panipat. The Road Officer removed the tomb. Another monument of this class was the Koil Minar, erected during the reign of the Pathan King Nasiruddin Mahmood, about 600 years ago, which was pulled down by the Magistrate of the District to furnish materials for a temporary tehsil.

But the most powerful agent of destruction has been the Railway contractor who cares for nothing on earth but the making of money. To him a temple is only a collection of ready squared stones or a heap of ready burnt bricks. Thus one Railway Contractor removed a whole temple from Tewar near Jabalpur in the time of Lord Canning and another pulled down about fifty small temples at Tigawar and collected the stones in a heap ready to be carried off on two hundred carts which he had brought to the place when he was stopped by the Deputy Commissioner of Jabalpur. But the mischief was already done as the temples had been utterly destroyed.

With an active and zealous curator, responsible for the preservation of all noble monuments which still exist, their safety would be ensured for the future against the vagaries of economic Magistrates, stolid Road Officers and rapacious Railway contractors.

I am glad to see that Sir Andrew Clarke has drawn attention to the vast superiority of good plain brick and terra-cotta over the mouldering plaster walls of the present day. I have lately visited a brick temple, which cannot be less than 1200 years old of which all the flowered mouldings, and pilasters (sic) are made of well-burnt bricks and still as sharp and fresh as when first put up. The bas reliefs also, many of them two and half feet high, are in terra-cotta with a high polish on the surface almost approaching to glaze. The lower part of his temple is rather dilapidated. One corner of it I repaired during my visit of two days at a trifling cost. I trust, therefore, that this unique specimen of ancient terra-cotta work may hereafter receive such repair as will secure it from tumbling down for centuries to come.

With regard to the preparation of a manual of Indian Architecture, I think that at present, we are scarcely in a position to draw up any standard work, as the amount of materials hitherto collected is too small to afford the best typical examples of so many different styles. This want however, has been steadily kept in view, as details of many hundreds of temples and their buildings have already been drawn and photographed, some of which will appear in volumes VII and VIII of the Archaeological Survey.

> I am of the opinion that the best fitted person, who is now available, is Captain Cole of Royal Engineers. The most difficult part of his duty, in my judgement, will be to determine the exact 'amount of restoration', which each building should receive. There will be no difficulty about the selection of buildings, which should be permanently maintained at the expense of the Government. These will, of course, be kept up in perfect order. But where buildings are partially ruined it will often be difficult to say how much repair should be made, and whether any of the fallen parts should be restored. Fortunately, Cole has had very favourable opportunities of seeing many different classes of Indian architecture and I think that the Government may safely rely on his judgement as to the nature and extent of the restorations that might be made with advantage, as well as to the repairs that might be absolutely required to secure the buildings from early ruin.[15]

John Strachey appreciated the efforts of Lord Lytton in ensuring proper conservation of monuments and supported the appointment of Captain Cole. He opined,

> even if our materials for the compilation of a manual of Indian Architecture were far more complete than they are, the Conservator would, I am convinced, have no leisure for the task in addition to the vast amount of work awaiting him in the ordinary sphere of duties which has been sketched out for him. But besides this, I would deprecate any attempt to place inventive genius and specially that of the natives of India, in leading strings or fetters and I can conceive no more effectual means to this end than the issue of standard designs – It will, no doubt, be impossible in a large majority of cases to decide how individual monuments should be dealt with or what proportion of the expenditure to be incurred on them should be Imperial, until after full consultation with the Local Governments and officers. But I think that some indication of how monuments should be classified and of the various sources to which we look for funds for their repair, would be useful to the Curator himself, to all local authorities and to the general public who will peruse the Resolution.

Strachey, however, felt that the draft Resolution should be sent to Secretary of State for India before its issue. He also proposed for Cole, a salary of an Under Secretary in the Public Works Department, viz., Rs. 1,100 per month along with an establishment for assisting him in his duties. He, however, recommended the name of James Fergusson for obtaining his expert opinion on the subject.[16]

Finally, on 15 March 1878, Lytton thanked the members of his Council and Cunningham for their valuable and useful comments,[17] and forwarded the Resolution to the Secretary of State for India on 18 March 1878. Lytton asserted that the "time has now arrived when the foundation in 1870 of the Archaeological Survey of India for purposes of research and record, may be supplemented by the appointment of an officer, with the designation of Curator of Ancient Monuments, to carry out under the Government of India a general system of conservation". The Government of India referred to the accompanying draft of a Resolution (to this draft was appended a very characteristic minute dated 25 August 1875 by Sir John Strachey when he was Lieutenant Governor of N.W.P.) (Appendix XV), which they proposed to publish in the *Gazette of India*. For the Curator's appointment, they considered a salary of Rs. 1,100 per month, which was the amount received by an Under Secretary to the Government of India in the Public Works Department and provision of an establishment to assist him in discharge of his functions.[18]

The opinion of J. Fergusson on the conservation of historical monuments of India was also invited and he gave his opinion to the Under Secretary of State for India in June 1878. He opined, "the time has arrived when it is necessary for Government to take steps to arrest the destruction of the numerous interesting monuments scattered over the length and breadth of the land. They are rapidly perishing from the effects of a most destructive climate and from the supposed exigencies of a uneducated community to appreciate historical or aesthetic considerations when brought in contact with the apparent immediate advantages that might be obtained by the removal of a disused monument or to comprehend the motives that would induce the better educated classes to spend money on its restoration". Further, he suggested that the Government should sanction the expenditure of a sufficient sum for ensuring the completion of any important repairs when once undertaken so as to prevent any fitful or spasmodic attempts, which may frequently do more harm than good. One of the greatest advantages of the creation of a separate office under a responsible chief, will be the continuity of the undertakings so directed instead of their being left, as heretofore, to the uncertain efforts of ever changing local authorities. He favoured the appointment of an officer with the designation "Curator of Ancient Monuments" who would be discharging his duties and functions in accordance with the stipulations as incorporated in the draft Resolution.

It appeared to Fergusson "that it would tend to the harmonious and efficient working of the scheme not only in the preparation of the lists but also in the execution of his duties as conservator. If the officer appointed for these purposes was placed under the same Department as the Archaeological Survey of India whose duties were in many respects so nearly identical with his. Fergusson, therefore, suggested that instead of holding the position of Under Secretary in the Public Works Department, he should be placed in a similar office in the Home Department, where his position would be freer from the trammels of existing organizations and more immediately under the control of the Committee whose creation was contemplated in the Draft Resolution. If this were done, in the event of questions of purely engineering character arising the Home Department would, as a matter of course, consult the Public Works Department, regarding them in the usual manner.

Fergusson was in total agreement with the plans regarding classification of monuments. He suggested that the Curator should coordinate the plan of action with regard to ensuring conservation and preservation of monuments. In this connection, he stated that the services of 'architectural historian' be enlisted who would ascertain the state of building and assess the repair works required for its conservation. Fergusson fondly hoped of "improving the working of a scheme which has my entire sympathy and warm approval".[19]

Gawthorne Hardy, later Viscount Cranbrook, Secretary of State for India also tendered his views on the state of archaeology in India and on appointment of Curator of Ancient Monuments. In his communication addressed to the Government of India on 31 July 1878, he stated that it was obligatory on the part of Government of India to preserve monuments and ensure that they are not neglected. Any neglect on the part of the Government would "entail lasting discredit on the English name". The selected incumbent for the post of Curator of Ancient Monuments should be given allowances and position equated to the Under Secretary either in Public Works Department or Home Department. The functions of the post of Curator should be placed under the "heads of classification and conservation". Besides, he should also be assigned the task of scrutinizing the list of accounts of ancient monuments which have already been compiled. He should prepare a list of "defective monuments" and sub-divide the monuments according to their importance and classify them further indicating their public and private ownership. The Curator should discharge his functions with close cooperation and collaboration with the Director General, Archaeological Survey of India and that "no final proposition shall be made without the concurrence of that Officer". He further suggested a Committee should be constituted comprising members of the Council in charge of Home, PWD and Director General, Archaeological Survey and that they should ensure all proposals and projects connected with architectural heritage and archaeological monuments be submitted by Curator to the Committee for ratification of the concerned proposal.

Viscount Cranbrook also stated that the delay in submitting his comments was primarily due to the fact that the Draft Resolution had to be modified with his proposal as mentioned, before it was approved and published in the *Gazette of India*. Gawthorne Hardy was assigned the task to protect the historic antiquities of India from further decay but he stated thus:

> something considerable seems to have been done of late years in the way of assignment of funds for that object, I shall learn with pleasure that expenditure on purposes of actual construction is maintained at its present rate or is even increased though our financial condition may probably not allow of a material increase for some time to come but I should not feel myself warranted in sanctioning just now additional expense for control and supervision especially as in the Archaeological Surveyor General's establishment we have very nearly all that is requisite for the latter purpose. As long, therefore, as that establishment is maintained on its present footing, there will, in my opinion, be no occasion for the appointment of a Curator in addition, there being among the functions assignable to such an officer hardly any which the Archaeological Surveyor General, with his existing staff, is not perfectly competent to perform. The time may come, and is probably not far off, when it will be expedient to replace the survey by a Curatorship.

Cranbrook felt that till such time the Government of India considered the modifications suggested by him, the appointment of Curator of Ancient Monuments might be deferred to a future date.[20]

In the meanwhile, a sum of Rs. 3,75,000 was requisitioned by the Government of North-West Provinces for the preservation and restoration of monuments of architectural significance and archaeological importance. Col. Alex Fraser, Secretary, Public Works Department, North-West Provinces justified his demand for the amount by stating that "the preservation of these buildings is not by any means a matter of mere local importance. On the contrary, it may almost be said that the whole world are interested in their preservation".[21]

The requisite amount of Rs. 3,75,000/- was sanctioned and conveyed to the Secretary, Public Works Department, North-West Provinces by R.B. Chapman, Secretary, Finance Department, Government of India on 20 December 1878.[22]

In place of Captain Cole, who was likely to be appointed as Curator of Ancient Monuments, Cunningham recommended his assistant, J.D. Beglar's name for conservation of monuments in Madras Presidency. Cunningham justified Beglar's appointment by stating that he had considerable experience of Indian architecture and "of conservation of the ancient buildings of the Madras Presidency".[23]

The Government of Bombay addressed its concern about the Government of India's attitude in not consulting them for their scheme of the publication with regard to preservation of monuments. Their protest was voiced by W.F. Sinclair, Bombay Civil Service in his communication dated 30 May 1878 addressed to the Under Secretary of State for India.[24]

However, a Resolution No. 924 dated 21 April 1879 (Appendix XVI) was issued by C. Robertson, Secretary, Government of N.W.P. and Oudh on the subject of the "preservation of antiquarian remains" in the N.W.P. and informed the Secretary, Government of India, Home, Revenue and Agriculture Department on 7 September 1879 about their efforts in this direction.[25]

NOTES AND REFERENCES

1. Home, Public A, August 1876, No. 40.
2. *Ibid.*
3. *Ibid.*
4. *Ibid.*
5. P.W.D., A.G., August 1876, Nos. 1-3.
6. P.W.D., Civil Works, Buildings, A, February 1878, Nos. 1-2.
7. P.W.D., Account-General, January 1877, Nos. 6-7, A.
8. Public, June 1877, No. 247.
9. Public, November 1877, No. 15.
10. Public, November 1877, Nos. 16-17.
11. Finance, Expenditure, December 1878, Nos. 570-74 and K.W.
12. *Ibid.*
13. *Ibid.*
14. *Ibid.*
15. *Ibid.*
16. *Ibid.*
17. *Ibid.*
18. Finance, Expenditure, December 1878, No. 570.
19. Finance, Expenditure, December 1878, No. 573.
20. Finance, Expenditure, December 1878, No. 572.
21. P.W.D., A.G., June 1879, No. 33.
22. P.W.D., A.G., June 1879, No. 34.
23. P.W.D., C,.W.B., June 1878, No. 11, B.
24. Home, Public, September 1878, No. 11.
25. Home, Revenue and Agriculture Department, Surveys – Archaeology, September 1879, No. 49.

CHAPTER VIII

H.H. Cole's Appointment as Curator of Ancient Monuments

The Secretary of State negated the proposal of appointment of Curator of Ancient Monuments on the ground that the Director General of Archaeology could execute scrutiny of projects in the provinces and further that the filling up of the proposed post of Curator of Ancient Monuments was not necessary. However, this proposal was revived under the tenure of Lord Ripon but in a modified form. In order to ensure conservation of ancient monuments of archaeological and historical interest in India, this post of Curator of Ancient Monuments was revived with a salary of Rs. 1,100/- per mensem.

Accordingly, a Draft Resolution was addressed to the Secretary of State, which detailed the historical retrospect of the appointment of Curator of Ancient Monuments for looking after the conservation work of the monuments in India. The officer who was to be designated should be equivalent to the rank of Under Secretary to the Government of India in the Public Works Department and to be paid a salary of Rs. 1,100 per month (Appendix XV). The Governor-General in Council in his dispatch to the Secretary of State while recommending the appointment of Cole as "Curator of Ancient Monuments" to oversee the work relating to conservation of monuments, reiterated his earlier proposal that the position of the incumbent should hold the position of Under Secretary to the Government of India in the Public Works Department. The Governor-General in Council was firmly of the view that conservation of monuments and archaeological survey of monuments were two aspects distinct from each other. He referred to the researches conducted in the field of archaeology by General Cunningham, and by Burgess in the field of conservation and preservation of monuments, especially his efforts to preserve Akbar's tomb at Agra. The Resolution of the Governor-General in Council stated that the archaeological research is one thing, the preservation of existing monuments is another". The Resolution underlined the need of preservation of monuments which had been neglected and could "entail lasting discredit on the English name". The Resolution also referred to the possibility of assigning the work of conservation to the Director General of Archaeological Survey, which is to be assigned presently to the Curator of Ancient Monuments. The Resolution also referred to employment of Burgess, who could not discharge his assigned functions due to the fact that the work of preparation of plans and estimates for repairs to the monuments was entrusted to the Public Works Department due to economy in expenditure. The Resolution emphasized the need of "Intelligent care" of monuments and referred to preventive conservation work undertaken at Agra to save the monuments from further ruin. This work was initiated by Sir William Muir and systematized by Sir John Strachey. The Resolution also lamented the neglected state of archaeological monuments of historical and architectural significance, which were in ruins at Punjab and Delhi.

The condition of Buddhist Stupa at Sarnath and demolition of monuments conducted by the contractors for constructing railways in the ancient city of Kannauj region was also incorporated in the Resolution.

The Governor-General in Council through the medium of this Resolution, emphasized the need of preservation of monuments and stated that Local Governments should be entrusted with the care and preservation of monuments and only under exceptional cases, the Government of India should directly involve itself to the work relating to the preservation of monuments. It was also proposed that Cole may be appointed initially on salary of Rs. 1,000 per month with annual increments ranging Rs. 1,000 to Rs. 1,500. An establishment comprising clerks and draughtsmen should also assist him.

Besides, the Governor-General in Council also recommended formation of a Committee for "projects involving issues of architectural or archaeological knowledge" would be submitted. The Resolution conclusively hoped "a step towards a better state of things and towards the removal of what has long been a serious scandal and a reproach to the British Government in India".[1]

On 11 November 1880, the Secretary of State replied to the Government of India and stated categorically that the work of conservation of archaeological monuments could be only carried out efficiently and on a permanent footing if various provincial and local governments carry it out. The Secretary of State suggested that if Cole was to be considered for an appointment as Curator of Monuments, he should visit the Provincial Governments and evolve a definitive policy for the monuments and should be sanctioned by each provincial government for the future course of action with regard to their conservation. As the definitive policy towards conservation of monuments is likely to take some time, steps should be initiated for eliciting a list of monuments and for documenting the details for "archaeological conservation". This work should be assigned to Captain Cole with the rank equivalent to that of Executive Engineer Ist Class with appropriate salary commensurating to his qualifications. The Secretary of State felt that this appointment should be made for three years and Cole should be appointed with immediate effect. Besides, the Secretary of State stated that a plan should be prepared indicating the annual expenditure involved and statements indicating expenditure to be recommended, which is to be borne by the local governments and administrations.[2] The copy of this communication was forwarded to the Public Works Department.[3]

On 19 January 1881, Alexander Fraser, Member of the Council expressed his doubts over the arrangements for conservation of monuments and overlapping of functions of Public Works Department and also assignments of Captain Cole. Fraser felt that since preservation of monuments and the repair and restoration work would have to be provided by the Collectors and Civil Officers in the Provincial Governments, the Public Works Department would have to provide the services in this regard. Cole should get clear orders from the Government in the Home Department in this regard. Fraser also felt that the Secretary of State was of the opinion that Cole should take up the survey of monuments in Punjab at the first instance and list out the priorities which would require his immediate attention. The work of survey normally should be undertaken and completed within three years.

FRASER'S GUIDELINES

Alexander Fraser also listed a set of eight guidelines to facilitate the work of survey of monuments in the provincial governments, which required immediate attention for repair and conservation which were as follows:

(i) that he should visit each Local Government in such order as may be thought desirable, the North-West Provinces might be left to the last, as that Government has the matter already well in hand; the Punjab should be the first to be dealt with I think.

(ii) that he should in communication with the Local Governments, make a list of all known requirements, which will be quite enough to occupy Captain Cole's immediate attention.

(iii) that having obtained this list, he should settle with the Local Government the works of interest to be taken in hand within, say, the next three years.

(iv) that he should visit each work, and with the local Executive Engineer, prepare an estimate of the probable cost involved in the restoration, repair of preservation of each.

(v) that he should put all the works noted in (iv) into a schedule showing the cost likely to be incurred in each Province within the next three years.

(vi) that the Local Government should review the proposals and submit to the Government of India, showing to what extent the Provincial Government or Administration requires help, it being understood that it is the primary duty of the Local Government to preserve ancient monuments within their jurisdiction.

(vii) The Government of India will then consider what assignment should be made to each Government of financial help the Provincial funds in bringing the chief monuments of interest into a satisfactory condition as possible.

(viii) The work required under (iv), to be locally carried out by Provincial establishments, subject to the approval of the detailed places by Cole or the Curator for the time being and subject to approval by the Curator on the completion of work. In important cases the Curator should visit the work while in progress, keeping, however, the Chief Engineer of the Province informed of his intentions in this respect.

Fraser was of the view that with this arrangement the confidence of Local Governments would be also ensured and the Local Officers' experience and knowledge would be ensured with regard to labour and material to be utilized for conservation work. Further, he was of the view that by designating Captain Cole as Executive Engineer 1st Class, there would be considerable heart burning amongst the senior officers in Public Works Department and, therefore, suggested that his functions should be transferred to the Home Department. He also opined that Captain Cole may have abilities in a particular specialized field but was deficient in the functions and duties normally assigned to an Executive Engineer. Fraser also suggested the payment plans for his salary and his rank vis-à-vis contemporary officers of the Public Works Department. He suggested that Cole should work in close collaboration with the local authorities which would afford him an opportunity to know the intricacies of archaeological monuments of importance, rather than military duties of forts with which he had been associated. He should also enlist cooperation of officers who could be beneficial in the proper discharge of his functions.

Finally, Fraser suggested that a Resolution should be issued in the Home Department with regard to Cole's appointment and should be forwarded to the Secretary of State for India for his concurrence. The despatch to the Secretary of State should be explicit in so far as changes made in the offer of appointment, especially with regard to emoluments.[4]

Another member of the Council, J. Gibbs also forwarded the views expressed by General Allexander Fraser and proposed that a Resolution of his appointment should be issued by the Home Department instead of Public Works Department. Gibbs also proposed that a report on the execution of the work plans proposed to be carried out by Captain Cole should be obtained.[5] Besides, C. Grant, Secretary, Government of India also opined on 27 January 1881 that Cole's salary should be Rs. 1,100, rising to Rs. 1,500 per month instead of the salary usually drawn by of an Executive Engineer Ist grade as Rs. 1,090 which was approved by Secretary of State.[6]

Finally, Captain H.H. Cole was appointed Curator of Ancient Monuments in India. In this respect, two notifications were issued, i.e., one by Public Works Department[7] and another by the Home Department.[8]

On 2 February 1881, a Resolution was adopted in Home, Revenue and Agricultural Department (Surveys), Nos. 1-30 to 42 through which the appointment of Captain Cole as a "Curator of Ancient Monuments in Home, Revenue and Agricultural Department whose duties will be to superintend under the Supreme Government the conservation of the most celebrated and important examples of national archaeology and architecture throughout India". The appointment of Captain Cole was notified in the Gazette of India on 29 January 1881. The copy of this Resolution was also forwarded "to all local agents and Administrations for information and guidance".[9]

A communication was addressed to Cole on 2 February 1881 by C.L. Tupper, Under Secretary, Government of India wherein he was requested to report on the **modus operandi** through which the survey and conservation work of archaeological monuments would be carried out in consonance with the instructions of the Secretary of State and Government of India and submit proposals for the "establishment you will require for the work".[10]

Captain Cole reported to the Government of India on 2 February 1881 about the survey and examination of monuments of archaeological interest at Lahore and Delhi, and submitted a report which detailed the comparisons between the restored and well-carved monuments at Agra and the neglected state of archaeological monuments at Lahore and Delhi. He stated that in order to know the extant of archaeological monuments in other parts of India, it was necessary for him to make on-the-spot assessment of monuments. He added that this work was to be completed without delay as his appointment was sanctioned for a period of three years. Cole also elaborated that it was not possible for him to undertake executive duties and that the actual operations and the officers appointed to carry them out should be directly under the provincial governments.[11]

This request of Cole was accepted by the Government and incorporated in the Resolution of Home, Revenue and Agriculture Department (Survey) No. 11-245/258, dated 8 June 1881. The position of Captain Cole, Curator of Ancient Monuments will be of head of a separate department under the Home, Revenue and Agriculture Department. His pay will be fixed at Rs. 1,100 for three years, the period for which the Secretary of State had sanctioned the appointment. The sanction would take effect from the 29 January 1881 upon which date the appointment of Captain Cole was notified in the Gazette of India. Besides, the Government of

India sanctioned an expenditure amounting to Rs. 24,552 towards Curator's establishment for 1881-1882.[12]

Thereafter, C. Grant, Secretary, Government of India on 12 August 1881 informed the local agents and underlined the objectives of the appointment of Captain Cole. He stated that the Local Governments would be benefited with professional expertise in restoration and conservation of monuments throughout India. He further stated that such schemes of restoration and conservation of monuments should be prepared in consultation with Captain Cole who will not be bestowed with the responsibility concerning preparation of estimates of expenditure, which would be the sole responsibility of the Local Governments. Besides, the Local Governments could requisite additional funds, which would be allocated exclusively for the purpose by the Government of India. Grant also prescribed the procedure for carrying out the restoration work of monuments by the Local Governments. He stated that the Local Governments were at liberty to carry out restoration and conservation work but Captain Cole should be consulted for the execution of such works.[13]

Grant also addressed a communication to Captain Cole on 12 August 1881 and informed that Rs. 50,000 would be exclusively earmarked by the Public Works Department for carrying out the restoration of ancient monuments by the Local Governments.[14]

It was decided on public grounds that the head quarters of the Curator's office should be located at Shimla because it was considered the best suitable place for conducting the whole operation throughout the country systematically.[15]

CAPTAIN COLE AND CONSERVATION

Captain Cole was a knowledgeable, industrious and enthusiastic officer. He had a thorough knowledge of his subject. Prior to his appointment as Curator of Ancient Monuments on 28 January 1881, he had been entrusted with the responsibility of examining the physical condition of the monuments at Lahore, Agra and Delhi. He had prepared a report on the work which was submitted on 10 May 1880. The report incorporated in the Memorandum on the "conservation of ancient and other architectural remains in India". The etymology of 'Conservation' had been succinctly defined by Cole in his Memorandum.

The salient features of his Memorandum are detailed below.

1. **Conservation** – He stated that conservation included "protection of works of art and for the production of permanent and convenient methods for facilitating their useful study". He further stated that the principal components of conservation were: (i) Custody, (ii) Preservation, (iii) Restoration, (iv) Illustration. Cole was of the view that while the Local Governments would satisfactorily undertake custody and preservation, work relating to restoration and illustration would require specialized and professional services of personnel.
2. **Custody** – Cole suggested enlisting the services of personnel locally, preferably retired policemen or soldiers. An intelligent and sleepy chowkidar would be no efficient guardian. He also suggested a corps of local personnel should be created in each district. The person entrusted with the responsibility should wear a badge with instructions indicated thereon.
3. **District Manuals** – Cole suggested that description of monuments should be prepared and printed in English and vernacular languages for creating awareness and interest in them.

4. **Buildings** – It might also be worthwhile to affix to some of the most important buildings on notice some imperishable material such as enamel or glazed pottery, giving the name and date both in English and other vernacular languages. Cole stated that this description would avoid wanton usage of monuments due to ignorance of history and would be enlightened by the importance of the edifice "because it possesses historical or artistic traditions".
5. **Preservation** – Cole suggested that the Local Governments should ensure –
   (i) cleanliness
   (ii) periodical removal of growth of vegetation and the removal of thick jungle without damaging the edifice.
   (iii) removal of debris from the precincts of monuments.
   (iv) repairing fallen portion of monuments.
   (v) collection of fallen carved and ornamental fragments.
   (vi) erection of enclosures for warding off cattle menace.
6. **Restoration** – The work regarding restoration should be undertaken after thoroughly investigating the plan of monuments. Since it is an important aspect of conservation, it should be left to the experts.
7. **Illustration** – The documentation on illustrations should be studied in detail for better appreciation of the art and architecture of India. In this connection, he referred to his note on the Industrial Art, which he submitted to the Government of India (Please see Appendix XVII).
8. **Duties of conservator of ancient and other architectural remains in India** – In order to ensure effective conservation of monuments, Cole suggested the appointment of a conservator who would liaise with the Local Governments with regard to custody and preservation of monuments. He would also arrange to publish manuals and inspect buildings with regard to advising the Governments for repair and restoration. The conservator would also supervise the work of draftsmen for collection of illustrations of Indian ornamental art. The Government also considered the recommendations of Cole for duties of conservator during the process of the appointment of Curator of ancient monuments.

   Cole referred to the constitution of a separate department or organization under the charge of Public Works Department in each province. This organization could be entrusted with the functions of repair, restoration and illustration, besides preservation of works of art and antiquity. He also stated that there was no better agency than public works in provinces to carry out restoration work other than the Public Works Department but it is only by those who take an interest in such work that it can be properly carried out.

   Mr. Gibbs of the Bombay Civil Service when Assistant Commissioner, under Sir Bartle Frere in Sindh, arranged for the repair of the Jama Masjid at Tatta and said in a Minute on the Bombay Archaeological Survey dated June 1873 that he got the work done by enlisting the sympathies of the Muslim community. It was afterwards estimated that the cost would have been four times the amount if the repairs had been done by the Public Works Department.
9. **Divisions for special repair and preservation** – In order to ensure execution of special repair works to monuments and to ensure the preservation and restoration of

illustrations, Cole suggested creation of divisions in various provinces. He also underline the need of inspecting various monuments with a view to estimate the expenditure involved for undertaking necessary repair and restoration.

10. **Civil authorities as custodians of artistic monuments** – Cole made suggestions that the civil authorities in the provinces should be entrusted with the responsibility of the custody of monuments under their respective jurisdiction. He also suggested that the monuments, which are under the charge of military authorities, should be immediately placed under the charge of Local Governments. He also referred to the charge of monuments in Agra under the charge of Executive Engineer of the Archaeological Division of the North-West Provinces and this arrangement presented no difficulty. In Madras, the monuments were under the jurisdiction of revenue officials and the repair works are entrusted to the Public Works Department. Cole lamented that there was no organization established in Madras, which could carry out the survey and conserve the monuments in the Presidency.
11. **Acts for the preservation of monuments** – As far as the discovery of buried ruins or works of art is concerned, the Treasure Trove Act of 1878 appears to furnish the civil authorities with all necessary power for dealing with valuable inscriptions, coins or other discoveries but in regard to the preservation of buildings and monuments, unless existing legislation is sufficient, an Act would seem requisite.[16]

When Cole was appointed Curator of ancient monuments in January 1881, special officers were engaged in the conservation pursuits. They were as follows:

(i) **Bengal** – Beglar, Executive Engineer, Bodh Gaya.
(ii) **North-West Provinces and Oudh** – Major Heath, Executive Engineer, Archaeological Division.
(iii) **Punjab** – Lt. Abbot, Assistant Engineer.
(iv) **Central India** – Major Keith, Assistant to the Curator of ancient monuments.
(iv) **Madras** – Mr. Black, Assistant Engineer.[17]

During his tenure as Curator of ancient monuments, Cole examined nearly all the important edifices both in British India and princely states. He also supervised the conservation work and gave his expert opinion in this regard. Besides, he also carried out restoration work in many monuments of intrinsic interest.

On monuments' restoration at Delhi and Lahore and other places at Punjab, the Government of India on 23 September 1882 issued a note of caution. The Government of India was of the opinion that the work of restoration of historical and buildings of significant archaeological importance should proceed with caution, judgement and artistic aesthetic sense. The work of restoration should be entrusted to an officer who should consider his sacred endeavour and such works should be normally done under the superintendence of Captain Cole.[18]

COLE'S PUNITIVE ACTION

Captain Cole took administrative measures to tackle lacdiasical and careless approach of the personnel engaged in repair and restoration of monuments. He took action against Niaz Ahmed, Draftsman, dismissed him from service and recommended forfeiture of his pay and allowances. Niaz Ahmed had damaged the mosaic work on the rear side of Diwan-i-Aam of Red Fort, Delhi and had also removed some of the inlaid stones from the walls. He also informed the Secretary,

Home Department on 19 April 1881 of his action against Niaz Ahmed. He also stated that the Superintending Engineer, Military Works Branch had shrugged off his responsibility in the superintendence of repair works and made an excuse that he was ignorant of the duties of Curator. Cole added that he was confident about the support of Inspector General of Military Works in his venture of repair and conservation of archaeological monuments. He also requested that unskilled workmen, who should be stopped forthwith, pending submission of proposals, normally execute the repairs to the archaeological monuments.

The Secretary endorsed the action taken by Cole that "you have acted rightly in punishing the man by dismissal and forfeiture of pay"[19] and issued instructions for restoration of Black Marble Mosaic which was damaged during the Revolt of 1857. The Secretary also referred to the plaque depicting orphans playing with wild beasts in the Indian Museum in London and stated that it should be brought back to India and restored to its resplendent glory. Further, the Secretary stated that repair work in painted putty should be replaced by mosaic work by qualified men, i.e., Agra stone workmen.[20]

Captain Cole always exercised caution and was forever alert in preserving monuments. His efforts in widening the entrance to the city is a good example in this direction. This was primarily done on account of some alterations made by the municipality of Delhi, on account of sanitation and traffic flow. Cole desisted every move to alter Kashmere Gate and the Government of India keenly supported him in this venture. The Secretary, Government of India had stated, "It would be a gross act of vandalism to tamper with the most interesting memorial." Captain Cole endorsed the views of the Government of India and stated, "The Cashmere Gate is in much the same state immediately after mutiny...I think that the Gateway and adjoining walls which show shot marks should certainly be preserved intact. The historical interest is alone sufficient reason, but the Gate has in addition an architectural interest of its own."[21]

Cole submitted a comprehensive scheme for monuments' preservation in Bengal and recommended Sher Shah's tomb should be taken up for preservation forthwith.[22] However, the circumstances in princely states were different and somewhat complicated. The problems of conservation of monuments were unique but complicated. Cole solved the problems with ease. It may be reiterated here that under the tenure of Cunningham, the entire country was divided into five circles, viz., Punjab, North-West Provines and Oudh, Bengal, Bombay and Madras.

However, nothing was done for the princely states. Explorations were conducted in certain points of Rajputana and Central India as is revealed through the annual reports of Archaeological Survey. Cole, as Curator of monuments, visited Rajputana, Central India and the princely states, viz., Hyderabad, Mysore and Kashmir. On his recommendations, the Government of India sanctioned a sum of Rs. 5,000 for the preservation of Gwalior Fort and Major Keith, a retired British Army personnel, was entrusted with the responsibility of work under the control of Major Cole. It was only after the appointment of Major Keith that there was steady augmentation of funds earmarked for the conservation of ancient monuments in princely states.[23]

On 21 April 1882, Lepel Griffin, Agent to the Governor-General wrote to the Secretary, Government of India that "there is abundance of work both in Native and British Territory and the Government of India has, till recently, done so little for Native art, that there are large arrears to make up. The appointment of Captain Cole as Curator is of little use unless supplemented by the labour of local assistants engaged on the practical work of conservation and restoration. Without these he has nothing to superintend, for experience has shown that artistic conservation of interesting buildings cannot be safely entrusted to the Department of Public Works".

Griffin further stated that he had done what he could in the way of inducing Native Chiefs to assist the work of architectural restoration and said, "The Maharaja Scindia has contributed Rs. 5,000 to the restoration of Jain Buildings in the Gwalior Fortress and both Dhar and Bhopal are ready to do what is reasonable with reference to the interesting remains in their respecting States, but they can hardly be asked to assist in the matter of salary and this would necessarily be a charge against the Government".[24]

On 1 June 1882, Grant had noted that the princely states should also actively contribute towards maintenance of monuments in their territories. He stated, "there are many reasons why they would not; their views are of course not so advanced in these matters as ours are or should be and expenditure on 'archaeology' means so much deducted from more agreeable objects." 'But some took deep interest. He referred to Amber Fort in Jaipur and the fortress of Chittor in Mewar. Besides, he also referred to deep interest taken by Bhopal State (Muslim Dynasty) in Buddhist ruins at Bhelsa. Grant mentioned that some states would extend help in this noble venture whereas others would "wish to please the paramount power and not to any enlightened archaeological sympathies". He further stated, "The question for us to decide is how far it is worthwhile to work on such a feeling as this for the purpose now in view. There are so many vitally important matters in which, we depend largely for the success on the cooperation of Native States that, for my part, I should be very loath to use up our influence by pressing for money for archaeological purpose." The Secretary also referred to the cooperation of some of the princely states and their pecuniary contributions in this regard. He particularly referred to efforts of the princes of Central India in the restoration of monuments. The Secretary proposed that a policy should be evolved for restoration of monuments in princely states with major brunt of expenditure to be borne by the British Indian Government, with subvention aid from the princely states.[25]

With regard to the quantum of funds coming from the princely states, Sir Lepel H. Griffin, Agent to the Governor-General for Central India reported to the Secretary, Government of India on 15 August 1882 and he stated that the Government of British India should not expect much from the princely states. He referred to an example of Sanchi Stupa and said that not much could be expected from the royalty of Bhopal under whose jurisdiction Sanchi was situated. He added that he could persuade Her Highness the Begam to contribute Rs. 5,000 towards restoration of the Stupa, but had fears that "the Nawab Consort, and his party would see the building destroyed with great pleasure".

He also referred to Bharahut situated in Rewa State where its ruler was a minor and assured that necessary expenditure to be borne for its preservation would be sent. Griffin also added that Maharaja Scindia has already subscribed Rs. 5,000 for the restoration of Gwalior Fort and for Mandu. Griffin felt that he was skeptical about the help the Raja would extend but through persuasion, he could be asked to contribute Rs. 2,000. He felt that sometimes it was beyond the means of a state to contribute any subvention towards the preservation of monuments in their respective territory, as it was beyond their financial means. Therefore, it was imperative that whatever financial contributions were forthcoming should be accepted and augmented with the funds from the budgetary grants of the British Indian Government. However, he concluded, "It would be more convenient for the Imperial Government to make a grant to be expended at the discretion of the Curator of Ancient Monuments."[26]

Thereafter, Charles Grant, Secretary, submitted to the Viceroy on 15 September 1882 that the monuments situated in Central India be in territories of rulers who have no religious or dynastic interest in their preservation. Therefore, the bulk of expenditure for the preservation of these monuments would have to be borne by the British Indian Government.[27]

Reacting to this suggestion, T.C. Tope opined on 30 September 1882:

> I trust the Home Department will see that too much of the Grant is not expended in Native States. There is in our own territory, a very large number of isolated monuments of great beauty and value e.g. the Roza at Mehmedabad in Kaira District, the Juma Mosque at Broach, also many in the South-West country which may be irreparably ruined if they do not receive early attention as well as great places like Ahmedabad, Bijapur and Mandu and for them is really required almost all the money we can spare.[28]

With the concerted efforts of Cole and a communication from the Agent to the Governor-General for Central India, A. Mackenzie, Secretary, Government of India recommended that grants towards restoration of important monuments in princely states should be made from the imperial funds and adequate provisions should be made in the budgets towards this expenditure. He requested Captain Cole to submit for the consideration of the Government of India, a statement showing what works should be undertaken for the year's budget grant. In the case of works situated in British India, such recommendation should be made in communication with the local governments and administrations and in Native States with the approval of the Political Agent; and in all cases the amount to be given by the Local Agent or Native Chiefs should be mentioned.[29]

In order to ascertain and report the amount of contribution by Central India, the agent to the Governor-General stated that the princely chiefs were not inclined towards contributions and felt that British Indian Government would have to bear the brunt of expenditure towards restoration and conservation of monuments in the princely states in Central India.[30]

The Government of India, however, agreed with the agent and in this connection, C. Grant addressed a communication to the Secretary, Foreign Department on 19 April 1883 requesting him to obtain aid and voluntary contributions from the princely chiefs wherever necessary.[31] A similar report for the conservation and restoration of monuments within the jurisdiction of Rajputana Agency was elicited from the agent to the Governor-General, Rajputana.

In reply, E.R.D. Bradford, the agent to the Governor-General in Rajputana, stated that most of the princely chiefs preferred to make their own arrangements for the preservation and repair of ancient monuments in their respective territories. However, Bradford underlined the need for proper restoration without hurting their sentiments. He, therefore, suggested that the Curator (Cole) could advise them in a variety of ways through personal visits, surveys and inspections, and communicate his recommendations through political officers. But he stated that cautious approach should be resorted and until and unless the princely chiefs are forthcoming to seek help in this direction, it should not be extended. Bradford, however, was appreciative of Cole's efforts but stated that technical help could not be forced on the princely chiefs as they were indifferent towards restoration efforts and often had preconceived notions and ideas. Bradford, however, offered to render assistance to Cole and also seek cooperation of officers under him to realize the desired objectives.[32]

The Government of India accepted the views expressed by E.R.C. Bradford, agent to the Governor-General in Rajputana, and addressed a communication on 12 June 1883 to Bradford, wherein he underlined the need to undertake the repair works as per plans of Cole and reiterated that princely chiefs should not ignore the restoration of monuments and they should be convinced of the need and importance of restoration of monuments falling under their jurisdiction by restoration plans of Cole.[33] He requested the agent to induce the princely chiefs without pressurising them.[34]

The princely states were willing to be guided by the Government archaeologists but objected to hand over the monuments requiring restoration to them.

Cole also made recommendations to the Resident of Hyderabad State on the preservation of frescoes at Ajanta Caves. He suggested that door frames should be secured with wire mesh so as to prevent the bees from damaging the fresco paintings. [35]

He addressed a letter to Kashmir State with regard to the preservation of ancient buildings in that State. The Kashmir Darbar, however, assured that the Maharaja was himself involved in preservation of old monuments and was "fully alive to the importance of conserving the specimens of ancient archaeological art".[36]

Thus, during the tenure of Cole, conservation of monuments got an impetus and the British Indian Government paid utmost attention towards the conservation of monuments in British India as well as the princely states. Cole tendered advice in the conservation of many monuments, prepared a detailed list of buildings of intrinsic nature, which were worthy of repair or restoration, and was submitted to the Government.

Bengal: Sher Shah's Tomb at Sasseram. The Golden Mosque at Gaur. The Adinah Mosque at Maldah. Temple at Sadri at Parisnath. Temples in the Puri District, Orissa.

The North-West Provinces and Oudh: The Jama Masjid at Badaun. Jama Masjid at Jaunpore. Atala Masjid at Jaunpore. Akbar's Palace at Fatehpur Sikri. Temple of Govind Deva at Bendrabun. Akbar's Tomb at Sikandra. Palace buildings in the Agra Fort. The Taj Mahal, Agra. Tomb of Itmad-u-Dowlah, Agra. Hall in the Fort at Allahabad. Temple of Vishveshwar at Benaras.

The Punjab: The Kutb Minar, Delhi. Humayun's Tomb, Delhi. Jama Masjid, Delhi. Palace Buildings in the Fort of Delhi. Golden Temple at Amritsar.* Tomb of Ranjit Singh at Lahore. Palace buildings in the Fort at Lahore. Tomb of Jahangir at Shahdara, Lahore. Shah Gardez in Mooltan. Shah Sham's Tabrez in Mooltan.

Rajputana: The Arhai-din-ka Jhompra, Ajmer. Tower of Victory at Chittore. Jaina temples at Mount Abu. Palace at Amber near Jeypore. Palace of Shah Jehan at Jugmunder, Udaipur.

Central India: Railing and Gateways of the Great Tope at Sanchi. Palace buildings in the Fort at Gwalior. Tomb of Muhamad Ghaus at Gwalior. Temples at Khajuraho. Jain temples at Gwalior.

Central Provinces: Remarkable Temple and Circular enclosure at Bheraghat. Ruins at Karanbel near Tewar. Fine Temples at Janjgir. Temples at Markundi.

Hyderabad: The Kylas at Ellora. Caves at Ellora. Caves at Ajunta. Temples at Maikur, Berar.

Mysore: Temples at Hullabid. Temples at Belur, Jaina Basties at Sravana Beluga.

Madras: The Seven Pagodas, Madras. Temple at Chillambaram, South Arcot. Pagoda at Tanjore. Tirumala Naik's Palace at Madura.

Bombay: Temple at Ambarnath, Buildings at Bijapur. Buildings at Ahmedabad Temples at Purudkal, Dharwar. Mosque and Tombs at Tatta, Sciende.[37]

* Cole: "The Sikhs contribute liberally towards the maintenance of this building and restoration are going on. When I visited the temple, the place was so thronged with natives that I had no opportunity of closely examining the building".

Cole had some valuable publications to his credit, viz., the Great Temple to Siva and his consort at Madura; Temples at Trichinopoly; Graeco-Buddhist sculptures from Yusufzai; Monuments of Agra and Gwalior; Great Buddhist Stupa at Sanchi; Maywar (Palace at Udaipur and Chittor); Golden Temple at Amritsar; Delhi (Diwan-i-Aam in the Red Fort); Tomb of Jahangir at Shahadra near Lahore; Buildings in Punjab; Illustrations of Ancient Buildings in Kashmir; The Architecture of Ancient Delhi; Illustrations of Buildings near Muttra and Agra; Catalogue of the objects of Indian art. Besides these publications, three voluminous reports with projected volumes were published in 1882, 1883 and 1885. He produced a series of preliminary reports on particular groups of monuments in Bombay, Madras, Rajputana, Hyderabad, Punjab and the North-West Provinces in 22 parts. These reports are considered as treatises on conservation.

COLE'S GENERAL OBSERVATIONS ON CONSERVATION OF HISTORICAL MONUMENTS

On 26 December 1882, Cole submitted to the Government of India his "General Observations of the Conservation of Historical Monuments". These observations are still considered unique.

The salient features of his observations are detailed below:

a. Investigation greatly encouraged.
b. Investigations on archaeological research.
c. Justifiable removal of remains.
d. Preservation of 'in situ' monuments in India.
e. Facsimiles of sculptures.
f. Stonehenge.
g. Conservation and custody.
h. Local interest in monuments.
i. Publication of drawings.
j. Experimental reproductions of drawings.
k. Imperial Budget Grants and methodology for applying Imperial Grants.
l. Local funds.
m. Principle for the allotment of Imperial Grants.

Cole was of the view that monuments of intrinsic nature had suffered due to neglect and apathetic attitude and continue to be neglected by the Government. The Government was more responsible than from the natural decay and ruins due to rain or vegetation in the jungle and deserted places. Cole felt that remedial measures taken for the monuments in Delhi and Lahore could definitely compensate the complacent attitude and neglect of the Government of British India during their early rule.[38]

Besides, Cole also prepared a list of "some Ancient and Modern Forts and citadels in India". Yet another achievement was the preparation of a list of some "Historical British Monuments and Memorial in India" which were worthy of preservation due to interest evinced in them by the general public. The list is still considered useful and undoubtedly a good source of information on British Monuments and Memorials in India (Appendix XVIII).

These facts only reveal that Cole was a successful Curator of ancient monuments in his short stint in office.

However, according to S. Roy, Cole suffered from a tendency to go beyond his special field of work and undertook activities which had no connection with conservation. He actually embarked on archaeological survey and excavation, and undertook a costly scheme of publication, which eventually was stopped under the orders of the Government of India. The material thus compiled contained fine illustrations of prominent edifices of archaeological interest, which were surveyed by him and were included in ten folio volumes without title page.

He was a difficult person to deal with and often got into rows with the Local Governments and the Government of India. He did not have cordial relations with Cunningham, Burgess and others. Besides, Cole used to interfere and meddle in others' affairs, which did not concern him.

Cole criticized the manner in which the Bodh Gaya temple had been restored. He particularly disliked the restoration work, which presented Bodh Gaya temple as a modern structure. He was of the view that modernization of ancient edifices should be avoided in future. He also criticized the removal of plaster, in parts, at Sher Shah's Tomb as clumsy. Besides, he criticized the makeshift approach across the task as inconvenient and incongruous and stated the new causeway as wretched low earth embankment with a hideous bridge in the middle. He also stated that in accordance with the orders of the Government of India in respect of monumental preservation, the Sher Shah project should not have been commenced before consulting him. He asked the Bengal Government to revise its orders in respect of the arrangements for preserving monuments and direct all concerned to consult him before sending in projects for sanction. Cole lodged a complaint with Col. S.T. Trevor, Officiating Secretary to the Government of Bengal, P.W.D. However, Trevor did not pay heed to Cole's complaints and he addressed a communication to the Secretary, Government of India on 30 June 1883 justifying the repair works carried out in Bodh Gaya and Sher Shah's tomb, thus ignoring Cole's justification. Regarding Sher Shah Tomb, Cole took no trouble to make himself acquainted with the facts of the case. No new causeway was made. The old causeway was exactly as it was. Only a small stone bridge of two spans was made in it to allow the circulation of water of the tank. As regards Buddha temple, the plaster was simply redone where it formerly existed, because there was no other way of carrying out the repairs.

Besides, Cole made repeated applications for having the estimates sent to him for approval by urging that he was a constituted adviser to all Local Governments and it was irregular to carry out any restoration without consulting him, Trevor added.

Trevor solicited the advice of the Government of India for effectively and systematically carrying out the repair and restoration work at Bengal. He opined,

> In fact Major Cole's contention is that Local Governments are to do nothing to preserve Ancient Monuments without his permission which is simply absurd and that some permanent archaeological organization is to be established in these provinces to work under his direction and supervision. If as the Lieutenant Governor feels confident must be the case, Captain (now Major) Cole is under some grave misapprehension as to the position he occupies and the nature of duties entrusted to him by the Government of India, I am to solicit such orders as will remove that misapprehension. It is intolerable that the Local Government should continue to receive doctoral letters from an officer in Major Cole's position.[39]

After examining the letter submitted by the Government of Bengal, A. Mackenzie, Secretary, directed on 18 August 1883 to convey their observations to Cole for his future guidance. The Secretary, Government of India conveyed the orders of the Governor-General in Council that Cole had incorrectly apprehended the scope and limit of the duties assigned to him as advisory and not executive. The Secretary also conveyed that it was incorrect on the part of Cole to seek assistance from the Local Governments in creation of temporary post of Curator of ancient monuments by each Local Government and insistence on Cole's part for seeking detailed estimates for his sanction. The Secretary of Government of India stated that the Local Governments were not under any obligation to submit either estimates or accounts of expenditure. However, the Curator could ask for progress and completion reports for their perusal and consideration. The Secretary felt that money should be accounted as a contribution to Provincial Public Works. The guidelines should be strictly adhered as per instructions laid down in the letter to the Secretary, the Government of India concluded.[40]

However, Cole continuously interfered in the matter of private endownments. An example of this could be mentioned when a communication was addressed by Cole to the Secretary, Government of India on 3 October 1883 in which he had a mention of a number about drawings that were meant for reproduction pertaining to the temples of Madurai, Rameshvaram in Madras and Wazir Khan's mosque at Lahore, in which the local communities had special interest and were supporting them. If the plans and illustrations of such buildings were published, interest could be instilled in general public, which could be used as an excuse for remedying their neglect.[41]

However, A. Mackenzie, Secretary, Government of India censured Cole and prevented him from interference in matters relating to private endowments until he had finished his assignments pertaining to all Government buildings. Mackenzie felt that the temples at Madura and Madras had been photographically documented and their plans had been prepared many times. As these endowments were in the jurisdiction of trustees, it would be improper on the part of the Government to invest money for illustrating or repairing them and, therefore, it declined to sanction the requisite expenditure. The money was required by the Local Governments for carrying out repair and conservation, which was to be granted without further delay and Cole was accordingly instructed to prepare a statement of disbursements on the lines suggested.[42]

COLE VERSUS BURGESS – THE CONTROVERSY OVER AMRAVATI MARBLES

In yet another example, Cole had interfered with the survey work at Madras and had altercations with Dr. James Burgess, Archaeological Surveyor for western and south India. Dr. Burgess took exception to this and lodged a complaint to the Secretary, Government of India on 20 January 1882, stating that Cole's duties were supposedly confined to matters relating to conservation. He also held that Cole should not interfere with architectural survey and detailed the delineation which rightly related to the duties of his department.

In September 1882, Captain Cole requested the Madras Government to obtain plans and illustrations as specified in his report for execution of repair works. In reply, the Madras Government advised Cole to execute the work in consultation with Burgess.

Captain Cole, however, did not reply to this letter of Madras Government. It was reported to the Madras Government that Cole had made arrangements for the survey of the Srirangam temple at Trichinipoly which was not under Government's control. Hence, the survey could not be essentially taken for conservation. The Government, however, felt that it was a needless public expenditure and was a direct interference with the survey undertaken by Burgess.[43]

A. Mackenzie, Secretary, Government of India, on 3 February 1882 invited the attention of Hon'ble Member on the letter of Dr. Burgess to form a judgement on the merits of the complaint of James Burgess. Mackenzie further noted that Cole's duties were defined and were confined to inspect the principal monuments and their historical and archaeological significance, which were brought under the ambit of archaeological survey for framing a scheme for their protection and conservation. On the other hand, Cole had launched an enterprise, which included the production of survey and plans of buildings by the Government of India irrespective of the fact whether consent of the Local Governments for their actual repair or conservation work was obtained.

The Secretary, Government of India further stated that when the Government of Madras expressed a fervent wish that Cole should consult Dr. Burgess, the former had diplomatically declined to do so. On the other hand, Dr. Burgess had condemned the survey work of Srirangam temples conducted by Cole as 'useless' since the temples were not under the administrative jurisdiction of the Government. The Secretary felt that Cole should not have had prepared the working plans for monuments let alone conserving them. Further, Cole should not interfere with the work, which was rightfully under the jurisdiction of Dr. Burgess. The Secretary finally concluded that Cole was 'most unbusiness-like head of a Department I ever came across'.[44]

J. Gibb, Hon'ble Member, however, expressed similar views on the conduct of Cole in his notings dated 11 February 1882, when he stated that in the opinion of Governor-General in Council, Cole's attention should in first place be confined to the monuments and the cost of repairs, etc. which will fall on the Local Governments and not on works like that at Srirangam which are in the possession of private persons and highly endowed. He should not in any way interfere with the duty of archaeological surveyors and it is no part of his duty to prepare illustrations or to publish works on the ancient temples and monuments of India. This is the work of the Archaeological Survey and Cole should place himself in communication with Dr. Burgess regarding any work he may see reason to undertake in southern of India; if this is not done, unnecessary expenditure may be incurred for both Departments working at the same moment.[45]

On 25 February 1882, A. Mackenzie, Secretary, Government of India addressed a communication to Cole and specifically advised him to confine himself to duties relating to the restoration and conservation of monuments, the cost of which was to be provided by Provincial and Imperial Governments through respective revenues, and should not interfere with the administrative arrangements of Local Governments. Besides, Cole was also restrained from interference with the duties of archaeological surveys, the only exception being plans and illustrations of the buildings could be published. Besides, Cole was also advised to carry out the survey work in South India in consultation with Dr. Burgess so as to avert unnecessary expenditure on the "same work at the same time".[46]

However, Cole clarified his position on 27 March 1882. He stated that the responsibilities "for survey, for conservation and for survey for archaeological research should be kept distinct and independent of each other". As regards Burgess' drawings, Cole stated and clarified that it was made for a specific purpose and drawing inferences and citing analogies on the drawings could not serve any purpose. He further stated that Burgess was not an architect and illustrations, which have appeared in the published reports pertaining to Western India, could be well suited for explaining the nuances of archaeology and could be considered artistic or perfect representations of architecture. Cole also clarified that he had no intention of interfering with the claim of Burgess and stated that Burgess was trying to monopolise the functions, which were peculiar to his department. On the other hand, Cole clarified that Burgess had levelled a charge with regard to the survey of temples of Srirangam and Trichinopoly which involved needless expenditure, as they were not under the administrative control of the Government and that the survey undertaken was without his knowledge which amounted to gross interference.

Cole clarified further that Burgess' approach was consistent with the Government's policy with regard to undertaking conservation work in princely states which are under the ambit of private property and he also referred to the orders of Supreme Government to keep the monuments in princely states under constant repair. Cole also stated that it was under the duties assigned to him to advise the Government of Madras for preserving the temples at Srinrangam, as he had done earlier when he advised the agent to the Governor-General in Central India and Rajputana on Sanchi Stupa and temples at Mount Abu, respectively. He also stated that it was his objective to prescribe remedial measures in the field of conservation of monuments and to facilitate the work of repair and conservation had the authority to call for the artistic drawings which are necessary for ensuring conservation of monuments. Besides, Cole also reiterated that he had no intention to trespass the functions and jurisdiction of Dr. Burgess in his capacity as archaeological surveyor in Madras. He stated that writing history through records and inscriptions of monuments was a subject which came under the ambit of functions assigned to Burgess, and the work of repair and restoration of monuments came under his jurisdiction. Cole wondered as to the reasons why the Government was relying on Dr. Burgess for the artistic delineation of the architectural monuments in Madras.

He elaborated that the objectives behind surveys undertaken at Srirangam were to induce the local populace for utilizing the state endowments for maintenance of monuments, and through artistic illustrations to highlight the neglected monuments which are in need of urgent attention and require immediate repair works. Thus, Cole concluded that Burgess and he should be free to utilize their own methods, for their functions and duties were independent of each other, especially in the case of the finest Madras temples.[47]

Finally, A. Mackenzie addressed a communication to Captain Cole on 26 April 1882 on the survey of private endowments for conservation of monuments with the help of Local Governments. He stated that there was an imperative need to induce all concerned, especially the trustees of the temples at Srirangam to arrange for funds to be expended on the repair and conservation of temples. Mackenzie admitted that the duties and functions assigned to Cole and Burgess were different and Cole should be left free to use his discretion independently and actual survey work in provinces should commence only after the receipt of permission from the Local Governments. Mackenzie added that plans prepared by Cole should be laid before the Local Governments concerned by whom they might be utilized in the manner desired by him for the purpose of conceiving the trustees of monuments and other persons interested in the restorations proposed by him and informing them of the nature and extent of any operations suggested.

Mackenzie expressed the hope of the Governor-General in Council that free communication will pass between all the archaeological survey parties and Cole in order that all measures should be taken to avoid unnecessary expenditure and clash of personalities on personal whims and fancies. He communicated to Cole that,

> There in all parts of India well-known monuments that it is desirable to have inspected and conserved. In the course of the operations of the Archeological Survey, other less famous monuments are frequently discovered and when the state of these appears to be such as to call for measures of conservation, the officers of the Archaeological Department should draw the attention of the Local Government to the fact, sending a copy of their letters to you direct. You will then be in a position to visit the sites in the course of your annual tours and to advise the Local Governments regarding the repairs of such buildings.[48]

Cole also clashed with Burgess on the matter pertaining to removal of marbles from Amravati as per report of Burgess submitted to Chief Secretary, Government of Madras on 30

December 1881. Burgess reported that marble slabs at the Stupa were pounded to pieces during the 'rough and ready' excavations commissioned in February 1880 and the information sought on the excavations thus carried was forever lost. He further suggested that some marble stones could be preserved if they were transported to Madras and requested an experienced officer to be deputed so that adequate directions could be given for their transport.[49]

On this issue relating to transport of marble stones from Amravati to Madras, Burgess addressed two communications to Chief Secretary, Government of Madras. In the first communication, he expressed his concern over the delay in transporting stones to Madras due to the sudden fall in flow of water in the river and canal and said that they should be removed forthwith.[50]

In yet another communication addressed to the Chief Secretary, Government of Madras, Burgess detailed the **modus operandi** of transporting the stones to Madras. He also referred to the visit of Horsefall, the Collector on the site where marbles were stored and reported that since 1880 "village boys and others were hammering on them with stones". Burgess also reported the dereliction of duties on the part of personnel who were entrusted with the responsibility of guarding the marble stones. He cited an example that

> there has been a man incharge for the last two years but when Government makes such arrangements, it is too often forgotten that the man is left altogether irresponsible. He draws his pay regularly and nobody goes near him for many months to learn whether he is attending to his duties or not. He is alone and goes to village to sleep and for his meals and it is expecting too much for such a man to suppose that he will be very regularly on his guard or prompt in reporting any damage. Indeed, he has perhaps not been instructed to make any such report or, if has, he knows there are no penalties for neglect of this or any other duty. When a man is placed in any similar charge, would it not be well to make him responsible for its proper performance and insure that performance by occasional official visits from some responsible Local Government officer who could stop his pay on the discovery of any neglect.

He also stated that people had different ideas and opinion about the worth of stones. "The native call them 'useless stones'. The Superintendent of a great National Museum such as those in London, Berlin or Vienna, would say that the probable depreciation in value of these slabs might be estimated at least at a good many hundreds of rupees." Burgess reiterated his earlier communication pertaining to the sanction of expenditure and keeping under the charge of responsible person so as to ensure their proper supervision. He stated that packing of marble stones for their transport to Madras was progressing satisfactorily in anticipation of sanction and approval of the Government.[51]

R. Davidson, Chief Secretary, Government of Madras approved the proposal of Burgess and instituted the Central Museum, Madras to initiate steps for the transportation of marble pieces from Amravati to Madras.

In the meanwhile, Cole addressed a communication to the Secretary, Government of India on 12 June 1882 enclosing his report in the form of a Memorandum on the Amravati Tope in Madras, and requested for a communication to be addressed to the Government of Madras for inspecting the ruins before the marble sculptures were transported to Madras.

Memorandum on the Present Condition of the Amravati Tope in Madras – 11 May 1882

1. *Dr. Burgess and the Amravati Tope*: Dr. Burgess has recently been to Amravati in the Kistna District and recommended the removal of the Buddhist sculptures to the Madras Museum.

The preservation of, or disposal of, these remains obviously a question appertaining to the subject of "Conservation" and not to "architectural research".

2. *Letter from the Collector, Kistna District*: I now learn from a letter written on 2nd April last by the Collector of the Kistna district, that Dr. Burgess was engaged at Amravati over a month this last cold season and packed up everything that he considered worth packing and has in fact ransacked the place of all valuable stones.
3. *Removal of Some Amravati Stones via Bezenada*: So much haste has been displaced in getting the Amravati stones removed under Dr. Burgess's auspices that the collections previously brought together at Bezurada were transferred by canal at once to Madras.
4. *Telegram from Collector*: My latest information from Collector by telegram dated the 23rd April, informs me that the Amravati marbles have been packed by Dr. Burgess and now in a shed close to the site waiting for the water to rise in the matter (i.e. render their transport to Madras possible).
5. *Conservation at Amravati*: The question of conserving the Amravati remains was one which I had taken up before Dr. Burgess had been appointed to Madras and both official and Demi-Official correspondence had passed between me and the Madras Government on the subject. When, however, Dr. Burgess arrived at Madras, his action as regards Amravati received the deliberate sanction of the Madras Government and it was not until I had personally represented to H.E. Governor how contrary this course was to the procedure sanctioned by the Government of India in respect to my office as Curator, that it was admitted that my report and opinion on the subject should have preceded any action.
6. *Duke of Buckingham's excavation at Amravati*: When I took up the Amravati case, excavation has been carried out under the orders of the Duke of Buckingham in 1880 and the Secretary of State was informed in March 1881 that "no demolition of the Tope had been taken place and that all that had been done was to remove the earth from the fallen marbles so as to expose them to view".
7. *Recommendation under present circumstances*: As explained, I have been unable this season to visit Amravati and intended postponing my report until I had seen the place, surveyed it and judged in the spell of all the arrangements for and against 'preservation in situ'. Under the circumstances described it is evident that the locality is on the brink of losing all its interesting traditions and that unless some "energetic action" is taken by Government it will lose them altogether. How far it may be possible now to restore any of the sculptures to their original positions is a question to which I cannot reply until all the facts are investigated; but I have no hesitation in counselling the preservation of the marbles (now at the Madras Museum and those lying packed) in a suitable manner on the site at Amravati. Even should it prove impossible to replace them as they stood, I recommended the erection of a small building where the carvings would be properly displaced and absolutely safe and the railing in the site of the great Buddhist Tope, securing as far as possible, all the existing masonry of the building.
8. *Interests of Museums and men of Science*: To meet the wants of the British Museum in London and Central Museum in Madras, at both of which places there are already several valuable marbles taken from Amravati.
9. *Ancient Monuments for India*: If all beautiful and valuable remains are to be ruthlessly torn from their ancient sites, the outlying districts of this country will be rapidly robbed of all

their interesting records. I believe, moreover, that the policy of preserving Ancient Monuments for India is a sounder one than carting them away to European Museums.

10. *'In Situ' principle*: It is generally agreed that monuments are most interesting 'in situ' and the inaccessibility of Amravati (now used as an argument against the 'in situ' principle) will probably cease in course of time.
11. *Sanchi Tope*: The great Sanchi Tope which together with the Amravati Tope, furnishes the subjects of Mr. Fergusson's large volume on 'Tree and serpent' worship, has escaped two great dangers, i.e. in 1853 when Cunningham advocated the removal of the fallen gateways to the British Museum and in 1868 when the Eastern Gate was merely carried off to Paris. Fortunately, a cast of the latter took the place of the original leaving the Tope and its sculptured gateways, now being restored and repaired to remain intact and 'in situ' for those who visit Sanchi by the new Bhopal State Railway.
12. *India's Communications and Visitors*: India is being opened up by communications of every kind. Travelers and savants from all countries visit her ancient cities and her temples and it seems to me a 'suicidal and indefensible policy to allow the country to be looted of original works of ancient art when there exist the means of making facsimiles scarcely distinguishable from the original'.
13. *Dr. Burgess's arguments (in Madras)*: Referring to the Amravati Marbles, Dr. Burgess writes in a letter to the Madras Government No. 153 of 16 February 1882, 'The Natives call them useless stones'.
14. *Opinion of Government of Madras*: In the other hand, the Hon'ble Governor-in-Council records in an order No. 985 of the 20th July 1881 that he is much pleased to hear that such cordial interest in Mr. Sewell's researches has been evinced by Natives of various classes.
15. *Dr. Burgess's arguments (in Bombay)*: In the matter of the 'in situ' principle, I find, however, that I am able to agree with Dr. Burgess in Bombay, although I cannot do in Madras. Writing from Edinburgh to the Bombay Government on 6 April 1881, he makes the following observations relating to the appropriation of the materials of certain old buildings at Ahmedabad.

> The principal argument for the appropriation appears to be that the valuable materials of such buildings are allowed to disappear gradually by theft, which it appears to be no one's business to report or detect and therefore it would be better to break up the stones into road metal. But the force of such reasoning is not quite clear. It is surely the duty of every Government officer to protect or report on the necessity of protecting the ancient public buildings in the district in which he is located. Had this been a little better attended to in the past, we should now have had to regret so many interesting monuments now utterly destroyed.
>
> The excuses for destroying these remains are always the same – they are desecrated; nobody cares for them. The destruction might begin with some that were of little or no interest, but all past experience shows it would not stop there.
>
> The fancy designs in perforated stone-work in the tomb and mosques near Betwa, which the Superintendent Engineer says are quite worth being preserved for future use, would be of very little interest anywhere else except in their original positions; and the Buildings and c. in which they are, thereby have a claim to protection.

Sd./- H.H. Cole

Conservator of Ancient Monuments[52]

Cole wanted to know whether conservation 'in situ' was possible. However, Cunningham was of the opinion that it was an utter impossibility to restore any portion of the tope 'in situ'. The great portion of the stones had been used for building in the neighbourhood transshipment to England and as regards the few stones left, it was better to be sent to Madras as the safest way to preserve them from destruction. Cole will only get amused for making such a suggestion.

A. Mackenzie, Secretary, Government of India took cognizance of the complaint with regard to removal of marbles from Amravati under the orders of the Madras Government on suggestion of Burgess and proposed eliciting a report from the Government of Madras on the matter. He suggested to put forth the proposal of transporting the marbles in abeyance till such time the Governor-General in Council had considered the whole question in totality. Lord Ripon in his minute supported the views expressed by Captain Cole and proposed that the Government of Madras should defer the proposal for removing the marbles till such time Cole had visited Amravati. "There can be no hurry about the removal." A. Mackenzie instructed the Government of Madras on 16 June 1882 that "steps for the removal of the sculptures could be suspended until Captain Cole had visited Amravati".[53]

It was felt by many that some stones were so much out of position that thier removal to Madras could do no harm. Others could be restored 'in situ'.

However, G.S. Master, Chief Secretary, Government of Madras clarified that transport of marbles on Burgess' suggestion was "delicate and perishable marble" and instructions were given to the local authorities to maintain status quo position till such time Captain Cole visits Amravati and gives his report.[54]

Burgess refuted the charges levelled against him by Cole. He further stated that

> Cole seems anxious that Government should regard the work of the Archaeological Survey as merely of a historical character and in a very narrow sense ignoring the very essence of archaeology as elucidative of the history of the Arts-Architecture, Sculpture, Painting and of Mythology. If Cole's own statement of 'the object of his department', be at all correct, his assumption that I 'to monopolize a ground peculiarly important to his department' is equally untrue and rash. No one could be more pleased than I was to learn that the Government of India had arranged to appoint an officer to superintend the conservation of Ancient Monuments and no one would have more willingly cooperated with the Curator and aided him to the utmost, had he only made it practicable by not keeping to trespass on my field of work.
>
> Cole's ignorance must be his excuse. Amravati has not been an 'Architectural Monument' for centuries. No two complete stones are together 'in situ', nor can three be found entire that were originally in juxtaposition. If anything in stone can be called Archaeological and not also Architectural, it is the scattered slabs and parts of slabs at Amravati so that even on Cole's narrow view of archaeology, it is an unjustifiable interference with my proper work to ask the Madras Government to countermand what they had arranged – an interference which, when Government knows the nature of it – they cannot honour allow. The Amravati Stupa has been so utterly destroyed and the remaining frequents are so few relatively to its original extent that the ablest living archaeologists differ in their views of its original form and as the villagers destroy and carry off the slabs to burn into lime any attempt at conservation on the spot would be futile, therefore, with the consent of Government, of arranged for transmission of the best of the exhumed sculptures to Madras.[55]

The officials of the Government of India were not in a position to take a decision with regard to the imbroglio over the removal of stones from Amravati to Madras and were particularly upset over the strife between Cole and Burgess over the methodology in transporting the marble stones, especially on account of river Krishna in spate and consequent navigational logistics in transporting on that account. The officials were also concerned about the "great delay will be caused and injury result to the delicate carvings".[56]

On 2 September 1882, F.C. Daukes, Under Secretary, Government of India addressed a communication to Cole wherein a request was made to Cole to visit Amravati at the earliest so that the stones could be transported in ensuing monsoons especially when the river Krishna would be in spate.[57]

In fact, the Government of India was eager to resolve the imbroglio and wanted that Cole, Burgess and Government of Madras to work out the convenient date of visit of Cole, because F.C. Daukes, Under Secretary, Government of India had submitted to the Secretary, Government of India on 12 September 1882 that "if we don't do this, they may throw the blame (if any injury occurs to the marbles) upon the Government".[58]

A Resolution (Home Department, Arch No. 3-167-81 dated 8 November 1882) was passed by the Government of India on "utilization and disposal of objects of archaeological interest which may be from time to time discovered in India". The Memorandum was prepared by Dr. Anderson, Superintendent of Indian Museum, on the management of his organization (Indian Museum). In this Memorandum, some concrete suggestions were made which are detailed below:

1. Arrangements should be made for the permanent deposit in the Indian Museum of archaeological collectors made by the officers of the Archaeological Survey of India.
2. The local governments and administrations should be instructed to furnish a list of Museums in their respective provinces with the details of the officials attached to each museum and statement of artifacts/objects for documenting the information and exchange of information and specimen objects held by the Indian Museum.

The Trustees of the Indian Museum invited particular attention to the above suggestions and requested the assistance of the Government of India in giving thereto.

2. The first suggestion involves the consideration of the question as to the proper manner of utilizing and disposing of objects of archaeological interest, which may from time to time be discovered in India and upon this question no definite orders appear hitherto to have been issued by the Government of India. The Governor-General in Council is of the opinion that the present opportunity may with advantage be taken to consider, in communication with local governments and administrations, the principles on which such objects should be dealt with and the circumstances under which they should either be preserved 'in situ' or exhibited in a central or other Museum where they would be readily available to the public for purposes of study and reference.

3. As regards the question of preservation in 'in situ' as opposed to the removal to and exhibition in a Museum, it may be observed that the great majority of the discoveries made by the Archaeological Survey of India consist of the remains of the buildings, massive pillars or inscribed blocks which cannot be removed and should for many other reasons be preserved where they stand. The case is, however, different with isolated figures, not 'in situ' especially if they are the remains of an extinct religion, such as Buddhist figures which are not infrequently mutilated by the people unless they happen to have been adopted by the Brahmins as belonging to Hindoo cults. In regard to such isolated figures and to others, which, although not mutilated, are lying neglected about the country, it appears to the Government of India that these might with propriety be removed to some safe place of deposit, such as the Indian Museum where

they could be seen and studied by all persons who take an interest in Indian art. The Governor-General in Council desires to make it clear that he is entirely opposed to the removal of any objects which are still 'in situ' such as the monoliths attached to Buddhist 'stupas' and Brahmanical temples; but, on the other hand, there seems no sufficient reason why isolated remains, such as a Capital which is found lying without a shaft or stray statues, the original site of which is unknown should not be removed to some museum in order to save them from further injury. To this class also belong the sculptures which have been found scattered about the Buddhist ruins of the ancient Gandhara now occupied by the Yusufzai Afghans, whose custom is believed to be to mutilate such remains unless this is prevented by their prompt removal to a place of safety.

4. In making the above remarks, the Governor-General in Council has not lost sight of the fact that it may be argued that the claim of the Government to objects of archaeological value rests upon no sufficient legal or other foundation. The Government, in fact, never claimed any indefeasible right of property in such objects, nor could such a right be asserted without legislation. Experience has, however, shown that the arrangements necessary for securing any object worthy of removal to a museum or for preserving it in any other way, can in most cases be made without difficulty by Local Governments or Local Governments or Local officers. This being so, it does not appear necessary to take any legal powers of compulsory acquisition.

5. As regards the place of deposit of objects of archaeological interest, the Governor-General in Council, as at present advised, considers it preferable that they should be concentrated, as far as possible, in some one Central institution such as the Indian Museum unless there are special reasons for preferring to deposit them at a Provincial Museum. On this point, it appears to the Government of India that small Local Museums, although doubtless of great utility for other purposes, can seldom reach a high standard of archaeological value, and would, therefore, without attaining any adequate object, interfere with the completeness of the archaeological series at the Imperial Museum which, for purposes of study and illustration, must always be of greater use to the public and should accordingly have a prior claim on archaeological discoveries of importance or general interest.

6. The above appear to the Government of India to be the general principles by which the disposal of objects of archaeological interest should be regulated in India but before issuing any definite orders, the Governor-General in Council would be glad to be favoured with any remarks which may have to offer on the subject.[59]

The response of this Resolution was encouraging. Lepel Griffin, agent to the Governor-General for Central India, addressed a communication to the Government of India on 8 January 1883 and expressed his satisfaction with the suggestions and directions of the Resolution. Griffin stated that he had on earlier occasions strongly pleaded for maintaining the objects of archaeological and historical importance at the site of monument concerned. He had stated that he was against the removal of objects relating to a monument to "a distinct museum like Calcutta" where it is difficult to correlate the objects of archaeological or historical importance with the monument concerned. However, he assured that the spirit of the Resolution will be observed throughout Central India.[60]

Cole also echoed similar views and was against the removal of archaeological finds connected with a particular monument to a distant place like Indian Museum, Calcutta. He, however, felt that duplicate specimens could be removed and displayed elsewhere.

Cole further added if the monuments and archeological objects were endangered due to religious reasons, viz., idol worship was not permissible under the religion, i.e., "Buddhist ruins of ancient Gandhara now occupied by the Yusufzai Afghans" under the circumstances, the sculptures and archaeological finds could be transferred to a place where they could be held secured. Further, Cole stated if there were harmonious relations between Hindus and Muslims, the archaeological finds and sculptures should be secured "in situ".[61]

In the meanwhile, Cole inspected Amravati Tope in December 1882. He submitted the following Memorandum of 24 November 1882 to the Madras Government on the state of the monument, and made concrete suggestions for ensuring its security and conserving remnants of its historical sculptures.

Memorandum of the present condition of the Amravati Tope, 24 November 1882

I have just returned from a careful inspection of the Buddhist ruins at Amravati and have had the advantage of conferring with Mr. Horsfall, Collector of Kistna District, who superintended the excavations ordered by the Duke of Buckingham in 1880. I also met Mr. Mackenzie, the sub-Collector, and Mr. Grant, the Executive Engineer at Amravati itself and am now able to give a description of the remains of the tope and its sculptures and to offer an opinion on the best means of preserving them.

x x x x x x x

3. **Dr. Burgess' work at Amravati**: Since then Dr. Burgess, Archaeological Surveyor for western and southern India, spent upwards of a month in examining the tope and in selecting and packing those sculptures which he considered worthy of removal to the Madras Museum. Those stones numbering 175, were carried to the River Kistna, about half a mile north of Amravati where they now are in a fenced enclosure and under the care of a Native Custodian. It is scarcely necessary to say that the stones comprise the finest sculptures and the most important historical records of the Great Tope. They appear to me in good condition and undamaged by the recent floods. They had been taken out of their cases to be freed from the straw which enveloped them and so far as I was able to judge, the action of the water had beneficially cleaned the carvings.
4. **Number of sculptures at Amravati**: The number of stone sculptures at Amravati are as follows:
   a. Sculptures of Dr. Burgess' selection on the rivers bank = 175
   b. Sculptures at the Tope –

In a shed to the north in boxes	...	8
... ... loose	...	43
... ... In situ	...	195
Total:		246 = **421**

5. **Removal of stones to Madras**: Dr. Burgess' intentions were to have removed the 175 stones – now taken half a mile away to the river bank – and to have deposited them at the Madras Museum. I do not know where they could be placed at the Madras Museum, which is already far too overcrowded unless they were displaced in the open grounds. Here, however, they would be subject to the more destructive atmospheric conditions of a town. As I have stated in my note on Amravati on the 11th May, casts are as good as originals for all scientific purposes; and if casting is undertaken, copies can be sent to as many museums in India as Europe as like to pay the cost of a set. The removal of the stones from Amravati has, I submit, but a single argument in its favour, viz., that Amravati is at present very inaccessible. Looking, however, to the future, are we justified in supposing

that Amravati and the fertile Kistna District will always be 150 miles from a railway? It is increasing in wealth and is now with its annual revenue of over forty lakhs of rupees, the third richest district in the whole of Madras. Should Hyderabad be connected as proposed with the East coast, the line of railway must pass near Amravati and so make it easily accessible to travelers and servants.

x x x x x x x

7. **Disposal of the sculptures at the river bank**: In regard to the 175 carved stones at the river bank, I should, if free to do what I thought best, take them back to the site of tope and send casts of them to Madras and other museums where Asiatic antiquities are appreciated. This course, I strongly commend to Government. The conservation of the structure will not be promoted by still further scattering its component parts, and I do not see what special benefit will be secured by removing the originals to the Madras Museum as proposed. The Amravati Tope is the most important and ornate Buddhist monument known to exist in the Madras Presidency and this will, I think, be most fittingly acknowledged by having casts of its best sculptures made for Museums in India and in Europe.
8. **Repairs**: Any attempt to restore the structure – unless it is possible to ascertain with certainty the former position of particular portions – is most undesirable, but the majority of the stones are easily identified as being parts of the railing or plinth, and their retention at the Amravati enclose would be an 'in situ' preservation even if they were not in their original structural positions and were merely placed on the ground so as to be easily inspected and examined.
9. **Photographs**: It would be expedient to have all the Amravati sculptures photographed and if the recommendations in this note are adopted, completion photographs should illustrate the condition of the tope and the beneficial effect of the remedies. It would, however, be necessary to employ a good professional photographer to take the negatives (which should become the property of Government for printing by a permanent process), as amateur work is usually unsatisfactory and not worth using for purposes of publication.[62]

The Government of India was accordingly informed regarding the above-mentioned Memorandum, and this was also referred to Burgess for an expression of opinion on Cole's recommendations and more especially on the question of preservation 'in situ' as opposed to removal to and exhibition in a Museum regarded from the point of view of archaeological research.

J. Burgess wrote (gave the opinion) to the Chief Secretary, Government of Madras on 9 March 1883 (No. 24), acknowledging Cole's Memoranda dated 11th May and 24th November relative to the Amravati Tope.

x x x x x x x

2. Before adverting to the main purport of the papers, I may notice two points: **First**: Major Cole has so emphasized his theory that "the real destroyers" of the Amravati Stupa were the Mohammedans, that it may be as well to observe that all the evidence is against him. When Colonel Mackenzie first unearthed the many slabs marked on his plan, the human figures were nowhere defaced in the way Mohammedans universally treat such imagery, nor is there a particle of a evidence to show that the rails had not been covered over by debris centuries before the birth of 'the Iconoclast Alamgir'. Again, of the stones excavated and left on the spot by Colonel Mackenzie, we know from the testimony of his own drawings and Sir Walter Elliot that all had disappeared between 1819 and 1848. We find others built into Hindu temples and wells

that were constructed between the time of the destruction of the Central Stupa by the Hindu zemindar in the latter half of the last century and that of the first visit of Colonel Mackenzie. All this and other evidence that I need not here adduce goes to shew that Major Cole is quite mistaken in his belief that "the prime ruin" was caused by the Mohammedans.

3. **Secondly** in paragraph 14 of his report, Major Cole tries to make out that I advocate different policies in Bombay and in Madras Presidency with respect to the preservation of remains 'in situ'. Nothing could be more inaccurate; the best reply to such a charge will be found in my correspondence with the Madras Government with reference to the Govindpuram Fort and Udaigiri temple.

4. As to the main question, I remark that Major Cole (in para 12 of his Memo of 24th November) rants that any attempts at restoration of any portion of the Amravati is impracticable and though (in para 11) he speaks of "the conservation of the structure", he admits that there is no structure to conserve. On his own showing, therefore, the remains do not come within the scope of his duties any more than the Stupas at Sopara or at Bharahut, or any of the remains excavated by Cunningham, or even my present excavations here. Such remains are entirely archaeological in character and are best left to the disposal of the Government and the Superintendent of the Archaeological Survey of the Presidency to which they belong. If Cunningham may arrange what is to be done at Bharahut or elsewhere without reference to Major Cole, it may be left also to the Madras Government and myself to arrange what is best to be done at Amravati. This view, I believe, would be fully supported by the Government of India. But if Major Cole is allowed to interfere in this instance, it may afterwards be used as a precedent for his interference with Cunningham's work as well as mine and considering the personal animus he has already manifested, this might lead to further difficulties.

5. On the simple ground alone of the remains being purely archaeological in character, Government need have no difficulty in deciding to carry out the operations begun last year under my recommendation of their propriety. I believe every one at all acquainted with the circumstances – such as the Collector Mr. J. Horsefall; the Sub-Collector, Mr. G. Mackenzie, the Engineer, Mr. Grant; former First Assistant Collector, Mr. R. Sewell – will agree without hesitation with me and if scientific opinion is required, the Government might ask General Cunningham's.

6. As to Cole's proposal to lift the fragments of the old terrace and relay the slabs on "concrete and in cement", I cannot refrain from entering a very strong protest against such a course. I would destroy the only portion of the original still left as the builders laid it down. Moreover, Major Cole is not aware that the construction of this terrace reveals a curious chapter in the history of the Stupa and all antiquarians would have cause to regret his ill-considered interference with it.

7. Major Cole's proposed masonry wall seven feet high round the sight might, I fear, be only a temptation to Telugu boys – natives of a hilly country – to climb over it. I have already informed Government that I intend requesting and making further excavations at Amravati and perhaps this wall might be delayed at least till I have done so.

8. For the preservation, as far as possible, if the slabs left on the site and not 'in situ', I would approve of the suggestion to erect a shed over them in the center of the area and to protect the place by means of a guardian.

9. A whole year has already been unnecessary lost and I would now respectfully submit the following for the approval of the Government.

(i) The Government should carry out the arrangements previously sanctioned, and how the stones packed removed to Madras as soon as the river and canal will permit. The slabs to be removed include those on the river bank, light in the small shed near the site and those from Jaggayyapet now at Bezwada.

(ii) The stones should only be unpacked at Madras under my own supervision, or orders as it is my intention to photograph them to scale and this can best be done and with least risk of injury as each is opened out.

(iii) If, as Major Cole hints, the whole of the slabs to be removed cannot be properly exhibited in the Madras Museum, some of them may be placed in the Government School of Arts where a few good specimens would be found most useful as models. But if the Museum is to serve its purpose as an educational agency, separate provision will have to be made for the natural products and the antiquarian collections, when there need to be no want of space for these slabs.

(iv) If Major Cole can induce other Governments to pay the expense of casts for their Museums, these might be made under the supervision of the Madras School of Arts. They could be made very much cheaper at Madras than at Amravati and the possession of the originals will save the Madras Government the expense of casts for their Museum.

10. Trusting that these suggestions will be approved and sanctioned by the Government".[63]

With regard to marble stones lying at Amravati, R. Sewell, Acting Sub-Collector, Chinglepet reported to the Chief Secretary, Government of Madras on 29 April 1883. He stated that the marbles were excavated more than three years ago under the orders of the Duke of Buckingham. The marbles, which were excavated by him, were lying unattended for the last six years since May 1877. Burgess had packed some of the specimens of the marble stones for onward transmission to Madras Museum, but they were lying unattended in the river bank as they had to be inspected by Cole. After the receipt of report on marbles from Cole, he had also stated that there was no damage caused to the marbles and these sculptures could be rehabilitated before they were further damaged due to summer heat and monsoons. He earnestly requested to take immediate steps to save them for further damage and deterioration and they were properly secured before the onset of next monsoons. He stated that they were not only beautiful objects and relics of rare artistic workmanship but they constituted almost the 'only known record' in the whole of India, whereby we could learn the manners, customs, costumes and religious habits of the inhabitants of this country in the early centuries.[64]

Besides, Cunningham also addressed a similar communication to the Chief Secretary, Government of Madras on 30 May 1883. He stated that there was hardly anything which remained in Amravati Stupa which would warrant restoration. He, however, asserted that he was a great proponent "for the conservation of all ancient building that actually exist and also for the restoration of such as can be restored". He also recalled his earlier suggestion in 1853 for removal of the gateway of Sanchi Stupa to British Museum, as his objective was towards their preservation. Cunningham also stated that ever since Cole was appointed as Curator, he had relentlessly advocated for complete restoration of the Sanchi Stupa.

With regard to sculptured stones at Amaravati, Cunningham was in agreement with the views expressed by Burgess to keep them under cover at the Madras Museum, where they would be safe and accessible. He also agreed with the opinion expressed by Cole that the ruins at Amravati should be secured under a shed and placed under the charge of a chowkidar; besides, photographs of specimens of marble pieces at Amravati and Madras should be taken. If casts of the specimens were to be taken as advised by Burgess, they should be commissioned at a loss at Madras rather than getting them done at Amravati.[65]

The Government of Madras, however, approved the proposals of the Archaeological Survey as enshrined in his letter dated 9 March 1883 and the Collector of Krishna District and Superintendent, Government Central Museum were advised accordingly.

On 8 June 1883, A. Mackenzie, Secretary, Government of India addressed a letter to Cole and emphasized the need of obtaining the approval of the Governor-General in Council before issuing general instructions to Local Governments on matters of archaeological interest. Besides, before taking any action with regard to removal of artifacts on objects of archaeological interest, the procedure of obtaining prior approval of the Governor-General in Council should be adopted. Mackenzie also instructed Cole to obtain the express approval of Local Governments concerned, before corresponding with "Executive Engineers and other officers subordinate to Local Governments".[66]

The Government of India issued a Resolution on 8 June 1883 in the Home Department. This Resolution intended to "regulate the utilization and disposal of objects of archaeological interest in India" and called for the opinion of local governments and administrations on the subject. The response received in this direction revealed that there was a difference of opinion expressed with regard to custody of archaeological objects 'in situ' and should be deposited in the Central Indian Museum or the Local Museum of the Province or District where it exists. However, the Local Governments were in agreement with the general principles as laid own in paras 3 and 4 of the Resolution. After consideration of the opinion expressed by the Local Governments, the Governor-General in Council felt the "difference of opinion will be reasonably met by compliance with following instructions".

DISPOSAL OF ANTIQUITIES

I. All discoveries of objects of archaeological interest made by Government officers (whether belonging to the Archaeological survey or not) should be reported by them to the head of the Local Government or Administration within which the discovery is made. When such a report is made, it will rest with the Local Government or Administration to issue orders for the preservation of the objects discovered 'in situ' or for their removal to a Provincial or Local Museum, where such exists, in accordance with the general principles set forth in the paras 3 and 4. Where there is no Local Museum, the objects should be sent to the Imperial Museum, if the Trustees, to whom information of the discovery should be conveyed by the local government and administration, should so desire.

II. The local governments and administrations will furnish the Trustees of the Indian Museum with lists of all Museums in the Province and with descriptive catalogues of their contents and will report to the Trustees all fresh discoveries dealt with under the preceding clause.

III. The Trustees will be at liberty to arrange with the local governments and administrations either for the transfer to the Indian Museum of any object the Trustees may require or for acquiring it by exchange or for obtaining casts or other impressions of it, any points as to which there is a difference of opinion being referred to the Government of India for final decision. In dealing with such application from the Trustees, the local governments and administrations will not fail to attach due might to the desirability of completing any particular archaeological series to which the Trustees of the Indian Museum may attach importance.[67]

Reacting to the stipulations of the Governor-General in Council, Cole addressed a communication to the Secretary, Government of India on 2 July 1883 on the antiquities and archaeological remains at Amravati, and suggested that the Government of Madras should be instructed to consider the case of archaeological remains at Amravati afresh, in light of the instructions of Governor-General in Council. Cole further submitted that the Government of Madras apparently had not received the orders of the Government of India. He, however, added that he would extend all possible help to Burgess with regard to Amravati sculptures. He also added that the purpose of "Archaeological Survey is to write Ancient History and not to go about the country pilfering tons of sculptures from well known monuments".[68]

The officials of the Home Department were in a dilemma to support Cole's contention with regard to Amravati ruins or approve the line of action as put forth by the Government of Madras. S.C. Bayley, Home Member, was not in favour of interference as the structure did not exist and the issue relating to sculptures was outside the purview of Cole's jurisdiction but was under the Archaeological Surveyor.[69]

At long last, Lord Ripon, the Governor-General approved the orders of the Government of Madras on the matter relating to marble structures of Amravati. A copy of the orders of Ripon were also forwarded to Cole with the remarks that "The Government of India see no reason to interfere with the orders of the Madras Government in the matter with whom the final decision rests."[70]

After an interval of two years, the Earl of Kimberley, Secretary of State addressed a communication to the Government of Madras on 12 March 1885. He referred to the suggestion put forth by the Secretary to the Trustees of the British Museum that Buddhist sculptures discovered at Amravati "should be presented to the national collection in this country". The Secretary of State felt that select sculptures should be presented to British Museum for the sake of "the history of which they illustrate".[71] The Government of Madras agreed to the request of the Secretary of State and assured that prompt action would be taken at "an early opportunity".[72] On 2 June 1885, the marbles were selected and shipped to London on board via **Goorkha** navigation steamer.[73]

Many officials felt that Cole's apprehension proved right that if the marbles were sent to Madras, they would be sent to England. Cole had also clashed with the agent to the Governor-General for Central India on the matter relating to certain photographic reproductions of Sanchi Stupa.[74]

In the meanwhile, the Government of India decided not to extend the tenure of Cole as Curator of Ancient Monuments (probably due to his nature), which was to be completed on January 1884. The Government of India decided to revert to the earlier practice of entrusting the task to Local Governments as the Government of India was seriously contemplating to issue a Resolution to the Local Governments in this regard. A. Mackenzie, Secretary, Government of India invited the views of Cole on this matter.[75]

On 22 September 1883, Cole expressed his views on the subject to the Government of India with emphasis on the following aspects:

1. First systematic organization in the N.W.P., 1875 by Sir John Strachey
2. Localisation necessitates several local architectural referees
3. Different areas under separate Governments
4. Objections to working the scheme under many advisers
5. Necessity for active steps for conservation admitted
6. A scheme binding on Local Governments involves complete surveys
7. Employment of Curator in 1881

8. Actual operations
9. No complete scheme ready to be binding on Local Governments
10. Advantages of concentrating information
11. Uniformity in treatment necessary
12. Continuity
13. Custody
14. Monuments in Native States
15. Advantage of one architectural referee
16. Principal Monuments
17. Economy
18. Indian architecture: An Imperial subject
19. Illustrations
20. The preliminary survey
21. Best practical measures
22. Provision of funds
23. Return for the outlay (Appendix XIX)

After the views of Cole were received by the Government of India, it adopted a Resolution on 26 November 1883 (No. 3) for the Local Governments.

Resolution

1. The Secretary of State sanctioned the appointment of Curator of Ancient Monuments in November 1880 for a term of three years only, in view to the settlement within that period by Local Governments of a complete scheme of conservation for each province. Major Cole has, since he took charge of his office in January 1881, visited most of the Local Governments, and in the notes and memoranda which form Appendices of his reports has indicated in respect of many of the principal monuments what measures of conservation are in his opinion required. It is important that the Local Governments should now settle, in communication with the Government of India, the general lines upon which their operations will in future be conducted. The lists of objects of antiquarian interest received from the different provinces show that very much information as to the number and character of existing monuments has been collected; and the Curator's memoranda and suggestions indicate sufficiently clearly the general direction which measures of conservation ought to follow.

2. The Governor-General in Council notices, however, that the Curator has to apparently place himself in such free communication with the officers of the Archaeological Survey as was desirable, and this is to be regretted. It is true the reports show that Major Cole has at times consulted General Cunningham; but as far as Madras and Bombay are concerned, he appears to have had no communication with Dr. Burgess whose great experience and sound knowledge, both archaeological and architectural, would have been of much service in preparing the necessary lists, and determining the mode in which repairs should be planned.

3. The Governor-General in Council desires that each Local Government will now, with as little delay as possible, take up the lists of ancient monuments for its province as given in Major Cole's Report for the year 1882-83, and, as regards Northern, Eastern and Central India, in communication with General Cunningham and as regards Madras and Bombay, in communication with the Archaeological Surveyor of Southern and Western India, prepare classified lists and a detailed report showing:

I. Those monuments which from their present condition and historical or archaeological value ought to be maintained in permanent good repair.

II. Those monuments which it is now only possible or desirable to save from further decay by such minor measures as the eradication of vegetation, the exclusion of water from the walls, and the like.

III. Those monuments which from their advanced stage of decay or comparative unimportance, it is impossible or unnecessary to preserve.

4. The monuments in classes I and II should be further subdivided, thus –

I(a) and II(a) – Monuments in the possession or charge of Government, or in respect of which Government must undertake the cost of all measures of conservation.

I(b) and II(b) – Monuments in the possession or charge of private bodies or individuals.

In respect of I(a) and II(a), the report should show what arrangements it is proposed to make for the due carrying out of the necessary measures of conservation. Definite provision should be made for the proper custody and upkeep of each monument in these classes. The Government of India do not wish to interfere in the details of these arrangements, but they desire to be satisfied that each Local Government has at its disposal, the means for the intelligent and judicious treatment of any questions that may arise in connection with the preservation of buildings of such importance. The Governor-General in Council considers that the cost of these measures is a legitimate charge upon the Public Works allotment of each province, but will be prepared to consider in very special cases whether any further assistance should be granted from Imperial funds.

In respect of classes I(b) and II(b), it should be reported what funds are available for their conservation; and whether the custodians can be induced to allow the inspection, direction, and control of Government officers in such matters. It may be advisable in some instances to offer small subsidies in view to securing the necessary amount of supervision, but this should only be proposed where the monument is one of primary importance, and its due conservation cannot be otherwise secured. In general, it may be hoped that the local officers and the Local Governments will be able to induce those interested to take proper steps for maintaining the buildings in their charge.

5. If hereafter it should become apparent that the Local Governments require advice or instructions with reference to the proper mode of preserving or treating any monument, the Government of India will be happy to arrange for procuring this from the best available authorities. Meantime, as above intimated, the Local Governments should, besides referring to General Cunningham and Dr. Burgess, freely consult the Curator of Ancient Monuments in the preparation of the lists and reports now ordered, remembering that Major Cole's services will not be available in that capacity after 28 January 1884, when the period for which his appointment was sanctioned by the Secretary of State will expire.

6. In the Annual Administration Reports of each province, full information should be given as to the measures of conservation carried out during the year and as to the condition of all monuments in classes I and II.[76]

It was also ordered that a copy of the Resolution was to be forwarded to the Local Governments and Cole was asked to visit monuments not yet seen by him before the expiry of his term, and also submit notes and recommendations to the Local Governments concerned.[77]

The Resolution was also approved by the Secretary of State for India and called for the Local Governments to conduct on "the general lines on which their operations will in future be conducted". It stated that "the cost of these measures is a legitimate charge upon the Public Works allotment for each province" and that Government "in special case will consider whether assistance can be granted from Imperial funds"; also that the best professional advice procurable will be obtained when asked for.[78] The guidelines/instructions as incorporated in the Resolution were sound and laid the foundation of the existing system of archeological conservation in British India. It also sought to classify monuments of each province.[79]

The following classification of monuments was indicated in several lists received. For the Punjab, the stage of classification had not reached then.

	I(a)	I(b)	II(a)	II(b)	III	Notclassed	Total
Madras	11	19	41	29	-	-	100
Bombay	66	74	67	109	-	-	316
Bengal	46	94	45	311	155	92	743
N.W.P and Oudh	62	171	43	571	605	-	1,452
Punjab	-	-	-	-	-	761	761
Upper Burma	-	-	-	-	-	44	44
Lower Burma	-	-	-	-	-	148	148
Central Provinces	5	5	12	29	-	-	51
Berar	2	2	3	6	-	-	13
Coorg	-	-	-	-	-	863	863

The statement only indicated information about the history of monuments rather than details of their present state of preservation. None of the provinces indicated in their list(s) thus forwarded the details with regard to taking up measures of conservation, which they were required to undertake. This was primarily attributed to the fact that the archaeological surveyors were not trained engineers but were of the draftsman class and there was lack of supervision by the departmental heads.[80]

It was also decided that since the lists were drawn up on dissimilar plans, the Government had to send them for being revised according to the prescribed format.

After the completion of Cole's tenure as the Curator of ancient monuments, the subjects and functions relating to repair of monuments was transferred from Home Department to Public Works Department. An amount of Rs. 50,000/- was earmarked for expenditure during the year 1884-85.[81] Out of this amount, Rs. 7,500/- was assigned for the restoration of marble pavilion at Daulat Bagh in Ajmer[82] and Rs. 10,000/- towards conservation of ancient monuments in Punjab.[83] The work pertaining to conservation now devolved on the local governments and administrations who were now required to approach General Cunningham for advice.[84]

In the princely states of Rajputana and Central India, the preservation and conservation of monuments were assigned to Dr. Burgess and General Cunningham. Monuments in Malwa, under the territory governed by, Maharaja of Holkar including those located in Udaipur and Jodhpur in Rajputana, were assigned to Dr. Burgess, the erstwhile Archaeological Surveyor of Western and Southern India, while all other states under the agencies were placed under General Cunningham.[85]

In 1884, Kashmir State was also approached by the Government with regard to the preservation of monuments.. The Kashmir Darbar in reply had stated that the Maharaja of Kashmir took personal interest in the preservation of all ancient monuments in state and was "fully alive to the importance of conserving the specimens of ancient archaeological art".[86]

However, to complete the survey of archaeological monuments of importance and attend to the pending work in hand, the Governor-General in Council sanctioned the extension of the tenure of Cole till the end of March 1884. The services of Cole were placed under the supervision of Public Works Department with effect from 28 January 1884, with instructions to the Public Works Department to allow Cole to discharge his functions and duties under the Home Department till 31 March 1884.[87]

The post of Curator held by Cole was, however, not revived by the Government of India, although the Secretary of State would have had allowed Cole an extension. The reason for not allowing Cole to hold on to the post of Curator was attributed to many controversies in which Cole was associated. He was considered as impracticable, uncordial and controversial officer, who was not amenable to discipline. He was charged with spending huge amounts on publication of reports, expenditure on which was unnecessary and which did not come under the purview of his assigned duties. It was thought best to allow his tenure of appointment lapse.

However, there was a word of praise from A. Mackenzie, Secretary, Government of India who noted on 26 September 1883 that his contribution in the field of preservation and conservation of archaeological monuments "may be classed as artistic and archaeological". Mackenzie also noted that Cole had penchant for the intricate details who had surpassed General Cunningham's contributions, especially archeological excavations in Yusufzai district in Afghanistan. Mackenzie, however, concluded that if Cole's appointment was extended, it would merely be "an arrangement for producing expansive, though interesting, illustrations of Indian architecture and Indian art".[88]

Besides, the Home Member S.C. Bayley was also of the view that the publications by Cole was, "distinctly archaeological work and not the duty of the Curator".[89]

Even after the abolition of the post of Curator, Cole continuously strived for employment relating to conservation work. The Governments of North-West Provinces, Punjab, Rajputana and Central India approached the Supreme Government for enlisting Cole's services towards archaeological repairs and Cole had fervently hoped that Government would support him for employment with the Governments, who sought his services.[90]

However, the Government of India did not wish to interfere in the matter concerning the arrangements proposed by the provincial and local governments in the "preservation of important building".[91]

As a corollary to his appreciation of Cole's contribution to the care of monuments, A. Mackenzie clarified the position of the Government of India in view of Cole's efforts in seeking employment with the Provincial and Local Governments. The fact was that only small allocations were available towards the conservation of monuments and further his work was not of high standard. His reports were of little or no value and his activities were very expensive for the class of work he had produced. Besides, he had been approaching the Local Governments for employment which was a matter not likely to be re-considered by the Government.[92] Mackenzie also stated as the Local Governments have to undertake the responsibility of conservation of monuments in their respective regions for the future with the advice of their archaeological surveyors and advisors and "they must make what arrangements they please for this purpose".[93]

Besides, the Local Governments expressed their inability to pay Cole from those respective budgetary fund allocations and also were not inclined to coordinate and cooperate with other Local Governments/Administrations with regard to payment towards salary for Cole. They were also unwilling to meet the expenditure of his office establishment.[94]

Finally, A. Mackenzie, Secretary, Government of India remarked, "Cole has been obstinate and subordinate to the last degree and we are well rid of him."[95]

NOTES AND REFERENCES

1. Department of Finance and Commerce, Accounts A, March 1881, No. 507.
2. Department of Finance and Commerce, Accounts A, March 1881, No. 509.
3. Department of Finance and Commerce, Accounts A, March 1881, No. 510.
4. Home, Revenue and Agriculture, Survey, February 1881, K.W. to No. 104.
5. *Ibid.*
6. *Ibid.*
7. Home Revenue and Agriculture, Survey, February 1881, No. 1
8. *Ibid.*
9. Home, Revenue and Agriculture, Survey, February 1881, No. 3.
10. Home, Revenue and Agriculture, February 1881, No. 4
11. Home, Archaeology A, August 1881, No. 1.
12. Home, Archaeology A, August 1881, No. 11.
13. Home, Archaeology A, August 1881, No. 12.
14. Home, Archaeology A, August 1881, No. 13.
15. Home, Archaeology, Conservation of A.Ms., A, September 1881, No. 21.
16. First Report of Cole on 'preservation of monuments for the year 1881-1882', Appendix Hii, pp. xxxiv-xxxviii; Department of Finance and Commerce, Salaries, March 1881, Proceedings No. 508.
17. First Report of Cole on 'preservation of monuments for the year 1881-82', p. 10.
18. Home, Archaeology and C.A.M., December 1882, No. 10.
19. P.W.D., C.W. Buildings, July 1881, Nos. 14-19, Pt. B.
20. *Ibid.*
21. Home, Archaeology B, August 1881, No. 23.
22. Home, Archaeology B, April 1883, Nos. 14-17.
23. K.W. to Home, Archaeology A, August 1881, Nos. 1-17.
24. Home, Archaeology A, July 1882, Nos. 13-15.
25. *Ibid.*
26. Home, Archaeology A, October 1882, No. 8.
27. Home, Archaeology A, October 1882, No. 6.
28. *Ibid.*
29. Home, Archaeology A, October 1882, No. 11.
30. Home, Archaeology A, Conservation of A.Ms., April 1883, No. 6.
31. Home, Archaeology, C.A.M., April 1883, No. 7.
32. Home, Archaeology A, C.A.M., June 1883, No. 71.
33. Home, Archaeology, C.A.M., June 1883, No. 82.
34. *Ibid.*
35. Home, Archaeology A, July 1882, No. 10.
36. Home, Archaeology A, February 1885, Nos. 1-26.
37. First Report of Cole on 'preservation of monuments for the year 1881-82', Appendix Hii, pp. xxxv-xxxvi.
38. First Report of Cole on 'preservation of monuments for the year 1881-82', pp. 11-20.
39. Home, Archaeology, C.A.M., August 1883, No. 10.
40. Home, Archaeology, C.A.M., August 1883, No. 27.
41. Home, Archaeology, C.A.M., October 1883, No. 26.
42. *Ibid.*
43. Home, Archaeology A, February 1882, No. 15.
44. *Ibid.*
45. *Ibid.*
46. Home, Archaeology A, February 1882, No. 18.
47. Home, Archaeology A, April 1882, No. 22.

48. Home, Archaeology A, April 1882, No. 27.
49. Home, Archaeology A, C.A.M., July 1882, No. 2.
50. Home, Archaeology A, C.A.M., July 1882, No. 3.
51. Home, Archaeology A., C.A.M., July 1882, No. 4.
52. Home, Archaeology A, June 1882, No. 8.
53. Home, Archaeology A, June 1882, No. 9.
54. Home, Archaeology A, June 1882, No. 8.
55. Home, Archaeology A, September 1882, No. 12.
56. *Ibid.*
57. Home, Archaeology A, September 1882, No. 13.
58. Home, Archaeology A, September 1882, No. 14.
59. Foreign, B General I, March 1883, Nos. 77-79.
60. *Ibid.*
61. Home, Archaeology, C.A.M., June 1883, No. 36.
62. Home, Archaeology, C.A.M., A, March 1883, Nos. 10-11.
63. Home, Archaeology, C.A.M., A, July 1883, No. 9.
64. *Ibid.*
65. *Ibid.*
66. Home Archaeology, C.A.M., A, June 1883, No. 70.
67. Home, Archaeology, C.A.M., A, June 1883, No. 68.
68. Home, Archaeology, C.A.M., A, July 1883, No. 11.
69. *Ibid.*
70. Home, Archaeology, Conservation of A. Monuments, A., July 1883, No. 12.
71. Home, Archaeology B, April 1885, Nos. 9-10.
72. Home, Archaeology B, June 1885, No. 4
73. *Ibid.*
74. Home, Archaeology B, October 1884, Nos. 12-18.
75. Home, Archaeology, C.A.M., December 1883, No. 3.
76. Foreign, B. General I, January 1884, Nos. 3-4.
77. *Ibid.*
78. Home, Archaeology, C.A.M., A., July 1884, Nos. 2-4.
79. Department of Revenue and Agriculture, Archaeology and Epigraphy, January 1901, No. 5.
80. *Ibid.*
81. Home, Archaeology B, February 1884, No. 6.
82. *Ibid.*
83. Department of Finance and Commerce, A., December 1884, Nos. 1135-1136; Salaries, B, April 1884, Nos. 763-67.
84. Home, Archaeology, A., December 1883, Nos. 3-6.
85. Home, Archaeology, A., June 1884, Nos. 12-15.
86. Home, Archaeology, A., February 1885, Nos. 1-26.
87. Home, Archaeology, C.A.M., A., January 1884, Nos. 17-19.
88. Home, Archaeology, C.A.M., December 1883, Nos. 3-6.
89. *Ibid.*
90. Home, Archaeology, C.A.M., July 1884, Nos. 2-4.
91. Home, Archaeology, C.A.M., April 1884, No. 3.
92. Home, Archaeology, C.A.M., July 1884, Nos. 2-4.
93. Home, Archaeology, C.A.M., April 1884, No. 9.
94. Archaeology, C.A.M., April 1884, No. 2.
95. Archaeology, C.A.M., A., June 1884, Nos. 1-3.

CHAPTER IX

Alexander Cunningham

After the tenure of Cole had come to an end, the Earl of Kimberley, Secretary of State approved the arrangements to "secure the numerous buildings of historical and archeological in India from further deterioration and decay".[1]

In this context, it is worthwhile mentioning that through a Resolution (No. 2129 dated 16 December 1884, Department of Finance and Commerce), the administration and expenditure relating to conservation of ancient monuments was transferred from the Home Department to Public Works Department.[2]

However, the Governor-General in Council revoked this Resolution and passed yet another Resolution (No. 5941, Department of Finance and Commerce dated 4 February 1885), in which the Home Department would be responsible for allocation of funds and expenditure on the conservation of monuments would be provided to Public Works Department.[3]

Meanwhile J. Gibbs, Member of the Council, had consulted Cunningham for the course of action to be adopted by the Government of India for the following:

1. Survey and conservation/curation of ancient monuments of India.
2. Acquisition and translation of the ancient inscriptions.

In the meantime, Cunningham agreed to give up his present appointment and expressed his desire that he would resign at any date convenient to the Government. Cunningham submitted a Memorandum on the Archaeological Department and the conservation of ancient monuments.

The Memorandum of Cunningham dilated on the future course of action with regard to conservation of monuments of archaeological importance. Cunningham was of the opinion that "No doubt many ancient monuments still remain to be discovered and many inscriptions still remain to be copied but I feel that the future work of exploration might be successfully carried on by a smaller and less expensive establishment." He proposed that the work relating to survey and exploration could be combined with the work of conservation. He stated that the archaeologist who has examined, measured and described the monument of different ages and is conversant with the style and dimension would be able to assess the conservation work thus involved and would be able to execute this work rather efficiently. He, therefore, pleaded that the functions and activities relating to distinct departments of exploration and conservation should be consolidated into one department. To implement the programme of conservation effectively, Cunningham proposed the creation of a separate division comprising officers to carry out conservation plans effectively. He opined that "with a divided authority there would always be the risk of a conflict of opinion as to the style in which certain repairs should be made and if this difference of opinion should occur frequently, a decision as to what ought to be done might sometimes cause embarrassment". In order to carry out the plans for ensuring conservation of monuments of archaeological importance, Cunningham favoured archaeological divisions, viz., Western, Eastern and Southern India.

1. Western or North-Western India would include the whole of Punjab and Sind with Rajputana and the western portion of the North-West Provinces and Central Provinces lying to the westward of the great lines of road running from Gonda and Fyzabad in Oudh through Allahabad and Satna to Jabalpur and Nagpur.
2. Eastern, or North-Eastern India might comprise the whole of the present Bengal Presidency with Assam and the South Eastern Provinces and the remaining portion of the North-West Provinces and Central Provinces lying to the eastward of the great lines of road mentioned above.
3. Southern India would include the whole of the Bombay and Madras Presidencies, with the Hyderabad and Mysore States and south-eastern portion of the Central Provinces along the lower course of the Godawari River.

Cunningham was of the view that for each of these divisions, an experienced officer as Director should be appointed as head. The reports of archaeological survey and conservation would be forwarded to the Local Governments concerned by these designated officers. Each Director might have two assistants, one of whom should possess some experience in building as well as some taste for archaeological enquiries. The other might be a local person, if one can be found suited for such work. He also proposed sanction of an establishment for the three divisions, i.e., 3 Directors, 3 First Assistants, 3 Sub-Assistants, 3 Head Draughtsmen and 3 Under Draftsmen.

Besides, he also proposed higher remuneration to the officers. He stated that the salaries of the Directors or Head Officers should be liberal, otherwise, each of them would always be on the look-out for a better paid appointment such as that of a Municipal Engineer and suggested that the salaries of the designated officers should range from Rs. 600/800. He was of the opinion that the cost of the proposed establishment would approximately be Rs. 75,000 per annum. The arrangement would effect considerable savings as compared to expenditure hitherto incurred through establishment of two separate departments. He was also of the opinion that the expenditure for maintaining each of the two divisions of North-Western and North-Eastern India would only amount to Rs. 22,500 or Rs. 45,000 for the two divisions, leaving Rs. 30,000 for the Southern Division under Dr. Burgess. Cunningham contended that he had purposely kept the allocations for Southern India on the higher side as he thought that the Government of India might like to retain the services of Dr. Burgess who at the present was engaged in the exploration of archaeological sites in Madras and Bombay Presidencies. He further contended that Burgess was competent to conduct the archaeological explorations in Southern India due to his valuable reports as well as his intimate acquaintance with all the architectural remains there. He also recommended increase of salary for Dr. Burgess who was currently drawing Rs. 1200 per month.

He was of the view that the great zeal and ability which was shown by Dr. Burgess in archaeological pursuits, he should be designated Director-General of the Archaeological Survey of Southern India and other officers could be designated Directors or Archaeological Surveyors of their respective divisions. In the concluding portion of the communication, Cunningham recommended an independent and a separate archaeological division for Punjab, North-West Provinces and Bengal. He recommended the following:

1. Sind and Rajputana should be added to the jurisdiction of Punjab.
2. Central India Agency and Central Provinces should be under the jurisdiction of the North-West Provinces.
3. Assam and Chota Nagpur might be included under the jurisdiction of Bengal.

Cunningham was of the view that this arrangement could increase the quantum of expenditure marginally by six to eight thousand rupees per annum, but the establishments being smaller, this would be better managed.[4]

However, J. Gibbs, Member, Governor-General in Council supported Cunningham's proposal for the administration of archaeological survey in India and suggested the following "manageable divisions":

1. Madras and Bombay as at present.
2. Punjab with Sind and Rajputana.
3. North-West Provinces, Central India Agency and the Central Provinces.
4. Bengal with Assam and Chota Nagpur.

Gibbs was of the view that with this arrangement, each surveyor would have a clearly demarcated district and prevent overlapping of problems/difficulties which are likely to be faced by another province. Gibbs also proposed a sum of Rs. 50,000 as Imperial grant-in-aid to the Local Governments.[5]

On 22 December 1884, W.C. Muir remarked that expenditure on archeological survey has become a part of Imperial expenditure from 1882-83. The earlier practice was that the expenditure was jointly met from the Imperial revenues as well as provincial revenues.[6] It was also contended that the grant-in-aid to Local Governments were subject to revision every five years.[7]

Another member of the Governor-General in Council remarked on 23 December 1884 that the expenditure on conservation was being carried out by the Public Works Department and a sum of Rs. 50,000 was being provided from Imperial budget for disbursing grant-in-aid to Local Governments towards conservation of monuments, and the Local Government concerned should provide additional funds if they could effect savings from their respective budgetary allocations.[8]

On 24 December 1884, the Member of Governor-General in Council contended that archaeology was serious science which required critical examination and wondered, "However, interesting the results may be, it is always a question whether it is worthwhile to pay large sums of money for them."[9]

However, J. Gibbs had noted on 22 January 1885 that there was a unanimity of opinion between Cunningham, Burgess and himself relating to combination of curation with survey work.

In this context, he proposed that the entire establishment of archaeology had to be reorganized.[10] He further was of the opinion that the functions of a Curator were to be merged with the archaeology and the monuments of archaeological importance would have to be conserved or restored by the Archaeological Survey. He also said that the actual repairs would have to be carried out by the Public Works Department of the various local governments and administrations, under the general supervision of the Archaeological Surveyor. The Archaeological Survey would be the central responsibility and there would be a proper coordination with local governments and administrations. Besides, it was laid down that the reports of all such survey would have to be submitted through Dr. Burgess to the Government of India after they are properly vetted by the concerned Local Governments.[11]

REORGANISATION OF ARCHAEOLOGICAL SURVEY

Thereafter, the Governor-General in Council had forwarded the proposal of reorganization of the Archaeological Survey Department to the Earl of Kimberley, Secretary of State on 17 February 1885 for his approval.[12] The Secretary of State approved this proposal and sent his assent through a telegram on 30 March 1885. The Secretary of State stated, "I entirely approve of the principle of the arrangements proposed by your Excellency. But, in present circumstances, I am unwilling to sanction an increase of expenditure not absolutely necessary even on an object so desirable as that of increasing the efficiency of the Archaeological Department."[13] Thereafter, a Resolution on the reorganization of Archaeological Survey Department was passed (Home Department Arch. 2/87-103 dated 6 June 1885).

> ...In accordance with the instructions contained in the Resolution No.649-650 dated 2 February 1871, General Cunningham has, year by year, submitted reports showing the nature and amount of the work done, the general result of which may be said to be that the greater part of the Northern India has now been explored either by the Director-General or by his Assistants. In spite, however, of this exploration, it cannot be doubted that many ancient monuments still remain to be surveyed or to be discovered and also many inscriptions to be deciphered. As General Cunningham has expressed his intention of shortly resigning his appointment, it has become necessary to consider the plan which should in future be adopted for the purpose of securing –
>
> (1) the further survey and conservation of the ancient monuments of India, and
> (2) The acquisition and translation of ancient inscriptions.
>
> 2. The work of conservation of ancient monuments was entrusted for a period of three years to a separate officer, Major H.H. Cole, whose appointment lapsed; and Home Department Resolution of the 26th November 1883 described the general plan of future operations recommended for adoption by Local Governments. After full consideration and consultation with General Cunningham, the Government of India has now come to the conclusion that it would be expedient to amalgamate in some measure the work of the conservation of monuments with that of the archaeological survey, experience having shown that work of the former description can best be directed by experienced archaeologists. The Governor-General in Council has accordingly decided that for the future, the two departments of exploration and conservation shall be consolidated to the extent and in the manner explained in following paragraphs.
>
> 3. On the retirement of General Cunningham, the appointment of Director General of Archaeological Survey would lapse; and the whole of India (exclusive of Madras and Bombay Presidencies, where present arrangements under Dr. Burgess will remain unaltered) will be divided into charges of comparatively limited extent, which can easily be undertaken by small independent survey parties. The apportionment which commends itself to the Government of India as most suitable is the following:
>
> 1. The Punjab with the Sind and Rajputana.
> 2. The North-West Provinces and Oudh, the Central India Agency, and the Central Provinces; and

3. Bengal with Assam, Orissa and Chota Nagpur.

The practical result of adopting these divisions will be to concentrate the operations of each party within a clearly demarcated district and to avoid the difficulties which have been found to arise from the operations in different parts of the same province having been entrusted to separate management. Experience may, however, show that for dynastic or other scientific purposes, a survey party should occasionally be allowed to go beyond the limits assigned to it, and the limits now laid down are in no way intended to interference with such an arrangement, if this should be considered necessary by higher authority. In the above apportionment, the territories of His Highness the Nizam and the Hyderabad Assigned Districts have not been provided for. This portion of the country is well known to Dr. Burgess and arrangements may probably be hereafter made that the Bombay party shall, after completing the work in that Presidency, move into Hyderabad.

4. With regard to the agency to be employed, it has been decided that the work in each of the three divisions indicated shall be entrusted to a Surveyor with a suitable establishment, Dr. Burgess, the Archaeological Surveyor of Southern and Western India, being constituted the head of the entire survey Department, but continuing, as at present, to carry on also the detailed work in the Madras and Bombay Presidencies. The duties of the surveyors will be, not only to conduct the work of survey, but also to advise to the various monuments or buildings of antiquity or interest which require to be preserved or restored, the necessary repairs being carried out by the Public Works Department of the several local governments and administrations, under the general supervision of the Archaeological Surveyors. The primary responsibility for conservation will remain, as at present, with the local governments and administrations in their Public Works Departments. The Surveyors will be on the footing of professional advisers to the Local Governments, with the right of initiating suggestions and calling attention to requirements. The strictly archaeological portion of their work should be kept entirely separate from that relating to conservation, and schemes for the preservation of restoration of monuments and c. should be submitted by them direct to the Local Government concerned, to be carried out by the Public Works department from such money as the Local Government can make available for the purpose, supplemented by any grant-in-aid which the Government of India may be in a position to contribute.

5. The surveyors will, as already indicated, be placed in direct communication with the Local Governments and Residents or Political Agents concerned, but their annual reports should be submitted to the Government of India through Dr. Burgess, after having been seen and reviewed by the Local Governments. Each surveyor will also be required to prepare in communication with Dr. Burgess and to submit for the approval of the Government of India through the Local Government concerned, before the commencement of each field season, a programme of the operations which he proposes to undertake, and at the end of each season, as soon after the close of the financial year as possible, an annual report of the work done by his party. In the yearly reports, a table should be added showing the schemes recommended to local authorities for the repairs or restoration of monuments and c. and the grants, if any, made from Provincial and Imperial revenues to carry them out. The Local Government, in forwarding the report, will see that this information is complete. Each report should contain an appendix showing in the 'vernacular characters' – in Devanagari for Hindu names, and in Persian for Muhammadan names – the correct native spelling of all names whether of places or a persons, tribes and c. mentioned in the report. In the reports themselves, no diacritical marks or accents should be used, except the authorized a for long a. All arguments and speculation based on the spelling of names and similar considerations as to the identity of persons, places, tribes and c. should be avoided. The reports should be restricted as much as possible to a clear and accurate account of facts and discoveries.

x x x x x

7. The Governor-General in Council has been pleased to fix the strength of each survey party on the following scale:

1 Surveyor on Rs. 600-25-700 a month
1 Assistant Surveyor on Rs. 300-25-400 a month
1 Draftsman on Rs. 180-10-220 a month
1 Writer on Rs. 50 a month

Each party will also have an allowance of Rs. 920 a year for contingencies and Rs. 2,000 for traveling allowances.

8. The above arrangements which have received the approval of Her Majesty's Secretary of State are sanctioned for a period of five years, on the expiry of which they willbe subject to reconsideration. They will come into operation from the 1st October next from which date the resignation of General Cunningham will take effect, and by which time it is hoped that the services of suitable officers to fill the appointment of Surveyors and Assistant Surveyors for the several divisions will have been secured.

9. The Governor-General in Council desires, in conclusion, to express his hope that Local Governments and others concerned will give their hearty cooperation for the furtherance of the objects set forth in this Resolution.[14]

In response of this Resolution, a few clarifications were sought by that local agents which were clarified by A. Mackenzie, Secretary, Government of India in his communication to the Secretary, Government of North-West Provinces and Oudh. He stated that the entire expenditure on archaeological survey would be borne by the Supreme Government through allocations in central budget. Whereas the preservation and restoration of monuments of archaeological interest would be provided by the Local Government from its own budgetary allocations, which could be further supplemented by the grant-in-aid contributions of the Government of India. He added that the archaeological surveyors will act as advisers to the Local Governments and render general supervision for operation concerning preservation and restoration by the Public Works Department concerned.[15]

Cunningham, in the meanwhile, submitted his resignation of the post of Director General, Archeological Survey of India to the Secretary, Government of India.[16] He gave an estimate of his services rendered (Please see Appendix XX).

Cunningham's retirement on 1 October 1885[17] deprived the Indian archaeological scene of a doyen amongst archaeologists whose contributions would be remembered in the annals of archaeology. In an address delivered at the meeting of the Indian Society of the Hague, on 14 November 1916, J.P.H. Vogel paid glowing tributes to Cunningham. He eulogized the role of Cunningham as "one of the first to stress the importance of field work, accurate description and precise measurement".[18]

However, Cunningham's tenure was also ridden with his controversial decisions in the field of conservation of monuments. He was held responsible for the destruction of many monuments during the course of his excavations. Lepel Griffin had received a complaint on the condition of Sanchi from Austin Mears, Superintendent, Public Works, Sehore that "the shaft 5 feet in diameter and 40 feet in deep sunk through the dome from its centre at the top by Cunningham and Lt. Maisey in search of relics. I have had solidly filled in. Should it prove to be the case and beginning of March will tell whether it be so or no. I hope the amount may be forthcoming, for the dome being put in through repair, there will be nothing to prevent its standing another 2000 years as it had hitherto done till wrecked by BLUNDERED ARCHAEOLOGISTS".[19]

Lepel Griffin had lodged a complaint to the Secretary, Government of India on 21 April 1882 on the injury inflicted to Sanchi Stupa by Cunningham, Director General, Archaeology for undertaking a search for coins and inscriptions, "A thousand years of time and weather have not so much injury to the invaluable tops at Sanchi as was caused by Cunningham, Director-General, Archaeology, years ago mined deep into the topes in the vain search of coins and inscriptions and never field in his excavations; reducing a quarter of this ancient and unique monument to complete ruin. This damage is being slowly and partially repaired but the building is irremediably injured."[20]

On 15 August 1882, Griffin again complained to the Secretary, Government of India about the difficulty in repairing the Sanchi Stupa as it was destroyed due to vandalism of archaeologists themselves and he pleaded for stopping the Archaeological Department from destroying the monuments further due to careless and ruthless excavations otherwise the Government but 'restore with one hand and they destroy with the other'.

He also referred to the removal from Bharhoot, the stone railings and carved gateway by the Director General of Archaeology to the Calcutta Museum, and requested its restoration to its original place from where it had been taken.[21]

He recommended a sum of Rs. 20,000 should be spent for restoration works and expressed fears of further vandalism in Sanchi in wake of extension of the Great India Peninsular Railway to Bhilsa would bring the line immediately below to Sanchi Tope; and unless measures be taken to enclose and conserve the monuments, its injury was probable, as railway contractors, who so far as ancient monuments were concerned, "are as destructive as Archaeologists" and the stone for restoration lying about could be used by the railway contractors, "as excellent material for the manufacture of lime".[22]

Cunningham was also criticized by H.H. Cole for going about searching for things to enrich museums. Neither Cunningham nor Burgess cared to keep 'in situ' and he stated that in the garb of sending relics of monuments to England, they have been vandalizing the monuments "by the extraction of their most valuable parts".[23]

Interestingly, Dr. Burgess who was recommended by Cunningham as his successor to the post of Director General of Archaeology, criticized Cunningham and his assistants for faulty excavation work. He charged Cunningham for not following the proper procedure in carrying out the excavations with the result that valuable data obtained from these excavations was lost forever. He cited the example of Amravati.[24]

However, Dr. J.P. Vogel summed up Cunningham's role that he was not entrusted with the preservation of ancient monuments. In his reports, he repeatedly mentions cases of vandalism committed upon old monuments or the plundering of ancient sites on a large scale especially in connection with the construction of railways. As an archaeologist, he must have felt deeply grieved but he regarded it, perhaps, as a fatality, which it was useless to strive against. Vogel stated that he was not aware, at any rate, that he ever suggested any means of combating the natural decay or wilful destruction of monuments except his collection of sculptures and inscriptions which were presented to the Asiatic Society of Bengal, leading to formation of a nucleus collection preserved in the Indian Museum, Calcutta. Cunningham was also responsible for the restoration of Buddhist shrines at Nirvana temple, Kushinagara, Mahabodhi temple at Bodh Gaya – where Sakyamuni experienced spiritual awakening which made him "The Awakened – the Buddha".

Beyond these solitary exceptions, Cunningham did not occupy himself with the preservation or restoration of monuments. Vogel was also critical of Cunningham's particularly apathetic attitude. He stated that he was particularly involved himself along with his assistants in excavation of archaeological sites,[25] and in the process he had spoilt many ancient structures in search for gold coins, gems, valuables, etc.

Although Cunningham was not directly involved in the preservation of ancient monuments, but his contribution to the other branches of archaeology has ensured him a permanent place in Indian archaeology. On his retirement on 1 October 1885, a notification No. 196 dated 30 September 1885 was issued, wherein A. Mackenzie had paid glowing tributes to Cunningham.

> ...During his tenure Major General Cunningham has made many interesting and important discoveries in Indian Archaeology which are recorded in the Reports of the survey brought out under his superintendence and in separate monographs which are recognized as authoritative on the subjects of which they treat.
>
> In notifying Major General Cunningham's retirement, the Governor-General in Council has much pleasure in tendering to that officer the thanks of the Government of India for the distinguished service rendered by him during an unusually long career and would venture to express a hope that he may in the leisure of his retirement be able to bring together in a permanent shape the numerous and valuable archaeological notes which he is understood to have collected during his service as Director General of the Survey.[26]

The Secretary of State granted Cunningham in 1887, a special pension of Rs. 2,000 per annum for the services rendered in the Archaeological Survey of India.[27]

BURGESS' MEMORANDUM ON THE REORGANISATION OF ARCHAEOLOGICAL SURVEY OF INDIA

The following Memorandum on the reorganisation of Archaeological Survey of India was submitted by Burgess to the Government of India on 29 July 1885.

> The general scheme laid down for the archaeological survey in the minute of the Government of India, Home Department No. 2-87-103 of 6 June 1885, is on the whole a good one and with some necessary modifications, it might be expected to work well if only three really qualified surveyors could be secured for the proposed three provinces or areas. At present, however, it would be difficult to find three men as qualified who could be secured for the small salaries offered. With really capable surveyors, the duties of the head of the survey would be comparatively light but with untrained men, it would be necessary that considerable supervision should be exercised either directly by the head or through a qualified deputy under his orders. Otherwise there would be the greatest danger of misdirected measures of conservation and of failure of worse in the purposes of research. On the basis supplied in the Minute, however, and strictly within the limits of estimated expense there laid down, I think, it would be quite possible to formulate a scheme which would be practicable and in the course of two or three years would work into the lines of the minute.
>
> To work out fully the exact from which such a scheme would take in all details so as to provide for differences of qualifications in the men available and to make the organization as clastic as seems desirable, requires time and care. What I have to say now relates more to its principles.
>
> A glance of some of the aims which I think a satisfactory archaeological survey ought to keep in view, may be helpful in indicating the sort of means required to accomplish them.
>
> Such a survey to the worthy of the country and of any expense bestowed upon it, ought to deal with the various branches of archeology on a comprehensive plan and not be confined to the investigation

Sir William Jones (1746-94).

Bust of James Prinsep (1799-1840) in Asiatic Society, Calcutta.

Lord Lytton (1831-91).

Marquess Curzon of Kedleston (1859-1925).

Elephant procession to Sanchi Tope. Visit of the Viceroy Lord Curzon to Sanchi, 1899.

Sir Alexander Cunningham (1814-93).

James Burgess (1832-1916)

From *Preservation of National Monuments in India,* Henry Hardy Cole (1843-1916), compiler.

Sir John Marshall (1876-1958).

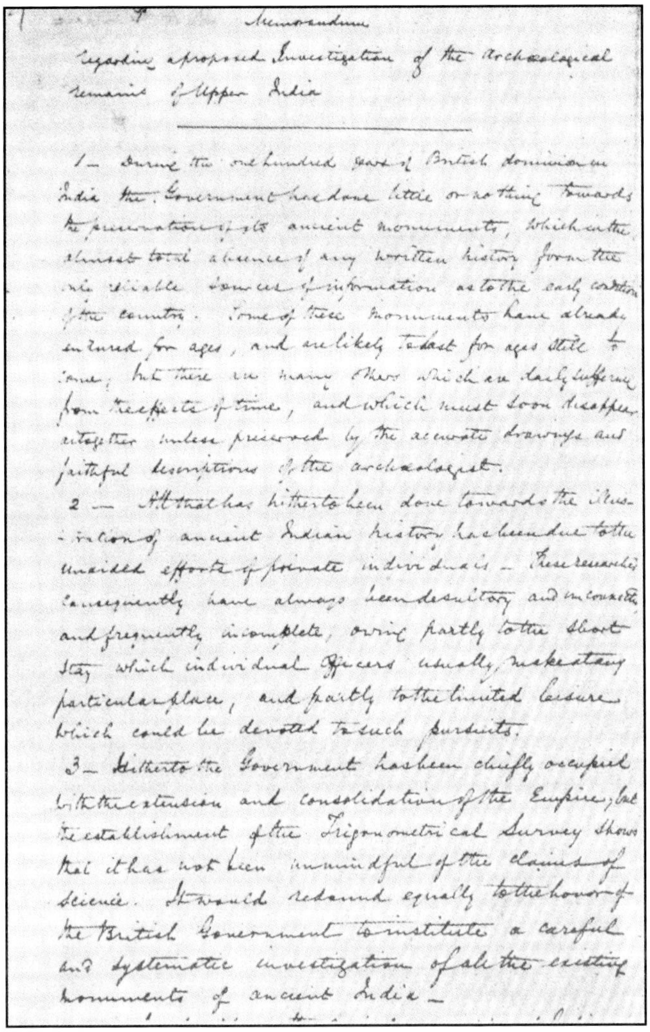
Memorandum

regarding a proposed Investigation of the Archaeological remains of Upper India

1 — During the one hundred years of British dominion in India the Government has done little or nothing towards the preservation of its ancient monuments, which in the almost total absence of any written history form the only reliable sources of information as to the early condition of the country. Some of these monuments have already endured for ages, and are likely to last for ages still to come; but there are many others which are daily suffering from the effects of time, and which must soon disappear altogether unless preserved by the accurate drawings and faithful descriptions of the archaeologist.

2 — All that has hitherto been done towards the illustration of ancient Indian history has been due to the unaided efforts of private individuals. These researches consequently have always been desultory and unconnected, and frequently incomplete, owing partly to the short stay which individual Officers usually make at any particular place, and partly to the limited leisure which could be devoted to such pursuits.

3 — Hitherto the Government has been chiefly occupied with the extension and consolidation of the Empire; but the establishment of the Trigonometrical Survey shows that it has not been unmindful of the claims of science. It would redound equally to the honor of the British Government to institute a careful and systematic investigation of all the existing monuments of ancient India —

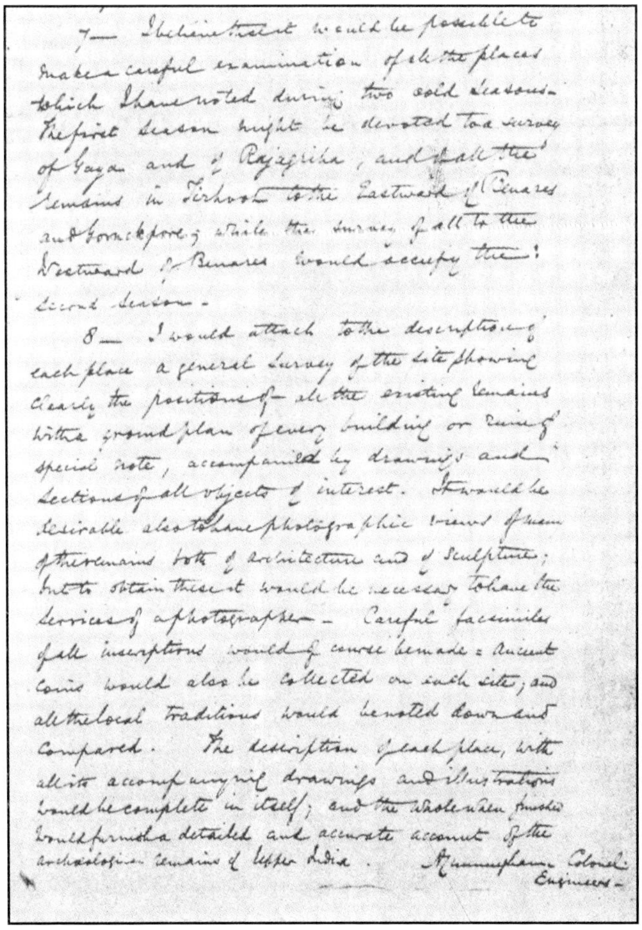
7 — I believe that it would be possible to make a careful examination of all the places which I have noted during two cold seasons. The first season might be devoted to a survey of Gaya and of Rajagriha, and of all the remains in Tirhoot to the Eastward of Benares and Gorruckpore; while the survey of all to the Westward of Benares would occupy the second season.

8 — I would attach to the description of each place a general survey of the site showing clearly the positions of all the existing remains with a ground plan of every building or ruin of special note, accompanied by drawings and sections of all objects of interest. It would be desirable also to have photographic views of many of the remains both of architecture and of sculpture; but to obtain these it would be necessary to have the services of a photographer. Careful facsimiles of all inscriptions would of course be made. Ancient coins would also be collected on each site; and all the local traditions would be noted down and compared. The description of each place, with all its accompanying drawings and illustrations would be complete in itself; and the whole when finished would furnish a detailed and accurate account of the archaeological remains of Upper India.

A Cunningham Colonel
Engineers

Memorandum by Cunningham on 'proposed archaeological investigations in India', November, 1861 (top: extract from first page; bottom: concluding paragraphs).

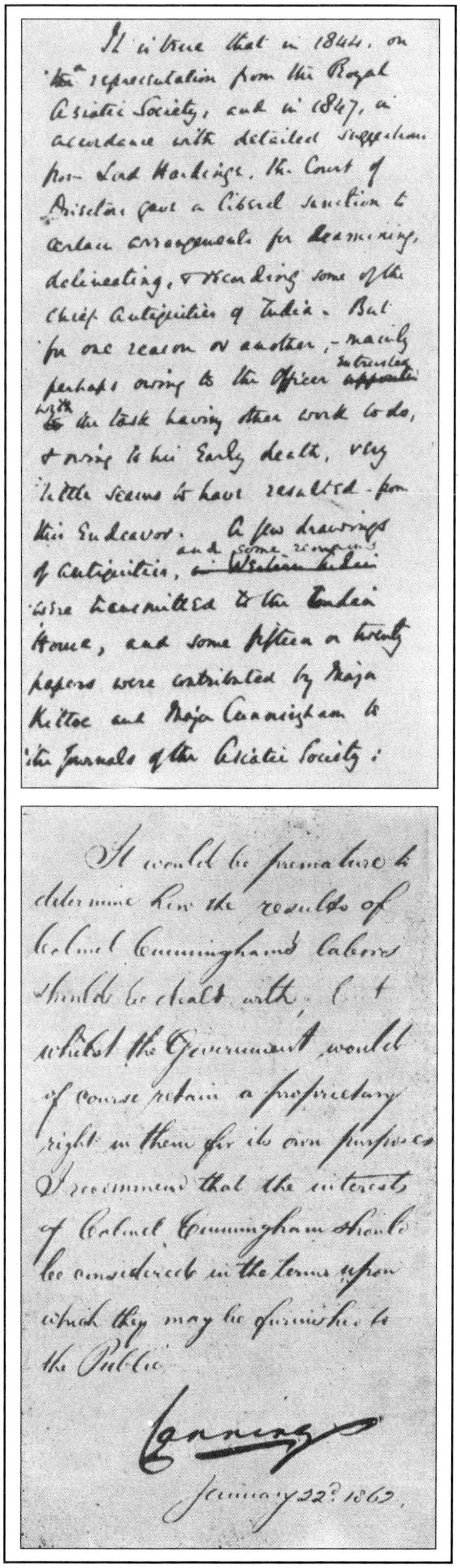

It is true that in 1844, on the representation from the Royal Asiatic Society, and in 1847, in accordance with detailed suggestions from Lord Hardinge, the Court of Directors gave a liberal sanction to certain arrangements for examining, delineating, & recording some of the chief Antiquities of India. But for one reason or another, – mainly perhaps owing to the Officer entrusted with the task having other work to do, & owing to his early death, very little seems to have resulted from this Endeavour. A few drawings of antiquities, and some remains, were transmitted to the India House, and some fifteen or twenty papers were contributed by Major Kittoe and Major Cunningham to the Journals of the Asiatic Society:

It would be premature to determine how the results of Colonel Cunningham's labors should be dealt with, but whilst the Government would of course retain a proprietary right in them for its own purposes I recommend that the interests of Colonel Cunningham should be considered in the terms upon which they may be furnished to the Public.

Canning

January 22d 1862.

Canning's Minute on the setting up of an archaeological survey, 20 January 1862 (top: extract showing additions made in his own hand; bottom: concluding portion).

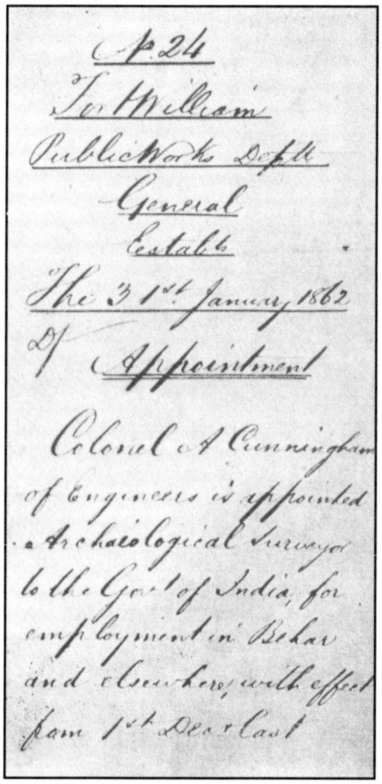

No. 24
Fort William
Public Works Deptt
General
Establt
The 31st January 1862
D/ Appointment

Colonel A Cunningham of Engineers is appointed Archaeological Surveyor to the Govt of India, for employment in Behar and elsewhere, with effect from 1st Decr last

Draft gazette notification announcing Cunningham's appointment as Archaeological Surveyor.

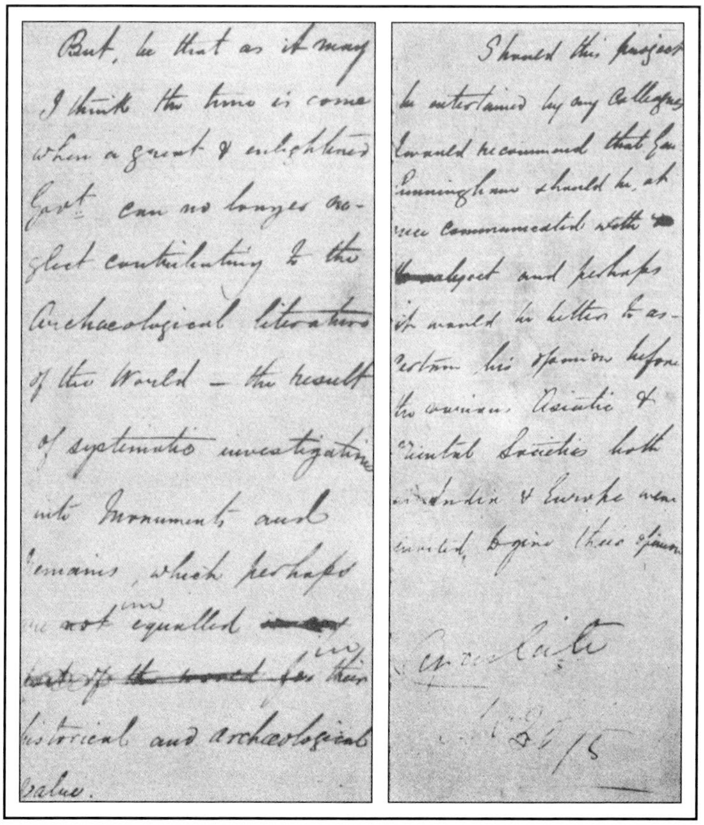

But, be that as it may I think the time is come when a great & enlightened Govt. can no longer neglect contributing to the Archaeological literature of the World – the result of systematic investigation into Monuments and remains, which perhaps are equalled by few for their historical and archaeological value.

Should this project be entertained by my Colleagues I would recommend that Genl Cunningham should be at once communicated with on the subject and perhaps it would be better to ascertain his opinion before the various Asiatic & Oriental Societies both in India & Europe were invited to give their opinion.

Mayo

An extract from Lord Mayo's Minute, dated 30 May 1870.

Taj Mahal, the most illustrious of all historical monuments in India, epitomises the splendour of Indian architecture. The opposite bank of the Yamuna river onto which the Taj backs is a popular vantage point for viewing the mausoleum, splendidly depicted here by Daniells. Aquatint by: Thomas & William Daniell, 1801.

Ruins of Martand, 1870.

The Great Stupa of Sanchi.

Filling in Breach in Great Dome, Sanchi, c. 1882. Photograph by: Lala Deen Dayal.

"Lions at South Gate, Sanchi Tope", in Lepel Griffin, *Famous Monuments of Central India* (1886), Plate XVII. Photograph by: Lala Deen Dayal.

of certain questions in ancient geography, epigraphy and a few other points, but ought to include also among its distinct aims the following:

1. A pretty full illustration and history of ancient and mediaeval architecture, down at least to the decline of the Mohammedan styles; nor need it exclude all that is best in the structural arts down to the present time. For, like Philosophy, it is now well recognized that archaeology covers a far wider field of investigation than the strict etymological sense of the term originally implied.

2. The illustration of decorative art and sculpture – whether mythological or other – with painting such as the frescoes of Bagh and Ajanta and the decorative coloured designs in use in Rajputana and the North-West.

x x x x x
x x x x x

5. The survey ought to be closely in rapport with the Indian Museum and the Local Museums of the different provinces and should help to secure the preservation in them of inscriptions on stone and copper, coins, sculptures and c. And in case of any officer in a Museum had special aptitude for research, it might be arranged to employ him occasionally and field work under the direction of the survey and on behalf of the Museum.

6. Besides these, there are other subjects of investigation such as – the ancient systems of Fortification employed in old forts as Gawilgarh, Asirgarh, Kamalaner and c., the ancient Geography of India not only of the Buddhist Pilgrims and Alexandrine Greeks, but also of the classical Sanskrit authors – a subject hitherto but little investigated; and other branches relating to the development of the civilization of the Indian people – all belonging to archaeology but which need not be further particularized.

7. Lastly and most important, the **Conservation of Monuments** is a matter of such importance in which an unskilled officer may so easily do irremediable harm, that very great care is required in the selection of men qualified by their architectural knowledge to advise the local Governments aright on all questions belonging to this branch of their duties. Too much stress can hardly be laid on this and most men require a special training to fit them for such work.

Now it might seem hopeless to get men qualified in all branches; but all are not equally important and some can be comparatively easily picked up by men who have been disciplined to study. And in view of the preceding, it would be well that the surveyors should be men of two classes – university men given to oriental studies and architects (not mere Engineers) – the one to complement the qualifications of the other. And I am personally acquainted at present with more than one young scholar of ability, deeply interested in oriental research who, I believe, would be willing to accept a very modest salary in this department. A few months training in one of my camps would perhaps be enough to fit such for the discharge of the duties of a surveyor only requiring occasional instructions. The employment of one or two such men, should help to propagate a scientific study of the subject to create a deeper interest in it while it would provide against any future emergency such as might arise from the death or resignation of the Head of the Survey or of the Epigraphical branch. Again, it would not be difficult to obtain the services of one or two young architects – like Mr. Rea, my assistant in Madras – with knowledge, taste and love of the work, who might be engaged for a term of 3, 4 and 5 years and who would very soon learn to conduct a survey and advise on conservation with reasonable success.

Finally, however much I might personally prefer to devote my attention almost exclusively to the Dekhan and southern India, for the first year or two, I am no strong probability of being able to leave the North without more direct supervision than is explicitly provided for. But after a year or two the superintendents ought to be able to carry on without much more supervision than the minute indicates. The men have first to be trained to the work, then they will be fit to act independently or nearly so.[28]

Under the new arrangement as enshrined in the Memorandum, archaeological excavations in Bengal were entrusted to the charge of J.D. Beglar, Cunningham's assistant who was designated Archaeological Surveyor. Beglar was a qualified archaeologist. He spoke Bengali fluently and had a stint in the Government of Bengal as a Conservator. Major J.B. Keith was assigned North-West Provinces and C.J. Rodgers was assigned Punjab, while Burgess continued to work in Bombay and Madras.

On 14 October 1885, Major Keith gave his views of archaeological survey in North-West Provinces and Rajputana. In a communication addressed to the Secretary, Government of India on 14 October 1885, Keith emphasized that:

> Coming to the subject matter of my letter, I would express the pleasure I feel in knowing that the Survey will have the invaluable assistance to Dr. Burgess. Aware that he will address Government on the duties of the various surveys, I hope some mean will be secured which, while it guards against misdirected zeal on the part of the surveyors, will protect industry, individuality and enthusiasm which constitute the life and soul of the work. This I understand the Government of India has done in making the surveyors. Assistants to the Local Government and not to a Department head, all who know the value of local knowledge, who can appreciate the differences of local details, will understand the wisdom of such an arrangement. Each surveyor ought to feel that he is working for the credit of a particular province, of a particular Local Government and not for the benefit of a particular Local Government and not for the benefit of a particular Department or a few European Orientalists. He ought above all things to try and awaken Native sympathy for the work – an aim that has hitherto escaped notice. In a large country like India where there are such divergences of style and so many peculiarities, it would be impossible to adopt one uniform system of work. The Archaeological Survey cannot be treated as either the Trignometrical or Geological surveys. Again I think it would be universe either to attempt or carry out too ambitious a programme or work. Few men will be found to unite in one person a large number of acquirements. Archaeology is the study of a life time and it is only men like General Cunningham who have obtained a multitude of facts and are in a position to generalize upon them. The abstruse portions of Archaeology, including numismatics, may be very safely left to those who have a particular knowledge of the particular branch of study. I have heard a good deal about a technical knowledge of architecture. Personally I cannot lay claim to much technical knowledge, for the greater part of my life has been passed as a soldier and not as an architect. What the Government of India and the public desire is good practical work and not arguments or learned theories. Monumental conservation, in my opinion is by far the most important branch of the newly organized Archaeological Survey of India which has no general history until the time of the Mohammedan conquest and any scattered facts prior to that time have been fully related in the works of General Cunningham and others. So long as there is any notable building or historical landmark unconserved, I think the other branches of Archaeology may be held subordinate to conservation. It is the only branch with which the Native public have any interest and the only one with which the general public sympathise.
>
> In past Native associated excavations with destruction, the search after valuables and the removal of sculptures. So long as they thus understood our proceedings, they saw no harm in carrying away temples for building purposes themselves.
>
> No sooner, however, did Government adopt the **in situ** principle than a very different interest was awakened. Men from long distances visited Gwalior and Sanchi in thousands and seemed much pleased with the work.
>
> The removal of the Elgin marbles from the Parthenon to the British Museum, the enrichment of Louvre after a similar fashion, at once gave sanction for the wholesale transfer of sculptures to central museums. Now, however, that we have Railways all over the country, there is no excuse for

robbing a neighborhood of a historical landmark. At one time there was a proposition to remove the Gateways of Sanchi to the British Museum and the Baharhut Stupa was actually transferred to Calcutta. This was done in the interests of safety, but the public would have much sooner welcomed a proposition for their conservation **in situ**. I noticed with regret several pieces of Indian sculpture at South Kensington. These, Mr. Pindon Clarke took away with him. He wanted in a similar manner to transfer two miniature temples from Gwalior, but this I steadily resisted why should the Natives be robbed of their own property and why should it be transferred to a place where not a fraction of the Native public can ever see it?

In Algeria, a French General Officer was marching through the country when he suddenly came upon the dilapidated tomb of a once distinguished Commander. Instead of plundering it for its mosaics, mirror, votive offerings and c., he piously ordered his men to repair it. A craze, however, for caskets, coins and c. have often induced our archaeologists to adopt a precisely opposite course and one very repugnant to the feeling of Natives. As I am more particularly interested in monumental conservation, indeed the one branch with which I have any real experience, I would propose on arrival in India to devote my first season to a careful survey of such buildings as are of sufficient importance to warrant repair.

Repairs can be carried out at great saving to the public if the debris which invariably surrounds old buildings is utilized instead of the expense of fresh quarrying. This also admits of investigation and research instead of independent investigations, which are too often attended with barren results. Preservation not restoration being the object in view, all carving is to be deprecated. Still a repair ought to be carried out so as to avoid all patch work and incongruity. The restoration of Buddha Gaya by Mr. Beglar has much exercised the savants of Albermarle Street. I have visited Buddha Gaya and while I would not presume to question the work of so zealous a brother officer as Mr. Beglar or work which has received the sanction of so high an authority as General Cunningham, I would mention that the restoration struck me as militating against that sentiment which belongs to age. Conservation to be thorough going ought not only to include an actual repair, but the buildings ought to be annually inspected so as to prevent the accumulations of lichen and vegetation. Native custodians at a small monthly stipend ought to be appointed so as to ensure cleanliness. A rough open store shed ought invariably to be set apart for sculptures and the Provincial Surveyor ought to be ex-officio the Secretary to the Local Museum. The latter Institution in contradistinction to great central Museums finds favour all over Europe. If properly managed, Local Museums ought to be places of instruction as well as recreation for the general public. So little did conservation in former times come within the scope of Archaeology that I found vandalism rife at Gwalior. Unless I had made an energetic protest, the whole of the Jain caves in the Urwahi valley and one or two of the splendid tanks on the Gwalior Esplanade would have been destroyed in order to save the pocket of a Public Works Contractor. I mention this in order to claim for conservation priority as the chief branch of Archaeology.

Expensive drawings are to be deprecated, but a record of ornament might prove highly useful, provided it is used for practical purposes and not buried in a report which never reaches the public eye. Eastern architecture is the architectonic expression of the Arts and its ornament should be at the service of the artisan class. Unless my liberty is fettered by hard-and-fast lines or impossible programmes, my ambition would be to impart an element of popularity into the work and so obtain Native sympathy. The surveys ought to word for their Provinces and the more rivalry imported into their work, the better. I have been sounded as to my qualifications not by the Government of India which has generously stood sponsor for the same, but in other quarters. I consider it, therefore, my duty to state at the outset that I lay no claim to scholarship or to an amount of technical knowledge which may be demanded. I have seen nearly every building of note in India, and if the same indulgence is extended to me as I received so generously at the hands of the Central India Administration, I will do my best to give satisfaction. The appointment I have accepted out of mere love for work and not for the remuneration which is, confessedly small for an officer of 28 years' service.[29]

Likewise, J.D. Beglar, Archaeological Surveyor, Bengal in his submission to the Secretary, Public Works Department, Government of Bengal emphasized that Archaeological Survey may be classified under the following heads of numismatics, paleography, ancient geography and ancient tradition which are valuable as a source material for compiling the moral, religious and political history of the past and coined a term "monumental archaeology" dealing exclusively with ancient art and architecture. He also lamented the loss of services of General Cunningham who was "the one man whose loss it is impossible to replace". Beglar referred to many published works on archaeology which revealed many forms and styles of art & architecture which were essential in prosecuting a scientific study of the subject. He also stated that pictures and photographs were useful for only supplementing the geometrical drawings. He requested the Government of India to provide him the services of a high caste "Brahmin" professional engineer for the examination and measurement of the interior of Hindu temples as his assistant so that he could be trained as an "active honest successor to myself when one is needed".[30]

The reaction of Beglar's proposal did not find favour in the Home Department of the Government of India, as they felt that he was unnecessarily leaning on engineering qualifications. F.C. Daukes, Under Secretary, Government of India felt that knowledge of archaeology and "inclination towards archaeological pursuits, seems essential in addition to technical knowledge of engineering".[31]

However, A. Mackenzie, Secretary to the Government of India observed that the Local Governments should be given autonomy to decide about conservation or restoration of monuments in their respective jurisdiction. He further suggested that the Archaeological Surveyors should submit their survey programmes to Dr. Burgess who would thereafter forward them to the Local Government with his own suggestions and advice in the matter. "If Burgess finds the surveyors giving foolish advice about conservation to the Local Government, he ought to have power to prevent its being followed".[32]

S.C. Bailey also agreed with Mackenzie's proposal and felt that Dr. Burgess should be entrusted with the responsibility for advice to the Local Governments.[33]

Besides, F.C. Daukes remarked that without increasing the pay and allowances to Dr. Burgess, he could be entrusted with the additional responsibilities especially with regard to "survey of Upper India". Daukes was of the view that concerned Local Governments should incur the additional expenditure as they would benefit from the advice of Dr. Burgess on matters relating to conservation and restoration of monuments in their respective jurisdiction.[34]

However, S.C. Bailey noted on 26 January 1886 that it was not possible for the Home Department to control the activities of Archaeological Surveyors in the absence of a departmental head. He also stated that Burgess would be entrusted with the responsibility of supervising the work of surveys and conservation of archaeological monuments which would be conducted in an economical manner.[35]

BURGESS' RECOMMENDATION ON CONSERVATION OF MONUMENTS

On 27 January 1886, Burgess had submitted his detailed recommendations on conservation:

> Conservation work is for the present practically at a standstill but this is a department in which an unskilled officer may so readily do irremediable harm, that only men qualified by large archaeological and architectural knowledge and experience can properly advise the Local Governments aright in questions of this kind. Too much stress can hardly be laid on this; and all three Provincial

> Governments have expressed a conviction that when conservation is resumed, all work of the kind should be approved by the head of the Department before it is undertaken; but the Surveyors should call attention to monuments requiring conservation and supply all requisite information to the Public Works Department and the head of the Survey. In special cases it might be necessary for the latter to inspect the building.
>
> Much necessary, if not wanton, destruction of ancient Stupas, mounds and other remains has been caused by unscientific excavation. Few have any proper knowledge how to conduct an excavation and like conservation, it ought not to be allowed to anyone without the permission of the Department. Surveyors should report to their respective Governments and the head of the Department all private cases of excavation and endeavour to prevent them.[36]

The Government of India decided that in future, the survey and conservation of monuments of archaeological importance should be undertaken under the guidance of Dr. Burgess and as S.C. Bayley agreed, "His views in regard to conservation are, I believe, considered to be sound and he is not the man to be likely to be led into a collison with Local Governments."[37]

DOCUMENTATION OF MONUMENTS

Besides, Burgess also detailed the list of drawings, plans and description of architectural monuments to the Secretary, Government of India. He stated that little or no attention had been paid to document the architecture of monuments during the survey of archaeological monuments in North India. Further, he mentioned that architecture should hold the foremost place in the field of archaeology. He also elaborated that religious and social history of any given region is best depicted by its monuments. In this context, he referred to the monuments at Ahmedabad, Agra, Delhi, Lahore and in Canara whose design, splendour and ornamentation could be compared with the masterpieces of early European Art. In order to disseminate the splendour of Indian art and architecture, it was necessary to procure detailed drawings of these splendours from the Public Works Department or else employ draftsmen to copy the drawing for being available to public for wider dissemination and appreciation. Burgess also desired a photographic representation of the archaeological monuments as an alternative documentation. He called for a report on the existing drawings from several depositories of the Government agencies to be used for reference purposes. He even brought forth in his suggestions the publications on Indian architecture. He extolled the published volumes on monuments of Agra, Delhi, Lahore and Mount Abu which could handle interest in Indian antiquarian studies and their effect on the readers would have more impact than the published works on Buddhist remains spread over India and Punjab.[38]

A. Mackenzie, Secretary, Government of India circulated the suggestions of Burgess on archaeological conservation to the Chief Secretaries of Bombay, Bengal, North-West Provinces, Punjab and Central Provinces on 8 January 1886, and invited their comments/suggestions for embarking upon a publication programme of this nature. He also requested these governments to furnish drawings, plans, photo negatives, etc. of archaeological monuments, and buildings of importance. Mackenzie was of the opinion that the list, thus furnished, should be comprehensive and should indicate the place where requisite information could be located or found. He also requested that the duplicate copy of the list should also be furnished to the Archaeological Survey Department for Western and Southern India where Burgess is presently the professional adviser of the Government of India on archaeological matters.[39]

NOTES AND REFERENCES

1. Foreign Department, B General I, May 1884, No. 321.
2. Home, Archaeological and Conservation of Ancient Monuments, February 1885, No. 50.
3. Home, Archaeology and C.A.Ms., February 1885, No. 51.
4. Home, Archaeology and C.A.Ms., July 1885, Nos. 5-9 Notes.
5. *Ibid.*
6. *Ibid.*
7. Finance, Accounts A, December 1878, No. 571.
8. Home, Archaeology and C.A.Ms., July 1885, Nos. 5-9 Notes.
9. *Ibid.*
10. *Ibid.*
11. *Ibid.*
12. Home, Archaeology and C.A.Ms., July 1885, No. 5.
13. Home, Archaeology and C.A.Ms., July 1885, No. 8.
14. Home, Archaeology and C.A.Ms., July 1885, No. 7.
15. Home, Archaeology and C.A.Ms., July 1885, No. 15.
16. Home, Archaeology and C.A.Ms., September 1885, Nos. 45-46
17. Home, Archaeology and C.A.Ms., July 1885, No. 9.
18. *Asiatic Review*, January 1912, p. 80.
19. Home, Archaeology B, March 1882, No. 1.
20. Home, Archaeology A, July 1882, Nos. 13-15.
21. Home, Archaeology A, October 1882, No. 8.
22. *Ibid.*
23. Home, Archaeology and C.A.M., December 1883, Nos. 3-6.
24. Home, Archaeology and C.A.M., July 1882, No. 2.
25. An address delivered by Dr. J.PH. Vogel, Late Professor of Laiden and Ex. Superintendent of Archaeological Survey of India, at a meeting of the Indian Society of the Hague, November 14, 1916; published in the *Asiatic Review*, January 1921, pp. 80-82.
26. Home, Archaeology and C.A.Ms., September 1885, No. 49.
27. Revenue and Agriculture, Archaeology, August 1887, No. 2.
28. Home, Archaeology and Conservation of Ancient Monuments (C.A.Ms.), July 1885, Nos. 5-9, Notes.
29. Home, Archaeology, C.A.Ms. November 1885, No. 11.
30. Home, Archaeology, C.A.Ms., August 1886, No. 23.
31. Home, Archaeology, C.A.Ms., August 1886, Nos. 22-37, Notes.
32. *Ibid.*
33. *Ibid.*
34. *Ibid.*
35. *Ibid.*
36. Archaeology, C.A.Ms., August 1886, No. 25.
37. Home, Archaeology, C.A.Ms., August 1886, Nos. 22-37, Notes.
38. Home, Archaeology, C.A.Ms., January 1886, No. 1
39. Home, Archaeology, C.A.Ms., January 1886, No. 2.

CHAPTER X

After Cunningham: James Burgess

In order make selection to the post of Director General, several names were considered. The Government of India desired that the incumbent to the post of Director General should be an able successor of Cunningham. Lewis Rice, Director of Public Instruction in Mysore and Coorg, was one of the applicants to this post. He was then engaged in collection and decipherment of inscriptions in the Government of Mysore. Rice was not associated with the conservation and work connected with archaeology. His application was rejected by A. Mackenzie, Secretary, Home Department on the ground that the selected persons should have both architectural and engineering skills along with archaeology which involved the work connected with conservation.[1]

Besides, Major Cole had also put forth his claim. J. Gibbs, Member of the Governor-General in Council was not in his favour. In his view, he was an impracticable person.[2] Cunningham also did not support him and gave reasons for rejecting his candidature. He contended that "Major Cole has shown but little aptitude as archaeologist". He stated,

> Cole rests his claim on the fact that his duties as Curator of Ancient Monuments gave him superior opportunities of becoming acquainted with Northern India and also of seeing many parts of Southern and Western India. No doubt he has had very good opportunities of seeking the finest remains of Indian architecture. But a man is not to be judged by the opportunities, which he has had of becoming fit, but by the use, which he has made of those opportunities. A man may travel from the Himalaya Mountains to Cape Comorin and return no wiser than when he set out. Such of believe to be Cole's case. To judge by the results of his published works and by his Annual Reports as Curator, I consider that Cole has shown but very little aptitude as an archaeologist. He is neither a discoverer nor an investigator of ancient remains. His works are mostly brief compilations from the writings of others, which add nothing to what was already known. He is not an oriental scholar, but he is a good draughtsman. He is a good designer not an archaeologist and poorly fitted for the post of a Director of Archaeology.
>
> Cole's proceedings also as a Curator of Ancient Monuments have shown a want of tact in dealing with the superior authorities with whom he was brought in contact. He mistook his proper functions as a Curator of Ancient Monuments. It appears to me that it is the special function of the

Archaeological Department to advise the Government in such matters. A conservator is a repairer; and in some case he may also become a restorer; but in case can he be considered as an archaeological authority to decide upon what buildings are worthy of being preserved. His proper province is to advise as to the nature and the extent of the repairs that should be made to such buildings as the Archaeological Department may think it desirable to preserve, either for their intrinsic value as historical monuments or for their beauty as specimens of Indian architecture".[3]

However, Cunningham recommended Dr. Burgess. Besides, in 1871, Cunningham had earlier also recommended him as "the only fit person to succeed me hereafter as Director, Archaeological Survey of India".[4]

It may be stated though Burgess had interest in various branches of archaeology, he was also equally interested in the field of conservation of monuments. In 1881 he had made certain observations which were valuable for utilizing the debris and material of certain old buildings at Ahmedabad. Further, he stated,

> had this been a little better attended to in the past, we should not have had to regret so many interested monuments now utterly destroyed. The excuses for destroying these remains are always the same, they are desecrated, nobody cares for them. The fancy design in perforated stone work in the tombs and mosques would be of very little interest anywhere except in their original positions and the buildings in which they are thereby have acclaim to protection.[5]

Cunningham's desire for Burgess becoming his successor, which he expressed in 1871, and which found expression in a Resolution No. 5-95-113 dated 15 March 1886, was passed by the Home Department on the appointment of Dr. Burgess as Director General, Archaeological Survey of India. In this Resolution it was stated,

> The Governor-General in Council is of opinion that so far as the actual work of survey is concerned, it will conduce the efficiency if Dr. Burgess is recognized as occupying the position of Director General of the department and the local surveyors are made directly subordinate to him. The cost of the survey is entirely imperial and it is in the interest of economy that there should be one executive head of the Department responsible to the Government of India for exercising a detailed professional check over the work done by the local surveys.
>
> As regards Conservation, it was observed in the Resolution of June 1885 that 'the duties of the surveyors will be not only to conduct the work of survey but also to advise as to the various monuments of antiquity or interest which require to be preserved or restored, the necessary repairs being carried out by the Public Works Department of the several local governments and administrations under the general supervision of the Archaeological surveyors. The primary responsibility for conservation will remain, as at present, with the local governments and administration in their Public Works Department. The surveyors will be on the footing of professional advisors to the Local Governments, with the right of initiating suggestions and calling attention to requirements. The strictly archaeological portion of their work should be kept separate from that relating to conservation and schemes for the preservation or restoration of monuments and should be submitted by them direct to the Local Governments concerned, to be carried out by the Public Works Department from such money as the Local Government can make available for the purpose supplemented by any grants-in-aid, which the Government of India may be in a position to contribute'.
>
> It must be clearly understood that the Archaeological surveyors are not to undertake the conservation of Ancient Monuments either with funds of their own or of the Public Works Department. A small provision not exceeding Rs. 50 monthly may be made in each surveyor's budget for clearing out jungle growth or performing such urgent petty works of conservation as may cost conveniently be carried out by his party when surveying a monument but the main work of conservation and repair

> is to be left to the Local Governments in their Public Department. It is desirable that the Local Governments should have the best available advice in respect of such matters and accordingly the Governor-General in Council is pleased to order that the communications addressed by the surveyors to the Local Governments regarding matters of conservation shall be sent under flying seal through Dr. Burgess who shall be at liberty to call for any further information that seems to him necessary and will, when the case is complete, forward it to the Local Governments with his own remarks, criticisms and suggestions. The responsibility of action will thereafter be entirely with the Local Government.[6]

In pursuance of the Government of India's Resolution, Dr. Burgess assumed the Office of Director General of Archaeology on 25 March 1886. The Secretary of State had approved a salary of Rs. 1,500 per month and £80 on his annual visit to England for six months during May-October.[7]

Sourindranath Roy was sceptical at the role of the Director General, who could only offer expert comments but took no decisions. The Government of India did not vest in the Office of Director General any power to take initiatives or decisions. The Director General of Archaeology had no authority to alter any programmes of conservation without reference to the Government of India.[8]

As this arrangement was likely to cause delay in transacting matters of urgent business, the Secretary, P.W.D., Government of Bengal addressed a communication to the Secretary, Government of India on 26 August 1886 wherein he conveyed the desire of the Lt. Governor, Bengal that the duties of Director General of Archaeology, as enshrined in the Resolution dated 15 March 1886, was not be to implemented in a satisfactory manner and requested that the Government of Bengal may be relieved of the responsibility of intervening in any way between the Director General of Archaeology and his subordinates. This would enable Dr. Burgess, the present Director General of Archaeology, the direct control on matters conserving archaeology. The Secretary made some concrete suggestions to amend the Resolution in a way that would bestow some powers to Dr. Burgess to function in an effective manner and requested the Government of India to issue orders afresh after taking the suggestions of the Lt. Governor into consideration.[9]

On 20 September 1886, A.P. MacDonell, Secretary, Government of India replied to the Secretary, P.W.D., Government of Bengal, and emphasized the role of Local Governments in effectively carrying out the conservation of archaeological monuments.

The Local Governments could play a pivotal role in liaising with the district offices and the Archaeological Survey for effective implementation of conservation programme of archaeological monuments of intrinsic value. The Secretary also impressed upon having cordial relations with the Local Governments, without whose cooperation the success of archaeological matters would be in jeopardy.[10]

Burgess had a positive approach towards the conservation of archeological monuments. He had emphasized this fact to A.P. MacDonell, Secretary, Home Department on 23 April 1886. He stated,

> survey work, if badly done, was wasted money and could be redone; but a monument ruined by ignorant conservation was for ever lost and if not modified and controlled, would almost certainly lead to the ruin of archaeology of most interesting monuments through ill advised conservation and restoration; and if by accepting the position offered I could prevent this – though I did nothing more – it would be a service of the highest ultimate value to that science we had so much interest in.[11]

Apart from Burgess, Keith who was Archaeological Surveyor in North-West Provinces also apprised the Secretary, Government of India about his views on conservation on 2 November 1886. He emphasized that personal supervision of conservation of monuments by Local Governments should be the centralized basis of archaeological activity. He also laid stress on monumental conservation as it would be a permanent sentiment of history. He stated that "Monumental conservation is so important that, if the records of the Archaeological Survey have been compiling for years were destroyed by fire, the monuments would remain to us." To prove his contention, Keith referred to the monumental volume, *The famous monuments of Central India*, which had given considerable attention to monumental conservation. Keith also made a reference to his correspondence with General Pitt Rivers, who inspected the English monuments at home, and the Society for Protection of Ancient Buildings, where considerable attention had been paid to conservation programmes of monuments of archaeological value. He emphasized similar treatment to be applied with regard to conservation plans of monuments in India. He believed that 'all the great monuments of India could be secured under an economical systematized plan but they ought to be regularly inspected. This is a duty for which the Public works have neither the taste nor time, but, if assisted by a Special Officer, much injury might be avoided by getting rid of the accretions caused by vegetation. Dr. Burgess cannot, under any circumstances, give this work his personal supervision.'[12]

The Government of India experienced great difficulties in increase of quantum of work in the Home Department, primarily due to annexation of Upper Burma, and the Government was seriously considering in reducing the burden of the Home Department.

It decided to transfer the business relating to Archaeological Survey and conservation of ancient monuments from Home Department to Revenue and Agriculture Department.

The issue relating to the transfer of business relating to archaeological survey and conservation of archaeological monuments was discussed in detail by the Home Department as well as Revenue and Agriculture Department, which had accepted in principle the transfer of business from the Home Department.[13]

Finally, the Government of India passed a Resolution in the Home Department (Public) No. 16-759A-759 dated 1887 that "It appears to the Governor-General in Council that all matters relating to Archaeological Surveys and the Conservation of Ancient Monuments can in future be more conveniently considered and disposed off in the Revenue and Agriculture Department which already deals with all other survey branches (except Marine Surveys) and with Museums."[14] (Appendix-XXI).

A sum of Rs. 10,000 was allocated in the budget estimates for 1887-88 towards grant-in-aid for conservation of ancient monuments.[15]

Burgess performed his assigned work sincerely and with great zeal and devotion. He visited far-flung areas and took extensive notes on the dilapidated condition of remote temples of Srisailam in Madras Presidency, which were rarely visited by Europeans. Burgess also submitted a note to the Chief Secretary, Government of Madras on 24 March 1886 before assuming the charge of the post of Director General of Archaeology. He referred to the vandalism of temples of Shankaracharya by a band of Rohillas and consequent damage to the shrines in search of jewels and other valuables. He attributed the unfortunate damages due to casual attitude of the temple officials for not affording security measures to guard the temple premises.[16]

Dr. Burgess also stressed the need for adoption of strict measures for preventing the destruction of objects of archaeological and historical interest. He also referred to vandalism committed by railway contractors who indulged in unauthorized removal of archaeological ruins without the knowledge of the Archaeological Department. He referred to correspondence relating to removal of archaeological ruins from Chandravati, erstwhile capital of Gujarat, on the foothills of Mount Abu in Sirohi State, where over 40,000 cubic feet of stones were removed for railway construction works. Dr. Burgess requested the Government of India for its intervention in the matter and refrain the Sirohi State from illegal removal of fragments of archaeological importance by the railway contractors. If possible, the services of railway officials, European contractors and engineers could be taken to stop the illicit removal of material of archaeological interest. He also referred to unwanton destruction of brick mounds and the sites of ancient villages or old stupas by railway and road contractors. The extracts of letter from Burgess were forwarded to the local governments and administrations to exercise vigilance during excavations conducted by private parties. Besides, Burgess was also apprised of the decision of Governor-General in Council that members of the Archaeological Department should confine themselves to reporting to their respective Governments and should abstain from interference in matters not concerning them, unless they have been specifically permitted by the Local Governments.[17]

On Burgess' report on the damages to Chandravati ruins caused by illegal removal of material by railway contractors, the Government of India was in favour of approaching the Public Works Department for restraining the contractors from illegal utilization of ruins of intrinsic interest and said that the consent of concerned Local Governments should be obtained who would consult the Director General, Archaeology to advise in cases of doubt or dispute.

The proposal of Dr. Burgess in this regard did not find favour with the Government of India who thought that this would amount to interference with the discretion of the Local Governments and also give grounds to mistrust. However, it was felt that the Foreign Department should be approached for taking up the matter with the political authorities of the concerned princely states.[18]

The Government of India was seriously contemplating to issue a circular for prevention of desecration of ancient monuments along with archaeological ruins in British India but was confronted with the problem of preventing the material of archaeological interest from being sold to contractors in princely states.[19]

Besides, the officers in the Revenue and Agriculture Department attributed vandalism of Chandravati ruins to the Archaeological Department.[20] However, the efforts of Burgess were not in vain. The Government of India issued a Circular Public Works No. 4 on 8 September 1886 for taking adequate measures to prevent the railway contractors and others on the illicit removal of stones of antiquarian interest for construction purposes.[21]

Copy of that important circular was issued not only to Local Governments and Residencies but also to the Inspector General of Military Works, Director General of Railways, Consulting Engineers to the Government of India for Guaranteed Railways, Calcutta, Lahore, Agra and Lucknow, and Director General of Telegraph in India for compliance.

Meanwhile, A. Rea, assistant to Burgess in Madras, submitted a report emphasizing the importance of photographs for the Archaeological Department. He stated,

> the great importance of photography in the scientific interests of archaeology is by no means overlooked and no opportunity is lost of employing it when the purposes of the survey will best be served by doing so; and there are many cases in which a photo shows a building or particular portion of it, much better than any drawing can. But in any case for the accurate survey of the building to show its architectural arrangements, structure and details – one or more plans, sections, elevations and detail drawings are always necessary whereas a photo showing a general view of the structure, with one or more others of certain features best shown by photography are sufficient.[22]

However, Burgess was not happy with the progress of work in all the archaeological circles. He, therefore, thought it prudent to report to the Secretary, Government of India on 16 March 1887 (252). He stated:

> I regret the necessity of laying the following report respecting the Archaeological Surveys in Upper India before Government. But I do not consider they are doing the work to be expected of them or are capable of doing that work and it becomes my duty, however painful, or bring to notice what I cannot undertake to be responsible for.
>
> The present organization was devised in 1885 and intended to continue for 5 years; but if, after 17 months' trial, it be found to be unsatisfactory, it may be as well to consider what is best to be done before more expenditure is incurred.
>
> Archaeology is a science requiring special knowledge and training, and it would be as reasonable to appoint the officers of the Geological or Trigonometrically Survey from the members of the Medical, Forest or Educational Service as to nominate the Archaeological Surveyors from like sources. Indian Archaeology is unfortunately as yet but little understood, but its principles can only be properly acquired on the basis of a high class education and a large acquaintance with the various sources of information existing, foreign as well as English. We cannot expect from men of few qualifications or acquirements, beyond a liking for curious of any sort, the intelligent management of a survey requiring an acquaintance with the progress of the lithic arts, of mythology, of paleography of early Indian History and Geography and c. A man with little knowledge of architecture cannot be expected to describe accurately early Hindu or Muslim buildings and remains and he must fail in fixing with any approximation to truth the dates of the monuments he meets with – one of the most essential and useful qualifications of the surveyors. So with Mythology, the 'dilettanti' sadly confound Hindu, Jaina and Buddha remains – apart from the map in shrines –.
>
> For the practical field duties of an archeological surveyor in India, there are two classes of qualifications: (1) a knowledge of what has been already done, with the ability of test the result arrived at and to prosecute research, implying an acquaintance with Sanskrit, Epirgraphy, History, Ancient Geography, Religions, Mythology and c. (2) such a knowledge of the development of architecture and art as will enable its possessor to relegate at once any monument to its proper place in the chronometrical scale, with the ability to select with judgement the drawings to be made correctly to illustrate any structure to describe it in accurate terms and to teach the draftsmen how to delineate in cases of special difficulty. If he can also photograph, it will be an advantage.
>
> Now it cannot be said that the staff of the surveys in Upper India were selected because of their fitness in either of these branches. With the exception of Dr. Fuhrer who is well qualified both by education and aptitude in the first, none of the others have had an equivalent to a university training nor possess in a marked degree any of the qualifications essential to an Archaeologist. Nothing therefore, can be expected from their five years' employment but the disappointment of crude work; the survey will be as far as from finished in 1890 as now. Even for an architectural and artistic survey only – this staff is unsuitable; the surveyors are not good draftsmen and do not select judiciously what ought to be done, while a single highly paid draftsman, as arranged for in the scheme, cannot be expected to do much work in a season. The Schools of Art would be encouraged by the surveys obtaining their draftsmen from them and with proper supervision, School of Art students make excellent draftsmen and can be got at a fourth of the salary proposed in the scheme; they also become fitted by this work for more highly paid appointment.[23]

Burgess was also not satisfied with the performance of Beglar. He lodged a complaint to the Secretary, Government of Bengal on 28 February 1887 in which he expressed his displeasure towards Beglar's work.[24] He found Beglar's report as incomplete, unsatisfactory, expensive and devoid of any photographic representation. He sought the opinion of the Lt. Governor in this regard before he could report the performance of Beglar to the Government of India.[25]

The Government of Bengal did not agree with the views of Burgess with regard to his report on the work performance of Beglar and his assistants. On the contrary, the Government of Bengal was of the opinion, "Mr. Beglar has now been employed for many years on archaeological work in Bengal and has always carried out the work entrusted to him with zeal and efficiency."[26]

Besides, Burgess had also lodged complaints against Major Keith, Surveyor, N.W.P. and Oudh Circle and also to the Secretary, Government of India on 16 March 1887. He had referred to the incapacity of Major Keith handling architectural work or antiquarian surveys. Besides, Burgess stated that Keith had no specialized knowledge of any branch of archaeology.[27] He also summarily criticized Rodgers, Punjab Surveyor, and stated that as he was not a knowledgeable person, his work and labour was not found useful in the field of archaeology. He stated that only in the Department of Numismatics, Mr. Rodgers was well versed.[28]

Burgess felt that the Archaeology Department was found on the wrong basis. It was an expensive organization without the basis of efficiency. In the absence of qualified staff, a creditable survey could not be expected. He favoured demobilisation of the present staff and deployment of temporary staff till such time basis for a better organization could be provided.[29]

On 6 April 1887, Burgess addressed a communication to the Secretary, Revenue and Agriculture Department and emphasized that, "Provincial boundaries cannot always be adhered to; when a survey party finds that monuments of the same age and style spread into adjoining territory, it is best that the whole group should be surveyed by the same staff; for example, the early temple of Mysore should be surveyed and published along with those of Dharwar."[30]

The Government of India responded to the suggestion of Burgess with regard to reorganization of the working of Archaeological Survey. W.R. Lawrence, Under Secretary, Government of India in his letter dated 27 April 1887 conveyed the views of the Governor-General in Council that since the views of Burgess were normally not accepted by the Local Governments, he called upon the details of the progress of work done by each surveyor and examine the quality of work done in comparison with cost involved.[31]

Burgess immediately replied on 2 May 1887 and stated that the surveyors did not possess the requisite essential qualifications for their prescribed duties. Besides, Major Keith and Beglar resented advisory functions in the field of archaeology particularly conservation of monuments. Burgess reiterated that the reason of emphasizing reorganization of Archaeological Department was to ensure introduction of efficiency in the organization.[32] E.C. Buck, Secretary, Government of India informed Burgess about the inability of the Government of India in effecting reorganization of the Department as suggested. Buck also conveyed to Burgess, the Government of India's concern about efficient working of the Archaeological Department whose Head of the Department was absent from India for six months each year and wondered why this practice should not be discontinued.[33]

On 9 November 1887, Burgess communicated to the Government of India, the reasons for his absence to England for six months each year. He stated that the annual visit to England was part of the contractual agreement of his appointment as Director General of Archaeology. Besides, he detailed flimsy reasons to justify his annual visit to England, viz., experience in consultation with great authorities in archeology, viz., James Fergusson, Edward Thomas, Dr. John Muir and other orientalists; consultation of published work in various libraries; and optimum utilization of services of draftsmen and staff while he was away.

In conclusion, he stated that since the Government of India was usually discouraging the good work done by him, he expressed his desire to retire in 1889 on the completion of 15 years of his service.[34]

The Secretary, Government of North-West Provinces and Oudh, gave an estimate of the duties of Major Keith on 3 November 1887, and expressed satisfaction over the performance of work done by him. The Secretary also conveyed the displeasure of the Lt. Governor over the tenor of the letter addressed by Burgess to the Government.

The Lt. Governor observed with regret that the tone of Burgess' letter was marked by a want of consideration and even of courtesy, towards an officer who, whatever might be his defects of technical training, he spared no pains in the face of difficulties and much discouragement to perform the work entrusted to him to the best of his knowledge and abilities.[35]

During the tenure of Burgess, emphasis was laid on the survey of Sharqui architecture of Jaunpur which was a notable work.[36]

Besides, conservation work was also undertaken though not on a large scale. Conservation work of the following was undertaken during his tenure: Ajanta Caves,[37] Baradari of Daulat Bagh at Ajmer,[38] Hasan Khan's Tomb and certain Muslim buildings at Sasaram,[39] conservation work of monuments in Baroda State[40] and Punjab,[41] and monuments of Islamic architecture at Bijapur.[42]

Burgess applied for 33 days' privilege leave to visit the museums and schools of art & architecture in Egypt and Athens, and interacting with archaeologists so as to acquire knowledge and experience which would be useful in discharge of his official duties.[43] This shows Burgess' consciousness towards archaeology.

A circular No. 5, P.W.D. dated 14 December 1887 was issued by the Secretary, Government of India in which instructions regarding prior consent of the Archaeological Survey of India had to be obtained before disposing the objects and ruins of archaeological and historical interest.[44] A similar Circular, P.W.D., No. 4 dated 8 September 1886, had also been circulated in 1886.

BURGESS AND CHECKING OF ANTIQUE TRADE AND MOVEMENT

Besides, Burgess was the first person to check the menace of touts masquerading as antique dealers or antiquarians. He include the clause in the Resolution No. 5-95-113 dated 15 March 1886 which debarred public officers from disposing antiquities acquired by them and also Public Works Circular No. 4 dated 8 September 1886 for bidding excavating ancient remains of any kind by obtaining prior consent of the Archaeological Survey. Burgess also made an amendment to the Treasure Trove Act, which would make it unlawful to export antiquities without an official permit.

Major Keith addressed a communication in this regard to the Under Secretary of State for India. He emphasized that some stringent measures need to be taken to prevent illicit export of antiques to Europe.

He stated that during his sojourn in India, he found private agencies actively at work in collecting art treasures. They were stimulated by no love of art but by the high price being offered for the unique archaeological speciments. In Calcutta, one gentleman assured him that he was in the habit of sending a monthly installment of sculptured heads to Europe. Similarly, an officer intimated to him that he had a box full of Greek heads from Hoti Mardan in the Punjab. After the Franco-Prussian war, Dr. Jagor from Berlin was allowed to take away from India as many antiquities as he could lay hands upon, thereby enriching Berlin at the expense of India.

Keith opined,

> the people of India have a right to feel aggrieved at the withdrawal from India of these antiquities. In a country, which boasts of a living art its chief value, is in reproduction. Indian art will never be revived through European agency, but European agency may drive a fatal blow at it by encouraging European copying. Only a Hindu who thinks as such can interpret Hindu art and presumably the best way to encourage it is by familiarizing the princes and artisans of India with the best examples of their own handicraft. This can never be done when the best examples are withdrawn.[45]

On this matter, Burgess also gave his advice to the Under Secretary, Government of India on 4 January 1889 (No. 12).

> 2. The allegation made to His Lordship on the appropriation by officers, civil and military, of the remains of Indian antiquities, sculptures, coins, engraved seals and gems are by no means exaggerated. That hitherto they have been chiefly carried off for sale, I am doubtful, though some, I believe, have been so. Officers collect them for their 'pals' and to present to distinguished tourists or to adorn the lobbies of houses and gardens at home at Simla and elsewhere.
>
> 3. The demand and prices now offered for such objects have become so great that natives are induced to search for them everywhere, both in our own territory and in Swat and Buner where some important Buddhist shrines must, not very long since have been dug up for sake of sculptures. Had no such demand existed, these remains would in all probability have been left undisturbed till some scientific exploration of them could have been made.
>
> 4. The present state of things is all the more to be regretted because no satisfactory exploration has yet been made of any of these very interesting Buddhist buildings. At Takht-i-Bahi, Jamalgiri and other sites which were excavated by sappers without skilled supervision, the work appears to have been done in a rough and ready way and sculptures sent off without any careful record of their relative positions or of all that most important detailed information which can only be secured while excavations are in progress, of which investigators like Dr. Schliemann and the German Archaeologists are always so very careful about. The sculptures from different buildings and places were inextricably mixed up; they lay, I believe, at the public works sheds at Lahore until two of the finest – quite unique – had disappeared; and then Major Cole divided them among different Museums – Lahore, Rangoon, Madras, etc. Their value largely depended on the completeness of the series for each place and building; but this division of the whole, without reference to original connexion – as if they had been so many independent 'curiosities' – broke up the different series and so destroyed this scientific value. With proper care during the excavation, the drums at least of several stupas and the connexion of the details in other structures might have been preserved almost entire: instead of which we have only disconnected panels without knowing whether any two or more belonged to the same building and still less the order in which they were arranged so as to tell the stories they had represented to every pilgrim to the shrines from which they have been removed. Could the remains in Swat and other frontier states and what still exists within our own borders be left undisturbed – though it were for fifty years – until a scientific survey could be carried out, we should learn much more than from the past excavations or any number of separate sculptures collected for private individuals, even if they were not distributed all over the world.
>
> 5. Some of the sculptures privately obtained do not leave the country but they are practically lost to science. In the mess-house of the Guides at Mardan, for example, are three very interesting figures of royal personages which not one scholar in a thousand has any chance of ever seeing. Two of them do duty at the jambs of the fire-places and the poor kings have been varnished or coated with Day and Mortin's blacking to make them shine! The third is placed in a niche of the wall. There are not very many such statues and it is to be regretted, these are not where they could be studied; they are evidently portraits. In the Lahore Museum, there is one somewhat similar to the third of these; and Dr. Stein and I agree that it bears a remarkable resemblance to the head of an early coin from the

frontier figured in the British Museum catalogue of Bactrian and Indo-Scythian coins. This suggests the comparison of all these regal statues with the heads of kings and kinglets represented on their coins. The identification of even a few would help to settle both the date of the sculptures and the domain of one or more series of these kings. But so long as these statues are in remote mess-houses or in the possession of officers, their friends and others, such study is impossible.

6. To stop the present traffic will perhaps now be a matter of some difficulty. Government can only appeal to the consciences of officers. The smaller and more important separate articles occasionally found – seals, rings and coins and c. – Government can bring within the Treasure Trove Act, by doing away with the absurd exception as to articles of small value. An officer finds, or has brought to him by the finder, an engraved sard, or a coin or an ancient brass ring and says – 'this stone, or coin, or ring, is of so little intrinsic value that it need not to be reported to Government', and thus important 'finds' are never made known and pass into private hands as 'curious'. The exception in the Act ought to be rescinded and the whole made less technical, speedier in setting with finders and more on the lines of the famous Danish Act which has been so largely adopted on the continent of Europe and with such excellent results.

7. The only suggestions I can offer to check the traffic in antiquities complained of are these:

(i) H.E. the Commander-in-Chief might be solicited to issue such orders to officers and persons connected with the Army as may seem calculated to stop their participating in the securing and appropriation of antiquities;

(ii) The Lieutenant Governor of the Punjab and N.W.P. should be consulted as to whether they would use official influence to prevent the private acquisition of such objects by civil officers whether for their personal pleasure or to present or sell to others. This should apply not only to Magistrates of every class, but to Engineers of all officers to the canal, salt, opium, ecclesiastical and Forest Department;

(iii) That all objects found in our own territories should be brought under the Treasure Trove Act which should make it illegal as in Greece, Italy and Denmark to export antiquities without an official permit from an officer specially authorized to grant such; and

(iv) Sculptures in private hands might be required by Government for the Museums where alone they can be of real importance. Separately they may gratify a half educated unscientific curiosity. They are not really of very high artistic merit, though there is a freedom and grace about their excavations and general style but anyone who compares them with even the late (perhaps contemporary) Greek sculptures excavated by Dr. Const at Pergamum, will see at a glance how ordinary is the 'art' of these Gandhara sculptures, though far superior to anything Hindu. Their chief value, as already stated, lies in groups of them, as complete and extensive as possible, illustrating the history, religious feeling and forms and art of the frontier provinces during the centuries immediately preceding and following the commencement of our era.

I would also be in favour of an appeal to officers and others now possessed of antiques which they have purchased, to give them up, at least for a reasonable remuneration so that they may be permanently preserved in Museums. Presents might not only be acknowledged but labeled in the Museum as presented by such and such a donor.

Trusting these remarks may be of some slight use for the information of Government.[46]

Besides, Sir George Birdwood, an authority on Indian Art and Archaeology, addressed a private letter to J.A. Godley, Permanent Under Secretary of State for India on 29 January 1889 on menace of export of antiquarian remains of India and squarely blamed the military officers for the illegal export of antiques. He suggested that representations should be made to Lord Lansdowne with a view to the restrictive orders which had been issued for the guidance of the Civil Service being extended – 'if the Government of India think fit – to the Army'.[47]

J.A. Godley forwarded the letter of Birdwood to J.C. Ardagh, Joint Private Secretary to Viceroy and requested him to take steps for curbing this menace.[48]

Burgess was also apprised of this correspondence. The outcome of the effort was that the Government of India decided to issue a Resolution Circular No. 24-4-2. Revenue and Agriculture (Arch.) dated 28 March 1889 in which attention of Local Governments to the relevant provisions of the Treasure Trove Act was called for implementation. In other words, it was an amendment of the Treasure Trove Act.[49]

However, S. Roy was of the view that though sincere efforts were made for this laudable endeavour, but the results were not worth the efforts made in this direction.[50]

THE ANCIENT MONUMENT CONSERVATION FUND

In the meanwhile, Beglar, the Archaeological Surveyor, Bengal had forwarded to the Secretary, Land Records and Agriculture Department on 12 July 1889, a scheme for the conservation of ancient monuments in India. He proposed contribution by the District Boards and Municipalities to contribute ¼ of its total income towards a fund which should be called "The Ancient Monuments Conservation Fund". The amount of the contribution in favour of Director General of Ancient Monuments and a trained engineer should be selected as its head. The selected officer should be conversant with the study of archaeology. He should be paid from the fund but should be an officer attached to the Government of India and the responsible head. The Director General should have exclusive control over the fund and the entire cost of conservation in each Province should be met from the fund. Besides, the expenditure should be supplemented by Imperial or Provincial aid if considered necessary. He further stated that the Secretary, Public Works Department of each province would be designated as ex-officio Director General in each province and would be vested with certain powers. The designated officer would also function as the President of the Provincial Board which would comprise of local people residing in the Provinces concerned, of which two-third of the members would be from the organizations which have contributed substantially towards the fund and one-third would be nominated by the Government. The Provincial Curator would be designated as ex-officio Secretary to the Board and would also direct the work relating to conservation. The Board would also transact the entire business relating to the conservation in the concerned Province. Besides, it would also consider the Budget estimate in the month of January each year. An annual report of the progress made would be submitted to the Government of India for information and orders.[51]

On 27 February 1890, Governor-General in Council reacted to this proposal and did not consider it practicable and expressed his inability to accept it and referred to a resolution formulated by the Government of India in consultation with Burgess which was soon issued.[52]

After Burgess relinquished his office in 1889, the post of the Director General was left vacant. This was primarily due to the fact that the Government of India followed a policy of retrenchment vigorously and the Archaeological Survey was the first to suffer since it was viewed by some officials 'a mere luxury'. In their opinion: "The Department is a luxury and judging from the recent account of the repair and renovation of a statue which appeared in the papers, its labours are not always well directed."[53]

But Auckland Colvin, Member of the Council remarked, "I am not prepared to say that the Archaeological Department is a luxury but I am quite sure that we cannot agree to recommend any increase to salaries connected with it. In my judgement we ought not to do so; and from repeated instances lately, it is evident that the Secretary of State will not listen to proposals of this kind of present."[54]

Sir Charles Aitchison, Member of the Revenue Department, noted on 14 September 1888 that if the post of Director General of Archaeology was considered as luxury, then it should be abolished.[55]

S.C. Bayley, Member of the Council, opined:

> The Department, it must be admitted, is to a certain extent a luxury, not a necessity. Its recent reorganization is a far from satisfactory plan and unlikely to work well in practice; without good professional supervision, it would certainly do more harm than good for none of our surveyors are qualified to work independently. Moreover, its work, so far as the protection of ancient monuments is concerned, depends entirely on the funds which can be allotted to this purpose. At present Local Governments who complain that they cannot keep their roads and public buildings in repair, are not likely to be able to spend anything on their ancient monuments and the Budget grant in our Department of Rs. 50,000 has this year been cut down to Rs. 10,000 so that in neither direction is there much prospect of the Archaeological Department being able to do useful work. All those considerations led me to doubt whether it was worth retaining the Department at all on its present footing.[56]

The Finance Committee was appointed by the Government of India in 1886 to examine the expenditure of the various organs of public service with a view to enforce retrenchment. The Committee, in particular, observed the mounting costs of the Archaeological Survey, which resulted in reduction of costs towards its establishment by the Government of India. However, it proposed that unnecessary expenditure during the "time of financial emergency perhaps ought to be retrenched".[57]

After considering the note of the Finance Committee on the Archaeological Survey Department, in the Revenue and Agriculture Department, W.R. Lawrence, the Under Secretary, informed the Department of Finance and Commerce on 16 May 1888 that the budget of the Archaeological Department had been considerably reduced. The post of surveyor of North-West Provinces, left vacant on the retirement of Major Keith, had been abolished and the annual visit of Burgess to England had since been curtailed. The Revenue and Agriculture Department felt that further reduction in the expenditure of Archaeological Survey Department was not possible. However, Lawrence concluded by stating that after the term of Archaeology Surveyor was completed, the reorganization of the Department would be considered.[58]

At the request of the Secretary, Revenue and Agricultural Department, Dr. Burgess prepared a note relating to the archaeological survey on 9 February 1889. In his note, he lamented the destruction caused to the monuments due to the deployment of unskilled personnel. He emphasized that "What is most essential is an Architect, skilled in the styles of architecture and who is also an antiquary to superintend and decide on all matters of conservation. It is lamentable to see what injury is done by unskillful but expensive repairs and restorations of ancient monuments carried out by the Engineers in India." He particularly referred to the responsibility entrusted to the Public Works Department of a particular province to carry out business in respect of archaeological conservation in a particular Local Government. He was of the opinion that in future only qualified architectural surveyors should be consulted and their approval obtained before it is submitted to the Public Works Department for carrying out necessary repairs. In his view, that was 'essential' to be preservation of ancient monuments as such. So far the whole of North India, he wanted an additional 'architectural archaeologist' who besides conducting minor surveys, would be responsible for conservation work.

Burgess recommended Rea and Cousens for carrying out the activities concerning conservation and survey of monuments on Peninsula. Rea might be deputed to Central Provinces or Hyderabad and Cousens to Rajputana and Sind or to Central India. Besides, Burgess recommended Dr. Fuhrer for work connected with conservation in North-West Provinces and Oudh. He also recommended that E.W. Smith could be retained for conservation work of monuments in Northern India with a small complement of staff. Burgess was of the opinion that Smith as an architectural surveyor was highly qualified and capable of giving sound advice in the field of conservation.

Burgess pointed that archaeology as the history of art, the surveyors were the exponents of history and are excellent judges of art and archaeology and that they could contribute substantially towards technical education.[59]

Another note was also submitted by Burgess on 20 February 1889 wherein he eulogized his own role in connection with conservation work at Ahmedabad, Bijapur, Ambernath, etc. where he had contributed substantially towards conservation at modest expenditure, wherein a saving of Rs. 10,000 was made. Similarly, the same procedure was adopted by him in Upper India where he carried out restoration works and utilized inexpensive measures of conservation. He was of the opinion that Jai Singh's observatory (Jantar Mantar) at Delhi could have been restored at a considerable outlay and the money spent on white-washing and restoration work on the monuments of lesser significance could have been easily avoided.

Burgess was further of the opinion that activities concerning conservation and excavations that do not come under the purview of the Government of India should be referred to a qualified Architectural Archaeologist which he had earlier proposed. He also contended that if the funds could not be secured, the post may be kept in abeyance until they can and "the best possible done with a material in hand".[60]

However, Burgess' proposals for a good "architectural archaeologist" was rejected on the ground that

> the good architectural archaeologist would no doubt be able to advise Local Governments on matters of conservation but as Government understands the position, the aim should be to reduce the staff and the expenditure to the lowest scale possible and compatible with the requirements of technical education. Both Rea and Cousens are competent architects. They can advise the Madras and Bombay Governments and when their work is over in those Presidencies, they can advise Northern India. The Government would, therefore, eliminate the good architectural archaeologist who would merely in a measure take the place vacated by Dr. Burgess. Rea and Cousens should be retained. We cannot support the appointment of a new architect and archaeologist. We can only deal with proposals to keep on a certain section of the Archaeological Department.
>
> As the Department will now have no one responsible head, it would be suggested that all the staff that is retained be placed under Rea and Cousens i.e. divided into two parties of which Mr. Rea should be at the head of one and Cousens at the head of the other. Each party would be placed under the orders and direction of the Local Government of the Province in which it is working.
>
> The aim of the reduced Department should be to make a survey and description of each monument or building of sufficient, architectural or archaeological interest in each province with suggestions for conservation. The provincial authorities should be responsible for conservation.[61]

On 1 June 1889, Burgess retired from Government service. This was a year earlier than his prescribed due date. He undertook the responsibility of completing the pending work on his publications. After his retirement, the Government of India did not approve his successor to head the survey. Madras and Bombay Governments retained the services of archaeological surveyors. The Government of North-West Provinces and Oudh was allowed to retain the services of Dr. Fuhrer, a German scholar, on reduced emoluments and small establishment. The Governments of Bengal and Punjab along with the princely states had no surveyors in their employment.

In order to justify its action with regard to curtailment of funds allotted towards archaeological and antiquarian research, the Government of India passed a Resolution No. 2-5-60, Archaeological Revenue and Agriculture dated 5 May 1890 in which the future of Archaeological Survey Department was highlighted.

> ...In view of the approaching termination of the 5 years period for which this scheme was approved, the Government has again had the work and constitution of the Archaeological survey under its consideration. The existing organization was commented on by the Finance Committee as unduly expensive and H.E. the Governor-General in Council has determined that the scale of expenditure is larger than is necessary or desirable. In some respects the results had hardly justified expectations; works under the different Surveyors had advanced unequally and a large quantity of unpublished material had accumulated. H.E. the Governor-General in Council is desirous that archaeological investigations should not be altogether abandoned till they have been brought to a satisfactory stage of completeness but he considers that as soon as is consistent with existing engagements and pledges, the Department should be reduced to the permanent minimum at which it is desirable to maintain it and that for some time to come, a considerable portion of the funds allotted to the archaeological budget should be devoted to the publication of the information already collected.
>
> Dr. Burgess's retirement took effect from the 1st June 1889 and the Government of India decided that the appointment of the Director of the Archaeological Survey should not be filled up.
>
> With regard to the rest of the establishment, the Governor-General in Council decided that the arrangements tentatively sanctioned in 1885 should, as far as possible under the altered circumstances created by Dr. Burgess' earlier retirement, continue undisturbed till the 1st October 1890. The only immediate steps resolved on affect the survey operations in Bengal and the Punjab. The Archaeological Surveyor of Bengal has already received instructions to close field operations and to devote himself to the completion of the reports on the field operations of past years. It was accordingly arranged that he should retire on the 31 March 1890, but his assistant will continue to work out in Northern Bengal a programme arranged by Dr. Burgess. The appointment of the Assistant Surveyor and staff will not be continued after the 1st October 1890. The Archaeological Surveyor of the Punjab has also been directed to close all field operations and to complete his reports thereon. His subordinate staff has been transferred to the N.W.P. and Oudh circle and he will be employed till the termination of his five years' agreement in numismatic work.
>
> The actual staff to be maintained after the 1st October 1890 should, the Governor-General in Council considers, be reduced to the following: H. Cousens, Archaeological Surveyor; H. Rea, Archaeological Surveyor, Dr. E. Hultzech, Epigraphist; A. Fuhrer for general antiquarian and epigraphical research in the N.W.P. and Mr. Smith, Architectural Assistant to Dr. Fuhrer.
>
> The archaeological survey as reduced will thus consist of two parties – one under Mr. Rea and the second under Mr. Cousens and it is considered that to these officers should be mainly entrusted to continuance of the Archaeological survey of the country until it has reached a satisfactory stage of completion. It is essential that these survey parties should be provided with a sufficient staff of native draftsmen as it has been found that much of the work executed hitherto has been unnecessarily expensive owing to the inadequate proportion of cheap drawing agency. The subordinate staff will, therefore, be increased to five draftsmen and one clerk, a suitable provision being allowed for contingencies. Both Surveyors will be ranked as gazetted officers and receive first class travelling allowance. The total cost of both survey parties is estimated Rs. 25,070 (Mr. Rea Rs. 12,200 and Mr. Cousens Rs. 12,870). As at present advised, the Government of India is of opinion that each of these parties should, as the work of the Province in which it is at present employed is completed, be

transferred to the next and placed under the general orders and direction of the Local Government of that Province, but a detailed programme for the several provinces will be prepared hereafter in communication with the Local Governments.

Dr. A. Fuhrer's appointment to the Archaeological Survey of the North-West Province Circle was part of the scheme, which comes to an end on the 1st October 1890. The Governor-General in Council is, however, of opinion that the services of this officer should be retained. He is, in addition to his other duties, in charge of the Provincial Museum at Lucknow which, it is understood, has greatly improved under his careful management. For this reason and also because it is expedient that there should be a qualified officer at hand to advise on questions of archaeological interest in the Upper Provinces, it is desirable that the appointment should be retained for a term of five years from September 1890. An application will be made to Her Majesty's Secretary of State accordingly and from the 1st October 1890, Dr. Fuhrer will carry out his duties under the immediate control and orders of the Government of North-West Provinces and Oudh. It has been ascertained that there is a considerable amount of work in the N.W.P. likely to require the services of a qualified architectural assistant to the survey during the next two years. With a view to the early and efficient performance of this work, the Government of the North-West Provinces has consented to bear during that period the charge of that portion of Dr. Fuhrer's pay which had hitherto been contributed from Imperial Revenues, on condition that Mr. Smith is retained at the charge of the Imperial Government for completion of the architectural works. The Government of India has accordingly agreed to retain Mr. Smith as an Assistant to Dr. Fuhrer until the 1st April 1892.

In conclusion, H.E., the Governor-General in Council desired that it should be understood that although, on consideration of the final resources available and the needs of the other branches of scientific enquiry, the Government of India has felt itself constrained to curtail the funds hitherto allotted to archaeological and antiquarian research which, so far as it falls properly within the functions of the State, has now been prosecuted to an advanced stage, the measures which have been decided upon are not intended to affect or impair the responsibility of Local Governments for conservation and maintenance of ancient monuments and buildings of historical or archaeological interest. This duty will rest as heretofore primarily with the Provincial Department of Public Works and H.E., the Governor-General in Council hopes that it will continue to receive careful attention throughout the country.[62]

However, the Government of India decided to continue the Archaeological Department on reduced scale for a term of five years w.e.f. 1 October 1890. Lord Cross, Secretary of State for India justified the retrenchment in his Despatch No. 50 dated 10 July 1890 and culled for regular submission of reports of progress in the field of survey and conservation of monuments. He further hinted in reduction of establishment concerning the Archaeological Survey Department in future. Besides, this scheme was also to be reconsidered in 1895.[63]

Sourindranath Roy, however, remarked that it was difficult to overestimate the services rendered by Burgess in the field of architectural survey and also the conservation of historical monuments.[64]

NOTES AND REFERENCES

1. Home, Archaeology B, September 1885, Nos. 51-53.
2. Archaeology, Conservation of Ancient Monuments, July 1885, Nos. 5-9, Notes.
3. *Ibid.*
4. Home, Public A, 11 February 1871, Nos. 152-153; 10 June 1871, No. 49.
5. Home, Archaeology A, June 1882, Nos. 7-9.
6. Foreign Department, Internal B, April 1886, Nos. 1-2.
7. Revenue and Agriculture Department, Archaeology, May 1888, Nos. 1-21, Notes.

8. *The Story of Indian Archaeology* by S. Roy, p. 65.
9. Home, Archaeology, Conservation of Ancient Monuments, September 1886, No. 24.
10. Home, Archaeology A, C.A.Ms., September 1886, No. 25.
11. Home, Archaeology, C.A.Ms., August 1886, No. 31.
12. Home, Archaeology A, January 1887, Nos. 5-11.
13. Revenue and Agriculture Department, Archaeology, May 1888, Nos. 1-21, Notes.
14. Home, Public, April 1887, No. 240.
15. Home, Archaeology A, February 1887, No. 15.
16. Home, Archaeology, C.A.Ms., June 1886, No. 7.
17. P.W.D., General A, October 1886, No. 16 Notes.
18. *Ibid.*
19. *Ibid.*
20. *Ibid.*
21. *Ibid.*
22. Revenue and Agriculture Department, Archaeology B, 1887, No. 8.
23. Revenue and Agriculture Department, Archaeology, May 1888, No. 2.
24. Revenue and Agriculture Department, Archaeology, May 1888, No. 1.
25. *Ibid.*
26. *Ibid.*
27. Revenue and Agriculture, Archaeology, May 1888, No. 2.
28. *Ibid.*
29. *Ibid.*
30. Revenue and Agriculture Department, Archaeology, May 1888, No. 3.
31. Revenue and Agriculture Department, Archaeology, May 1888, No. 4.
32. Revenue and Agriculture Department, Archaeology, May 1888, No. 6.
33. Revenue and Agriculture Department, Archaeology, May 1888, No9.
34. Revenue and Agriculture Department, Archaeology, May 1888, No. 14.
35. Revenue and Agriculture Department, Archaeology, May 1888, No. 16.
36. *The Story of Indian Archaeology 1784-1947* by S. Roy, 1961, p. 66; *Revealing India's past* edited by Sir John Cumming, 1939, pp. 65-66.
37. Home, Archaeology B, May 1886, Nos. 23-38; A, May 1886, Nos. 35-41.
38. Home, Archaeology A, August 1886, Nos. 5-6.
39. Archaeology, December 1886, Nos. 16-17; R&A, Archaeology B, July 1889, Nos. 48-51.
40. Home, Archaeology, Conservation of Monuments A, February 1887, Nos. 6-10.
41. *Ibid.*, Archaeology B, August 1887, Nos. 41-43.
42. Revenue and Agriculture Department, Archaeology, July 1888, Nos. 1-2.
43. Home, Revenue and Agriculture, Archaeology B, May 1887, Nos. 21-23.
44. Public Works Department, General A, October 1891, No. 153.
45. Revenue and Agriculture Department, Archaeology A, April 1889, No. 1
46. Revenue and Agriculture Department, Archaeology A, April 1889, No. 3.
47. Lansdowne Papers, N.A.I., Accession No. 1650, Letter No. 28.
48. *Ibid.*
49. Revenue and Agriculture Department, Archaeology A, April 1889, No. 4.
50. *The Story of Indian Archaeology, 1784-1947* by S. Roy, p. 67.
51. Revenue and Agriculture Department, Archaeology B, April 1890, Nos. 64-65.
52. *Ibid.'*
53. Archaeology and Conservation of Ancient Monuments, August 1886, Nos. 22-37, Notes.
54. *Ibid.*
55. K.W. of A Salaries, September 1888, Nos. 503-505; Revenue and Agriculture Department, Archaeology A, July 1898, Nos. 10-29, Notes.

56. Archaeology, Conservation of Ancient Monuments, August 1886, Nos. 22-37, Notes.
57. Revenue and Agriculture Department, Archaeology, July 1887, Nos. 4-6, Notes.
58. Revenue and Agriculture Department, Archaeology, May 1888, No. 37.
59. Revenue and Agriculture Department, Archaeology, June 1890, Nos. 1-30, Notes.
60. *Ibid.*
61. *Ibid.*
62. Foreign Department, Internal B, May 1890, No. 348.
63. Revenue and Agricultural Department, Archaeology A, June 1890, Nos. 1-30; Revenue and Agricultural Department, Archaeology A, July 1891, Nos. 35-48.
64. *The Story of Indian Archaeology, 1784-1947* by S. Roy, p. 71.

CHAPTER XI

A Decade of Official Apathy towards Care of Monuments

After retirement of James Burgess as Director General, Archaeological Survey in 1889, the activities relating to the care and conservation of ancient monuments in India came down to a virtual standstill. No new Director General was appointed and there was no official who was entrusted with the responsibility of preservation. All that was little accomplished for the care of monuments was primarily on account of localized efforts in various provinces. As far as conservation was concerned, nothing substantial was achieved after the retirement of Burgess. Sporadic efforts in conservation work were reported, viz., Fatehpur Sikri in North-West Provinces. The conservation work was hardly encouraging in other parts of the country. The activities relating to excavation and epigraphy were given low priority. The budgetary allocations under archaeology were expended primarily on publication of data that had been since compiled. The Government of India was confronted with the problem of reorganization of administrative structure of Archaeological Department. The period following Burgess' retirement "was one of the almost unrelieved gloom during which archaeology found itself caught up again in stagnant waters".[1]

However, the Government of India discussed and considered measures on the state of monuments periodically but in a continuous fashion. On 29 January 1891 (No. 7 Public), Viscount Cross, Secretary of State for India brought to the notice of the Government of India, the deplorable state of archaeological remains in Bombay and stressed the need of cooperation with officers of Archaeological Survey of Western India so as to enable them to prevent the neglect and destruction of archaeological monuments of interest and reiteration of Resolution No. 4 dated 8 September 1886 of the Public Works to follow the stipulations incorporated therein in letter and spirit.[2]

In pursuance of the above orders of the Secretary of State, a circular No. 4 (Public Works) was addressed by the Public Works Department, Government of India on 21 May 1891 to all Local Governments / Administrations and political officers, inviting their attention to the necessity of preservation of buildings of historical and architectural interest and added that "this subject has been brought to notice on previous occasions. As, however, there is some possibility especially in connection with the prosecution of new public works, that standing orders of this nature may be overlooked". He further stated that His Excellency in Council desired to draw special attention to paragraphs 74 and 75 of Chapter III and paragraph 6 of Chapter XI of the P.W.D. Code, Volume I of 1886 (Appendix XXII) and to impress upon local governments and administrations, the necessity of seeing that these orders are thoroughly carried out.[3]

Meanwhile, Hallam Murray, an English traveller, in his communication addressed to his father, John Murray. His father, incidentally, was a friend of Viscount Cross and discussed the prevalent state of architecture in India particularly Fatehpur Sikri. He gave a detailed account of the architectural features of the monument. Besides, he gave an account of the efforts of Mr. Smith, an archaeologist in the field of survey and reporting the detailed plans of conservation of this monument. Hallam Murray was critical of the lackadaisical attitude of the Government of India towards conservation plan of the archaeological monuments in India. He particularly referred to the decisions of the Government of India in abolishing the posts of the Archaeological Survey Department. Murray recommended that Smith should be held back in Fatehpur Sikri monument to supervise its conservation plans. He also pleaded that the Government of India should provide adequate funds to carry out repair works in Fatehpur Sikri. Murray concluded that "it is a miserable pity to see such splendid buildings and such storehouses of art falling into ruin for the want of a word and few rupees. The Engineer won't do, he has no sympathy with and feeling for the place; it must be an Archaeologist and one Architect, a man who will respect every original stone".[4]

John Murray promptly forwarded this letter of his son to Viscount Cross on 1 April 1891, with a request to support the concern of his son for saving the "magnificent architectural remains of India which are daily attracting English travellers to visit that country". Cross assured that he would intervene in the matter and do his best.[5]

Around the same time, E.C. Buck, Secretary, Revenue and Agriculture Department addressed a communication to Col. J.C. Ardagh, Private Secretary to Viceroy on 11 May 1891 and forwarded to him a note on archaeological survey and conservation of ancient monuments. The letter was in fact a retrospect of the activities and efforts of the Government of India and Archaeological Department, in particular, in the field of survey and conservation of archaeological monuments. The note also referred to the various administrative safeguards taken by the Government in preservation of monumental edifices in India.

Buck felt that the Local Government and provincial administration might not be able to provide funds that were necessary for the preservation of buildings of architectural and historical interest. He fervently pleaded that an allocation of Imperial funds should be made and granted to the Local Administrations/Provincial Governments towards maintenance and preservation of monuments in their respective jurisdiction. This measure would give a greater hold on the provincial governments, but he feared that the Financial Department, both Imperial as well as Provincial, would not favour such a proposal.[6]

Besides, an important Circular No. 2002 G.P.W.D. (General) dated 27 July 1891 was issued in consequence of the attention of Government having been called to the destruction of ancient remains to provide materials for railway works. G.H.D. Walker, Under Secretary to Government of India, stated therein that the attention of officers employed on the construction and maintenance of Guaranteed and Assisted Railway Companies as well as State Railways may be specially directed to the necessity of discouraging and prohibiting the destruction of such remains either by their own workmen or by contractors and their agents.[7]

An article on the state of ancient monuments was published in *The Times of India* on 15 May 1893 which deplored the state of ancient monuments, entitled "Ruin of Indian Architecture":

> Dr. Le Bon whose "Les Monuments de 1'inde" we noticed lately, observes that the ruin of Indian architecture dates from the English Conquest. It is the fashion to give the English credit for more of good and of ill than they have done to India and perhaps people who believe that the English have introduced alcohol into India can bring themselves to believe also that we are responsible for the destruction of its ancient monuments. Doubtless, the Public Works Department has much to answer for in the way of deleterious example, though we suspect that the Princes of India are less given to copying British work than Dr. Le Bon takes them to be. So far, however, as the ruin of Indian architecture deplored by Dr. Le Bon is the result of destructiveness and carelessness, it is a mistake to charge the mischief upon us. The offenders are to be found elsewhere. There is abundant and tangible proof that the greatest havoc committed amongst Hindu remains all over the country was caused by the Mohammedans when, flushed with victory, these iconoclasts first swept down upon the country. We find the earliest mosques built almost and in many cases entirely, of Hindoo temple material. In scores of cases the builders have just adapted the Hindoo temple itself with a few alterations and the necessary defacement of forbidden figure sculpture to their own uses. The Mohammedans who blew up the shrine with gunpowder wrecked the temple in Northern Gujarat, Surya at Modhayra. Their gunpowder, accidentally also demolished one of their own buildings – one of the finest in the Deccan – the Madressa in Bidar. Organized expeditions were sent out by the Mohammedan rulers of Gujarat on several occasions to destroy the temples in Kathiawar and the neighbouring country and evidence of how well they did their work is not wanting. Among the Mohammedans there is a strict rule against demolishing, for any purpose, a religious building once built to their faith and the Hindus and Jains knowing this had miniature *idghas* built upon different parts of their own temples as a protection to them against Moslem violence and there they still are. The Hindus in turn when they got the upper hand often paid back the Mohammedans in their own coin. At Patan, in Gujarat, for instance, the Mohammedans destroyed every temple in the place for material; but their finest mosque, the great Adina Musjid built of such materials, was subsequently completely destroyed and carted away to help to build the present walls of the town, in which most of the material of scores of fine Hindu buildings now finds an ignominious resting place. The many marble buildings, save a few beautiful pillars now in the *katcheri*, have completely disappeared, having been burnt for lime. The days when contractors and others bought up temples and other ruins wholesale for their material is quite a thing of the past and though much is to be deplored, need not be continually brought up anew. Had the people themselves cared ought for the buildings this could never have happened. One great drawback to conservation is the stolid apathy of the native. He will use some of these old shrines, covered with delicate work, but desecrated, as storehouses for cow dung cakes and any dirty lumber, while he will plaster the former to dry all over the sculptured walls. Worse than this, such a shrine has been seen in use as a latrine. The real rescuers of the ancient buildings of the country are the rulers whom it is the fashion to call foreign but who have done more for the preservation of the architectural wealth of India than the natives themselves.[8]

Later in August 1888, sanction was accorded for the removal of the Lahore Gate at Delhi on the request of the Government of Punjab. The Deputy Commissioner, Delhi had stated that the Kabul and Mori Gates has since been removed. With regard to Lahore Gate, it was stated that it was totally unconnected with the Revolt of 1857 and was not having any architectural significance.

When this case was referred to the Defence Committee, the Commander-in-Chief did not offer any objections to the Lahore Gate. Besides, Punjab Government proposed to grant building bases on certain unoccupied ground immediately outside the Lahore Gate, the intention being that the Gate should be removed and a square with shops laid out beyond it. It was promptly reported that no objections would be put forth by His Excellency to any improvement proposed in the vicinity of Lahore Gate.[9]

On 18 May 1893, the Office of the Private Secretary's Office, communicated to Buck that ancient landmarks should be preserved for posterity as vandalism had been permitted in Delhi and stressed the need for preservation of monuments instead of destroying them. He particularly lamented on the decay of monuments in Delhi and stressed timely measures to prevent further damage to the monuments. He stated that all the antiquities he visited around Delhi were decaying and he did not see a sign of any effort to prevent it, since apparently some very long time ago when something was done.[10]

It was noted on 19 May 1893 by referring to the existence of two Lahore Gates in Delhi, the first one at the Red Fort and the other in the outer precincts of the city. The latter had no architectural interest, except for the fact that "armies come out of when marching northwards". This Gate was apparently constructed during the reign of Shah Jahan. He added that the Gate blocked the view of north end of Chandni Chowk and could be pulled down.[11]

E.C. Bayley also remarked on 21 May 1893 that Local Governments should be entrusted with the responsibility of maintaining the edifices, which were certified by the archaeological surveyors as "worth preserving". He, however, was of the view that since the Department had no control over the administration of Local Governments, the best course of action should be to take measures for preventing demolition and also take care that fortifications and gates constructed for logistic reasons by the Military Department should not be pulled down without their permission. He further elaborated that from the archaeological point of view, we can take decisions and issue orders accordingly, but cannot take decisions in individual cases in the Secretariat of the Department. Besides, implicit trust should be reported in the Local Governments for actions initiated in this direction.[12]

With the sanction accorded by the Military Department for the removal of the Lahore Gate and earmarking the square for construction of shops,[13] the Hon'ble Member remarked on 8 July 1893, "I think the demolition of the Lahore Gate and the formation of the proposed square may be allowed to proceed." He even quoted from the volume of Kaye and Malleson's *History of the Indian Mutiny*, p. 384, "The Lahore Gate has no special interest."[14] Finally, the Viceroy in his order dated 9 July 1893 allowed the demolition of Lahore Gate.[15]

The Civil and Military Gazette datelined 10 April 1894 carried a report on the transport of stones of ancient monuments found near Peshawar to Paris for deciphering the inscription thereon. This incident was taken up for discussion in a meeting of the Asiatic Society of Bengal held on 6 December 1893. It was deliberated in the meeting that stone inscriptions at Peshawar were sent to Mr. Senart, French Epigraphist for decipherment. As the finder was a Government official, the members of the Asiatic Society made discreet enquiries whether he was officially authorized by the Government of India to send the stone inscriptions out of the country. The members felt that it was a grave matter especially when the experts in inscription were available within the country, viz. Government epigraphist at Bangalore, Dr. Fuhrer, known epigraphist at Lucknow, J. Fleet at Poona, Aurel Stein at Lahore and R. Hoenle at Calcutta. The members of the Society felt that the appropriate course of action would be to return the stone inscriptions to Lahore Museum after decipherment of inscriptions by Senart.[16]

However, the Secretary, Revenue and Agriculture Department drew the attention of the Government of Punjab on 28 April 1894 and pointed out that rules regarding deciphering of publication of Indian inscriptions circulated on 27 June 1893 (R&A No. 36/8) were not observed by the officials; that no original stone of Ancient Monuments should be sent out of country. He warned that the rules laid down should be strictly adhered by the concerned officers.[17]

Meanwhile, an International Congress of Orientalists was held at Geneva in September 1894. G.A. Grierson, Philological Secretary of Asiatic Society of Bengal was deputed to represent the Government of Bengal. While Dr. Burgess went as representative of the Government of India, Dr. G. Buhler of Vienna and M.E. Senart* of Paris also participated in the Congress.

After participating in the Congress, Grierson sent his report to the Government of Bengal on 23 September 1894. In the conference, Grierson highlighted the efforts made by the Trustees of the Indian Museum in preservation of Ashoka inscriptions. In this connection, a Resolution was adopted by the Congress which thanked the Trustees for their efforts in inviting the Government of India's attention. He also added that as Secretary and delegate of the Asiatic Society of Bengal and the Trustees of the Indian Museum, he was able to report to the Congress the accurate information on Ashoka inscriptions.[18]

However, Grierson's Report on the proceedings of International Congress of Orientalists was also submitted to the Government of Bengal. Besides, Buhler's contribution to the Congress on historical and linguistic value of Ashokan inscriptions was also significant. He had strongly pleaded for preparation of facsimile of these inscriptions and also for the formation of an Asoka Gallery where casts could be collected and made accessible to students. These inscriptions were lying exposed to the weather and they had suffered considerable injuries both from neglect and from iconoclasts or relic-hunting tourists. They were also inconveniently situated, some in the extreme North-West, others in Orissa, in Mysore, in Gujarat, in Central India and in Nepal. Even when approached, some of them were so placed that they could not be read without using scaffolding. The delegates of the Congress, viz., Weber Burgess, Senart, Bhownagree, Lord Reay and Buhler supported this proposal.[19]

This report was also sent to Henry H. Fowler, Secretary of State for India and after examining the report, the Secretary of State in his Despatch of 25 April 1895 to the Governor-General in Council appreciated the efforts of the Trustees of the Indian Museum for the preservation of Asoka inscriptions in many ancient monuments in India. The Secretary of State also referred to decay of Bharahut sculptures in the custody of Indian Museum and appreciated the efforts taken for their preservation. He stated that "the importance of taking steps to prevent further deterioration or destruction of Ancient Monuments whose historical and linguistic value cannot be overstated, will not I trust be lost sight of". He was equally appreciative of the measures being taken for preparation of facsimile casts of the Ashoka inscriptions in India.[20]

MEMORANDUM OF PRESIDENT OF THE ROYAL INSTITUTE OF BRITISH ARCHITECTS

On 19 February 1894, the President of Council of the Royal Institute of British Architects forwarded a Memorandum** of the classification and conservation of the historical monuments of India to Earl of Kimberley, Secretary of State for India for his consideration.

> The attention of the Royal Institute has for some time been directed to the very important work initiated and carried on by the Government during the last 20 years in the matters of the systematic classification and preservation of the Ancient Monuments of India. The Council while fully aware of the difficulties of carrying out such work in a country like India, desired to express on behalf of the architectural profession and expressed their sense of gratitude and obligation for the valuable and efficient work done and their appreciation of its unrivalled importance from an artistic, antiquarian and historic point of view.

* Specialist in deciphering Ashoka inscriptions.

** This memorandum was signed by Mr. J. Macvicar Anderson, President, Mr. Aston Webb, one of the Vice Presidents, Mr. Edward Gunning, a Member of Council and William Emerson, Honorary Secretary with the corporate seal affixed on it.

While sensible, however, of the value of the work already accomplished and the labour and cost necessarily entailed, they nevertheless beg respectfully to draw attention to the following defects:

I. That the classified lists of ancient monuments of Bengal and Madras and the Punjab, need revision and that systematic and exhaustive lists have yet to be made of the monuments of Mysore, Hyderabad and Rajputana and the Central Provinces of Berar.

II. That while there are certain archeological officers in various parts of India, they would appear to be hardly numerous enough to exercise an efficient supervision over works necessary for the preservation or reparation of outlying monuments, the importance of which from an historic and antiquarian stand point, renders such supervision imperative, the natives themselves either doing more than is necessary or inventing too much. The Council of the Royal Institute beg permission, therefore, to offer the following suggestions:

SUGGESTIONS OF ROYAL INSTITUTE REGARDING CONSERVATION

A. It would be very advantageous if no restoration works at all were permitted to be undertaken or estimates sanctioned, without the approval of the Archaeological Survey officers having been previously reported.

B. That a greater number of skilled independent archaeologists might advantageously be employed to advise how far restoration should go and to superintend the same, the work being carried out by natives whose guilds have usually very correct traditional knowledge. Such European supervision is advisable to prevent the limits of proper conservation being exceeded.

C. That if the Government could see their way to making further yearly grants for the purposes of completing the classification of the monuments of the whole of India and of undertaking such repairs and restorations as are absolutely necessary in many instances, to prevent the disappearance and damage by neglect of important relics, they would earn the gratitude of all lovers of art, archaeology and history.

The immense importance of the subject, and the unequalled interest of the architecture and history of this portion of the British Empire is the sole excuse the Council of the Royal Institute of British Architects feel it necessary to put forward for troubling your Lordship with this Memorial. Trusting that it may be found worthy of some consideration.[21]

On 25 April 1894, Sir Arthur Godley, Under Secretary of State for India, gave a retrospect of the Archaeological Survey Department and its reorganization plans in 1885. He stated that Rs. 6,000 was being expended on the functions of Archaeological Survey of India and an equal amount was also spent on conservation.[22] With regard to the memorial of Royal Institute, H.H. Fowler, Secretary of State for India (Earl of Kimberley's successor), addressed a communication to the Governor-General in Council on 26 April 1894 and stated that remedial measures could be got effected through Archaeological Departments, and the Local Governments should be entrusted with the responsibility relating for disputes of to survey and ownership of monuments without involving any additional financial burden.[23]

George Birdwood, one of the members of the Royal Institute, was not a signatory to the memorial as he felt that a memorial was not necessary. He stated this position to A.H. Hallam Murray on 7 March 1894. Birdwood praised the efforts of the Government of India for undertaking systematic conservation of the historical monument of India. He also stated that the conservation measures conducted by the Government of India was detailed, comprehensive and thorough. He referred to the problem of ownership of historical monuments which was confronted by the Government of India. He also stated that there were innumerable monuments of lesser interest and of no historical character, for which the Government of India should not take responsibility with regard to their ownership. He mentioned categorically that no Government anywhere in the world takes "more intelligent, zealous and fruitful care of the historical monuments for which it should be held to be properly responsible than the Government of India."

Birdwood explained the reasons behind not signing the memorial as he thought it was prudent to be sympathetic with the Government, which was "under the weightiest obligation to the patient, long-suffering people of India, to consider every possible means of financial retrenchment". Birdwood hoped that the archaeological activities specially in matter of archaeological monuments, should be thrown open to independent scholars and felt that ever since monuments came under the purview of the Government, the academic pursuits emanating from the studies of archaeology had languished. He, therefore, felt that revival of interest in archaeological studies could be done under the guidance of learned bodies, viz., Royal Asiatic Society of Great Britain and its branches in India, the Society of Biblical Archaeology and the Society for the Promotion of Hellenic Studies, etc.[24]

THE MEMORIAL ENTITLED "THE PRESERVATION OF ANCIENT MONUMENTS IN INDIA" PRESENTED TO SECRETARY OF STATE FOR INDIA

Another memorial relating to archaeological monuments in India was presented by the Royal Academy of Arts, the Society of Antiquaries of London, the Society for the Preservation of Ancient Buildings and the Royal Archaeological Institute. The Memorial entitled "The Preservation of Ancient Monuments in India" was presented to Henry Hartley Fowler, the Secretary of State for India in September 1894. The memorial listed their recommendations on the preservation of ancient buildings in India.

'We beg respectfully to call your attention to a memorial presented twenty years ago to H.M.Secretary of State for India in Council by certain gentlemen interested in the history and antiquities of India, on the preservation of ancient buildings in that country.

We need not repeat what was then said as to the importance of these buildings both historically and archaeologically and we gratefully acknowledge that much has been done since that time by the Government of India for the furtherance of the objects of the Memorial; much, however, still remains to be done to meet the necessities of the case and to preserve the ancient buildings of India – unrivalled for their historic and artistic interest – from the frequent depredations of tropical rains, from the overpowering effects of jungle growth, and sometimes from destruction by Civil Officers, railway contractors and others and we venture to refer to the recommendations then made and apply them to the altered circumstances of the present day.

RECOMMENDATIONS

The first of the recommendations was for the classification of the different monuments in India on a defined system. That proposal the Government of India has carried out fully in the case of Bombay, the N.W.P. and Oudh while it is understood that similar valuable work is being prepared for Central India and the Central Provinces by Dr. Fuhrer and Mr. Cousens who in the course of their investigations have brought to light fresh treasures of ancient art and ornament and have made plain and intelligible much that before was unknown or obscure. The lists for the Provinces of Madras, Bengal, the Punjab and the States of Rajputana are, however, still very defective and we would suggest the extreme importance of completing them before it is too late and causing detailed lists of the architectural remains to be compiled for each Province under the direction of an Archaeological Surveyor similar to those drawn up by Dr. Fuhrer for the North-West Provinces. Such volumes would be of the utmost value.

The second recommendation of the memorial of 1873 was the employment of officers charged with the conservancy of historical monuments whose business it would be not only to survey and catalogue the monuments most worthy of attention but to visit them periodically and to be responsible for the apportionment and expenditure of any grant made by Government for the purpose of keeping them in repair.

We would respectfully submit that this suggestion has not been carried out in the way intended. The execution of almost all repairs has, very naturally, been entrusted to the Public Works officers but unfortunately, except in Bombay, the advice of the Superintendents of the Archaeological Surveys has not hitherto been systematically taken. The archaeological or architectural training and the knowledge of the history, age and style of the buildings, which they possess, is necessarily of a more complete nature than can be expected from a Public Works Engineer or Civil Officer.

The work requires much technical skill and experience and for want of this, mistakes have been made and much injury unwittingly done to important monuments(*)(**) at the cost of quite unnecessarily large expenditure. In some cases a building is restored at great expence and made completely solid and permanent but unless the restorer understands the intention of the building and possess some little veneration for the art it displays, the result is almost always unsatisfactory and any interest or value which it may originally have possessed is hopelessly destroyed. While in other cases the neglect of small and inexpensive repairs at the right moment has led to lamentable ruin.*** We would, therefore, recommend that no substantial interference with monumental remains of any kind, particularly by way of restoration, should be permitted except when the proposal has the full sanction of the Superintendent of Archaeological Survey (to be

* An illustrative case occurred not long since at Bijganagar where the Collector noticing that the base of the stone car, or "Rath", in front of the Vithal Temple showed cracks and signs of decay, reported it to the Government and the Public Works Engineer being instructed to deal with it, the whole of the brick superstructure – 400 years old – was at once pulled down. Thus an old and interesting memorial of the end of the 15th century was summarily destroyed, without reference to the Archaeologist who might at least have secured complete drawings of it, if, as a trained architect, he could not have devised some means of preserving it.

** We are informed that the sleeping apartments of the great Akbar at Fatehpur Sikri form a distinct building in themselves. They possess various points of interest, amongst others a private doorway, which gave the Emperor access to his Record Office and enabled his Prime Minister to visit him without public observation. An Engineer was sent to Fatehpur Sikri to make some repairs and for reasons best known to himself, built up this doorway. At the same time he built up open work screens in another building, where blind screens had been before – and viceversa – and removed a staircase from one part of a palace to another for no sufficient reason.

*** As an instance of such a catastrophe has been averted we give the following: In 1891 of the domes of the Hummum at Fatehpur Sikri had a role in it, about the size of a Coconut. The ceiling of the dome is covered with exquisite designs in stamped plaster work unique of their kind and if the hole had been allowed to remain until the monsoon, the rains would have washed through it to the further ruin of the dome and the plaster work and designs would have been for ever lost. There is no found at the command of the Archaeological Surveyor for the repair and preservation of these buildings and it is Sir the duty of no one in particular to look after them. A note, however, from a stray traveller to the Secretary to the Department who happened to be interested in archaeology calling his attention to the condition of the Hummum, brought a workman to the spot; with a little plaster and a piece of zinc and for the cost of a few rupees the dome was satisfactorily repaired and the delicate plaster work preserved.

appointed) through whom Collectors, Public Works Officers and others should in the first place report. He should also inspect and report on all conservation works carried out.

The third suggestion of the memorial of 1873 was that a fixed sum should be annually allocated to the conservation of these buildings. We venture to substitute for this a recommendation that each Government should be asked to assign in its Public Works budget a yearly sum for inspection and conservation of buildings to be applied only after the Archaeological Surveyor has inspected the monuments and checked or approved of the detailed estimates prepared under the instructions by the Public Works Department in each case. This would prevent injury and insure economy".[25]

There were other prominent personalities also who were in sympathy with the Memorial's object and gave their signatures to this Memorial. They were: Vincent Cross, Lord Aberdare, Lord Stanmore, Earl of Carlisle, Sir A.H. Layard, Sir E. Burne-Jones Bart, Sir F.W. Burton, A.S. Murray, George Seharf, Duke of Argyll, Professor Max-Muller, Frederick Milner Bart M.P., Sir West Ridgeway, General Sir G. Chesney M.P., James C. Stevenson, M.P., Lord Roberts, Lord Kinnaird, Sir John Evans, R.H. Benson, Stanley Lane Poole, Sir C.W. Wilson, Rowland E. Prathero, Major-General Sir E.F. Du Cane, Arthur Lucas, Herbert Marshall, R.W.S., Sir John Lubbock Bart M.P., Sir James D. Linton, Hon. George N. Curzon M.P., Sir William Markley, Lady Markley, Lord Knutsford, Lord Llangattock, Lord Lawrence, Sir George Grove, James Burgess, Hon. D. Naoroji M.P., W.S. Caine M.P., T. Herbert Warren President of Magdalen College, Oxford, Hon'ble Leonard Courtney M.P., Honourable A.J. Mundella M.P., Benjamin L. Cohen M.P., Harry R. Graham M.P., Hon'ble T.H. Huxley, Wilson Noble, M.P., Earl Stanhope, Sir Frederick Pollock Bart, Lord Tennyson, Sir M. Monier Williams, Sir Arthur Sullivan, J. Lockwood Kipling, Sir Colin Scott Moncrieff, Viscount Midleton, Sir William J. Farrer, Edward J. Poynter, Miss Broadwood, Sir F. Seymour Haden, Sir Donald Mackenzie Wallace, Sir S.C.E. Pollock, Sir J.D. Hooker, Colonel Charles E. Stewart C.B., Professor Pelcy Gardner, Sir Theodore C. Hope, Sir Arthur J. Otway Bart, Sir Bartle C. Frere Bart, A.H. Hallam Murray.[26]

The Secretary of State promptly forwarded the memorial to the Governor-General in Council on 27 September 1894 for his consideration and further necessary action.

Protests from different sections of society prompted the Government of India to resolve the issue. On 14 May 1891, Viscount Cross, Secretary of State for India had already addressed to the Government of India on the proposal of entrusting work relating to the preservation of monuments in India to the Asiatic Society of Bengal and assisting their work in the direction by granting a subvention from the Government of India. The Secretary of State felt that with this arrangement, the work of preserving the monuments of archaeological interest would be performed efficiently and at a lesser cost rather than maintaining a separate establishment under a distinct department.[27]

Acting on the suggestion of the Secretary of State, the Government of India made a move to transfer the entire work relating to the preservation of archaeological monuments to the Asiatic Society of Bengal. The Government of India prevented itself from taking this move as it felt that a lot of work pertaining to preservation of archaeological monuments remained to be done. However, the Society was requested by the Government of India to take up the responsibility as per the suggestion of the Secretary of State who thought that the work could be done more efficiently and more cheaply by the Society, but the Society was unwilling to take up the entire responsibility. This fact was communicated by C.R. Wilson, Honorary Secretary, Asiatic Society of Bengal to the Secretary, Department of Revenue and Agriculture. The Secretary further contended that:

> The Asiatic Society of Bengal is a body of fluctuating character which, though it contains among its members persons of special attainments in the subject of Archaeology, has not that unity of control and sustained acquaintance with the work which has been done and which remains to be done, which are necessary to be direction of the prosecution of Archaeological research in a systematic and methodical manner. Members who take interest in the subject go away or are absorbed in other business and have not the leisure to give to the consideration of projects for further operation.
>
> We are aware that our President, the Lt. Governor of Bengal proposed to appoint an archaeological expert from Europe and undertook to provide to his salary and his establishment and we much regret that the Government of India were unable to sanction this scheme. We would urge now that it should be favourably reconsidered. Such an expert while under Government control would receive valuable aid in the direction of his researches from the Trustees of the Indian Museum. The Trustees include among their number representatives of the Asiatic Society of Bengal. They are a continuous body and they are accustomed to researches in various departments connected with the work of Museum. These considerations seem to point to the Local Government aided by the Museum Trustees and not to this Society as the proper body to which should be committed the control of researches of the kind under discussion.
>
> Next only to the conservation of notable monuments, excavation is the main business of the Archaeological Department. It is of little use to print off bulky lists of ancient sites, if the sites are never to be examined and without excavation, any real examination of old sites is impossible. Nothing could be more erroneous than the belief that this work could be left in India to private enterprise. Excavations and explorations of ancient sites made by private explorers without archaeological or scientific knowledge are positively detrimental. The work is done recklessly and selfishly. Valuable memorials of the past are in this way mutilated, destroyed or abstracted from the country. Private enterprise has no doubt done a great deal in Egypt and Palestine; but the inducements for private work in these countries are very much greater than in India and the circumstances under which the explorations are carried on are quite different. There can, in the opinion of the Asiatic Society, be no doubt that in India funds ought to be provided by the State for this class of operations and that the work itself should be supervised by the Government.[28]

The Government of India conveyed its thanks to the Asiatic Society of Bengal for their help in the work of the Archaeological Survey of India.[29] Besides, E.C. Buck, Secretary, Government of India remarked that the Asiatic Society of Bengal should be approached and their advice sought continuously on archaeological and epigraphical matters. However, C.R. Wibson, Honorary Secretary of the Society stated that society should act as referee and adviser to the Trustees as well as the Local Governments. C.J. Lyall, President of the Asiatic Society, also suggested that the Government of India could prescribe the working arrangements with regard to Secretary handling of archaeological scheme. He particularly wanted the society to be a "consultative, suggesting and criticizing agency".[30]

At long last, a scheme for the revision of the Archaeological Survey Department was proposed. The Honorable Members of the Department of Revenue and Agriculture as well as Denzil Ibbetson, Secretary, Government of India gave their considered opinion in support of this scheme. J. Westland, Honorable Member remarked that "there is not at present an Archaeological Department in the same sense as a Geological one". Lord Elgin, the Viceroy, also favoured retaining full powers of supervision in conservation and excavation activities. He made this observation in his minute dated 10 May 1895 and was not in favour of entrusting the work to private agencies. He referred to the similar practices prevalent in Germany and Greece.[31]

Considering all the facts and suggestions, a circular (No. 21-40-1 dated 27 June 1895, Revenue and Agricultural Department) was issued regarding reorganization of the Archaeology Survey Department and forwarded to all local governments and administrations for their opinion.

The reorganization of the Archaeological Survey Department effected by the Resolution of the Government of India in this Department No. 2/5-60 dated 5 May 1890 received the approval of the Secretary of State in Lord Cross' Despatch No. 50 dated 10 July 1890. In sanctioning the scheme which was to be reconsidered in 1895, His Lordship remarked 'It seems not unreasonable to expect that, within the next five years, the work of Archaeological Survey of India generally, so far as the Government is concerned, will have been completed but this will become more apparent when a detailed programme for the several provinces shall have been prepared'.

No such programme was prepared, but the replies to the letters from this Department No. 1385-86-27-8 dated 11 July 1891 sufficiently indicate that the operations of the Archaeological Survey Department cannot be terminated within the period suggested by Lord Cross and indeed, it is doubtful whether the Government of India can ever properly dispense with professional assistance in the matter. Assuming, then, that State aid to archaeology is still required, it is necessary to consider what arrangements should be made from October next to carry on the work. I am directed to set forth, for consideration and criticism, the general lines upon which the Government of India, as at present advised, think that the matter should be treated and the proposals which they suggest for recommendation to the Secretary of State and to ask for the assistance of – in dealing with a subject in which the learned world of Europe is interested.

2. That the operations hitherto carried out by the Archaeological Survey have not been in all respects satisfactory, is mainly due to the enormous extent of the field for research and the infinite number and variety of the questions for investigation. The work was begun without system and continued in a desultory manner. But since 1885 the field for action has been gradually narrowed and made more definite and it is still in this direction that the Government of India desire to proceed.

3. The possible functions of an Archaeological Survey may be divided into two main branches – the conservation of existing material and its examination. In some cases (e.g. inscriptions) the two are almost identical; but where this is not the case, conservation is the first duty; since, if the material is duly conserved, it can be examined at leisure, and by such agency, paid or unpaid, as may be available. Especially is this the case with respect to buildings of architectural or historic interest, the preservation of which is a duty which we owe to the civilized world.

4. The first object, then, to be aimed at is to ensure effective conservation. Past experience shows that for this purpose to continuous inspection and advice of experts in archaeology is essential; though it is believed that the desired object can be secured at a very moderate cost. The staff that is maintained for the purpose of conservation will naturally to a certain extent examine and publish information regarding the material it conserves; but the possibility of any further examination to be made at public expense must depend upon the funds available for its prosecution. In view of the present state of Indian finances and of the fact that branches of scientific inquiry which directly tend to develop the resources of India are unavoidably restricted because money is not available for their extension, the Government of India have reluctantly come to the conclusion that they would not be justified in spending large sums of money on work which, however, great in its scientific interest and importance, can never be productive of any material benefit to the country. They are, however, ready and anxious to offer all facilities to private enquiry by competent persons and they are not without hope that when once it is understood that the Government will rigidly confine itself to the conservation of existing material, private individuals and the learned societies of Europe will come forward to investigate it, which they are far less likely to do so long as Government profess to undertake this task, however, inadequately.

5. For effective conservation, the first essential is to know what material exists and what portions of it are best worth preserving. The manner in which the Government of India has endeavoured to ascertain this, so far as buildings are concerned, is indicated in the previous circulars/orders. These circulars/orders prescribed the preparation of classified lists of the archaeological objects of interest in each province, as a basis upon which conservation was to proceed. The lists are, however,

not yet complete and some of the earlier ones are defective and unsatisfactory. It will perhaps seldom be possible to publish a really satisfactory list in the first instance and the first thing necessary is to complete the lists in their initial form. When this has been done and a decision arrived at as to what buildings should be preserved through the Agency of the Public Works Department, it will still be necessary to maintain a small staff of archaeological experts to assist and advise the engineers in their work.

6. Their 'primary' duty will be to advise upon, assist in, and secure the effective preservation of the buildings, which it may be decided to preserve. This, however, will not fully occupy their time and their second duty will be to revise and perfect the existing lists of remains where those lists are still unsatisfactory. Such leisure as may still remain to them may very properly be employed upon archaeological research.

7. In carrying out this last branch of their duties, much must depend upon the inclination and capacity of the individual; but three suggestions may be offered for their guidance. The first suggestion is, that the material, which is not to be conserved, should form the first subject of enquiry wherever it possesses any real archaeological interest. It is, 'ex hypothesis', of minor importance; but it will disappear and such results as can be obtained from it should be recorded before this has happened. The second suggestion is that of the buildings which are to be conserved, those of which reasonably sufficient descriptions have already been published should not ordinarily form the subject of further research, even although those descriptions may leave much to be desired, until other major buildings have been exhausted. There has been observable in past years a strong tendency to go over the same ground again and again; a tendency which is natural as the ground first taken up is generally the most attractive, but one which it is essential to check in order to obtain the best results from the limited means at our disposal. The last suggestion is that while the architectural and still more the artistic side of the subject can be examined by competent experts from Europe, whether amateurs or agents of societies, as effectively as by Government agency in India, there is a wide field for archaeological research of the greatest and importance which can only be explored effectively by men acquainted with the vernacular and with the ways of the country. They as may remain to the Archaeological staff after performing the duties specified in the preceding paragraph might well employ such leisure in this direction.

8. The numbers of cases in which experts will have to advise in each year will be small but skilled inspection will always be necessary and the large area to be inspected will probably require the permanent services of at least five Archaeological Surveyors. They should be, not architects with a knowledge of archaeology, but archaeologists with a knowledge of architecture. They might be employed as follows: (1) for Bombay, Berar, Sindh and Baluchistan; (2) for Madras and Coorg; (3) for the Punjab and the North-West Provinces and Oudh; (4) for Bengal and Assam; and (5) for the Central Provinces and Ajmere. This last officer might also exercise such supervision (as an adviser) over the more celebrated monuments of Hyderabad, Central India and Rajputana as the Durbars concerned might consent to. These surveyors would be under the control of the Local Government; the expenditure being provincialised either at once or at the next revision of contract, as recommended by the Finance Commission. The pay of each appointment might be fixed at Rs. 350-30-500 per mensem, personal allowances being given for the present where the surveyor is already in receipt of a higher salary. When two or more Local Governments are concerned, each would have a fixed share of the Surveyor's time.

13. A great deal still remains to be done in the way of excavation and the results would probably be of extraordinary interest in many cases. The Asiatic Society of Bengal which was consulted in regard to the future of Archaeological work in India, has pointed out the danger of excavation by skilled hands. It should be the aim of Government to prevent the destruction of valuable material; and if in any case it becomes necessary for Government to disturb an ancient site, no excavation will be permitted except under the supervision of the Local Archaeological Surveyor. Indeed, no such excavation should in any case be allowed without the consent of the Local Government. But

all possible encouragement and assistance should be offered to private explorers whose archaeological competence is ascertained.[32]

The Local Governments did not agree with this contention and stated that these directed to 'conservation', the scheme of which was approved by the Local Governments.

After ascertaining the views of Learned Societies and Local Governments, the Governor-General in Council submitted a proposal to Lord George Hamiton, Secretary of State for India on 16 June 1898 (No. 31 R&A, A.E.) regarding reorganization of the Archaeological Survey Department.

In the year 1890, our views as to the Constitution of the Department during the next five years were embodied in Resolution No. 2-5-60 dated 5 May in the course of which we observed that although we were anxious that archaeological investigations should not be altogether abandoned till they had been brought to a satisfactory stage of completeness, yet the Archaeological Survey Department should, as soon as might be practicable, be reduced to the permanent minimum at which it was desirable to maintain it. This Resolution was forwarded with our despatch No. 6 dated 13 May 1890 and in despatch No. 50 dated the 10 July 1890, your Lordship's predecessor communicated his sanction to the scheme recommended. In commenting upon our proposals Lord Cross remarked that it seemed not unreasonable to expect that within the next five years the Archaeological Survey of India would be brought to completion, so far as it lay within the functions of Government though it was impossible to make an accurate forecast till detailed programmes for the several Provinces had been prepared. But it should be observed that an entire withdrawal of State aid was not contemplated by us nor apparently by the Secretary of State for though in a later despatch No.46, Public (Records) dated the 14 May 1891, Lord Cross suggested the desirability of entrusting work of this nature to the Asiatic Society of Bengal, he admitted that a subvention from Government would probably be required. This suggestion was laid before the Asiatic Society in our letter No. 2747 dated the 19 June 1894, but the Society in its letter No. K-7 dated 5 January 1895, while expressing its sympathy with the efforts of the Government of India to advance the cause of archaeological research, regretted that it was not in a position to assume the control and direction of Archaeological Surveys and Epigraphy. We have reluctantly come to the conclusion that effective control by the Asiatic Society or any other similar body is impossible and that the work must be continued by Government, if it is to continue at all.

3. We have been in communication with Local Governments on the subject and their replies sufficiently indicate that the operation of the Archaeological Survey Department cannot be terminated within the period suggested by Lord Cross. We are indeed doubtful whether archaeological research in this country can at any time dispense with State direction and control. The papers sent to us with Sir Henry Fowler's Despatch No. 52 Revenue dated 26 April 1894 and No.139, Revenue 27 September 1894, your Lordship's Despatch No. 43, Revenue dated 23 April 1896 and representations from such authorities as the Royal Asiatic Society, London, the Indian Museum, Calcutta, Mr. Tawney and Dr. Buhler, constitute a strong plea for the continuance of archaeological work in India and we are forced to the conclusion that there is still much work which should be done by Government and may rightly be included amongst its responsibilities and that moreover to withdraw from archaeological research would lay the Government open to general condemnation in scientific circles.

4. Assuming then that State aid is to be continued, there remains for determination the general basis upon which work should be conducted in the future. The scheme which we suggested for the consideration of Local Government is set forth in a circular addressed to them in June 1895, of which a copy forms an enclosure to this despatch. The replies received showed that the programme of archeological work proper there suggested is generally approved but although it is admitted that CONSERVATION must be the first object, regret is very generally expressed that a more prominent

place cannot be given to the exploration of archaeological remains, more particularly in the way of excavating the sites of ancient cities. We are, however, disposed to affirm the draft programme of work and to insist that the first thing to be done is to conserve our material and that the first and most essential step towards this end is to take stock of it and decide what is worth preserving. In para 6 of our circular we described original investigation as ranking last among the surveyor's duties. We have no wish, however, to discourage original work, nor do we undervalue what has been and is being done in this direction by the officers of the Survey and we are completely in accord with the further proposition that every facility and encouragement should be given to any individual or Society who will undertake work of the kind under proper control. In doing so we are pursuing the course that can claim to show the best results in the past and we are desirous that an assurance of the kind may be given to the English memorialists. But we consider that the limited sum, which we are justified in spending upon archaeological work, should primarily be devoted to the conservation of existing material.

6. The draft scheme provided for five circles with an Archaeological Surveyor for each. After considering the replies of local governments and administrations, we are of opinion that the five circles should be constituted as follows: (1) Bombay (including Sindh) and Berar, (2) Madras and Coorg, (3) Punjab, Baluchistan and Ajmere, (4) North-West Provinces and Central Provinces, (5) Bengal and Assam.

7. The machinery of the Government of India being generally unsuited for executive control, we propose that the surveyors in charge of these circles should be placed under the general control of the Local Governments whose names occupy the first place in the circle designations given below. But any of the Provinces in the circle would have the right to call on the surveyor for special assistance and advice at any time and work in each province would be done under the orders of the Local Government concerned. Under such an arrangement the expenditure would be more conveniently charged to Imperial than to Provincial revenues and we propose to accept it as an Imperial charge, saw in the case of Madras where it is now a Provincial charge and may continue to be such.

...

11. The amount involved is in itself not large and we think that, considering the importance of archaeological research, Rs. 91,000 odd is not an excessive expenditure for the whole of India. It is sometimes thought that archaeological work can wait almost indefinitely but this is certainly not true in India where decay is often exceptionally rapid. Moreover modern improvements such as railways, water-works and sanitary reforms appeal to other considerations and are often carried out by men without special archaeological knowledge and most valuable monuments are apt to disappear at their approach. This danger is imminent at the present stage of progress in India and any action to counteract it ought not be deferred. This view was shared by Sir H.Fowler, who in his Despatch No.28, Public (Records) dated 25 April 1895 wrote 'the importance of taking steps to prevent further deterioration or destruction of ancient monuments whose historical and linguistic value cannot be overstated, will not, I trust, be lost sight of'.[33]

The Foreign Department, Government of India suggested that the course of action to be taken for conservation and upkeep of archaeological monuments in princely states should be left to the Foreign Office. The scheme of reorganization of Archaeological Department in princely states should not form the reorganization plans that was recommended to Secretary of State for sanction.[34]

On 18 May 1899, George Hamilton, Secretary of State sanctioned the scheme for five years and called for a report on the progress made and the work remaining to be done in the archaeological survey and conservation of monuments under the Government of India. The Secretary of State felt after a five years term, "devolution of some of the archaeological work upon private societies or persons" could be considered.[35]

It was also decided by the Government of India through their Circular No. 2628-41-6 dated 2 August 1899 for making the service in the Archaeological Survey Department would be pensionable in the case of all persons appointed to the Department as on 18 May 1899.[36]

However, according to S. Roy, the scheme suffered from a number of defects. It completely ignored the value of excavation and left all initiative and responsibility in respect of conservation of archaeological monuments under the supervision of Local Governments. The survey was devoid of any proper direction.[37]

NOTES AND REFERENCES

1. *Story of Indian Archaeology* by S. Roy, 1784-1947, p. 72.
2. Revenue and Agriculture, Archaeology A, August 1891, No. 1.
3. Revenue and Agriculture, Archaeology, A, August 1891, No. 2.
4. Lansdowne Papers, N.A.I., Microfilm Acc. No. 1651, No. 16.
5. *Ibid.*
6. Lansdowne Papers, N.A.I., Microfilm, Acc. No. 1655, No. 505.
7. P.W.D., General A, October 1891, No. 153.
8. Revenue and Agriculture, Archaeology, Part-C, August 1893, No. 1.
9. *Ibid.*
10. *Ibid.*
11. *Ibid.*
12. *Ibid.*
13. *Ibid.*
14. *Ibid.*
15. *Ibid.*
16. Revenue and Agriculture Department, Archaeology, Part-C, April 1894, No. 1.
17. *Ibid.*
18. Home, Public, February 1895, No. 194.
19. Home, Public, February 1895, No. 199.
20. Public A, May 1895, No. 330.
21. Revenue and Agriculture, Archaeology B, June 1894, Nos. 19-22.
22. *Ibid.*
23. *Ibid.*
24. *Ibid.*
25. Revenue and Agriculture, Archaeology B, October B, No. 24.
26. *Ibid.*
27. Revenue and Agriculture Department, Archaeology, June 1891, No. 7.
28. Revenue and Agriculture Department, Archaeology and Epigraphy, January 1895, No. 3.
29. Revenue and Agriculture Department, Archaeology and Epigraphy, January 1895, No. 4.
30. Revenue and Agriculture Department, Archaeology A, January 1895, 1-5, Notes; June 1895, 19-22.
31. Revenue and Agriculture Department, Archaeology A, July 1895, Nos. 6-13 Notes.
32. Revenue and Agriculture Department, Archaeology and Epigraphy, July 1895, No. 6.
33. Revenue and Agriculture Department, Archaeology and Epigraphy, July 1898, No. 29
34. Revenue and Agriculture Department, Archaeology and Epigraphy, Nos. 10-29.
35. Revenue and Agriculture Department, Archaeology and Epigraphy, January 1900, No. 1.
36. Revenue and Agriculture Department, Archaeology and Epigraphy, January 1900, No. 6.
37. *The Story of Indian Archaeology* by S. Roy, p. 76.

CHAPTER XII

Curzon's Concern towards Care of Monuments (1899-1905)

The intervening period between the retirement of James Burgess and the assumption of Lord Curzon as Governor-General and Viceroy in 1899 has been described by Sourindranath Roy as a "bleak interlude" in his monumental treatise *History of Archaeology*.[1] However, Dilip K. Chakrabarty holds a different view. He was firmly of the view that this was not the correct assessment of the period. Firstly, he was of the view that the Government of India was fully alive to its responsibility towards archaeology. In fact, the Government had proposed to the Secretary of State for India for the creation of five archaeological circles in the country under a Surveyor who was to be responsible to the Local Governments. The Government of India clearly pointed out that it could not circumvent its responsibility towards archaeology without being taken up for adverse comments. Secondly, although there was lack of coordination from the administration and lack of supervisory control over the regional surveyors, the fact remained that a good deal of conservation work and archaeological research was conducted successfully during this period. It may be stated that a list of archaeological and antiquarian remains was prepared in various Presidencies which was primarily done at the behest of the Government of India. Besides, the Local Governments also took keen initiative in this direction. The annual progress reports in the archaeological field of the Government of North-West Provinces and Oudh during this period amply testifies the seriousness of the Government in this field and the amount of seriousness was not visible elsewhere. However, Chakrabarti admitted that "the lack of a centralized direction was no doubt the major problem in this context".[2]

The historians' opinions notwithstanding in archaeology, it was pertinent fact that no concrete work in archaeology, conservation of monuments in particular, was done. Towards the care of ancient monuments, a sum of Rs. 2,20,814 was expended during the period 1892-1898 in the entire country (Appendix XXIII).

This period of apathy and inactivity came to an end towards the close of 19th century. A new era ushered in with the assumption of Lord Curzon as Viceroy on 6 January 1899.[3] Curzon gave utmost importance to the promotion of archaeological research and the preservation of ancient monuments as a "part of our Imperial obligation to India". It was Lord Curzon as Viceroy of India who had established the archaeological service and had organized preservation of monuments effectively. Before coming to India, Curzon was keenly interested in archaeology, besides the art and literature of India. He was quite concerned over the conservation of ancient monuments of India when he assumed Viceroyalty. He exchanged correspondence with persons who were keen in the conservation of monuments of archaeological importance and took effective measures on the care of monuments.

On 26 November 1898, Lord Reay, formerly Governor of Bombay, addressed a letter to Lord Elgin, the Governor-General on the issue pertaining to preservation of monuments, inscriptions and documents which could be "secured efficiently" in India through a government agency.[4] Reay felt that if the Viceroy took keen interest in this direction, the adequate funds needed for the conservation would be easily forthcoming and the local people would easily give their consent for the purpose.

This letter impressed Curzon a great deal. He evinced personal interest in archaeology in general, and care and preservation of monuments in particular.

M. Ee-mile Haveloque, wife of A.E. Haveloque, the Governor of Madras, addressed a communication to Lord Curzon on 15 March 1899 wherein she detailed the vandalism which was prevalent throughout India in Delhi Fort, Akbar's Tomb and Sikandra at Agra.

She felt,

> archaeologists rarely possess an artistic sense and Indian ones are certainly no exception. But the general principles relating to the preservation of historical monuments are sufficiently known by this time. Some agreement ought, therefore, to be come to easily, some general rules were laid down by common consent for the guidance of Engineers and municipalities. The general ignorance of both and the destruction worked as much (or even more) by their mistaken zeal as by their neglect, have filled me, I must confess with extreme indignation. My testimony might seem prejudiced. I can only refer you to what Fergusson, in his *Indian Architecture*, says about the Fort of Delhi and Agra. His language is stronger than any I should dare to use. Unless the English are to pass as the master vandals of Indian rulers, something ought to be done and rapidly. There seems no other way than the stringent enforcement of the rules prevailing e.g. in the Commission des Monuments Historiques of France – a State Board as you know – or the similar institutions in Italy.
>
> ...It is all the more sad to see Indian things drifting to ruin everywhere, that very large sums are spent by Government in praiseworthy efforts to preserve a memory of them – e.g., the different archaeological surveys, such admirable looks as Smith's Fatehpur Sikri and c. But a general direction is needed and some general principles; some elementary truths have to be taught to men full of zeal, but untrained or badly trained who are not sufficient in touch with European archaeologists and comparative methods; above all, who have not in any degree that rarest of gifts among Englishmen, the aesthetic family. A no light can be hoped for, unfortunately, from Natives nobles whose taste seems utterly vitiated. If they could be led back to an intelligent appreciation of good Hindu work in the past, a love for it, a desire it should live in the future, more would be done for Indian industrial arts and architecture than by all the art schools in the world which will no more produce art than compulsion virtue. If your Excellency could make the taste of influential Hindus Hindu and a living thing, an appetite he would have deserved well of lovers of beauty all the world over.[5]

Lord Curzon, therefore, addressed a communication to Sir W. Mackworth Young, Lt. Governor, Punjab on 25 April 1899 and was horrified at the conversion of Moti Masjid, Lahore to a treasury by Sikhs and that of vandalism was in their agenda "I think unpardonable in us".[6]

He wrote to Sir A.P. MacDonell, Lt. Governor of North-West Provinces and Oudh on 2 July 1899 and stated that, "I am not altogether satisfied with the general supervision of Ancient Monuments in India and this again is one of the subjects which I am waiting as soon as I can find the spare hour, to raise."[7] In yet another letter of Curzon addressed to Sir A.P. MacDonell about the Stupa at Sarnath, he particularly lamented the archaeological finds pertaining to Buddhist sculptures which were housed in the Benaras College in a total neglect. He was of the opinion that a temporary shelter or covered verandah may be erected and the archaeological finds of Buddhist specimens should be kept properly classified and shown to visitors.[8]

On 10 August 1899, Sir J. Woodburn, Lt. Governor of Bengal informed Curzon about the ruins at Gaur and Pundua in Bengal lying buried in forests uncared. Woodburn pleaded to "preserve these beautiful monuments of the past".[9]

In a similar communication, R.B. Stewart, Acting Secretary, Government of Bombay addressed a communication to the Secretary, Revenue and Agriculture Department, Government of India on 17 August 1899 and pointed out the neglect of archaeological remains in Western India. He also referred to monuments and archaeological remains in Western India which should be preserved in the best possible manner. Stewart lamented that in India, the interest taken in archaeology by individuals was negligible or limited as compared to such practices in Europe. Stewart strongly pleaded for the deployment of an Archaeological Surveyor in Bombay Presidency.[10]

Curzon promptly addressed a communication to Sir Arthur Godley, Under Secretary of State for India, on 7 December 1899.

> I take a very keen interest in Archaeology and hold strong views about our obligations as custodians in India of what are, on the whole, the noblest series of monuments in the world. In the past we have scandalously neglected this duty and are only now tardily awakening to it. I am, therefore, personally going round, with the Director of archaeology of the Province, not merely every one of the principal monuments but every nook and cranny of everyone of them and am giving orders as to what is to be done. I do this at every place I visit and I hope at the end of five years to have effected a very perceptible change. I happen to take the keenest interest in architecture as well as Archaeology; and in my Eastern Travels to have made a close study of the Arabian style in particular so that I have some confidence in taking the matter in hand. I cannot find that since Lord Northbrook any Viceroy has troubled himself much about it.[11]

Taking immediate cognizance of this communication, Sir Arthur Godley addressed a communication to Lord Curzon on 29 December 1899 and study of English church architecture and the photographs of finest specimens of Indian architecture which prompted him to undertake a tour of India. He appreciated Curzon's concern for archaeological remain in India and for their preservation and conservation in right earnestness.[12]

On 15 January 1900, Curzon addressed a letter to W. Mackworth Young, Lt. Governor, Punjab in which he highlighted the apathy towards monuments by the British Indian Government but referred to the good work done in North-West Provinces in this regard. He lamented and pointed to dismally low allocations elsewhere in the other provinces which he stressed required increased allocation.[13]

Curzon delivered a comprehensive address at a meeting of the Asiatic Society, Calcutta on 7 February 1900, where he highlighted the Government's efforts in the preservation of monuments and archaeological ruins which required the Government's attention. Few excerpts of his brilliant speech have been detailed below:

> I hope that there is nothing inappropriate in my addressing to Society a few observations upon the duty of Government in respect to ancient buildings in India. The Asiatic Society of Bengal still, I trust, even in these days, when men are said to find no time for scholarship and when independent study or research seems to have faded out of Indian fashion, retains that interest in archaeology, which is so often testified to in its earlier publications and was promoted by so many of its most illustrious names. Surely here, if anywhere, in this house which enshrines the memorials and has frequently listened to the wisdom of great scholars and renowned students, it is permissible to recall the recollection of the present generation to a subject that so deeply engaged the attention of your early pioneers and that must still, even in a breathless age, appeal to the interest of every thoughtful man.
>
> In the course of my recent tour, during which I visited some of the most famous sites and beautiful and historic buildings in India, I more than once remarked, in reply to municipal addresses, that I regarded the conservation of ancient monuments one of the primary obligations of Government. We have a duty to our forerunners as well as to our contemporaries and our descendents – nay, our duty to the two latter classes in itself demands the recognition of an obligation to the former, since we are the custodians for our own age of that which has been bequeathed to us by an earlier and since posterity will rightly blame us if, owing to our neglect they fail to reap the same advantages that we have been privileged to enjoy. Moreover, how can we expect at the hands of futurity any consideration for the productions of our own time – if, indeed, any are worthy of such – unless we have ourselves shown a like respect to the handiwork of our predecessors? This obligation which I assert and accept on behalf of Government, is one of an even more binding character in India than in many European countries.

And a little further:

> If there be anyone who says to me that there is no duty devolving upon a Christian Government to preserve the monuments of a pagan art, or the sanctuaries of an alien faith, I cannot pause to argue with such a man. Art and beauty and the reverence that is owing to all that has evoked human genius or has inspired human faith, are dependent of creeds, and, in so far as they touch the sphere of religion, are embraced by the common religion of mankind.
>
> To us the relics of Hindu and Mohammedan, of Buddhist, Brahamin and Jain are, from the antiquarian, the historical and the artistic point of view, equally interesting and equally sacred. One does not excite a more vivid and the other a weaker emotion. Each fills a chapter in Indian history. Each is a part of heritage which providence has committed to the custody of the ruling power.

With regard to the claims of "research" and "preservation" to support from the Government, he remarks:

> Epigraphy should not set behind research any more than research should be set behind conservation. All are ordered parts of any scientific scheme of antiquarian work. I am not one of those who think that Government can afford to patronize the one and ignore the other. It is, in my judgement, equally our duty to dig and discover, to classify, reproduce and describe, to copy and decipher and to cherish and conserve. Of restoration I cannot, on the present occasion, undertake to speak, since the principles of legitimate and artistic restoration require a more detailed analysis than I have time to bestow upon them this evening. But it will be seen from what I have said that my view of the obligations of Government is not grudging and that my estimate of the work to be done is ample.

CURZON ENDS HIS ADDRESS

> For my part, I feel far from clear that Government might not do a good deal more than it is now doing, or than it has hitherto consented to do.

I certainly, cannot look forward to a time at which either the obligations of the State will have become exhausted or at which archaeological research and conservation in this country can dispense with Government direction and control. I see fruitful fields of labour still unexplored, bad blunders still to be corrected, gaping omissions to be supplied, plentiful opportunities for patient renovation and scholarly research. In my opinion, the taxpayers of this country are in the last degree unlikely to resent a somewhat higher expenditure – and, after all, a few thousand rupees go a long way in archaeological work and the total outlay is exceedingly small – upon objects in which I believe them to be as keenly interested as we are ourselves. I hope to assert more definitely during my time the Imperial responsibility of Government in respect of Indian antiquities, to inaugurate or to persuade a more liberal attitude on the part of those with whom it rests to provide the means and to be faithful guardian of the priceless treasure – house of art and learning that has, for a few years at any rate, been committed to my charge. (Appendix XXIV)

The speech of Lord Curzon received appreciation from all quarters. He also forwarded a copy of the address to Sir Arthur Godley, Under Secretary of State for India on 8 February 1900 and observed that neglect of monuments in India was apparent. He squarely blamed his predecessors and stated that due to the apparent apathetic attitude of British Indian Government, the neglect of the archaeological monuments had been continuous discussed in the Indian Press and hoped that "my statement will evoke an outburst of universal approval, both from Europeans and natives. **The Englishman** has already led off this morning".[14]

Sir Arthur Godley acknowledged the receipt of Curzon's address on 2 March 1900 and stated, "Many thanks for your archaeological paper which I read with interest and sympathy. How do you find time for all these things."[15]

Besides, Curzon acknowledged the letter of appreciation from Dr. P.Goethals, Archbishop of Calcutta and stated that, "I hope that I may be able to do something for Indian Archaeology in my time."[16]

Sir John Strachey, Ex Lieutenant Governor, North-West Provinces, praised the speech delivered by Curzon and hoped that "British Government shall become a more faithful guardian of her priceless treasure-house of art". Strachey also referred to architectural splendours of Mughals especially reflected in the Delhi's Red Fort, and lamented the destruction of the edifices of the Fort by the Military Engineers in fortifying the fort and destroyed the wall and gateway.[17]

Curzon had praised Lord Northbrook for his efforts in the conservation and care of ancient monuments. He told him on 22 February 1900, "You are so far as I can make out, the only Viceroy who has taken much interest in Ancient Monuments."[18]

Besides, Curzon also addressed a letter to Lord Hamilton, Secretary of State for India on 20 December 1900 stating:

... As regards the temple of Somnath what Lord Ellenborough did was to claim that he had brought back from Ghazni the historic Gates which were alleged to have been carried off from Somnath by Mahumud of Ghazni many hundred years before. Now Somnath is an old Hindu Temple and its doors, if such ever existed and if Mahmud carried them off, must have been Hindu in character and style, while from the still standing doorways their probable dimensions are known. On the other hand, the gates that Lord Ellenborough carried off from Gazni where I have seen the mosque from which they were taken, are doors of a Mohammedan character, and of a late and corrupt style, some centuries posterior to Mahmud himself. The fraud was discovered before the pompous procession and restitution to Somnath which had been planned by Lord Ellenborough, could be carried out and the unhappy gates now repose in an apartment of one of the Mogul Palaces in the Fort of Agra where I saw them last year.[19]

On the question of archaeological reform, Lord Curzon wrote to G. Hamilton that:

> In any case do let me entreat you to save from their devastating and pernicious activity the proposals which we are sending home to you this week for appointing Director or Inspector-General of Archaeology and for sending a little more money for a few years on the conservation of ancient buildings. A few years ago there were two such officers – a Curator of Ancient Monuments and a Director-General of Archaeology. Now there is neither. There is no supervision, no control. One province, like the N.W.P. spends a lot upon restoration and repairs. Another like the Punjab spends nothing. Beautiful remains are tumbling into irretrievable ruin, all for the want of a directing hand, and a few thousand rupees. The Archaeological Surveyor whom you sanctioned in Elgin's time are so humbly paid that we can only get inferior men. From time to time they perpetrate atrocious horrors partly from ignorance, still more because there is no one to guide them. I can do a great deal in my five years if only you will allow me. As it is, sooner than wait or have a squabble, I am doing a good many things myself. The Native Press is unanimous about the conservation of ancient Buildings and if we spent 5 lakhs a year upon it, you would not have a protest.[20]

Meanwhile, the Government of India received a communication on 13 March 1900 from Dr. M.A. Stein on the future appointment of Archaeological Surveyors. Stein stressed the need of appointing surveyors who were well versed with the history and archaeology of the province concerned, especially in Punjab. If an Archaeological Surveyor was to be appointed in Punjab, the incumbent should have considerable knowledge of ancient Indo-Aryan culture and literature, and should be trained in Indian historical and philosophical research. This would enable him to carry out his assigned functions in the "critical methods and results to the investigation of such Ancient monuments as are preserved come to light from time to time". He also stressed that some English scholars/students should be encouraged to prosecute archaeological and antiquarian studies in Indian context.

Stein further added, "In India, I believe, it will not be possible to find at present a native scholar thoroughly qualified from a scientific point of view and at the same time likely to accept the post on the terms offered. But it appears to me probable that one or the other Sanskrit scholar in England anxious to prosecute his studies under the favourable conditions offered by such an appointment may be attracted to it."[21]

It may as well be mentioned that the Government of India while appointing the Archaeological Surveyors in future took recommendations of Dr. Stein into consideration.

By now, Curzon had understood the nuances of archaeological monuments in India. He had thoroughly studied the problems of Indian archaeology and acquired the knowledge of archaeological ruins and the state of conservation of ancient monuments in India. He, therefore, embarked on a concrete and positive policy for the conservation and preservation of monuments of archaeological importance, which were in ruins.

Curzon, undoubtedly, was concerned with the apathetic attitude of the Government towards monuments and was determined to infuse life and blood in the Archaeological Survey Department so as ensure its effective functioning. He recorded an important minute in this direction on 23 September 1900 thus:

> I deliberately say Imperial responsibility, since I cannot conceive any obligation more strictly appertaining to a Supreme Government than the conservation of the most beautiful and perfect collection of monuments in the world or one more likely to be scamped and ignored by a delegation of all authority to provincial administrations.
>
> The way in which the Government of India, sometimes in obedience to, sometimes in collusion with, the Secretary of State has hitherto discharged or rather failed to discharge, this responsibility is, in my judgement, both sad and discreditable.

First in 1871, we appointed a Director-General of Archaeological Survey whose work was to be directly limited to research, record and description. Conservation was not considered to be a part of his duties.

When Lord Lytton, in 1878, first suggested a Curator of ancient monuments for the latter purpose, the idea was scouted as superfluous by the Secretary of State.

A little later, more generous counsels prevailed and a Curator was appointed in 1880 experimentally for a period of three years.

He was a very energetic and capable man. But he quarreled both with the Government of India and with the Local Governments and when his term was up, no fresh appointment was made.

A few years later an attempt was made to combine the functions both of research and conservation in a single individual; but since Dr. Burgess' retirement in 1889, there has been no head of their department, neither Curator of Ancient Monuments nor Director-General of Archaeology.

Thus, having originally started with the contention that one chief was sufficient and having next found that two were necessary, we have ended by having none at all.

Archaeology accordingly in India now rests upon the frail and impossible basis of the provincial system. This means that though the Imperial Government pays the cost of the entire establishment – which according to the estimate last sanctioned by the Secretary of State – amounts only to the paltry sum of Rs. 88,450 per annum – any expenditure whatever that is incurred upon exploration, upkeep, record, or repair is entirely dependent upon the volition of Local Governments who may as they please, spend much, little or nothing at all.

It is impossible to conceive a system more chaotic or futile in practice. I have made it my object to examine its operation for the last year and a half in every Province in India. The whole country is supposed to be divided into five circles with an Archaeological Surveyor for each. The geographical arrangement of these circles is fantastic in the extreme. Sind is lumped together with Bombay and Berar. Baluchistan is tacked on to the Punjab; and Ajmer is casually thrown in. The Central Provinces are added to the North-West Provinces which require the uninterrupted services of the best available man. In practice it is found that, till a week ago, the Punjab had never succeeded in appointing a surveyor at all and has only now 'faute de mieux' succeeded in persuading a young German philologist, who is willing to put up with a small salary to accept the charge of its incomparable monuments. Bengal, so far as I know has no surveyor. The surveyors in the remaining circles, instead of being scholars or even engineers are merely as their name implies – Surveyors who make drawings and write reports but can only at considerable risk be entrusted with the task of renovation or repair.

In practice, too, the most whimsical difference prevails between the policy adopted in different provinces. No Local Government is 'per se' interested in archaeology. It is occupied with grosser and more material concerns. The result is that the progress or suspension of archaeological work, the decay of priceless treasures of art, the restoration, sometimes involving the prostitution, of exquisite palaces and halls – all depend upon the taste of interest or caprice of the Local Governor who, if in a few rare cases, he exerts himself on the cause of art and good taste, may on the other hand if he chooses, leave an indelible and fatal mark upon the monuments of his province or more frequently be content with leaving no mark at all.

Thus it has come about the owing to the absence of any central and duly qualified advising authority, not merely are beautiful and famous buildings crumbling to decay but there is neither principle nor unity in conservation or repair while from time to time horrors are still committed that make the student shudder and turn grey.

A Local Government, moreover, can always plead its poverty or the pressure of other claims as an excuse for doing nothing; and as a matter of fact in the majority of palaces (the North-West Provinces under Sir A. Mac-Donnell are a notable exception) nothing whatever is done.

The continuance of this state of affairs seems to me little short of a scandal. Were Germany the ruling power in India, I do not hesitate to say that she would be spending many lakhs a year on task to what we have hitherto rather plumed ourselves on our generosity, Rs. 61,000 raised only a little more than a year ago to Rs. 88,000. Somewhere, indeed in the notes I have come across the astounding remark that if India assigned not more than Rs. 50,000 a year to the duty, she would still be doing the thing very handsomely.

When I reflect upon the sums of money that are gaily dispensed for the construction of impossible forts in impossible places which are to sustain an impossible siege against an impossible foe, I do not venture to hope that so mean a standard may not again be pleaded at any rate in my time.

It remains to be considered what we should do. I hold –

(1) That we ought to re-appoint a Curator of Monuments or Director-General of Archaeology in India. I rather prefer the latter little: because the former would seem to limit his obligatory duties to curation whereas he ought, in my opinion, to exercise a general supervision over all archaeological work in the country whether it be that of excavation or preservation or repair of epigraphy or registration or description. I think we should pay him a handsome salary and appoint him, say, for a period of five years. He should be a scholar and a student and if possible a trained explorer with some engineering knowledge, into the bargain. If we could not find him in England we might have to go to the continent.

(2) That the Local Governments should be called upon to set aside a minimum annual sum, to be fixed in some ratio to their resources and to the character and number of their archaeological treasures, for the work of the circle in question.

(3) That a fixed annual grant of say one lakh of rupees should be placed at the disposal of the Director-General to be assigned as grant-in-aid, upon application to and with the sanction in each case of the Imperial Government, to any particular object or task, demanding early or immediate execution and proved to be beyond the financial capacity of the Local Government.

(4) That he should visit all the circles in succession and the more important ones, so far as possible in each year; that he should coordinate and bring up to date the local surveys and reports and should, if necessary, present an annual report to Government upon his own work.

I think that in time a re-arrangement of the circles would be found necessary. But to begin with, I would not ask for too much; and I should be content if we could get what I have pleaded for.

I shall be glad of the opinion of Public Works Department and Finance Department on these proposals.[22]

The Public Works Department agreed to the proposals of Lord Curzon as enshrined in his minute of 23 September 1900. A.C. Trevor, Secretary, Public Works Department, however, recorded his doubts for selection of an officer from the cadre and establishment of a Public Works Department. He felt that it was possible to select an officer who had knowledge of engineering skills and could carry out the conservation and repairs to the monuments of archaeological importance but should possess adequate skills in the field of archaeology. Trevor further added that as per the Viceroy's proposals, the Local Government could be asked to allocate a fixed sum annually towards conservation of monuments and also attend to their repair works. However, Trevor added that such allocations from Imperial grants should work better. For this, he proposed that a fixed grant should be allocated under the budgetary grants of the Director General of Archaeology for being additionally provided to the Local Governments towards carrying out the repair works of monuments within their respective jurisdiction.[23]

However, the Financial Department expressed its eagerness to agree to the stipulations contained in the minute of Lord Curzon dated 23 September 1900. E.P.G. Law, Secretary, Financial Department, however, was of the view that an appointment of suitable staff and establishment for the preservation and restoration of monuments was absolutely essential to carry out the wishes of Lord Curzon. He suggested that the staff and establishment should be under the administrative purview of the Imperial Government. Law proposed that till such time the sanction of establishment for the Archaeology Survey Department was received, the question of increased allocation should be held in abeyance. Law regarded this expenditure was a "Luxury".[24]

After considering all the facts, contentions and suggestions, the Governor-General in Council communicated its remarks through a despatch to Lord George Hamilton, Secretary of State regarding the proposed appointment of a Director General of Archaeology. Before sending this despatch to procure support for the contentions included in the despatch for Secretary of State's considerations, Curzon expressed his desire to T.W. Holderness for procuring the signature in this despatch of "as many Honourable Members as may be. There is no hurry and the more signatures the better". In this despatch, the Governor-General in Council gave a retrospect of the efforts. In this dispatch, the efforts put in by Captain Cole towards the cause of archaeology was amply highlighted and the budgetary allocations in provincial governments was also highlighted. The **modus operandi** of the Archaeological Survey Department to exercise, "a general supervision over all the archaeological work of the country whether it be that of excavation, of preservation or repair, of epigraphy or of the registration and description of monuments and ancient remains, he could coordinate and bring up to date local surveys and reports and he should, if necessary, present an annual report to us of his own work".[25]

The Governor-General in Council enclosed the speech delivered by Lord Curzon at the Asiatic Society of Bengal at Calcutta on 7 February 1900 and requested the Secretary of State that "in this view we take of the responsibilities of the Imperial Government was foreshadowed and laid down and we trust that our proposals for carrying out the pledge that was then given may receive your Lordship's approval.[26]

However, no reply was received from the Secretary of State. Lord Curzon, therefore, reminded him on 1 April 1901 to expedite sanction of grant and appointment of a Director General of Archaeology, "If you give us the money and the man we asked for, the whole thing will be systematized."[27]

The Secretary of State on 14 May 1901 sent a telegram conveying the sanction of the post of the Director General of Archaeology for a period of five years on an experimental basis. The Secretary of State also proposed the appointment of Vincent Smith, formerly N.W.P. and Oudh to the post of Director General of Archaeology on an annual salary of Rs. 20,000 and "free passage to India in addition to present pension".[28] The telegram was followed by a despatch from the Secretary of State replicating the proposals contained in the telegram. The Secretary of State was of the view that,

> Vincent Smith is a zealous and laborious archaeologist and would undoubtedly make a suitable director of exploration and surveys including the publication of any results obtained. It is less certain that he possesses the executive ability and artistic taste which are needed for the control of the repair and restoration of buildings. But his knowledge of the country and of the ways of Government, would be much in his favour and would perhaps make his efforts more immediate fruitful than those of a stranger to the country.[29]

The members of the Governor-General in Council were not in the favour of Smith's appointment to the post of Director General and stated, "we doubt if he would be a suitable selection, we think that Secretary of State ought to have no difficulty in finding a better man".[30]

Reacting to the suggestion of Secretary of State's dispatch on the suggestion for appointment of Vincent Smith, Curzon sought the confidential opinion of Lt. Governor, North-West Provinces and Oudh. The Viceroy had stated, "Can you favour me with your confidential opinion as to his qualifications? My impression is that he is deficient both in expert and artistic knowledge and in energy."[31]

The Lt. Governor, North-West Provinces, replied to the Viceroy immediately the next day, i.e., 27 May 1901 through a telegram and stated that Vincent Smith was not suitable for appointment to the post of Director General of Archaeology and stated "... Your Excellency desires to control and coordinate provincial operations connected with, first, monumental archaeology and secondly, Epigraphy on neither subject is Mr. Vincent Smith an expert. Indeed I believe he knows nothing of architecture. He is merely an amateur in antiquarian researches with Indian History and religious growth. As Director General of Archaeology, I fear he would be found wanting."[32]

Thereafter, Curzon taking all the facts into consideration informed G. Hamilton, Secretary of State, on 12 June 1901 that:

"Vincent Smith is not at all the man that we want for the new Director General of Archaeology. He is an amateur and a dilettante, we want a man of science." Besides, Curzon also apprised the Secretary of State about the position regarding funds for the work pertaining to preservation and conservation of monuments of archaeological importance: "The man will be powerless without the fresh grant." He further stated, "It is almost entirely consumed in salaries and establishment and we have no money to conduct archaeological work of any kind."[33]

In the meantime, the name of John H. Marshall emerged for the post of the Director General of Archaeology. Curzon addressed a communication to Sir Arthur Godley on 8 November 1901 and stated, "The Indian Paper say that you have selected an archaeologist of the name of Marshall who hails from explorations in Crete and they are denouncing this wanton sacrifice of India's interests. If he be your man I have little doubt that he is good one. But so far I have heard nothing about it."[34]

After considering the Despatch of the Governor-General in Council of 20 December 1900, George Hamilton, the Secretary of State, sent a Despatch to the Governor-General on the appointment of John Marshall as Director General of Archaeology and also underlined the future policy to be adopted by the Government of India with regard to the archaeological work in India.

> ...In that letter it is stated that the present organization of the Archaeological Department is defective in that, while providing a staff of archaeological surveyors whose services are placed at the disposal of Local Governments, it makes no provision for their control and guidance by a competent central authority, nor gives to your Excellency's Government any means of informing itself as to what measures are being taken for the proper preservation of ancient buildings, or as to whether the Local Governments are sufficiently alive to the duties which, under the present Constitution of the Archaeological Department, devolve in this respect upon them. You consider that the ultimate responsibility for the preservation of the great historical monuments of India necessarily rests with the Government of India and urge that you should be placed in a position to effectively discharge this responsibility. You propose that the Director-General should exercise general supervision over all the archaeological work of the country including research as well as the conservation, that he

should coordinate and bring upto date local surveyors and that he should, if so required, submit an annual report on his own work. You further propose to make provision in the Imperial estimates, to the extent of at least one lac of rupees a year; for grants-in-aid to provincial Governments for archaeological work of special importance and magnitude.

I am in complete sympathy with your Excellency's desire that the great historical buildings of India should be preserved so far as may be practicable from decay and as your Excellency's Government is of opinion that there is no security that this will be done unless a special officer be appointed for a term of years to take stock of the position and to advise the responsible authorities and guide the provincial surveyors, I have decided to sanction the appointment of a Director of Archaeology for a term of five years and to approve your proposal to provide in the estimates an annual sum not exceeding one lac from which grants-in-aid of archaeological work may be made to Local Governments. I desire, however, to express my concurrence in the view set out in the Marquess of Hartington's Despatch No. 43 (Public Works) dated 11th November 1880 (Surveys A, Progs, February 1881, No. 1) that no efficient and permanent system for the preservation of ancient monuments is possible unless it be taken up by the several Local Governments and I trust that this principle will be observed in any arrangements which may be made during the continuance of the office of Director. It should, I conceive, be the primary aim of the Director to establish harmonious relations with the provincial Governments and to work through them.

I regret to learn that cases have come within Your Excellency's observation "in which beautiful or famous fabrics are crumbling in ruin". Or are diverted from their original purpose to civil uses. I find that in the past considerable sums have been expended by Local Governments from provincial resources on the maintenance of the more celebrated monuments of antiquity in their respective territories. In view of this evidence of practical sympathy and also of the wide interest, which the monuments of India excite, I imagine that in many of the cases to which Your Excellency refers the damage must be of old standing and the decay far advanced rendering conservation a difficult and costly affair. I think, your Government will agree with me that it would be improper to expend large sums of money in the attempt to conserve buildings which are in an advanced stage of ruin and which are not of more than local importance. With regard to mosques and temples and other similar edifices that have been diverted from their original purpose to civil uses, I am under the impression that such misappropriation of this kind as still exists in British India originated in many instances under Native rule, and is consequently of ancient date. I think that questions of expediency as to the restoration of such buildings to their original uses may reasonably arise when the desecration occurred under Native rule, has been acquiesced in for a number of generations and cannot be remedied without considerable expenditure of public inconvenience. I make these remarks not as a criticism on the views held by your Excellency's Government, but because I consider that there are limits of financial and administrative, to the work of conservation which it is proposed to entrust to the Director of Archaeology and also because it is possible that some of the instances of apparent neglect which you ascribe to remissness of the Local Governments may be due to the existence of such limits.[35]

The Secretary of State for India on the appointment of John Marshall, who was to be appointed for a period of five years on a salary of Rs. 1,600 per month, requested the Governor-General in Council to send periodically the progress reports of the work done by the Archaeology Survey Department under the Director Generalship of John Marshall. The Secretary of State for India also forwarded the letter dated 30 September 1901 received from Marshall detailing his special qualifications and achievements[36] (Appendix XXV).

Similarly, Sir Arthur Godley, Under Secretary of State for India, addressed a communication to Lord Curzon on 31 December 1901 wherein he attributed the selection of Marshall to Maunde Thompson of the British Museum who recommended the incumbent. He further stated that Marshall was a distinguished scholar from Cambridge and had a stint in Greece and Crete in the archaeological pursuits. Godley also recommended the "compensation allowance" for Marshall.[37]

Besides, T.W. Holderness, Secretary, Revenue and Statistics, India House also addressed a similar communication to Curzon on the appointment of Marshall on 31 January 1902 and stated, "This is Marshall's present ideal and hope he will keep to it and that his five years of probationary service may prove sufficiently valuable to ensure his being permanently retained. He is fully determined to master Sanskrit as being an indispensable aid to his work."[38]

RESOLUTION

A Resolution [Department of Revenue and Agriculture No. 7-6-12 (Archaeology and Epigraphy) dated 11 February 1902] was adopted which defined the duties of the new Director-General and detailed the policy of the Government of India relating to work on archaeology in India. The Resolution stated:

> The conservation of the ancient buildings which provide so splendid a record of Indian history and so interesting an illustration of the artistic and religious feelings of the past is a task that should appeal powerfully to the sympathy of the Government of this country and that must be regarded as a responsibility for the due discharge of which it will properly be held to account. For some time past the attention of the Governor-General in Council has been directed to the question of securing the recognition of a liberal policy in this matter and of increasing the efficiency of the organization, which exists for carrying it into effect. Under a scheme, which was introduced in 1898, the provinces of British India were grouped into five circles to each of which an Archaeological Surveyor was appointed, to be paid from the Imperial revenues but to be controlled by the Local Government within whose jurisdiction his head-quarters were situated. He was charged with the duties of cataloguing archaeological remains, of advising the Local Government concerning the preservation of such of these remains as merited care and generally, with the prosecution of archaeological research. Responsibility for the effective conservation of such monuments as it was decided to maintain was left with Local Governments, which were to employ the agency of the Provincial Public Works Departments in carrying out necessary measures of conservation and repair. This responsibility has led in some provinces to a liberal and well-judged expenditure and the Governor-General in Council recognizes that the local interest and pride in the public monuments of province, which are thereby developed, should furnish the most effective security against their neglect. But the organization has been shown to be imperfect in so far as it has left the Archaeological Department without an expert Head who could assist local effort with authoritative advice and guidance and maintain a continuous record of the archaeological needs of the various provinces and of the action taken to meet them. In the absence of such a central authority, the attention that is given to the conservation of ancient monuments of the country and to archaeological questions in general must depend partly upon the attractiveness which these subjects may possess for particular Heads of local governments and administrations partly upon the sufficiency of available funds. With a view to introducing greater uniformity as well as greater liberality of treatment, the Governor-General in Council has determined with the approval of the Secretary of State to appoint tentatively for a term of five years a Director General of Archaeology and Mr. J.H. Marshall has been selected for the post. In name, the appointment will be a revival of that held by Major-General Cunningham and Dr. Burgess between the years 1871 and 1889. But the duties of the incumbent will extend considerably beyond the direction and control of archaeological research to which these officers mainly directed their attention. It will be most important of his functions to secure that the ancient monuments of the country are properly cared for, that they are not utilized for purposes, which are inappropriate or unseemly, that repairs are executed when required, and that any restorations which may be attempted are conducted on artistic lines. In this respect his position will be generally similar to that occupied by the Curator of Ancient Monuments who held office from 1880 to 1883. But his

> duties will extend to the exercise of a general supervision over all the archaeological work of the country whether it be that of excavation or preservation or repair or of the registration and description of monuments and ancient remains or of antiquarian research; he will assist the Provincial Surveyors in ascertaining and formulating the special requirements of each province; and he will advise the Government of India as to the operations for which special subsidies may be allotted from Imperial funds. He should visit all the circles in succession and the more important ones, so far as, impossible in each year succinctly reporting the general results of his tour to the Local Governments and each province visited and offering any suggestion that he may have to make in connection with the buildings which he has inspected. He should co-ordinate and bring up to date the local surveys and reports and he will be expected to submit annually to the Government of India a brief report on the progress effected during each official year.
>
> The Governor-General in Council desires to make it known that the creation of this appointment is in no way intended to weaken the responsibility of Local Governments for the care of the ancient monuments of their provinces. Their duty in this respect will remain unimpaired but it is hoped that a stimulus may be lent to its continuous and effective discharge by the offer of expert advice and, where required, of practical assistance. The present arrangements under which repairs and restorations are carried out by the Provincial Departments of Public Works will remain unaltered and the Government of India are indeed of opinion that in the interests of continuity of administration, it is desirable that each Local Government should fix an annual minimum sum to be expended on these purposes. The Governor-General in Council is prepared to emphasize its own responsibility in the matter and to facilitate the prompt undertaking of necessary works reserving annually a sum of one lakh of rupees to be distributed for particular objects demanding early execution and shown to be beyond the financial capacity of Local Governments. It is further in contemplation to take powers by legislation for the more efficacious protection and repair of ancient buildings in which case these subsidies will prove of special assistance to those administrations whose archaeological responsibilities will thereby be enhanced.[39]

John Marshall assumed the charge of his duties as Director General of Archaeology on the forenoon of 22 February 1902. A notification for his appointment was issued on 20 March 1902.[40]

J.B. Fuller, Secretary, Department of Revenue and Agriculture, addressed a communication to John Marshall on 25 March 1902 wherein he detailed the administrative arrangements on the compliance of orders by the Archaeological Surveyor and the Epigraphist to take their orders from the Provincial Government concerned and their functions would be advisory in character. However, he was authorized to correspond with them on all technical matters.[41] Besides, the Government of India decided to have his permanent headquarters at Simla.[42]

Vogel gave an estimate of the performance of John Marshall in the field of archaeology. He stated,

> Marshall was entrusted with the charge of both archaeological research and conservation of monuments and the hitherto neglected field of conservation was given priority by Marshall. The Director General was to function differently from what he had been functioning earlier. Though his appointment was viewed by orientalists with suspicion but the office was entrusted to Marshall who was the "right man in the right place". He succeeded in improving and developing both the conservation of monuments and archaeological research. He showed himself to be a man of good taste and sound judgement and a man of great intelligence and extensive knowledge. He applied the strict scientific methods that he had acquired in Crete.[43]

Besides, Curzon also addressed a communication to Hamilton, Secretary of State on 17 April 1902 about Marshall's competence in the field of archaeology and advised him to "learn

Sanskrit at once in order to be able to deal with inscriptions, one of the most important branch of Indian archaeology".[44]

Again, in the next week dated 23 April 1902, praising Marshall, Curzon wrote to the Secretary of State:

> The work of Agra Monuments that has been done there since my first visit as Viceroy nearly 3 years ago is really wonderful. Sir A. MacDonnell was very sympathetic to archaeological restoration and the Government has plenty of money. The crimes of earlier vandals have one by one been obliterated; repair and renovation have, on the whole, been most judiciously applied; the whole of the principal mosques, tombs and c. have been surrounded with exquisite gardens to parks and by the time I leave India, I believe it may be said with truth that the Agra Monuments will be best tended, just as they are also the most beautiful body of architectural remains in the world. I have supervised and given orders upon every single detail myself; for the local engineers who have to carry them out are destitute of the faintest artistic perception and if left to themselves; will perform horrors that make one alternately laugh and weep. In future, I hope that Marshall, the Archaeologist whom you sent out to me and by whom I have been quite favourably impressed will relieve me of a good deal of this labour and will supply the controlling and coordinating hand.[45]

Curzon again wrote to the Secretary of State on March 1903 that:

"The best of the men whom you have sent out to me in my time has been Marshall, the Archaeologist. He has taken very kindly to his work and will, I think be a really valuable man."[46]

John Marshall proved himself as a competent archaeologist. With the support and cooperation of Lord Curzon, he did a wonderful work in the field of archaeology and made valuable contribution in the field of care of ancient monuments. Marshall had taken a number of administrative decisions, which has a considerable bearing on the conservation of monuments in India. Before taking charge of the post of Director General of Archaeology, John Marshall had approved a scheme for the conservation of ancient monuments in princely states.

Towards this objective, J.B. Wood, Under Secretary, Foreign Department, Government of India had addressed a communication on 29 June 1900 to the local governments and administrations and to political officers. This communication was sent primarily with a view to effect reorganization of the Archaeological Survey Department with reference to the princely states under their respective jurisdiction. This letter detailed the policy towards care of monuments in princely states and the propagation of the Government's policy on archaeological matters. Wood also emphasized the need of obtaining the advice of archaeological surveyors appointed in five circles for seeking expert opinion in the conservation of monuments. It was categorically indicated that funds would not be elicited from the Princely States in the field of conservation and preservation of monuments for carrying out effective repair works.[47]

This scheme was approved by the local governments, administrations and also by the princely states. However, the scheme was adopted with slight alterations. J.B. Wood, Under Secretary, Government of India, Foreign Department, informed this decision to the Governments of Madras, Bengal, Bombay and Punjab on 4 June 1901. The areas of the archaeological circles were earmarked for the purpose of advising the princely states on matters of archaeological interest and conservation of monuments. The archaeological circles along with the details of princely states covered are as hereunder:

Punjab, Baluchistan and Ajmere Circle: Kashmir, Rajputana and the Native States in the Punjab and Baluchistan. The surveyor may also correspond with the political officers in tribal territories, such as the Political Agent for Dir, Swat and Chitral at Malakand with reference to archaeological remains in such territory outside British India.

Bombay and Berar Circle: Baroda, Central India, Hyderabad and the Native States within the political jurisdiction of the Government of Bombay.

Madras Circle: The Native States within the political jurisdiction of the Government of Madras.

Bengal and Assam Circle: The Native States in Bengal and the Manipur State.

The archaeological surveyors were instructed to avoid confrontation and misrepresentation of aims and objectives of the Government of India which might embarrass or offend the princely chiefs. A set of guidelines were formulated for discharging their respective functions. The archaeological surveyors were specifically instructed to refrain from giving any orders to the princely states and any suggestion should be conveyed to the princely states through "the medium of political authorities". Wood also conveyed the intention of the Government of India for appointment of qualified archaeologists by princely states, as was appointed by the Mysore State and to "enlist sympathies of the native states in the task of preserving the monuments of archaeological and historical interest within their territories".[48]

Even Marshall gave his opinion with regard to the archaeological care of monuments in the princely states. He stated that in pursuance of the Government's policy in helping the princely states in the field of care and conservation of monuments, the princely states, viz., Hyderabad, Udaipur, Bhopal, Dhar had accepted the advice and undertook serious measures with regard to conservation of archaeological heritage. Besides, several princely states, viz., Hyderabad, Kashmir and Gwalior had instituted archaeological departments by placing them under "charge of qualified officers obtained from the Archaeological Department of India".[49]

In 1902, a decision was taken by the Government of India for appointing an Architect – Archaeologist for Islamic buildings in North India (United Provinces) which had fallen vacant due to the death of E.W. Smith. The Government of India also utilized this opportunity to effect some changes in the organizational structure of Archaeological Survey especially for conservation of monuments in Agra which was also linked with conservation of monuments in Delhi and Lahore. The Government felt that conservation of these monuments forms a special branch of archaeology and was distinct from the study of Hindu and Buddhist archaeology or for that matter distinct even from epigraphical and numismatic research. The Government, therefore, felt that these monuments should be grouped in a circle which should be formed and placed under the charge of a "Surveyor with special architectural and other qualifications". [50]

The Local Governments accepted this proposal and the Governor-General in Council informed Lord Hamilton, Secretary of State for India, on 29 January 1903 accordingly.

The Governor-General in Council in his dispatch to the Secretary of State stated that it was imperative for the surveyor that he should be well versed with art and architecture of both Hindu and Islamic styles, and also mixed styles of architecture so as to impart guidance and training to the Local Governments under the supervision of the Director General, Archaeology so as to ensure "to do justice to so responsible a task".[51]

The Governor-General in Council further added in his dispatch to the Secretary of State to deploy an architect to train the surveyor attached to the Punjab circle, in order to ensure paper preservation and conservation of monuments in Delhi and Lahore besides Agra, and also requested to extend the jurisdiction of the Surveyor of Punjab to United Provinces to archaeological work besides architecture. The Governor-General in Council contended that the Punjab surveyor was well qualified to carry out the archaeological investigations in epigraphy, numismatics and other allied disciplines. This proposal resulted in organizational changes which was effected for the archaeological work in provinces. As Rajputana was under the jurisdiction of Punjab circle and Central Provinces was under the United Provinces, the Secretary of State was accordingly apprised by the Governor-General in Council that the archaeological circle of Rajputana and Central Provinces were attached to Bombay circle and an assistant to the Archaeological Surveyor was attached to the Bombay circle. The Secretary of State was also informed that the proposal of the Government of India was accepted by the concerned Local Governments. [52]

The Secretary of State, however, accepted the proposal of the Government of India.[53] J.O. Miller, Secretary, Government, in his recommendations in the form of a note had stated Shepherd, who was from Oxford, could be entrusted with the job profile of an architect in the Archaeological Department, United Provinces. He stated that he was a restorer rather than a repairer. Besides, it was also noted that the upkeep of principal monuments in United Provinces would be the responsibility of architect-archaeologist under the guidance of the Director General, archaeology. Besides, in the United Provinces Circle, especially for the monuments of Agra, Delhi and Lahore, the jurisdiction of work of the surveyors, viz., Shepherd and Dr. Vogel was also proposed. Shepherd was hitherto entrusted with the responsibility of Islamic monuments with Dr. Vogel, who was entrusted with the responsibility for upkeep of Hindu and Buddhist monuments. Besides, Dr. Vogel would also be entrusted with functions relating to epigraphy and numismatics. The responsibility of Public Works Department was limited to execution of repair works of the monuments along with their upkeep.[54]

Marshall, however, stated that Shepherd was more competent than Vogel and that the former could be entrusted with the conservation of all monuments of Islamic architecture, whereas Vogel would be entrusted with the upkeep of monuments bearing Hindu and Buddhist architecture but with the amalgamation of the zonal circles, the services of Maulvi and Pandit would have to be utilized both by Shepherd and Vogel jointly and Maulvi would also render his services to Shepherd as most of monuments were situated in Punjab.[55]

On 1 July 1903, J.O. Miller, Secretary, Government of India apprised the Secretary, Public Works Department, Government of United Provinces detailing the duties assigned to Vogel and Shepherd. He elaborated that Vogel would be entrusted with the responsibility of overseeing the functions relating to epigraphy, numismatics and excavations connected with monuments of Hindu and Buddhist architecture. He further laid down that the Archaeological Surveyor would be under the administrative control of the Government of United Provinces but would have to obtain advice with regard to conservation work from the Director General of Archaeology before he transmits them to the Local Government for its approval. On the other hand, the Archeological Superintendent would function under the Government of Punjab "but either Government may address these officers direct in matters falling within each officer's sphere of work. The two officers will also communicate direct with one another on all professional matters".

Miller concluded by stating that the Annual Reports should be drawn by each officer in the amalgamated circle, "copies of which will be submitted to each of the Local Government concerned".[56]

In June 1902, R.G. Hardy, Officiating Secretary, Government of India, addressed a letter to John Marshall on the scheme for conservation of monuments of archaeological interest. He emphasized preparation of lists of ancient monuments as a basis for carrying out the work of conservation. Hardy gave a retrospect for the guidance of Marshall. He reiterated the following points:

1. A rough initial catalogue of all ancient remains and building in each district to be prepared by district officials assisted by archaeological officers,
2. A revision of the initial list by archaeological officers and a preliminary classification of ancient monuments according to their archaeological or historical value, their condition and the possibility or desirability of preserving them;
3. A final revision and classification under the orders of the Local Governments.

Hardy also indicated the progress made towards the preparation of lists by the Local Governments and emphasized that "Archaeology would continue to require skilled supervision and that the operations of the Archaeological Survey Department could not be terminated at an early period." Besides, he referred to a Circular dated 27 June 1895, which enunciated the principles to carry out effective preservation of monuments of archaeological importance. It declared that the primary duty of archaeological officers is 'to advise upon, assist in and secure the effective preservation of the buildings which it may be decided to preserve' and their second duty 'to revise and perfect the existing list of remains where those lists are still unsatisfactory'.[57] Hardy also added that it was an opportune time to review the progress in the field of archaeology, particularly monuments preservation. He felt that action should be initiated to carry out systematically the scheme of conservation of archaeological monuments.

Hardy emphasized the need to document and centralize information available on archaeology, particularly conservation of monuments, in various libraries at Calcutta and Delhi. He desired that a "Catalogue Raisonne" of this material should be prepared. He concluded by stating, "All this will take time but I am to ask you not to lose sight of the subject".[58]

Later in 1902, the matter pertaining to preservation **in situ** of archaeological objects arose when it was decided by the Government of Bombay to remove the collection of archaeological objects at Bijapur and shift them to Poona.[59]

Reacting to this matter of intrinsic interest, Marshall felt that archaeological remains of Bijapur should not be shifted and emphasized that it should be preserved "on their original site as suggested by the Collector and Executive Engineer at Bijapur". He referred to archaeological objects that were shifted to Lucknow Museum from Mathura. This resulted in confusion, as many of these objects could not be identified and the provenance of these objects of archaeological interest could not be traced. Marshall felt that if the archaeological remains from Bijapur were to be shifted to Poona, it would become a precedent for further centralization of archaeological objects in future.[60]

R.G. Hardy, Officiating Secretary, Revenue and Agriculture Department, Government of India agreed with the opinion of Marshall and stated that "it will be a pity to remove the Bijapur antiquities at all".

However, Lord Curzon gave his opinion in a note dated 30 May 1902 thus:

> The question raised is one of principle and it involves a much wider range of application than the limited case of Bijapur. It is the question whether we are to encourage local collections or museums in India in connection with the localities or neighbourhoods where the objects have been found or whether we should for the reasons named by Bombay and by Hon'ble Member centralize in capital cities or larger towns. To my mind, there can be no doubt that the former is the sound and the latter the faulty principle. I am acting or advising upon the former basis throughout India. I have persuaded Sir J. Woodburn to start a small Exhibition or Museum at Malda of the sculptured stones and enameled bricks etc. from the ruins of Gaur and Pandua. At present they are lying about uncared for or have been purloined for private houses and gardens. The visitor to Gaur and Pandua must start from Malda and will see the remains there whereas the odds are that they would be entirely

overlooked (apart from the expence of removal) in a corner of the Imperial Museum at Calcutta. Again I have instructed Colonel Deane to start a Local Museum at Peshawar, and if he can, to recover some of the last objects of his Province, from the Museum at Lahore.

Similarly I got Sir F. Fryer to start a Local Museum for the stamped and enameled bricks, the Buddha figures, etc. at Pagaha.

Why should we surrender this principle – all for the sake of a few rupees – at Bijapur? If 'there has never been any one there who has taken much or any interest in it' – that is the fault of the Local Government which has not itself shown the least interest and has not instructed its officers and if 'most officials have looked upon it as so much lumber and rubbish' – that only illustrates the stupidity of the Bombay officials.

It is a very good thing that there should be a Museum at Poona or if the Governor prefers at Bombay for the collection of scattered slabs, stones and archaeological objects in general from different parts of the Province though I very much question whether a room or rooms in the Town Hall are the proper sort of place for the purpose.

But where a collection already exists, in connection with a famous group of buildings or remains, that attracts visitors on its own account, and represents the architecture or sculpture of a particular epoch or style, then I think it a great pity to sever these objects from their natural surroundings, in order to add to the size or the symmetry of central collection.

If the plea be raised that it is necessary for their conservation, the answer would seem to be that nothing is required beyond the orders of Government and a slight outlay for their proper conservation at Bijapur. It is pitiable to hear a Local Government say that the collection will be at the mercy of future Collectors and Assistant Engineers when the present fortuitous combination of local intelligence has disappeared; while, if the contents are as reported at present unsafe then the Local Government cannot possibly be acquitted of blame for not making them safer.

I think we might reply in this general sense, though not, of course, verbatim in the above terms and might say that the Government of India having adopted the policy of encouraging local collection, in places where the conditions that I have described exist, they would be most reluctant to sanction a departure from them in such a case as Bijapur and that it would be in their opinion far better to issue such orders as would ensure the proper custody and the conservation of these objects at Bijapur itself than to carry them off to Poona or Bombay.[61]

However, R.G. Hardy, Secretary, Government of India addressed a communication to the Secretary, Government of Bombay on 16 June 1902 and emphasised that archaeological antiquities and remains should be preserved **in situ.** However, scattered stones, isolated figures and objects of archaeological interest could be deposited in a Central Museum. He stated that the policy of encouraging local collections in places where they exist had been accepted by the Government of India and departure from this accepted policy should not be accepted. The Government of Bombay should, in fact, sanction a small outlay for the conservation of archaeological antiquities at Bijapur rather than shifting them to Poona or Bombay. "If the Government of Bombay attaches serious importance to this matter of archaeological importance, the officials of Bijapur and that successors would effectively preserve the archaeological relics with interest and devotion."[62]

Curzon, however, closely monitored the work of archaeological surveyors. He enquired from Lord Ampthill, Governor of Madras regarding the protection of Asoka inscriptions at Purushottampur in Madras and steps taken by Rea, the Archaeological Surveyor in Madras. Ampthill replied on 4 April 1902.

"I have written to Mr. Rea who I confess with shame, I had never even seen or heard of. You will be surprised to hear that neither of my colleagues nor a single member of our Secretariat has ever seen Mr. Rea or heard of his work. I shall make a point of finding out what he has done and is doing now."[63]

Lord Ampthill addressed yet another communication to Lord Curzon on 12 April 1902, wherein he criticized the working of Rea, Archaeologist and stated that he "does not display much enthusiasm or give much information but I have given to Public Works Department to prepare an estimate for a protecting roof and railing to the Asoka inscription".[64]

Curzon immediately apprised George Hamilton, Secretary of State, of the indifferent and apathetic attitude of Rea as informed by Ampthill in the preservation of an Asokan inscription.[65]

Lord Hamilton in his communication addressed to Curzon on 15 May 1902 had appreciated his efforts in preservation of ancient monuments of archaeological importance in India especially at Agra which had been attended with utmost care. He further stated, "The story you tell of the Madras Government being in ignorance of their official archaeologist is a very good comment upon our rule in India and elsewhere I do not know how it is possible to infuse imagination or artistic taste into the prosaic beings who constitute the great mass of the governing class in India and the colonies."[66]

In June 1902, Curzon once again addressed a letter to Ampthill, Governor of Madras in which he lamented at the state of affairs of archaeology in Madras.

He stated:

> It is rather staggered to hear that none of your leading men knew Mr. Rea. It illustrated the disrepute and obscurity into which archaeology has fallen in India. I hope to send down the new Director-General, Archaeology to see your principal antiquities to make the acquaintance of Mr. Rea, to consult with you and to frame a plan for putting Archaeology in Madras on a firmer and more scientific footing. He is keen and competent and I am sure that you will give him every assistance in your power.[67]

It may as well be stated that right from the beginning, Marshall emphasized the need and importance of a good library for undertaking the study of various aspects of archaeology especially ancient monuments. On 20 August 1902, he had submitted a proposal to the Government of India for establishment of a Central Archaeological Library at Simla. Marshall proposed that:

> Central Archaeological Library which in the primary instance with comprise books immediately needed by the Archaeological Surveyors in the several circles and which they cannot readily obtain elsewhere.
>
> Subject to the approval of the Government of India, I beg to propose that a sum of Rs. 6,000 be sanctioned from the lakh of rupees provided in the budget estimates for archaeological purposes during the current year for the purpose of:
>
> (a) Books specially required at present by the Archaeological Surveyors and which cannot be obtained readily from elsewhere.
> (b) Government publications on Indian Archaeology which cannot otherwise be procured.
> (c) Sets of Journals of the leading Societies which specialize on Indian Archaeology.
> (d) Recent European publications on the subject (the lack of which is greatly felt by the Archaeological Surveyors).
> (e) Photographs of Archaeological value.
> (f) The cases and shelves necessary to receive the books and photographs.[68]

The Government of India sent its approval for the establishment of Central Archaeological Library at Simla. J.O. Miller, Secretary, Government of India through his communication dated 17 September 1902 sanctioned "a sum of Rs. 6,000/- from the grant of one lakh provided for archaeological work in the budget estimates of the Archaeological Survey Department during the current year to meet expenditure connected with the scheme."[69]

A provision of Rs. 4,000/- was made for the library in 1903-04 and Marshall hailed it as "the best archaeological library in India, perhaps in Asia".[70] Later, the library was shifted from Simla to New Delhi.

Sourindranath Roy, commenting on the Indian archaeological scenario, had stated that, "the programme of conservation naturally received the greatest emphasis during the Curzon's regime and in pursuing it the Governor-General was well served by Mashall. The latter brought to bear on his task a scientific approach and an aesthetic understanding never encountered before in the history of Indian archaeology".[71]

MARSHALL'S NOTE ON 'THE OPERATIONS AND FUTURE CONDUCT OF THE ARCHAEOLOGICAL SURVEY'

Thereafter, on 6 April 1903, Marshall had submitted an important and useful note to the Government of India entitled "**The operations and future conduct of the Archaeological Survey**" which he prepared on 29 March 1903, in which he formulated definite principles about every field of archaeology, particularly conservation of monuments. He mainly focussed and emphasized on the care of monuments:

> I have now, in the course of eight months' traveling visited all the archaeological circles with the exception of Burma. Thus I have constantly had the opportunity of discussing the conditions regulating the existence of the survey in the majority of the provinces and of receiving or offering suggestions for its future conduct.
>
> 2. The Office of Director General is advisory only and carries with no direct control over any of the provincial surveys nor does any experience up to the present lead me to believe that direct control would be an advantage. In the capacity of Adviser to the Government of India, I shall probably be able to do more towards promoting the effectiveness of the survey than I could if charged with executive duties. The exercise of administrative interference involving a constant attention to routine work would absorb most, if not all, of my energies and prevent me applying myself to gathering together the experiences of the different circles and shaping from them a general and uniform policy to keeping in touch with archaeology in other countries and introducing where there is need, more up to date and approved methods to devising plans for the future and to collecting the literature requisite for reference and research. I have already found that mere routine work may develop rapidly and consume an undue proportion of my time and I have consequently asked local Governments to refrain from making a practice of sending all archaeological estimates to me for correction and counter-signature. Only in the United Provinces which since the death of Mr. Edmund Smith have been without a Superintendent, I am still revising the estimates and moreover in this case have obtained the consent of the Local Government to issue instructions direct to the draftsman in charge of the current duties of the Archaeological Office, in order that we may avoid the delay consequent upon referring requests to Government. Without authoritative control, I realize that my influence with the surveys must depend largely upon the friendliness existing between myself and the Superintendents and that any friction would be a stumbling block in the way of forward progress. Of this, I think there is little danger. All the officers with whom I am acquainted will, I venture to believe, concur with me in saying that our relations are completely harmonious. They have shown themselves thoroughly sympathetic and ready to accept any modification of action in

their own circles which might help to uniformity in the work and constitution of the survey as a whole.

3. What I have especially tried to bring about is that more prominence should be given to conservation and less to survey work. It is needless to recapitulate here the orders on this point contained in the Government Circular No. 21 of 1895 (A, July 1895, 6-13) and confirmed in the Despatch No. 31 of 1898 (A, July 1898, Nos. 10-29) and again in your letter of instructions to this Office No. 1823-16-3 of the 10 June 1902 (A, August 1902, 10-14). The purport of these orders seems scarcely to have been realized. In the Bombay and Madras Presidencies and in the United Provinces where surveys were established prior to the reorganization of 1898, and have not since been discontinued, the old order of things has remained unchanged, save only the complement of draftsmen was reduced to the number then prescribed. In the two former circles we must look to the lack of funds especially for the cause of this conservation. Without work to assist in, or the hope of the where-withal to give effect to their suggestions, it was not to be expected that conservation would have the first claim upon the time of the archaeological surveyors. In the Punjab and Bengal, the surveyors have been appointed subsequently to the reorganization and it might have been thought that they would be chosen with a special view to conservation work. It was, however, found impossible to obtain men trained in architecture as well as in epigraphy and it was decided that the latter qualification was on the whole more essential than the former. Thus one cause or another has interfered in each of the circles to stultify the main objects of the reorganization of 1898. I have myself lately explained how matters stand to the Madras and Bombay Governments and mapped out certain plans of action with the surveyors themselves but a general resolution reminding Local Governments of the aims of the survey would I think be useful.

4. Relative duties of the Archaeological and P.W.D.'s officers towards ancient building: I have frequently discussed the duties of both archaeological surveyors and officers of the Public Works Department towards ancient monuments and have found that the opinions of the provincial authorities differ widely as to how the duties should be defined. The most prevalent is that the onus of reporting on dilapidations and suggesting measures for the protection of ancient monuments rests with the Archaeological Department and there is practically no responsibilities attaching to officers of the Public Works department except in the actual execution of repairs. This, I believe, is wholly erroneous and I have already suggested to the Government of India that the Public Works Department might be asked to emphasize again the duties of Executive Engineers as defined in their Code Regulations in respect of ancient buildings. It is impossible for an archaeological surveyor to make regular and comprehensive inspections of all the monuments in the large areas under his charge nor has this ever been held to be an essential part of his duties. In 1898 when the archaeological surveyors for the Punjab, Bengal and Native States were disbanded, it was expressly pointed out that 'the measure did not affect or impair the responsibility of the Local Governments for the conservation and maintenance of ancient monuments. This duty will rest, as heretofore, primarily with the Provincial Department of Public Works, and should continue to receive careful attention throughout the country'. I have tried therefore to arrange with the Provincial Public Works for a systematic annual or even more frequent inspection to be made by Executive Engineers of the monuments in their circles but I confess to not being sanguine that my attempts will bear fruit until further pressure is brought to bear.

5. Duties of the Archaeological Officers in respect of conservation: In this connection, it remains to explain more detailed interpretation which I have ventured to put on the orders dealing with the duties of the archaeological surveyor himself: (i) He should revise and offer suggestions for the annual programmes and proposed repairs submitted by Superintending Engineers. The value of these programmes will depend largely upon the fullness of the returns sent in by Executive Engineers but it should be the duty of the archaeological surveyor to assign to each measure contemplated its relative importance and to draw up an order of precedence for all the works in the province. This order should be observed by the Public Works Department and the work taken in hand according

to the funds at their disposal, (ii) He should countersign the estimates after they have been passed by the Public Works Department approving only and noting on the character of the works proposed and not concerning himself with the estimated cost, (iii) He should record by photography or if necessary by coloured drawings, the essential details of a building before repairs are commenced. To this end the Public Works Department should inform the archaeological surveyor when they intend to start work upon any monument and ask him to prepare any drawings or photographs which he may consider necessary other than the usual working plans and elevations which belongs to an engineer's province, (iv) He should make frequent visits to the monuments under repair and be ready to assist the engineer with his advice. Such assistance would gladly be welcomed and to judge from past relations with the Public Works Department, there is no need to anticipate any friction, (v) In certain measures of repair calling for very careful or artistic handling, the draftsmen attached to the Archaeological Office might be employed actually to carry out the work. Their training fits them peculiarly to technical undertakings of this kind and it is, perhaps, more important to utilize their skill in repairing originals than in producing copies for publication. Where it is possible, I am suggesting that the assistance of the schools of art might be invoked. This I have discussed with several of the directors and have been assured that they would welcome any proposal to put the labour of their pupils to a practical purpose, (vi) He might be permitted to carry out any urgent petty works (e.g. the clearance of jungle growth) without reference to the public works and for this purpose a small provision not exceeding fifty rupees monthly might be made in the conservation budget, effect thus being given to the resolution No. 5-59-13 of 15th March 1886.

With the limitations mentioned above, the archaeological officers should have nothing to do with the actual execution of conservation works. It has indeed been proposed to organize a special archaeological section in the Public Works Department. Such an organization could not, I think, work successfully. It would of necessity be on a very small scale and its officers under the disadvantage of moving from district to district and of having to arrange for works without any special knowledge of local conditions or the labour market and without the means at their disposal ordinarily possessed by an engineer stationed in one spot.

6. Survey drawings: Here we may add also our interpretation of the wishes of Government in respect of survey drawings. The attention of the superintendents is merited first for the preparation of the records mentioned in paragraph 3 of the preceding paragraphs. Secondly and in accordance with the instructions of the Government of India No. 21-40-1 of 1895 (A July 1895, No. 6-13) for the survey of buildings of archaeological value which were not to be conserved – 'These monuments are, **Ex Hypothesi**, of minor importance but they will disappear and such results as can be obtained from them should be recorded, before this has happened'. It is not proposed that the elaborate surveys of, per exemplum, the Agra and Lahore forts, which are now well advanced should be dropped but they must be made subservient to more pressing needs and in the case of the Bombay and Madras circles they ought certainly to be postponed until the completed surveys of past years have been published.

7. Relations of this office with the Public Works Department: I have constantly had enquiries from the Provincial Departments of Public Works as to what measures should be taken with this or that building and I have had to point out that I am not empowered to issue orders or make suggestions except through the Government of India. The system involves certain unavoidable delays but I should be sorry to have it changed. I am, myself, too little acquainted with the ways of the local administrations not to wish for all the guidance which can be vouchsafed to me and my office, being new, requires a backing of well-known authority. During my tours in the last rainy season, I followed the plan of submitting my recommendations for conservation without waiting for the estimates of the work proposed and leaving these for the Public Works Departments to settle afterwards. I have since found that except in the case of Native States, it is more satisfactory and expeditious in the long run to procure the estimates from the executive engineers as soon as possible after our joint inspection of the building and submit all those relating to one province EN BLOC to

Government after I have completed my tour there. It necessitates my delaying the report for some time but on the other hand the estimates are likely to come to quicker than they would, if the matters had already passed through the hands of the Government and the details being fresh in engineer's mind, they are likely to be more accurate. When orders have been passed on the reports, some questions usually arise concerning the execution of the work and additions or alterations may have to be made involving a good deal of correspondence. With these details I do not think that there is, as a rule, need to trouble you. The main outlines and salient features having been settled and approved, I shall be able to arrange for the rest satisfactorily through the provincial surveyors in the Archaeological Department.

Restoration Policy

8. Limits of legitimate restoration: Before leaving the question of conservation, I desire to explain as briefly as possible and without trying to analyse the underlying principles, what in my opinion are the limits to be set to legitimate restoration.

Hypothetical restorations are unwarranted unless they are essential to the stability of a building.

Every original member of a building should if possible, be preserved in tact. Demolition and rebuilding is to be undertaken only, if the structure cannot be otherwise.

I should be reluctant to accept this as exhaustive. We rebuilt some of the approaches to the Taj (dalans, etc.) from nothing because we were certain of the originals – CURZON maintained or if it can only be maintained at the price of unsightliness, out of proportion to be result gained.

The restoration of carved stone or brick stone and of carved wood or plaster mouldings should only be undertaken if the artisans employed are able to attain approximately to the excellence of the originals, and this only, if the originals have been destroyed or are in such disrepair, as actually to disfigure the buildings. If this condition cannot be fulfilled, architectural members necessary for the stability of the building should be restored without carvings or mouldings.

In none, except extreme cases, should any attempt be made to recarve mythological or other scenes in which the figures of deities or living beings occur. This point marks, I think, a certain distinction which we should generally observe, in our treatment of Mohammedan remains on the one hand, and Hindu or Buddhist on the other. In the latter classes we are met at nearly every point in the surface decoration by divine and human figures, each of which has its own sculpturesque qualities, its own attributes, its own significance. We could scarcely ever hope to restore it with certainty as to all of these three points. Could we know its attributes and significance, we could not escape technical mistakes and anachronisms of style destined possibly to confuse the archaeologist of the future. In respect of the older types of Hindu and Buddhist sculptures moreover, the traditions of its artificers have long since perished and the methods and rules which governed its production are no longer understood.

It is different with Mohammedan carving; we find often that the descendants of the old stone and marble workers are still carrying on their trade in ancient centres like Agra and Jaipur. There has been no failure of continuity in their traditions. The workmen can, if they like, execute their copies as well today as they could be originals three or four hundred years ago. The designs seldom consist of anything but a repetition of geometrical patterns reproduced mechanically and admitting of little or no individuality. Their restoration is unlikely to give rise to errors as that of Hindu sculptures might do and need not therefore, I think, be objected to. The above distinction we put forward as a broad principle only and not one to which exceptions may not be made.

No previous attempts in the restoration of tilework in Indian buildings can be said to have met with success and until we have solved and difficulties of reproducing the original tints, we may consider that this class of restoration is precluded.

In painting sufficient advance has now been made to warrant us in improving on some of the unhappy restorations of past years and in executing minor repairs, such, for instance as the filling in of designs on the plaster patches that so often disfigure Mohammedan frescoes.

9. During my tours I have made a point of visiting a selected few of the most important monuments in each district in company with the provincial surveyor and of satisfying myself by practical inquiry and observation as to his ideas of the lines on which conservation should be carried out. Generally, I have found them diffident of attempting to do more than patch up a building here and there and leave the rest for future years. In such cases I have thought it expedient to suggest the adoption of more radical measures and together we have compiled notes for the use of the engineers detailing as far as possible such item of the work and the methods to be employed in carrying it out. Next I have asked for general estimates from the Public Works Department and after ascertaining the approximate cost of all the work to be undertaken in each province or Native State in the immediate future, I have approached the Local Governments with a view to discovering whether they could be persuaded to bear the whole expense or whether they would need any subsidy from the Imperial Government. Everywhere that I could, I have taken the opportunity of discussing the question of conservation personally with the Governors, head of departments, native chiefs or local officials and have, I think, met with some measure of success in the promises of active support which they have given.

10. List of monuments: Closely connected with actual consideration is the preparation of the classified lists of monuments. It would be out of place here to explain the stage which each of these lists has reached. I have been into the question pretty thoroughly and will submit an account of them in connection with the report called for by the Secretary of State at the close of this year. The lists for the Central India States and Rajputana are not yet begun and there is still much to be done for the completion of those in the Punjab. The two former will fall to Mr. Cousens' province and he is of opinion that they will take at least 5 years to complete. Subject, therefore, to your approval I propose to relieve him of the initial part of the cataloguing in Central India. My plan which will be explained to you later is to take advantage of an opportunity which offers itself just now of working in conjunction with Captain Luard, the Gazetteer officer and of simplifying thus the collection of our material.

11. General principles to be followed in regard to original research: The general principle which is to be followed in the field of original research and in accordance with which original investigation on the part of members of this survey must be circumscribed is explained in pages 4 and 12 of the Government of India Circular No. 21-40-1 of the 27th June 1895 (A, July 1895, No. 6-13). "It is the duty of the Government to conserve the materials only, it is for private scholars to compare, collate and draw conclusions from them"; we do not favour any modification of this principle, the fact that so much more is now possible in conservation must draw the limits of original research even more closely than before. But I take it that under the head of conservation we are to include the unearthing and protecting of the most promising of our buried sites and the collecting and housing in museums of scattered antiquities. I take it also that it is the duty of the survey to register and catalogue the material and if possible publish it in a simple form for the information of scholars to whom it is not accessible.

x x x x x

18. Annual Reports: It has been decided to issue fresh regulations concerning the provincial reports. Each superintendent is to publish two parts, the first purely official and the second archaeological and descriptive. These reports are for local use and the number of copies to be printed and their distribution will be settled by the Provincial Governments. I, at first, expressed the opinion that there would be no need for Part II of the provincial report but in the light of wider experience agree that it would be a mistake to risk the possibility of killing provincial interest in the reports.

Your instructions concerning my own reports were given some time ago. The same principle of dividing up the material is to be adopted. Part I will be a formal record of the work of the Department, Part II is designed to provide both the Government and the general public with an adequate record simplified by photographic illustrations, of the progress made in the conservation of ancient monuments in each province and in all other branches of archaeological work and investigation. By its means it is hoped to create an interest for Indian archaeology in people who do not profess any great scientific knowledge of the subject; whatever has been done in India during the last thirty years, has been done, as it were in secret. Everybody has known that nothing is likely to be heard of it for fifteen or twenty years and no one has cared to help with his support. In Egypt, Greece or Italy, volumes appear, year by year, embodying the outcome of the previous season's work. They are not kept back until some great specialist has assimilated everything that can be known and can write with certainty his full and deliberate conviction. The result has been that while the work going on in Egypt, Greece or Italy has been watched with intense interest by every European country and while, therefore, the societies engaged are supplied with funds which enable them to carry on the excavations and print their volumes, the labours of the Indian archaeological departments have fallen invariably dead and lifeless. By keeping the public constantly informed of our progress in India, we are likely to bring new adherents to the Royal Asiatic Society and the Indian Exploration Fund and so generally strengthen the cause of Indian Archaeology both in the country and in Europe (A, July 1898, 31-32).

I had thought that a general volume of this kind dealing with a variety of archaeological subjects might command a slightly larger circulation than the highly specialized works of the Imperial series and suggested that 700 copies might be printed instead of 500. I have since gathered that there is seldom any call for more than the 200 copies distributed gratis by Government and conclude therefore that the usual number should not be exceeded. As regards the binding to be employed, I am inquiring the opinions of the Superintendents and will submit the designs for your opinion at a later date.

19. Volumes belonging to the New Imperial Series: There has been much confusion in the numbering of the volumes of the New Imperial Series of reports owing to the unsatisfactory system of assigning numbers to volumes before they were ready for publication. As soon as the catalogues of antiquities for the Punjab and Rajputana are ready, the two remaining blanks in the lists hitherto published will be filled, viz., Nos. XXVII and XXVIII and no numbers will henceforth be allotted until the volumes are in the press. Up to date 30 reports in this series have been published and there are enough drawings in the possession of the survey to produce at least 20 more volumes. Many of these date back for five and twenty years and until the majority of them have been published, I feel that a check ought to be put on the preparation of elaborate drawings. The delay has no doubt been due, in the main to Dr. Burgess' procrastination but it may be doubted if many of the volumes in his hands could have been published earlier by Mr. Cousens or Mr. Rea; both have had their hands full with other volumes with which Dr. Burgess has had no connection and the regular duties of an archaeological surveyor leave little time for writing. I hesitate now to believe that if all the material asked for by the Madras Government is placed in Mr. Rea's hands, he will be able to publish it satisfactorily during the next eight years. It is, of course, highly important to reserve it from the confusion of Dr. Burgess' library and assure ourselves that he can account for all the drawings and manuscript copy sent from India. This done we might return to him two volumes to work upon; one for the Bombay and one for the Madras circle.

The following list will show the subjects the volumes now in course of preparation: (1) Dakhan or Hemadpanti temples, (2) Temples in Kathiawar, (3) Mosques and tombs of Sindh, (4) Chalukyan temples, (5) Bijapur, (6) Ahmedabad, Volume II, Architecture subsequent to 1510, (7) Dilwara temples of Mount Abu, (8) Temples of Conjeveram, now in the Press, (9) Seven Pagodas, (10) Madura, (11) Buddhist remains in the Nellore and Kistna Districts, (12) Vijaynagar, (13) Prehistoric antiquities in the Tinnevelly district, (14) List of archaeological remains in the Punjab, (15) List of archaeological remains in Rajputana, (16) List of archaeological remains in Central India, (17) Chamba State inscriptions, (18) Tilework in Lahore Fort, (19) Gandhara antiquities, (20) Reliefs on the tower of victory at Chitor, (21) Akbar's tomb at Secundera, (22) Guide to Fatehpur Sikri, (23) Buildings in Agra Fort, (24) Catalogue of sculptures from the Gandhara district, (25) Catalogue raisonne of Indian archaeological material, (26) List of antiquarian remains at Pagan, Mandalay.

x x x x x

21. Distribution of circles: I have above referred to the necessity of a redistribution of the circles. The present arrangement was never considered other than a temporary makeshift and adequate for our needs. Our chief difficulties have been in the Punjab and Bombay circles, both of which are unwieldy and insufficiently equipped. In the former Rajputana, in the latter Central India, have received no attention for several years past (A, February 1903, Nos. 1-6). To meet our needs, I have proposed that a new surveyor should be appointed with a small staff but that instead of creating a new circle, he should be placed under Mr. Cousens' direction and Rajputana transferred to Bombay circle. This arrangement will give us all the assistance we want and will have the additional advantage of enabling us to preserve by tradition the results of Mr. Cousens' experience gained during twenty-seven years of practical work. I have recommended, moreover, that to meet the need of architectural assistance in the Punjab, that circle might be amalgamated with the United Provinces and the duties divided between Dr. Vogel, the Punjab Surveyor and a purely architectural surveyor who will succeed to Mr. E. Smith's post in the United Provinces.

x x x x x

23. Expenditure of the lakh provided for Archaeology: The disbursement (A, February 1903, Nos. 37-50) of the lakh provided for archaeology during 1902-03, has had to depend almost exclusively upon the recommendations which I could make on the strength of my own observations and as I have previously had occasion to explain, I was unable to inaugurate any measures until my tour in the rainy season. These were confined to the Punjab, the United Provinces and Rajputana. The archaeological surveyors in the other provinces had no suggestions to offer. Accordingly, I issued a circular to the Local Governments asking if any grant-in-aid from Imperial funds was needed. All the replies received were in the negative. I shall make my recommendations for the division of most of the money before the end of June in each year. For 1903-04, a small sum will be required, as in the present year, for excavations, the purchase of antiquities and the library. In the apportioning of the remainder, the claims which we shall put first will be those of the small Native States which cannot be expected to draw largely upon their own resources. The ruins of Mandu and Dhar, for instance, will call for a very considerable subsidy. Next in rank we must consider the provinces where conservation is most backward. These are the Punjab and the Madras Presidency and in a less degree Bombay. The larger Native States will perhaps be able to look after themselves. Gwalior has promised to see the works which I have recommended, carried through, and other States also convince an active desire to fall in with the wishes of the present Government.

24. Archaeological Library for the Survey: I do expect that the library will be in working order until the beginning of 1904 or some three or four months after I have taken up my quarters in the new Government Offices. After June next, however, I hope to be able to send out on loan a number of volumes immediately needed by the provincial surveyors. So far our progress has not been rapid. The first step was to find out what books, if any, could be supplied from the Home Department's spare copy Room and the Metacalfe Hall as a nucleus for the library. The final orders about them reached me only in the latter end of December last but I had by that time settled upon the books which were most urgently wanted in the survey and had communicated with several firms in India, England and elsewhere with a view to completing the purchases, if possible, before the end of the financial year.

First in the list of books, I have ranked those dealing expressly with Indian archaeological subjects and among them the complete series of the journals of the Royal Asiatic Societies of London,

> Bombay and Colombo and of the Bengal Asiatic Society and Indian Antiquary numbering in all some three hundred volumes. Many of these have been supplied by the Societies at about half of their original cost. A particularly welcome gift has come from Sir E. Maunde Thompson who has presented a complete set of the British Museum's archeological publications including the twenty-seven volumes on the numismatics of Rome, Greece, Asia Minor, Persia, India and China some of which it is now impossible to buy.
>
> Secondly, I have purchased a fair number of volumes in connection with special lines of work in one or other of the circles but not procurable in the provincial libraries. Such, for instance, as Avebury, Chabas, Hutchinson, Lubbock, Evans, Munnro, Nadaillac, Westropp and Wilson on prehistoric antiquities for Mr. Rea in reference to his discoveries in the Tinnevelly district. Besides, these, I have secured some general historic, philological or literary works and a representative selection of the most up-to-date writers on European archaeology.[72]

This note had a far reaching impact on the Indian archaeology in particular, thus charting a new course of action plan for the preservation and conservation of monuments.

Meanwhile, Marshall had addressed yet another letter to the Secretary, Revenue and Agriculture Department, Government of India on 14 May 1903 wherein he had raised the issue relating to duties to be defined for the provincial Engineers of the Public Works Department in respect to the preservation of monuments of archaeological interest. Marshall stated that there was erroneous opinion prevailing amongst the provincial Public Works Department, that the onus of reporting and suggesting measures for the conservation of public monuments of archaeological or historical interest lies on the officers of the Archaeological Department and not with the Executive Engineers and he suggested that the Public Works Department should be instructed to adhere to standing orders of their code. The duties of Executive Engineers in respect of public buildings or monuments were made explicit in the code and that the inspection of the monuments formed part of their duties as was made expressly clear in the earlier instructions of June 1890 vide A, June 1890, Nos. 1-30. The order stated that "the measure did not affect or impair the responsibility of the Local Governments for the conservation and maintenance of ancient monuments", that "his duty would rest as heretofore primarily with the provincial departments of Public Works and should continue to receive careful attention throughout the country".[73]

He also stated that earlier this was stressed by Holderness in his un-official note dated 18 March 1899 but Marshall stated "any action which may then have been taken as yet proved ineffectual".[74]

On 12 May 1903, E.G. Stanley, Under Secretary, Public Works Department, after obtaining the views of the Revenue Agriculture Department addressed a communication to all Local Governments and Chief Commissioners, requesting them to reiterate the orders as incorporated in the Public Works Department Code Volume I, paragraphs 318, 319, 1046 (Appendix XXVI) to the attention of all Superintendents and Executive Engineers and "they may be instructed to take every opportunity of performing their duty in respect to preservation of monuments of archaeological interest".[75]

In the Resolution No. 7-6-12, dated 11 February 1902, it was stated the sum of Rs. one lakh would be reserved annually from the Imperial Fund to be distributed for particular objects connected with the repair or restoration of buildings of historical interest which demanded early execution and which are shown to be beyond the financial capacity of the Local Government.

The Government of India prescribed a procedure for submitting the proposals for allotment of special archaeological grant. A Resolution No. 51-61-9, dated 19 December 1902, was circulated by the Revenue and Agriculture Department in which the details of the accounting procedure were also laid down.

(1) The Government of India, in the Department of Revenue and Agriculture, will allot funds to Local Governments from the provisions made in India Estimates and Communicate a copy of the orders of the Comptroller India Treasuries.

(2) The expenditure incurred against the allotment will, after audit by the Examiner of Public Works Accounts in the province concerned be passed on to the Comptroller, India Treasuries, by the Examiner if he has a direct account with the Comptroller, India Treasuries and through the Provincial Civil Account Office if not, for adjustment against the provision made in India Estimates.[76]

Besides, J.O. Miller, Secretary, Revenue and Agriculture Department, Government of India also issued a Circular (No. 29-63-1) dated 20 July 1903 to all local governments and administrations. This circular laid down the guidelines for ensuring uniformity of procedure with regard to distribution and expenditure of the special archaeological grants.

> With a view to secure uniformity of procedure and to ensure that this special archaeological grant is distributed and expended to the best advantage, the Governor-General in Council has now decided that all applications by Local Governments for allotments from the grant should, in the first instance, be addressed to the Director-General, Archaeology who is in the best position to consider the comparative urgency of the requirements of the various provinces.
>
> 2. The submitting an application for an allotment from the fund, it should be stated what archaeological works are likely to be undertaken during the year, what provision has been made for them in the provincial budget and the extent of the assistance required. Information should, if possible, be given as to whether the total amount of the allotment asked for can be spent during the financial year. The Director-General of Archaeology will then after considering the requirements of the various provinces from which applications are pending or are likely to be put forward or in which he considers that assistance is required, submit his recommendations to the Government of India stating the amount of the subsidy asked for by the Local Government and the amount which he recommends should be given. The procedure to be adopted in regard to the allotments of funds and the accounting of the expenditure will be prescribed in the Department's Circular No. 51-61-9 dated 19 December 1902.
>
> 3. The Governor-General in Council desires to take this opportunity to make it clear that the special grant of one lakh provided by the Government of India is not intended to relieve Local Governments of the necessity for making proper provision in their provincial budgets for expenditure upon archaeological objects. The intention is that the allotments from the special grant should supplement the money available from provincial source in special cases where Local Governments are unable to find the funds required from their own resources.[77]

Taking cognizance of the note of Marshall dated 29 March 1903, the Government of India adopted a Resolution R.A. No. 26-28-2 on 7 July 1903. This Resolution was forwarded to all local governments and administrations. Through this Resolution, the Government of India communicated detailed instructions for the preparation of the annual reports submitted by the Archaeological Officers of various circles and also defined their duties and responsibilities.

> The Governor-General in Council having decided that the Director-General Archaeology should publish annually a report or summary of the progress of archaeological surveys and the conservation

of ancient buildings, it has become necessary to lay down more detailed instructions for the preparation of the annual reports submitted by the Archaeological officers of the various circles. The opportunity is taken to call attention to certain other matters connected with the duties and responsibilities of Archaeological officers in regard to which it would appear that further explanation is advisable.

2. Under existing orders Archaeological Officers in charge of circles are required to submit annually to the Local Governments to whom they are subordinate, a report of the work carried out by them during the year and a programme of the tours and work to be undertaken during the ensuing season. The reports and programmes are forwarded to the Government of India by Ist August. No detailed instructions have been issued regarding the form and matter of the annual reports, which vary greatly in the scope, and arrangements for their contents. Most of them include in addition to formal departmental matters, detailed descriptions and historical accounts of the buildings examined and occasionally remarks on the ethnology, religion and folklore of the localities visited. The annual report to be prepared by the Director-General Archaeology will consist of two parts, each of which will be printed and published separately. The first will be purely official and deal with the working of the Department. The second part will have a wider scope and will aim at supplying the public and students of Archaeology with interesting and readable accounts of the progress of archaeological research in India. It will contain clear and accurate accounts of the work of restoration and preservation of important buildings and sites of excavations and fresh discoveries and will be illustrated. It will also give a resume of the epigraphical, numismatic, exploratory and other works of the Department compiled from special reports of the Provincial Surveyors and from personal observation. The Government of India consider that it will be convenient and desirable that the same principle of separating the record of departmental routine from the account of the work accomplished should be adopted in the preparation of the annual reports of the provincial officers though in the case of these latter, the two parts will be printed and published together. If the introduction of any change in the form of the reports would delay their submission in the present year, the change should be postponed.

3. The first section of the report should contain a brief and formal statement showing how the archaeological staff was occupied during the year and the work accomplished. It should mention the time spent in touring and inspection work, the tours made, the buildings and sites examined and any recommendations for conservation or excavation submitted to Government. The progress made in the preparation of the provincial lists of ancient remains where these have still to be finally completed should be stated and any detailed surveys or excavations undertaken should be recorded. A list should be given of, the drawings prepared, photographs taken, publications issued, and of the inscriptions, copper plates, coins, seals and other such antiquities discovered or acquired. The manner in which any inscriptions were dealt with or disposed off should be noticed. Any contravention of standing orders regarding conservation, excavations or disposal of finds should also be noticed in this part of the report. A clear statement omitting detailed descriptions should be given of all conservation work proposed, carried out or in progress and of the expenditure incurred on them. On these heads it will be necessary to obtain information from the Department of Public Works. Finally, the report should include the usual notice of subordinates and their work and any changes in **Personnel** and give an abstract account under main heads of the expenditure of the survey. Many of particulars above indicated can be exhibited with a saving of space in the form of lists and tables appended to the report and this arrangement should be adopted as far as possible, brief explanatory remarks where necessary being added in the body of the report.

4. Part II of the Provincial reports should deal with the progress of archaeological research in the Province concerned, on the lines laid down in paragraph 2 above regarding the corresponding part of the Director-General's report but need not be illustrated. The second part of the latter report will largely consist of contributions from Provincial officers on special subjects selected as the result of communication between those officers and the Director-General. These contributions will, it is

intended, appear in the names of the officers furnishing them and it is hoped that the opportunity offered by the general report for the publication of archaeological researches in an illustrated and attractive form will not be overlooked. An account will, as at present, be given in the provincial reports of all important discoveries made or information collected by Provincial officers and of their bearing on questions of historical research but in cases in which such discoveries or researches have been made the subjects of special contribution to the general report, it will be necessary to do more than refer to them briefly in the Provincial report.

5. Among the other matters calling for notice, the most important is the duties of Archaeological Officers in regard to conservation. In the circular letter No.21-40.1 dated 27 June 1895 in which Local Governments were consulted on the scheme for the reorganization of the Archaeological Survey Department, it was stated that it would be the **Primary** duty of archaeological officers to advise upon, assist in and secure the effective preservation of the buildings, which it may be decided to preserve. The views of Local Governments on the scheme and the conclusions at which the Government of India finally arrived and in which the Secretary of State for India concurred, are summed up in the following extract from their despatch of 16 June 1898:

'The scheme which we suggested for the consideration of Local Governments is set forth in a circular addressed to them in June 1895 of which a copy forms an enclosure to this Despatch. The replies received show that the programme of archaeological work proper there suggested is generally approved but although it is admitted that conservation must be the first object, regret is very generally expressed that a more prominent place cannot be given to the exploration of archaeological remains more particularly in the way of excavating the sties of ancient cities. We are, however, disposed to affirm the draft programme of work and the assist that the first thing to be done is to conserve our material and that the first and most essential step towards this end is to take stock of it and decide what is worth preserving. In paragraph 6 of our circular we described original investigation as ranking last among the surveyor's duties. We have no wish, however, to discourage original work nor do we undervalue what has been and is being done in this direction by the officers of the Survey and we are completely in accord with the further proposition that every facility and encouragement should be given to any individual or society who will undertake work of the kind under proper control. In doing so we are pursuing the course that can claim to show the best results in the past and we are desirous that an assurance of the kind may be given to the English memorialists. But we consider that the limited sum which we are justified in spending upon archaeological work should primarily be devoted to the conservation of existing material'.

It appears to the Government of India that the responsibility laid upon Archaeological officers by the above quoted orders for efficiently supervising the work of conservation is not yet generally recognized. In some instances it appears to be regarded as sufficiently fulfilled by casual visits to the buildings under repair and in others to be subsidiary to the work of exploration and discovery. They consider it necessary therefore to lay down more precise instructions on the subject which should be strictly adhered to unless, for special reasons to be reported for their information, any Local Governments should be of opinion that a departure from them is necessary.

6. It should be the duty of the Provincial Archaeological Officer:

(1) To advise on the proposals for conservation or restoration works submitted by the officers of the Public Works Department and to recommend the order of precedence in which these as well as any works suggested by themselves should be undertaken.

(2) To submit proposals for the conservation or repair of ancient buildings of interest requiring preservation which have come to their own notice during their tours. This work should be carried out **Pari Passu** with the preparation of the list of remains referred to in the Government of India circular No.12-28 dated 24 August 1891 where these have not yet been completed and should not await their final completion.

(3) To pass plans and estimates for all work of conservation and repair whether suggested by himself or by the Public Works Department. It will not be the duty of the Archaeological officer to criticize rates but to approve and advise on the character of the works to be carried out.

(4) To assist in the supervision of the works of conservation while they are in progress. The degree of assistance required must depend upon the nature and importance of the work. It will be the duty of the Archaeological officer to assist the Engineer with his advice and to bring to the notice of the proper authority any alterations or repairs which in his opinion are likely to affect the architectural or historical interest of the building.

The manner and extent to which the Archaeological officers carry out these duties should be clearly stated in the first section of their annual progress reports. It should be understood that in prescribing them the Government of India do not intend to relieve Public Works officers of the responsibility which also rests upon them under the standing orders to which attention was called in the letter from the Public Works Department No.644-C.W-B dated 12 May 1903. It is impossible for an archaeological surveyor to make regular or systematic inspections of all the monuments in the large areas under his charge and this duty will rest as heretofore primarily with the Public Works Department who should endeavour to arrange for a systematic annual or even more frequent inspection to be made by Executive Engineers of the monuments in their circles. But notice of any measures that may be suggested by officers of the Public Works Department for the protection or conservation of any monument should invariably be communicated to the Provincial Archaeological officer before they are carried out in order that he may have an opportunity of expressing his opinion as to their suitability. Similarly no repairs or removal of ancient buildings or remains should be undertaken by District or Municipal authorities without previous report to the Provincial Archaeological officer who should also be kept informed of any intended demolition or defacement of ancient buildings, inscriptions or other antiquities in private possession which may come to their knowledge.

7. In some of the reports under consideration, reference is made to intended excavations or ancient sites. In the circular of the 27 June 1895 already quoted, it was laid down that 'if in any case it becomes necessary for Government to disturb an ancient site, no excavation will be permitted except under the supervision of the local archaeological surveyor. Indeed, no such excavation should in any case be allowed without the consent of the Local Government. But all possible encouragement should be offered to private explorers whose archaeological competence has been ascertained'. The Government of India trust that Local Governments will prevent any such excavation being undertaken by thoroughly competent persons. The history of many such undertakings has proved that no one without training in the approved methods of digging can avoid losing much of the evidence which an excavation under more experienced supervision might bring to light and it is infinitely better to leave antiquities underground till such supervision is available than the destroy in digging out half the evidence which they might afford.

Drawings

8. Another noticeable feature in the provincial reports is the extent to which the time and energies of the subordinate staff are observed in the preparation of detailed drawings and the comparatively small use made of photography. Having regard to the large number of unpublished drawings which have accumulated in the Archaeological Offices, it appears to the Government of India that some restriction should be placed upon their further multiplication. No useful purpose is served by drawings which accumulate unpublished. Their preparation should continue slowly and methodically and the Arcaheological Surveyor should be prepared to give them to the public as soon as they are finished.

PHOTOGRAPHY

> 9. These objections to the too frequent employment of the laborious and expensive process of hand drawing do not apply to photography where the taking of photographs can be arranged for. Photographs are not only less expensive and more easily reproduced but they are more reliable than drawings; they are indeed the only illustrations now accepted as conclusive evidence by archaeologists in Europe. This process should, therefore, be freely employed for the illustrative work of the survey. For purely architectural purposes it may sometimes be necessary to elaborate carefully drawn plans and elevations but as a rule, only such architectural features should be drawn as cannot be reproduced equally well or better by photography and the practice should be discontinued by employing draftsmen to sketch statuary and other antiquities at great pains and considerable expense. Whenever scaffolding is erected to carry out repairs to a building, the opportunity should be taken to photograph any architectural details which would otherwise be inaccessible to the camera. A complete series of photographs should also be made of both the exterior and interior of buildings selected for extensive repair before the work of conservation is concerned. In the case of structures of a perishable nature or in an advanced stage of decay, it is specially desirable that complete photographic illustrations should be obtained without delay for future reference. It should further be the aim of the Department to make its photographs freely available to students of Archaeology for which purpose a catalogue of them should be published periodically.
>
> 10. It will be observed from the foregoing remarks that the Government of India attach much importance to the free use of photography in archaeological work but they recognize the difficulty of arranging with the existing staff for any extensive resort to the process. They will be glad, however, if Local Governments will consider whether some steps cannot be taken in the direction indicated without any great additional expense. [78]

This Resolution was also communicated to the Director General of Archaeology in India, Public Works, Foreign and Military Departments for information and guidance.

Besides, James Burgess in his letter dated 4 January 1889 brought to the notice the rampant sale of archaeological remains by the local population in North-West Frontier India, especially at Swat and the Government of India could not take any action to curb this menace of cultural vandalism. However, Resolution (Arch and Epi) No. 24-4-2 dated 28 March 1889 was issued which empowered the Government of India to acquire articles of archaeological interest "emphasizing the steps to be taken to prevent the despoiling of archaeological remains".[79]

This matter was under the active consideration of the Government when in 1895 Surgeon Major Wadell was sent on deputation to Swat. He was placed under the services of Chitral Relief Force with the sole objective of conducting archaeological research in the Swat Valley. In his report, Wadell had mentioned that several archaeological sites were being clandestinely excavated by the private individuals in Chakdra Valley. These sites in fact had Buddhist monasteries and stupas, and the illegal excavations were made to obtain best of the Buddhist sculptures. He also reported that many officers had excavated and completely destroyed "the structural designs of the buildings and made no record whether of what they saw".[80]

Wadell also reported that the officers had also taken away the Buddhist relics of archaeological importance and most of these relics could be seen at Takht-i-Bahi near Hoti Mardan. These relics were heavy in weight and size which would hence require the bullock carts to transport them. He lamented that "officers, as a rule, have neither the leisure on field service nor the means necessary to remove such articles".[81]

In this connection, permission was also granted by the Government of Bengal to depute Alexander E. Caddy, Officer on Special Duty, for the sole purpose of collection of Asoka inscriptions to locate and survey the Buddhist archaeological remains in the Swat Valley Dargai in the North-West Frontier India. He sent his report to the Secretary, Government of Bengal on 16 December 1895.

> ...During my travels in this country, I had opportunity for observing how the country abounds in remains of the works of these ancient people. There are many sites of ancient cities with their walls still standing, of towers, monasteries, abbcys and other structure where intelligent and scientific exploration will in every probability yield a rich harvest of Greeko-Scythian and Greeko-Asian art treasures.
>
> It is important that the Government of Bengal should acquire these relics for the Imperial Museum where they would be immediately available for reference and study even if they did divert their accumulation in a local museum.
>
> One of the dangers of delay lies in the greed of the natives of the country. They will remove objects of the value piecemeal to sell the British officers and others or with the Mohammedan in their iconoclastic zeal, they will destroy of deface "Buths" wherever they see them. I noticed this among many of the objects from the Morah pass where the soft slate images were often mutilated in a most vicious manner.
>
> It often happens that a stupa is broken up and dispersed or the remains disturbed while it is yet possible for a record of its construction to be made were an expert to see it with its structural and artistic objects **in situ.**
>
> At present, the only known representation of a stupa of this type is the small votive stupa from Gandheri (a village just north of Peshawar) which I was fortunate to have given me by Major Deane and Mr. Waterfield for the Government of Bengal which I have been able to set up temporarily in the Museum not quite correctly but as nearly so as available materials would permit.[82]

The Secretary, Revenue and Agriculture Department, Government of India claimed at the situation arising out of rampant sale of Buddhist remains at Rawalpindi and addressed a communication to M.W. Fento, Secretary Revenue Department, Government of Punjab on 23 July 1897 in which he requested to take urgent steps "to prevent as far as possible, the undue appropriation by private persons of such antiquities".[83]

Fento apprised the Government of India on 13 August 1897, the position in this regard and the possible steps to be taken to curb this menace. He stated:

> So far as the Lieutenant-Governor is aware, the only action which can be taken by the officers of this Government to prevent such appropriations is that which is permissible under the Treasure Trove Act, 1878 and the Commissioner of Peshawar will be asked to see that the Act is rigorously enforced in the case of the finds of antiquities in British territory under the jurisdiction of this Government. There is reason to believe that in some cases sculptures found in the Peshawar District are accounted for as having been brought in from Swat and the Political Officers will be directed to investigate, as far as possible, cases in which there are grounds for suspecting the truth of such allegations.
>
> But most of the antiquities now being appropriated by private persons do no doubt come from Swat and the Lieutenant Governor would be glad to receive from the Government of India further instructions as to the action to be taken in regard to these. As the Government of India are aware, the Swat Political Agency is under the direct jurisdiction of the Government of India but even if the tract were under the control of this Government, the Treasure Trove Act does not apply to it, the Lieutenant-Governor is unable to suggest any way by which the appropriation of traffic in Buddhist sculptures can be prevented. If it is no criminal offence to appropriate such funds in trans-border territory, there does not seem to be any provision of law by which interference is possible when the antiquities are brought into British Territory. No doubt the Government of India in exercise of the jurisdiction

> which it has over British subjects, European or Indian, wherever they may be or could through the Political Agent Swat adopt stringent prohibitory measures but such measures, the Lieutenant Governor thinks, must be taken before the sculptures leave Swat and come into the Punjab as neither can their import into the Peshawar District be legally forbidden by the officials of that District nor can their sale in Rawalpindi be prevented.[84]

The Governor-General in Council in its Despatch dated 6 January 1898 informed George Hamilton, the Secretary of State, about the measures taken by the Government of India to prevent the rampant vandalism in North-West Frontier Province and for ensuring the preservation of Buddhist antiquities in Swat.

> The case of objects of antiquarian interest discovered beyond the limits of our jurisdiction is more difficult. In 1895, Surgeon-Major Waddell was placed on deputation with the Chitral Relief Force for the purpose of archaeological research in the Swat Valley and a rule was laid down that on the occasion of an expedition crossing the frontier, the attention of all Military and Political officers should invariably be drawn to the importance of preserving antiquarian remains and of preventing their removal except by duly authorized persons and their assistance in doing so requested. Orders to this effect were issued to the Chitral Force and at the same time the Punjab Government was instructed that the claims of Government should take precedence of those of individuals in respect of all antiquities removed from Chitral by Government officers and it was asked to endeavour to prevent the undue appropriation of valuable antiquities. Collections of sculpture were eventually made by a few officers and presented to the Indian Museum, Calcutta and the Lahore Museum.
>
> Thus, all that was possible was done to preserve archaeological remains in the Swat Valley from removal and dispersion. But your Lordship is aware that it is difficult or impossible wholly to prevent the removal of antiquities by private persons. As regards British Territory, it is impossible to go beyond the provisions of the Treasure-Trove Act, VI of 1878 and beyond the frontier executive action alone can be taken; while in both cases the main difficulty lies in the fact that neither duty nor interest leads private persons to inform officials of cases in which their interference is called for so that the removal of sculpture is too often heard of, it at all, only when it is too late to prevent.[85]

Besides, James Burgess also brought to the notice of the Government of India the steps taken by him to prevent illegal excavations during his tenure as Director General, Archaeology. In his communication addressed to the Secretary, Department of Revenue and Agriculture Department dated 9 February 1899 from Edinburgh, he recounted the steps taken to curb this menace.

> I venture to submit confidentially the following for the consideration of Government and I can hardly doubt that if brought to the notice of His Excellency the Viceroy, he would take a personal interest in the matter.
>
> It has always been deplored by scholars that the very ancient Buddhist remains in the north of the Punjab and on its frontiers containing so many remarkable and beautiful sculptures were dug up in a haphazard way and no note taken of the find spots of each, still less of the relative positions of figures found at the same place by which they might have been interpreted. They have also been scattered in the most reckless way: A few have reached the British Museum through General Sir A. Cunningham and others; a considerable number particularly from Swat are in the Konigl Museum at Berlin and others are at Bombay, Madras and even Rangoon. Of course, the largest collections at Lahore and Calcutta.
>
> When in the Archaeological Survey, I appealed against the mischief done by Europeans and others digging out ancient sites for sculptures and curios. To some extent this vandalism was stopped but not till infinite loss had been incurred. But still it goes on in a furtive way. Native traders and European amateur collectors all through the north of Punjab – though less openly than they used to

> do – still carry on the destructive work. Quite recently a police officer from the Hazara district brought home some Buddhist sculptures dug up by his men somewhere on the right bank of the Indus (he has not given the find spot) and sold for about £ 12 to the Fitzwilliam Museum at Cambridge.
>
> Government could survey, do something effective for the protection of such sites. With fact and decision the wrest European offenders might be brought to realize the great harm they are doing unwittingly perhaps and as to traders among the natives a few drastic measures would suffice for a long time.
>
> Excavations of ancient sites should be carried out with the skill shown at Pergamum where sculptures broken in hundreds of pieces have been restored. The only amateur I have ever seen who seemed to know what he was about was Major Deane, Political Agent Dir, Swat and Chitral who enriched the Lahore Museum with a complete drum of the Sikri Stupa about 1887.
>
> Trusting some attention will be directed to this subject as excavations may still be going on across the Indus from Hazara as well as elsewhere to the north-west.[86]

Reacting to this communication from James Burgess, E.H.S. Clarke, Assistant Secretary, Foreign Department issued orders to the Political Agent in Swat and Chitral as well as the Resident in Kashmir on 2 May 1899. He stated:

"You will take executively such steps as may be possible to prevent the practices desired by Dr. Burgess. There is no law whereby objects of antiquarian value could be stopped at the frontier and confiscated but a good deal could probably be done by concerted action with the inhabitants of the territories where such objects are found."[87]

Similarly, with a view to ensure preservation of Buddhist archaeological remains, Captain A.N. Mac Mohan, Political Agent for Swat and Chitral addressed a communication to the Secretary, Foreign Department on 28 May 1900.

> The question of the preservation of Buddhist antiquities is one on which considerable attention has always been bestowed by my predecessor Major Deane and also by myself both in this Agency and formerly when in charge of the Yusufzai Sub-Division of the Peshawar District. Both Major Deane and I have done our best to prevent the destructive excavation of Buddhist sites and strict orders have been for some time in force in this Agency prohibiting this. The sale and export of Buddhist relics are also prohibited in this Agency. All that it is possible to do to enforce these orders has been done.
>
> The difficulty of effectively enforcing this prohibition lies in the fact that as long as British officers and the general public are willing to pay large sums for coins, Buddhist sculpture, carrying, etc., the ready and remunerative market afforded for such articles tempts trans-frontier natives to risk detection and punishment in procuring them to preserve Buddhist remains in trans-frontier tracts; it is necessary to prevent the import and sale of Buddhist relics in British India. The only routes on which export of archaeological treasures can be effectively checked from here are the passes leading from Swat to India. The routes most used for such export lie through Boner and across the Indus to Hazara or through Khundu Khel and Gadun country to the Peshawar District.
>
> Nothing is done to check such export by these routes and a case has recently come to my notice in which a man caught excavating in this Agency was in possession of a letter from the Native Police Officer in charge of a Punjab post watching one of these routes directing the country people to assist him in excavation.
>
> The great majority of purchasers and receivers of such articles are Government officers and officials – Their case can be met by a Government order prohibiting the purchase of acceptance (This is necessary to meet the case of relics now largely brought in by native soldiers and civil

> subordinates as presents to their superior officers) by them of archaeological relics without Government sanction ordering them to report to Civil District Officer any person who may come to their notice as offering such for sale.
>
> The case of Native traders who purchase relics or employ their own men and agents in collecting them across the border is a more difficult one to deal with. They sell largely to European travelers and agents of European Museums and Societies who are beyond the scope of the Government order suggested above. One of the worst offenders in this line is one Mulchand (one Mir Chand is also well known, but Mir Chand and Mulchand may be one and same man) a trader in Rawalpindi who has his men and agents employed all over this country specially in Boner in collecting relics. The amount of destruction caused by these men to ancient sites and ruins is lamentable.[88]

For the protection of archaeological remains in British India, the Law Member of the Legislative Department mentioned that Section 19 of the Sea Customs Act could be effectively applied for preventing the import of Buddhist relics and other antiquarian objects from Swat and Boner into British India.[89]

The Commissioner, Peshawar Division also expressed similar views and addressed a communication to the Revenue and Financial Secretary, Government of Punjab on 7 September 1900. He stated:

> ...the knowledge that ancient sculptures, carved stones, inscriptions and other relics of bygone times find a ready sale in India may lead to the spoliation of ancient buildings which were better preserved intact.
>
> As regards sites of ancient buildings beyond British India, it would of course be better that they should remain intact until they can be visited, surveyed, photographed and reported on by experts and a permanent record taken of their place, arrangement and architecture. But the day seems far distant when such exploration can be carried out or when buildings so excavated can be preserved from destruction by weather or by the mischievous hands of the inhabitants of the country.
>
> Most of the sites likely to be fertile in ancient remains lie beyond British India and beyond our control; such absolute prohibition might put off all further discoveries to an unknown age. If Government could itself arrange for systematic exploration or excavation on such places, the case would be difficult, as it is, these valuable relics lie in the possession of ignorant practically barbarous people whose first thought when they see a stone Buddha or sculptured frieze is to mutilate the faced or, if possible, knock it to pieces. In some parts of the stones of old buildings are utilized by the villagers in the construction of their own huts or defences. It seems to me questionable whether it is not better that an inscribed stone or a frieze illustrating perhaps some episode in the life of Buddha should find its way to India to the hands of those who know its value and may cause it to be deciphered or properly described.
>
> It appears to me, therefore, that it may be useful to direct servants of Government to repress anything like a trade in old sculptures which may encourage or hasten the violent and unintelligent spoliation of ancient monuments but that it would be going too far to prohibit the sale of such relics or as is suggested to treat them as contraband articles liable to seizure like arms or ammunition or excisable drugs.
>
> I think it may be fairly said that much of our present knowledge of past dynastics in Bactria of the Scythians and other invaders after the time of Alexander has been pieced together from coins, seals and inscriptions picked up beyond India and acquired by Collectors in this country. If there were a Parthenon in Upper Swat or Bijaur, it seems to me better that its friezes or architecture should find their way into India even in pieces to be put together and restored in the Museum at Calcutta than that they should remain whether they are useless to the historian and likely to be defaced and destroyed before their original home can come under civilized control.

> On the other hand, I quite agree that within India and outside of it so far as our political officers can exercise effectual control, excavation of old ruins and buildings should be prohibited without permission of Government.[90]

The Settlement Collector, Jhelum[91] and the Commissioner, Rawalpindi Division[92] also expressed similar views and stated that an order should be issued by the Government that Government officials, whether civil or military, should be prohibited to purchase Buddhist sculptures, inscriptions and other objects of archaeological importance. It was also proposed to issue instructions for bringing to the notice of the Government all genuine relics that could be conveniently acquired for the Government.

The Foreign Department issued a notification on 22 February 1901 (No. 438-F) banning trade in archaeological relics. The notification also prohibited import of relics to British India from "Dir, Swat and Chitral Agency, Gilgit Agency or from any of the tribal areas which lie between those Agencies and border of British India, of any Buddhist sculptures, carvings or inscriptions save under the authority in writing of chief political officer of the said territories".[93] This notification provided the requisite legal authority for the seizure of antiquarian treasures.

In this connection, it may as well be mentioned that Marshall addressed a letter to the Chief Commissioner, North-West Frontier Province on 20 December 1902 on the preservation of ruins at Takht-i-Bahi and Jamalgarhi. Marshall requested for the conservation of these monuments on priority basis which required "resetting many of the loose and fallen stones in protecting the tops of wall and, if necessary strengthening them with invisible or inconspicuous cement in cleaning out the accumulated debris from the courts and passages".[94]

The letter from Marshall was forwarded to the Chief Commissioner, North-West Frontier Province by REV Arbuthnot, Under Secretary, Government of India on 6 February 1903 with a request to take necessary action for saving the monuments and archaeological remains at North-West Frontier Province.[95]

ELEVENTH CONGRESS OF ORIENTALISTS AT ROME AND INDIAN EXPLORATION FUND

In 1898, the Eleventh Congress of Orientalists held at Rome proposed an establishment of an "Indian Exploration Fund". This was proposed as most of the delegates to the Congress had seen the decadence of monuments in India. In this connection, Lord Reay, President of the Royal Asiatic Society, who was also a delegate to this Congress, addressed a letter to Lord Elgin, Viceroy on 26 November 1898 and stated civil officers in India were over-burdened with their assigned duties and those officers who take active interest in archaeological pursuits should be given due encouragement. He further stated that princely states had earlier given their support and British Indian Government should also do the same. He added that if monuments are continuously neglected, the British Indian Government being trustees of these treasures should be universally criticized for neglect of edifices of archaeological importance. Lord Reay requested that "A circular to Provincial Governments placing funds at their disposal would probably have the desired effect and I am sure you will find at Calcutta men interested in this important branch of administration".[96]

A Memorandum was prepared for the scheme for an establishment of an "Indian Exploration Fund" by T.W. Rhys Davids, Secretary, Royal Asiatic Society.

> The Royal Asiatic Society have carefully considered the scheme for an "Indian Exploration Fund". As it is contemplated to obtain the approval of the Government of India for any exploration, which

may be initiated, and to obtain the cooperation of that Government, the Society wishes to give its cordial support convinced of the great importance of all well regulated activity in this direction.

As the Central Council would be domiciled in London, and as it would be the Executive of the Fund, there is no danger of undue foreign interference. As the delegates of the Government of India and of the English National Committee would represent on the Central Council a number equal to that of the foreign delegates, this would amount to control of the Fund by the English Members.

The Society has reason to believe that its Secretary, Professor Rhys Davids will be appointed Hon'ble Secretary of the Central Council and they welcome this selection as a further guarantee of success. The Society is quite prepared to appoint four or five delegates to the English National Committee on which probably the Government of India will desire to be represented (as well as on the Central Council).

The Society will also place its rooms in Albermarle Street at the disposal of the Committee for the first meeting.

An obvious advantage would accrue from this International control because it would give the Government of India security for the selection of the explorers (in foreign countries) and various National Committees would exercise due care in sending out experts and archaeologists.

In conclusion, the Society wishes to lay stress on the fact that the interest taken by foreign orientalists in the preservation and discovery of Indian antiquities is disinterested and complimentary. There is no alternative but to cordially accept the offered assistance. The question of funds will have to be considered by the National Committee after it has been constituted.

These observations are obviously not intended for the foreign initiators of the scheme but they are meant to remove any doubts which might arise in the minds of those who are chiefly concerned in Great Britain and in India in giving their support to a scheme which, if judiciously carried out, may prove most beneficial in expending our knowledge of the treasures which are scattered all over our Indian Empire.[97]

INTERNATIONAL ASSOCIATION FOR ARCHAEOLOGICAL RESEARCH IN INDIA

This proposal for the "Indian Exploration Fund" was forwarded to the Secretary of State for India for their concurrence on 31 March 1898. The Asiatic Society also sought views of the Government of India for the establishment of an "International Association for Archaeological Research in India.[98]

The Government of India welcomed the proposal of the establishment of an "International Association for Archaeological Research in India" on certain conditions. Accordingly, the Government of India in its Despatch to the Secretary of State for India clarified on 14 July 1898 as:

The Scheme is one which we most heartily welcome. It will provide for antiquarian exploration and records under the most competent guidance of a nature and to an extent, which we have reluctantly decided that we should not be justified in undertaking at the public cost. It will moreover, strengthen our hands in dealing with a class of cases which will probably become more and more frequent where private travellers as to whose knowledge or competence we have no means of judging apply for permission to explore.

The proposed Association, if constituted, will receive all kind of assistance in our power. Two stipulations are, however, in our opinion necessary.

In the first place, no exploration must be undertaken without our previous consent. The condition is essential. Many of the most interesting fields of archaeological research lie on or beyond portions

> of our frontier which separate us from not the least susceptible among our neighbours while within our borders, the religious susceptibilities of our own subjects must be protected from possible injury. In the second place we understand that in Greece and Italy and perhaps in other countries of Europe it is now the established rule that all objects of archaeological or historical importance by whomever discovered belong to the Government of the country though duplicates may be removed. We are strongly of opinion that the same rule should be enforced in India subject to the payment of such compensation to the owner of the place. Where they are found and to the finder when he is not exploring with the permission of Government as may appear reasonable.
>
> We have no information as to the precise regulations, which govern this matter in countries such as Greece and Italy. Your Lordship, however, will be able to ascertain their nature and we shall be glad to receive any information that may be obtainable about such conditions as may appear proper and necessary in accordance with the principle which we desire to enforce.
>
> The information will enable us to consider in what respects the provisions of the Treasure-Trove Act (VI of 1878) require to be amended or supplemented so as to make them apply to all classes of articles of archaeological or historical interest discovered in British India and to secure to the Government ample power to acquire such objects or to prevent their sale and removal. It may further throw light on some other questions closely connected with the subject which are not without difficulty. One is as to the extent to which power should be taken by the Government to enter upon private property for the purpose of making explorations. Another is as to the propriety or practicability of preventing exploration from British India of articles of archaeological or historical interest already in private hands, or of securing to the Government the right of preemption. Another is the possibility of regulating archaeological exploration in native States or tribal territory within or near our borders with a view of preventing the destruction or the removal for commercial purposes, of sculptures and other similar objects such as those which were found in the Swat Valley in the recent occupation. We have not arrived at any conclusions on these points and we shall be glad to see whether the practice in the countries which we have mentioned will afford us any assistance in the manner."[99]

However, Lord George Hamilton, Secretary of State for India in its Despatch dated 10 November 1898 to the Governor-General in Council had forwarded copies of Parliamentary Papers (C-8443 of 1897) concerning "European Laws and Rules for the preservation of Ancient Monuments".[100]

Lord Curzon, however, vehemently opposed the Government of India's participation in the "Indian Exploration Fund". In his letter to Lord Reay on 8 February 1900, he stated, "I saw Professor Rhys Davids about M. Senart's proposal for an Indian Exploration Fund paid for and run by foreigners. I am not in favour of it, since I do not want French and German Savants running about this country except in our employ and since I think that we ought to do the thing not with M. Senart's money but with our own".[101]

On 12 July 1901, Lord Northbrook also sent his views to Lord Curzon on the proposal of the Asiatic Society for the establishment of an "International Fund for the Archaeological Exploration of India". He stated that:

> I received a short time ago a paper from the Asiatic Society asking me to join a scheme for starting Executive Committees in America, Austria, France, Germany, Italy and England to manage an International Fund for the Archaeological Exploration of India. I said that I could not join the movement without knowing whether you approve of it – being doubtful whether you would like an incursion of archaeologists scattered about India with all sorts of proposals and I know you have taken a great interest in these questions. The whole thing does not seem to me to be very practical; for the archaeologists are by no means millionaires and I doubt if any subscriptions of consequence will be forthcoming – some say you can tell me what you think of it."[102]

Curzon replied to Northbrook on 16 November 1901 thus:

> In your last letter, you kindly asked for my opinion about a proposal to send a motley crew of international archaeologists rampaging about India. My predecessor unfortunately gave his sanction to the scheme. I have not the slightest intention of admitting them to the country. Anything that remains to be done – and there is a great deal – we are prepared to undertake ourselves and I am just re-establishing the post of Director General of Archaeology and setting out a man from home. I do not at all want a polyglot crew of Germans, French and so on digging about India hammering the natives and carrying off our spoil. The project will probably languish for want of funds and it will certainly meet with no encouragement from me.[103]

Earl of Northbrook replied on 12 December 1901:

"I thought you would not like international interference with your Archaeology which made me hesitate in my answer after what you say I shall have nothing to do without it."[104]

NOTES AND REFERENCES

1. *The story of Indian Archaeology, 1784-1947* by Sourendranath Roy; 1961, p. 72.
2. *A History of Indian Archaeology* by Dilip K. Chakrabarti; 1988, p. 120.
3. *I.R.D., List of Heads of Administrations in India and of the India Office in England*, published in 1921, p. 5; Home, Public, January 1899, No. 161.
4. Revenue and Agriculture, Archaeology and Epigraphy, January 1901, No. 5 Notes.
5. Curzon Papers, N.A.I. Acc.No. 1636, Mss Eur F.111/199, No. 116.
6. Curzon Papers, N.A.I. Acc.No. 1636, Mss Eur F.111/199, No. 116.
7. Curzon Papers, N.A.I. Acc.No. 1637, Mss Eur F.111/200, No. 3.
8. Curzon Papers, N.A.I. Acc.No. 1637 Mss Eur F.111/200, No. 121.
9. Curzon Papers, N.A.I. Acc.No. 1637, Mss Eur F.111/200, No. 37.
10. Revenue and Agriculture Department, Archaeology and Epigraphy, January 1900, No. 9.
11. Curzon Papers, N.A.I. Acc No. 1630, Mss Eur F.111/158, No. 60.
12. Curzon Papers, N.A.I. Acc No. 1630, Mss Eur F.111/158, No. 78.
13. Curzon Papers, N.A.I. Acc No. 1637, Mss Eur F.111/201, No. 11.
14. Curzon Papers, N.A.I. Acc No. 1631, Mss Eur F.111/159, No. 8.
15. Curzon Papers, N.A.I. Acc No. 1630, Mss Eur F.111/159, No. 14.
16. Curzon Papers, N.A.I. Acc No. 1637, Mss Eur F.111/201, No. 11.
17. Curzon Papers, N.A.I. Acc No. 1635, Mss Eur F.111/181, No. 98 a.
18. Curzon Papers, N.A.I. Acc No. 1635, Mss Eur F.111/181, No. 65.
19. Curzon Papers, N.A.I. Acc No. 1631, Mss Eur F.111/159, No. 77.
20. *Ibid.*
21. Revenue and Agriculture Department, Archaeology and Epigraphy, October 1900, No. 2.
22. Department of Revenue and Agriculture, Archaeology and Epigraphy, January 1901, No. 5, Notes.
23. *Ibid.*
24. *Ibid.*
25. Department of Revenue and Agriculture Department, Archaeology and Epigraphy, January 1901, No. 5.
26. *Ibid.*
27. Curzon Papers, NAI Acc.No. 1631, No. 32.
28. Department of Revenue and Agriculture, Archaeology and Epigraphy A, May 1901, No. 4.
29. *Ibid.*
30. *Ibid.*, Notes.
31. Curzon Papers, NAI Acc.No. 1638, Mss Eur, F.111/203, No. 159.
32. Curzon Papers, NAI Acc.No. 1638, Mss Eur, F.111/203, No. 161.
33. Curzon Papers, NAI Acc.No. 1631, Mss Eur, F.111/160, No. 39.

34. Curzon Papers, NAI Acc.No. 1631, Mss Eur, F.111/160, No. 82.
35. Revenue and Agriculture Department, Archaeology A, May 1902, No. 1.
36. *Ibid.*
37. Curzon Papers, NAIi Acc.No. 1631, Mss Eur, F.111/160, No. 84.
38. Curzon Papes, NAI Acc.No. 1635, Mss Eur, F.111/182, No. 62.
39. Department of Revenue and Archaeology A, May 1902, No. 3.
40. Revenue and Agriculture Department, Archaeology and Epigraphy A, May 1902, No. 8.
41. Department of Revenue and Agriculture, Archaeology and Epigraphy, May 1902, No. 9.
42. Department of Revenue and Agriculture, Archaeology and Epigraphy, Part B, August 1902, No. 8.
43. *Asiatic Review 1921*, pp. 90-91.
44. Curzon Papers, NAI Acc.No. 1632, Mss Eur, 111/161, No. 29.
45. Curzon Papers, NAI Acc.No. 1632, Mss Eur, 111/161, No. 30.
46. Curzon Papers, NAI Acc.No. 1632, Mss.Eur, 111/161, No. 13.
47. Foreign Department, Internal A, July 1901, No. 69.
48. Foreign Department, Internal A, July 1901, No. 88.
49. *The Asiatic Review*, January 1921, p. 100; *Marshall's Indian Archaeological Policy*, p. 10, Govt. Publication, 1916.
50. Department of Revenue and Agriculture, Archaeology and Epigraphy A, February 1903, No. 2.
51. Department of Revenue and Agriculture, Archaeology and Epigraphy A, February 1903, No. 6.
52. *Ibid.*
53. *Ibid.*
54. Department of Revenue and Agriculture, Archaeology and Epigraphy, October 1903, Nos. 1-16, notes.
55. *Ibid.*
56. Department of Revenue and Agriculture, Archaeology and Epigraphy, October 1903, No. 10.
57. Department of Revenue and Agriculture, Archeology and Epigraphy A, August 1902, No. 12.
58. *Ibid.*
59. Archaeology B, June 1901, Nos. 1-2.
60. Revenue and Agriculture, Archaeology and Epigraphy, A, August 1902, No. 2, Notes.
61. *Ibid.*
62. Revenue and Agriculture, Archaeology and Epigraphy A, August 1902, No. 2.
63. Curzon Papers, NAI Acc.No. 1638, Mss Eur 111/205, No. 147.
64. Curzon Papers, NAI Acc.No. 1638, Mss Eur 111/205, No. 156.
65. Curzon Papers, NAI Acc.No. 1632, Mss Eur, F.111/161, No. 30.
66. Curzon Papers, NAI Acc.No. 1632, Mss Eur, F.111/161, No. 43.
67. Curzon Papers, NAI Acc.No. 1638, Mss Eur, F.111/205, No. 149.
68. Department of Revenue and Agriculture, Archaeology and Epigraphy A, September 1902, No. 4.
69. Department of Revenue and Agriculture, Archaeology and Epigraphy A, September 1902, No. 5.
70. *Revealing India's past* edited by Sir John Cumming (1939), p. 31.
71. *The Story of Indian Archaeology, 1784-1947*, by Sourendranath Roy (1961), p. 86.
72. Department of Revenue and Agriculture, Archaeology and Epigraphy, August 1903, Nos. 11-12.
73. P.W.D., C.W. Buildings, May 1903, Nos. 23-24, Part B.
74. *Ibid.*, A, January 1901, No. 5.
75. P.W.D., C.W. Buildings, May 1903, Nos. 23-24, Part B.
76. Revenue and Agriculture, Archaeology and Epigraphy, A, February 1903, No. 44.
77. P.W.D., A-G, August 1903, No. 4.
78. Revenue and Agriculture, Archaeology and Epigraphy, August 1903, No. 13.
79. Revenue and Agriculture, Archaeology and Epigraphy, April 1889, Nos. 1-5.
80. Archaeology, Part C, December 1895, No. 1, Notes.
81. *Ibid.*

82. Foreign Department, Frontier B, February 1896, No. 51.
83. Revenue and Agriculture, Archaeology and Epigraphy, B, July 1897, No. 5.
84. Revenue and Agriculture, Archaeology and Epigraphy, B, September 1897, No. 10.
85. Revenue and Agriculture, Archaeology and Epigraphy, A, January 1898, No. 2.
86. Revenue and Agriculture, Archaeology and Epigraphy, B, April 1899, Nos. 6-7.
87. Revenue and Agriculture, Archaeology and Epigraphy, B, May 1899, Nos. 1-2.
88. Foreign, Frontier A, March 1901, No. 11.
89. Foreign, Frontier A, March 1901, No. 11, Notes.
90. Foreign, Frontier A, March 1901, No. 15.
91. *Ibid.*
92. *Ibid.*
93. Foreign, Frontier A, March 1901, No. 16.
94. Revenue and Agriculture, Archaeology and Epigraphy, February 1903, No. 9.
95. Revenue and Agriculture, Archaeology and Epigraphy, February 1903, No. 20.
96. Revenue and Agriculture, Archaeology and Epigraphy, January 1901, No. 5 Notes.
97. Revenue and Agriculture, Archaeology and Epigraphy, July 1898, Nos. 31-32, Notes.
98. Revenue and Agriculture, Archaeology and Epigraphy, July 1898, No. 32.
99. Revenue and Agriculture, Archaeology and Epigraphy, July 1898, No. 32.
100. Revenue and Agriculture, Archaeology and Epigraphy, November 1901, No. 1.
101. Curzon Papers, NAI Acc.No. 1635, Mss Eur, F.111/181, No. 62.
102. Curzon Papers, NAI Acc.No. 1635, Mss Eur, F.111/182, No. 2a.
103. Curzon Papers, NAI Acc.No. 1636, Mss Eur, F.111/1832, No. 34.
104. Curzon Papers, NAI Acc.No. 1635, Mss Eur, F.111/1832, No. 44.

Chapter XIII

Ancient Monuments Preservation Act of 1904

The conditions relating to the condition of ancient monuments, exploitation of archaeological remains in Swat Valley, India Exploration Fund, apathetic attitude of some archaeologists and unstable Archaeological Survey Department led Curzon to review the archaeological policy and give the Archaeological Survey Department a right and dynamic direction for ensuring that the ancient monuments remained in good condition.

The major step in this direction was the enactment of '**The Ancient Monuments Preservation Act,** 1904 (VII of 1904)'. Cole, the Curator, had earlier recommended the enactment of an act in the Memorandum 'on the conservation of ancient and other architectural remains in India' published in his first report for the year 1882. Curzon consulted many learned persons in this regard. He studied the Parliamentary Paper (C-8443 of 1897) concerning the European laws and rules for the preservation of ancient monuments which were forwarded to him by George Hamilton, Secretary of State, on 10 November 1898 (Despatch Revenue No. 203).[1]

He sought information from various governments of the countries where Legislation or Ancient Monuments Preservation Act had come into force. Apart from Great Britain and Ireland, France, Germany, Italy, the Austrian Empire, Belgium, Holland, Switzerland, Denmark, Norway, Sweden, Russia, Finland, Spain, Portugal, Greece, Turkey, Egypt, Algeria and Tunis were the principal countries.

At the advice of Curzon, a draft Bill was prepared which was sent on 5 November 1901 (Circular No. 30, Department of Revenue and Agriculture, Archaeological and Epigraphy) to all local governments and administrations for their opinion:

> The Government of India have had under consideration the expediency of taking measures to preserve to the country ancient monuments of historical or artistic interest and other valuable relics of antiquity and I am directed to forward for the opinion of – a draft bill embodying provisions which the Governor-General in Council after a careful examination of this question, considers to be such as might be reasonably adopted for the purpose in view. Within the past few years,

arrangements have been made to secure that the attention of the Archaeological Department is systematically given to the condition of the more important of the buildings which link present history with the past and provision is made for the expenditure of public funds in the maintenance and repair of certain of them. But these arrangements fall short of desirable completeness in that they are liable to be defeated by the indifference or opposition of private persons into whose hands such buildings may have fallen and it is notorious that this country has lost, and is now losing, monuments of great artistic and archaeological interest owing not merely to neglect but to deliberate destruction. The Government of India are of opinion that these circumstances warrant the intervention of the State to prevent further injury and to carry out such necessary measures of protection and repair as the owners are unwilling to undertake and they are not without hopes that legislation for this purpose may, by awakening public interest, render the interference of Government less necessary than it appears to be at present.

2. The main provisions of the Bill are concerned with buildings. The line of action which it is proposed to follow in order to secure proper maintenance and repair may tend rather to the encouragement of private effort than to its supersession. The owner or manager of a building which merits greater care than it has been receiving, will be invited to enter into an agreement for its protection and upkeep, a breach of the agreement entailing a penalty. In the event of his refusing to come to terms, the Government may itself take the necessary measures, the expenditure thus incurred being met from public funds except in cases where an endowment exists to which it may reasonably be charged. Power is taken to acquire buildings compulsorily but only in cases where no other course will serve the object in view and with the express exception of buildings which are used for religious worship. The Government will also have right of pre-emption in cases of transfer.

3. Clauses 11 and 12 of the Bill are concerned with moveable objects of historical value. The former authorises the Government to place restrictions upon the traffic in things of this class, in order to prevent their export from the country or in order to obviate such spoliation of archaeological remains as has recently occurred in Swat and Buner. Under clause 12 it will be possible to prohibit the removal from their site of sculptures, bas-reliefs and the like and to acquire them if acquisition is necessary in order to ensure their preservation or retention in India.[2]

The replies received were exceedingly voluminous and the opinions given were of very varying value. The opinions were discussed and T. Raleigh and Denzil Ibbetson, members of Council, making some alterations, prepared a revised draft. Curzon considered it a good draft.[3]

The Draft Bill was forwarded by the Governor-General in Council (Curzon, Kitchener, T. Raleigh, E.F.G. Law, E.R. Elles, A.T. Arundel, Denzil Ibbetson) to Lord George F. Hamilton, Secretary of State (Department of Revenue and Agriculture, Archaeology and Epigraphy, No. 24) dated 28 May 1903:

In 1898 Lord Elgin's Government, when addressing your Lordship on the subject of antiquarian exploration and research in this country, requested that information might if possible be obtained as to the regulations in force in such countries as Greece and Italy for the protection of objects of archaeological or historical importance (Despatch No. 39 dated 14th July 1898). Your Lordship, in reply, forwarded a Parliamentary paper concerning the European laws and rules for the protection of ancient monuments and we have since had under our consideration the expediency of legislating for the same purpose in India (Revenue Despatch No. 203, dated 10 November1898). We are much impressed by the necessity of taking measures which will strengthen our hands in our endeavour to preserve to India its ancient monuments and other valuable relics of antiquity; which will enable us to prevent, by the infliction of adequate penalties, the wilful destruction or defacement of such monuments and relics; and which will confer on us the power to control the traffic in antiquities, and to prevent the excavation of sites of historic interest by ignorant or unauthorized persons. While the subject was under our consideration, the necessity for taking some further power for the attainment of these objects was brought prominently to our notice in connection with the rifling of the Buddhist remains in the Swat Valley, and with the attempt made shortly afterwards by a German adventurer, under pretext of a mission from a scientific society of Berlin, to remove certain valuable frescoes from one of the famous Buddhist pagodas at Pagan in Burma. After making further enquiry from other countries, we decided that legislation was required to enable us to discharge effectually our responsibilities in this matter. We therefore drafted a brief bill, based on the existing English Acts, and embodying certain provisions which have found a place in recent legislation in regard to antiquities in Greece and Italy. This bill we circulated for the opinion of Local Governments. The replies which we have received show that our proposals in their main lines meet with almost unanimous approval, criticism being directed almost entirely against some of the details of the Bill. The Government of Bengal had indeed independently taken up the question of legislating on the subject. We have revised and somewhat expanded the Bill in the right of the criticisms received, the changes being mainly in the direction of defining more clearly the relation between the owners of private monuments and Government officers, and we now forward the Bill as thus amended for your Lordship's approval.

2. The first portion of the Bill deals with the protection of ancient monuments. The definition of this term is a matter of some difficulty and your Lordship will observe that this Bill will apply only to ancient monuments (as defined in clause 2(1) of the Bill) which have been expressly brought within the compass of the Act by a notification issued under clause 2(7). The chief object of this part of the Bill is to secure the better preservation of monuments which are in private ownership. The greater number of the more famous and beautiful buildings are indeed already in the possession or under the control of Government. But there are others, whose preservation is very desirable, which have unfortunately either already been partially destroyed, or which are fast falling into decay owing to the apathy or ignorance of the private owners to whom they belong and with whose actions we have at present no power to interfere. We appreciate the difficulties that may attend executive action in such cases, and the risk of offending the prejudices and susceptibilities of the people whose religious buildings are concerned. But on the other hand, we feel strongly that there are cases in which we are bound, as guardians of the public interests, to interfere to such extent as may be feasible for the purpose of securing the preservation of such buildings. The principle of interference for such a purpose is not new. It is in accordance with the policy formally enunciated in Section 23 of the Religious Endowments Act XX of 1863, which expressly recognizes the right of Government to "prevent injury to, and preserve buildings remarkable for their antiquity and for their historical or architectural value or required for the convenience of the public". But the power of Government to intervene is at present limited to cases which arise under the Regulations (Bengal Regulation XIX of 1810, Section 3; Madras Regulation VII of 1817, Section 3) referred to in that Act, while the manner in which the power of interference should be exercised is at present somewhat obscure, and requires to be more clearly defined and described. In the proposals which we have embodied in the Bill, we have aimed at enlisting the good-will and securing the active cooperation of the owners of the buildings in question in the beneficent designs of Government, and we are not without hope that the line of action which it is proposed to follow may tend rather to the encouragement of private effort than to its suppression. The owner or manager of a building which merits greater care than it has been receiving, may be invited to enter into an agreement for its protection and upkeep, and in the event of his refusing to come to terms the Collector may, if there is an endowment, move the Courts to secure its proper application to the repairs of the monuments; or he may, if necessary for its preservation, proceed to acquire the monument compulsorily, with the express exception of buildings which are used for religious observances. We have made it clear that there is to be no resort to compulsory acquisition until the owner has been given the opportunity of entering into an agreement. The Bill also secures to Government a right of pre-emption in cases of the transfer of ancient monuments or their sites. The sentiment of the people is guarded by the express provision that a monument maintained by Government under the proposed Act shall not be used for any purpose inconsistent with its character or with the purposes of its foundation, and that, so far as is compatible with the object in view, the public shall have access to it free of charge. These proposals

have met with almost unanimous approval on the part of the officers whom we have consulted, and we believe that we shall be supported in our efforts by the more enlightened section of the native public.

3. There is one provision in this part of the Bill which appears to call for further explanation. By the third proviso to Section 11 it is laid down that in assessing the value of a monument for the purpose of compulsory acquisition, the archaeological, artistic, or historical merits of the monument shall not be taken into account. We believe that this proviso is fair and reasonable. It may indeed be argued that the owner is entitled to receive a return for the archaeological or historical value of the monument, and objection may be taken to this clause on the ground that it will enable Government to take possession of monuments in British India at a price greatly below their real value. The argument however omits to take into account the circumstances of the purchase. The object of Government in purchasing is to preserve, at its own expense, an ancient monument with all its historical or archaeological associations, for the benefit of the public who will have free access to it; and we do not think that in such circumstances Government should pay for the value of these associations. Moreover, such value, when admitted in other countries, depends mainly on the right of the proprietor to fence round the monument or building and to levy a charge for admittance. We doubt whether, if such right can be held to exist in India, any profit could be derived from its exercise. Your Lordship will observe that the section will apply only when compulsory acquisition is necessary in order to preserve the monument.

4. The second portion of the Bill deals with moveable objects of historical or artistic interest. Such articles fall into two classes. The first class consists of arms, enamels, silver and copper vessels, Persian and Arabic manuscripts, those articles in short which are generally termed curios. These articles are mostly portable and consequently difficult to trace; they generally possess an artistic rather than a historic interest; and it would be impossible in practice, even if it were desirable, to prevent a dealer from selling or a traveller from buying. We should not in ordinary circumstances think it necessary to interfere with the disposal of articles of this class. But there is another class of articles, such as sculptural carvings, images, bas reliefs, inscriptions and the like, the value of which mainly depends upon their local connection, and the possession of which enriches the archaeological or ethnological treasures, which ought properly to remain in India, where museums in which they can be preserved exist at the provincial capitals. Of such a character are the Buddhist sculptures which were discovered in such numbers a few years ago in Swat and Yusufzai, and a large number of which were smuggled out of the country. Many of these antiquities – those in Swat furnish a case in point – are found outside the confines of British India or in Native States. As was pointed out in our Despatch No.1, dated the 6th January 1898, it is impossible, as regards British territory and under the existing law, to go beyond the provisions of the Indian Treasure-Trove Act, 1878 (VI of 1878), while we cannot, by our legislation, provide for anything to be done outside British India. The powers which we propose to take in the present Bill will not only enable us to prevent the removal from British India of any antiquities which we may desire to retain in the country, but further, by preventing the importation of antiquities from foreign territories into British India, and thus putting a stop to traffic in such articles, will enable us to protect against spoliation a number of interesting places situated outside the limits of British India. The enforcement of the prohibition will, it is true, involve in some cases a customs or police inquisition. But inquisition of some kind is necessary, since by no other means is it possible to enforce a law which restricts the sale of moveables. The power will be exercised only in rare cases, and our proposals do not go beyond what has been found necessary in Italy and Greece. In clause 19, we have endeavoured to provide for antiquities, such as sculptures, inscriptions and the like, which belong to a particular place, and ought therefore to be kept **in situ** or sent to local museums. Clause 20 provides for the compulsory purchase of such antiquities if such purchase is necessary for their preservation, but it will be observed that articles from which the owner is unwilling to part on personal or religious grounds are expressly excepted from the operation of the clause.

5. Finally, the Bill gives power to prohibit or regulate that excavation by irresponsible persons of ancient sites, by which so much evidence that might have proved of immeasurable value to trained archaeologists has in the past been irretrievably destroyed or impaired.

6. We have been careful in legislating on this subject to take no greater powers than are necessary to enable us to exercise due control over the preservation of the archeological treasures of the country. We desire, as far as possible, to avoid all resort to compulsory proceedings and we think that the Bill which we have prepared will enable us to attain the objects in view without any recourse to action that might be resented as appressive.[4]

Accordingly, a Draft Bill was submitted to the Secretary of State which was as follows:

"A Bill to provide for the Preservation of Ancient Monuments and of objects of Archaeological, Historical or Artistic interest

Whereas it is expedient to provide for the preservation of ancient monuments, for the exercise of control over traffic in antiquities and over excavation in certain places, and for the protection and acquisition in certain cases of ancient monuments and of objects of archaeological, historical or artistic interest; it is hereby enacted as follows:

I. Short Title, Extent and Commencement

(1) This Act may be called the Ancient Monuments Preservation Act, 1903.
(2) It extends to the whole of British India inclusive of British Baluchistan, the Sonthal Parganas and the Pargana of Spiti; and
(3) It shall come into force at once.

II. Definitions

In this Act, unless there is anything repugnant in the subject or context –

(1) "ancient monuments" means any structure, erection or monuments, or any tumulus or place of interment, or any rock-sculpture, inscription or monolith, which is of historical, archaeological or artistic interest, or any remains thereof, and includes –
   (a) the site of an ancient monument;
   (b) such portion of land adjoining the site of an ancient monument as may be required for fencing or covering in or otherwise preserving such monument; and
   (c) the means of access to and convenient inspection of an ancient monument.
(2) "antiquities" include any moveable objects which the Government, by reason of their historical or archeological associations, may think it necessary to protect against injury, removal or dispersion.
(3) "Commissioner" means the chief revenue officer of a division, and includes any officer authorized by the Local Government to perform the duties of a Commissioner under this Act.
(4) "excavation" means any removal or disturbance of the soil for the purpose of searching for buried ancient monuments or for antiquities or for treasure as defined by the Indian Treasure-Trove Act, 1878;
(5) "maintain" and "maintenance" include the fencing, covering in, repairing, restoring and cleansing of a protected monument, and the doing of any act which may be necessary for the purpose of maintaining a protected monument or of securing convenient access thereto;

(6) "land" includes a revenue-free estate, a revenue-paying estate, and a permanent transferable tenure, whether such estate or tenure be subject to encumbrances or not; and

(7) "protected monument" means any ancient monument which the Local Government may, by notification in the local official Gazette, declare to be subject to the provisions of this Act.

III. Evidence that any structure, etc., is an Ancient Monument

An order writing, signed by a Secretary to the Local Government, and stating that any structure erection, tumulus, place of interment, sculpture, inscription or monolith is an ancient monument within the meaning of this Act, shall be conclusive evidence of that fact.

ANCIENT MONUMENTS

IV. Acquisition of rights in or Guardianship of an Ancient Monument by Commissioner

(1) The Commissioner may, with the sanction of the Local Government, purchase or take a lease of any protected monument.

(2) The Commissioner may, with sanction of the Local Government, accept a gift or bequest of any protected monument.

(3) The owner of any protected monument may, by written instrument, constitute the Commissioner the guardian of the monument, and the Commissioner may, with the sanction of the Local Government, accept such guardianship.

(4) When the Commissioner has accepted the guardianship of a monument under sub-section (3), the owner shall, except as expressly provided in this Act, have the same estate, right, title and interest in and to the monument as if the Commissioner had not been constituted guardian thereof.

(5) When the Commissioner has accepted the guardianship of a monument under sub-section (3), the provisions of this Act relating to agreements executed under section 5 shall apply to the written instrument executed under the sub-section.

V. Preservation of Ancient Monument by agreement

(1) The Collector may, with the previous sanction of the Local Government, propose to the owner to enter into an agreement with the Secretary of State for India in Council for the preservation of any protected monument in his district.

(2) An agreement under this section may provide for the following matters, or for such of them as it may be found expedient to include in the agreement –

(a) the maintenance of the monument;

(b) the custody of the monument, and the duties of any person who may be employed to watch it;

(c) the restriction of the owner's right to destroy, remove, alter and deface the monument;

(d) the facilities of access to be permitted to the public or to any portion of the public and to persons deputed by the owner or the Collector to inspect or maintain the monument;

(e) the notice to be given to the Government in case the land on which the monument is situated is offered for sale by the owner, and the right to be reserved to the

Government to purchase such land, or any specified portion of such land, at its market-value;

(f) the payment of any expenses incurred by the owner or by the Government in connection with the preservation of the monument;

(g) the proprietary or other rights which are to vest in the Government in respect of the monument when any expenses are incurred by the Government in connection with the preservation of the monument; and

(h) any matter connected with the preservation of the monument which is a proper subject of agreement between the owner and the Government.

(3) An agreement under this section may be executed by the Collector on behalf of the Secretary of State for India in Council, but shall not be so executed until it has been approved by the Local Government.

(4) An agreement under this section may be terminated by the Collector or by the owner on giving six months' notice in writing.

VI. Owners under disability or not in possession

(1) If the owner is unable, by reason of infancy or other disability, to act for himself, an agreement under section 5 may be made and executed by the person legally competent to act on his behalf.

(2) If a protected monument belongs to joint-owners, one of whom is invested with powers of management on behalf of the others, an agreement under section 5 may be executed by such managing owner, after giving one month's notice in writing to the other owners.

(3) In the case of village property, an agreement under section 5 may be executed by the headman or other village-officer exercising powers of management over such property.

VII. Variation and Enforcement of Agreement

(1) The terms of an agreement under Section 5 may be altered from time to time, with the consent of the owner or of the persons competent to make an agreement under that Section.

(2) If the Collector has reason to apprehend that the owner or occupier of a monument intends to destroy, remove, deface or imperial the monument in contravention of the terms of an agreement for its preservation under Section 5, the Collector may make an order prohibiting any such contravention of the agreement.

(3) If an owner who has entered into an agreement for the preservation or maintenance of a monument under Section 5 refuses or neglects to do any act necessary to such preservation or maintenance, the Collector may authorize any person to do any such act, and the expense of doing any such act or such portion of the expense as the owner may be liable to pay under the agreement may be recovered from the owner as if it were an arrears of land-revenue.

(4) A person aggrieved by an order made under this Section may appeal to the Commissioner, who may cancel or modify it and whose decision shall be final.

VIII. Purchaser, etc. bound by instrument executed by owner

Every person who purchases, at a sale for arrears of land-revenue or any other public demand, or at a sale made under the Bengal Patni Taluks Regulation, 1819, an estate or tenure in which is situated a monument in respect of which any instrument has been executed by the owner for the time being, under Section 4 or Section 5, and every person claiming any title to a monument from through or under an owner who executed any such instrument, shall be bound by such instrument.

IX. Application of endowment to repair of an Ancient Monument

If any owner fails to enter into an agreement proposed to him under Section 5 for the preservation of a protected monument, and if any endowment has been created for the purpose of keeping such monument in repair, or for that purpose among others, the Collector may institute a suit in the Court of the District Judge, or, if the estimated cost of repairing the monument does not exceed one thousand rupees, may make an application to the District Judge for the proper application of such endowment or part thereof.

X. Pre-emption of Ancient Monument in case of sale

(1) If any protected monument, or the land on which any such monument is situated, is about to be sold, the owner shall send a written notice to the Collector, stating the price at which he is willing to sell the monument or the land, as the case may be, and the Government shall have a prior right to purchase such monument or land at its market-value.

(2) Sub-section (1) shall not apply in any case where an offer to sell is addressed only to members of the family or of any religious association to which the vender belongs.

(3) If the effect of a purchase made by the Government under Sub-section (1) is to diminish the market-value of any land offered for sale, other than the land purchased by Government; the vendor shall be entitled to compensation, the amount of such compensation to be ascertained in the manner provided by the Land Acquisition Act, 1894.

XI. Compulsory purchase of Ancient Monument

The preservation of a protected monument shall be deemed to be a "public purchase" within the meaning of the Land Acquisition Act, 1894:

Provided, 'first', that the powers of compulsory purchase conferred by that Act shall not be exercised in the case of –

(a) any monument which or any part of which is periodically used for religious observances; or

(b) any monument which is the subject of a subsisting agreement executed under Section 5.

Providing, 'secondly', that, in any case other than the cases referred to in the first proviso, the said powers of compulsory purchase shall not be exercised unless the owner has failed, within a reasonable period, to enter into an agreement proposed to him under the said Section.

Provided, 'thirdly', that, when making an enquiry under the said Land Acquisition Act as to the value of a monument, the Collector shall be assisted by two assessors one of whom shall be nominated by the Collector and one by the owner or, in his default, by the Collector.

Provided, 'fourthly', that in assessing such value the archaeological, artistic or historical merits of the monument shall not be taken into account.

XII. Maintenance of certain protected Monuments

(1) The commissioner shall maintain every monument in respect of which the Government has acquired any of the rights mentioned in Section 4 or which the Government has acquired under Section 10 or Section 11.

(2) When the Commissioner has accepted the guardianship of a monument under Section 4, he shall, for the purpose of maintaining such monument have access to the monument at all reasonable times, by himself and by his subordinates and workmen, for the purpose of inspecting the monument, and for the purpose of bringing such materials and doing such acts as he may consider necessary or desirable for the maintenance thereof.

XIII. Voluntary contributions

The Commissioner may receive voluntary contributions towards the cost of maintaining a protected monument and may give orders as to the management and application of any funds so received by him.

Provided that no contribution received under this Section shall be applied to any purpose other than the purpose for which it was contributed.

XIV. Protected Monument not to be diverted to unsuitable purpose

A monument maintained by the Government under this Act shall not be used for any purpose inconsistent with its character, or with the purpose of its foundation, so far as the same can be ascertained.

XV. Relinquishment of Government Rights in a Monument

With the sanction of the Local Government, the Commissioner may –

(a) where rights have been acquired by Government in respect of any monument under this Act by virtue of any sale, lease, gift or will, relinquish the rights so acquired to the person who would for the time being be the owner of the monument if such rights had not been acquired, or

(b) relinquish any guardianship of a monument which he has accepted under this Act.

XVI. Access to certain protected Monuments

(1) Subject to such rules as may after previous publication be made by the Local Government, the public shall have a right of access, free of charge, to any monument maintained by the Government under this Act.

(2) In making any rule under Sub-Section (1), the Local Government may provide that a breach of it shall be punishable with fine which may extend to twenty rupees.

XVII. Penalties

Any persons other than the owner who destroys, removes, injures, defaces or imperils a protected monument, and any owner who destroys, removes, injures, defaces or imperils a monument maintained by Government under this Act or in respect of which an agreement has been executed under Section 5, and any owner or occupier who contravenes an order made under Section 7, Sub-Section (2), shall, on conviction by a Magistrate of the first or second class, be punishable with fine which may extend to one thousand rupees, or with imprisonment which may extend to one month, or with both.

TRAFFIC IN ANTIQUITIES

XVIII. Power to control traffic in antiquities

(1) If the Governor-General in Council has reason to apprehend that antiquities are being sold or removed to the detriment of India or of any neighbouring country, he may, by notification in the Gazette of India, prohibit or restrict the bringing or taking by sea or by land of any object or objects described in the notification into or out of British India or any specified part of British India.

(2) Any person who brings or takes or attempts to bring or take any such object into or out of British India or any part of British India in contravention of a notification issued under Sub-Section (1) shall, on conviction by a Magistrate of the first or second class, be punishable with fine which may extend to five hundred rupees.

(3) Every object in respect of which an offence referred to in Sub-Section (2) has been committed shall be liable to confiscation.

(4) An officer of customs, or an officer of police of a grade not lower than Sub-Inspector, duly empowered by the Local Government in this behalf, may search any vessel, cart or other means of conveyance, and may open any baggage or package of goods, if he has reason to believe that goods in respect of which an offence has been committed under Sub-Section(2) are contained therein.

(5) A person who complains that the power of search mentioned in Sub-Section (4) has been vexatiously or improperly exercised may address his complaint to the Local Government, and the Local Government shall pass such order and may award such compensation, if any, as appears to it to be just.

PROTECTION OF SCULPTURES, INSCRIPTIONS, CARVINGS, ETC.

XIX. Control over removal of sculptures, etc.

(1) If the Local Government considers that any sculptures, carvings, images, bas-reliefs, inscriptions or other like objects ought not to be removed from the place where they are without the sanction of the Government, the Local Government may, by notification in the local official Gazette, direct that any such object or any class of such objects shall not be removed unless with the written permission of the Collector.

(2) A person applying for the permission mentioned in Sub-Section (1) shall specify the objects or object which he proposes to remove, and shall furnish, in regard to such object or objects, any information which the Collector may require.

(3) If the Collector refuses to grant such permission, the applicant may appeal to the Commissioner, whose decision shall be final.

(4) Any person who removes any object in contravention of a notification issued under Sub-Section (1), shall, on conviction by a Magistrate of the first or second class, be punishable with fine which may extend to five hundred rupees.

(5) In the case of any moveable object comprised in a notification under Sub-Section (1), the Local Government shall, on the requisition of the owner, purchase such object, and in the case of any immoveable object so comprised, if the owner proves to the satisfaction

of the person appointed as hereinafter provided that he has sustained any loss by reason of such object being so comprised, the Local Government shall pay compensation in respect of such loss.

The price or the compensation to be paid by the Local Government under this Sub-Section shall be assessed by a competent person appointed by the Local Government with the consent of the owner.

XX. PURCHASE OF SCULPTURES, ETC. BY THE GOVERNMENT

(1) If the Local Government has reason to apprehend that any object mentioned in a notification issued under Section 19, Sub-Section(1), is in danger of being destroyed, removed, injured or allowed to fall into decay, the Local Government may direct the Collector to purchase such object, and the Collector shall thereupon give notice to the owner of the object to be purchased.

(2) The Collector shall consider any claim and any evidence of value which may be presented on behalf of such owner and shall assess the value of the object to be purchased.

(3) The owner may appeal to the Local Government against the Collector's assessment, and the Local Government, after considering such further evidence (if any) as may be presented on behalf of the owner, may pass such order as it thinks fit.

(4) The property in the object to be purchased shall be vested in the Government on payment of six-fifths of the value assessed by the Collector or by the Local Government, as the case may be.

(5) The power of compulsory purchase given by this Section shall not extend to –

(a) any image or symbol actually used for the purpose of any religious observance, or

(b) anything which the owner desires to retain on any ground personal to himself or to any of his ancestors, or to any member of his family.

EXCAVATIONS

XXI. POWER TO CONTROL EXCAVATION

(1) If the Local Government is of the opinion that excavation within the limits of any local area ought to be restricted or regulated, the Local Government may, by notification in the local official Gazette, make rules –

(a) fixing the boundaries of the area to which the rules are to apply; and

(b) prescribing the authority by which, and the terms on which, licenses to excavate may be granted.

(2) The power to make rules given by this section is subject to the condition of the rules being made after previous publication.

(3) A rule made under this section may provide that any person committing a breach thereof shall, on conviction by a Magistrate of the first or second class, be punishable with fine which may extend to two hundred rupees.

(4) If any owner or occupier of land included in a notification under Sub-Section (1) proves to the satisfaction of the Local Government that he has sustained any loss by reason of such land being so included, the Local Government shall pay compensation in respect of such loss, and the amount of such compensation shall be assessed by a competent person appointed by the Local Government with the consent of the owner.

GENERAL

XXII. Power to make Rules

(1) The Governor-General in Council or the Local Government may make rules for carrying out any of the purpose of this Act.
(2) The power to make rules given by this Section is subject to the condition of the rules being made after previous publication.

XXIII. No suit in respect of Acts done in exercise of powers given by Act

No suit or other legal proceedings shall lie against any person in respect of any act done, or in good faith intended to be done in the exercise of any power conferred by this Act.[5]

Lord George Hamilton, Secretary of State, addressed a communication to the Government of India on 14 August 1903 (No. 121 dated Revenue) and appreciated the efforts for enacting the Legislation.

> Your Excellency's Government has devoted great attention to the subject and I am in sympathy with your desire to preserve to India its ancient monuments, to control the traffic in antiquities, and to prevent the excavation of sites of historical interest by ignorant or unauthorized persons. You state that in preparing the measure you have been careful to take no greater powers than are necessary for the object which you have in view, that you desire to avoid all resort to compulsory proceedings, and that you think that in applying the law it will be possible to avoid recourse to action which might be resented as appressive. I desire to express my concurrence in the policy thus described. I observe that after consulting the Local Governments, it was found possible to abate, in some matters, the stringency of the provisions of the draft Bill on which their opinions had been invited. I have no doubt that during the progress of the Bill in the Legislative Council your Excellency's Government will consider carefully, and will endeavour to meet, any reasonable representations which may be made on behalf of private interests with regard to particular provisions of the Bill now before me. I refer more particularly to the fourth proviso to clause 11, which introduces a novel and apparently inequitable principle into the provisions of the Land Acquisition Land; to clause 19, which renders the owner of private property, if he remove such property without permission, liable to a criminal prosecution, while it places no obligation on the State to purchase the property from him; and to clause 20, which empowers a Local Government to acquire certain classes of antiquities of prices finally fixed by its revenue authorities. With regard to clause 21, it is a matter for consideration whether it should apply to operations of the nature of an "excavation" undertaken on private land by or on behalf of the owner of it.[6]

He sanctioned the introduction of the Bill into the Legislative Council.

Forwarding the above-mentioned Secretary of State's despatch, the Revenue and Agriculture Department sent an Office Memorandum (No. 3240-75) dated 19 September 1903 to the Legislative Department requesting for necessary steps should be taken for the introduction of the Bill in the Council of the Governor-General for making Laws and Regulations.[7]

Denzil Ibbetson prepared a **Statement of Objects and Reasons** on 19 October 1903.

> The object of this measure is to preserve to India its ancient monuments, to control the traffic in antiquities, and to prevent the excavation by ignorant or unauthorised persons of sites of historic interest and value.
>
> 2. In 1898 the question of antiquarian exploration and research attracted attention, and the necessity for taking steps for the protection of monuments and relics of antiquity was impressed upon the Government of India. It was then apparent that legislation was required to enable the Government effectually to discharge their responsibilities in the matter, and a Bill was drafted on the lines of

existing Acts of Parliament, modified so as to embody certain provisions which had found a place in recent legislation regarding the antiquities of Greece and Italy. This draft was circulated for the opinions of Local Governments, and the replies submitted showed that the proposals incorporated in it met with almost unanimous approval, the criticisms received being directed, for the most part, against matters of detail. The draft has since been revised; the provisions of a draft Bill prepared by the Government of Bengal have been embodied, so far as they were found suitable, and the present Bill is the result.

3. The first portion of the Bill deals with the protection of "ancient monuments", an expression which has been defined in clause 2. The measure will apply only to such of these as are from time to time expressly brought within its compass through being declared to be "protected monuments". The great number of the more famous buildings in India are already in the possession or under the control of the Government; but there are others worthy of preservation which are in the hands of private owners. Some of these have already been injured or are fast falling into decay. The preservation of these is the chief object of the clauses of the Bill now referred to, and the provisions of the Bill are in general accordance with the policy enunciated in Section 23 of the Religious Endowments Act, 1863 (XX of 1863), which recognises and saves the right of the Government "to prevent injury to, and preserve, buildings remarkable for their antiquity and for their historical or architectural value, or required for the convenience of the public". The power to intervene is at present limited to cases to which Section 3 of Bengal Regulation XIX of 1810 or Section 3 of Madras VII of 1817 applies. In framing the present Bill, the Government have aimed at enlisting the interest and good-will and securing the cooperation of the owners concerned and it is hoped that the line of action which it is proposed to take may tend rather to the encouragement than to the suppression of private effort. The Bill provides that the owner or manager of a building which merits greater care than it has been receiving, may be invited to enter into an agreement for its protection, and that, in the event of his refusing to come to terms, the Collector may proceed to acquire it compulsorily, or, if there is an endowment, move the Courts to secure its proper application. It has been made clear that there is to be no resort to compulsory acquisition in the case of a monument used in connection with religious observances, or in any other case until the owner has had an opportunity of entering into an agreement of the kind indicated above; and it is expressly provided that a monument maintained by the Government under the proposed Act shall not be used for any purpose inconsistent with its character or with the purposes of its foundation, and that, so far as is compatible with the object in view, the public shall have access to it free of charge. By the fourth proviso the clause 11 it is laid down that, in assessing the value of a monument for the purposes of compulsory acquisition under the Land Acquisition Act, 1894 (I of 1894), its archaeological, artistic or historical merits shall not be taken into account. The object of the Government as purchaser being to preserve, at the public expense and for the public benefit, an ancient monument along with all its associations, it is considered that the value of these associations should not be paid for.

4. The second portion of the Bill deals with moveable objects of historical or artistic interest, and these may be divided into two classes. The first consists of arms, enamels, silver and copper vessels, Persian and Arabic manuscripts and curios generally. These are for the most part portable and consequently difficult to trace; they are as a rule of artistic, rather than historic, interest; and it would be impracticable, even were it desirable, to prevent a dealer from selling, or a traveller from buying, them. But sculptural carvings, images, bas-reliefs, inscriptions and the like form a distinct class by themselves, in that their value depends upon their local connection. Such antiquities may, as in the case of those of Swat, be found outside the confines of India or in Native States, and these the legislature cannot reach directly; while, as regards British territory and under the existing law, it is impossible to go beyond the provisions of the Indian Treasure-trove Act, 1878 (VI of 1878). In these circumstances, it is proposed, by clause 18 of the Bill, to take power to prevent the removal from British India of any antiquities which it may be deemed desirable to retain in the country, and at the same time to prevent importation. By thus putting a stop to traffic in such articles, it is believed that it will be possible to protect against spoliation a number of interesting places situated

without and beyond British territory. Clause 19 aims at providing for antiquities, such as sculptures and inscriptions, which belong to a particular place and ought, therefore, to be kept **in situ** or deposited in local museums. The removal of these it is proposed to enable the Local Government to prohibit by notification; and the clause also provides that if the object is moveable, the owner may require the Government to purchase it outright, and that, if it is immoveable, the Government shall compensate the owner for any loss caused to him by the prohibition. Clause 20 deals with the compulsory purchase of such antiquities, if that is found to be necessary for their preservation and the owner is not unwilling, on personal or religious grounds, to part from them. In such cases it is proposed that the price to be paid should be assessed by the Collector, subject to a right of appeal to the Local Government; but it is for consideration whether the Land Acquisition Act of 1894 should be followed and a reference to the Courts allowed.

5. The third portion of the Bill deals with excavations, and gives power to make rules to prohibit or regulate such operations.

6. A general power to make rules is given by clause 22, and clause 23 is intended to protect acts done, or in good faith intended to be done, under the law which it is now proposed to enact.[8]

Councils of the Governor-General of India met for the purpose of making laws and Regulations under the provisions of the Indian Councils Act, 1861 and 1892 (24 and 25 Vict, C.67, and 55 and 56 Vict, C.14).

It met at the Viceregal Lodge, Simla, on Friday, the 23 October 1903.

The Hon'ble Sir Denzil Ibbetson introduced a Bill to provide for the preservation of Ancient Monuments and of objects of archaeological, historical or artistic interest. He stated:

My Lord, during the past three quarters of a century, Archaeology, which has been defined as the study of the material remains of the human past, has received an enormous impetus, if indeed it may not be said to have sprung into existence in Europe. The aesthetic value of works of ancient art has always been recognised, though never studied with such intelligent care as now-a-days. But the civilised world has only lately learnt that what has come down to us from the past has a value and a lesson for us independent of its beauty, and that there is hardly any object of antiquity which may not teach us something about the people who made and used it.

In pursuance of this belief, almost every nation with any pretensions to civilisation has recently taken measures to conserve its ancient buildings and to protect from dissipation, loss or injury the archaeological material contained within its territories, and has founded or enlarged museums in which objects of archaeological interest are collected and displayed for the information of the intelligent and for the study of the learned. Moreover, the buried relics of the past are being systematically explored under the guidance and supervision of the most competent scholars; and within the last thirty years excavation has become a science, and has added enormously to our knowledge of the history of the human race. In furtherance of the objects which I have indicated, legislation has everywhere been found necessary. At the present moment there is hardly a country in Europe which has not made legal provision for the protection of objects of artistic, historical or archaeological interest, even Turkey and Crete having followed the example of their neighbours. The laws are in all cases based upon the recognition of the principle that the nation possesses on interest in such objects, even although they may be the property of private persons. They are, as might be expected, most stringent in Greece and Italy, as being the two countries which have most to protect. In Greece the law goes so far as to declare that 'antiquities possessed by private persons, either in their collections or situated on their property, are considered as national property'; and if an ancient building is in danger owing to the neglect of the owner, the Government will step in and repair it, in which case the building becomes the property of the public. In Italy the owner of an old picture cannot sell it without the permission of Government, even though it may have been in the possession of his family ever since it was painted, and no antique or artistic object can be taken out of the country without obtaining leave. In both countries the Government has powers of compulsory acquisition, and excavation is strictly regulated by law, the State having the first claim to what is found.

My Lord, India is surpassed by few countries in the beauty, the importance and the interest of her ancient monuments, or in the wealth of archaeological material which she possesses. There are very many buildings in this country of which the whole Indian people may be justly proud; there are some which the world could ill afford to spare. As at any rate one of the cradles of the Aryan race, India's early history possesses an absorbing interest for European as well as for Indian scholars, while the fact that the genius of her people has never turned in the direction of history, renders us peculiarly dependent upon survivals from the past for information regarding events previous to the Mohammedan invasion. Yet India alone, or almost alone, among civilised countries, has made no legislative provision for the protection of her priceless treasures. The principle upon which such legislation must rest is indeed not unknown to the Indian Statutes, since Section 23 of Act XX of 1863 expressly recognises the right of Government to 'prevent injury to and preserve buildings remarkable for their antiquity, or for their historical or architectural value'. But no effective provision has yet been made for the performance of this duty.

The reason certainly is not because our antiquities stand in no need of protection. The history of India has not been of a nature to promote the conservation of her ancient monuments, or to foster a regard for them in the minds of her people; and every traveller must have been struck with the frequent sight of buildings of the greatest beauty, or interest, or both, crumbling to decay, simply because nobody is interested in their preservation. Irreparable injury has in many cases already been done by such neglect. Nor is the injury always merely passive. In 1899 some foreigners visited one of the ancient capitals of Burma, and not content with removing detached objects of interest, chiselled from the walls unique tiles and frescoes illustrative of events in the life of Buddha, many of which they destroyed in the process, but some of which they succeeded in carrying to Europe. This was no doubt an exceptional instance of barefaced and dishonest vandalism; but wanton or ignorant disfigurement of ancient monuments is by no means uncommon.

Again when in 1895 our troops marched through the Swat Valley, which lies beyond our border, sculptures and inscriptions of the greatest archaeological interest and value were discovered in considerable numbers. Some of them were removed by those who might have known better; and as soon as it became apparent that a value was attached to them, enterprising Punjabis made a business of importing and offering them for sale on a very extensive scale, while some years later, a considerable collection of sculptures from Swat and Yusufzai was exhibited in one of the capitals of Europe. This, again, is only an aggravated instance of a process which has been steadily going on, on a smaller scale, for very many years past. It is common for the land surrounding an ancient building in India, to be strewn with figures, carvings, and inscriptions which have once formed portions of the building or its appanages; and similar objects are often discovered on ancient sites. Such fragments, if collected and preserved in the immediate vicinity of the building or site to which they appertain, or, if that is impossible, removed to a museum with full information as to the place from which they came and the position in which they were found, may shed invaluable light upon the history of the site or building and of the people by whom it was inhabited or erected. Yet there is no one of us but has seen such objects in the hands of private individuals, where, in the absence of all definite information concerning them, they degenerate into mere curiosities; while many of them are taken out of the country or even disappear altogether.

So again, the buried sites of deserted towns and buildings are common all over India; and there can be little doubt that systematic excavation under competent guidance would cast a flood of light upon the ancient history of the country, as it has done in Europe; and indeed results of value have already been obtained in this country when such operations have been undertaken with knowledge. But at present these sites lie at the mercy of the villager, who digs in them for bricks with which to build his houses, or for soil impregnated with nitre to spread upon his fields; or, even worse, of the enthusiastic but ignorant amateur, who destroys in his well-meaning but misguided efforts, evidence which, in competent hands, might have been of the utmost archaeological value.

It is in order to supply the deficiency in our statute Book which I have indicated, and to prevent a repetition of occurrences such as I have described, that the Bill which I am about to ask leave to introduce has been drafted. As long ago as 1898 proposals for legislation were made to Lord Elgin's Government, and the Secretary of State was asked to supply us with information as to the law on the subject in European countries; but it was not till 1900, when your Lordship took the matter up, that any real progress was made. Such legislation as is proposed is especially appropriate, and especially desirable, now that, at your Lordship's personal initiative, so much more has been done than ever was done before to conserve and restore precious monuments of Indian history and architecture. Within the past few years systematic attention has been paid to the condition of the more important of those buildings which link the present with the past; and in the Imperial and Provincial Budgets of the current year, no less than Rs. 4,68,000 are provided for the conservation of Ancient Monuments.

Some further information was procured from Europe, and at the end of 1901 our first draft of the Bill was referred to Local Governments for opinion. There was a good deal of criticism on points of detail, but the general principles found universal acceptance, while the Bengal Government sent us a draft of a Bill which it had been preparing independently with the same object, from which we have borrowed several valuable suggestions.

The details of the present Bill are so fully discussed in the statement of Objects and Reasons that I need not notice them at any length. The Bill is divided into four distinct Parts: The first Part deals with Ancient Monuments: a term which includes, not all ancient buildings, but only those which possess a historical, archaeological or artistic interest. But, as a matter of fact, its provisions relate, not to all ancient monuments, but only to such of them as Government declares to be Protected Monuments; that is to say, monuments, the importance of which is such that their preservation is a public interest. This Part of the Bill is framed upon the model of the English Act, which is said to be working well, and to have prevented a great deal of mischief. The idea upon which it rests is to depend in the main upon the voluntary action of the owner. It is hoped that the owner of a building such as we are considering will not infrequently be willing to make it over to the guardianship of a high official, on condition that it is managed as a public trust, that it is maintained at the cost of Government, that it is not used for any purpose inconsistent with its character or object, and that the public shall have free access to it. When the owner is not prepared to go so far, it is hoped that Government will often be able to come to an understanding with him as to the conservation of the monument on terms which are fair to both parties.

When neither of these courses is possible, the Bill provides two methods whereby the building maybe preserved from destruction. If an endowment exists for the purpose of its maintenance, the Collector may invoke the aid of the Civil Court to enforce its application to that purpose. And in the last resort, when all other means have failed, when the owner has refused to enter into an agreement, and when, but not until, it appears that the intervention of Government is necessary in order to the preservation of a Protected Monument, the Government may acquire the monument under the Land Acquisition Act, subject, however, to the important exception that no monument of which any part is periodically used for religious observances can be so acquired. The Part further confers upon Government the right of pre-emption whenever a Protected Monument is being sold otherwise than within the family of the owner, or within any religious association to which he may belong. Finally, provision is made for the enforcement of agreements under this Part of the Act, and a penalty is provided for damaging or defacing a Protected Monument.

The second Part of the Bill deals with antiquities of a moveable nature, and is intended to provide for the case of sculptures, carvings, inscriptions and the like, to which I have already alluded. It

> empowers the Governor-General in Council, whenever he has reason to believe that antiquities are being sold or removed to the detriment of India or of any neighbouring country, to prohibit or restrict the importation into or exportation out of any part of British India of any specified class of antiquities. It is not proposed to follow the example of Italy, and to attempt to prevent the removal from India of all antique or artistic objects; for it is recognised that in the case of large classes of such objects, while their value to the country is great and their removal from it to be deplored, it would be impossible to enforce a prohibition, while an attempt to do so would involve inquisitorial measures which the circumstances of the case would fail to justify. The definition of antiquities, therefore, makes no mention of artistic value, but is confined to objects which, by reason of their historical or archaeological interest, Government deems it proper to protect. Even this definition will cover certain objects of the sort to which I have just alluded, and with which it is not ordinarily intended to interfere. The main object of the provision is to enable us to deal with the case of archaeological remains.
>
> The third part of the Bill also deals with these remains, whether moveable or immovable, and is designed to prevent their removal from the vicinity of the site or building to which they belong, and upon their connection with which their value to the student depends, and to protect them from injury or decay. The Government may prohibit the removal of any such objects, on condition of being compelled to purchase them, if moveable, at the option of the owner, and of compensating him for any loss that may result from the prohibition in the case of an immovable object. A power of compulsory purchase is also vested in Government when it appears that any object notified under the Part is in danger of injury or destruction; subject, however, to the important exception that the power shall not extend to anything used for the purpose of religious observance, or to any object which is rendered valuable to the owner by family associations.
>
> The fourth Part of the Bill deals with excavation, which it empowers Government to restrict or regulate within any local area, subject to payment of compensation for any resulting loss. The necessity for such powers I have already explained.
>
> Such, my Lord, are the provisions of the Bill which I propose to lay before the Council. That some such powers are desirable in the public interest, I think few will be found to deny. They necessarily involve a certain degree of interference with private property. But the man who is fortunate enough to be the owner of a monument of national importance owes a duty to the public; and we have endeavoured to confine the powers of interference which we propose to confer upon Government to cases in which they can be justified upon public grounds, to restrict their exercise where religious feeling or family associations are involved, and to little them to what is essential in order to secure the public end in view.[9]

Sir Denzil Ibbetson introduced the Bill. He moved that the Bill, along with the statement of Objects and Reasons relating, should be published in the Gazette of India and in the local official Gazettes in English and in such other languages as the Local Governments think fit. The motion was introduced and adopted.

The copy of the Bill with statement of 'objects and reasons' which was introduced in the Council of Governor-General was forwarded by J.M. Macpherson, Secretary, Legislative Department forwarded (No. 2057-2069 dated 27 October 1903) to local governments and administrations for opinion.[10]

Some Governments submitted their opinions and suggestions (they were voluminous not possible to mention here) and they communicated their approval of the Bill and considered it suitable.

Besides, the Registrar, High Court replied (No. 3439 dated 1 December 1903) that the Judges 'have no observations to offer on the provision of the Bill'.[11]

BADRI DASS MEMORANDUM

Apart from local governments and administrations, some organisations also forwarded their opinion. For example, Rai Bahadur Budree Dass and four hundred and twenty others submitted a memorial on behalf of the Jain Community of India to Curzon on 7 January 1904.

> That your Excellency's memorialists appreciate with feelings of gratitude the efforts of your Excellency's Government for the preservation of the ancient monuments of India, and cordially welcome the introduction of a Bill for that purpose in your Excellency's Legislative Council.
>
> 2. That the community to which your memorialists belong, have the honour to be in possession of and directly concerned in, as places of public religious worship, some of the most ancient and valued monuments yet extant in India; and your memorialists and their co-religionists visit such places in large numbers and offer worship therein in accordance with the injunctions of their faith.
>
> 3. That your memorialists acknowledge with thankfulness the desire of Your Excellency's Government to safeguard the interests of the various religious communities in India; and encouraged by the solicitude shown by Your Excellency's Government not to disturb the practice and observance of their religion by the people. Your memoralists venture to submit the following observations for the consideration of Your Excellency's Government.
>
> (a) That a provision of a general character be embodied in the Bill on the lines of proviso (1)(a) to clause 11 laying down that no monument of the nature referred to in the proviso, namely, which or any part of which is used for any religious purpose, shall be either compulsorily acquired, or otherwise brought under the operation of the Act except under an agreement voluntarily made by the owner, or all the owners acting conjointly, where there are several owners.
>
> (b) That when the Government has acquired under this Act a right to maintain a monument which is used for any religious purpose, provision be made to safeguard it from pollution or desecration by entry into it or into any part of it, of any person, who is prohibited by the religion or the religious usage of the worshippers of the said monument except under conditions agreed to by those in religious charge of the said monument.
>
> (c) That the Bill goes much too far in providing for the vesting of proprietary rights in Government for payment of expenses incurred by it for the preservation of any monument and the realization thereof as arrears of land revenue.
>
> (d) That words be added in clause 14 providing that in case of a monument used for any religious purpose, nothing be done to it, which is inconsistent with the dictates of the religion of the worshipper at it.
>
> 4. That your memorialists most respectfully submit that if the suggestions herein made are given effect to, all apprehension of any possible interference with the religious observances of the people will be removed from their mind."[12]

MEMORIAL ON BEHALF OF MEMBERS OF THE 'KASHI SUJAN SAMAJ' OF BENARAS

Chhamlol Saj and others submitted another Memorial on 16 January 1904 to Curzon on behalf of members of the 'Kashi Sujan Samaj' of Benaras:

> That your Excellency's memorialists respectfully appreciate with feelings of gratitude the desire of your Excellency's Government to preserve ancient monuments, and cordially welcome the introduction of the Bill into the Supreme Legislative Council. The Samaj sincerely hope that it will soon be followed by some enactment for the better administration and regulation of the charitable and religious endowments concerning temples and mosques.

> The Kashi Sujan Samaj most humbly beg to suggest that in the Act some provision be added that monuments connected with religious worship or sanctity must not compulsorily be taken or anyway desecrated without voluntary agreement on the part of their owners or the people of the faith to which the monuments belong. And for this your memorialists shall ever pray.[13]

The Council once again was convened at Government House, Calcutta on Friday, the 4th December 1903. Sir Denzil Ibbetson moved the Bill to be referred to a Select Committee, consisting of the Hon'ble Mr. Raleigh, the Hon'ble Rai Sri Ram Bahadur, His Highness the Agha Khan, the Hon'ble Mr. Lely, the Hon'ble Mr. Adamson, the Hon'ble Mr. Morison and the mover. He said, "I should explain that neither with regard to this Bill nor to another Bill respecting which I am about to make a similar motion have the opinions of all the authorities consulted been received but it is thought desirable to Constitute the Committee at once in order that they may be in a position to begin work as soon as the papers are ready."[14]

The motion was adopted.

The Council met at Government House, Calcutta on Friday, the 19th February 1904. Sir Denzil Ibbetson said, "His Highness the Agha Khan has unfortunately been obliged to leave Calcutta for a while and as we propose to proceed at once with the Ancient Monuments Bill, his services will not be available on the Select Committee. I, therefore, move that the Hon'ble Nawab Saiyid Muhammad be added to the Select Committee on the Bill to provide for the preservation of Ancient Monuments and of objects of archaeological, historical or artistic interest."[15]

The motion was put and agreed to.

The Bill was submitted to Select Committee (Denzil Ibbetson; T. Raleigh; Sri Ram; Syed Mohammed; F.P. Lely; H. Adamson; Theodore Morison) and which gave its report on 2 March 1904 after considering it.

"We the members of the Select Committee to which the Bill to provide for the preservation of Ancient Monuments and of objects of archaeological, historical or artistic interest was referred, have considered the Bill and the papers, and have now the honour to submit this our Report, with the Bill as amended by us."[16]

The Bill was amended by Select Committee and came in its second stage.

Sir Denzil Ibbetson presented the Report of the Select Committee to the Council on 4 March 1904.[17]

Members of the Governor-General in Council (E.F.G. Law: A.T. Arundel; Denzil Ibbetson; E.R. Elles; Kitchener; T. Raleigh) also saw the report and Curzon in its 11 March 1904 noting remarked that:

"the Bill as amended by the Select Committee be proceeded with at the Legislative Council to be held at 18th instant."[18]

Meeting of the Imperial Legislative Council held on the 18th March 1904 at which the Report of the Select Committee was considered and the Bill passed.

The Hon'ble Sir Denzil Ibbetson moved that the Report of the Select Committee on the Bill to provide for the preservation of Ancient Monuments and of objects of archaeological, historical or artistic interest be taken into consideration. He said,

> When I introduced this Bill at Simla, I explained the objects of the Bill and its provisions at considerable length. In Select Committee we made some substantial alterations, and I think improvements; but they in no way touched the principles upon which the Bill is based, and they were mainly directed towards providing still further safeguards for the right of private property and in individuals the religious feelings of the public. I therefore think it unnecessary to add any further remarks now.[19]

The motion was put and agreed to.
The Hon'ble Sir Denzil Ibbetson moved that the Bill, as amended, be passed.
The Hon'ble Nawab Saiyed Muhammad said:

My Lord, I venture to congratulate Your Lordship's Government on this Bill of which the motive and object will commend themselves to all interested in the preservation of ancient monuments which are of manifold value. These monuments will serve in future as landmarks of the various civilizations and Governments that existed in this country from time immemorial. The various provisions of this Bill are chiefly protective and not penal, and without any unnecessary encroachment upon private or individual rights seek to preserve from ignorant, careless or wanton destruction ancient buildings and monuments of historic and antiquarian value which may not be known to people living in the neighborhood or in actual possession of the same. The amendments made in the Select Committee are, on the whole, such as will meet with the approval of the public, and are calculated to minimise proceedings of a vexatious nature. Considering the immense advantage which the country derives by the preservation of these monuments, the tax-payer, I think, is not likely to complain about any expenditure that may be incurred in acquiring and preserving them.[20]

His Excellency **The President** said:

In a session which embraces a good deal of contentious business, it will, I think, be a pleasure to all of us to pass into law a Bill which has been received without a discordant note by all classes of the community, to which no one has come forward to move an amendment, and which will presently take its place, to use the classical phrase, **nemine contradicente**, on the Statute-book. The principle of the Bill is the sound, and as I think, irrefragable, proposition that a nation is interested in its antiquities – and interest which is based on grounds alike of history, sentiment, and expediency, and that it is reasonable and proper to give statutory sanction to the maintenance of this principle by the State. In the somewhat frigid language of the preamble, the object of the measure, more specifically stated, is 'to provide for the preservation of ancient monuments, for the exercise of control over traffic in antiquities, and over excavation, and for the protection and acquisition of ancient monuments and of objects of archaeological, historical, or artistic interest'. In pursuing these ends we have endeavoured, as far as possible, to enlist private co-operation, to exercise the minimum of interference with the rights of property, to ensure a fair price in the event of compulsory purchase, and to pay most scrupulous deference to religious feelings or family associations. The Bill will require to be administered with sympathy and discretion. But I trust the awakened conscience of all sections of the community in respect of our duty to the past to save us from friction or trouble, and I believe myself that private effort will gladly combine with Government for the furtherance of objects in which both are equally concerned. For the individual owner is as much the trustee for his particular archaeological possession as the Government is the general trustee on behalf of the nation at large.

The Bill is, however, even more than its stipulations imply. It is in reality the coping-stone of a policy in respect of archaeology and the remains of the past which the Government of India have pursued with fits and starts throughout the past half century, but with sustained and unremitting ardour during the past few years. I had been in India more than once as an ordinary traveller before I came out as Viceroy, and had observed the state of its antiquities with pain and regret. Fresh as I then was from my university days, I remember thinking how pertinent to India, and to my countrymen in India, were the words of reproach in which the Roman poet, Horace, had addressed his countrymen in what he thought the decadent and indifferent days of the early Empire; and at the risk of being so unfashionable as to quote a language which is said to be now tabooed in public life, I must cite the passage –

> Delicta majorum immeritus lues,
> Romane donec templa refeceris,

Edesque labentes deorum, et
Foeda nigro simulacra fumo.

In India it was not so much a case of recovering the favour of the Gods – for our theology is not quite the same as that of the Romans – as it was of expiating the carelessness of the past, and escaping the reproaches of posterity. But the obligation was just as strong and urgent; that this Council, while giving the authority of law by its vote of today to the culminating phase, may like to hear something of the manner in which we have interpreted its remaining injunctions.

It seemed to me, when I began to enquire exhaustively into the matter five years ago, that the Government of India had made three mistakes. In the first place, they had not recognised that any obligation lay upon them. They had devolved it entirely upon Local Governments, leaving to the latter to spend much or little or nothing at all, and contenting themselves with paying for an inadequate supervisory staff. Secondly, they had set no standard to which Local Governments ought to conform. There was neither co-ordination, nor system, nor control. In one province an enthusiastic administrator might do his duty by the archaeological treasures temporarily committed to his care. In another, there was no idea that archaeology existed as a science or, if it did, that Government had anything to do with the matter. The third mistake was that conservation, or the task of preserving the memorable relics that we still possess, had been forgotten in the task of research for those that no longer exist, or of writing about objects that were fast falling into decay. Our first step, accordingly, was to revive the post Director-General which had been in abeyance since 1889, and to procure a competent person to fill it. The next was to set an example to Local Governments, which are undertook to do by the grant of sums aggregating a lakh per annum, to supplement the local expenditure of which their own funds might permit. The third step was to stimulate them and the Native States also to renewed efforts by a definite programme of conservation and repair. By the end of 1900 our proposals had gone home to the Secretary of State. A year later his answer was received, and a Director-General, Mr. Marshall, who has since thrown himself with scholarly energy and enthusiasm into his task, was on his way out to India; and in February1902 we were in a position to publish a Resolution in the Gazette defining our policy, and foreshadowing the programme of work that lay before us as well as the legislation which we are carrying to completion today. Two years have passed since that date, and the new system is now firmly established, and has already justified itself by its fruits. I can, perhaps, bring home to the office Council the extent to which we have advanced by giving the concrete figures of then and now. In the year 1898-99, the total expenditure of the Government of India upon archaeology was less than £3,000, and this was almost exclusively devoted to salaries; the total expenditure of all the Local Governments added together was only about £4,000 in the same year. A sum, therefore, of £7,000 per annum represented the total contribution of the Government of 300 millions of people towards the study or preservation of the most beautiful and precious collection of ancient monuments in the Eastern world. The Government of India is now spending upon this object 2½ lakhs per annum, and the Local Governments 3 lakhs per annum, or a total of some £37,000 a year. Thus, not little by little, but by leaps and bounds, are we catching up the errors of the past, and purging our national reputation of this great strain.

It is given to but few to realize, except from books and illustrations, what the archaeological treasures of India are. I know of civilians who have spent a life-time in the country without ever seeing Agra, and who make a pilgrimage to visit it when their thirty-five years are done. A governor-general's tours give him a unique chance, and I should have been unworthy of the task which I undertook at the first meeting of the Asiatic Society that I attended in Calcutta five years ago, had I not utilized these opportunities to visit all the great remains or groups of remains with which this country is studded from one end to the other. As a pilgrim at the shrine of beauty I have visited them, be as a priest in the temple of duty have I charged myself with their reverent custody and their studious repair.

Our labour may be said to have fallen into four main categories. First there are the buildings which demanded a sustained policy of restoration or conservation, with most diligent attention to the designs of their original architects, so as to restore nothing that had not already existed, and to put up nothing absolutely new. For it is a cardinal principle that new work in restoration must be not only a reproduction of old work but a part of it, only reintroduced in order to repair or to restore symmetry to the old. Of such a character has been our work at all the great centres of what is commonly known as the Hindu-Saracenic style. We have, wherever this was possible, recovered and renovated the dwellings in life and the resting-places in death of those master builders, the Mussulman Emperors and Kings.

The Taj itself and all its surroundings are now all but free from the workmen's hands. It is no longer approached through dusty wastes and a squalid bazar – A beautiful park takes their place; and the group of mosques and tombs, the arcaded street and grassy courts that precede the main building, are once more as nearly as possible what they were when completed by the masons of Shah Jehan. Every building in the garden enclosure of the Taj has been scrupulously repaired, and the discovery of old plans has enabled us to restore the water-channels and flower-beds of the garden more exactly to their original state. We have done the same with the remaining buildings at Agra. The exquisite mausoleum of Itmad-ud-Dowlah, the tile-enamelled gem of Chini-ka-Rauza, the succession of Mogul palaces in the Fort, the noble city of Akhar at Fatehpur Sikri, his noble tomb at Sikandra, – all of these have been taken in hand. Slowly they have emerged from decay and in some cases desolation, to their original perfection of form and detail: the old gardens have been restored, the old water-courses cleared out, the old balustrades renovated, the chiselled bas-reliefs repaired, and the inlaid agate, jaspar, and cornelian replaced. The skilled workmen of Agra have lent themselves to the enterprise with as much zeal and taste as their fore-runners three hundred years ago. I have had there the assistance of two large-minded and cultured Lieutenant-Governors in the persons of Sir Antony MacDonell and Sir James La Touche. Since I came to India we have spent upon repairs at Agra alone a sum of £40,000 and £50,000. Every rupee has been an offering of reverence to the past and a gift of recovered beauty to the future; and I do not believe that there is a taxpayer in this country who will grudge one anna of the outlay. It will take some three or four years more to complete the task, and then Agra will be given back to the world, a pearl of great price.

At Delhi and Lahore we have attempted, or are attempting, the same. The Emperor Jehangir no longer lies in a neglected tomb at Shahdera: his grandfather, Humayun, is once again honoured at Delhi. The Military authorities have agreed to evacuate all the principal Mogul buildings in the Delhi Fort, and the gardens and halls of the Emperors will soon recall their former selves. I might take you down to Rajputana and show you to restored bund along the Ana Sagar Lake. There a deserted stone embankment survived, but the marble pavilions on it had tumbled down, or been converted into modern residences. Now they stand up again in their peerless simplicity, and are reflected in the waters below. I might bring you much nearer home to Gaur and Pandua in this province of Bengal, in the restoration of which I received the enthusiastic co-operation of the late Sir John Woodburn. A hundred and twenty years ago the tombs of the Afghan Kings at Gaur were within an ace of being despoiled to provide paving stones for St. John's Church in Calcutta. Only a few years back these wonderful remains were smothered in jungle from which they literally had to be cut free. If the public were fully aware of what has been done, Malda, near to which they are situated, would be an object of constant excursion from this place. We have similarly restored the Hindu temples of Bhubaneswar near Cuttack, and the palace and temples on the rock-fortress of Rohtasgarh. At the other end of India I might conduct you to the stupendous ruins of the great Hindu capital of Vijaynagar, one of the most astonishing monuments to perished greatness, or to Bijapur, where an equally vanished Mohammedan dynasty left memorials scarcely less enduring. If I had more time today, I might ask you to accept any guidance to the delicate marble traceries of the Jain temples at Mount Abu, or the more stately proportions of the mosques at Jaunpur – both of which we are saving from the neglect that was already bringing portions of them to the ground: or I might take you across the Bay of Bengal to Burma, and show you king Mindon's Fort and Palace at Mondalay, with their timbered halls and pavilions, which we are carefully preserving as a sample of the ceremonial and domestic architecture of the Burmese Kings.

A second aspect of our work has been the recovery of buildings from profane or sacrilegious uses, and their restitution either to the faith of their founders or at least to safe custody as protected monuments. Here we have a good record. The exquisite little mosque of Sidi Sayid at Ahmedabad with the famous windows of pierced sandstone, which I found used as a tehsildar's cutcherry when first I went there, is once more cleared and intact. The Moti Masjid in the Palace at Lahore, into which I gained entrance with difficulty because the treasury was kept there in chests beneath the floor, and which was surrounded with a brick wall and iron gates, and guarded by sentries, is once more free. The Choti Khwabgah in the Fort is no longer a church, the Diwan-i-Aam is no longer a barrack, the lovely tiled Dai Anga Mosque near the Lahore Railway Station has ceased to be the Office of a Traffic Superintendent of the North Western Railway, and has been restored to the Mohammedan community. At Bijapur I succeeded in expelling a dak bungalow from one mosque, the relics of a British post office from another. The mosque in the celebrated fort at Vellore in Madras is no longer tenanted by a Police Instructor. The superb **Mantapam** or Hindu temple in the same fort is now scrupulously cared for. A hundred years ago the East India Company presented it to George IV, when Prince-Regent, for erection in the grounds of the Pavilion at Brighton, and only failed to carry out their design, because the ship, which had been charted for the purpose, very happily went to the bottom (Laughter). Next it was used as an arsenal, and finally commissariat bullocks were tethered to its pillars. At Lucknow I recovered a mosque, which had been used for years as a dispensary. At Ahmedabad I have already mentioned that the marble **Baradari** on the bund is no longer the dining-room of the Commissioner's house. At Mandalay the Church and the club are under notice of removal from the gilded throne-rooms of the Burmese sovereigns.

In this policy, which I have so far described in relation to monuments in British territory, I have received the most cordial support from the Indian Princes in their own States. The Nizam of Hyderabad was willing to do all that I asked him – I only wish that it had been a quarter of a century earlier – for the unique caves of Ajunta and Ellora. He undertook the cataloguing and conservation of a most interesting collection of old China, copper ware, and carpets that had been lying neglected for centuries at Aurungabad in the tomb of the wife of the Emperor Aurungzeb. The Maharana of Udaipur has willingly undertaken the restoration of the exquisite Towers of Fame and victory on the hill fort of Chitor, one of which could hardly have survived for many more years. The Maharaja Scindia threw himself with characteristic zeal into similar works in his magnificent fortress at Gwalior. The Begum of Bhopal did all that was required at the Sanchi Tope. Finally, there stands in the remote state of Dhar the huge rock-fortress of Mandu, certainly one of the most amazing natural spectacles in the world. Rising to a height of 1,500 feet above the Nerbudda plain, it carries upon its summit, which is thirty miles round, a splendid group of disserted Mohammedan fortifications, palaces, and tombs. These we are assisting the state, which is not rich enough to assume the entire responsibility itself, to place in order. They were fast perishing, victims to the ravages of the jungle, and to unchallenged decay.

There is yet another aspect of the work of conservation to which I hope that the Bill that we are about to pass will lend a helping hand. This is the custody in collections or museums of rare or interesting objects that have either been torn from their surroundings or whose surroundings have disappeared. Hon'ble Members will be familiar with the larger museums in the capital cities of India, where are collections not without value, but, as a rule, sorely mutilated, often unidentified and uncatalogued, and sometimes abominably arranged. The plan has hitherto been to snatch up any sculptured fragment in a Province, or Presidency, and send it off to the provincial museum. This seemed to me when I looked into it, to be all wrong. Objects of archaeological interest can best be studied in relation and in close proximity to the group and style of buildings to which they belong, presuming that these are of a character and in a locality that will attract visitors. Otherwise, if transferred elsewhere, they lose focus, and are apt to become meaningless. Accordingly we have started the plan of a number of local museums, in places of the nature that I have described. I may instance Malda in Bengal, Pagon in Burma, the Taj at Agra, Bijapur in Bombay, and Peshawar, as localities where these institutions are being called into being, and I hope that in future any local fragments that may be discovered in the neighbourhood of such places, instead of being stolen, packed off, or destroyed, will find their way into these minor collections. Of course the larger provincial museums will continue to attract all classes of objects that do not easily find a local habilitation.

These remarks will, I hope, give to Hon'ble Members an idea of the scientific and steadfast policy upon which the Government has embarked in respect of archaeology, and which they are invited to assist by passing this Bill today.

By rendering this assistance all will join in paying the debt which each of us owes to the poets, the artists, and the creators of the past. What they originated, we can but restore; where they imagined we can but rescue from ruin. But the task though humble is worthy, and the duty though late is incumbent. A hundred and thirty years ago Samuel Johnson in England used to keep up a correspondence with Warren Hastings in Bengal, and in one of his letters the philosopher thus addressed the Governor-General – 'I hope that you will examine nicely the traditions and histories of the East, that you will survey the corridors of its ancient edifices, and trace the vestiges of its ruined cities, and that, on your return, we shall know the arts and opinions of a race of men from whom very little has hitherto been derived'. It is in this spirit that my archaeological coadjutors and I have worked. All that there is beauty in India in abundance. I like to think that there is reverence also: and that amid our struggles over the present we can join hands in pious respect for the past. I like to think, too, that this spirit will survive, and that the efforts of which I have been speaking will not slacken in the hands of our successors, until India can boast that her memorials are as tenderly prized as they are precious, and as carefully guarded as they are already, and will in the future be even more, widely known.[21]

The motion was adopted.

The Bill was passed and **'The Ancient Monuments' Preservation Act, 1904 (VII of 1904)'** came into existence (Appendix-XXVII).

Curzon forwarded a despatch (No. 16 of 24 March 1904) to R.H. St. John Brodrick, Secretary of State for India, and transmitted an authenticated copy of this Legislation:

"In conformity with the provisions of Section XXI of the Indian Councils Act, 1861, I have the honour to forward herewith an authentic copy of the Law (Act No. VII of 1904) to provide for the preservation of ancient monuments and of objects of archaeological, historical or artistic interest which has been passed by the Council of the Governor-General of India for making Laws and regulations and to which I have signified my assent."[22]

G. Baldwin Brown, Professor of Fine Art in the University of Edinburgh, remarked:

"It is noteworthy that it is fully equipped with the compulsory clauses, prohibitions, and penal sanctions, of which people in the mother country are so shy. This illustrates once again the fact already noticed, that in less advanced communities it is more easy to pass stringent monument laws than in states where the individual citizen is accustomed to stand stiffly by his rights."[23]

The Act is a landmark in the history of archaeology in India, particularly in the field of care of monuments.

NOTES AND REFERENCES

1. Department of Revenue and Agriculture, Archaeology and Epigraphy, A, November 1901, No. 1.
2. Department of Revenue and Agriculture, Archaeology and Epigraphy, A, November 1901, No. 2.
3. Legislative Department, March 1904, Nos. 114-150, Notes.

4. Legislative Department, March 1904, No. 114.
5. Legislative Department, March 1904, Nos. 114-150, Appendix A 104; Department of Revenue and Agriculture, Archaeology and Epigraphy, A, October 1903, No. 33.
6. Legislative Department, March 1904, No. 115.
7. *Ibid.*
8. Legislative Department, Proceedings, March 1904, Nos. 114-150, Appendix A 105; Department of Revenue and Agriculture, Archaeology and Epigraphy, October 1903, No. 33.
9. Legislative Department, Proceedings, March 1904, Nos. 114-150, Appendix A, 106.
10. Legislative Department, Proceedings, March 1904, No. 118.
11. Legislative Department, Proceedings, March 1904, Appendix A, 108.
12. Legislative Department, Proceedings, March 1904, Appendix A, 120.
13. Legislative Department, Proceedings, March 1904, Appendix A, 122.
14. Legislative Department, Proceedings, March 1904, Appendix A, 124.
15. Legislative Department, Proceedings, March 1904, Appendix A, 125.
16. Legislative Department, Proceedings, March 1904, Appendix A, 126.
17. Legislative Department, Proceedings, March 1904, Appendix A, 128.
18. Legislative Department, Proceedings, March 1904, Nos. 114-150, Notes.
19. Legislative Department, Proceedings, March 1904, Nos. 114-150, Appendix A, 129.
20. *Ibid.*
21. *Ibid.*
22. Legislative Department, Proceedings, March 1904, No. 150.
23. *The Care of Ancient Monuments* by G. Baldwin Brown; Cambridge 1905; p. 235.

CHAPTER XIV

The Archaeological Survey Department on Permanent Footing

After the enactment of the Ancient Monument Act, yet another important task before the Government of India was to give the Archaeological Survey Department a permanent basis. It was necessary to get the Act implemented in an effective manner. In June 1904, the scheme that had a validity of five years was to expire. In order to obtain further sanction, J. Wilson, Secretary, Revenue and Agriculture Department addressed a letter on 28 March 1904 to John Marshall, Director General, Archaeology for renewal of term.

The Secretary of State for India conveyed the sanction and desire, on the expiry of term of sanction, a full report on the progress made and the work which remains to be done by the Government. Besides, the Secretary, Government of India also requested the Director-General that the Memorandum should be recast and confined to statement of work accomplished and the remaining to be accomplished especially under the field of surveys, conservation and epigraphical research. The possibilities of entrusting archaeological work to private persons or societies and the measures taken to train and employ natives as archaeologists should be noticed. The proposal should be all-encompassing and include recommendations for the establishment of a permanent Archaeological Department in India. Then it could be forwarded to the Secretary of State.[1]

By this time, it had become sufficiently clear that problems relating to archaeological survey were too gigantic and complex to be tackled in a short span of five years and until the Archaeology Survey Department was reorganized on permanent footing, the working problems could not be solved.[2]

Accordingly, Marshall prepared a note on 18 April 1904, which detailed the progress made by the Archaeological Department during five years along with a statement of work which remained to be done. This report had been considered a milestone on the constitution of the Archaeological Survey Department on a permanent basis (Appendix XXVIII).

Marshall submitted the requisite report to the Government of India on 19 April 1904. The report was approved by the Government of India and forwarded to John Brodrick, Secretary of State for India on 26 May 1904 for consideration. The Report had proposals for continuance of staff till 1907, when the term of Director General would expire along with proposals for establishment of Archaeological Survey Department on a permanent basis.

It was also reported that the work of archaeological survey or exploration and research was far from complete. However, substantial work had been accomplished and further the work in some places was fragmentary and desultory. Many gaps were to be filled and fresh survey would be undertaken after completion of survey, which is being carried out. The excavations of buried sites still remain to be done. As those areas have remained untouched, it was expected that if the excavations were initiated, it would shed light on the early history of India and of the races which have inhabited the country in early times. In order to accomplish this work, deployment of trained band of archaeologists was essential. Besides, it was proposed that proper application of the recently enacted law, Ancient Monuments Act, which had conferred powers and prescribed duties on the part of the Government was essential. It was also expected that matters connected with the acquisition and preservation of antiquities should be given priority by the Government.

Marshall referred to the dispatch of George Hamilton, Secretary of State who expressed his desire that the archaeological work should be entrusted to learned societies and scholars. This policy was applicable in Europe. The same proposed policy could not be applied in Indian context where the responsibility of the Government of India for the preservation of national antiquities has been recognized since long. For the creation of the post of Director General of Archaeology, the Government of India was of the view that few measures were taken by the regional communities to ensure restoration and guarding the ancient relics at the public expense. This task is one, which no private body in India is competent to perform and which rests with the Government. The Government was ready to accept the cooperation and help of the private societies and archaeologists in the field of survey and exploration. It was also contemplated that students having an aptitude for antiquarian research were few in numbers and the local residents with an exception of a few have not been inclined to prosecute this field of study. However, the Government of India was aware of these problems and was taking adequate steps for training the locals for enlistment in work pertaining to survey and conservation of monuments of archaeological importance.

The Government of India requested for constituting the Archaeological Survey Department on a permanent basis. It also requested to accord sanction to the temporary extension of establishment, which was going to expire in the current year. It was also reported that the total budgetary expenditure for the Archaeology Department was Rs. 1,79,800, which was exclusive of the annual provision of Rs. 1,00,000 towards conservation of monuments considering the vast area of the country and the great number and variety of monuments to be dealt with. This can not be regarded as an extravagant outlay, especially in view of the fact that the necessity for the greater part of it has risen from neglect of our duties in the past. To curtail or reduce the work in progress and outlay would be constrained as grave mistake. Besides, if the entire archaeological operations are suspended, it would be abnegation of public duties, more especially at the present juncture, when Lord Curzon had provided impetus to the restoration work and conservation of monuments through his personal interest and devotion towards the area of preserving relics of importance.

In conclusion, the Government of India contended that expenditure involved was being met from the Imperial revenues. Besides, to economize on the expenditure front, only one Surveyor was placed in each Province to attend the work of both survey and conservation of archaeological monuments, which are to be carried out under the supervision of the Local Governments, and provincial control and accountability are taken care in full measure.[3]

It was, therefore, trusted that the proposal would receive the Secretary of State's approval.

St. John Brodrick, the Secretary of State, sanctioned the extension of the Archaeology Survey Department vide the despatch dated 29 July 1904 (Revenue, No. 114). The Secretary of State felt that the Archaeology Survey Department should be made permanent as the work of restoring and conservation of ancient monuments would continue for years to come as the work was far from complete and that the work of archaeological exploration and research also was far from complete. With the promulgation of the Preservation of Ancient Monuments Act, new powers and duties necessitated a complement of trained archaeologist at the disposal of the Government of India. The Secretary of State stated that these could not be made over to private societies and scholars and the Government of India must continue to support the noble venture. However, the Secretary of State sanctioned temporary extension of the appointment to a further period and requested the Government of India to forward concrete proposals for the establishment and complement of staff required for the Archaeological Department.

The Secretary of State also referred to the contention of John Marshall in which he had categorically stated that the work pertaining to archaeological survey would come to a logical conclusion within a span of 10-15 years. Most of the extensive operations for the conservation of the principal ancient monuments of India would have been brought to a conclusion and the archaeological lists of the several provinces completed. The Secretary of State felt that if that stage was achieved, then a smaller complement of staff would be sufficient that would augur well with the economy in expenditure and the establishment of the Archaeological Survey Department would be progressively on a reduced scale.[4]

This matter was further reviewed after a year and the Governor-General in Council addressed a communication to John Brodrick, Secretary of State on 9 November 1905 and proposed constituting the Archaeological Survey Department on permanent basis. The Governor-General in Council pointed towards the necessity of constituting the Department on permanent basis by referring business of the Archaeological Survey Department as following:

1. The restoration and maintenance in thorough repair of monuments of first rate historical or architectural importance.
2. The conservation of those monuments, which we cannot undertake to restore, but which, in view of their historical interest and associations, ought to be saved from further decay.
3. The prosecution of archaeological exploration and research.
4. The administration of the Ancient Monuments Act.

The Governor-General in Council contended that the first activity of operations could be completed within next fifteen or twenty years. The Council added that 'but even when this stage has been reached we should hesitate to entrust the further repairs which will from time to time be necessary to be agency of the ordinary Public Works officers without the assistance of competent archaeological experts. The Buildings in question are of worldwide reputation and any solecism that might be perpetrated by an ill informed engineer would attract immediate attention in Europe and would redound to our lasting discredit. In respect of the buildings of the second class, the task to be discharged is of a more difficult and delicate character and we cannot conceive that it will ever be possible to leave it to unskilled hands'. As to archaeological research, it was proposed to have documentation on all known sites of antiquarian interest and materials collected for the use of scholars. This was only possible after all the sites of archaeological interest have been exhaustively expired. Even then the maintenance of the various local museums will demand the care and attention 'which only an expert can give'. With regard to Marshall's proposal on the application of Ancient Monuments Act, it was necessary to seek competent advice of a skilled archaeologist. However, the Government of India was not in favour with the reduction of strength in Archaeological Survey Department. The Government of India contended that it was unlikely that reduction of staff strength was possible within the next 20 years. However, the progress of survey and conservation of archaeological monuments progressed satisfactorily; the possibility of not filling up the vacancies could be considered. The Government of India recommended increasing the salaries of the officer-in-charge of each circle. It was proposed to be designated as 'Superintendent of Archaeological Survey'.[5]

John Morley, who at that time was the Secretary of State, approved the proposal of the Government of India on 26 January 1906 (Despatch-15-Revenue).[6] In pursuance of this Despatch of the Secretary of State, the Government of India in its Resolution dated 28 April 1906 (Nos. 134-136 Home, A&E) stated that the survey was placed on a permanent and improved footing. The Archaeological Service was made permanent and definite improvements were made in the salary structure and status of the officers connected with it.[7]

Thus, the Archaeological Survey Department on a permanent basis was an important landmark in the history of Indian archaeology.

NOTES AND REFERENCES

1. Department of Revenue and Agriculture, Archaeology and Epigraphy, May 1904, No. 30.
2. *The Story of Indian Archaeology*, 1784-1947, by Sourindranath Roy, 1961, p. 89.
3. Department of Revenue and Agriculture, Archaeology and Epigraphy, May 1904, No. 32.
4. Department of Revenue and Agriculture, Archaeology and Epigraphy, March, 1905, No. 3.
5. Home, Department, Archaeology and Epigraphy, November 1905, No. 19.
6. Home Department, Archaeology and Epigraphy, July 1906, No. 21.
7. Home Department, Archaeology and Epigraphy, July 1906, No. 23.

CHAPTER XV

Tribute to Lord Curzon

The book would be incomplete without enumerating Curzon's contributions in the field of archaeology and care of monuments in particular. Though there may be many instances of exemplary care of ancient monuments, Lord Curzon was perhaps the only English statesman who was genuinely interested in the conservation of ancient monuments and archaeological sites in India. Curzon was not only instrumental in the enactment of Ancient Monument Act, 1904 – a most comprehensive legislation at that point of time – but he also worked relentlessly to lay the foundation stone of Archaeological Survey on an improved basis and permanent footing. It was Lord Curzon, the Viceroy of India, who had fairly established the archaeological service with a vision and regulated the system for conservation of ancient monuments in an efficient manner.

Most often, Lord Curzon would personally accompany the Director General of Archaeology to inspect the archaeological sites and historical monuments. He had a keen insight and organized surprise visits and observed minutest details in a particular monument. He addressed a communication to Sir C.M. Rivaz, Lt. Governor of Punjab on 1 May 1902 and gave details of incidents he had witnessed. He referred to his visit to Wazir Khan's mosques which was littered with pigeon's droppings and urged upon him to give instructions to the concerned officials to keep the **imambara** clean. At Badshahi Mosque, he found squalor and filth and kerosene lamps, which, earlier presented by Curzon to the mosque, were kept in dingy rooms and were not properly lit. Curzon was particularly perturbed on being informed by the **mutawali** that funds were not given by the Committee for the upkeep of lamps. He also informed that he preferred to visit the mosque **in cognito** and "if they had known my visit, I should have found none of these things, but that is the merit of surprise incursion". Curzon was also outraged at the growth of vegetation and weeds all over the Badshahi Mosque and ordered their immediate removal. Besides, he also noticed an advertisement of a dentist inscribed on the entrance gateway to the mosque and requested for immediate removal.

Curzon also wanted the restoration of the Moti Masjid, Diwan-i-Aam and the church. He particularly complained about the orders in this respect which were issued three years ago when he had visited the Lahore Fort, but apparently nothing seems to have been done for carrying out repair works. He stated, "It is this sort of delay that leaves me in despair, for when I have gone, who will care about these things? I fancy that your German Archaeologist has furnished some reports on all these subjects. Would you kindly send them to me?" Curzon was of the opinion that with little initiative, the restoration work in the Fort could be done in two years and sought the cooperation of Lt. Governor in the matter.

At railway mosque at Lahore, Curzon appreciated the old façade of the mosque – Kashi work – but its "present use or abuse is a crying shame". He stated that if the charge of the mosque is handed back to Muslims, a guarantee would have to be obtained from them that they would arrange funds for its restoration. Besides, the restoration work would have to be done under the supervision of Marshall, new Director General of Archaeology. He stated, "Its present use is indefensible but at least the tile work is protected and I am not going to give this over to destruction, I am confident that in all these matters I may rely upon your help."[1]

It was an irony of fate that Lord Curzon decided to resign due to his disagreement with Lord Kitchener, the Commander-in-Chief on the issue relating to military administration. No sooner his decision of resignation was made public, letters and telegrams of farewell, regret and appreciation constantly flowed expressing dismay over his decision of resignation. Curzon's resignation had a far reaching impact on the care of monuments and many projects relating to the preservation of monuments had come to abrupt standstill.

Majority of these reactions in the form of letters and telegrams were from non-official individuals and agencies. Some of such examples have been highlighted in subsequent paragraphs.

John Marshall, Director-General, Archaeology sent a telegram to his Secretary on 22 August 1905:

"I only heard last evening the news of the Viceroy's intention to resign and I need not to tell you how deeply I deplore it. Will you, please, convey to His Excellency the expression of my profoundest regrets and, may I respectfully add of my sincere sympathy?"[2]

Maharaj Kumar Prodyot Coomar Tagore, of Pathuriaghata, Calcutta sent a telegram dated 22 August 1905:

> It is with deepest regret that I have learnt the news of His Excellency's resignation. His Excellency was pleased to show the Tagore family every consideration during His Viceroyalty...we had hoped that His Excellency receive Their Royal Highnesses the Prince and Princes of Wales in Calcutta and inaugurate the ceremony of laying the foundation stone of the Victoria Memorial Hall, which owes its very inception to His Excellency's broad-minded love of Indian Art and antiquity and in which he took so warm an interest, but it is not known if his successor would take quite as much interest in a national gallery which the thinking portion of His Majesty's loyal Indian subjects are proud to possess.[3]

Babu Jyotiprakash Sen, 59-3, Bhawani Charan Dutta's Street, Calcutta sent a letter on 26 August 1905:

> May it please Your Excellency – on behalf of my venerable grandmother, the mother of the late Babu Keshab Chander Sen, the religious reformer of Bengal and other members of the Sen family, we beg respectfully to tender our extreme regret at the termination of your Excellency's Office as Viceroy of

India and to applaud and thank you for the exceptional services Your Excellency has rendered to Hindustan. You Excellency's excellent service, that is the preservation of old monuments will be remembered forever in India. Our grandmother offers her sincere blessings to Your Excellency and Lady Curzon and that grand lady prays to God for your Excellency's peace, happiness and prosperity.[4]

The Viceroy's Office acknowledged some of the letters. A glaring example was a letter addressed to Jyotiprakash Sen on 2 September 1905:

His Excellency the Viceroy was very pleased to receive so kind a message of farewell from yourself and the other members of the family of that great social and religious reformer, the late Babu Keshab Chander Sen. His Excellency appreciates your reference to his labours for the preservation of old monuments and is glad to think that they meet with the approbation of educated Indians. Their Excellencies specially thank your venerable grandmother for her kind words.[5]

The Chairman, Municipal Board, Agra city sent a telegram dated 30 August 1905:

"At a meeting of Municipal Board of Agra, the following Resolution passed – 'that the Board has heard with deep regret of the resignation of H.E. Lord Curzon and desires to put on record its high appreciation of, and gratitude for, the interest His Excellency ever showed in the Progress of Agra and the restoration of its historical buildings'."[6]

A reply telegram of same date was received by the Chairman, Municipal Board, Agra:

"Among the happiest episodes of his work in India has been the revival of the artistic and archaeological glories of Agra; and H.E. believes that this task has now reached a point at which its permanence is absolutely secured."[7]

Haji Sheikh Qudir Bukhsh, Khan Bahadur, Hony Magistrate and Vice Chairman, District Board, Fyzabad, sent a telegram on 6 September 1905:

"Mohammedans are grateful for Lord Curzon's interest in Aligarh College and restoration of old Mohammedan buildings."[8]

A reply telegram dated 7 September 1905 was sent from the Viceroy's office;

"The attention to Mohammedan buildings has throughout been a labour of love of His Excellency."[9]

On 25 September 1905, the President and Members of the Bombay Branch, Royal Asiatic Society addressed to H.E. the Viceroy regarding the work of archaeological preservation and repair done throughout India during the term of his viceroyalty.

At the recent centenary meeting of this Society, during the sitting of the Archaeology Section, various speakers gave expression to the obligation under which you have placed this country on account of your services in the matter of Monumental Preservation and a vote of acknowledgement was unanimously passed and is reported in the published proceedings.

In full agreement therewith the Managing Committee desire, before you leave the scene of your memorable administration to tender their sincere thanks for all that you have done in the cause of Indian Archaeology and Archaeological Research during the term of your Viceroyalty; and more especially for the unremitting attention that you have paid to the conservation of India's ancient monuments, culminating the much desired Act for their effectual preservation. Your interest and sympathy in the matter has not been the mere passing duty of office but a personal solicitude which prompted you, upon the first opportunity lay in your power, to introduce measures which have removed, we hope for all time, a standing reproach, more or less deserved, regarding the neglect of those old relics committed to our care.

By the passing of the Ancient Monuments Preservation Act, anxiety for the proper care and custody of our monuments has been dispelled and we shall longer fear the ruthless hand of the utilitarian

> or vandal. We devoutly trust that the great impetus given to the work of preservation by Your Excellency and the various measures inaugurated for the more systematic prosecution of Archaeology in general, will not be diminished in the future and that Your Government's generous provision for the work year by year will be continued.
>
> We cannot but express our admiration of the thorough grasp of the subject which you have had from the beginning and still more of the untiring capacity for the work which you have shown when you have been able amid the multifarious duties and more exigent business of your high office to pay so much attention to these matters. And we feel sure that on whatever sphere of action your Lordship may hereafter enter, you will continue to use your influence, if need be, to press the continuance in their integrity of the measures you have so successfully brought into operation.[10]

To this, Curzon replied on 4 October 1905 that:

"Permit to tender to you my sincere thanks for the testimony, as gratifying as it was unsolicited which you have been good enough to offer to the work of archaeological preservation and repair throughout India that has occupied so much of my time and interest during the past seven years. The obligation is one that has always been recognized by Civilized Governments but for the proper discharge of which continued vigilance and enthusiasm on the part of those who are in authority are required. Otherwise the task is neglected, subordinate officers plead want of time for attending to what is apt to be regarded as a work of supererogation rather than one of duty and beautiful buildings crumble into irreparable decay.

The principal work of the past seven years has been to revive this spirit of enthusiasm and duty among officers of all classes, to provide, firstly by legislation and secondly by the strengthening of establishments and provision of funds, for the proper supervision and discharge of archaeological work and thirdly to take in hand without delay every considerable group of archaeological remains of India and to place them with regard to the canons of reverent and cautious restoration in a proper state of repair.

The time has fortunately been long enough to admit of these objects being very generally carried out. A visit to Agra for instance would be one of the most fascinating surprises to anyone who had not seen that place for ten years. In your own Presidency, where the undertaking has received the powerful and energetic patronage of successive Governors and has been in the hands of a most competent expert in Mr. Cousens, similarly good work has been done at Ahmedabad, Bijapur and other places.

What is now wanted to continuity of interest and expenditure? The building and monuments of a continent of the size of India cannot be overhauled in the space of a few years or kept in repair without a continuous outlay. In so far as the Government of India are responsible in both these respects, there will, I am confident, be no falling off. I firmly trust that a similar spirit will animate the Local Governments whose responsibility is not less great and whose power of doing good is in some respects greater.

I have often stated my opinion that in the range, the variety, the historical interest and the artistic beauty of its ancient monuments, India stands first of all countries in the world. As time passes they will attract increasing crowds of visitors from abroad. It has been one of my ambitions – now I hope in course of realization – that when these come, they will think the Government of India entitled to a similar place among Governments for the manner in which it has interpreted its duties of conservation, custody and repair."[11]

Munshi Abdul Karim, General Secretary, Anjuman-i-Ahbab, Bombay, sent his feeling on 13 October 1905:

"...We also beg to state that we are highly indebted to Your Excellency for the keen interest taken by Your Excellency in restoring the ancient Monuments of the past Mohammedan grandeur and of architectural feature and historical interest."[12]

Shri Runga Deva Rayalu, Raja of Anagondi, wrote on 23 October 1905:

"... my personal heartfelt gratitude towards the preservation of the relics and memorials of ancient greatness ..."[13]

M. Karim Baksh, Editor and Proprietor 'Anwar-ul-Islam', Sialkot wrote on 25 October 1905:

"... I, on behalf of the Mohammedan community of Sialkot, desire to convey to Your Excellency the profound and the most sincere regret at your approaching departure and the keen appreciation of the benefits you have conferred on the Mohammedans of India such as the restoration of ancient buildings and Mosques."[14]

The President and Members of the Anjuman-i-Islamia, Punjab wrote from Lahore on 28 October 1905:

> ... Your Excellency's work in retaining and preserving old historic buildings deserves our special gratitude, the Anjuman-i-Islamia being the custodian of important Mohammedan WAKFS in the capital of the Province. Early in your administrative career, Your Excellency announced that it was the duty of the British Government to preserve from decay and disintegration of old relics of past Indian Empires including the Muslim and most desirable change in the attitude of the Government towards their preservation was promised. Right well has that promise been fulfilled and among other places, Lahore has cause to be grateful to Your Excellency for the unremitting labour, watchful vigilance and keen interest which you have all long displayed in the redemption of some of the local historic monuments from the sacrilegious purposes for which they were used and in effecting much needed repairs to others.[15]

J.H. Marshall, Director-General, once again, wrote to Curzon on 15 November 1905:

> ... Within the last few days I have received letters and telegrams from all our Archaeological Officers in India and Burma asking me to express to His Excellency the deep gratitude which they feel for all that he has done for Archaeology and to offer to him the good wishes of their Departments on his return to England.
>
> To me, it is difficult to realize as yet that the happy chapter of the last few years has finally closed and that we can no longer look to Lord Curzon to guide and inspire us in our efforts. His Excellency knows well how deeply sensitive we are of the obligation under which his labours for Archaeology have placed us and how keen are our regrets at the severance of the tie which has bound him so long to India. Those regrets are tempered only by the thought that he will still continue to mould the destinies of this country in the new sphere to which he is going.
>
> On behalf of my colleagues and myself I would wish Their Excellencies God-speed on their journey and every good gift that fortune can bring them.[16]

Finally, Lord Curzon resigned on 18 November 1905.[17]

Celebrities also have always appreciated his work. Field Marshall, the Duke of Connaught after visiting Gwalior, Agra, Bharatpur, Jaipur and Bikaner wrote to Lord Curzon from Bombay on 19 February 1903 that:

"May I say how much I have admired and appreciated what you have done to keep up and restore the splendid antiquities in India which also had been too long left neglected."[18]

Appreciation of his work towards Archaeology particularly, care of monuments, continued even after his leaving India. A meeting of the East India Association was held on 22 November

1920 at the Caxton Hall West Minister, S.W., which discussed the preservation of ancient monuments in India. Members of the Association expressed their valuable views on the subject particularly praising Lord Curzon on his devotion to his work during his Viceroyalty. Noteworthy members who expressed their views were Mr. G.S. Dutt, I.C.S.; Lady Muir Macknezie; Mrs. Villiers Stuart; Sir Aurel Stein; Dr. Pollen and Mancherjee Bhownaggree. We can mention here views of some members.

According to Dr. Pollen:

> ... No one has done more for the preservation of Ancient Monuments in India than his Lordship. I remember some thirty odd years ago crossing the Indus with him between Sukker and Rohri. He was then the Hon. George Nathaniel Curzon, a traveling M.P. I draw his attention to the new railway-bridge then under construction across the Indus at Sukker and spoke of it as 'one of the wonders of the World'. But he turned away from it at once and gazed at the beautiful tombs of the seven sisters on the Rohri side., expressing regret that they had been allowed to crumble into ruins. I do not suppose he had then any idea that he would become Viceroy, but years afterwards as I stood behind him at the Apollo Bunder in Bombay – when he was making his first speech as Governor-General – elect on Indian soil. I recalled his Indus crossing and his care for Indian monuments. A few weeks after landing in Bombay he spoke out about the promotion of archaeological research and our imperial obligation to India in this matter and by his energy and determination he succeeded in rousing Government officers to a sense of their duty. In this connection, as in many others, India owes a deep debt of gratitude to Lord Curzon. I always foretold that sooner or later Indians would recognize the debt they owe to him.[19]

Sir Aurel Stein, the famous Central Asian explorer, expressed his views at this meeting:

> Historical students all over the world, not only in India, owed a very great debt of gratitude to Lord Curzon. It was very encouraging to know that apart from that love of antiquity and love of art, which he had amply shown. Every Viceroy who had since held office had shown a full appreciation of the duties which England owed to India in regard to its ancient monuments. It was a piece of very good fortune that Lord Curzon went out to India as a statesman prepared by his historical studies for understanding the past of more than one oriental Empire and that for six years he had that full scope which a Viceroy's power could give in the days gone by.[20]

B. Krishna, a member of the Association, opined at this meeting that:

> ... they were most highly indebted to Lord Curzon for the initiation of the policy of preservation of monuments, since it was due to his inspiring ideal that students and scholars had been able to learn something definite and concrete of ancient Indian history. As a student of history I express my indebtedness to the Government for the useful work they had done from the year 1900. I am sure that during this period specimens of ancient art and culture had been brought more and more before the people of India and undoubtedly a great impetus had been given to historical research by this policy of the preservation of monuments in India. There was a great cause for them to be highly indebted and for them to pay their tribute so far as they could in words, to the wise policy that had been initiated by Curzon.[21]

Appreciating Curzon's views and policy towards the preservation of old monuments, Mrs. Villiers Stuart, a member of the Association, put her thought at the meeting:

> Indians should be members of the Surveys and that it should not be left solely to England and Europeans to study the monuments of India because with Europeans there was always the danger that their interest would be historical only and that the living relations of the Indian monuments to the life of the country would be to a certain extent missed.[22]

Lady Muir Mackenzie, a Member, said that:

> I have always been a great admirer of Lord Curzon as I follow my footsteps all these wonderful restorations and preservations that he had the privilege to bring about. Personally, I have never seen anything more wonderful than the caves in India and I am glad to be able to say that they also have been preserved in an excellent way and perhaps the Ellora Caves were better preserved than any other monument I had the pleasure of seeing in India. I am delighted to be able to add my small tribute to Lord Curzon's wonderful care of ancient monuments of India.[23]

This was one of the landmarks amongst the many, which distinguished his Viceroyalty, one of those activities of his career in India that bore fruit in future. R. Vasudeva Poduwal rightly says, "For the recognition of the importance of the conservation of the national antiquities in India we owe much to Lord Curzon who declared that the preservation of the ancient monuments of India was essentially an imperial duty of Government."[24]

On 4 April 1905, he wrote to his wife Mary, that even if he had not achieved anything else in India, his name was carved in inerasable letters because of the preservation of the archaeological monuments, which was enough to earn him praise and ensure his place in history.[25]

Even after leaving India, Curzon continued to stay in touch with India through his contacts. He was always concerned about the archaeological projects started by him and took a personal interest in all matters related to them.[26]

The glowing tributes were also paid by Pandit Jawaharlal Nehru at Archaeological Survey of India at Mandu that "Curzon will be remembered because he restored all that was beautiful in India".[27]

NOTES AND REFERENCES

1. Curzon Papers, Mss, Eur, F. 111/205, N.A.I., Acc. No. 1638, No. 100.
2. Curzon Papers, Mss, Eur, F. 111/420, N.A.I., Acc. No. 1643.
3. *Ibid.*
4. Curzon Papers, Mss Eur, F. 111/420, N.A.I. Acc. No. 1643, No. 144.
5. *Ibid.*
6. Curzon Papers, Mss Eur, F. 111/420, N.A.I. Acc. No. 1643, No. 144.
7. *Ibid.*
8. *Ibid.*
9. *Ibid.*
10. Home, Archaeology and Epigraphy, October 1905, No. 15, deposit; Curzon Papers, Mss Eur, F. 111/420, N.A.I., Acc. No. 1643, No. 319.
11. *Ibid.*
12. Curzon Papers, Mss Eur, F. 111/420, N.A.I., Acc. No. 1643, No. 319.
13. *Ibid.*
14. *Ibid.*
15. *Ibid.*
16. *Ibid.*
17. *List of the Heads of Administrations in India*, Government of India Publication, 1921, p. 5.
18. Curzon Papers, Mss Eur, F. 111/207, No. 55, N.A.I. Acc. No. 1639.
19. *The Asiatic Review*, January 1921, p. 109.
20. *The Asiatic Review*, January 1921, pp. 109-110.
21. *The Asiatic Review*, January 1921, p. 111.

22. *Ibid.*
23. *The Asiatic Review*, January 1921, p. 112.
24. 'The Care of Ancient Monuments'; Broadcast from Trivandrum Radio Station on 19 September 1947; Published in 'Radio Talks by R. Vasudeva Poduval' at Trivandrum in December 1948; pp. 54-55.
25. 'Curzon-Nama, Autocrat Curzon, unconquerable India' by Pramila Sharma, p. 62.
26. *Ibid.*
27. Quoted in Gordia, Nayana. *Lord Curzon: The Last of the British Moghuls*, O.U.P., Delhi 1993, C.f. list of Illustrations No. 33, p. xi.

Appendix-I

A. KYD'S COMMENTS ON STEEL'S REPORT ON REPAIRS REQUIRED FOR THE PRESERVATION OF THE TAJ MAHAL AND VARIOUS BUILDINGS IN THE VICINITY OF THE TAJ MAHAL*

1 AND 2. REPAIRS REQUIRED TO THE ROOF OF THE TAJ INCLUDING THE LARGE CENTER DOME, THE FOUR SMALLER DOMES, THE FLAT TERRACE WITH PARAPET WALLS

It does not appear, that any of the marble slabs which compose the exterior coating require to be removed for the purpose of extirpating the grass and plants from the joints which since the rape ladders have been fixed has already been done by the Daroga of the Taj; all that is required is to have the joints well pointed with marble chunam and the surface well cleaned. The terrace roof between the Domes as well as the interior plastering of the Parapet appear to be in very good repair and should not be broken up but the few cracks filled up with fresh strong mortar. The greatest expense in making the above repair will be in erecting a scaffolding to the small of the Dome, above which the whole may be most conveniently done by a spices of cradle used for such purpose in this country, but as the scaffolding for the whole repairs is separately estimated, the expense of cleaning and painting the joints will be confined to workmanship and a very small quantity of marble chunam, which in my judgement should not exceed Rs. 5,000.

3. FOR REPAIRING THE KULLIES OR COPPER GILT ORNAMENT ON THE TOP OF THE LARGE DOME

The part of this ornament which remains appears very firm and should not be removed. The upper part which has been blown down is so much bruised, that it must be renewed and new copper used. The difference of price between the new and old copper cannot be great and the expense will principally be in the workmanship. To regild the whole is a matter of calculation by establishing the expense of gilding a square fool of copper. This I have not at present the

---

* Judicial, 24 November 1809, Nos. 8-10.

means of doing but by making a liberal allowance, the expense of repairing and regilding this ornament should not in my opinion exceed Rs. 3,000.

4. For repairing the exterior body of the Taj

Several of the marble slabs which compose the coating of the body of the Building are broken and many of the ornaments of inlaid coloured stone have tumbled out. All this can be easily repaired by lowering the above-mentioned cradles from the Parapet. Instead of filling up the vacancies in the ornaments with coloured chunam, I should recommend that first pieces of coloured stone should be inserted. The expense of this repair will Chiefly be in workmanship as a very small quantity of marble chunam will be required and abundance of coloured stone and small pieces of marble can be procured from the dilapidated building without the great square which it is not proposed to be repaired. I think that Rs. 7,000 will be abundant for the repair.

5. For repairing the upper Marble Terrace

Few or none of the marble slabs of this paved terrace are broken or displaced and I should conceive the expense of cleaning and painting them to be trifling but the exact expense of this might be ascertained in a few days by ordering 100 square feet to be done. The spents had better be of marble stone as those of metal would soon be stolen. Rs. 1,500 should I think fully suffice for this repair.

6. For repairing the four marble Minarets

To completely clean and paint the marble coating of these minarets and to repair the parapets of the exterior Galleries, several of which are broken, will require I think Rs. 4,000.

I would not recommend the filling up of the arcades which support the cupolas of their most elegant pillars as I do not think it would contribute to their solidity and it would certainly substract very much from their beauty.

7. For repairing the fronts of the raised marble platform

The fronts of this platform appear to be in very good repair and only require being completely cleaned and partially painted. The cracks in the walls and arches of the various apartments under the platform occasioned by the shock of an Earthquake cannot now be effectively repaired. All that can be done is to wedge small bricks into the cracks and to fill in the interstices with strong mortar. To effect this repair and to clean and paint the four fronts of the platform should not I think, cost more than Rs. 2,000.

8. For repairing the Chequered Pavement round the Base of the Platform

Many of the stones of the edges of this pavement are displaced and some are broken. Some of the marble and stone slabs are broken. To repair this will I think cost Rs. 1,500.

REPAIRS OF THE MUSJID AND BUILDINGS ON THE LOWER TERRACE

1 & 2. Repairing the Domes of the Musjid and braking up the terrace

There appears no necessity for removing any of the marble coating of the Domes of this Building to root out the grass. They only require cleaning and painting. The inlaid ornaments of the neck of the Dome are almost all fallen out. As they are not seen from below, they had better be filled up with mortor and the whole neck plastered of one colour. The flat terrace between the Domes is in a very bad state and requires being broken up and a new surface of Terrace laid to effect both the above purposes, I should think Rs. 5,000 would suffice.

3. For repairing the stone facing on the front sides of the above building

The stone coating of this building is very much broken and in many places entirely fallen off. The interior of the building requires considerable repair particularly the Dome. The stones of which are much **exfoliated** and must in such cases be covered with Plaster of the some colour as the stone. To give the body of this Building a substantial repair, it strikes me will cost at least Rs. 10,000.

4. The repairing of the marble Domes of the two Boorjis or Pavillions

To put these buildings in complete repair will require about Rs. 3,000.

5. For repairing the Jemyut Khana (Jemyd Khanah)

This building is similar in plan and dimensions to the Musjid but is somewhat more out of repair and may require about 16,000 rupees to put it in a good state.

6. For repairing the lower stone Terrace and cleaning the Domes

The terrace is very much out of repair. Many of the paving stones are quite exfoliated and decayed and will require to be renewed. Under the terrace are the covered drains for the whole building which are reported to be choked. To clean and repair them is the very first thing that should be done. As the water being allowed to find another passage may endanger the foundations of the buildings and in the end would certainly be the means of ruining them until these drains are broken up. It appears quite impossible to form and idea of the expense of cleaning and repairing them but to repair the stone pavement of this terrace will at least cost Rs. 4,000.

7. For repairing the connecting wall on the river side

The great wall to the river side is a most solid well built work apparently in very good repair and will only require the weeds and grass to be removed from the joints of the stones and to be painted where necessary. This I think should be done for Rs. 1,500.

8. Repairing the walls and arches supporting the Platform

The whole of the arches of the extensive aqueduct and reservoirs for supplying the garden and fountains with water are much out of repair, to effect which cannot cost less than Rs. 8,000.

9. Timbers of all sizes, Ropes and for Scaffolding

It does not appear that a great quantity of scaffolding will be required and as I presume each building will be done successively. The same scaffolding will certainly answer – the first o be used is that to the smell of the great dome of the mausoleum which I imagine will be enough for the Musjid and every other building in succession. In my opinion, Rs. 6,000 will amply provide timber for scaffolding rope.

I have gone all over the buildings at the Taj which it appears you directed Lt. Steell to examine and Estimate. I cannot help, however, submitting to you the propriety of repairing the principal gate to the garden which I estimate will cost about 6,000 rupees. This is a very magnificent structure and were it allowed to go to ruin, much would be lost of an impression of wonder and delight which every beholder must feel in approaching this splendid monument which for magnificence and taste and costliness of materials far exceeds anything of the same kind that is probably in the universe. The repairing and keeping in order of which will reflect 'such credit on the British Government through every part of Industan'.

Rewari
24 November 1808

Sd/- A. Kyd
Acting Chief Engineer

ABSTRACT OF AN ESTIMATE FOR REPAIRING THE TAJ MAHAL, AGRA

		Rupees
1&2	Repair requisite to the roof and domes	5,000
3.	To the Kullus or Copper ornament	3,000
4.	The exterior Body of the Taj	7,000
5.	Upper Marble Terrace	1,500
6.	Four Menarets	4,000
7.	Fronts of the great Platform	2,000
8.	Chequered Pavement round Do	1,500
1&2	Roof of the Musjid	5,000
3.	Exterior and Interior of Do	10,000
4.	The two Boorjis or Pavilions	3,000
5.	Jemyd Khanah	16,000
6.	Lower Stone Terrace and cleaning the Drains	4,000
7.	Great front wall River side	1,500
8.	Aqueduct and Reservoirs	8,000
9.	Scaffolding and Rope	6,000
10.	Grand Gate	6,000
		Rs. 83,500

Rewari
24 November 1808

Sd/- A. Kyd
Acting Chief Engineer

Appendix-II

REPORT OF THE COMMITTEE OF SURVEY (TAJ)*

Description of Works	Remarks
1.	2.
The Roof, Large Dome and Four Small Ones.	The large Dome and four small ones appear now in complete repair. They have had their surfaces thoroughly cleaned of the crust which had been forming upon them in the course of nearly two centuries, the whole of the marble slabs forming the coating are in their proper situations and although this item of the work has been complete upwards of three years, it is at present in the most thorough repair and appears most substantially executed. The roof has been broken up and a new surface given to it. This part of the work was completed a short time after the Dome and it still wears the appearance of having been just executed.
The Kullus on Copper Gilt Ornament at the Taj	This ornament which from its size must be of great weight (its height being 30 feet) appears to be firmly fixed and has been newly gilded.
Exterior Body of the Taj	The whole of the outer surface of the Body of the Taj has been thoroughly repaired and cleaned; the stones which had fallen out have been replaced and the mosaic work completely renewed, new Kullis have been given to several of the small minarets and others have been regilt.

* Revenue, 26 January 1815, No. 66.

The Upper Marble Terrace	Has been cleaned and repaired and 336 marble spouts have been made and fixed.
The Four Marble Minarets	Repairs to the arcades which support the Cupolas have been well executed.
The Marble Platform with the Rooms Beneath	Have been cleaned and repaired; the cracks (occasioned by an earthquake) in the rooms beneath have been well stopped up with the best cement and bricks firmly wedged in.
The Chequered Pavement Round the Platform	Those pieces of marble and red stone which were wanting have been replaced.
The Musjeed	The Domes have been cleaned on the outside and the whole of slabs forming the outer coating of them are now regularly laid and the marble ornaments in the neck of each have been renewed where wanting the interior of each of the necks has been newly plastered and the tops of the lower Domes have been newly terraced. The whole of the Roof has been broken up and a new terrace laid down. The parapet walls have been repaired. The interior of the Building has been plastered where it was found necessary and the whole of the ornaments restored to their original state. The stones which had fallen from the front and sides have been replaced, also some of the marble ornamental parts. Several new Cullis have been made and gilded for the small gooldistan on minarets; the whole is now completely repaired.
The Two Boorjes Pavilions on the River Face	The Domes of these pavilions have been repaired and cleaned and the roots of trees have been completely extracted. The whole of the wall has been repaired and painted and the Jawlies (stone net work) has been renewed where required. The river flowing continually against the N.W. Bastian was likely to have injured the foundations but this has been remedied by throwing down large stones and rubbish to break its force. This has now settled and appears to be a considerable service.
The Jemynd Kanah	The same remarks apply to this which were made to the Musjid.
The Lower Stone Terrace and Drains	The Drains have all been opened and cleaned and the Bottom and sides have been relaid. Also a new variegated stone pavement have been laid over the whole of them. The Terrace has also been renewed where it is required.
The Great Wall on the River Face	Appears in a complete state of repair. It has been represented to the Committee by the Engineer who had charge of the works

that this particular item was in a very ruinous state. A great part of the face was covered with the peeple tree. Some of the roots of the tree which were taken out had penetrated upwards of ten feet into the wall and were above 16 feet in length; also of very considerable thickness. Had they not been extracted completely, they would to all appearance have soon brought down the wall and eventually much injured the Building.

The Aqueduct and Reservoirs

The supporting wall of the Bullock walk has been repaired, painted and strengthened. The whole of the arches have been made new. The walls of the aqueduct have been completely repaired, painted and those of the Reservoir strengthened so as to enable it to bear nearly two-thirds more water than it was want to do. The whole of the interior of the Reservoirs has been replastered and covered with a coat of polished marble chunam.

The Great Gate of Entrance

The several small Domes, Goooldistans, Roof and Sides have been completely repaired and several new cullis fixed. The Terrace of the Roof has been broken up and a new one laid down. The interior rooms and passages have been thoroughly repaired. The great doors covered with copper and brazen ornaments have also been repaired and are now in complete order. The stones which had fallen from the exterior fronts and sides have been replaced and the whole of this building is brought to its original state.

The Channels of the Fountains under the Great Terrace

Appear in thorough repair.

The Jawlies or Stone Net Work.

Are in excellent order.

The Channels for Water for Fountain in the Garden

Have been repaired and the fountains are now in good order.

The Bowlee Boorje

The Dome and walls of the Building are in complete order and Jawlies which were broken and carried away have been renewed. The Bowlee has been cleaned out and a small parapet wall has been built up at each of the Doors. To prevent falling into a new kullies has been given.

The Bastion South of Jemynd Khanah

With the exception of what regards the Bowlee or well, the same remark applies to this Bastion as to the preceding.

Pavilion East of the Garden	The Dome of this has been entirely rebuilt in a most substantial manner. A new kullis has also been given. The walls have been thoroughly repaired and painted and a great deal of new Jawlies or net work has also been made.
Pavilion West of the Garden.	It is in complete repair.
(Sd) J. Taylor **Lieutenant of Engineers**	(Sd) D. Macleod, Major, President " W. Tallemach, Captain and Member " A. Owen, Captain and Member " I. Land, Lieutenant and Member " Dingwall Fordyce, Lieutenant and Member

Appendix-III

ESTIMATE DRAWN UP BY LOCAL AGENTS IN CONSULTATION WITH CAPTAIN PHIPPS, BARRACK MASTER FOR THE REPAIRS OF TAJ MAHAL AND ADJACENT BUILDINGS, MOTI MASJID IN THE FORT OF AGRA, MAUSOLEUM OF AKBAR AT SIKANDRA AND DURGAH OF SALIM CHISTI AT FATEHPUR SIKRI*

STATEMENT-I

1. The Taj and its Adjacent Buildings

The munificence of the Government in authorizing the repairs of this splendid Edifice has been duly appreciated and gratefully acknowledged by all classes of its subjects and it would be matter of extreme regret that the work should be discontinued in its present imperfect state.

The whole of the interior of the Building to be cleaned without injuring the polished surface of the marble. The Rooms and Staircases to be repaired ... Rs. 2,500

Doors

Two pair of stout seasoo Doors coated with copper sheet ornamented with Brass mouldings at the staircase leading to the marble terrace. Copper and Brass to be supplied from the Magazine.

2 Pair of Doors	= Rs. 50		
Workmanship for coating	= Rs. 150		
	Rs. 200	...	Rs. 2,00

Five pair of Doors for the lower apartment of the Building to be coated with silvered copper and ornamented with Gilt moulding ... Rs. 2,000

* Revenue, 28 April 1815, No. 50 B.

Brought forward	...	Rs. 4,700
4 pair of stout painted saul Doors for the interior stair cases with fastening and complete.	...	Rs. 100
Boundary Wall		
The binding stones round the interior face of the ramparts and on the Terraces in front of the southern arcades to be replaced and the ornamental line round the ramparts to be repaired	...	Rs. 300
Southern Arcades		
A substantial parapet wall faced with stone and appropriately ornamented to be built round the interior faces of each arcade	...	Rs. 2,000
The terraced roofs of both the buildings and of the small arcades attached to them facing outwards to be broken up and relaid.	...	Rs. 1,700
The small arcades to the North and South of the west leading into the outer square and those on the western and northern sides of that square which are in tolerable order to be repaired. The remains of the arcades to the East and South of the square and to the North and South of the eastern entrance to be pulled down and the rubbish removed.	...	Rs. 1,000
The Turrets at the South-East and South West angles of the Garden to be rebuilt – estimated by Lt. Taylor	...	Rs. 10,000
Total:		**Rs. 19,800**
The total amount of the estimate for completing the repairs of the Taj, to the full extent that seems to be desirable, is	...	Rs. 19,800
Remaining (surplus amount already kept in deposit) to be applied of former grant	...	Rs. 2,565
Now total remains	...	**Rs. 17,235**

STATEMENT-II

2. Moti Masjid

The terraced roofs of the Musjid and cloisters to be broken up and relaid	...	Rs. 800
The spires to be furnished. The Domes and Cupolas to be cleared of trees and grass. All roots to be extracted and the seams throughout to be pointed with marble chunam	...	Rs. 1,200
6 small square turrets to be taken down and rebuilt; several new brackets to be supplied – 150 each	...	Rs. 900
The whole of the marble inside and out to be well cleaned without injuring the Polish	...	Rs. 300
The red stone wall to be repaired and painted	...	Rs. 160
A stone fence to be placed on the outer edge of the staircase	...	Rs. 200

The entrance doors to be repaired. Copper and Brass from the magazine workmanship ... Rs. 200

Marble slabs forming the pent house of the arcades to be replaced ... Rs. 200

Total: Rs. 3,960

STATEMENT-III

3. Mausoleum of Akbar at Secundra

One marble cupola on the summit to be rebuilt.

The Domes of the remaining 3 to be repaired.

The terraced roof of the marble arcade to be dug up and relaid – roots to be extracted and the Parapets repaired.

The Cenotaph to be cleaned.

The pavement on which the Cenotaph is constructed to be repaired with stone taken from the arcade, those to be replaced by marble. The Domes of the Cupola throughout the building to be repaired.

All roots to be extracted where it can be done without great expense or injury to the superstructure.

The seams throughout the stone part of the building to be pointed.

The Jalies or net work which surrounded the floor of each story to be replaced viz on the first story by a parapet wall, on the 2nd and 3rd by a stone panelled fence.

The lower grand arcade to be repaired and plastered.

Three pair of common stout Doors for the Entrance of the lower tomb of 2nd stair cases, the marble net work throughout the building to be cleaned.

Total Cost Required ... Rs. 20,000

STATEMENT-IV

4. Durgah at Fatehpur Sikree

As it has appeared to us on, superficial observation, that the dilapidations are by no means extensive, we may hope to persuade the ministerial officer in charge of the endowments, at the expense of the fund assigned to him, such repair to the Gateway and Mosque as may appear to be requisite and to allot a small sum annually towards the preservation of further injury to the Edifice.

The pecuniary aid of grant is, therefore, not called for.

Sd/- A. WRIGHT
G.W. BLUNT
C. MACSWEEN
Local Agents

Agra
4 March 1815

Appendix-IV

REPORT OF "SPECIAL COMMITTEE OF SURVEY" APPOINTED ON 11 DECEMBER 1823

The President along with the members of the Special Committee met at Agra on 20 January 1824 and proceeded to examine the actual state of Taj:

First the exterior body of the Taj which from the basement to as high as it is possible to examine the same without the aid of scaffolding. They find on all sides in a very considerable state of dilapidation from parts of the mosaic work having fallen out. Much of the repaired work still remains perfect. What deterioration has taken place by the falling of the pieces of coloured cement, the Committee strongly recommends to be immediately repaired with coloured stone as originally constructed.

The Committee next proceeded to examine the four Minarets, each of which exhibits considerable want of repair to the pointing done with black cement and which has fallen out and ought in like manner with the body of the Taj to be immediately repaired and that with black stone of which its joints were originally filled up. The Committee cannot with any certainty or accuracy exactly state to what extent this repair may be required but from the examination they gave to it; it may be estimated at little or nothing short of one half. The Committee could not detect any injury in the blocks of the Minarets or the marble squares of which they are composed and the whole repairs are consequently confined to the pointings.

The Committee prosecuted their examination by inspecting the upper roof together with the neck of the dome and the dome itself; the faces of the marble Platform with the rooms beneath – The four faces of this Platform composed of large slabs of white marble and jointed with black stone exhibit deficiencies in the pointings which whether of cement or stone have fallen out and require to be renewed. The Committee observe that a doorway to the western side of the staircase from the lower to the upper terrace has been closed with brick and faced with red stones which are falling out. This the Committee recommend to be immediately opened, the passage restored and a new door made. The rooms in the East, South and West sides are in good order.

The chequered Pavement around the Platform – The whole of this area of pavement composed of red stone, is in good order and perfect.

The Musjid – This building shows on its principal face as well as both ends abundant instances of dilapidation of its structure as well as in the red stone work as in the mosaic ornaments, the Orcades, Pinnacles and other parts forming the attic buildings of the body of the Taj, all of which appear to the Committee to be in excellent condition and perfect repair. Some tufts of grass and weeds have shown themselves on the surface of the Dome. These ought to be immediately destroyed and particular attention given to prevent the future growth of fresh grass. Some very trifling and inconsiderable repair is required to a particular part of the Parapet which was pointed out to the Darogah of the Taj.

The Committee having thoroughly examined the Taj internally as well as externally are led to make the following observation:

That in all parts, Chunam and marble cement has been employed instead of white marble to fill up all deficiencies or broken parts and that coloured cements have been used at least as far as the vacant joints demonstrate instead of coloured stones or marbles from every appearance of the work executed.

The upper marble Terrace – This part appears in good condition. Those parts that are deficient have been undoubtedly filled up with coloured cements.

The Roof (terrace) is in a perfect state but the mosaic ornaments and work of the fillet and cordon round the upper neck of the Domes are in almost every part deficient and Grass and weeds are growing out of the domes in a few places. Many of the Pinnacles or small minarets are in a state of dilapidation and are out of the perpendicular.

The interior is in good order.

The two Boorjes on the River face – These appear generally to be in tolerable repair. Here and there pieces have fallen out of the coloured cement that has supplied the place of the former marble pointing.

The Jumyind Khanah – The building in all its faces exhibits similar deficiencies in the mosaic work and pointing. The Terrace roof is in a less perfect state than the Musjid. The mosaic fillet cordon of white and black marble round the upper part of the neck or drum of the Dome is almost entirely without filling up. Several of the Pinnacles are in a similar state and in bad condition.

The lower stone Terrace and drains – These do not afford any cause for particular remarks. They appear generally in good condition. Excepting on the water face from the Taj to the angle nearest the Jumyind Khanah, the Terrace seems to have sunk and water lodges to remedy which the pavement must be taken up and relaid.

The great wall on the River face – Its exterior face appears to be in good repair.

The Aqueduct and Reservoir – This appears in good condition. It does not require any particular remarks.

The channels of the Fountains under the great Terrace – These are in good repair as the fountains appear to play without any sort of impediment or defect.

The Jaalies or stone net work and rails round the Grand Terrace – These are all in good order and perfect.

The channels for the water for the Fountains in the Garden – These are apparently in good order as the fountains appear to play freely.

The Bhowlie Boorje – The same notice may be applied to this building generally as all the others. The pointing originally of white marble has been replaced with marble lime which has fallen out and leaves the joints open. The Jaalies or balcony rails of open work have been renewed and are complete and the Bhowlie apparently very clean and in good order.

Bastion south of the Jumyind Khanah – In general good repair.

Pavilion east side of the Garden – This Building is in a good repair excepting the fillet round the upper part of the drum of the Dome of Mosaic work which is nearly all deficient. The Terrace is in general good repair.

Pavilion west side of the Garden – The foregoing remarks are generally applicable to this Building, excepting in the fillet of mosaic work, which is a very small part only, is deficient.

Copper gilt ornaments on the Domes – The whole of the copper gilt appears perfect and in good order.

The Great Gate of Entrance – The exterior and interior external faces of this Gateway are in a similar state of dilapidation in the mosaic work and some trifling parts of the red stone which had been repaired with a red cement has been fallen out as well as much of the white pointings which has been made with white cement. All this should be replaced certainly with white marble.

The Roof, Dome, Arcades, Pinnacles and Parapets are in good order. The mosaic work round the small minars in some places are deficient. In some places the grass is growing in the small domes which crown the arcades of the exterior and interior area of the Gateway.

Appendix-V

ABSTRACT OF THE SPECIAL COMMITTEE'S REPORT ON AGRA FORT DATED 10 MARCH 1810 SUGGESTING REPAIRS, ALTERATIONS, ERECTIONS AND DEMOLITIONS, ETC.*

1. Recommended that Brick on edge Ramps be substituted as the Trucks of the Garrison carriages with heavy ordnance mounted on them require a very hard substance such as Brick-work or Puckah Terrace.
2. Curtain between Shaw and Tully Burge – The inner parapet or retaining wall which is in Ruins and requires repairs.
3. Tully Burge curtain between that and Sheme Sheer Burge – The retaining wall along the interior face requires cutting down to the height laid down for those walls.
4. Shum Sheer Burge – On the shoulder of the curtain is a Guard Room for Sepoys which Committee recommended to be removed and built Puckah at the fort of the Ramp in the interior of the Garrison.
5. Curtain between Shum Sheer Burge and Nando Burge – The slopping and repairs of the Terreplain is required.
6. Curtain between Nundoo Burge and Jaffer Bux – The inner retaining wall requires cutting down plastering and c.
7. Jaffer Bux Burge – The taking down of the curtain here and the small room as a magazine at the head of the Ramp and the disposal of the platforms in the Bastion was required.
8. Curtain between Jaffer Bux Burge and the Delhi Gate – The slopping and dressing of the Terreplain. Removal of the Cavalier and old Blocks of Masonry. Battlements require repairs and stone Flags to be replaced at the Top.
9. Great stair case leading off the Rampant into the interior of the Garrison – This staircase which is a principal one requires to be rebuilt throughout as it is in a very ruinous and dangerous state.

---

* Military, 24 November 1810, Nos. 70-74.

10. Curtain between Delhi Gate and Yallumaddet Burge – There is in front of the left of this curtain and adjoining to the Delhi Gate way an old Ruin tumbling down, that ought undoubtedly to be removed.

....

The company having now terminated their survey of the upper part of the work of the Body of the Place proceed to examine and report on the interior or lower part of these works.

Casements in the Curtains and Bastions

Committee was unanimously of the opinion that the casements under the Ramparts of the wall will deserve the notice of the Board to have them repaired and filled up as Barracks or accommodation for Native Troops in the event of a siege to afford shelter for the number of Troops which would be necessary to throw in the Garrison for its defence.

Parts of the arches in the interior retaining walls can be easily repaired.

The Committee now proceed to enumerate the number of those arches in each casement above and below each of which has a Circular Dome within; the whole is built of solid stone and chunam.

Shaw Burge – Under this Bastion are rooms which with some repairs and alterations in the temporary partition walls of the archways could be converted into very excellent Guard Room.

Omar Singh's Gate and outworks

An inner parapet wall round the Terrace will be required.

The outworks in front of Omar Singh Gate-way.

As there is a regular passage for Troops and Ordnance from the Area of the Body of the place to the Terreplain of the Rampart of this work and good broad stair cases require repairs. Committee recommended that the entry and winding passage from the Body of the place to the great Gate below be filled up on the inside by a strong retaining wall of the stone.

The Committee recommend that the spaces between the Battlements be filled up.

Rownee curtain to the left of the Shaw Burge – As a general remark, the Committee wish to call the attention of the Board to the necessity of immediately ordering those Ramparts to be cleared of Jungle Grass, weeds and filth for they are made use of by the Native Troops and inhabitants of the Garrison as Princes at present as are (The Committee are concerned to observe) most of the outworks.

Circular Bastion under the small Bastion outwork of the Delhi Gate

Lower Rownee left of Delhi Gate – The parapet requires repairs and plastering some old temporary Buildings. The apertures in the Parapet require to be filled up leaving proper loopholes sufficient to depend the Bridge.

Right Bastion under the left Bastion of Delhi Gate outworks – Requires the alterations and repairs of the curtain.

Rownee curtain front of the Palace – The whole of this Parapet is crumbling away into complete decay. A new parapet wall must be constructed with Loopholes only or solid with a Banquette.

Semi-circular Bastion and Traverse to the body of the Palace – Parapet wall and Loopholes require considerable repairs. A stair case on the centre of the Rampart requires to be filled up.

Delhi Gate – Their defences and Outworks

The work which joins the inner and outer lower Gates – The spaces between the Battlements require filling up. Three stair cases require small repairs; also a Building over the outer Gate. The jungle and weeds should be immediately removed.

Apartment over the Inner Gate – Three rooms and two passages leading into the Inner upper outwork of this Gate require small repairs and clearing as they are in a most filthy offensive state.

The slopping passage from the lower to the Upper Gate – The two large Arches in the walls of this passage at the foot of it, close to the Gate have parts of old Blocks of loose Bricks and stones laying in them meant to fill them up which ought to be removed.

Inner Gates in the Body of the Palace – There are two Banks of Earth and Stones raised in the Hexigen Area of this Gateway on each side of the counter passage which ought undoubtedly to be removed. They are in a ruinous state.

Repair work in front of the outer Delhi Gates

Interior of the Garrison – The high road leading from the Delhi Gate to the Berkey Magazine requires a retaining on wall each side to hold the Earth which may be done from the stones of the ruins to be thrown down.

There are several old ruinous walls and fragments of buildings near to Salim Ghur which ought on every account to be thrown down and levelled and their materials applied where wanting.

The Akbar Mahal – There are two Gateways adjoining the large one leading to the great square with ruins about them all of no use as Buildings which ought to be pulled down and their materials used where wanting.

Many small ruins and broken banks require to be laid down and the area levelled.

Upper Roomed House in the Centre of the Garrison

Requires a straw chopper to be taken down and some slight repair and cleaning out.

Salim Ghur

Upper apartments require small repairs. It is at present like all the other old buildings in a very dirty filthy state. The door leading into the square will require stone pillars at the sides and flat stones at top to support the wall over now held up by some slight wood work.

(Sd/-) H.G. GRACE
Lt. Col. and President
G. PENNINGTON
Captain Horse, Artillery
(Sd/-) G.S. BROWN
Lt. Col. Commanding Agra

(Sd/-) H.W. GREENE
Captain, Artillery
H. STARK, Captain

Appendix-VI

REPORT OF A COMMITTEE OF SURVEY ASSEMBLED IN OBEDIENCE TO GOVERNMENT ORDERS OF THE 14TH MARCH 1829 FOR THE PURPOSE OF SURVEYING THE REPAIRS OF KUTUB MINAR*
PRESIDENT – CAPTAIN I. WILSON, 17TH REGT. NATIVE INFANTRY

LIEUT. MACKESON, 14th REGT. N.1 – (MEMBERS) ENSIGN C. BLACK, 17th REGT. N.1

Description of Buildings	Measurement of Work	Remarks by the Engineer	Remarks by the Committee
1.	2.	3.	4.
Kutub Minar	**In the ground on 1st story of Minar-average** 186 feet length and 16th feet breadth of red stone re-newed and fixed with from branch and bad work done outside. 10 Ditto and 2ft Do of Red stone Do Do 8 Ditto and 4ft Do of Red stone Do Do 3 Ditto and 2ft Do of Red stone Do Do 3 Ditto and 2ft Do of Red stone Do Do	The work executed on the Minar is no longer new. The nature of the repair being intricate and unsafe to attempt much of at once has occupied a length of time and as it was studied from the commencement to assimilate the repairs as much as possible with the old work, it is difficult to verify the repairs to the extent to which they have been executed.	The whole appears as described by the Executive Engineer.

* Political, 25 April 1829, No. 18.

1.	2.	3.	4.
	150 feet length and 10 feet breadth of gray quarts stone fixed with from Iron Branch and lead of the centre pillar. 220 feet Do and 10 Do of common stone Do 56 feet Do and 6 ft of Do inside steps 144 feet Do and 3½ ft high of new Red Stone Balcony Balustrade fixed with Iron branch and lead. 144 feet Do and 4½ ft Do of Red stone balcony floor repaired. **2nd Story of Minar** 110 feet length and feet Breadth of Red stone of renewed outside. 55 feet 6 Do and 6 Ft Do Red Stone work done on the inside. 114 feet length and 3 ft 1½ inch Breadth of new Red Stone Balcony Balustrade fixed with iron cramp and lead. 64 feet length and 1½ ft Breadth of Red Stone Terrace repaired **3rd Story of Minar** 104 feet length and 4 ft Breadth of Red Stone fixed with Iron Cramp and Lead Work done outside. 52 feet length and 2 ft Breadth of Red Stone fixed with Iron Cramp and Lead work done inside. 100 feet length and 3 feet high of Red Stone Balustrade Balcony fixed with Iron cramp and lead.	The Great Fissures and dangerously dilapidated parts of the lower story have been carefully rebuilt and all the lost and defective parts of the numerous sculptured inscriptions perfectly restored. The like repair is effected through all the stories and their parts to the top of the old pillar including in it the almost entire reconstruction of the spiral stair of the upper stories of the column which had fallen in a manner most dangerous to the stability of all the upper part of the Building. Interly new Balcony Balustrades of Red Stone have been added to four lowest stories of the column and a light Iron and Brass open Rail added to the 5th story. The pavilion or 6th story entirely new composed of Red Stone fluted columns supporting an enriched cornice covered with a Dome and Turrets of the same material. The whole being surmounted with an upper cupola octagonal top of Sissoo-wood supporting a Flag staff. The former Rude and fractured Entrance Door of the Base of the column repaired and improved with new mouldings frieze and repair of the Inscription Tablet. The external pavement of the west base of the Pillar newly formed into a Drain for taking off the water.	The whole appears as described by the Executive Engineer.

1.	2.	3.	4.
	26 feet length and 2½ ft. Breadth Red Stone Terrace repaired		
	4th Story of Minar 11 feet length and 2 feet Breadth of Red Stone fixed with Iron Cramp and lead work done outside. 24 feet length and 7½ feet Breadth and Red Stone fixed with Iron cramp and Lead work done on inside. 85 feet length and 6 feet ditto 58 feet length and 3 feet high of new stone Balcony Balustrade fixed with Iron Cramp and Lead. 60 feet length and 7 inches Breadth of red stone cornice fixed with Iron cramp and lead.	The Eastern angle of the ancient colonnaded enclosure called the Bhood Kannah which had fallen down opposite the Entrance Door of the column is rebuilt and the whole of the area of the Kannah and of all the ranges of ancient buildings near the pillar so thoroughly cleared out of the mud buildings of rubbish and accumulated Incumbrance of ages as to lay the whole open to a free access and along with this improvement. The field of ruin and incumbered ground at the foot of the column on all sides has been completely converted into open space, new and good roads of access and communication with all parts of the neighbourhood are established, and the vast quantity of incumbent rubbish has been collected into ornamental mounds and seats of view. In combination with planning of about 2,000 trees and shrubs which are thriving on all the adjoining grounds. The whole of the above clearance and improvements to this public place of resort have with the exception to the repairs of column itself been effected extra and without surcharges on the estimated expense for the restoration of Kutub-Minar.	The whole appears as described by the Executive Engineer.
	5th Story Minar 41 feet length and 7¾ feet Breadth of red stone fixed with Iron Cramp and Lead outside. 6 feet length and 1 feet breadth of white marble fixed with Cramp and Lead outside. 24 feet length and 7 feet breadth of gray quarter stone fixed with iron cramp inside. 52 feet length and 4 feet breadth Do Do. 58 feet length and 3 feet high of new iron railing fixed with iron cramp and lead with 3 coats of white paint. 58 feet length of brass kurb on the railway.		

1.	2.	3.	4.
	6th Story of Minar 8 Pillars of red stone each ½ length 8 Arches of red stone fixed with iron cramp and lead on pillars. 18 feet length of Arches vault roof of red stone and fixed with iron cramp and lead. 22 feet of red stone cornice Do Do 26 feet length and 3 feet height of new red stone railway fixed with grom cramp and lead. 8 Parapet spearhead blocks of red stone. 25 feet length fixed with grom cramp and lead. **The 7th Story Pavilion of Sisso wood supporting the Flag staff** 8 Pillars of carved Sissoo 2 each feet length. 17 feet of length of covering and fixed with iron on the pillars. 1 Flag staff of saul wood. 55 feet long fixed with iron in solid red stone black sheet.		

REPAIRING THE OLD SURAI NEAR THE KUTUB MINAR

Remarks by Engineer

The ruined arcade and *kootries* of the Surae capable of being restored have been rebuilt principally on the east-west and south sides of the square. The roofs composed of good stone and bricks masonry vaults. The area and *kootries* generally cleared of rubbish, the ground leveled and cross roads made. The east and west gates restored from their ruined bases by new superstructure and new solid arched roofs. The south front central ruin cleared and formed into a spacious opening to the meanor with substantial gate pillars and side apartments plastered and terraced. The mosy and angular towers restored the whole of the parapets reconstructed with repair of painting/pointing to the walls and the jungle cleared.

Attending the Committee

(Sd/-) Robert Smith, Major
Superintendent Kutub and other works

(Sd/-) John Wilson, Captain Resident
(Sd/-) F. Mackeson, Lt. & Member
(Sd/-) C. Black, Ensign & Member

Appendix-VII

(EXTRACT FROM BENGAL REGULATION OF 1810)
AD 1810 REGULATION XIX

A Regulation for the due appropriation of the rents and produce of lands granted for the support of mosques, Hindu Temples, colleges and other purposes, for the maintenance and repair of Bridges, Serays, Kittras and other public buildings; and for the custody and disposal of Nuzzool property or escheats – passed by the Governor-General in Council on the 14th December 1810.

1. Whereas considerable endowments have been granted in land by preceding Governments of this country and by individuals for the support of Mosques, Hindu temples and other beneficial purposes, and whereas there are grounds to suppose that the produce of such land is in many instances appropriated, contrary to the intentions of the donors, to the personal use of the individuals in the immediate charge and possession of such endowments and whereas it is important duty of every Government to provide that all such endowments be applied according to the real intent and will of the grantor, and whereas it is moreover essential to provide for the maintenance and repair of buildings which have been erected either at the expense of the Government or of individuals for the use and convenience of the public and also to establish proper rules for the custody and disposal of Nazul property… the following rules have been erected to be in force …
2. The general superintendence of all lands, granted for the support of Mosques, Hindu Temples, and for other pious and beneficial purposes and of all public buildings such as bridges … and other edifices, is heavily vested in the Board of Revenue.
3. It shall be duty of the Board of Revenue to take care of all endowments made for the maintenance of establishments of the above description and which be duly appropriated to the purpose for which they were destined by Government or individual by whom such endowments were granted.

   In like manner, it shall be the duty of the Board of Revenue to provide with the sanction of the State Government for the due repair and maintenance of all expenses of the former or present Government or of individuals and which either at present are or can conveniently be rendered conducive to the concurrence of the community.

4. In those cases in which any of the buildings in question have fallen to decay, and cannot, from that or other causes be conveniently repaired, or are not calculated if repaired to afford any material accommodation to public, the Board shall recommend that they be sold on public account or otherwise dispose off as may appear most expedient.
5. Under the foregoing rules it will, of course, be incumbent on the Board of Revenue and Board of Commissioners to prevent any lands which have been granted for the support of establishments of the above description from being converted to the private use of individuals or appropriated in any other mode contrary to the intent and will of the donor, and likewise to prevent all edifices from being usurped by individuals and falling into the possession and exclusive use of private persons.
6. Whereas the Board of Revenue and Board of Commissioner may be of opinion that if any of the above-mentioned edifices require repair, they shall obtain the necessary estimates of the expense required for the execution of work and forward them to the State Government for approval.

Appendix-VIII

(EXTRACTS FROM MADRAS REGULATION VII OF 1817)
AD 1817, REGULATION VII

A Regulation for the appropriation of the Rents and Produce of Lands granted for the support of Mosques, Hindu temples and Colleges or other Public Purposes, for the maintenance and repair of bridges, choultries or chuttrums and other public buildings and for the custody and disposal of Escheats, passed by the Governor-in-Council of Fort St. George on 30 November 1817.

1. Whereas considerable endowments have been granted in many or by assignment of land or of the produce or portions of the produce of land by the former Government of this country and the individuals for the support of mosques, Hindu temples, colleges, etc. and for other pious and beneficial purposes, and whereas there are grounds to believe that the produce of such endowments in many instances have been appropriated contrary to the intentions of donors to the perusal of the individuals in immediate charge and possession of such endowments, and whereas it is the duty of Government to provide that all such endowments be applied according to the real will and intent of the grantor and whereas it is more expedient to provide for the maintenance and repair of the bridges and other buildings which have been erected at Government expense or of individuals for the use and convenience of public and also to establish proper rules of custody and disposal of escheat, the Rules have been framed.
2. The general superintendence of all endowments, in land or money granted for the support of mosques, Hindu temples or colleges, or for other pious or beneficial purposes and all public buildings ... is hereby vested in the Board of Revenue.
3. It shall be the duty of the Board of Revenue to take such measures as may be necessary to ensure that all endowments made for maintenance of establishments of the description above-mentioned are duly appropriated to the purpose for which they were destined by the Government or the individuals by whom such endowments were made. In like manner,

it shall be the duty of the Board to provide with the sanction of Government for the due repair and maintenance of all public edifices which have been erected at the expenses either of the former or present Government or of individuals and which either are or can be rendered conducive to the convenience of the community.

4. In those cases, however, in which any of the buildings specified in the preceding section have fallen to decay and cannot be conveniently repaired, or are not calculated, if repaired to afford any material accommodation to the public, the Board of Revenue shall submit (to the State Government) their opinion as to the most expeditious mode of disposing of such buildings and they shall be sold on the public account or otherwise disposed off, as the (State Government) may determine.

Appendix-IX

A list of the Senapur Caves,* commonly called 'Ajanta Caves', describing their present state as found on examination:

Cave No. 1: Dimensions 74′ x 60′ and it has 22 pillars. More than two-thirds of the paintings in it have been destroyed by wasps and swallows' nests and of the remainder only a few retain their colours and the others defaced and faded.

Cave No. 2: Dimensions 63′ x 48′. Pillars 12. Stone figure in good order. The left arm of the large figure was broken. Half of the paintings in it were completely destroyed and some only retained their colours.

Cave No. 3: Dimensions 105′ x 85½′. Pillars 20. The stone images in this cave were in good order, but they were filled with earth and rubbish. There were no paintings.

Cave No. 4: Completely filled up with earth.

Cave No. 5: Two stones. 18 pillars. The right arm of the large stone figure was broken. The upper story was in good order. Dimensions 72′ x 48′ with 14 pillars. Only slight remains of paintings to be seen in it.

Cave No. 6: Dimensions 60′ x 45′. Pillars broken. The right arm of the large stone figure was broken. No painting in it.

Cave No. 7: Completely filled up with earth.

Cave No. 8: Dimensions 46½′x 30′ with 22 pillars, of which 12 were broken. No figure in this cave. The paintings in it were completely destroyed.

Cave No. 9: Dimensions 87′ x 69½′. The cave is partly filled up with earth.

Cave No. 10: Dimensions 36′ x 36′, with four pillars broken. The large stone figure in this cave was also broken.

Cave No. 11: Filled up completely with earth.

Cave No. 12: Dimensions 15′ x 12′. No figure traces of painting in it.

---

* Public, 22 February 1845, No. 10.

Cave No. 13: Dimensions 60′ x 36′ with six pillars broken, partly filled up with earth. No stone figures, nor traces of painting in it.

Cave No. 14: Completely filled up with earth.

Cave No. 15: Dimensions 75′ x 70′ with 6 pillars, of which 5 were broken on the exterior face. There is an inscription but illegible. Many of the paintings are in a faded state.

Cave No. 16: Dimensions 64′ x 60′ with 22 pillars and partly filled up with earth. Slight remains of paintings were perceptible.

Cave No. 17: Dimensions 51′ x 22′ with 17 pillars, one of which was broken. No stone figure in it; slight remains of paintings are only perceptible in it.

Cave No. 18: Dimensions 27′ x 24′ pillars broken, paintings completely destroyed.

Cave No. 19: Dimensions not taken, pillar broken, slight remains of paintings were traceable. The cave was partly filled up with earth.

Cave No. 20: Dimensions 24′ x 15′ with two pillars; paintings completely destroyed.

Cave No. 21: Dimensions 48′ x 43½′ with 12 pillars, 3 of which were broken. Paintings completely destroyed.

Cave No. 22: Dimensions 66′ x 63′ with 4 pillars broken. No stone figure or traces of paintings in it.

Cave No. 23: Dimensions 39′ x 30′ with two pillars broken. One stone figure is lying on one side of the cave and partly buried in earth. A few of the paintings in this cave were in good order and a great deal of earth was collected in it.

Cave No. 24: Dimensions 66′ x 30′ with 30 pillars. No stone figures or paintings in it.

Cave No. 25: Dimensions 42′ x 30′ with pillars broken.

Appendix-X

MEMORANDUM BY PREOFESSOR ORLEBAR*

"As you have desired me to give my opinions to you on the best manner in which you as an artist could best plan out the execution of the design of Government in having delineated antiquities of western India. I must first consider the subject which it seems to embrace.

The whole work appears to divide itself into three parts:

1st – Cave remains – Buddhist and Brahminical.

2nd – Comparatively recent Hindoo Temples and other ancient structures.

3rd – Mussulman remains.

Each of these again may be subdivided into these classes of relative importance so that we may consider nine different classes of work.

1st – The large monastic excavations of Ajunta, Kennery and Jooner and Brahminical excavations of Ellora.

2nd – The Hindoo Cave Temples of Bedamer and Elephanta and more important although small Buddhist excavations (which bear some relative to those of the first class as priories to monasteries) for instance Carli, Nasik, Bearia (Beira) Mhar.

3rd – Numerous Buddhist Cells in Mountains and obscure places and Hindu excavations known as Ambolee in Salsette.

4th – The Hindu temples throughout the country have been but little noticed. They however are rich in sculpture and their architecture correctly delineated and studied will connect the cave with that of the Mussulman period. This would contain the more important buildings as those at Somnath, Palitana and Aboo.

5th – Smaller and less important Hindu Temples and whose antiquity is not doubtful but whose age must be decided by comparisons of drawings from them with one another and those of the fourth class.

* Public, 20 September 1845, No. 65.

6th – Hindu Buildings of more uncertain date, but the sculpture or architecture of which seems deserving of preservation.

7th – The Extensive Mussalman remains at Beejapur and Ahmedabad.

8th – Isolated tombs or Mosques of peculiar interest as the tomb of Auragzeb's daughter at Aurangabad and the tomb at Mohmoodabad near Kaira.

9th – Small tombs scattered over the country many of which contain beautiful architectural work and drawings from which may supply facts to fill up gaps in the history which may be declined from the other two divisions of Mohammedan remains.

xxx xxxx xxxxx

It will be impossible to enter into a detached explanation of the manner in which I would recommend you to proceed with work, without writing almost a pamphlet. I shall therefore be as brief as possible in my reasons and clear as possible explaining my plan.

I would recommend you to commence them according to the period of the year with one of the 1st class, if possible this should be Ajunta.

Ajunta you will find a very difficult work. The object of greatest importance are the frescoe paintings both on account of their historical value and an account of their exposure to destruction. These will find partly buried with earth which has accumulated on the floor and which must be removed in order fully to obtain the idea of the pieces represented for a whole history which seems generally to occupy aside of a square excavation. Buddhist excavations are of two kinds – temples and residences, the latter of which are cut square or oblong, the former are apsidal. On the walls of the latter, I remember nothing but pictures of Boodhs in various costumes and varying ethic characteristics. But on the walls of the former are delineated 'Historic Scenes' which you will have carefully and laboriously to discover and Metre on Evidence to use an untranslatable expression.

The labour referred to consist first in carefully removing from the surface of the frescoe, the innumerable little wasp nests which in many caves have totally destroyed the paintings and secondly in carefully bringing out the colours which are as you may suppose greatly faded.

The importance of well considering the labour which you will have in this unraveling the intention of the original composer will be evident from the following fact. On one wall is represented the siege of a town. This I made out after nearly a whole day dubbing, cleaning, noting and sketching. I sketched off a group which I thought most characteristic of the military tactics, dress and armour of the time for I had but little time to spend on this interesting locality and therefore could do no more but it was quite enough to induce Mr. Wathen to send up a draftsman at his own expense. Of course it could not be expected that a mere draftsman would take the requisite pains. But finding my group pretty well cleaned be copied it, but not taking the necessary trouble instead of a group of human soldiers desperately struggling for honour and country he has made a group of demons fighting in the air. He was made a Myth of history and has I believe with these similar errors quite misled Dr. Bird in his long promised work the idea of which originated in the above little sketch.

I would say that it would be impossible for you to do yourself or the Company Justice in working out the paintings in that one little room in less than a month and anything but a complete work will deceive European literati.

I do not know whether Ajunta would be a safe locality all the year round, but supposing that it would. I could not say less than eighteen months would be adequate to make drawings of all frescoes friezes statuary and architecture. I should think it more likely that three years will be found barely sufficient.

If Ajunta would not be safe all the year, through you would probably find abundance of employment in the neighbourhood in filling up the details of the other classes of antiquities ... some Hindu temples in a hasty ride to Junnar to Ajunta and I feel quite certain that these must be Buddhist temples subordinate to Ajunta along the escarpment of the chandore range of this you will be able to obtain information, but I think that if Ajunta is your first headquarters that neighbourhood should not be left until it is well explored and drawings taken of everything of apparent interest.

Supposing, however, that you could not well remain in one place during the whole year, then you should take some other central position of the 1st, 4th, or 7th class and whilst laboring principally at that should make enquiries about studying any building of the 2nd, 3rd, 5th, 6th, 8th and 9th classes within moderate distances.

The whole country might thus be paralled out into geographical districts, each containing a centre of operation which in order of importance I would thus suggest:

1. Ajunta, 2, Ellora, 3. Kenenery, 4. Junnar
5. Aboo, 6. Palitana, 7. Beejapur, 8. Ahmedabad.

I do not mention this as a complete list but these with their neighbourhoods would give a complete series of Indian antiquities.

Within the limits of Ellora, I would comprehend of the –

4th class, the temple of Shiva in the town of Ellora.
3rd class, the fort of Dowbalabad
8th class, the tomb of Aurangazeb's daughter at Aurangabad.
9th class, thé tomb at Rosa.

Within the limits of Junnar, I would comprehend of the 2nd class Cave Temples of Nasik, Carlie and Bara (Beira).

3rd numerous caves along the Ghats.
6th temple of Rama at Nasik and probably some of the sculptures.

With Peshwa's places would by value to History.

These two examples will, I think, suffice to explain my meaning.

Besides these great centres, there can be many places of secondary importance which would require special visits not being at a convenient distance from any of the centres, for some would throw great light on the present state of the country. For instance, there is a curioius old temple to the Devi of Kolhapur at Devaliyaum, 12 miles north of Satara. Again the caves at Mhar are very much out of the way of anything of primary importance.

The longer you continue at the work, the easier it will become – for both sculpture and architecture will appear in duplicate in many places. The same figures of the Boodhthesuine legends will be found sculptured over and over again.

Supposing, however, that I have not overlooked (as I doubt I have) several important centres of artistic operation in western India, yet allowing an average of four years to each of my districts (which is little enough considering that I allow 3 years to each of my districts, which is little enough considering that I allow 3 years to Ajunta Caves independent of the neighbourhood which I reckon will never be less than double the work), it would take thirty-two years (32 years) to complete the whole independent of the numerous Ceutteirs to which I have referred above.

I would, therefore, suggest that the Government should appoint a competent Committee who should decide for you what centres should be first taken and when you have completed one set of drawings, that is, of one of the first class buildings or caves, they might be sent down for examination to the same Committee and when approved of by them sent to the Court of Directors.

If you like to forward the above to Lieutenant Nash, you are quite welcome and he is at liberty to make any use that he pleases of it. And I shall have much pleasure in giving any explanations which may be desired or in any way to forward so great and so useful a work as that contemplated by the Government."

Appendix-XI

EXTRACTS FROM THE RELIGIOUIS ENDOWMENTS ACT, 1863
ACT NO. XX OF 1863

PASSED BY THE GOVERNOR-GENERAL OF INDIA IN COUNCIL
(Received the assent of the Governor-General on the 10th March 1863)

An Act to enable the Government to divest itself of the management of religious endowments.

Preamble: Whereas it is expedient to relieve the Boards of Revenue and the local agents, in the Presidency of Fort Williams in Bengal and the Presidency of Fort St. George, from the duties imposed on them by Regulation XIX-1810 of Bengal Code (for the due appropriation of the rents and produce of lands granted for the support of Mosques, Hindu Temples, Colleges, and other purposes; for the maintenance and repair of Bridges, Serays, Kuttras, and other public buildings; and for the custody and disposal of Nuzzool Property or Escheats) and Regulation VII-1817 of the Madras Code (for the due appropriation of the rents and produce of lands granted for the support of Mosques, Hindoo Temples and colleges or other public purposes; for the maintenance and repair of Bridges, Choultries, or Chuttrums, and other public buildings; and for the custody and disposal of Escheats), so far as those duties embrace the superintendence of lands granted for the support of Mosque and Hindoo temples and for other religious uses; the appropriation of endowments made for the maintenance of such religious establishment; the repair and preservation of buildings connected therewith, and the appointment of Trustees or Managers thereof; or involve any connexion with the management of such religious establishments; and whereas it is expedient for that purpose to repeal so much of Regulation XIX 1810 of the Bengal Code, and Regulation VII 1817 of the Madras Code, as relate to endowments for the support of Mosques, Hindoo Temples, or other religious purposes; ...

....

Clause (3): In the case of every mosque, temple or other religious establishment to which the provisions of either of the Regulations specified in the preamble of this Act are applicable, and the nomination of the Trustee, Manager, or Superintendent whereof, at any time of the passing of this Act, is vested in, or may be exercised by, the Government or any public Officer; or in which the nomination of such Trustee, Manager, or Superintendent shall be subject to the confirmation of the Government or any public officer, the Local Government shall, as soon as possible after the passing of this Act make special provision as hereinafter provided.

....

Clause(23): Nothing in this Act shall be held to affect the provisions of the Regulations mentioned in this Act, except in so far as they relate to Mosques, Hindoo Temples and other religious establishments; or to prevent the Government from taking such steps as it may deem necessary, under the provisions of the said Regulations, to prevent injury to and preserve buildings remarkable for their antiquity, or for their historical or architectural value, or required for the convenience of the public.

Appendix-XII

MEMORANDUM SUBMITTED BY CUNNINGHAM REGARDING THE LIFE-SIZE STATUES DISCOVERED INSIDE THE DELHI PALACE*

On the information furnished to me by Mr. Cooper, Deputy Commissioner of India, I went to the Palace to inspect the fragments of two human statues in red stone, and of two statues of Elephants in black stone, which had lately been found in clearing away some old buildings inside the area of the Palace walls.

2. The two human Statues which are of lifesize are formed of single blocks of the well-known reddish chocolate colored sandstone of Futtehpore Sikri; one of the heads is missing and the other is separated from the Statue, having been broken at the neck. The head dress is that of a royal personage, such as is seen in the pictures of the Kings of Delhi and such as is now worn by all Rajput Princes. But the figure is certainly that of a Hindu, as the dress is represented with its opening over the right breast. Both figures are squatted in the native fashion. They were probably colored originally to represent the real figures as the spot of the stone are not visible anywhere on the surface, but only at the points of fracture.

3. The Elephant Statues are each formed of many pieces of hard black stone, which were originally built up with thick square bars of wood inside the legs, the pieces being joined together by fine lac. One forefoot measures 6 feet 5 inches in girth, and another measures 6 feet 2 inches. If the height accorded with the well known proportion of twice the girth of the forefoot, these Statues would have been colossal, or not less than 12 feet, but I believe that the legs of these figures as is usual in all Indian Statues of Elephants were made somewhat stouter than nature to obtain actual stability, as well as to give an appearance of sufficient strength. The number of pieces of these Statues is very great and many of them are much injured; but I think that are complete Statue, or very neatly complete, might be built up with a little care and trouble. I recognized the following pieces.

---

* Public Works, April 1863, Nos. 31-33.

1st – **Top of Head** to below the eyes, in 2 pieces, which were joined perpendicularly.

2nd – **End of Trunk**, holding a chain and resting on the ground.

3rd – **Two Ears** – each 3 feet long.

4th – **Piece of Back** towards the rail.

5th – **Piece of Stomach** – hinder portion.

6th – **Several pieces of a Howda**. The chains (which no doubt supported bells) are formed of yellow stone and let into the black stone of the Howda. Similarly, the cotton ropes, which fastened the Howda, are formed of white marble.

7th – There are also several pieces with straight-lined ornamentatioin in white and yellow stone, let into the black stone which I presume must have represented the decorated borders of the Jhul or cloth napping, which is usually embroidered in gold and silver.

8th – A doubtful piece with a deep round socket. This may I think have been part of the jaw for the insertion of a tusk, which would of course have been made of white marble.

4. From this brief account, it is evident that in these broken Statues of men and elephants we possess something quite unique in Indian sculpture. The human figures are of lifesize and although the less of the elephants are rather massive, I believe that their Statues were also of the usual height. Small Statues of elephants are not uncommon and may be seen in many Indian temples; but with one simple exception I am not aware that the Hindu artists have ever attempted so large a piece of sculpture as a full size figure of an elephant. The exception which I refer to was the great elephant Statue which once stood on a pedestal outside of the upper gate of the fort of Gwalior, which was accordingly called Hathiya-Paur or "Elephant Gate": a name which it still bears, although the Statue has long ago disappeared. This Statue was of lifesize, and bore on its back three human figures, namely, Raja Man Singh of Gwalior, with his mahout and his attendant umbrella bearer. Raja Man Singh died during the siege of Gwalior by Ibrahim Lodi. The group was soon afterwards seen by the Emperor Babur who describes it fully in his memoirs. It is afterwards noticed by Abul Fazl in his *Ain-i-Akhari*, written in the 40th year of Akbar's reign and it was last noticed by an English merchant, who visited the Fort of Gwalior in the reign of Shah Jahan. That is was removed during the reign of his son and successor bigoted, Aurangzeb. I have little doubt, as it is omitted in his minute account of Gwalior by Hiraman, a Hindu Munshi, in the employ of Aurangzeb's Mohammedan Governor of the fortress.

5. Now it seems to me possible that the Statues just discovered in Delhi may have been brought from Gwalior, for tradition says that there was formerly second lifesize elephant in the Gujari Mahal at the foot of the fort of Gwalior. That it was usual to remove such objects to Delhi, we have a proof in the case of the brass Statue of a Bull which was obtained by Ibrahim Lodi on his capture of the Badilgarh outwork of the Fort of Gwalior. The brazen Statue according to Ferishta was carried to Delhi, and thrown down before the Bagdad Gate of the city.

6. I know of only one objection to this identification of the Delhi Statues with Man Singh's missing group from Gwalior, namely, the probability that all the Statues would have been formed of the durable light-coloured sandstone of Gwalior. But as a black stone was selected for the elephants, it seems probable that the designer may have purposely made use of the reddish brown sandstone of Futtehpore Sikiri for the human figures for the special purpose of giving the group as nearly as possible the actual colours of real life. This idea is further carried out in the white and yellow marbles of the rapes and chains. It is only a surmise, however, that these Delhi figures may possibly be the very group that once adorned the upper gate of the fortress of Gwalior. Perhaps someone of the three authorities when I have quoted as making mention of

the Statue, may have noticed some peculiarity of colour that may settle this point. I have no means of reference at present in camp and am writing from memory, as I have only a few books with me.

7. But whether these Delhi Statues be identical with the Gwalior Group or not, their value as unique specimens of Indian sculpture is undoubted. I would therefore most earnestly recommend that immediate steps should be taken for their preservation and that an attempt at least should be made to reconstruct one of the elephant statues. If one statue should be found complete or nearly so, it should, of course, be preserved; but even if the fragments should be found insufficient for one statue, I think that an attempt might still be made to complete with the aid of brick and mortar coloured black, if only for the purpose of having the group photographed.

8. Perhaps Lt. Macsween of the Engineers would be able to set up one of these statues at a small expense, say of 50 rupees, in about one fortnight.

Appendix-XIII

INDIAN MUSEUM

ARRANGEMENT OF ARCHAEOLOGICAL REMAINS*

The Archaeological remains belonging to the Indian Museum consist of five distinct classes – the ABORIGINAL, the BUDDHIST, the BRAHMANICAL, and the MUHAMMADAN, each of which should be kept quite separate from the others.

I. ABORIGINAL REMAINS

The ABORIGINAL REMAINS, now in the Museum, consist chiefly of implements of stone and bronze, which take up very little space. But accommodation should be provided for large objects, such as stone coffins, menhirs and few typical specimens of dolmens; many of these are of small size and could be easily transported to Calcutta.

II. BUDDHIST REMAINS

The BUDDHIST REMAINS are not only the most numerous, but they are also the most important class of Indian antiquities. They consist chiefly of sculptures and inscriptions of various dates from the time of Asoka (BC 250), down to the Mohammedan conquest of Bengal in AD 1200. To the earliest period belong the inscription of Asoka from Bairat, and all the great sculptured railway from Bharahut. As the remains of the railing are sufficient to set up one gateway with a portion of railing on each side, complete with pillars, rail-bars and coping, I would recommend that this magnificent work, which is by far the most valuable specimen of Indian art yet discovered, should be erected in the middle of the courtyard of the Museum under a glass-house. This house need not be more than 60 feet in length by 40 feet in breadth, with a height of 35 feet in the centre over the gateway. I have shown the arrangement of the gateway with a portion of railing on each side under a glass shed of these dimensions. To make the place quite accessible in rainy weather, it would be necessary to have two passages leading to it from the verandahs of the courtyard. There

* Home, Public A, August 1876, No. 40.

would be sufficient room in the four corners of this house to display all the remains of the Asoka period which the Museum at present possesses. As the total height of the gateway is about 25 feet, it would be impossible to set up inside the building. I, therefore, strongly recommend the erection of the small glass-house which I have proposed above for the display of this splendid specimen of Indian art. If this cannot be done, the only alternative that I can see is to send the whole of the Bharahut railing to the Indian Museum in London.

The next series of BUDDHIST REMAINS consists of a number of inscribed bases of pillars and of numerous specimens of Buddhist railings from Mathura of the time of the Scythians, or from BC 50 to AD 100. To these may be added a very fine capital with human-headed bulls which I have deposited at Allahabad, and a number of sculptures and inscriptions which I have deposited in the Fort of Agra. A large collection of sculptures of this period has also been made by Mr. Grouse of Mathura, all of which I have reason to believe might be obtained for the Indian Museum.

The third period of Buddhist sculpture is chiefly represented by the large collection which I made at Sarnath, Benaras and presented to the Asiatic Society in 1836. These sculptures range through the whole of the Gupta period from AD 79 to 319 and onwards about AD 600.

The fourth period of Buddhist sculpture is easily represented by the numerous specimens procured in Behar, with a few from Benaras, Sankisa and other places. These range from AD 700 down to AD 1200.

Modern Buddhism is represented only by Tibet, Nepal and Burma. There are several specimens from these countries in the Museum already; but others may easily be procured to complete the series of figures required to illustrate the present forms of worship.

III. JAINA REMAINS

The JAINA REMAINS consist almost entirely of the statues of the 24 Jaina Pontiffs. Some of the Jaina works are difficult to distinguish from those of the later forms of Buddhism; but the chances of confusion are much lessened by the occurrence of the well known Buddhist creed " Ye dharmma" & c., on the latter, and of some easily recognized Jaina symbol on the former.

IV. BRAHMANICAL REMAINS

The BRAHMANICAL REMAINS consist chiefly of sculptures and inscriptions. The latter may be kept together and placed chronologically. But the sculptures should be arranged according to their subjects, of which five principal groups may be formed, namely,

1. General subjects as the TRIMURTI, the NAVARATNA (or nine planets), the ASTASAKTI (or Eight Female Energies) & c.
2. Statues of Brahma, Saraswati & c.
3. Statues of Vishnu, Lakshmi, the Ten Avatars, and bas-reliefs relating to their legends.
4. Statues of Siva, Parbati and Ganesha and bas-reliefs relating to their legends.
5. Sculptures of other subjects, not religious, whether figures, scenes, or simple ornaments.

V. MUHAMMADAN REMAINS

The MUHAMMADAN REMAINS consist chiefly of inscriptions, glazed tile, ornamentation and trellis-work. Each of these should be arranged according to locality as well as according to date; for the workmanship of two distant provinces often differs just as much as that which is separated by two distant dates. Thus, the niggling patterns of the glazed tile-work of Gaur have nothing in common with the bolder pattern of Northern India.

SIMLA
The 21st July 1876

A. CUNNINGHAM, MAJ. GEN.
D.G., Archaeological Survey

Appendix-XIV

EXTRACTS FROM INDIAN TREAURE TROVE ACT, 1878*

INTERPRETATION CLAUSE TREASURE

Section 3. In this Act:

"Treasure" means anything of any value hidden in the soil, or in anything affixed thereto.

Collector

"Collector" means (1) any Revenue Officer in independent charge of a district, and (2) any officer appointed by the Local Government to perform the functions of a Collector under this Act.

Owner

When any person is entitled, under any reservation in an instrument of treasure of any land or thing affixed thereto, to treasure in each such land or thing, he shall, for the purpose of this Act, be deemed to be the owner of such land or thing.

Section 4

Procedure on Finding Treasure Notice by Finder of Treasure

Whenever any treasure exceeding in amount over the value of ten rupees is found, the finder, shall, as soon practicable, give to the Collector notice in writing –

(a) of the nature and amount or approximate value of such treasure;

(b) of the place in which it was found;

* Act No. 6 of 1878, Legislative Department, Legislative A, February 1878, No. 86-137.

(c) of the date of the finding; and either deposit the treasure in the nearest Government Treasury, or give the Collector such security as the Collector thinks fit, to produce the treasure at such time and place as he may from time to time require.

Penalties on the finder failing to give notice, etc.

If a finder of any treasure fails to give notice or does not either make the deposit or give the security required by Section 4, or attempts to alter such treasure so as to conceal its identity, the share of such treasure or the money in lieu thereof to which he would otherwise be entitled, shall vest in His Majesty; and he shall, on conviction before a Magistrate be punished with imprisonment for a term which may extend to one year or with fine, or both.

Appendix-XV

DRAFT RESOLUTION BY THE GOVERNMENT OF INDIA, FINANCIAL DEPARTMENT*

The preservation of ancient monuments of historical or archaeological interest is an essential duty of every civilized Government. The Government of India has received from its predecessors an inheritance of such monuments which, for variety, extent, completeness and beauty, is perhaps unequalled, but certainly unsurpassed, throughout the world. So vast, indeed, has been this inheritance, that the full magnitude of it can only be gradually ascertained: but a few years ago, the first authorities on the subject were of the opinion that only one-half of the remains known to exist had been explored; while the result of the recent excavations at Gandhara and Bharahut indicates the value and variety of the sculpture, the art-treasures, and the pictures of social life in ancient days, which further research is likely to recover from the numberless buried cities of this Empire.

2. The Government of India, moreover, is unhampered by the political necessity of removing from the eyes of the people the memorials of fallen dynasties hostile to its own, and is free from the religious obligation of desecrating or destroying the shrines of any faith not professed by itself. Secure on the basis of unrestricted toleration, it can extend, without fear of misconstruction, its influence and aid to the preservation of all that is historically or archaeologically precious throughout the land, without reference to the character of the monument or to the dynasty or creed in honor of which it was erected.

3. During the earlier period of British administration in India, the establishment of internal tranquility, the organization of Civil Government, and the development of national resources, necessarily engaged primary attention; but the servants of the State were not backward in devoting their leisure to the investigation of local antiquities, and the Government did not refuse its aid in arresting the progress of any decay to which its notice was specially attracted. Of such individual labours, the names of Jones and Colebrook, Tod and Court, Wilson and Prinsep,

* Finance Department, Expenditure (Minor Department), December 1878, No. 571.

Buchanan and Kittoe in Bengal and Northern India, of Mackenzie and Elliot in Madras, and of Sykes, Forbes, Wilson and Bhau Daji in Bombay, will be handed down as illustrious examples; while to the discriminating liberality of the Marquis of Hastings, Lord Amherst, Lord Auckland, Lord Canning and others, some of the most beautiful monuments of Indian antiquity owe their present state of preservation.

4. The necessity of investigating the history and condition of the archaeological remains of India in a systematic manner was formally recognized in 1844 on a representation from the Royal Asiatic Society; and in 1847 the Court of Directors "gave a liberal sanction to certain arrangements for examining, delineating, and recording some of the chief antiquities". Circumstances deprived this endeavour of any very appreciable results; but in 1862 (now Major-General) Cunningham, who as early as 1835 had opened and described Sarnath and its vicinity, was appointed by Lord Canning as the Archaeological Surveyor to the Government of India. During the four subsequent years, this officer made extensive researches, which have been published as Volumes I and II of the Records of the Archaeological Survey of India. In 1867-68 the field of inquiry was extended by instructions to every Local Government to compile lists of all remains or works of art existing in each district and to obtain photographs of them at the expence of the State wherever it was possible to do so. The preparation of these lists has involved great labour, but though not yet complete, they are in an advanced state. Subsequently, four separate parties were organized for Madras, Bombay, Bengal and the Upper Provinces to take casts and photographs of all important ancient buildings, a portion of the expense being defrayed by the Department of Science and Art in London in return for copies to be supplied to them. In 1870, the Secretary of State suggested the expediency of directing the researches in a more systematic and deliberate manner than had been practicable at the outset, and of concentrating in one department the supervision of the entire system. The result was the appointment in 1871 of Major General Cunningham to be Director-General of the Archaeological Survey of India. Major General Cunningham has since been employed with the aid of a competent staff, in the survey of Upper and Central India. Five volumes of his proceedings have already been published; four more are about to issue from the press, while seven others are in various stages of preparation, illustrating and recording the numerous interesting and important discoveries which he and his assistants have been so fortunate as to make. In Bombay the survey has for the last four years been carried on, under the immediate direction of the Local Government, by Mr. J. Burgess, who has published two illustrated volumes of his researches. In Madras, the survey is unfortunately still in abeyance, owing chiefly to difficulties in obtaining competent supervision, which will, it is hoped, soon disappear.

5. Simultaneously, with these efforts of the Government to gauge the extent and ascertain the condition of the archaeological remains of India, private persons have pursued the same object with unremitting zeal and with marked success. During the earlier portion of the century, the Journals of the Asiatic Society of Bengal and of the Royal Asiatic Society with its branches in Bombay and Madras were the chief channels of publicity on the subject, but the increase of general interest in, and acquaintance with, such matters gradually stimulated the issue of independent works. In 1846, Mr. James Fergusson produced his first work on the caves of western India; and in 1848 appeared his *History of Architecture*, which, in its successive enlarged editions, has probably done more than any other individual effort to popularise Indian architecture in both this country and Europe. About the same time, a long series of elaborate treaties has been issued on special subjects or localities, from General Cunningham's *Temple of*

Cashmir and *Bhilsa Topes* to Babu Ranjendralala Mitra's splendid work on Orissa. Photographic art has also been impressed into the service with marked success. The contributions of isolated amateurs and professional enquiries throughout India have afforded to the student opportunities of comparison which are quite invaluable. As regards western India, such works as Mr. Fergusson's *Cave Temples*, Mr. Hope's series on Ahmedabad, Beejapore, Dharwar and Gujarat, Mr. Burgess's Palitana, Junagarh, Elephanta and Southern Mahratta country, have furnished admirable models for the illustration of selected localities by means of photographs specially made for architecture purposes with a good explanatory letter-press. The system thus introduced has been successfully adopted by Captain Cole as regards Cashmir, Delhi and Muttra; and the application of it to other parts of India is all that is now needed for the completion of an adequately instructive literature respecting the architectural remains of this Empire.

6. Upon a review, thus briefly epitomised, of the progress made in archaeological research and record, His Excellency the Governor-General in Council is of the opinion that the measures taken by the State, in furtherance of these objects, will require but little development to render them sufficient for all present purposes, as soon as the Archaeological Survey of Madras has been organized.

7. In the no less important branch of the conservation of monuments, admitted to be worthy of the tenderest and most jealous care, it must, however, be confessed that the progress attained has not been equally satisfactory. The Government of India has not, indeed, been remiss in the issue of instructions generally conducive to this end, or in sanctioning grants for repairs in special cases which have from time to time been brought to its notice. In 1868, all local governments and administrations were instructed to insert in their annual administration reports a chapter on archaeology, and to notice the condition of works of art mentioned in the lists they had been requested to prepare. In 1873, they were reminded of the existing orders, which enjoin due attention to buildings and monuments of historical or architectural interest; and it was then directed that all such monuments "should be cared for as a matter of duty without the intervention of any special order from Government". Analogous instructions have been issued during the present year. These measures have not been altogether without fruit. Many important buildings throughout India have been repaired at the expense of the State, and many more by native gentlemen or communities, under the suggestions of European officers or the general stimulus imparted by reviving interest in the subject. The zeal of Native Chiefs in co-operating for the discovery and preservation of the relics of the ancient art of their country was in 1870 noticed with satisfaction by the Secretary of State for India. But, notwithstanding these encouraging symptoms, it is to be feared that from year to year many monuments of beauty or interest fall into irremediable decay, or premature dissolution, for want of trifling care and timely expenditure; and even that the demand for materials to construct railways, roads and buildings, private as well as public, created by the rapid advance of India in material prosperity, has occasioned the wanton demolition of many more such monuments by their native owners or by European officials.

8. To this general neglect or defacement of ancient monuments, however, a striking exception exists in the judicious conservation of those which belong to the North-West Provinces. The Honourable Sir John Strachey, when Lieutenant-Governor of those Provinces, clearly recognized, and ably discharged, the duty incumbent on those who administer any portion of Her Majesty's Indian Empire, to preserve with reverent care its ancient monuments and historical remains. To him belongs the credit of having founded and set in motion a definite organization for repair

and conservation. His proposals, put forth in a minute of exceptional interest which is herewith republished for general information, resulted in the formation of a separate Engineer's Division of the Public Works Department, "for the preservation of works of art and antiquity in the North-West Provinces", in the appropriation of a sum of Rs. 5,16,239 from Provincial balances towards measures of preservation then urgently required, and in the grant of Rs. 35,000 per annum by the Government of India, from Imperial Funds, to promote the objects in view.

9. But, throughout the rest of India, there is still no satisfactory organization for archaeological conservancy. Such conservancy is, indeed, rendered peculiarly difficult by the enormous number of monuments more or less interesting and important; the absence of any authoritative classification, distinguishing those worth preserving (by greater or minor measures) and indicating who is to be responsible for their preservation; the great expense which really adequate conservation would involve, as also the difficulty of apportioning the burden between Provincial and local resources; and finally, the want of an officer or department specially charged with the duty of perfecting and supervising a system laid down by the Government of India.

10. His Excellency the Governor-General in Council is of opinion that the time has now arrived when the foundation in 1870 of the Archaeological Survey of India, for purposes of research and records, may with advantage be supplemented by the appointment of an officer, with the designation of "Curator of Ancient Monuments", to carry out under the Government of India a general system of conservation. It is essentially necessary that this officer should be under the Government of India, for as was explained by His Excellency in January last, "the preservation of the national antiquities and works of art ought not to be left exclusively to the charge of Local Governments, which may not be always alive to the importance of such a duty. Lieutenant-Governors who combined aesthetic culture with administrative energy are not likely to be very common, and I cannot conceive of any claims upon the administrative, initiative and financial resources of the Supreme Government more essentially Imperial than this one".

In this measure, the Secretary of State has expressed his entire concurrence.

11. The first duty of the Curator will be to scrutinize all lists and accounts of ancient monuments which have been compiled under existing orders, and to procure, by correspondence, and even by personal conference with the Local Governments when necessary, all information which may be wanting in them. He will then classify all the monuments on the following principles.

12. The monuments should, in the first place, be divided (in accordance with the suggestions made in a memorial presented to the Secretary of State in 1873 by an influential body of noblemen and gentlemen) into three classes, viz.,

(a) those which should be kept in permanent good repair;
(b) those the further decay of which should be arrested by the eradication of trees and the exclusion of water from the walls, but which would need only occasional subsequent attention.
(c) those which, from their advanced stage of decay or comparative unimportance, it is impossible or unnecessary to undertake to preserve.

Upon the approval by the Government of India of this classification, the connection of the Curator with class (c) will terminate by his transferring the list of monuments to the Director-General of the Archaeological Secretary, who will collect and record any further particulars which he deems necessary regarding any of them.

13. The monuments placed in classes (a) and (b), respectively, the Curator should then subdivide according to –

I. whether they are in the possession and charge of Government or of private individuals.
II. whether, in the latter event, grants of land or money, and if so of what amount, are held from the State on condition of their maintenance in good repair.
III. whether grants are required or not for annual maintenance or special repair, and if they are, whether the charge ought to be borne by Provincial Funds or by Local and Municipal Funds, or whether the monument is of such imperial importance that it ought to be maintained, wholly or in part, by the Government of India. The propriety and possibility of obtaining contributions from the local chiefs, landowners, or community should also be noted.
IV. whether the monument is of such architectural merit that no repairs or restoration should be effected without the approval of the Government of India, such approval being assumed to be necessary in the large majority of cases falling under class (a) and the more important of those falling under (b).

The classified statement should also indicate the designation of the local authority, whether Collector, Deputy Commissioner or Executive Engineer to be held responsible for attending to and reporting the condition of every monument classed as (a) or (b).

14. In preparing the classification of monuments, the Curator will act in close communication with the Director-General of the Archaeological Survey of India and no final proposition should be made without the concurrence of that officer.

15. The Government of India will consider the classified statement and propositions in communication with the Local Governments, and will be prepared to guarantee to each of the latter a 'minimum' annual contribution in aid of local resources, the amount of which will be fixed for five years and subject to revision at the end of each such period, and will look to those Governments to provide from other sources the rest of the funds which may from time to time be necessary for the preservation of their ancient monuments.

16. His Excellency in Council has every confidence that the Local Governments will cordially co-operate in a matter so directly affecting the national reputation of the governing power, and that the people, if frankly invited to come forward as members of local Committees, will not be found slow to aid in preserving what is most beautiful or venerated in their native land. The Local Governments will be left free to administer all grants and funds, and to effect all executive measures, in the manner they may deem best, subject only to the obligations of notifying to the Government of India in a tabular form all repairs or restorations effected to the monuments consigned to their charge of noticing fully in their administration reports (as required by the orders of 1868), the condition of the classified monuments, and of submitting for previous sanction of that Government all projects for the repair or restoration of monuments with regard to which that course may be prescribed.

17. The Curator of Ancient Monuments will be an officer specially selected for engineering combined with archaeological acquirements, and he will hold the position of an Under Secretary to the Government of India in the Public Works Department. Upon the final sanction of the scheme for any Governments, his duty will be to carry on all correspondence between that Government and the Government of India, to examine the tabular reports of repairs and restorations and to advise and take the orders of the Government of India upon all projects submitted for previous sanction. Regarding sanctions of new expenditure, he will communicate

with the Financial Department. All projects, issues of architectural taste or archaeological knowledge should be submitted by him to a Committee, of which the Members of Council in charge of the Home and Public Works Departments and the Director-General of the Archaeological Survey will be ex-officio members, and to which other persons possessing special qualifications will from time to time be appointed.

18. This announcement of the course which the Government of India have decided on pursuing with reference to ancient monuments would be incomplete without notice of the fact that some of the most beautiful and ancient monuments in India are situated within the territories of Native Princes. In such cases, it will be the duty of the Political Officers accredited to those States to keep the Government of India, through the Curator, periodically informed of the condition of the more important examples, and to make to the chiefs such representations as, after reference to the Foreign Department, may be deemed appropriate. His Excellency the Governor-General in Council, in view of the liberality and enlightenment which as noticed above the chiefs of India have hitherto displayed in such matters, has every confidence that such representations will rarely be needed, and will never fail to elicit adequate response.

Dated 25 August 1875

MINUTE – By the Hon'ble Sir John Strachey – Lt. Governor,* North-West Provinces

In its orders of the 13 February 1873, Public Works Department, the Government of India assigned to the Local Governments the duty of caring for the preservation of all buildings and monuments of historical or architectural interest. In some places in these Provinces, and especially, as I shall notice presently, at Agra, much has been done during the last few years towards removing the reproach which has frequently been thrown upon our Government, that it is allowing admirable works of art to perish from neglect and age, or to be ruined by more active causes of destruction. It cannot be denied that such reproaches have been well deserved, and I desire to see such measures taken as shall render it impossible hereafter that, so far as the North-West Provinces are concerned, they should be repeated.

Everyone knows that there are many buildings in these Provinces which in beauty or in interest can hardly be surpassed in the world. It is very far from complete, and it is not pretended that everything named in it is worthy of preservation, but it will serve to show that the objects which demand attention are very numerous.

Independently of the magnificent architectural works which are to be found at such places as Agra, Sikandra, Fatehpur Sikri, Bindraban and Jaunpur, many of them unhappily in a state of lamentable disrepair and dilapidation, there are scattered, more or less uncared for, over many parts of these Provinces, remains of antiquity, which is the duty of a civilized Government to protect.

It may be stated in general terms that it is only at Agra and at Bindraban that serious measures have hitherto been taken to preserve the ancient buildings from further injury.

At Agra, extensive works of restoration and repair have, during the last few years, been undertaken under the orders of Lord Mayo, of Lord Northbrook, and of my predecessor, Sir William Muir, and they have been actively continued since I became Lieutenant-Governor. The results have, I think, been highly satisfactory. I visited Agra last winter, and I was surprised and delighted with the change from the state of things which existed a few years ago.

---

* Financial Department, Expenditure (Minor Department), December 1878, No. 571 A.

In 1871, the beautiful buildings in the Palace, the Diwan-i-Khas, the Khas Mahal, and the Machi Bhawan were in a ruinous state. In 1873, the Superintending Engineer, writing of the Saman Burj, stated that "nearly every marble was broken more or less, and the verandah and marble roofs are only kept from falling by masonry pillars and props lately put up". The great Hall of Audience, the Diwan-i-Aam, with "its three ranges of arcades of exquisite beauty", was still in the state in which it was described by Mr. Fergusson. It was used "as an arsenal, and reduced to as near a similarity as possible to those in our dockyards". "A brick wall had been run up between its outer colonnades with windows of English architecture, ... and internally, whatever could not be conveniently cut away, was carefully covered up with plaster and white-wash, and hid by stands-of-arms and deal fittings".

The Jahangiri Mahal, described by Mr. Fergusson as the Palace of Akbar, had fallen into a lamentable state of decay. He wrote that "having escaped the fate of so many of the palaces of India, time has only softened, without destroying, the beauty of its features". In 1872, matters had changed very much for the worse. The Superintendent Engineer then reported that the buildings were "rapidly crumbling away; many of the lintels are broken, and are giving way, and unless speedy and judicious measures are taken, there is every probability of this beautiful palace falling entirely into ruins".

A similar story might be told of other fine architectural remains. I remember the time, not many years ago, when even the Taj, although it had not suffered structurally to the same extent as the buildings in the Fort, was in a state that was very far from satisfactory.

Although a great deal remains to be done, the work already accomplished has been excellent, and its execution reflects much credit on Mr. Alexander, the Executive Engineer, on Mr. Haupt, Supervisor, and on the other officers to whom it has been entrusted. I was especially pleased to find how well the fatal error had been avoided of attempting to do too much. As Mr. Keene, whose knowledge and good taste have been of great service, has observed – "No restoration in the suspicious sense of the word has been attempted." When I remember the ruin that has been brought by so-called restorers upon many admirable works of ancient art, I am almost inclined to be thankful for the barbarous neglect with which many of the buildings at Agra and elsewhere were formerly treated.

During the last three years the Diwan-i-Khas, the Khas Mahal, the Saman Burj, and other buildings, have been restored to a condition of more or less complete security against further injury. Much work has been done, and is still going on, for the preservation of the Jahangiri Mahal. The Diwan-i-aim has been opened out; it has ceased to be an armoury, and the disfigurements which Mr. Fergusson described with just indignation have been swept away. The last vestiges of white-wash will soon have disappeared. There still remain near the Diwan-i-Aam some unoccupied gun-sheds and other hideous buildings, which will not, I hope, last much longer.

Great attention has been given to the Taj. The restoration of the eastern façade has been almost completed. The broken marbles of the walls and vaulted openings have been replaced by new slabs, and the renovation of the inlaid work has been steadily going on. The interior of the buildings is now in an almost perfect condition. The great gateway has been repaired, and its pinnacles, which had fallen or been blown down, have been re-erected. Notwithstanding all this, it will take several years of careful and patient labor before the Taj and its surrounding buildings can be placed in a thoroughly safe and satisfactory state.

At Fatehpur Sikri, the arches at the south-each corner of the Dargah, which had shown signs of failure, have been strengthened. I am sorry to say that the great gateway; perhaps the grandest building of its class in existence, is said to require much care. Both at Fatehpur Sikri and at Akbar's tomb at Sikandra, a great deal has to be done.

Since 1871-72, up to 31 March 1875, a little more than one lakh of rupees had been expended on the works to which I have referred. About Rs. 53,000 had been spent on the palace and other buildings in the Agra Fort, and about Rs. 45,000 on the Taj. In 1872-73, the Government of India made an additional grant for these works of Rs. 5,000; and in 1873-74, a further sum of Rs. 50,000 was similarly given. The rest of the funds have been provided from the provincial revenues.

Another work of great interest, which had been undertaken, is the preservation of the temple of Govind Deva at Bindraban. This building, of which Mr. Fergusson has written in terms of high admiration, and which is certainly one of the most magnificent remains of ancient art existing in these Provinces, had fallen into a lamentable condition of decay.

When Mr. Fergusson wrote, "the interior was complete and in perfect preservation", but in 1873 Mr. Growse reported to the Government that "unless immediate steps are taken for its preservation, it will almost certainly be an utter ruin in the course of a few more years". Sir William Muir declared that "it would be a national disgrace if the structure were allowed to fall to pieces". Active measures were taken under his orders to prevent further decay; they have been continued since I became Lieutenant-Governor, and are still going on. The work has been carried on under the skilful superintendence of Mr. Growse, and the acknowledgments of the Government are due to him for the care and the good taste with which he has conducted it. A sum of about Rs. 18,000 has been already expended on this temple; of this amount Rs. 5,000 was given by the Maharajah of Jaipur, and the rest has been furnished from provincial revenues. Considerable further expenditure will be necessary to complete the work.

With the exceptions which I have mentioned, very little has been done for the preservation of works of art and antiquity in these Provinces; and there can be no doubt that many ancient buildings of great beauty and interest are falling rapidly into a worse and worse condition of decay. I may give as examples which have lately come under my own observation, the beautiful Atala Masjid at Jaunpur, and other buildings in the same town which urgently demand attention.

I find a good illustration of the process of destruction which is going on in Mr. Growse's account of what has happened almost under his own them eyes to the temple of Hari Deva at Gobardhan near Muttra. In 1873 Mr. Growse wrote as follows:

"When I came into the district three years ago, the companion temple (Mr. Growse had just mentioned the temple of Gobind Deva at Bindraban) of Hari Deva was perfect, so far as the interior was concerned; from want of a little timely care, the roof – the earliest vaulted roof that the Hindus ever constructed, and therefore of special interest in the history of architecture – has now all fallen in, with the exception of one Compartment."

Mr. Growse has given, in his Memoir on the district of Muttra, the rest of the history.

> While the authorities were considering what ought to be done, a Bania from the neighbouring town of Aring, by name Chhitar Mal, hoping to immortalize himself at a moderate outlay, came to the relief of the temple proprietors, and undertook to do all that was necessary at his own private cost. He has accordingly ruthlessly demolished all that yet remained of the original roof, breaking down at the same time not a little of the curious cornice, and in its place is simply throwing across, from wall to wall, rough and unshapen wooden beams, of which the best that can be said is that they may, for some few years, serve as a protection from the weather. But all that was unique and characteristic in the design has ceased to exist; and thus another of the few pages in the fragmentary annals of Indian architecture has been blotted out for ever.

It is hardly for us, when we remember what Englishmen have done, to throw a stone at Chhitar Mal. We are not, I hope, so barbarous as we were. The time has, I trust, passed for ever in which English gentlemen might have been seen at a picnic at the Taj, seated on the tomb of Shah Jahan, at work with hammer and chisel, and presenting agates and cornelians to the ladies of their acquaintance.* Worse things than this, however, have occurred within my own recollection. I cannot for example forget the vandalism which has ruined the Palace at Delhi. Neither can I forget other facts which show that the danger of further and deliberate destruction can hardly be said with confidence to have passed away. Take, for instance, the almost incredible fact that after the capture of Delhi in 1857, the Jama Masjid, one of the most magnificent buildings in India, had the narrowest possible escape of being razed to the ground. It was Lord Lawrence who saved us from this national disgrace, sanction to which was urged upon him as an act of righteous vengeance for Muhammadan atrocities. Only a few years ago, when I was a Member of Council, I recollect a proposition which came to the Government of India, backed by a great weight of authority, urging the necessity, on sanitary grounds, for cutting off the noble battlements and reducing by I forget how many feet the height of outer wall of the Delhi Fort and Palace, one of the most striking architectural objects in India. It fortunately happened that the opinions of the Doctors, who had declared this measure to be necessary for the maintenance of the health of the troops, were controverted by others of the same profession, who were equally strongly convinced that it was due solely to this wall that malaria of a fatal kind was shut off from the interior of the Fort. This happy conflict of medical theories relieved the Government from what threatened to be a serious difficulty.

I might give instances in which even during the last few years, irreparable injury has been deliberately inflicted on valuable remains of artistic or archaeological interest. I might tell, for example, how the great pillar at Aligarh, called the Koil Minar, erected in AD 1253, to commemorate the victories of Sultan Nasir-ud-din, was completely demolished a few years ago, to make room for some municipal improvements "and for a row of shops which have never yet been let". I might tell another story, unfortunately true, of a zealous district officer, who not long ago actually pulled down the sculptured columns from a well-known temple of great antiquity and extreme beauty, with the object of decorating a temporary triumphal arch through which the Viceroy was to pass!** Stranger stories than this might be told. Within the last few months, cases have come under my notice which have shown me that there are still in India English gentlemen, holding positions which might give practical importance to their opinions, who sympathize with the feelings of the old iconoclasts, and who pride themselves on openly declaring that a Christian Government violates a sacred duty when it helps to preserve the idolatrous monuments of heathen art.

I have, I think, said enough to show that more systematic and more comprehensive measures are required for the protection of our ancient monuments. Until they are taken, it is not possible for the Government of these Provinces properly to discharge the duty which was imposed upon it by the Government of India in the orders of the 15th February 1873, to which I have referred in the first paragraph of this Minute. While I fully acknowledge the excellent work which in particular cases has already been performed, I feel that I have no means at my disposal by

* A late distinguished member of the Civil Service told me that story, and assured me that in his youth, now perhaps 40 years ago, this was a common practice.

** This temple is the famous Arhai-din-ka Jhompra at Ajmer.

which I can secure that general and constant attention to the subject which I consider essential. I now propose the following measures:

I would establish a new division of the Public Works Department, Provincial Branch, which might be termed the "Division for the preservation of works of art and antiquity in the North-West Provinces".

An Executive Engineer specially qualified would be appointed to the charge of this division.

He would be placed directly under the Chief Engineer, and his work would be carried on under the immediate orders of the Lieutenant-Governor, issued through the Chief Engineer.

His first duty would be, in communication with the local authorities, to prepare a list of all works of art and antiquity in the North-West Provinces, and when it was determined which of them deserved preservation, he would proceed to organize the necessary measures. The more important works would be illustrated by plans and architectural drawings or photographs, and these would be accompanied by reports showing any existing means of maintenance in the shape of endowments or otherwise. When necessary, projects would then be prepared to secure the permanent protection of the buildings from the weather and other causes of decay, and for maintaining any establishments required to preserve them from mutilation or disfigurement.

Care would be taken to utilize all existing agency. For instance, I should endeavour, both in the preparation of the lists and in the actual execution of work, to retain the co-operation of officers like Mr. Keene and Mr. Growse, who have already rendered so much assistance.

The headquarters of the Engineer-in-charge of the Division would be at Agra, where he would take over the works now going on with the establishment employed under Mr. Haupt. The Engineer's salary would be Rs. 650, and the ordinary permanent establishment would cost, say, Rs. 500 per mensem.

In regard to the provision of the funds necessary for putting this scheme into operation, I should hope that the Government of India, which has repeatedly expressed a strong interest in the subject, and which has liberally contributed towards the expense of the works which have been in progress at Agra, will consent to relieve the Provincial revenues from at least a portion of the charge. This proposal seems proper on the ground not only that the object is one of national interest, but because when the new system of provincial assignments was established, the necessity of this expenditure was not contemplated. It will be gathered from what I have already said, that nothing could be further from my wish than to undertake any extensive work of structural or decorative restoration. I should look upon this as even more barbarous than doing nothing. What I desire is to preserve what exists. It fallows that I do not wish to incur any great expenditure of money. I think that if, for some years to come, we can continue to spend an amount not much larger than that which we have been spending during the last few years, or about Rs. 70,000 a year, it will be sufficient. Since 1872-73, the Government of India has given us an annual grant of Rs. 5,000. I would ask that this sum be raised to Rs. 35,000, and that the Provincial revenues bear the rest of the charges which might probably amount to an equal sum. The additional amount now asked for is therefore Rs. 30,000 per annum.

In regard to the manner in which I propose to carry out these measures, I have perhaps said enough already. I feel that the danger of doing too much will be one of the most serious dangers to be guarded against. It is often difficult to determine the limits within which the operations necessary for preserving ancient architectural remains should be confined. As a general rule, 'it is clear that there should be no attempt to restore the buildings to what we choose to suppose may have been their original appearance. Our duty is simply one of preservation against further injury. It is only in those rare instances in which it is really impossible to maintain the structural stability of a building without the partial re-construction of its existing features, that any extensive restorations should be attempted'.

I will conclude by quoting some remarks made by Mr. Fergusson on the study of Indian architecture in 1866, and which I believe to be equally true at the present time. I think that the measures which have now been proposed would enable us to take an important step in the direction which he has pointed out:

> I need no apology for concluding by saying that if Indian architecture is worthy of study, it is worthwhile that something should be done to obtain the materials requisite for that purpose; and I do hope that some sort of organization may be got together to collect and bring such representations of Indian buildings as may render the study easy and accessible to all. A good deal has been done lately, but it has been done without system. Those temples only have been photographed which are situated near where some artist with the necessary apparatus happened to reside. Many of the most important are still unrepresented. In no instance except one have they been accompanied with the plans or measurements or descriptions necessary to make them intelligible, without at least a very disproportionate amount of study. By organization all these difficulties might be avoided and with it, I think, the results would be such as would surpass the most sanguine anticipations.
>
> If anything is to be done, it ought to be done quickly, for in a tropical country like that of India, 'decay's effacing fingers' work much more rapidly than in a temperate climate. Vegetation is also an active power, always tending to tear down temples, and destroy the most elaborate buildings.

Mr. Fergusson adds something, which I hope has now ceased to be true, although unhappily it was quite true once, and I quote it as a warning:

"There is a third power," he says, "more perniciously active than either, in the shape of the barrack department, which is fast obliterating beauty in the land. Within the last few years one-half of the Palace at Delhi has been pulled down to make way for a regimental barrack. The Fort of Gwalior has still more recently been handed over to the department. Everywhere, from the causes above mentioned, destruction is stalking over the land; and unless something is done, and done quickly, to perpetuate by representation the forms of those beautiful buildings, it may be too late, and their memory pass away for ever."*

– JOHN STRACHEY

---

* Finance Department, Expenditure (Minor Department), December 1878, No. 571 A.

Appendix-XVI

PRESERVATION OF ANTIQUARIAN REMAINS IN THE N.W.P. AND OUDH*

NO. 924 OF 1879

RESOLUTION

GENERAL DEPARTMENT

DATED NAINITAL, 21 APRIL 1879

OBSERVATIONS

The subject of protecting from injury buildings which are interesting on account of their antiquity, their artistic qualities, or their historical associations is one that has on several occasions engaged the attention of the Government, and no effort has been spared to impress on district officers the necessity of taking adequate measures to secure this desirable object. In the orders (P.W.D., Resolution No. 950 B.R./C dated 6 July 1876), they were directed to prepare complete lists of such buildings and to report what steps were considered necessary for their preservation. A yearly grant is made for the restoration of those structures which are falling into a ruinous condition, or require protection from the ravages of time. Having thus evinced the importance which is attached to the preservation of antiquarian remains, it is with painful surprise that His Honor has read the papers by Mr. H. Rivett-Carnac. If it is still possible that the spoliation and destruction of valuable remains of ancient art can go on with impunity to the extent described; if sculptures and carvings may be removed from old buildings; if such structures as the Sarnath Tope are left to perish for want of a little care and attention; and if the mounds of ruined cities may be excavated and the objects unearthed may be appropriated or destroyed without hindrance or without information reaching the Collector of what has occurred; then it must be

* Home, Revenue and Agriculture, Survey-Archaeology, September 1879, No. 49.

admitted that the orders hitherto issued have failed of their object, or that new dangers have arisen that require to be specially guarded against. The considerations urged in the Chief Engineer's note induce His Honor to believe that the extent of the mischief at Kanauj has been rather exaggerated. The matter is one which requires strict investigation by the district authorities and this will be at once ordered. But even if this should prove on full enquiry to be the case, it is desirable that once for all such arrangements for protecting and preserving the remains of ancient art should be made as will furnish the Government with the assurance that in future the wilful destruction of what it desires to preserve is rendered impossible.

The subject naturally divides itself into two branches:

I. The protection of buildings which are still standing, or the ruins of which are above ground and visible.

II. The preservation of antiquarian remains now buried in the ground, which are discovered in the course of excavation.

In regard to objects of the first class, the duty of district officers is clear; but to prevent any misapprehension, the following instructions are issued for their guidance:

(a) District Officers should at once assure themselves that the list of old structures of interest is complete, and that every object is entered in them which, as a specimen of ancient work, it is desirable to protect.

(b) Definite arrangements should be made for the protection of each work entered in the list.

(c) In some cases, there are special guardians interested in the protection of the buildings, to whose care they may be left. But where there are none, the district officer should endeavour to enlist the services of the principal proprietor or proprietors of the land on which the building or the ruins stand; should impress on them the importance attached by the Government to their preservation and endeavour to obtain from them an arrangement to prevent molestation or injury; the village police should be made to understand that they are responsible for reporting any attempt at spoilation, or the occurrence of anything which is likely to endanger their stability.

(d) There may be special cases in which these measures will not be adequate to prevent mischief and in which the importance of the building may justify some expenditure on the part of the Government for due protection. In each cases, the district officer should submit his recommendation, through the Commissioner, for the orders of the Government.

(e) The more important buildings should be inspected and reported on annually by an officer of the Public Works Department, in order that, if necessary, suitable measures may be taken to prevent their falling into a ruinous condition.

In regard to remains of the second class, other arrangements must be made. His Honor considers that valuable remains of old buildings or objects of art, which are buried in the ground, may properly be held to come within the scope of the definition of treasure, under Act VI of 1878; and that when they are discovered, they ought to be dealt with under the provisions of that Act, as far as they are applicable. It is impossible to catalogue all the places in which excavation is likely to lead to the discovery of interesting remains; but there are certain well known places in many districts, the sites of old ruined cities and buildings, which have this character. A list of such sites should now be prepared and unauthorized excavation should be prohibited and steps taken to prevent it. The proprietors of the soil of the chaukidars of neighbouring villages should be informed of the prohibition and required to give information of any attempts to disregard it. It should be made generally known to the police, the revenue officials and the people generally, that the Government considers it of importance that old works of art, sculptures, inscriptions & c, discovered in excavating the soil, should be reported and preserved, until at least they have been examined by competent persons and further that, if they are found to be of value, a small reward or some mark of the favour of Government will be bestowed on the finder or the informer.

When contracts are given for making excavations for large public works, special care should be taken to remind contractors of their responsibility for reporting the discovery of any such remains and preserving them from injury.

Sd/- C. ROBERTSON,
Secretary, Government of N.W.P.

Appendix-XVII

NOTE ON THE INDUSTRIAL ARTS IN INDIA
By
H.H. Cole*

1. Although influences have been long active tending to deteriorate the original character of Indian ornament, no great attention has been drawn to the subject until within the last few years.

2. Changes have been wrought so gradually that they have received little notice from those whose daily occupations have been to minister to the more urgent and practical wants of this country. It is only by comparing the manufactures of 30 or 40 years ago with those of to-day that a full estimate can be formed of the harm that has been done.

3. Owen Jones, Sir Digley Wyatt, Redgrave, Lubke, Langles, Dr. Royle, Taylor, Forbes Watson and Birdwood have at various times drawn attention to the peculiar merits of indigenous Indian ornament as applied to works of utility, but the first concentrated effort to bring together the facts of the subject as at present known was made when in 1874, the task of compiling a descriptive catalogue of the Indian objects exhibited in the South Kensington Museum fell upon myself.

4. The opportunity I then had of examining both the collections there and at the Indian Museum served to strengthen and stimulate the interest I have always taken in the general subject of Indian architecture and art.

5. As Archaeological Surveyor in the North-West Provinces from 1868 to 1870, my observations were mostly directed to old temples and buildings in Kashmir, at Agra, Delhi and at Sanchi in Central India; but architecture is the parent of industrial ornament, and the latter is often to be valued not alone for its intrinsic beauty but for the interest it possesses in a recognizable architectural origin.

* First Report of Cole on preservation of monuments, Appendix G, xvii-xix.

6. The collections of Indian art in the Indian Museum and at South Kensington are the results of various Exhibitions held in London and abroad. Many of the best specimens of modern art industries that have been collected in this country for the international gatherings of 1851, 1855, 1862, 1867, 1870-74 and 1878, have eventually been secured for one or other of those institutions.

7. From those, it is curious to trace gradual introduction of European forms of ornament which have not ceased to import a debasing and impure character to the ornament and colouring employed in the industrial arts. The degradation has of late and specially since the last Exhibition at Paris, excited much comment; but if the corruption of Indian art by the uncontrolled mixture of styles meets with no approval in Europe, how much more should dissatisfaction and disapproval be felt among those who are in the country, and in whose hands lies the power of rending help?

If the debasement appears in the collections at home, it certainly is much more apparent in the objects daily produced and sold to us in this country.

8. I know of no example so deplorable as the present condition of Aligarh pattery. In former days, this industry was noted for graceful well-modelled shapes. Today it is detestable for its worthless imitation of English jugs covered with vine leaves. I quote this case of Aligarh pottery as collections are displayed for sale at the Railway station at Aligarh and always excite in me feelings of regret at what I consider to be an industry completely ruined.

9. There are, however, many examples of handicraft more or less debased by our western tastes and styles – some so much as to damage the demand for them.

It is often difficult to tell pieces of Delhi from vulgar Birmingham jewellery. The kuft metal work of Gujarat and Siolkot loses its flavour in the application to inkstands, picture frames and small objects, instead of to shields and arms. Carpets are now often woven on designs furnished by tasteless English dealers; embroideries are applied to English instead of Indian fabrics; and the patterns in Kashmir shawls are no longer the so splendid specimens of pure Indian colouring and outline that has made them famous in the years gone by.

10. The importance of helping Indian industries to recover their old characteristics should, I think, be considered in connection not only with the value from an educational point of view, but with the view to a direct benefit which may arise to the craftsmen themselves and ultimately to the Government.

11. The love of decorative art is very much on the increase in Europe, and is diffusing itself all over England. People formerly content to accept anything from India as a mere "curiosity", are now more discriminating as to purity of style. They know something of Hindu forms and mythology and of the exigencies of the Mussalman creed forbidding the imitation of human or animal shapes. A demand may not instantly result from such growing knowledge but in tracing the possible future of Indian arts. The tastes and knowledge of patrons and buyers are worthy of consideration.

12. Museums and art schools have been established in this country but not with any very precise aims as regards Native Art (The schools want ample means and special opportunities for studying Indian art – H.H.C. 18-7-72). To render them of use, they should be accessible and attractive to Natives and well stored with objects of the best indigenous art.

13. Instruction in European styles confuses the Native student and unfits him for the development and advancement of his own craft. With the best wish to adopt our forms, he fails, for want of sympathy and understanding. He reverts, however, with readiness to his own traditional ornament.

14. To bring this back to him requires ample illustrative material, in the collection of which lies the main spring of the power of Government to render assistance. Give a clever workman a good Native pattern and he works willingly and with success; but he is incapable of correctly interpreting European forms.

15. The varieties of ornamental manufactures in India are numerous; some alive, some dying, some dead and some perverted. To revive and preserve can, I think, be best accomplished by taking stock of the best ancient and modern work and making it easy of referee to Natives.

16. I believe that a series of illustrations collected from the best types would not be very difficult or costly to produce. The sources from which they could be obtained are:

(a) architectural flat and carved ornament;
(b) ancient work of industrial art; and
(c) from existing illustrations of varieties of Indian art in English and foreign books on the subject.

17. The drawings published in single plàtes could be purchased by Natives, or in some cases distributed free of cost; schools of art and museums should have on view and for sale a complete set.

18. I believe that a simple process of giving illustrations will accomplish much good, and after it proves itself to be successful, the scope of museums and schools of art may be extended.

19. As an example of where good patterns seem to be wanted, I may mention the case of pottery made at Multan. Two Natives know the secret of making the two shades of blue, by means of which they produce beautiful effects in the limited sphere of their traditional foliation. They apply this with great success to plates, tiles for mosques, vases and c., but they have no access to the thousand varieties of ornamental outline existing in the enrichments of old Hindu and Mohammedan buildings. They also want more knowledge of the old pottery shapes which India can supply from its three corners. Encouragement would extend this industry which does not confine to Multan but is still alive in Sind.

20. There exist throughout India many thousand craftsmen able to produce admirable saleable works in textiles, pottery, metal, wood and stone and I cannot but think that it would be more profitable to encourage these people in industrial pursuits rather than they should be left to labour in the fields.

21. To keep up the interest among work people who still produce good manufactures, the establishment throughout India of industrial order of merit, say a medal or certificate, would be of great good. It would be necessary to show care in the award of such recognitions; but there are many civil and military officers possessed of good taste from whom local judging committees could be formed. The labour to them would alone be a relief in the dull monotony of official work and would excite an interest, not only in India, but amongst their friends in England.

22. To collect the necessary materials for producing illustrations of the best known ancient and modern art industries will require the cooperation of local governments and administrations; but with such assistance and with a small grant from imperial funds, a staff of clever native craftsmen may be organized to carry out the work.

Appendix-XVIII

LIST OF SOME HISTORICAL BRITISH MONUMENTS AND MEMORIALS WORTHY OF PRESERVATION ON ACCOUNT OF THEIR PUBLIC INTEREST DATED 13 JULY 1882*

Prepared by H.H. Cole

BENGAL

1. The Ochterlony monument on the Calcutta maidan; but in 1825 in honour of Sir David Ochterlony. The column is of plastered brick.
2. Pedestrian statue of Lord William Cavendish Bentinck, Governor-General; erected in 1835 in front of the Calcutta Town Hall; bronze.
3. Pedestrian statue of George, Earl of Auckland, Governor-General; erected in 1848; inside the Eden Gardens, Calcutta; bronze.
4. Pedestrian statue of Sir William Peel, Calcutta; white marble.
5. Equestrian statue of Henry, Viscount Hardinge, on the Calcutta maidan; bronze.
6. Equestrian statue of Sir James Outram (by Foley, 1874).
7. Statue of the Marquess of Hastings (in the Dalhousie Institute), Calcutta.
8. Statue of Lord Lawrence, Calcutta.
9. Statue of Lord Mayo, Calcutta.
10. Lady Canning's tomb in Barrackpore Park.
11. Cenotaph in Barrackpore Park, erected by the Earl Minto containing the following mural tablets: to the memory of officers who fell at the conquest of Java, 1810-12; also to the memory of officers who fell at the conquest of the Isle of France 1810; and to the memory of the officers who fell at Maharajpore, 1843.

---

* *First Report of the Curator of Ancient Monuments in India,* 1881-1882, pp. cvi-cxii.

12. Cenotaph close to the Judge's Kutcherry at Bankipore, erected in memory of Major Knox who in 1760 relieved Patna when besieged by the Emperor Shah Alum.
13. Tall stone shaft in Patna city, erected in memory of 48 servants of the East India Company and 100 European soldiers massacred by Mir Kassim Ali, Subedar of Bengal, when the British were marching to the rescue of their countrymen in Patna n 1763. Among the victims were Mr. Ellis (Resident of Patna) and Messrs. Hay and Lushington (Members of Council).
14. Two monuments at Bhagalpur to the memory of Mr. Augustus Cleveland, Collector of Bhagalpur; one of brick, erected by the district landholders, and the second of stone, sent out by the Court of Directors from England.
15. A small cross in the disused burial ground enclosed in the Bhagalpur race course, erected to the memory of officers and men of Her Majesty's 3rd Buffs, interred in 1828.

NORTH-WEST PROVINCES

16. Monument at Aligarh to the memory of officers and men who fell at the taking of Aligarh in 1803.
17. Tomb at Aligarh of Major Robert Nairn, 6th Bengal Cavalry, who fell at the siege of Kutchowra in 1803.
18. Monument at Aligarh to the memory of officers and men who fell during the Mutiny, 1857.
19. Two memorial pillars erected to the memory of the officers who fell at the storming of the Kalinga Fort in 1814, Dehradun.
20. Monument at Fatehgunj near Bareilly to the memory of the officers and men who fell near Fatehganj against the Rohillas in 1794.
21. Tomb of the late Mr. Thomason, Lt. Governor, North-West Provinces in the Churchyard of Christ Church, Bareilly.
22. Tomb of Lt. Governor the Hon'ble John Russell Colvin at the Palace of Agra.
23. At Goverdhun, a massive monolith bearing an inscription setting forth that colonel Seymour, C.B., will punish any soldier who shoots game in the neighbourhood.
24. Monument at Aligarh to the memory of Ensign Marsh and others killed on the Agra and Aligarh road in 1857.
25. Tombs at Shewalaghat, Benaras, of three British officers who were killed in the disturbance of Rajah Cheyt Singh.
26. Memorial cross at Fatehgarh in memory of those who fell during the Mutiny, 1857.
27. Tomb in Cawnpore Memorial Church compound erected to the memory of Major Vibrat and 70 officers and men who escaped from the massacre at Cawnpore in June 1857 and were captured and murdered at Sheorajpur.
28. Tomb near the Cawnpore Church erected by the Memorial Church Committee over the remains of those that were first killed in the entrenchment in June 1857.
29. Well in the Memorial Church compound covered with a stone and inscription.
30. Large stone cross at the barracks, Cawnpore, erected over the well in which those that lost their lives in the entrenchment were buried in 1857.
31. Statue (by Marochetti) and enclosure over the well in the Memorial Gardens, Cawnpore.
32. Memorial at Azamgarh erected to the memory of the officers and men who were killed in the battle of Azamgarh.

33. Mausoleum of Lord Cornwallis at Ghazipur by Flaxman.
34. Monuments at Jhansi in memory of those killed in the Mutiny, 1857.

Oudh, Lucknow

35. The space in front of the Tarawali Kothi, where two parties of Europeans were murdered in 1857; a memorial has been put up to commemorate these massacres almost on the spot where they occurred.
36. On left of "Goosainganj" Road about ¾ mile from "Dilkoosha", and on this side of bridge, over "Pangri" Nullah – Lieutenant Percy C. Smith, 97th Regiment.
37. About fifty yards on the left flank of "Dilkoosha" in an enclosure, Major the Hon'ble Barrington R. Pellew and Ensign L.E. Cooper, 2nd Ballalion, Rifle Brigade.
38. In rear of the General's house, Captain Charles William Mc Donald, 93rd Highlanders; Lt. Lowick Emilius Cooper, 2nd Battalion, Rifle Brigade; Lt. Charles Warden Sergison, 93rd Highlanders, and Charles Evans, 93rd Band.
39. In the "Belatibagh", Captain H. Hutchinson, 9th Royal Lancers, Sergeant S. Newman, 9th Royal Lancers, and Mr. Henry B. Garvey, Acting Mate, Her Majesty's S.S. 'Shannon'.
40. In rear of the right flank of "La Martiniere" – Captain W.S.R. Hodson of Hodson's Horse; Captain L. D'Acosta, 56th Native Infantry.
41. Under a tree on the left of the road going from "La Martiniere" to "wingfield Park Bridge" – Lt. Augustus Otway Mayne, Bengal Artillery.
42. About fifty yards on the left of "Secundrabagh" – Lt. Francis Dobbs, and 5 Privates of 1st Madras Fusiliers.
43. Off the road between "Mushidzadi's Tomb" and the Kaiserbagh – Captain T. Clarke, R.E., Lt. E.P. Brownlow, R.E., Corporal F. Morgan, Lance Corporal J. Davies and 12 Sappers.
44. Dt. "Secundrabagh" bridge on the left bank of "Gumti" – Lt. W.R. Moorsom, 52nd Light Infantry, Deputy Assistant Quarter Master General, 1st Division.
45. About 2½ miles on and close to the left of "Fyzabad" road – Captain W.F. Thyme, 2nd Battalion, Rifle Brigade.
46. About 150 yards off the right of the "Fyzabad" road, at 50 yards beyond the bridge over the "Gokral" Nullah-Charles Sanford, late Captain of the 3rd Bengal Light Cavalry.
47. Old Cantonment Cemetery, 3 miles on the "Sitapur" road to the right – Lt. F.G. MacDonald, Adjutant, 2nd Punjab Cavalry; Lt. H.G. Richards, 3rd Battalion, Rifle Brigade, the Lt. Robert Daly Synge, 90th Light Infantry.
48. About 50 yards to the right of the "Sitapur" road at the 4th milestone, the 46th Regiment Cholera Graveyard – Private W. Aston, 46th Regiment.
49. At the "Musabagh" – Captain T. Wale, 1st Sikh Irregular Cavalry.
50. About ½ mile off the "Malliabad" road between it and "Musabagh" – Major John Griffiths Price, 2nd Dragoon Guards (Queen's Bay).
51. The 97th Regiment Graveyard on the river road, 1 mile from the Fort, Ramiki Darwaza – Sergeant W. Smith and Sergeant G. Smith, 97th Regiment; Assistant Surgeon W. Dumbreck 97th Regiment.
52. Steeple monument on the top of "Hazratganj" near "Kaiserbagh" – Sir Mountstuart Jackson, Bart, Captain Patrick Orr, Lt. G.J.H. Burns, 1st Bombay European Fusiliers, Sergeant – Major Morton; on other side G.P. Carew, Esq., Mr. Greene, Miss Jackson and others, victims of 1857.

53. In the "Alambagh" – Major T. Perrin, Lt. N.G. J.J. Munn, and M. Preston, 90th Light Infantry, Lt. Dundas W. Gordon, Bengal Artillery, Henry Ayton, 84th Regiment, Major-General Sir H. Havelock.
54. Tomb about 3¾ miles off the left side of the "Sitapur road between the 7th and 8th milestones".
55. Old "Murriaon" cemetery and Raman Catholic Cemetery in rear of the "Pussunt" (Revenue or Customes) "Kaiserbagh".
56. Two tomb-looking enclosures – one close to the right side of "Seetapore road", about the 8th milestone, nearly opposite the Traveller's Bunglow; the other on the Artillery side of the road, running between their lines and the Lancers.
57. Lawrence's tomb – Residency.
58. Cross to those who fell in the defence – Residency.
59. Memorial to the faithful sepoys of the Bailey Guard, outside the Bailey Guard.
60. The "Sher Darmaza", where Neill fell.
61. Tomb of Mr. Ravenscroft, murdered at Bhinga, Oudh, 1825.

PUNJAB

62. Mackeson's Obelisk – Peshawar.
63. Bilaspore monument to Captain Showers, four or five hundred yards to the East of Ruttem Ghar, 1-19th Bengal Native Infantry, storming the Malown Heights, 15th April 1815.
64. Also to Lt. Lawtis, R.E., rude tomb of stones; a monument was erected to him in the Cathedral Church of Calcutta.
65. Lt. Thackery, 26th Native Infantry, killed at the siege of Jeytuk; his tomb on the bank of a tank at Nahun. This monument is a lofty pyramid on a pedestal without any inscription; there are three other graves.
66. In front of the Delhi Church is a massive marble cross, sacred to the memory of those who were massacred in May 1857.
67. The Delhi magazine rendered famous by the intrepid Willoughby.
68. John Nicholson's grave in the cemetery, Delhi, facing the Kashmir Gate.
69. Flag-staff Tower, Delhi.
70. The monument on the Ridge, Delhi.
71. Monument and fountain in memory of General John Nicholson, who fell at Delhi, 1857, at Margulla between Rawalpindi and Attock.
72. Memorial monument of the siege of Delhi, 1857, Delhi.
73. Battle-field monument at Mudki, Ferozpur.
74. Battle-field monument at Ferozeshah.
75. Battle-field monument at Sobraon.
76. Tomb of Sir Henry Durand at Dera Ismail Khan.
77. Tomb of Lord Elgin at Dhurmsalla.
78. Monument in memory of those killed at Hissar in 1857.
79. Memorial at Montgomery of Leopold Oliver Fitzhardinge Berkely, Extra Assistant Commissiner, killed in 1857.
80. Monument over the bodies of officers killed at Chatrian, Sirsa District, 1857.
81. Battle-field obelisk at Gujrat.

82. Battle-field obelisk at Chilianunalla, and graves of men who fell in 1849.
83. Battle-field obelisk at Aliwal, Ludhiana.
84. Monument erected in memory of Mr. Vans Agnew and Lt. William Anderson, at Mooltan in the Fort.

MYSORE

85. Equestrian Statue of Lt. General Sir Mark Cubbon Commissiner of Mysore and Coorg (by Marochetti) in front of the Mysore Government Offices, Bangalore, bronze.
86. Cenotaph of the officers who fell at the siege of Bangalore 1792.

BOMBAY

<table>
<tr><td>87. Statue of Sir Charles Forbes.</td><td rowspan="8">In the Town Hall, Bombay</td></tr>
<tr><td>88. Statue of Hon'ble Mountstuart Elphinstone.</td></tr>
<tr><td>89. Statue of Sir John Malcolm.</td></tr>
<tr><td>90. Statue of John, Lord Elphinstone.</td></tr>
<tr><td>91. Sitting statue of Mr. Stephen Babington.</td></tr>
<tr><td>92. Statue of Sir Bartle Frere.</td></tr>
<tr><td>93. Sitting statue of Mr. Charles Norris.</td></tr>
<tr><td>94. Sitting statue of Sir Jamsetjee Jejeebhoy.</td></tr>
</table>

<table>
<tr><td>95. Statue of Lord Cornwalis.</td><td rowspan="2">Garden enclosure of the Elphinstone Circle, Bombay</td></tr>
<tr><td>96. Sitting statue of the Marquis of Wellesley.</td></tr>
</table>

97. Sitting statue of Her Majesty Queen Victoria in the Esplanade, Bombay.
98. Statue of the Prince of Wales.
99. Statue of Prince Albert.
100. Statue of the Hon'ble Jugganath Sunkersett, in the Fort.
101. Statue of Sir Jamsetjee Jejeebhoy, Bart, Jamsetjee Jejeebhoy Hospital, Byculla.
102. Memorial marble tablets of the officers and men who fell in the Afghanistan and Sind campaigns on the walls of the apse and chancel of St. John's Church at Colaba.
103. Old Dutch tombs at Ahmedabad.
104. Monument in the wall of the town of Ahmadnuggur, naming those who fell at the storming of the city in 1803.
105. Monument at Koregaun, near Poona, to the 2nd Bombay Grenadiers.
106. Grave in Kanera of Lord St. Mour, son of the Duke of Somerset, killed in 1865 by a bear at Kirwatty near Yellapur.
107. Grave in Kanara of Lt. Carpendale who died at Yellapur while surveying the Arbyle Ghaut Road.
108. Memorial cross at Poona to Lord Frederick Fitzclarence.
109. Monument at Kawulkad, Kanara, in memory of Lt. John Edgar Leslie, Madras Native Infantry, who died in service on 20th March 1845.
110. Tomb at Murkwad, Kanara, in memory of Lt. Mortlock.
111. Monuments at Aden over the officers and men who fell at the capture of Aden in 1839.
112. Tomb of John Thackeray, Collector and Political Agent, killed at Kittur in 1824, during the insurrection at Kittur in Dharwar.
113. Wooden cross with metal tablet bearing Latin inscription in the "Mula's Ward" of Surat – marks site of ancient capuchin chapel.

114. Oxenden Mausoleum, Surat.
115. Tombs at Surat of Gerald Angier (supposed) Bernard Wyche, F. Breton, H. Gary and B. Harris; former Presidents and merchants of Surat.
116. Tomb of Van Reede, Dutch President of Surat, and other Dutch tombs of same epoch, near the preceding.
117. Tom Coryat's tomb – old European burial ground, Swali, near Surat.
118. Vaux's tomb on right bank of Tapti, not far from its mouth – near Surat.
119. Tomb of Brigadier David Wedderburn, killed at siege of Broach, 1772, near North-Western bastion of Fort Broach.
120. Tomb of Captain William Sempil, killed at Broach, 1803, near the village of Pejalpur, Broach.
121. Tomb of M. Francais Montreaux, a Portuguese Officer, who seems to have taken part in siege of Broach, 1803, near the Preceding.
122. Dutch tombs – about one mile west of Pejalpur, Broach.

SIND

123. Tomb of Edward Cooke, with peculiar inscription, 1743 – Tatta in Sind.
124. Old European burial ground on Bandar Road, Karachi.
125. Napier Obelisk (1853) in memory of Sir Charles Napier – Napier Mole Rod – Karachi.
126. Monument bearing names of officers and men who fell on the battle-field of Miani, Hyderabad, Sind.
127. Monument erected by Sir C. Napier to memory of officers and men, 22nd Regiment, who fell in Sind Campaign – in Government House Grounds, Karachi.

RAJPUTANA

128. Bust and inscription of Ajmer of the late Colonel Sutherland.

CENTRAL PROVINCES

129. Monument and tombs in the Sitabuldi Hill Fort to the memory of officers killed at the battle of Sitabuldi in 1817.

BRITISH BURMA

130. Graves at the Shive-Dagsu Pagoda, Rangoon, of officers and men killed at the storming of the Pagoda in 1852.
131. Graves at the Botatoung Pagoda, Rangoon, of officers and men who fell or died in the second Burmese War, 1852.

ASSAM

132. Memorial at Cherra Punji to the memory of David Scott, B.C.S., Agent to the Governor-General, who died on 20th August 1831.

MADRAS

133. Equestrian statue of General Neill, 1st Madras Fusiliers – Mount Road; bronze.
134. Equestrian statue of Sir Thomas Munro, once Governor of Madras, middle of island; bronze.

135. On the parade ground facing the Council House, stone canopy covering a large pedestrian marble statue of the Marquis of Cornwallis on a marble pedestal, decorated with groups of figures in alto-relievo representing the surrender of the sons and suite of Tippu Sultan.
136. White marble statue of Sir Thomas Munro – Fort Church.
137. Cenotaph to the Marquis of Cornwallis, enclosed by an iron railing cast from the Cannon taken at the siege of Seringapatam, 1799, by the troops under his command – Mount Road.
138. Cenotaph to Colonel Dallrymple – Parade Ground, St. Thomas' Mount.
139. Obelisk in memory of General Sydenham – St. Thomas' Mount.
140. Granite Column to Colonel Noble, C.B., erected by the men of the Horse Artillery – St. Thomas' Mount.
141. A half length marble bust (by chantrey) to Colonel Noble, C.B., placed by the officers, Royal Horse Artillery, in the Church, St. Thomas' Mount.
142. Madras Memorial Hall erected by public subscription in memory of the Madras Presidency not joining in the Sepoy Mutiny of 1857.
143. "Lal Bagh" Seringapatam, a mausoleum built by Tippu Sultan for his father, and in which he also was buried. The folding doors, inlaid with ivory, were the gift of Lord Dalhousie and the mausoleum is supported at Government expense.

Appendix-XIX

AN EXPRESSION OF COLE'S VIEWS ON THE CONSERVATION OF MONUMENTS AS DESIRED BY THE GOVERNOR-GENERAL IN COUNCIL*

22 September 1883

First systematic organization in the North-West Provinces, 1875 by Sir John Strachey

No systematic organization was set on foot until 1875 when Sir John Strachey, a Lieutenant Governor of great exceptional taste, established the Archaeological Division in the North-West Provinces. As I have pointed out at page 10 of the Report for 1882-83, no system could have been better. An Engineer of general ability having been appointed, Sir John Strachey issued instructions after personal and attentive scrutiny of each individual structure. The taste to discern what was necessary directed the operations, which were carried out in a workmanlike manner. Sir John Strachey was succeeded by Sir George Couper who took less interest in monumental preservation, but the foresight of its originator had secured the requisite funds for completing certain definite operations and momentary indifference passed harmlessly.

Localisation necessitates several local architectural references

If local governments and administrations are to 'independently' undertake the worthy maintenance of important monuments, 'each area' should have its Superintending Architect, with the necessary knowledge of Native architecture, as well as an Engineer, to carry out the actual operations, a course involving considerable cost, or there must be a consulting Architect with the Government of India, a course which practically reverts to the present scheme.

Different areas under separate Governments

The areas to be considered are the two great Presidencies, Madras and Bombay; the three Provinces, Bengal, the North-West Provinces and Oudh, and the Punjab; the four Administrations,

---

* Home, Archaeology and Conservation of Ancient Monuments, December 1883, No. 4.

the Central Provinces, Berar, Burma and Assam; and the Native States of Rajputana, Central India, Hyderabad and Mysore.

Objections to working the scheme under many advisors

The separate working of the scheme under many advisors would, independently of cost, possess the following objections:

(a) want of uniformity in remedies throughout India;
(b) want of connection between administrative areas and the areas of architectural styles;
(c) the activity of any one local direction would to a great extent be dependent on the personal taste of the administrative chief;
(d) small areas, such as the Central Provinces, Assam, Mysore & c. would probably be left without any organization.
(e) work in any one area being complete, and the special organization broken up, the interest would be liable to fade away.

Necessity for active steps for conservation admitted

The absolute necessity for active steps being taken for the conservation of many monuments of historical interest is freely admitted in the dispatch of the Secretary of State dated, the 11th November 1880. The 'best practical measures' for the attainment of the object in view were therein considered and the duties of the Curator were defined 'as being to assist in framing a definite scheme, embracing the determination of the monuments which it is most important to secure, with an estimate of the supervising staff and of a moderate expenditure on work, such a scheme to be binding on Local Governments'. It was considered that, for the purposes indicated, the appointment should be limited to three years. The Secretary of State, in his dispatch of the 9th March 1882, again observed that, 'as far as he could see at that time', the arrangements with reference to the Curator's office should be limited to three years.

A scheme binding on Local Governments involves complete surveys

Any scheme to be binding on Local Governments involves a complete survey of monuments with specifications of the requisite remedies. It will be seen from the Annual Reports that a very large amount of work is at present 'untouched', and much work already in hand remains to be completed.

Employment of Curator in 1881

I have endeavoured since January 1881 to make the best use of my time and to promote work in each of the Provincial and Administrative areas. Out of the 428 important places enumerated in the Report for 1882-83, I have visited and have personal knowledge of only 121, being a little over one-fourth the recorded buildings and objects of interest. Of these 121, about one-half have been surveyed or reported on, whilst out of 768 rough field drawings only 437 have been faired out.

Actual operations

As regards actual operations, Mr. Black, Assistant Engineer, has been appointed since December 1882 for work in Madras. Mr. Heath, Executive Engineer, Archaeological Division, N.W.P., has been at work since 1875. Lieut. Abbot, Assistant Engineer has been appointed since November

1882 for work in the Punjab. The Local Governments direct these three officers to prepare their projects in consultation with me, and invite my inspection of their work during actual operations. Major Keith has been temporarily appointed my Assistant for Central India since October 1882 and has worked directly under my orders by request of the Agent to the Governor-General, Mr. Beglar, Executive Engineer has since 1880 been employed at Buddha Gaya and Sasaram in Bengal; but the Local Government has not placed him in communication with me. No special officer has been appointed in Bombay; but I hope the want will be met before long.

Administrations and Native States

No special organizations exist for Central Provinces, Berar, Assam, Rajputana, Hyderabad, Mysore, & c. The system I advocate is to temporarily employ an Engineer for the British districts to carry out such projects as are agreed on and accepted by the Administrations concerned. In the case of Native States, projects can be framed by me for the Political authorities – important structures like the Sanchi Tope can be repaired by a special grant.

No complete scheme ready to be binding on Local Governments & c.

If the work of my office is now discontinued, there is nothing on record to bind Local Governments in respect of two-third of the monuments that it is desirable to maintain in British territory and there would be no survey of monuments in Native States or of buildings in the possession and use of Native Communities, of which two classes of buildings there are 123 entries in the lists of Annual Report for 1882-83. Rajputana, which is specially rich in fine buildings, is under a number of Native Rulers who have agreed to maintain their own ancestral monuments and the Supreme Government has recently determined to induce the Durbars through the British Political official officers to carry out such repairs and remedies as I may recommend to the Agent to the Governor-General. The survey and examination of the Rajputana monuments will alone take several years to complete.

Advantages of concentrating information

In addition to the preparatory surveys and specifications for repairs and remedies, which are at present the initial duties of the Curator under the Supreme Government, the advantages of concentrating information* are as follows:

(a) Economy in having one architectural referee instead of several;
(b) Uniformity in remedies throughout the country is assured.
(c) Continuity in operations is rendered more probable.
(d) Systematic custody throughout the country is constantly advocated.
(e) Attention is invited to monuments in Native States.
(f) The best structures of their class in India are recommended for treatment.
(g) Economical expedients are suggested and experience reaped in one province is made available for the benefit of other provinces.
(h) Indian architecture is recorded and dealt with as a whole, and not illogically, by provincial or political areas;
(i) Illustrations can be produced of the general subject of architecture.

* The Science and Art Department in London is a Central Department under the British Government and has to deal with all kinds of local interests.

Uniformity in treatment necessary

In respect of uniformity, which it is most desirable to secure in the treatment of monuments, a number of incongruous measures have been carried out in various parts of India, which require to be constantly brought to notice. Amongst others I may mention –

1. The modern custom in Madras of periodically whitewashing and painting beautiful stone sculptures in temples.
2. The conversion of a handsome mosque at Bijapur into a dak bunglow.
3. Conversion of the beautiful mosque of Sidi Sayed at Ahmedabad, Bombay, into a mamlatdar's Kacheri.
4. The recent maltreatment by Natives of the Buddhist Caves at Karli.
5. Whitewashing of the handsome palace buildings at Amber for the Viceroy's visit in 1882.
6. Occupation of a beautiful pavilion in the Agra Fort by the Provost Sergeant.
7. Annual whitewashing of Akhar's palace in the Allahabad Fort.

Continuity

In respect of continuity, each set of operations once agreed on should be seen to a logical conclusion. The best arrangement is for some officer to have the time and the means for advising the Government on the subject.

Custody

Systematic custody of the most important examples is best assured by one officer arranging and conferring with local authorities all over India.

Monuments in Native States

As regards Native States, there are two classes of monuments – those which Native Rulers will repair at their own entire cost, and those for which Imperial help in money is required. For the former surveys and specifications suffice; for the latter special arrangements and special grants have to be provided; but it would be impracticable to provide a special officer for each great political division.

Advantage of one architectural referee

In respect of architectural referees for each Local Government, it would be difficult at the present time to find officers who knew their subject thoroughly. Mr. Fergusson and General Cunningham have an extensive knowledge of Indian architecture and archaeology, but very few have their opportunities or their devotion, and no exhaustive work has yet been published by means of which a young officer could master the subject. I feel myself to be only on the threshold, and repairs to no one important building have as yet been completed under my advice. It is, therefore, better in the interests of economy and expediency, to look to one architectural referee instead of to several.

Principal monuments

It is obviously right to repair the best monuments of their class at the outset, but how are those typical examples to be selected without a central aspect of the architecture of the Empire?

Economy

Economical expedients in repairs are important, as the available funds should be made to do the greatest amount of good. Instances are quoted in the Report 1882-83, in which a total savings of over one lakh of rupees was effected in two estimates for renewing the ceilings of two of the Agra palaces. The experience reaped on this occasion was useful in a similar class of repairs in the Daolat Bagh pavilion at Ajmer.

Indian architecture on Imperial subject

It is most important to deal with Indian architecture as a whole. The areas of Buddhist, Jain, Brahminical and Mohammedan styles overlap each other, intermingle, and overrun the provincial and other divisions, and to treat the subject by such divisions would be illogical.

Illustrations

I have, at the Annual Report for 1882-83, touched on the importance of illustrations of Native architecture, firstly, to indicate actual repairs; secondly, as the only means of preserving a knowledge of certain classes of buildings that for various reasons cannot be touched; and, thirdly, as the best means of reviving the knowledge and application of Indian architecture and art. I have been permitted to publish some of the more finished drawings made in my office, and those show what a valuable series can be collected.

Preliminary survey

The 'preliminary survey' with specifications and the 'actual operations' are of course distinct and could be kept distinct. The architectural referee might confine his attention to simply preparing surveys and submitting his plans and reports for the use of the local authorities. This system would have the advantage of providing a number of projects which would be ready to hand when wanted, but to do the work best the executive officer should be in communication with the architectural referee (like an architect and builder in England). It often happens that buildings are so covered with debris and ruin that the executive officer has to first clear them of overgrowth and rubbish before the needful remedies are apparent. Again, progress of work should be watched and modifications suggested when necessary.

Best practical measures

The best practical measures for securing the objects laid down by the Secretary of State are, I submit, as follow:

1. Local Governments and local authorities should be responsible for estimates, expenditure and work.
2. An architectural referee or consulting architect should be with the Government of India to prepare surveys of buildings.
3. This officer should report what buildings in India merit and require remedies, submitting his plans and specifications through the Government of India, and stating when the local circumstances make a grant-in-aid necessary.
4. The detailed estimates should be drawn out by the executive officers of Local Governments and local authorities in unofficial communication with the actual referee as far as the 'work provisions' of the estimates are concerned.

5. The architectural referee should visit works in progress and assist the Local Governments and their local officers with suggestions and experience reaped in other parts of India. His official reports should be submitted to the Government of India for communication to the authorities concerned.

Provision of funds

As regards the provision of funds, it is important that some arrangement should be made to prevent money lapsing. Hurry in spending a grant would often affect the quality of work, which in repairs to monuments of value should be as good as possible.

Return for the outlay

I also respectfully point out that outlay on work of the kind, like grants for educational purposes, produces a return in the improved taste which a revival of ancient Indian art is sure to produce in modern works. An improvement in designs for Indian manufactures would increase their demand, and an increase in trade means a direct benefit to Government.

Appendix-XX

SERVICES OF MAJOR-GENERAL A. CUNNINGHAM, ROYAL ENGINEERS, BENGAL*

I entered the service of the Government of India as a Lieutenant of the Bengal Engineers on 9th June 1831. My first public employment was as Aide-de-camp to the Governor-General, a post which I held for three-half years, from 1836 to 1840.

I served in four separate campaigns as an Engineer, at first with the Sappers, and afterwards as a Field-Engineer.

In 1842-43, I was with an army of 5,000 men employed on a campaign in Bundelkhand for the capture of the rebel Raja of Jaitpur.

In 1843-44, I was with the army of Gwalior, at the battle of Punniar, where I turned the captured guns of the enemy against themselves, as recorded in General Grey's dispatch, dated 30th December 1843, and G.O.G.G. dated 4th January 1844.

In 1845-46, I was with the army of the Sutlej and I was selected by Lord Hardinge to accompany the troops as Political Officer to take charge of Kangra.

In 1848-49, I was with the army of the Punjab, in the battles of Chillianwala and Gujarat. I was again mentioned in the Commander-in-Chief's dispatch, as published in G.O.G.G., dated 1st March 1849, and at the same time I was made a Brevet Major.

I have been three times employed by Government of Kashmir and Ladak.

In 1839, I was sent by the Governor-General through the hills from Simla to Ladak and Kashmir.

In 1846, I was deputed by Government, with Mr. Vans Agnew, to arrange the boundary between the Ladak territories of Kashmir and China.

In 1847, I was again deputed by the Government along with Lieutenant H. Strachey and Dr. Thompson on the same duty. On my return I drew up a detailed account of the Temples of Kashmir and a long report on Ladak. The latter obtained for me from Lord Dalhousie the compliment that I had "well deserved the thanks of Government". After its publication by the Court of Directors I received for it the "honourable mention" of the French Geographical Society.

---

* Home, Archaeology and Conversation of Monuments, September 1885, No. 46.

While I was Executive Engineer of Gwalior, in 1851, I explored in Company with Lieutenant Maisey the ancient Buddhist buildings of the Bhilsa District, and the results were published in my work, entitled "The Bhilsa Topes, or Buddhist Monuments of Central India".

After spending upwards of three years as Executive Engineer of Multan, I was appointed Chief Engineer in Burma by Lord Canning, whose thanks I afterwards received for my administration, and at the end of two years, in 1858, I was promoted to be Chief Engineer of the North-West Provinces.

After attaining my Regimental Colonelcy, in the end of 1861, I resigned the service, and obtained from Lord Canning a new appointment as Archaeological Surveyor. This work I carried on from December 1861 till February 1866. I then returned to England, and towards the end of 1870 I was offered by Lord Mayo the higher appointment of Director-General of the Archaeological Survey of India. This appointment I have now held from December 1870 up to the present time or for more than 14 years.

During my employment as an Archaeologist I have been fortunate in making many interesting and important discoveries. These have been described in the Reports of the Archaeological Survey, which have now reached to 22 volumes, and which will exceed 25 volumes when complete.

I have identified the sites of many of the chief cities and most famous places of ancient India; such as the Rock of Aornos, the city of Tarila, and the fortress of Sangala, all connected with the history of Alexander the Great. In India, I have found the sites of the celebrated cities of Sankisa, Sravasti, and Kausambi, all intimately connected with the history of Buddha. Amongst other discoveries I may mention the Great Stupa of Bharahut, on which most of the principal events of Buddha's life were sculptured and inscribed. I have found three dated inscriptions of King Asoka, and my assistants have brought to light a new Pillar of Asoka and a new text of his Rock Edicts in Bactrian characters, in which the whole of the 12th edict which is wanting in the Shahbazzarhi text, is complete.

I have traced the Gupta style of Architecture in the Temples of the Gupta Kings at Tigowa, Bilsar, Bhitargaon, Kuthera and Deogarh and I have discovered new inscriptions of this powerful dynasty at Eran, Udayagiri and other places.

The illustration of my explorations and discoveries I have published the following works:

1. The Temples of Kashmir
2. The Bhilsa Topes or Buddhist Monuments of Central India.
3. Ladak, physical, statistical and historical.
4. Geography of Ancient India.
5. Coins of Alexander's successors in the east.
6. Corpus Inscriptionum Indicarun, Volume I, Inscriptions of Asoka.
7. Stupa of Bharahut.
8. Book of Indian Eras, with tables for the calculation of dates.

The Stupa of Bharahut was received with great approbation by the learned orientalists of Europe and was very favourably noticed by all the Reviews. At the same time it was proposed, as stated in the TIMES, the ATHENOEUM, the BUILDER and other papers in 1876, to reward me with the distinction of a K.C.S.I., the companionship of the order having already been granted to me in 1871, on the recommendation of Lord Mayo. This reward, however, was withheld at the time, as I was still engaged in the service of Government as the Head of the Archaeological Department.

– MAJOR-GENERAL A. CUNNINGHAM
Director-General
Archaeological Survey of India.

15 February 1885

Appendix-XXI

ARCHAEOLOGY AND CONSERVATION OF ANCIENT MONUMENT BRANCH*

Prior to July 1879, the subject relating to 'Archaeology' was dealt with in the Public Branch of the Home Department. On the Constitution of the Home Revenue and Agricultural Department on 1 July 1879, the subject was taken over by this department in its Survey Branch. The Home, Revenue and Agricultural Department was bifurcated into two separate departments on 6 July 1881, viz., (i) Home Department and (ii) Revenue and Agricultural Department and a new independent Archaeology and Conservation of Ancient Monuments Branch was created under the Home Department to deal with the subject (Home, Public, A, July 1882, No. 157). However, on 13 April 1887, the work relating to this branch was transferred to the Revenue and Agricultural Department and the branch was named as Archaeology Branch (Revenue and Agricultural, Archaeology A, April 1887, No. 1). In 1895, the name of the branch was again changed to Archaeology and Epigraphy Branch. On 1 May 1905, this branch was transferred to the Home Department (Revenue and Agricultural Department, General A, May 1905, Nos. 15-17).

The Education Department was created on 9 December 1910, and the Archaeology and Epigraphy Branch was taken over by this Department (Home, Establishment, A, February 1911, Nos. 246-247). The Education Department was designated as Education and Health Department on 5 August 1921 and Education, Health and Lands Department on 16 April 1923, and the work relating to "Archaeology Epigraphy" was transferred to its Education Branch.

The records on "Archaeology" are indexed under the heads of the following departments:

(i) Prior to 1879 - Home Department
(ii) 1879-1881 - Home, Revenue and Agricultural Department
(iii) 1881-1887 - Home Department
(iv) 1887-1905 - Revenue and Agricultural Department
(v) 1905-1910 - Home Department
(vi) 1910-1921 - Education Department
(vii) 1921-1923 - Education and Health Department
(viii) 1923 onwards - Education, Health and Lands Department

* Guide to the Records in the National Archives of India, Part IV, 1980, pp. 121-122.

Appendix-XXII

P.W.D. CODE, CHAPTER-III, PARAS 74 AND 75 (PAGE 76 VOLUME I OF 1886*)

PARA 74

It is the duty of an Executive Engineer to suggest public improvements and to prepare detailed design for them, as far as he may be able to do so, without permitting any interference with the persecution of those designs or works especially ordered by the superior departmental authority. He is also required to report on, and suggest measures for the protection of any public monument or building of architectural or historical interest which appears likely to fall into decay and he will be responsible for any neglect or destruction which he has failed to report (see also Chapter XI, para 6).

PARA 75

The term "public monument or building of architectural or historical interest" above is intended to include all works of this class, whether public or private property. In the latter case, it will be for the Local Government to decide whether the Government shall take any further steps than those of endeavouring to influence the owners.

CHAPTER XI, PARA 6 (PAGE 253)

All buildings and monuments of historical and architectural interest should be carefully attended to as a matter of duty, and Executive and Superintendent Engineers should keep the Government fully informed as to their condition (see also Chapter III, paras 74 and 75).

---

* Revenue and Agricultural Department, Archaeology B, May 1891, No. 28.

Standing Order No. 52 dated 29 September 1891, P.W.D. Code, Volume III, 3rd Edition*

78 A – The rules to be observed in connection with the preservation of buildings of historical or architectural interest are contained in Chapter III, paras 74 and 75 and Chapter XI, para 6, Volume I, P.W.D. Code.

As it is understood that ancient remains have on certain occasions been destroyed to provide materials for railway works, the attention of all officers employed in the construction and maintenance of Railways, should be specially directed to the necessity of discouraging and prohibiting the destruction of such remains either by their own workmen or by contractors and their agents.

* P.W.D., General, October 1891, No. 155.

Appendix-XXIII*

Abstract of outlay incurred on the preservation of buildings of arcaheological interest by public works department and other public bodies from 1892-93 to 1897-98 (excluding buildings used for public purposes or as residences of government officers).

Province	1892-93	1893-94	1894-95	1895-96	1896-97	1897-98	Total
Rajputana (Ajmer and Merwara)	6,049	6,292	-	-	278	37	12,656
Coorg	1,547	1,928	351	1,510	2,506	2,220	10,062
Central Provinces	-	-	-	288	564	190	1,042
Assam	352	342	350	547	488	314	2,393
Bengal	4,103	726	1,280	3,280	3,629	2,576	15,594
North Western Provinces and Oudh	1,441	8,308	8,,081	15,178	16,285	7,402	56,695
Punjab	8,279	7,311	4,492	5,430	4,452	7,664	37,628
Madras	1,244	9,161	4,934	1,005	779	457	17,580
Bombay	14,291	16,098	14,077	10,715	8,039	3,944	67,164
Total (Rs.)	**37,306**	**50,166**	**33,565**	**37,953**	**37,020**	**24,804**	**2,20,814**

* Department of Revenue and Agriculture, Archaeology B, January 1901, Nos. 6-7.

Appendix-XXIV*

ANCIENT MONUMENTS IN INDIA

SPEECH DELIVERED BY HIS EXCELLENCY THE VICEROY AND GOVERNOR-GENERAL OF INDIA (LORD CURZON) AT A MEETING OF THE BENGAL ASIATIC SOCIETY AT CALCUTTA, ON THE 7th FEBRUARY 1900

I hope that there is nothing inappropriate in my addressing to this Society a few observations upon the duty of Government in respect of ancient buildings in India. The Asiatic Society of Bengal still, I trust, even in these days, when men are said to find no time for scholarship, and when independent study of research seems to have faded out of Indian fashion, retains that interest in archaeology which is so often testified to in its earlier publications, and was promoted by so many of its most illustrious names. Surely here, if anywhere, in this house which enshrines the memorials, and has frequently listened to the wisdom of great scholars and renowned students, it is permissible to recall the recollection of the present generation to a subject that so deeply engaged the attention of your early pioneers, and that must still, even in a breathless age, appeal to the interest of every thoughtful man.

The Preservation of Historic Buildings

In the course of my recent tour, during which I visited some of the most famous sites and beautiful or historic buildings in India, I more than once remarked, in reply to municipal addresses, that I regarded the conservation of ancient monuments as one of the primary obligations of Government. We have a duty to our forerunners, as well as to our contemporaries and to our descendants; nay, our duty to the two latter classes in itself demands the recognition of an obligation to the former, since we are the custodians for our own age of that which has been bequeathed to us by an earlier, and since posterity will rightly blame us if, owing to our neglect,

---

* Proceedings, Department of R&A, A and E, January 1901, pp. 21-27 (Calcutta copy).
Some authors have mentioned that the speech was delivered on 6 February 1900.

they fail to reap the same advantages that we have been privileged to enjoy. Moreover, how can we expect at the hands of futurity any consideration for the productions of our own time – if, indeed, any are worthy of such – unless we have ourselves shown a like respect to the handiwork of our predecessors? This obligation, which I assert and accept on behalf of Government, is one of an even more binding character in India than in many European countries. There abundant private wealth is available for the acquisition or the conservation of that which is frequently private property. Corporations, societies, endowments, trusts provide a vast machinery that relieves the Government of a large portion of its obligation. The historic buildings, the magnificent temples, the inestimable works of art, are invested with a publicity that, to some extent, saves them from the risk of desecration or the encroachments of decay. Here all is different. India is covered with the visible records of vanished dynasties, of forgotten monarchs, of persecuted and sometimes dishonoured creeds. These monuments are, for the most part, though there are notable exceptions, in British territory and on soil belonging to Government. Many of them are in out of the way places, and are liable to the combined ravages of a tropical climate, an exuberant flora, and very often a local and ignorant population, who see only in an ancient building the means of inexpensively raising a modern one for their own convenience. All these circumstances explain the peculiar responsibility that rests upon the Government in India. If there be anyone who says to me that there is no duty devolving upon a Christian Government to preserve the monuments of a pagan art or the sanctuaries of an alien faith, I cannot pause to argue with such a man. Art, and beauty, and the reverence that is owing to all that has evoked human genius or has inspired human faith are independence of creeds, and, in so far as they touch the sphere of religion, are embraced by the common religion of all mankind. Viewed from this standpoint, the rock temple of the Brahmans stands on precisely the same footing as the Buddhist Vihara, and the Muhammadan **Masjid** as the Christian Cathedral. There is no principle of artistic discrimination between the mausoleum of the despot and the sepulcher of the saint. What is beautiful, what tears the mask off the face of the past, and helps us to read its riddles, and to look it in the eyes – these, and not the dogmas of a combative theology, are the principal criteria to which we must look. Much of ancient history, even in an age of great discoveries, still remains mere guess work. It is only slowly being pieced together by the efforts of scholars and by the outcome of research. But the clues are lying everywhere at our hand – in buried cities, in under ciphered inscriptions, in casual coins, in crumbling pillars, and penciled slabs of stone. They supply the data by which we may re-construct the annals of the past, and recall to life the morality, the literature, the politics, the art of a perished age.

The Age of Indian Monuments

Compared with the antiquity of Assyrian or Egyptian, or even of early European, monuments, the age of the majority of Indian monuments is not great. I speak subject to correction, but my impression is that the oldest sculptured monument in India is the Sanchi Tope, the great railing of which cannot possibly be placed before the middle of the third century before Christ, although the top itself may be earlier. At the time the palaces of Chaldaea and Nineveh, the Pyramids and the rock tombs of Egypt, were already thousands of years old. We have no building in India as old as the Parthenon at Athens; the large majority are young compared with the Coliseum at Rome. All the Norman and the majority of the Gothic Cathedrals of England and of Western Europe were already erected before the great era of Moslem architecture in India had begun. The Kutub Minar at Delhi, which is the finest early Muhammadan structure in this country, was built within a century of Westminster Hall in London, which we are far from regarding as an ancient monument. As for the later glories of Arabian architecture at Delhi, at Agra, and at Lahore, the Colleges of Oxford and Cambridge, which we regard in England as the last product of a dying architectural epoch, were already grey when they sprang, white and spotless, from the hands of the masons of Akbar and Shah Jahan; while the Taj Mahal is only one generation older than Wren's Renaissance fabric of modern St. Paul's.

Exotic Antiquities

There is another remarkable feature of the majority of Indian antiquities – of those at any rate that belong to the Musalman epoch – that they do not represent an indigenous genius or an Indian style. They are exotics, imported into this country in the train of conquerors who had learnt their architectural lessons in Persia, in Central Asia, in Arabia, in Afghanistan. More than a thousand years earlier, a foreign influence had exercised scarcely less marked, though more transient, influence upon certain forms of Indian architecture. I allude to the Greek types, which were derived from the Graeco-Bactrian kingdoms, that were founded upon the remains of Alexander's conquests, and which in the centuries immediately preceding the Christian era profoundly affected the art and sculpture of North-West India and the Panjab. Indian sculptures or Indian buildings, however, because they reflect a foreign influence or betray a foreign origin, are not the less, but perhaps the more, interesting to ourselves, who were borne to India upon the crest of a later but similar wave, and who may find in their non-Indian characteristics a reminiscence of forms which we already know in Europe, and of a process of assimilation with which our own archaeological history has rendered as familiar. Indeed, a race like our own, who are themselves foreigners, are in a sense better fitted to guard, with a dispassionate and impartial zeal, the relics of different ages, and of sometimes antagonistic beliefs, than might be the descendants of the warring races or the votaries of the rival creeds. To us, the relics of Hindu and Muhammadan, of Buddhist, Brahman, and Jain, are from the antiquarian, the historical, and the artistic point of view, equally interesting and equally sacred. One does not excite a more vivid, and the other a weaker, emotion. Each represents the glories or the faith of a branch of the human family. Each fills a chapter in Indian history. Each is a part of the heritage which Provindence has committed to the custody of the ruling power.

If, however, the majority of the structural monuments of India – the topes, and temples, the palaces and fortresses, and tombs – be of no exceeding antiquity in the chronology of architecture, and even if the greater number of those at any rate which are well known and visited are not indigenous in origin, it remains true, on the other hand, that is, in the exploration and study of purely Indian remains, in the probing of archaic mounds, in the excavation of old Indian cities, and in the copying and reading of ancient inscriptions, that a good deal of the exploratory work of the archaeologist in India will in future lie. The later pages of Indian history are known to us, and can be ready by all. But a curtain of dark and romantic mystery hangs over the earlier chapters, of which we are only slowly beginning of lift the corners. This also is not less in obligation of Government. Epigraphy should not be set behind research any more than research should be set behind conservation. All are ordered parts of any scientific scheme of antiquarian work. I am not one of those who think that Government can afford to patronize the one and ignore the other. It is, in my judgment, equally our duty to dig and discover, to classify, reproduce, and describe, to copy and decipher, and to cherish and conserve. Of restoration I cannot, on the present occasion, undertake to speak, since the principles of legitimate and artistic restoration require a more detailed analysis than I have time to bestow upon them this evening. But it will be seen from what I have said that my view of the obligations of Government is not grudging, and that my estimate of the work to be done is ample.

The Work of Iconoclasts

If, then the question be asked – How has the British Government hitherto discharged, and how is it now discharging, its task? – what is the answer that must be returned? I may say, in preface, that, were the answer unfavourable, – and I will presently examine that point – we should merely be forging a fresh link in an unbroken historic chain. Every, or nearly every, successive religion that has permeated or overswept this country has vindicated its own fervour at the expense of the rival whom it had dethroned. When the Brahmans went to Ellora, they hacked away the features of all the seated Buddhas in the rock chapels and halls. When Kutub-ud-din commenced, and Altamsh continued, the majestic mosque that flanks the Kutub Minar, it was with the spoil of Hindu temples that they reared the fabric, carefully defacing or besmearing the sculptured Jain images, as they consecrated them to their novel purpose. What part of India did not bear witness to the ruthless vandalism of the great iconoclast Aurangzeb? When we admire his great mosque with its tapering minarets, which are the chief feature of the river front at Benaras, how many of us remember that he tore down the holy Hindu temple of Vishveshwar to furnish the material and to supply the site? Nadir Shah during his short Indian inroad effected a greater spoilation than has probably ever been achieved in so brief a space of time. When the Maratha conquerors overran Northern India, they pitilessly mutilated and wantonly destroyed. When Ranjit Singh built the Golden Temple at Amritsar, he ostentatiously rilled Muhammadan buildings and mosques. Nay, dynasties did not spare their own members, nor religions their own shrines. If a capital or fort or sanctuary was not completed in the lifetime of the builder, there was small chance of its being furnished, – there was a very fair chance of its being despoiled, – by his successor and heir. The environs of Delhi are a wilderness of deserted cities and devastated tombs. Each fresh conqueror, Hindu or Moghal or Pathan, marched, so to speak, to his own immortality over his predecessor's grave. The great Akbar in a more peaceful age first removed the seat of Government from Delhi to Agra, and then built Fatehpur Sikri as a new capital, only to be abandoned by his successor. Jehangir alternated between Delhi and Agra, but preferred Lahore to either. Shah Jahan beautified Agra, and then contemplated a final return to Delhi. Aurangzeb marched away to the south and founded still another capital and was himself buried in territories that now belong to Hyderabad. These successive changes, while they may have reflected little more than a despot's caprice, were yet inimical both to the completion and to the continuous existence of architectural fabrics. The British Government are fortunately exempt from any such promptings, either of religious fanaticism, of restless vanity, or of dynastic and personal pride. But in proportion as they have been unassailed by such temptations, so is their responsibility the greater for inaugurating a new era and for displaying that tolerant and enlightened respect to the treasures of all, which is one of the main lessons that the returning West has been able to teach to the East.

Archaeological Research by English Officials

In the domain of archaeology, as elsewhere, the original example of duty has been set to the Government of India by individual efforts and by private enthusiasm; and only by slow degree has Government, which is at all times and seasons a tardly learner, warmed to its task. The early archaeological researches, conducted by the founders and pioneers of this Society, by Jones, Colebrooke, Wilson, and Prinsep, and by many other *clarum et venerabile nomen,* were in the main literary in character. They consisted in the reconstruction of alphabets, the translation of manuscripts, and the decipherment of inscriptions. Sanskrit scholarship was the academic cult of the hour. How these men laboured is illustrated by the fact that Prinsep and Kittoe both died of overwork at the age of 40. Then flowed an era of research in buildings and monuments, the pen was supplemented by the spade, and, in succession, descriptions, drawings, paintings, engravings, and in later days photographs and casts, gradually revealed to European eyes the precious contents of the unrifled quarries of Hindustan. In this generation of explorers and writers, special honour must be paid to two names, to James Fergusson, whose earliest work was published in 1845, and who was the first to place the examination of Indian architecture upon a scholarly basis, and to General Sir A. Cunningham, who only a few years later was engaged in the first scientific excavation of the Bhilsa Topes. These and other toilers in the same field laboured with a diligence beyond praise; but the work was too great for individual exertion, and much of it remained desultory, fragmentary, and incomplete.

Meanwhile the Government of India was concerned with laying the foundations and extending the borders of a new Empire, and thought little of the relics of old ones. From time to time a Governor-General, in an access of exceptional enlightenment or generosity, spared a little money for the fitful repair of ancient monuments. Lord Minto appointed a Committee to conduct repairs at the Taj. Lord Hastings ordered works at Fatehpur Sikri and Sikandra. Lord Amherst attempted some restoration of the Kutub Minar. Lord Hardinge persuaded the Court of Directors to sanction arrangements for the examination, delineation, and record of some of the chief Indian antiquities. But these spasmodic efforts resulted in the little more than the collection of a few drawings, and the execution of few local and perfunctory repairs. How little the leaven had permeated the lump, and how strongly the barbarian still dominated the aesthetic, in the official mind may be shown by incidents that from time to time occurred.

The Desecration of Historic Buildings

In the days of Lord William Bentinck, the Taj was on the point of being destroyed for the value of its marbles. The same Governor-General sold by auction the marble bath in Shah Jahan's Palace at Agra, which had been torn up by Lord Hastings for a gift to George IV, but has somehow never been dispatched. In the same *regime* a proposal was made to lease the gardens at Sikandra to the Executive Engineer at Agra for the purposes of speculative cultivation. In 1857, after the Mutiny, it was solemnly proposed to raze to the ground the Jama Masjid at Delhi, the noblest ceremonial mosque in the world, and it was only spared at the instance of Sir John Lawrence. As late as 1868, the destruction of the great gateways of the Sanchi Tope was successfully prevented by the same statesman. I have read of a great Muhammadan pillar, over 600 years old, which was demolished at Aligarh, to make room for certain municipal improvements and for the erection of some *banias'* shops, which, when built, were never let. Some of the sculptured columns of the exquisite Hindu-Musalman mosque of Ajmer were pulled down by a zealous officer, to construct a triumphal arch under which the Viceroy of the day was to pass. James Fergusson's books sound one unending note of passionate protest against the barrack builder and the military engineer. I must confess that I think these individuals have been, and, within the more restricted scope now left to them, still are, inveterate sinners. Climb the hill top at Gwalior and see the barracks of the British soldier and the relics, not yet entirely obliterated, of his occupation of the Palace in the Fort. Read in the Delhi guide books of the horrors that have been perpetrated in the interests of regimental barracks and messes and canteens in the fairy-like pavilions and courts and gardens of Shah Jahan. It is not yet thirty years since the Government of India were invited by a number of army doctors to cut off the battlements of the Fort at Delhi, in order to improve the health of the troops, and only desisted from doing so when a rival band of medial doctrinaires appeared upon the scene to urge the retention of the very same battlements, in order to prevent malarial fever from creeping in. At an earlier date, when picnic parties were held in the garden of the Taj, it was not an uncommon thing for the revelers to arm themselves with hammer and chisel, with which they whiled away the afternoon by chipping out fragments of agate and cornelian from the cenotaphs of the Emperor and his lamented Queen. Indeed, when I was at Agra the other day, I found that the marble tomb of Shah Jahan in the lower vault, beneath which his body actually lies, was still destitute of much of its original inlay of which I ordered the restoration.

The Era of Vandalism Not Yet at an End

That the era of vandalism is not yet completely at an end is evident from recent experiences, among which I may include my own. When Fergusson wrote his book, the *Diwan-i-Aam*, or Public Hall of Audience, in the Palace at Delhi was a military arsenal, the outer colonnades of which had been built up with brick arches lightened by English windows. All this was afterwards removed. But when the Prince of Wales came to India in 1876 and held a Darbar in this building, the opportunity was too good to be lost, and a fresh coat of whitewash was plentifully bespattered over the red sandstone pillars and plinths of the Darbar Hall of Aurengzeb. This, too, I hope to get removed. When His Royal Highness was at Agra, and the various pavilions of Shah Jahan's Palace were connected together for the purposes of an evening party and ball, local talent was called in to reproduce the faded paintings on marble and plaster of the Moghal artist two-and-a-half centuries before. The result of their labours is still an eyesore and a regret. When I was at Lahore in April last, I found the exquisite little Moti Masjid, or Pearl Mosque, in the Fort, which was erected by Jehangir exactly three hundred years ago, still used for the profane purpose to which it had been converted by Ranjit Singh, viz., as a Government treasury. The arches were built up with brick work and below the marble floor had been excavated as a cellar for the reception of iron bound chests of rupees. I pleaded for the restoration to its original state of this beautiful little building, which I suppose not one visitor in a hundred to Lahore has ever seen. Ranjit Singh cared nothing for the taste or the trophies of his Muhammadan predecessors, and half a century of British military occupation, with its universal paint pot and the exigencies of the Public Works Engineer, has assisted the melancholy decline. Fortunately, in recent years something has been done to rescue the main buildings of the Moghal Palace from these two insatiable enemies. At Ahmedabad I found the mosque of Sidi Sayed, the pierced stone lattice works of whose demilune windows is one of the glories of India, used as a tahsildar's *kachahari*, and disfigured with plaster partitions and the omnivorous whitewash. I hope to effect the re-conversion of this building. After the conquest of Upper Burma in 1885, the Palace of the Kings at Mandalay, which, although built for the most part of wood, is yet a noble specimen of Burmese art, was converted by our conquering battalions into a club house, a Government office, and a church. By degrees I am engaged in removing these superfluous denizens, with the idea of preserving the building as the monument, not of a dynasty that has vanished never to return, but of an art that, subject to the vicissitudes of fire, earthquake, and decay, is capable of being a joy for ever. There are other sites and fabrics in India upon which I also have my eye, which I shall visit, if possible, during my time, and which I shall hope to rescue from a kindred or a worse fate.

Efforts Made by the Government

These are the gloomy or regrettable features of the picture. On the other hand, there has been, during the last forty years, some sort of sustained effort on the part of Government to recognize its responsibilities and to purge itself of a well merited reproach. This attempt has been accompanied, and sometimes delayed, by disputes as to the rival claims of research and of conservation, and by discussion over the legitimate spheres of action of the Central and the Local Governments. There have been periods of supineness as well as of activity. These have been moments when it has been argued that the State had exhausted its duty or that it possessed no duty at all. There have been persons who thought that, when all the chief monuments were indexed and classified, we might sit down with folded hands and allow them slowly and gracefully to crumble into ruin. There have been others who argued that railways and irrigation did not leave even a modest half lakh of rupees per annum of the requisite establishment to supervise the most glorious galaxy of monuments in the world. Nevertheless, with these interruptions and exceptions, which I hope may never again recur, the progress has been positive, and, on the whole, continuous. It was Lord Canning who first invested archaeological work in this country with permanent Government patronage by constituting, in 1860, the Archaeological Survey of Northern India and by appointing General Cunningham in 1862 to be Archaeological Surveyor to Government. From that period date, the publications of the Archaeological Survey of India, which have at times assumed different forms, and which represent varying degrees of scholarship and merit, constitute, on the whole, a noble mine of information, in which the student has but to delve in order to discover an abundant spoil. For over twenty years General Cunningham continued his labours, of which these publications are the memorial. Meanwhile, orders were issued for the registration and preservation of historical monuments throughout India; local surveys were started in some of the subordinate Governments, the Bombay Survey being placed in the capable hands of Mr. Burgess, who was a worthy follower in the footsteps of Cunningham, and who ultimately succeeded him as Director-General of the Archaeological Survey. Some of the Native States followed the example thus set to them, and either applied for the services of the Government archaeologists or established small departments of their own.

In the provinces, much depended upon the individual tastes or proclivities of the Governor or Lieutenant-Governor, just as at headquarters the strength of the impetus varied with the attitude of successive Viceroyalty. Lord Northbrook, who was always a generous patron of the arts, issued orders in 1873 as to the duties of Local Governments; and in his Viceroyalty Sir John Strachey was the first Lieutenant-Governor to undertake a really noble work of renovation and repair at Agra – a service which is fitly commemorated by a marble slab in the Palace of Shah Jahan. The poetic and imaginative temperament of Lord Lytton could not be deaf to a similar appeal. Holding that no claim upon the initiative and resources of the Supreme Government was more essentially Imperial than the preservation of national antiquities, he contributed in 1879 a sum of Rs3¾ lakhs to the restoration of buildings in the North-West Provinces; and proposed the appointment of a special officer, to be entitled the Curator of Ancient Monuments, which, while it did not receive sanction in his time, was left to be carried out by his successor, Lord Ripon. During the three years that Major Cole held this post from 1880 to 1883, much excellent work in respect both of reports and classification was done; and large sums of money were given by the Government of India, *inter alia,* for repairs in the Gwalior Fort and at Sanchi Tope. But at the end of this time succeeded a period of some reaction, in which it appeared to be thought that the task of the Central Government, in the preparation of surveys and lists, was drawing to a close, and that Local Governments might, in future, be safely entrusted with the more modest, but, I may add, not less critical, duty of conservation. More recently, under Lord Elgin's auspices, the archaeological work of Government has been placed upon a more definite basis. The entire country has been divided into a number of circles, each with a surveyor of its own, and, while the establishment is regarded as an Imperial charge, the work is placed under local control and receives such financial backing as the resources of the Local Governments or the sympathies of individual Governors may be able to give it. In the North-West Provinces, where I was recently touring, I found Sir A. MacDonell worthily sustaining in point of generous and discriminating sympathy, the traditions that were created by Sir John Strachey.

For my part I feel far from clear that the Government might not do a good deal more than it is now doing, or than it has hitherto consented to do. I certainly cannot look forward to a time at which either the obligations of the State will have become exhausted, or at which archaeological research and conservation in this country can dispense with the Government's direction and control. I see fruitful fields of labour still unexplored, bad blunders still to be corrected, gaping omissions to be supplied, plentiful opportunities for patient renovation and scholarly research. In my opinion, the tax-payers of this country are in the last degree unlikely to resent a somewhat higher expenditure – and, after all, a few thousand rupees go a long way in archaeological work, and the total outlay is exceedingly small – upon objects in which I believe them to be as keenly interested as we are ourselves. I hope to assert more definitely during my time the Imperial responsibility of Government in respect of Indian antiquities, to inaugurate or to persuade a more liberal attitude on the part of those with whom it rests to provide the means, and to be a faithful guardian of the priceless treasure-house of art and learning that has, for a few years at any rate, been committed to my charge.

Appendix-XXV*

TESTIMONIAL-MARSHALL

14, ALLEYN PARK
WEST DULWICH
30 SEPTEMBER 1901

Dear Sir Edward Thompson,

I enclose copies of one or two testimonial which were written for me some time ago when I was thanking of applying for the professorship of Greek at Sydney University. Since that time I have worked in Greece, Southern Turkey and Crete – in the general exploration of the eastern half of that island. Perhaps a direct record of my Cambridge Career is of more avail to you than testimonials; I therefore append it:

Senior scholar, King's College, Cambridge, 1894
Porson University, Prizeman
First Class Classical Tripos.
Undergraduate Scholar, King's College
First Class Archaeological Tripos, Part II.
Student at British School of Athens
Prendergast Fellowship for Greek, Cambridge
Cravan student for Archaeology.

– J.H. Marshall

Sir Edward Thompson
Director, British Museum

* Department of Revenue and Agriculture A, May 1902, 1-6.

1. From Professor W. Ridgeway, Professor of Archaeology in the University of Cambridge; Fellow of Gonwille and Caivs College; late Professor of Greek in Queen's College, Cork; Author of "The Origin of Metallic Currency", etc.

FEN DITTON
CAMBRIDGE

I have very great pleasure in testifying to the great ability and attainments of Mr. J.H. Marshall, B.A. of King's College, Cambridge. Mr. Marshall was my pupil during the whole of one academic year and I have therefore had every opportunity of forming an opinion of his intellectual range. He is an admirable young scholar, bright, enthusiastic for his subjects, independent in thought and self-reliant. These fine natural qualities are equipped with a very wide range of knowledge; he has read both widely and wisely. He has studied classical Archaeology in Greece itself and at the present moment is the holder of the Prendergast Traveling Fellowship.

Mr. Marshall's university career is a sufficient proof of his training in all the accuracy of verbal scholarship which is a distinctive feature of Cambridge.

As he is thus a good linguistic scholar and at the same time is deeply interested in the history and literature of the ancient authors, he will be a most admirable addition to the staff of any university of college. I look forward to seeing Mr. Marshall producing original work in classicial Archaeology of a very high order. May I add that I found Mr. Marshall a most pleasant pupil and I am of the opinion that he would make an equally pleasant colleague.

– WILLIAM RIDGEWAY

---

2. From D.G. Hogarth, M.A., Fellow of Magdalen College, Oxford, late Director of British School of Archaeology at Athens. Author of "Devia Cypria", "Philip and Alexander", etc.

23, Alexander Square, S.W.
October 27, 1900.

Sirs,

Mr. J.H. Marshall was a student of the British School at Athens in 1898-99 and there showed great sympathy with, and grasp of, Greek Archaeology on all its sides. Indeed, his promise there was superior to that of any other student of the year and fully prepared me for his subsequent brilliant performance at Cambridge.

As to his pure scholarship his university tutors will speak but so far as I had opportunity of judging it was very great.

– D.G. HOGARTH

Appendix-XXVI

P.W.D. CODE*

Chapter III, Para 318-300, pp. 101

It is the duty of an Executive Engineer to suggest public improvements and to prepare derailed designs for them as far as he may be able to do so without permitting any interference with the prosecution of those designs or works specially ordered by superior departmental authority. He is also required to report on, and suggest measures for the protection of any public monument or building of architectural or historical interest, which appears likely to fall into decay and he will be responsible for any neglect or destruction; which he has failed to report.

Chapter III, Para 319-301, pp. 101

The term "public monument or building of architectural or historical interest", above is intended to include all works of this class whether public or private property. In the latter case, it will be for the Local Government to decide whether the Government shall take any further steps than those of endeavouring to influence the owners.

Chapter X, Para 1046-897, pp. 288-289

All buildings and monuments of historical or architectural interest should be carefully attended to and it will be the duty of Executive Engineers to arrange for a systematic annual or even more frequent inspection of the monuments in their divisions and of all Executive and Superintending Engineers to keep the Government fully informed as to the condition of those monuments and to prepare estimates for the repair. It will be the duty of the Archaeological Officers:

* P.W.D. Code, 1907, Volume No. 1.

1. To advise on the proposal for conservation or restoration works submitted by the officers of the Public Works Department and to recommend the order of precedence in which these as well as any works suggested by themselves should be undertaken.
2. To submit proposals for the conservation or repair of ancient buildings of interest requiring preservation which have come to their own notice during their tours. This work should be carried out PARI PASSU with the preparation of the list of remains referred to in the Government of India, Department of Revenue and Agriculture Circular No. 12-28, Archaeology dated 24 August 1891 where these have not yet been completed and should not await their final completion.
3. To pass plan and estimates for all works of conservation and repair whether suggested by himself or by the Public Works Department. It will not be the duty of the Archaeological officer to criticize rates but to approve and advise on the character of the works to be carried out.
4. To assist in the supervision of the works of conservation while they are in progress. The degree of assistance required must depend upon the nature and importance of the work. It will be the duty of the Archaeological officer to assist the Engineer with his advice and to bring to the notice of the proper authority any alterations or repairs, which in his opinion are likely to effect the architectural or historical interest of the buildings.

N.B.

Towards 1907, John Marshall prepared guidelines for those entrusted with the responsibility of conservation and repair of ancient monuments. The guidelines in the form of a pamphlet entitled "CONSERVATION OF ANCIENT MONUMENTS" was also got published in 1907 by Marshall. This pamphlet, according to Marshall, would aid in rehabilitating the monuments in an authentic way. He was of the opinion that the authentic specimens of monuments was to be collected and utilized towards execution of repair work rather than "rebuild or renew them; and not so much to add new work in imitation of what the original is thought to have been, as to preserve what is left of it".

For carrying out the conservation work, Marshall emphasized the need of selection of monuments for conservation and its history, and architectural details should be documented. He also laid stress on the preparation of estimates for repair and conservation.

The pamphlet also contained guidelines for the preservation of remnants of the monuments before the repair work was effected. Besides, guidelines also emphasized the "replacement of missing architectural details". The pamphlet also contained instructions with regard to effacement of traces of old designs, new stone work, roofs and walls, cement and pointing, brickwork, clamps and dowels, broken lintels, plaster stucco details, carvings, weather stains, images, whitewash, decorative tile work wooden buildings, etc.

Marshall also laid stress on sprucing up of the premises of monuments after completion of its repair works. The pamphlet concluded with instructions to this effect: "No mortar wheels, mortar heaps, brickbats and the like should be left behind."

Appendix-XXVII

THE ANCIENT MONUMENTS PRESERVATION ACT, 1904 (VII OF 1904)*

PASSED BY THE GOVERNOR-GENERAL OF INDIA IN COUNCIL (RECEIVED THE ASSENT OF THE GOVERNOR-GENERAL ON THE 18th MARCH 1904)

An Act to provide for the preservation of Ancient Monuments and of objects of archaeological, historical or artistic interest.

WHEREAS it is expedient to provide for the preservation of ancient monuments, for the exercise of control over traffic in antiquities and over excavation in certain places, and for the protection and acquisition in certain cases of ancient monuments and of objects of archaeological, historical or artistic interest; It is hereby enacted as follows:

Short Title and Extent

1. (i) This Act may be called the Ancient Monuments Preservation Act, 1904.
   (ii) It extends to the whole of British India, inclusive of British Baluchistan, the Sonthal Parganas and the Pargana of Spiti.

Definitions

2. In this Act, unless there is anything repugnant in the subject or context, –
   (i) "ancient monument" means any structure, erection or monument, or any tumulus or place of interment, or any cave, rock-sculpture, inscription or monolith, which is of historical, archaeological or artistic interest, or any remains thereof, and includes –
   (a) The site of an ancient monument;
   (b) such portion of land adjoining the site of an ancient monument as may be required for fencing or covering in or otherwise preserving such monument; and;
   (c) the means of access to and convenient inspection of an ancient monument.

* Legislative Department, Proceedings, March 1904, Nos. 104-150 – Appendix A 130.

(ii) "antiquities" include any moveable objects which the Government by reason of their historical or archaeological associations, may think it necessary to protect against injury, removal or dispersion:

(iii) "Commissioner" includes any officer authorized by the Local Government to perform the duties of a Commissioner under this Act:

(iv) "maintain" and "maintenance" include the fencing, covering in, repairing, restoring and cleansing of a protected monument, and to doing of any act which may be necessary for the purpose of maintaining a protected monument or of securing convenient access thereto:

(v) "land" includes a revenue-free estate, a revenue-paying estate, and a permanent transferable tenure, whether such estate or tenure be subject to encumbrances or not; and

(vi) "owner" includes a joint owner invested with powers of management on behalf of himself and other joint owners, and any manager or trustee exercising powers of management over an ancient monument, and the successor in title of any such owner and the successor in office of any such manager or trustee:

Provided that nothing in this Act shall be deemed to extend the powers which may lawfully be exercised by such manager or trustee.

Protected Monuments

3. (i) The Local Government may, by notification in the local official Gazette, declare an ancient monument to be protected monument within the meaning of this Act.

(ii) A copy of every notification published under sub-section (1) shall be fixed up in a conspicuous place on or near the monument, together with an intimation that any objections to the issue of the notification received by the Local Government within one month from the date, when it is so fixed up will be taken into consideration.

(iii) On the expiry of the said period of one month, the Local Government, after considering the objections, if any, shall confirm or withdraw the notification.

(iv) A notification published under this section shall, unless and until it is withdrawn, be conclusive evidence of the fact that the monument to which it relates is an ancient monument within the meaning of this Act.

ANCIENT MONUMENTS

Acquisition of Rights in or Guardianship of an Ancient Monument

4. (i) The Collector, with the sanction of the Local Government, may purchase or take a lease of any protected monument.

(ii) The Collector, with the like sanction, may accept a gift or bequest of any protected monument.

(iii) The owner of any protected monument may, by written instrument, constitute the Commissioner the guardian of the monument and the Commissioner may, with the sanction of the Local Government, accept such guardianship.

(iv) When the Commissioner has accepted the guardianship of a monument under sub-section (3), the owner shall, except as expressly provided in this Act, have the same estate, right, title and interest in and to the monument as if the Commissioner had not been constituted guardian thereof.

(v) When the Commissioner has accepted the guardianship of a monument under sub-section (3), the provisions of this Act relating to agreements executed under section 5 shall apply to the written instrument executed under the said sub-section.

(vi) Where a protected monument is without an owner, the Commissioner may assume the guardianship of the monument.

Preservation of Ancient Monument by Agreement

5. (i) The Collector may, with the previous sanction of the Local Government, propose to the owner to enter into an agreement with the Secretary of State for India in Council for the preservation of any protected monument in his district.

(ii) An agreement under this section may provide for the following matters, or for such of them as it may be found expedient to include in the agreement:

(a) the maintenance of the monument;

(b) the custody of the monument, and the duties of any person who may be employed to watch it;

(c) the restriction of the owner's right to destroy, remove, alter or deface the monument or to build on or near the site of the monument;

(d) the facilities of access to be permitted to the public or to any portion of the public and to persons deputed by the owner or the Collector to inspect or maintain the monument;

(e) the notice to be given to the Government in case the land on which the monument is situated is offered for sale by the owner, and the right to be reserved to the Government to purchase such land, or any specified portion of such land, at its market value;

(f) the payment of any expenses incurred by the owner or by the Government in connection with the preservation of the monument;

(g) the proprietary or other rights which are to vest in His Majesty in respect of the monument when any expenses are incurred by the Government in connection with the preservation of the monument.

(h) the appointment of an authority of decide any dispute arising out of the agreement; and

(i) any matter connected with the preservation of the monument which is a proper subject of agreement between the owner and the Government.

(iii) An agreement under this section may be executed by the Collector on behalf of the Secretary of State for India in Council, but shall not be so executed until it has been approved by the Local Government.

(iv) The terms of an agreement under this section may be altered from time to time with the sanction of the Local Government and with the consent of the owner.

(v) With the previous sanction of the Local Government, the Collector may terminate an agreement under this section or by giving six months' notice in writing to the owner.

(vi) The owner may terminate an agreement under this section on giving six months' notice to the Collector.

(vii) An agreement under this section shall be binding on any person claiming to be owner of the monument to which it relates, through or under a party by whom or on whose behalf the agreement was executed.

(viii) Any rights acquired by the Government in respect of expences incurred in protecting or preserving a monument shall not be affected by the termination of an agreement under this section.

Owners under Disability or Not in Possession

6. (i) If the owner is unable, by reason of infancy or other disability, to act for himself, the person legally competent to act on his behalf may exercise the powers conferred upon the owner by section 5.
   (ii) In the case of village-property, the headman or other village-officer exercising powers of management over such property may exercise the powers conferred upon an owner by section 5.
   (iii) Nothing in this section shall be deemed to empower any person not being of the same religion as the persons on whose behalf he is acting to make or execute an agreement relating to a protected monument, which or any part of which is periodically used for the religious worship or observances of that religion.

Enforcement of Agreement

7. (i) If the Collector apprehends that the owner or occupier of a monument intends to destroy, remove, alter, deface, or imperil the monument or to build on or near the site thereof in contravention of the terms of an agreement for its preservation under section 5, the Collector may make an order prohibiting any such contravention of the agreement.
   (ii) If an owner or other person who is bound by an agreement for the preservation or maintenance of a monument under section 5 refuses to do any act which is in the opinion of the Collector necessary to such preservation or maintenance, or neglects to do any such act within such reasonable time as may be fixed by the Collector, the Collector may authorize any person to do any such act, and the expense of doing any such act or such portion of the expense as the owner may be liable to pay under the agreement may be recovered from the owner as if it were an arrear of land-revenue.
   (iii) A person aggrieved by an order made under this section may appeal to the Commissioner, who may cancel or modify it and whose decision shall be final.

Purchasers at Certain Sales and Persons Claiming through Owner Bound by Instrument Executive by Owner

8. Every person who purchases at a sale for arrears of land-revenue or any other public demand, or at a sale made under the Bengal Patni Taluks Regulation, 1819 (VIII of 1819), an estate or tenure in which is situated a monument in respect of which any instrument, has been executed by the owner for the time being under section 4 or section 5, and every person claiming any title to a monument from, through or under an owner who executed any such instrument, shall be bound by such instrument.

Application of Endowment to Repair of an Ancient Monument

9. (i) If any owner or other person competent to enter into an agreement under section 5 for the preservation of a protected monument, refuses or fails to enter into such an agreement when proposed to him by the Collector, and if any endowment has been

created for the purpose of keeping such monument in repair, or for that purpose among others, the Collector may institute a suit in the Court of the District Judge, or, if the estimated cost of repairing the monument does not exceed one thousand rupees, may make an application to the District Judge for the proper application of such endowment or part thereof.

(ii) On the hearing of an application under sub-section (1), the District Judge may summon and examine the owner and any person whose evidence appears to him necessary, and may pass an order for the proper application of the endowment or of any part thereof, and any such order may be executed as if it were the decree of a Civil Court.

Compulsory Purchase of Ancient Monument

10. (i) If the Local Government apprehends that a protected monument is in danger of being destroyed, injured or allowed to fall into decay, the Local Government may proceed to acquire it under the provisions of the Land Acquisition Act, 1894 (I of 1894), as if the preservation of a protected monument were a "public purpose" within the meaning of that Act.

(ii) The powers of compulsory purchase conferred by sub-section (1) shall not be exercised in the case of –

(a) any monument which or any part of which is periodically used for religious observances; or

(b) any monument which is the subject of a subsisting agreement executed under section 5.

(iii) In any case other than the cases referred to in sub-section (2), the said powers of compulsory purchase shall not be exercised unless the owner or other person competent to enter into an agreement under section 5 has failed, within such reasonable period as the Collector may fix in this behalf, to enter into an agreement proposed to him under the said section or has terminated or given notice of his intention to terminate such an agreement.

Maintenance of Certain Protected Monuments

11. (i) The Commissioner shall maintain every monument in respect of which the Government has acquired any of the rights mentioned in section 4 or which the Government has acquired under section 10.

(ii) When the Commissioner has accepted the guardianship of a monument under section 4, he shall, for the purpose of maintaining such monument, have access to the monument at all reasonable times, by himself and by his agents, subordinates and workmen, for the purpose of inspecting the monument and for the purpose of bringing such materials and doing such acts as he may consider necessary or desirable for the maintenance thereof.

Voluntary Contributions

12. The Commissioner may receive voluntary contributions towards the cost of maintaining a protected monument and may give orders as to the management and application of any funds so received by him:

Provided that no contribution received under this section shall be applied to any purpose other than the purpose for which it was contributed.

Protection of Place of Worship from Misuse, Pollution or Desecration

13. (i) A place of worship or shrine maintained by the Government under this Act shall not be used for any purpose inconsistent with its character.

(ii) Where the Collector has, under section 4, purchased or taken a lease of any protected monument, or has accepted a gift or bequest or the Commissioner has, under the same section, accepted the guardianship thereof, and such monument, or any part thereof, is periodically used for religious worship or observances by any community, the Collector shall make due provision for the protection of such monument, or such part thereof, from pollution or desecration:

(a) by prohibiting the entry therein, except in accordance with conditions prescribed with the concurrence of the persons in religious charge of the said monument or part thereof, of any person not entitled so to enter by the religious usages of the community by which the monument or part thereof is used, or

(b) by taking such other action as he may think necessary in this behalf.

Relinquishment of Government Rights in a Monument

14. With the sanction of the Local Government, the Commission may –

(i) where rights have been acquired by the Government in respect of any monument under this Act by virtue of any sale, lease, gift or will, relinquish the rights so acquired to the person who would for the time being be the owner of the monument if such rights had not been acquired; or

(ii) relinquish any guardianship of a monument which he has accepted under this Act.

Right of Access to Certain Protected Monuments

15. (i) Subject to such rules as may after previous publication be made by the Local Government, the public shall have a right of access to any monument maintained by the Government under this Act.

(ii) In making any rule under sub-section (1), the Local Government may provide that a breach of it shall be punishable with fine which may extend to twenty rupees.

Penalties

16. Any person other than the owner who destroys, removes, injures, alters, defaces or imperils a protected monument, and any owner who destroys, removes, injures, alters, defaces or imperils a monument maintained by the Government under this Act or in respect of which an agreement has been executed under section 5, and any owner or occupier who contravenes an order made under section 7, sub-section (1) shall be punishable with fine which may extend to five thousand rupees, or with imprisonment which may extend to three months, or with both.

TRAFFIC IN ANTIQUITIES

Power to Governor-General in Council to Control Traffic in Antiquities

17. (i) If the Governor-General in Council apprehends that antiquities are being sold or removed to the detriment of India or of any neighbouring country, he may, by notification in the Gazette of India, prohibit or restrict the bringing or taking by sea or

by land of any antiquities or class of antiquities described in the notification into or out of British India or any specified part of British India.

(ii) Any person who brings or takes or attempts to bring or take any such antiquities into or out of British India or any part of British India in contravention of a notification issued under sub-section (1), shall be punishable with fine which may extend to five hundred rupees.

(iii) Antiquities in respect of which an offence referred to in sub-Section (2) has been committed shall be liable to confiscation.

(iv) An officer of customs, or an officer of Police of a grade not lower than Sub-Inspector, duly empowered by the Local Government in this behalf, may search any vessel, cart or other means of conveyance, and may open any baggage or package of gods, if he has reason to believe that goods in respect of which an offence has been committed under sub-section (2) are contained therein.

(v) A person who complains that the power of search mentioned in sub-section (4) has been vexatiously or improperly exercised may address his complaint to the Local Government, and the Local Government shall pass such order and may award such compensation, if any, as appears to it to be just.

PROTECTION OF SCULPTURS, CARVINGS, IMAGES, BAS-RELIEFS, INSCRIPTIONS OR LIKE OBJECTS

Power to Local Government to Control Moving of Sculpturs, Carvings or Like Objects

18. (i) If the Local Government considers that any sculptures, carvings, images, bas-reliefs, inscriptions or other like objects ought not to be moved from the place where they are without the sanction of the Government, the Local Government may, by notification in the local official Gazette, direct that any such object or any class of such objects shall not be moved unless with the written permission of the Collector.

(ii) A person applying for the permission mentioned in sub-section (1) shall specify the object or objects which he proposes to move, and shall furnish, in regard to such object or objects, any information which the Collector may require.

(iii) If the Collector refuses to grant such permission, the applicant may appeal to the Commissioner, whose decision shall be final.

(iv) Any person who moves any object in contravention of a notification issued under sub-section (1), shall be punishable with fine which may extend to five hundred rupees.

(v) If the owner of any property proves to the satisfaction of the Local Government that he has suffered any loss or damage by reason of the inclusion of such property in a notification published under sub-section (1), the Local Government shall either –

(a) exempt such property from the said notification;

(b) purchase such property, if it be moveable, at its market-value; or

(c) pay compensation for any loss or damage sustained by the owner of such property, if it be immovable.

Purchase of Sculptures, Carvings or Like Objects by the Government

19. (i) If the Local Government apprehends that any object mentioned in a notification issued under section 18, sub-section (1), is in danger of being destroyed, removed, injured or allowed to fall into decay, the Local Government may pass orders for the compulsory

purchase of such object at its market-value, and the Collector shall thereupon give notice to the owner of the object to be purchased.

(ii) The power of compulsory purchase given by this section shall not extend to –
   (a) any image or symbol actually used for the purpose of any religious observance; or
   (b) anything which the owner desires to retain on any reasonable ground personal to himself or to any of his ancestors or to any member of his family.

Excavations

Power to Local Government to Control Excavation

20. (i) If the Local Government is of the opinion that excavation within the limits of any local area ought to be restricted or regulated for the purpose of protecting or preserving any ancient monument, the Local Government may, by notification in the local official Gazette, make rules –
   (a) fixing the boundaries of the area to which the rules are to apply; and
   (b) prescribing the authority by which, and the terms on which, licenses to excavate may be granted.

(ii) The power to make rules given by this section is subject to the condition of the rules being made after previous publication.

(iii) A rule made under this section may provide that any person committing a breach thereof shall be punishable with fine which may extend to two hundred rupees.

(iv) If any owner or occupier of land included in a notification under sub-section (1), proves to the satisfaction of the Local Government that he has sustained any loss by reason of such land being so included, the Local Government shall pay compensation in respect of such loss.

General

Assessment of Market-value or Compensation

21. (i) The market-value of any property which Government is empowered to purchase at such value under this Act, or the amount of compensation to be paid by Government in respect of anything done under this Act, shall, where any dispute arises touching the amount of such market-value or compensation, be ascertained in the manner provided by the Lord Acquisition Act, 1894, (1 of 1894), sections 3, 8 to 34, 45 to 47, 51 and 52, so far as they can be made applicable.

Provided that when making an inquiry under the said Land Acquisition Act, 1894, the Collector shall be assisted by two assessors, one of whom shall be a competent person nominated by the Collector, and one a person nominated by the owner or, in case the owner fails to nominate an assessor within such reasonable time as may be fixed by the Collector in this behalf, by the Collector.

Jurisdiction

22. A Magistrate of third class shall not have jurisdiction to try any person charged with an offence against this Act.

Power to Make Rules

23. (i) The Governor-General in Council of the Local Government may make rules for carrying out any of the purposes of this act.
(ii) The power to make rules given by this section is subject to the condition of the rules being made after previous publication.

Protection to Public Servants Acting Under Act

24. No suit for compensation and no criminal proceeding shall be against any public servant in respect of any act done, or in good faith intended to be done, in the exercise of any power conferred by this Act.

This Bill was passed at a meeting of the Council of the Governor-General of India for the purpose of making Laws and Regulations on the eighteenth day of March, 1904.

(Signed) CURZON
President

I assent to this Bill.

(Signed) CURZON
Viceroy and Governor-General
The 18th March 1904

(An authentic copy)

(Signed) J.M. MACPHERSON
Secretary to the Government of India
Legislative Department

Appendix-XXVIII

NOTE BY THE D.G.A. ON THE WORK OF THE A.S.D. IN INDIA*

Progress made by the A.S.D. in India during the past 5 years of future employment of the survey staff.

CONSERVATION

Speaking generally, there has been during the past five years a conspicuous and rapidly increasing interest shown by Local Governments in the monuments under their charge. Some administrations have, it is true, been more backward than others in responding to the appeals of the Imperial Government in the matter – a backwardness doubtless due for the most part to the pressing exigencies of local finance – but a comparison of the provincial allotments made to archaeology during 1903-04 with those of 1898-99 will serve to show that the responsibility has now been uniformly accepted, and has at last led to the general adoption of a sufficiently liberal policy. The allotments from the various provinces are as follow:

				1898-99	1903-04
Madras	...	...	...	919	18,542
Bombay	...	...	...	8,285	18,000
Bengal	...	...	...	9,670	44,374
United Provinces	...	...	...	11,530	1,13,513
Punjab	...	...	...	7,888	40,000
Central Provinces	...	...	...	—	10,000
			Total:	**38,292**	**2,44,429**

In addition to the above sums, the Government of India has set aside a lakh of rupees yearly since 1902, from which subsidies have been given in aid of special archaeological objects

---

* Proceedings, Department of Revenue and Agriculture, May 1904, Nos. 31-32, pp. 111-122.

shown to be beyond the financial capacity of the local administrations. The beneficial effect of the action of the supreme Government in thus assuming direct responsibility has been most apparent in the stimulus it has imparted to local endeavour.

Almost the whole of the provincial grants and of the subsidies made since 1902 from imperial sources have been denoted to conservation, comparatively insignificant sums only being reserved for exploration of other archaeological purposes. In the following general account of the works which they have rendered possible, only those operations which may be considered of first-rate importance can here be noticed, and that too but very briefly. To detail them fully and exactly, or to refer to all the miscellaneous repairs carried out by the survey, can be tedious in the extreme. Minor works, it is true, constitute the bulk of the last five years' work in more than one Province, but a description of these undertakings, however necessary they may have been to the preservation of the buildings, would entail a mere repetition of measures like the clearing away of overgrowing jungle, the erasing of hideous whitewash and the resetting of crumbling masonry, associated with long lists of monuments, of the archaeological value of which the mere names would convey little or no idea.

Undoubtedly, the greatest achievement of the last five years has been the restoration of the Agra group of monuments – greatest not only by reason of the superlative importance of the monuments themselves which have been saved from impending ruin, but by reason also of the exceptional skill of the local masons which has enabled them to copy the original carvings with scrupulous fidelity, and thus restore to many of the monuments the full measure of their ancient symmetry. The Taj Mahal, in particular, with its gardens and surrounding buildings can hardly have looked more effective in the days of the Mughal Emperors than it now does. Squalid bazaars have been cleared away from its very gates, the colonnades flanking its approach have been opened out and repaired, and the untidy quadrangle that precedes its main entrance has been converted into a well-grassed and peaceful Court. Within the precinct of the tomb itself, the gardens with their water-courses, fountain and flower beds have been restored more exactly to their original condition, and the stately mosque and jawab have been structurally repaired and beautified by the renovation of their encrusted ornaments and sculptured panels.

In the Fort, the complete restoration of the imposing river frontage of the Jahangiri Mahal has been effected and the dilapidated brick supported Kiosk standing on the south bastion flanking the great front has been rebuilt. The quaint Square Pavilion known as the Salimgarh, which adorned the highest point of Agra Fort, was until quite recently used as a canteen, and the better to adapt it to that ignoble purpose, the fine arches which open the pavilion on all four sides, had been bricked up and fitted with mistri-made doors and windows, while a barrack room verandah had been built up against the sun. Today the canteen has been wiped out of sight and the pavilion has regained its former beauty. In the square surrounding, the Diwan-i-Aam or Hall of Public Audience which the visitor used to remember only as an arsenal yard littered with debris and a convenient stand for carriages, the military authorities have allowed the hideous modern casemates to be demolished and the ancient arcades which they screened from view to be restored in their entirely. The debris has been cleared away, and the old roads and pavement, where the assembled audience stood before the Emperor, brought to light and repaired. Other ancient buildings in Agra have received their full share of attention. The exquisite tomb of Itmad-ud-daulah on the further bank of the Jumna is crowned again with its graceful balustrade of perforated marble, and much of its inlay of precious stones has been repaired; while hard by it the crumbling fabric of the Chini-ka-Rauza, than which no finer specimen of tile work exists in the Province, has been skillfully saved from further decay. At Sikandarah in the main gatehouse of the Mausoleum of Akbar, the bold designs of coloured stone work have been renewed and another of the gates – which would inevitably have fallen in a few more years – has also passed into the repairer's hands. Equally systematic and equally successful have been the repairs to the numerous buildings in the city of Akbar at Fatehpur Sikri.

In Rajputana, at the Jain temples at Mount Abu, whose lace-like traceries are the triumph of Indian marble carving, the difficulty of saving their domes from collapse without taking away from their beauty has been skillfully overcome and the marks of former rough usage or neglect have been removed.

On the side of the Ajmer lake, the stately marble embankment of Shah Jahan has been carefully restored and the ugly modern offices and bungalows, which offended every sympathetic eye, have been made to yield place to the exquisite marble pavilions of the Mughal Emperor – white and spotless as when first erected. At Ajmer also, the Arhai-din-ka Jhompra Mosque, which according to some is the finest specimen of the Mohammedan mosques that now exists, has been rescued from a sad state of dilapidation. The domes have been replaced, the tenements of squatters have been bought up and cleared, the cloister walls have been strengthened and many of the missing pillars have been restored.

Within the fortress of Chitor, the well known Tower of Fame has been saved from untimely destruction. For several years its crowning had been in imminent danger of collapse, and the Darbar had started the work of falling down the Tower to its foundations, with the idea of building it afresh and recarving any of the exquisite sculptures that might have been defaced or broken in the process. Happily they were diverted in time from their purpose and the Tower is now being repaired – for repair is all that is needed – with scrupulous care.

In another native state – that of Dhar in Central India – the rock fortress of Mandu, overlooking the sacred Nerbudda, the ancient capital of the Kings of Malva, is still in the process of being reserved from the undeserved oblivion into which it had fallen. In the whole of India there is no capital of antiquity which occupies a nobler site and no group of monuments more impressive in their lonely grandeur or more romantic in their decay. It is strange indeed that no previous attempt was ever made to rescue them from the rank jungle which for centuries has been encroaching and tearing their masonry to pieces. The operations which have now been undertaken have already borne remarkable fruit not only in the successful preservation they have effected of some of the most beautiful of the buildings above ground but in the discovery also of fresh monuments of first-rate importance – notably of the Victory Tower and tomb of the Great Mahmud – buried deep in their own accumulated debris.

No longer is the mosque of the slave nobleman Sidi Sayed at Ahmedabad perverted to mean utilitarian uses. The many deformities which were perpetrated in order to convert it into a modern district treasury and which, incredible though it may seem, were allowed to obscure the exquisite beauty of its demilune windows, have been removed, while the precincts have been dedicated to their original purpose. For many years, debarred by the stringent rules observed in all treasury buildings from crossing the official threshold, the public once more enjoys free access to the interior, and Ahmedabad has regained an acquisition to its architectural attractions which alone would reward the visitor for his journey there.

From the finely proportioned mosque of the Gol Gumbaz at Bijapur, the unsightly dak bungalow has been summarily obliterated and the building with its noble façade and slender graceful minars, has been rescued from rapid decline. At this tomb also the bold and highly ornate eaves that served by contrast to set off the grand simplicity of the building are being restored, and a like work is being done, in the same capital, at the Ibrahim Rauza and the Jami Masjid.

In the Punjab, great effort has been and still is being made, to make up for the neglect of past years and to do for the monuments of Delhi and Lahore what has already been done for those of Agra. At Delhi, a whole succession of buildings dating from an age before the Mohammedan conquest until the latest Mughal times – all of them among the finest representatives of their class – have come into the repairer's hands. The graceful Hindu colonnades incorporated by Altmash into his stupendous mosque at the Qutab, and the famous façade which he himself added; the masjid within the old fort of Sher Shah with its richly coloured encrustrations; the massive Mausoleum of the Emperor Tughlak Shah; the gem-like tomb of Atgah Khan, the foster father of Akbar, with its delicate reliefs and inlaid Kashii titles; and the pretty grave of Jahanara, the devoted daughter of Shah Jahan – all these have been restored to their former beauty or put into a thorough state of repair and defence against their natural enemies. Around the tomb of Humayun, a barren wilderness is being converted into a stately garden, that shall be worthy of the glorious resting place of so great an Emperor. Hard by, the tomb of Isa Khan also has been rescued from the squalor of its surroundings by transplanting a whole village of dirty huts from its quaint octagonal enclosure, and this monument has already taken rank among the great attractions of Delhi.

Coming to the city and fortress of Shah Jahan, the military authorities have agreed to evacuate all the principal Mughal buildings that now exist within the Fort, and already the work of digging out the marble tanks and reservoirs long buried beneath the soil, and of restoring the famous Hayal Bakhsh Garden and its marble pavilions to some semblance of their former beauty has made good progress. Here also have been restored in the throne of the Great Mughal those mosaiced panels – among them the well-known picture of orphans fiddling to a group of listening animals – which were carried off to England at the time of the Mutiny.

Outiside the Fort, the Zinat-ul-Masjid, used within recent years as a bakery for the British troops, has been converted once more to a holier purpose.

So too at Lahore, the Moti Masjid in the Fort, built round with battering walls of British brick and made strong with iron bars when it was turned into a treasury, once more resembles its former self and displays to the light of day the full purity of its glistening marbles. The Chhoti Khwabgah, or sleeping hall of Shah Jahan, that was covered in with an ugly modern roof and appropriated as a Church for the soldiers, has all but been restored to its original beauty. And the tile-enamelled mosque of Dai Anga has been freed from the mass of railway offices, in which it had been literally buried.

At Shahdra, the tomb of the Emperor Jahangir has received most careful attention, and hands have been at work arresting the decay in many of the surrounding buildings.

In Bengal, a whole series of important projects have been taken up. Asoka's broken pillar near Rampurwara, the separate pieces of which lay buried in a swamp, has been raised from its grave and re-erected on the site where there is very reason to suppose that the great Buddhist monarch originally set it up. The weird Jain Caves at Khandagiri, crumbling away under their burden of age, have been protected against the further ravages of heat and rain; and the two stone elephants which lay broken in confused fragments close by, have been repieced and placed upon their feet again, flanking the front of the Ganesa Gumpha, where they once formed a guard of honour. On the summit of the deserted hill of Mundesvari, the queer octagonal temple which lay half smothered in its own ruin – the whole heap overgrown to the roof with the rank vegetation of the jungle – has been brought back to the civilized light of day, and though the structure cannot now be restored to the form it bore twelve continues ago, efforts are being made to preserve all the essential features. Similarly, the numerous temples at Bhubaneswar, some of the which are in their own way quite unique, have been rescued, not, it is true, from the same advanced stage of disintegration, but still from a condition of more than incipient decay. Portions of the building which by the loosening of stones had become unsafe have been dismantled and rebuilt as far as possible with the ancient material. The magnificent and costly temple of the Sun God, known as the Black Pagoda, strangely reared six hundred years ago on what is now at any rate a desert of sea sand at Konarak, had sunk into a state sadly different from that which still delighted the world in the time of Abul Fazl, who wrote it that "even those whose judgement is critical and who are difficult to please stand amazed at the sight". Much has now been done to remedy the inroads of time and mischief. The plinth of the temple, which was buried in sand, has been laid upon and is now seen to be full of startling carvings including representations of processional horses and chariot which – sure symbols of the glorious Sun God.

Among the Mohammedan buildings in Bengal – relics for the most part of the independent Sultans who had their capitals at Gaur and Panduah between the 14th and 16th century – there has been, and still is, much room for protective and restorative energy. It is the misfortune of these curious buildings, with their soft brick facades chiseled as elaborately as if of sandstone, that the glazed tiles which form their crowning ornament have excited general covetousness. Much of the spoliation was wrought by Hindus in the early days of the East India Company, but happily those days are now passed, and in place of destruction we now have reconstruction and the sedulous preservation of all that has been spared. At Panduah, the striking five-storied minar, evidently an imitation of the Qutub-minar at Delhi, had lost its topmost storey and its pinnacle, but these have now been carefully restored. Finally, the famous hill fort of Rohtasgarh and the many curious buildings on the Rohtasgarh plateau, which constitute the only specimens of Mughal civil architecture in Bengal, have come into the scheme of conservation, mainly because of the interesting example they afford of the conditions of military life in those unrestful days.

Passing rapidly on to Southern India, the vast ruins of Vijaynagar have been subjected to a critical examination; the relative merits of each of the numerous monuments there have been weighed, and a carefully thought-out scheme for preserving all those that are most worthy of preservation is now being vigorously pushed forward. In Vellore Fort, the old Hindu temple – one of the most perfect examples of Dravidian architecture – has been saved from the ruin with which it was threatened by the flooding in of the water from the surrounding moat. One of its pillared halls or "mandapas" which had subsided to a dangerous extent has been rebuilt, and the shrine itself skillfully refaced in places where it had become honey-combed by the exhaling moisture. Much attention also has been given to the Chennakesavasvami temple at Sompalle, but in the floriated style with its beautifully carved four-pillared marriage canopy, under which the nuptials of the celestials are solemnized, and to the re-excavation and clearance of the cave temples in the Fort rock at Trichinopoly.

In concluding this brief account of the progress of conservation, it will be appropriate to refer also to the steps that have been taken to secure the preservation of minor and moveable antiquities by instituting small museums in some of the main centres of archaeological interest and by stimulating local officers to assist in bringing together any objects of value upon which they may chance. This is one of the most important aspects of conservation, in as much as many of the smaller monuments scattered about the face of the country are incapable of preservation on the spot where they have been found and often too bulky to be removed to the larger museums which exist only in the capital cities of India; and even if their removal were practicable, there are few local officers with sufficient general interest in the preservation of antiquities to take the trouble to dispatch them to some far off Museum, where they themselves may never have the opportunity of viewing them again. The Museums which have been created during the past five years – all, it should be added, at the instigation of H.E. the Viceroy – are at Malda, at Pagan and Mandalay in Burma, at Bijapur in Bombay, at Sarnath near Benaras, at the Taj in Agra, and at Peshawar in the Frontier Province. The districts in which these Museums are placed are sufficient guarantee that they will be rapidly stocked with interesting and valuable antiquities. Already in Pagan the efforts of one native assistant and the outlay of a few rupees have brought together a collection of inscriptions, ideals, terracotta plaques, enamelled tiles and the like, well worthy of a place in the first Museums of Europe. By the institution of such collections, the attraction of visitors to these localities will be greatly increased; fresh light will be thrown on the groups of monuments with which they are connected, and the minor antiquities themselves, which go to make up the collections, will be studied to a greater advantage on the actual spot where they have been discovered, than they could be, if dissociated from their surroundings in some distant Museum.

I come now to the future of conservation work in India, and in this connection, I may refer at the outset to an illusory belief to which expression has often been given that a time would soon come when the Archaeological Survey might be disbanded, and the work of conservation if not complete, accomplished through the agency of P.W.D. That time has receded further year by year and the phantom might now, once and for all, be laid to rest. The fact is that the work of the survey never can be finished, nor will the P.W.D. ever be in a position to undertake it. So far as their conservation is concerned, the monuments claiming the attention of the Archaeological officers may be divided into two classes. In the one class are those of first-rate historical or architectural importance which are to be restored and kept in a permanent state of thorough repair. In the other are those which are to be saved from further decay and not restored in any way.

As regards the former class, it is indeed possible that after a certain number of years (always supposing of course that the present generous policy towards Archaeology is uniformly maintained in British India, and continuously stimulated in the Native States), the Government will be able to assure itself that all the large undertakings at any rate throughout the country have been brought to a satisfactory finish, and that there will be need only of a comparatively small annual outlay to provide for the efficient maintenance of these monuments in the future. But that time cannot be for fifteen or twenty years yet. In the United Provinces, Bengal and Bombay, where there has been a fairly well-sustained policy for some years past and perhaps in Burma also, it may be that this estimate is too high, but in the Punjab and Madras and in the Natives States of Rajputana and Central India, it will take all those years of patient labour to carry through the most moderate scheme of restoration. And while this is going on, there will be need for the most scrupulous care and patient supervision on the part of the Archaeological Department. Those who have been the round of Indian buildings must know well what incongruities have been perpetrated through unskillful restoration in the past. The truth is that the successful repair of any monument demands an accurate knowledge of its architecture, knowledge of the history of the building and the events associated with its erection, and the knowledge,. gained only by experience, of what repairs are appropriate and what are not. And with this knowledge must be combined sound artistic judgement and some measure of engineering skill. As an instance in point I may cite the case of the Tower of Fame at Chitorgad, to which I have previously referred. Its crowing cupola was in a dangerous condition and had to be restored, but the body of the Tower was sound enough save for a few cracks caused by lightning. The State Engineer however decided, and another Engineer supported him, that it would be safer to pull it down so far as its foundations and rebuilt it entirely. Doubtless it would! The same might be said, and more forcibly, of half the monuments of antiquity! But what of its inimitable carvings which were to be replaced by new ones, if broken in the hazardous process of demolition? And what of the time worn beauty of the Tower; which no amount of skill could restore? I do not hesitate to say that timely advice has in this instance saved one of her most cherished monuments for India, and an outlay of a lakh of rupees or more for the Native Darbar.

Turning to the second class of monuments, namely, those that stand in need of protective measures only, the handling which they require is equally delicate; and the artistic taste of the repairer should be equally good. And in the case of these monuments, it should be noted, conservation is an ever-recurring factor, however, judiciously the repairs may have been executed in the first instance. The destructive forces of a tropical climate are year by year working some havoc in masonry which can neither be seen or prevented. Our experience has taught us that difficulties are for ever cropping up in connection with buildings that were thought to have been already completely and effectively repaired, and it is useless spending money now unless it is intended that the monuments shall be, as far as is practicable, permanently maintained. So far, therefore, as this class of work is concerned, the task before the Archaeological Department may be said to be an unlimited one.

Act – There is yet another branch of work connected with conservation which may be expected to increase materially the duties of the Archaeological Department in future. It relates to the application of the various sections of the "Ancient Monuments Act". In the event of interference with any buildings in private possession, or in the event of their compulsory purchase, or the purchase of moveable and minor antiquities, it will be the task of this Department to help in assessing their market-value and in securing a general uniformity in the amounts of compensation paid, and it will be their task to keep the Government informed of the removal or sale of any antiquities of value or the despoiling of any ancient sites of excavation. This means a great deal. It means that we must possess thoroughly up to date knowledge of the market prices of every class of antiquities; that we must keep in touch with the channels through which the traffic in them passes; that we must periodically inspect any monuments of importance in private possession as well as those in possession of the State, and that we must preserve a record of any transaction connected with the application of the new Act.

When I was in Greece and Italy, I used to see a good deal of the illicit traffic in antiquities and measures taken to prevent it, and I used to hear much about the difficulties connected with the compulsory purchase of monuments. The laws in those countries are of course far more stringent and lead constantly to difficulties such as there is no need to anticipate in India. But there the regulations in force are the outcome of long experience, and here it will take many years for them to be developed and reduced into a systematic form, and whereas in those countries expert advice is ready at every turn, if the Government require it, in India there is no agency through which it can be obtained, except the Archaeological Department.

Survey Work – In the account which is to follow of the progress made in the record of Archaeological material, the work of the survey will, for convenience sake, be divided under two heads. Under the first will be considered the compilations of the general lists of antiquarian remains and under the second, the preparation of elaborate survey drawings or other illustrations of particular monuments.

1. The several divisions of India where the antiquarian remains had already, previously to 1899 been catalogued with some degree of finality were the Madras Presidency, Coorg, Bombay (including Baroda) Central Provinces and Berar and the North-West Provinces and Oudh. Besides these, the monuments in the Punjab had been very briefly and superficially catalogued, and rough lists had been prepared by the P.W.D. of the remains in Bengal and British Burma. The areas still entirely unsurveyed in 1899 were Rajputana, Central India, H.H. The Nizam's territory, Kashmir, Baluchistan and the Frontier Province, and in addition, the survey had before it the task of revising and re-editing the lists for Bengal, and of practically compiling afresh those for the Punjab and Burma.

During the past five years, the remains in H.H. The Nizam's territory have been very completely listed and the publication issued in its final form. In Bengal, the work of preparing a fresh edition of the old list published by the P.W.D. is almost complete. All the most important the P.W.D. is almost complete. All the most important monuments have now been visited by the Archaeological Surveyor; many omissions and errors in the old catalogue have been rectified and much fresh informationin added by him. In the Punjab, a complete catalogue of the monuments in the Delhi and Lahore districts has been published with full literary references, but without descriptive narrative, and a list of the inscriptions in the same districts is ready for the press. Similar lists for the Kangra districts also are now in hand.

In the Frontier Province, the catalogue of monuments in the Peshawar region is practically finished.

In the United Provinces, the old catalogue published in 1891 was found to be deficient and a specially revised list of the antiquities in the Agra District has therefore been drawn up. Throughout the rest of the Province, a considerable amount of fresh material has also been collected from local officials, chiefly with a view to fixing more closely the responsibility for the preservation of the various classes of monuments. A like revision of the old lists has been going on in Behar and Madras, where fresh touring on the part of the Archaeological Officers has given them the opportunity of inspecting many of the monuments previously.

In the new edition of the old lists and in the fresh lists now under preparation, a special effort is being made to include, in addition to the descriptive history of the monuments in the past, a further statement of their present condition of the measures necessary for their effective conservation. The effect of this will be to provide a more useful basis for a working programme for the survey staff and the officers entrusted with the actual duties of conservation, and thereby to enhance the value of the lists for administrative purposes.

2. In accordance with the provisions of the reorganization of 1898, the systematic surveys of important sites and monuments, which until then had constituted the main task of the survey, has had to give away to conservation. But, amid the increasing duties which conservation has imposed, occasional opportunities have been found to continue the survey work of former years. Of the Imperial series of Survey Reports, one volume illustrating the Mughal colour Decoration of Agra was brought out by the late Mr. E. Smith, and another of the same series dealing with the antiquities of Northern Gujarat by Dr. Burgess and Mr. Cousens. Mr. Cousens has also prepared an elaborate series of drawings and photographs of the Dilwara temples at Mount Abu, and a portfolio of exquisite coloured reproductions of Sind tile work. He has surveyed also many miscellaneous monuments in Berar and other parts of the circle of Western India and has

accomplished a most useful work in taking a complete set of 225 photographs to scale of the Sanchi Stupa. In Madras many additional drawings of monuments in the Kistna, Anantpur, North Arcot and Madura districts have been made for the purpose of completing a report on their architecture, which has for some time been under preparation. An extended and minute survey of the whole of the Vijaynagar site spreading over many miles of country and including many hundreds of monuments has been carried out, and besides this is a full series of illustrations has been made for a Report on the architecture of the Malabar district, which is unique of its kind in the Southern Peninsula. In the United Provinces, the illustrations for another volume relating to the Mausoleum of Akbar at Sikandrah are ready for publication and wait only for some further revision of the letterpress accompanying than. The majority of the palace buildings in the Agra Fort have been surveyed and the illustrations, when completed, will form one of the handsome publications yet issued. A similar survey of the Lahore Fort is also in progress, and some beautiful facsimile copies of about half the scenes represented in the unique tile ornamentation on the face of the Fort have been prepared under the supervision of the local Superintendent.

It should be added that many other miscellaneous monuments have been surveyed in parts of the Punjab, United Provinces, Baluchistan, Bengal and Assam, many of them being buildings which for one cause or another it has been decided not to conserve.

Future of Survey Work – The most important survey work waiting to be done in the immediate future is that connected with the listing of ancient remains. This is an all important task, because it is the first step towards conserving them, and it is impossible to formulate any effective scheme of conservation until the lists have been completed. Making allowances for possible delays and hindrances, it will take some six or seven years more to compile the new lists and revise the most imperfect ones among the old. PARI PASSU with this work, drawing and photographs will be prepared for those monuments which are to be allowed to fall to decay. This is a work which cannot be postponed, as many of the monuments in question are rapidly disappearing. The surveys of some of the most famous sites will also go forward – particularly of the vast collection of ruins at Delhi (of which not even a plan yet exists) and of those at Lahore, Agra, Mandu, Chitor, Gaur, Panduah, Mandalay, Pagan and of certain classes of monuments in Southern India and Bombay. But the progress of these more elaborate surveys must be slow, as they can only be taken up during the time that can legitimately be spared from other duties.

Conclusion

Enough perhaps has now been said to indicate that the work of the Archaeological Officers is of a kind which cannot be discharged by any other existing Department of Government or through any private agency, and that it can only cease if the Government ceases to admit its responsibility for the preservation of the ancient remains of the country.

If monuments are to be conserved or their restoration attempted, skilled supervision will always be necessary. If they are to be consigned to natural decay, a full record must be kept of whatever may be of interest in the future. The preliminary listing of the materials to be conserved is a task of but temporary duration, which will be completed in a few more years, but while it lasts, great discretion will be needed in selecting the monuments that are worthy of being maintained, and when it has ended, the task of conserving these monuments will take its place. Public and private monuments alike will have to be watched and cared for. Large tracts of the country will have to be searched for inscriptions, and the inscriptions themselves (not a few of them in scripts or languages, of which European scholars profess no knowledge) will have to be deciphered. Antiquities will have to be brought together into museums, and assistance given in cataloguing and arranging them. The exploration, too, of buried remains must form part of the programme; and lastly, the results of the work should periodically be published, and no efforts spared to widen public interest in India's splendid treasure-house of relics.

The Government cannot yet look to private enterprise to discharge any one of these tasks. In India the genius of the people has not yet turned in the direction of the scientific archaeology or of veneration for the monuments of the past. In Europe, it is true, an international society was started more than five years ago for the purpose of exploration in India, but few adherents have yet been found to support it, and there is little hope, I believe, of the enterprise bearing fruit for many years to come. Even allowing that the society achieved its purpose and sent out excavators at its own expense, it would not thereby appreciably diminish the task before the Archaeological Survey. For the Government would always find it necessary to exercise the closest supervision over private excavations of that kind, and to constitute the Archaeological Department as a sort of Ephoralty on lines similar to those followed in Greece.

Whether the natives of India can be trained to take the place of Europeans upon the survey is still an open question. We have now three well-trained native epigraphists on the staff, whose work, so far as it goes, is of a thoroughly good quality but carries them no further than the decipherment of inscriptions; and there are no other native archaeologists possessed of sufficient artistic feeling or discrimination to be placed in charge of important monuments. One has only to read a few native art criticisms to realize the truth of this statement. Perhaps this is due to the fact that they have never had an opportunity of being trained in the other, and the more artistic, fields of archaeology. But, whatever the cause may be, serious attempts are now being made to put their capabilities in these fields to test, and to see to what extent they can be developed. Two scholarships have lately been created and the number, it is hoped, will afterwards be increased, which will enable, us to select men of the best scholarly tendencies and to do our best of train them to the sceintific methods followed in Europe. They are to be trained in each of the circles in succession in those subjects in which the respective European superintendents have had most experience – in architecture, in sculpture and in epigraphy, in excavations, numismatics and the minor arts, and in a technical knowledge of drawing and photography, and they will have the advantage withal of extensive travelling and the opportunity of educating their comparative faculties to the fullest degree. In another direction also, we are endeavouring to promote the employment of native archaeologists. One has recently been appointed as an assistant in the circle of Western India, and we are making it our special object to instruct him in the highly mechanical processes connected with Archaeology, which Mr. Cousens – the Superintendent of that circle – has raised almost to the level of a fine art, and in other respects also to make him instrumental in keeping alive and transmitting to others the results of Mr. Cousen's long years of experience. When we have given these attempts a sufficient trial, we ought to be in a position to say whether it will be possible to allow much of the archaeological work to devolve upon natives of this country, or whether we can only look to them to serve upon the survey as they have hitherto done, in the capacity of epigraphists or subordinate assistants.

– J.H. MARSHALL
D.G.A.

18th April 1904

Bibliography

ORIGINAL SOURCES (RECORDS)

NATIONAL ARCHIVES OF INDIA, NEW DELHI

Public Branch of Home Department 1784-1856
Public A Branch of Home Department 1867-1895
Archaeology A Branch of Home Department 1881-1887
Archaeology B Branch of Home Department 1881-1887
Archaeology, Conservation of Ancient Monuments Branch of Home Department 1881-1887
Archaeology and Epigraphy Branch of Home Department,1905-1906
Revenue and Agriculture Branch of Home Department 1881
Public Letters from Secretary of State 1867.
PWD – Military Governor General Papers of Home Department 1858
PWD – Governor-General Papers of Home Department 1858
Judicial Letters from Court of Directors 1813-1820
Legislative Department , Act XX of 1863
Legislative Department Proceedings 1904
Legistlative A Branch of Legislative Department 1878
Archaeology and Epigraphy Branch of Revenue and Agriculture Department 1887-1904
Archaeology B Branch of Revenue and Agriculture Department 1887-1902
Archaeology C Branch of Revenue and Agriculture Department 1893-95
Land Revenue Records 1838
General A Branch of Public Works Department 1862-1891
Buildings and Roads, Civil Buildings of Public Works Department 1873
Civil Works Buildings Branch of Public Works Department 1878-1903
Accountant General Branch of Public Works Department 1876-1903
Public Works Department Despatch from Secretary of State 1864-1866
Department of Finance and Commerce Series 1878
Accounts A Branch of Department of Finance and Commerce Series 1878
Salaries B Branch of Department Finance and Commerce 1884

Accounts A Branch of Finance Department 1878
Salaries A Branch of Finance Department 1888
Expenditure(Minor Department) Branch of Finance Department 1878
Political Branch of Foreign Department 1804-1860
Secret Branch of Foreign Department 1857-1858
General A Branch of Foreign Department 1862-1868
General B Branch of Foreign Department 1862-1868
B General I Branch of Foreign Department 1883-1884
Internal A Branch of Foreign Department 1901
Internal B Branch of Foreign Department 1886-90
Frontier A Branch of Foreign Department 1901
Frontier B Branch of Foreign Department 1896
Political Series 1829-1846
Military Department Series 1810-1815

Residency Records

Central India Agency 1804-1910
Bundelkhand Agency 1804-1905
Chhattishgarh Agency 1901-1905
Hyderabad Residency 1779-1910
Mysore Residency 1799-1905
Rajputana Agency 1805-1830
Punjab States Agency 1850-1900
Western India States Agency 1864-1910

West Bengal State Archives, Calcutta

Judicial Series 1809-1813
Revenue Series 1813-1817

PRIVATE PAPERS (MICROFILMS), NATIONAL ARCHIVES

Curzon Collection 1899-1905
Lansdown Collection 1889-1895
William Bentinck 1835
Lytton,1st Earl 1883-1914
Additional Manuscripts 29196, 1b-2 (photocopy) – Original in British Museum

PUBLISHED MATERIALS

Journals

Ancient India
Journal of Asiatic Society 1838-1906
Asiatic Review 1921
Bengal: Past and Present 1907-1909
Calcutta Review 1844
Modern Review 1911-1913

Books

The Care of Ancient Monuments by G Baldwin Brown, 1905
Dara Sukoh by K.R. Qaunungo, 1935

Travellers' India: An Anthology, edited by H.K. Kaul, 1979
History of India Under the Company and the Crown by P.E. Roberts, 1958
Colloquies on the Simples and Drugs of India by Gracia d aorta, 1913
Delhi and Agra: A Travellers' Companion, selected and introduced by Michael Alexander
The Asiatic Society of Bengal and the Discoveries of India's Past by O.P. Kejariwal
The Story of Indian Archaeology, 1784-1947 by Sourendra Nath Roy, 1961
Early Travels in India, 1583-1619, edited by William Foster
A History of Indian Archaeology by Dilip K. Chakrabarti, 1987
Travels in India during the Years 1780-83 by William Hodges
History of India by Wilson
Revealing India's Past, edited by Sir John Cumming,1939
Radio Talks by R.Vasudeva Podwal, published at Trivandrum, 1948
Curzon Nama: Autocrat Curzon, Unconqurable India by Pamela Sharma
Administrative History of India by B.B. Mishra
Golden Adventure Book of Archaeology by Eva Know Evans, 1962
Protection, Conservation and Preservation of Indian Monuments by Shanti Lal Nagar, 1993
Hampi Ruins edited by A.H. Longhurst, 1917
History of Kumaon by Badri Dutt Pandey, 1937
Story of Delhi Iron Pillar by R. Balasubramaniam, 2005
Prayag Pradeep by Shaligram Bhargava
Factors in Indian History by K.A. Nilakanta Sastri, 1949
The Penguin Guide to the Monuments of India by George Michell, 1989, Vol. 1, Budhist, Jain, Hindu
The Penguin Guide to the Monuments of India by Phillip Davies, 1989, Vol. 2, Islamic, Rajput, European

Government Publications

General Memorandrum on the "Development of British Administration in India and on the origin of functions of the India Government" by W.S. Meyer, C.I.E, I.C.S Decentralization Committee for the Royal Commission on Decentralization, 1907.
Public Works Department Codes
Delhi Gazette, 1847
National Guides, National Archives of India
Guide to the Records in the National Archives of India, Part 1 to 11
First Report of the Curator of Ancient Monuments in India for the Year 1881-82
Indian Record Department; Lists of Heads of Admininistration in India and of the India Office in England, 1921.
Fort William-India Office Correspondence 1748-1800

Unpublished Material

'Sir John Marshal's Contribution to Indian Archaeology', Dissertation presented by Ritu Paul Bammi, National Archives of India, 1998-99.

Index